Business Ethics

Decision Making for Personal Integrity and Social Responsibility

Business Ethics

Decision Making for Personal Integrity and Social Responsibility

Second Edition

Laura P. Hartman
DePaul University

Joe DesJardins
College of St. Benedict/St. John's University

McGraw-Hill Irwin

The McGraw-Hill Companies

McGraw-Hill Irwin

BUSINESS ETHICS: DECISION MAKING FOR PERSONAL INTEGRITY AND SOCIAL RESPONSIBILITY, SECOND EDITION

Published by McGraw-Hill, a business unit of The McGraw-Hill Companies, Inc., 1221 Avenue of the Americas, New York, NY 10020.

This book is printed on acid-free paper.

1 2 3 4 5 6 7 8 9 0 DOC/DOC 1 0 9 8 7 6 5 4 3 2 1 0

ISBN: 978-0-07-813713-6
MHID: 0-07-813713-6

Vice President & Editor-in-Chief: *Brent Gordon*
Vice President EDP/Central Publishing Services: *Kimberly Meriwether David*
Publisher: *Paul Ducham*
Managing Developmental Editor: *Laura Hurst Spell*
Editorial Coordinator: *Jonathan Thornton*
Associate Marketing Manager: *Jaime Halteman*
Project Manager: *Erin Melloy*
Buyer: *Kara Kudronowicz*
Design Coordinator: *Brenda A. Rolwes*
Cover Designer: *Studio Montage, St. Louis, Missouri*
Senior Photo Research Coordinator: *Jeremy Cheshareck*
Cover Images: *Winding Road: © Imagestage Media (John Foxx); Fork in the Road: © Chase Jarvis/Getty Images; Signpost in New York: © Image Source; Intersecting Railroad Tracks: © Steve Crise/Corbis; Fork in Desert Road: © Stockbyte/PunchStock; Commuting: © Ingram Publishing/SuperStock*
Media Project Manager: *Balaji Sundararaman*
Compositor: *Laserwords Private Limited*
Typeface: *10/12 Times New Roman*
Printer: *R.R. Donnelley*

Library of Congress Cataloging-in-Publication Data

Hartman, Laura Pincus.
Business ethics : decision making for personal integrity and social responsibility/ by Laura P. Hartman and Joseph DesJardins.—2nd ed.
p. cm.
Includes bibliographical references and index.
ISBN 978-0-07-813713-6 (alk. paper)
1. Business ethics. I. DesJardins, Joseph R. II. Title.
HF5387.H3743 2010
174'.4—dc22

2010011965

www.mhhe.com

To Rachel and Emma.

—Laura Hartman

To Michael and Matthew.

—Joe DesJardins

About the Authors

Laura P. Hartman *DePaul University*

Laura P. Hartman is Vincent de Paul Professor of Business Ethics and Legal Studies in DePaul University's College of Commerce, serves as Special Assistant to the President with a focus on DePaul's Haiti Initiative and is also Research Director of DePaul's Institute for Business and Professional Ethics. Hartman represents DePaul University on the steering committee for Zafen.org, a microfinance organization seeking to enhance economic development in Haiti to benefit Haitians living in poverty. In her work in the private sector, she manages external partnerships for Zynga.org, the social initiative component of Zynga Game Network. She has been an invited professor at INSEAD (France), HEC (France) the Université Paul Cezanne Aix Marseille III, among other European universities, and previously held the Grainger Chair in Business Ethics at the University of Wisconsin–Madison. Her other books include *Rising above Sweatshops: Innovative Management Approaches to Global Labor Challenges, Employment Law for Business, Perspectives in Business Ethics,* and *The Legal Environment of Business: Ethical and Public Policy Contexts.* Hartman graduated from Tufts University and received her law degree from the University of Chicago Law School.

Joe DesJardins *College of St. Benedict/St. John's University*

Joe DesJardins is Associate Provost and Academic Dean, as well as Professor in the Department of Philosophy, at the College of St. Benedict and St. John's University in Minnesota. His other books include: *An Introduction to Business Ethics, Environmental Ethics: An Introduction to Environmental Philosophy, Environmental Ethics: Concepts, Policy & Theory* (McGraw Hill, 2000); *Contemporary Issues in Business Ethics,* (co-editor with John McCall), and *Business, Ethics, and the Environment: Imagining a Sustainable Future.* He is the former Executive Director of the Society for Business Ethics, and has published and lectured extensively in the areas of business ethics, environmental ethics, and sustainability. He received his B.A. from Southern Connecticut State University, and his M.A. and Ph.D. from the University of Notre Dame. He previously taught for twelve years at Villanova University.

Preface

We began writing the first edition of this textbook in 2006, soon after a wave of major corporate scandals had shaken the financial world. Headlines made the companies involved in these ethical scandals household names: Enron, WorldCom, Tyco, Adelphia, Health-South, Global Crossing, Arthur Andersen, ImClone, KPMG, J.P. Morgan, Merrill Lynch, Morgan Stanley, Citigroup Salomon Smith Barney, and even the New York Stock Exchange itself. At the time, we suggested that, in light of such significant cases of financial fraud, mismanagement, criminality and deceit, the relevance of business ethics could no longer be questioned. Sadly, the very same issues are as much alive today as they were several years ago. Consider the rash of problems associated with the financial meltdown in 2008–09 and the problems faced by such companies as AIG, Countrywide, Lehman Brothers, Merrill-Lynch, Bear Stearns and of the financier Bernard Madoff. Once again, we have witnessed financial and ethical malfeasance of historic proportions and the inability of market mechanisms, internal governance structures, or government regulation to prevent it.

As we reflect upon the ethical corruption and financial failures of the past decade, the importance of ethics is all too apparent. The questions today are less about whether ethics should be a part of business strategy and by necessity the business school curriculum, than about which values and principles should guide business decisions and *how* ethics should be integrated within business and business education.

This textbook provides a comprehensive yet accessible introduction to the ethical issues arising in business. Students who are unfamiliar with ethics will find that they are as unprepared for careers in business as students who are unfamiliar with accounting and finance. It is fair to say that students will not be fully prepared, even within traditional disciplines such as accounting, finance, human resource management, marketing, and management, unless they are sufficiently knowledgeable about the ethical issues that arise specifically within and across those fields.

While other solid introductory textbooks are available, several significant features make this book distinctive. We emphasize a **decision-making approach** to ethics and we provide strong **pedagogical support** for both teachers and students throughout the entire book. In addition, we bring both of these strengths to the students through a pragmatic discussion of issues with which they are already often familiar, thus approaching them through subjects that have already generated their interest.

New to the Second Edition

Our goal for the second edition remains the same as for the first: to provide "a comprehensive yet accessible introduction to the ethical issues arising in business." We have retained the focus on decision making as well as the emphasis on both personal and policy-level perspectives on ethics. We continue to provide pedagogical support throughout the text. The most noticeable changes involve a thorough updating of distinct items such as Reality Checks, Decision Points, and readings to reflect new cases, examples, and data.

Among these changes:

- Twenty-five new end-of-chapter readings, averaging more than two new readings for each chapter;
- New readings offering international and global perspectives;
- New cases to serve as Chapter Opening Decision Points;
- New readings on Stakeholder theory;
- Extremely timely and expanded textual coverage of such topics as corporate culture, leadership and gender, cultural diversity, stakeholders, social entrepreneurship, sustainability, the 2009 Genetic Information Non-Discrimination Act, sweatshops, living wages, green-washing, corporate governance, and the agency problem;

Finally, we have made numerous small editorial changes in each chapter to make the text more readable, to clarify concepts, to better integrate theory and practice, and to improve end-of-chapter questions to better support assessment of student learning, group projects, and classroom discussion.

Why a Decision-Making Model?

Ethics is all about making decisions: What should we do? How should we act? What type of life should we live? What type of organization and society ought we to create? Who should we be? By providing a decision-making model early in this text and revisiting and reinforcing this model through Decision Points and discussions of case studies in each chapter, we hope to accomplish several important goals.

First, an emphasis on decision making avoids the nagging challenge of relativism without succumbing to dogmatic preaching. Our decision-making model teaches students to think for themselves and to build a case in support of their own conclusions, conclusions that are rationally defensible precisely because they are the result of a rational decision-making process. In this way, students become active learners by taking responsibility for their points of view.

A decision-making emphasis also offers the promise of lifelong lessons. Long after students have forgotten the specific content of this course, the reasoning skills and habits developed here will continue to influence their everyday personal and professional lives. The purpose of the text is to encourage readers to explore their own values and then to apply a logical process to reach a well-reasoned conclusion regarding an appropriate course of action. This process will be relevant no matter the circumstances, profession involved, or stage in life as students proceed beyond the course within which it is taught.

The significance of the decision-making model also makes this text inherently compatible with diverse and global perspectives in a way that could not be achieved by a discussion that focused only on specific ethical values and principles. This inclusivity allows the model greater power of application across borders, subjects, and even time, than a value-based orientation would allow.

Finally, the decision-making model introduced here is easily transferred into other contexts and other courses. Many scholars now realize that business ethics should be integrated across the entire range of business disciplines. The strength of our decision-making model is that students and teachers can use it in any business course as a means for addressing ethical issues that arise in other fields. This is not a text that students will leave on the bookshelves. This is one that they will need to consult for each of their courses and, one would hope, for each of the issues they might also face in the business environment outside of the educational environment as well.

Pedagogical Support

Business ethics creates distinct challenges for both students and teachers. One would naturally assume that business ethics requires familiarity with the concepts and categories of two diverse fields, business and ethics. For many business students, a class in ethics will be unlike any other class in their experience. Faculty trained in business disciplines are challenged to master ethics; and those trained in ethics are equally challenged to master business concepts. This challenge will be increasing as more and more business school faculty are asked to teach ethics as part of the recognition of the critical importance and consequent integration of ethics in the business school curriculum. This evolution demands a textbook that provides strong pedagogical support for both student learners and teachers.

As if the challenge of teaching an interdisciplinary field is not enough, accrediting agencies are increasingly requiring that faculty demonstrate student learning, and the assessment of student learning will be required at both the program and individual instructor level.

This text offers a range of pedagogical elements to support both students and teachers. Each chapter is introduced with a **Decision Point**, a short case that raises issues that will be introduced and examined in the chapter. The Decision Point provides a topic through which to begin discussion and to ease students into the issues to follow, and it also includes a set of questions that demonstrate how to explore each decision using the ethical decision-making model proposed early in the book. A follow-up discussion of these Decision Points concludes each chapter, offering the opportunity to reflect on the opening case as a means to summarize and reflect upon the chapter. Decision Points are also sprinkled throughout each chapter as a way to help refine students' critical thinking skills.

Each chapter begins with a specific list of **Chapter Objectives**, which serve as the student learning goals as well as the organizational framework of the chapter, and concludes with a list of **Key Terms** introduced within the chapter. Key Terms are in color in the chapter text where they first appear, then included with comprehensive definitions at the end of the book in a full glossary.

Also integrated within each chapter are **Reality Checks**, which highlight real-life situations of business applications. They are examples of how these particular processes are applied in a timely, straight from the headlines business situation. The Reality Checks provide another application of the text material and keep students aware of issues and questions they will need to grapple with in this course.

The end-of-chapter material contains **Discussion and Project Questions** that go beyond recall questions to also include further research and application. The end-of-chapter **Readings** present a variety of provocative takes on the issues just raised in each chapter so that students become familiar with new perspectives, the subtle ethical implications of business actions, and the need for clarity of vision in engaging in business activity.

The **Online Learning Center** for this book, ***www.mhhe.com/busethics2e***, has two portals: instructors can download the IM, Video Files and Notes, Weblinks to related research sites, PPT files, and Sample Syllabi. Students can access the Glossary pages, Weblinks to Suggested Resources, and Chapter Review Quizzes.

By striving to speak to the students in language that is accessible to them, providing them with a framework within which to respond to even the most complicated ethical challenges, and by equipping them with theories that allow them a breadth of perspective and insight, the text offers the support that students need to ensure their voices will be heard in the business environment they are entering or have entered. Articulate, persuasive students with integrity and conviction will be business leaders of action. Our objective is to provide students with the tools they will require to ensure their action is effective, valuable, and sustainable.

Acknowledgments

A textbook should introduce students to the cutting-edge of the scholarly research that is occurring within a field. As in any text that is based in part on the work of others, we are deeply indebted to the work of our colleagues who are doing this research. We are especially grateful to those scholars who graciously granted us personal permission to reprint their materials in this text:

Denis Arnold
Norm Bowie
Martin Calkins
Michael Cranford
Jon Entine
Andrew Kluth
Philip Kotler
Dennis Moberg
Lisa Newton
Mark Pincus
Tara Radin
Ed Romar
Penelope Washbourne
Patricia Werhane

Our book is a more effective tool for both students and faculty because of their generosity. In addition, we wish to express our deepest gratitude to the reviewers and others whose efforts served to make this manuscript infinitely more effective:

Rikki Abzug,
Ramapo College of New Jersey
Carolyn Ashe,
University of Houston
Lia Barone,
Norwalk Community College
Marilyn Byrd,
University of Mary Hardin-Baylor
Elizabeth Evans,
Concordia University
Charles Foley,
Columbus State Community College
Denise Kleinrichert,
San Francisco State University
Lisa Knowles,
Saint Thomas University
Elias Konwufine,
Keiser University
Donneia Lawson,
Herzing College

Our thanks also go out to the team at McGraw-Hill/Irwin who helped this book come into existence:

Brent Gordon,
Editorial Director
Paul Ducham,
Publisher
Laura Hurst Spell,
Sponsoring Editor
Jonathan Thornton,
Editorial Coordinator
Suresh Babu,
Media Project Manager
Jaime Halteman,
Marketing Manager
Faye Schilling,
Project Manager
Erin Melloy,
Production Supervisor
Brenda Rolwes,
Designer

Brief Contents

Table of Contents

Chapter 1

Ethics and Business

Good people do not need laws to tell them to act justly, while bad people will find a way around the laws.

Plato

It is difficult to get a [person] to understand something when his [or her] salary depends upon . . . not understanding it.

Upton Sinclair

Profit is not the explanation, cause or rationale of business behavior and business decisions, but rather the test of their validity.

Peter Drucker

No snowflake in an avalanche ever feels responsible.

Voltaire

Opening Decision Point[1] *The Meaning of "Good"*

The term "business ethics" includes both words: ethics ***and*** business. The "ethics" element refers to the application of values within a business context. In the for-profit environment, the business context means that a firm must (usually) earn a profit in order to survive and to serve its mission. Therefore, does a firm have an ethical obligation to ensure that it makes money in everything it does, even when it tries to do "good"?

Let us take a look at a challenge that faces both local and global businesses alike. Cemex is a large Mexican building materials company that sells cement, cement blocks, and other supplies necessary to build homes and additions. The Guadalajara division has not been the most profitable; its clients represent some of Mexico's poorest residents. However, although the average sale to these low-income customers is extremely small, the Guadalajara division is one of Cemex's largest. Therefore, it is considered to be one of the more stable ones and less subject to fluctuations in the economy.

There is no question that those living in poverty in Guadalajara have a severe need for Cemex's products. Most of the houses are not large and have only one or two rooms per *family.* Journalist Kris Herbst reports:

> Such crowding aggravates tensions that accompany life amidst poverty. The quality of the relations between family members will determine a family's future. Imagine one room with ten persons living together, yelling and fighting all day long. So the children are propelled out into the streets at a young age. What do they learn in the streets? Vicious delinquency, theft, and prostitution. If the first thing in your life is contact with the street, your future will be the street, with its related risks.[2]

Cemex knows that there are marvelous business opportunities here. Sales in the Guadalajara division potentially could offset its losses during challenging times, and they could make Cemex more competitive overall. If only it could figure out a way to overcome a few minor hurdles, Guadalajara could become a significant profit center. In fact, it accounts for approximately 40 percent of cement consumption in Mexico and has the potential to be a market worth $500-600 million annually.

Cemex seeks to do "good" by these clients and by everyone else with a stake in its decisions. Listed below are the major challenges that Cemex confronts. Are they insurmountable? Consider how you might resolve some of them. In this chapter, we will introduce a process by which to examine these types of dilemmas and then we will return to these questions at the end of the chapter.

1. These purchasers are part of an informal economy. When they wish to purchase goods, they cannot pay for them outright and, yet, they do not have a regular paycheck from which the company can make deductions.
2. The social culture of this rung of the ladder does not currently foster an environment of saving. In fact, there is a culture fighting against it—"In the tradition of many poor communities, social status comes not from what you own, but what you contribute to the social life of the community. This means parties," Herbst explains. Much of their money goes to weddings and other celebrations.

(continued)

(*concluded*)

3. Because of number 2, above, there is an intense resignation about how long it would take to afford any improvements at all. On average, it currently takes four years to finish one room and 13 years to finish a small four-room house (kitchen, bathroom, bedroom and second bedroom/living area).
4. The legal status of property ownership is not always clear and documentation is not present or available with regard to assets or sources of income.
5. Finally, as in many informal economies, clients generally try to form savings groups (typically made up of women) called *tanda*. Each member of the *tanda* is supposed to contribute a small amount of money each week, such as US$10, for a specified period of time. Each week, one member of the *tanda* gets to take the entire amount. These *tandas* might be the company's saving grace since many of the women who participate in *tandas* are saving money to construct improvements on their homes. But only 10 percent actually spend the money on building materials. The *tandas* often fall apart when everyday issues arise during the course of the week, before each woman has received her share, such as the need for clothing, health care, basic shelter (as opposed to improvements), or even food.

Chapter Objectives

After reading this chapter, you will be able to:

1. Explain why ethics is important in the business environment
2. Explain the nature of business ethics as an academic discipline.
3. Distinguish the ethics of personal integrity from the ethics of social responsibility.
4. Distinguish ethical norms and values from other business-related norms and values.
5. Distinguish legal responsibilities from ethical responsibilities.
6. Explain why ethical responsibilities go beyond legal compliance.
7. Describe ethical decision making as a form of practical reasoning.

Introduction: Making the Case for Business Ethics

Even though years have passed and other scandals have occurred, we still refer to the 2001 Enron Corporation collapse as the watershed event in this century's business ethics news; since that time ethics and values have seldom strayed from the front pages of the press. Whether we are referring to government scandals such as Illinois governor Rod Blagojevich's alleged attempt to auction President Obama's senate seat to the highest bidder or to the federal bailout following the mortgage crisis, the list of leaders that have been involved with legal and ethical wrongdoing is, sadly, incredibly long. Reflect for a moment on the businesses that have been involved in scandals or, at least, in flawed decision making: Siemens, Enron, Halliburton, AIG, WorldCom, Tyco, Adelphia, Cendant, Rite Aid, Sunbeam, Waste Management, HealthSouth, Global Crossing, Arthur Andersen, Ernst & Young, Imclone, KPMG, JPMorgan, Merrill Lynch, Morgan Stanley, Bear Stearns, Fannie Mae, Countrywide Financial Corp., Citigroup Salomon Smith Barney, Marsh & McLennan, Credit Suisse First Boston, and even the New York Stock Exchange itself. Individuals implicated in ethical scandals include Kenneth Lay, Jeffrey Skilling, Andrew Fastow, Dennis Kozlowski, Bill McGuire, Bob Nardelli, John J. Rigas, Richard M. Scrushy, Martha Stewart, Samuel Waksal, Richard Grasso, and Bernard Ebbers. Beyond these well-known scandals, consumer boycotts based on allegations of unethical conduct or alliances have targeted such well-known firms as Nike, McDonald's, Carrefour, Home Depot, Chiquita Brands International, Fisher-Price, Gap, Shell Oil, Exxon-Mobile, Levi-Strauss, Donna Karen, Kmart, and Wal-Mart.

This chapter will introduce business ethics as a process of responsible decision making. Simply put, the scandals and ruin experienced by all the institutions and every one of the individuals just mentioned were brought about by *ethical failures.* If we do, indeed, reflect on those institutions and individuals, perhaps they should remind us of the often-repeated Santayana admonition, "Those who cannot remember the past are condemned to repeat it."[3] This text provides a decision-making model that, we contend, can help individuals to understand these failures and to avoid future business and personal tragedies. As an introduction to that decision-making model, this chapter reflects on the intersection of ethics and business.

Ethical decision making in business is not at all limited to the type of major corporate decisions with dramatic social consequences listed above. At some point, every worker, and certainly everyone in a management role, will be faced with an issue that will require ethical decision making. Not every decision can be covered by economic, legal, or company rules and regulations. More often than not, responsible decision making must rely on the personal values and principles of the individuals involved. Individuals will have to decide for themselves what type of person they want to be.

At other times, of course, decisions will involve significant general policy issues that affect entire organizations, as happened in all the well-known corporate scandals. The managerial role especially involves decision making that establishes organizational precedents and has organizational and social consequences. Hence, both of these types of situations—the personal and the organizational—are reflected in the title of this book: *Business Ethics: Decision making for Personal Integrity and Social Responsibility.*

As recently as the mid-1990s, articles in such major publications as *The Wall Street Journal,* the *Harvard Business Review,* and *U.S. News and World Report* questioned the legitimacy and value of teaching classes in business ethics. Few disciplines face the type of skepticism that commonly confronted courses in business ethics. Many students believed that "business ethics" was an oxymoron. Many also viewed ethics as a mixture of sentimentality and personal opinion that would interfere with the efficient functioning of business. After all, who is to identify right and wrong, and, if no law is breached, who will "punish" the "wrongdoers?" However, this approach has left business executives as one of the lowest ranked professions in terms of trust and honesty, according to a 2008 Gallup poll.[4]

Leaders realize that they can no longer afford this approach in contemporary business. The direct costs of unethical business practice are more visible today than perhaps they have ever been before. As discussed above, the first decade of the new millennium has been riddled with highly-publicized corporate scandals, the effects of which did not escape people of any social or income class. Moreover, we saw the economy begin a downward spiral into one of the largest financial crises of the last 80 years, driven significantly by questionable sub-prime mortgage lending practices at the banks, as well as the widespread trading of risky mortgage-backed securities in the markets. These lending and trading efforts encouraged bad debt to appreciate beyond levels that the market could bear. The inevitable correction caused real estate values in most markets to decline sharply, domestic credit markets to freeze, and the federal government to intervene with a rescue package.

If the key (or not so key) decision makers who contributed to the bubble bursting had acted differently, could these unfortunate consequences have been avoided? Well, suffice it to say that it is a bit of a vicious circle. Economic turmoil incites misconduct; there is an 11 percent *bump* in observed workplace misconduct during times of economic challenges. In turn, misconduct based on fraud alone causes an estimated 7 percent loss of annual revenues, equivalent to more than $1 trillion of the 2008 gross domestic product in the United States (or $70,000 for every $1 million of revenue). These ethical failures are responsible for over half of all quality costs or 5–15 percent of all operating costs (and can be the single largest quality cost item in many firms).[5]

Personal retirement accounts like 401k's, institutional investments like pension funds, federal, state, and municipal retirement funds, and major insurance companies are heavily invested in corporate stocks and bonds, as well as pooled securities of every size, shape, and order. As a result, these costs of Wall Street failures on Main Street families and businesses become larger and more noticeable by the day.

The questions today are less about *why* or *should* ethics be a part of business; they are about *which* values and principles should guide business decisions and *how* ethics should be integrated within business. (A persuasive case for *why* this shift has occurred can be found in the reading "Value Shift," by Lynn Sharp Paine.) Students unfamiliar with the basic concepts and categories of ethics will find themselves as unprepared for careers in business as students who are unfamiliar with accounting and finance. Indeed, it is fair to say that students will not be fully prepared, even within fields such as accounting, finance, human resource management, marketing, and management, unless they are familiar with the ethical issues that arise within those specific fields. (See Figure 1.1, to which we will refer again in later chapters.)

FIGURE 1.1 **In 2007, global consulting firm Kroll and *The Economist* together surveyed 892 executives worldwide and found the following results. Note that the two areas of greatest "heat" or concern are *corruption and bribery* and *information theft, loss or attack.* We will be examining these issues and the means by which to respond to these challenges throughout the text (*see chapter 7*).**

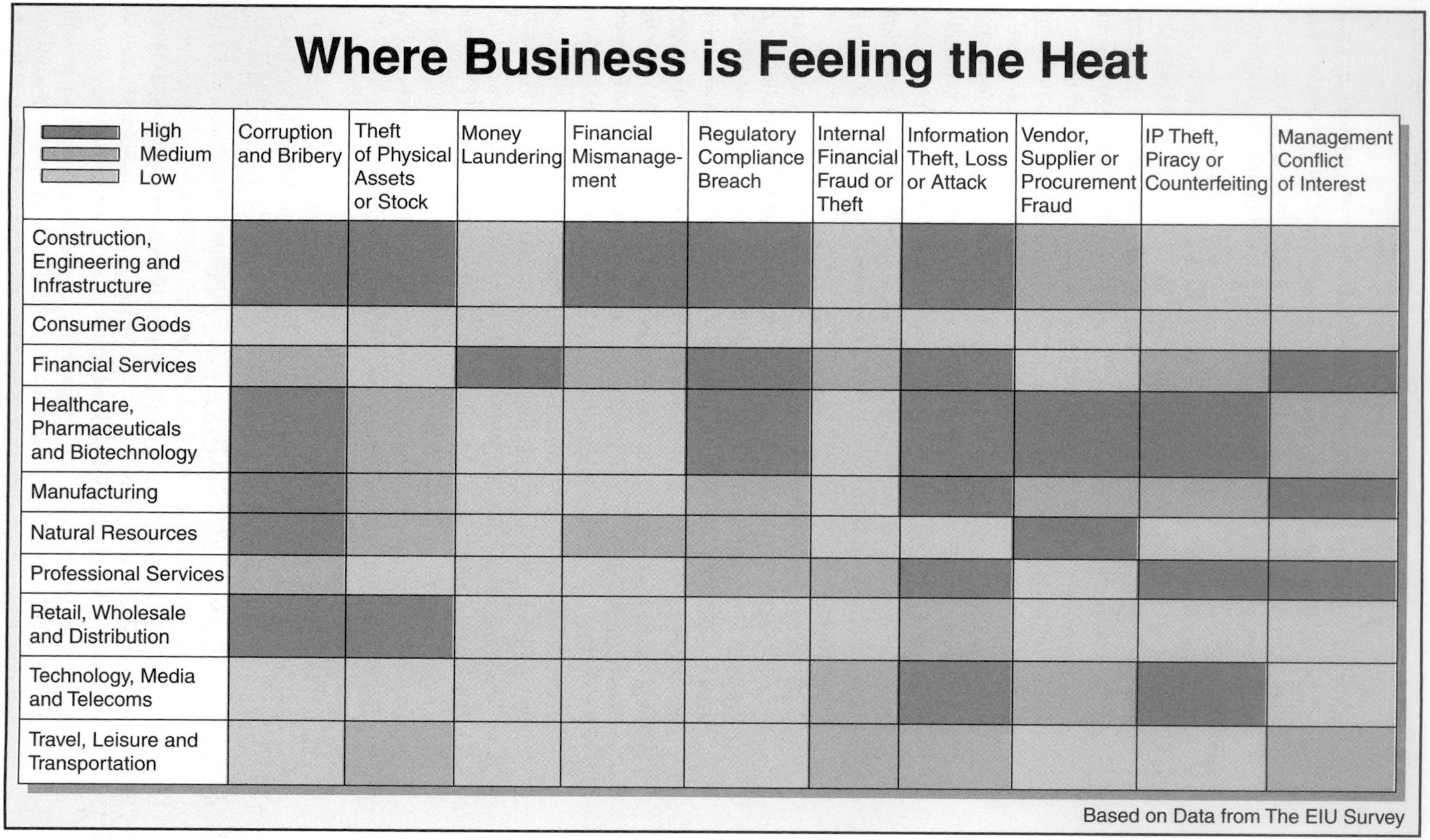

Source: Marshall, A., "Where Business is Feeling the Heat," *in* Krielstra, P., Kroll and Economist Intelligence Unit, *Global Fraud Report* (2007/2008).

1 OBJECTIVE

To understand the origins of this shift from *whether* ethics or values should play a role in business decisions to the almost frantic search for *how* most effectively (and quickly!) to do it, consider the range of people who were harmed by the collapse of Enron. Stockholders lost over $1 billion in share value. Thousands of employees lost their jobs, their retirement funds, and their health care benefits. Consumers in California suffered from energy shortages and blackouts that were caused by Enron's manipulation of the market. Hundreds of businesses that worked with Enron as suppliers suffered economic loss with the loss of a large client. Enron's accounting firm, Arthur Andersen, went out of business as a direct result. The wider Houston community was also hurt by the loss of a major employer and community benefactor. Families of employees, investors, and suppliers were also hurt. Many of the individuals directly involved have since suffered criminal and civil punishment, up to and including prison sentences for some. Indeed, it is hard to imagine anyone who was even loosely affiliated with Enron who was not harmed as a result of the ethical failings there. Multiply that harm by the dozens of other companies implicated in similar scandals to get a better idea of why ethics is no longer dismissed as irrelevant. The consequences of unethical behavior and unethical business institutions are too serious for too many people to be ignored.

This description of the consequences of the Enron collapse demonstrates the significant impact that business decisions can have on a very wide range of people. Both cases dramatically affected the lives of thousands of people: employees, stockholders, management, suppliers, customers, and surrounding communities. For better or for worse, the decisions that a business makes will affect many more people than just the decision maker. As we will discuss throughout this text, in order to sustain the firm, ethically responsible business decision making must move beyond a narrow concern with stockholders to consider the impact that decisions will have on a wide range of **stakeholders.** In a general sense, a business *stakeholder* will be anyone who affects or is affected by decisions made within the firm, for better or worse. Failure to consider these additional stakeholders will have a detrimental impacton those stakeholders, on stockholders, specifically, and on the firm's long-term sustainability as a whole. This perspective is articulated effectively by Whole Foods Supermarket's "Declaration of Interdependence."

> Satisfying all of our stakeholders and achieving our standards is our goal. One of the most important responsibilities of Whole Foods Market's leadership *is to make sure the interests, desires and needs of our various stakeholders are kept in balance.* We recognize that this is a dynamic process. It requires participation and communication by all of our stakeholders. It requires listening compassionately, thinking carefully and acting with integrity. Any conflicts must be mediated and win-win solutions found. Creating and nurturing this community of stakeholders is critical to the long-term success of our company. (Emphasis added.)[6]

Whole Foods has maintained this priority structure over a period of 10 years, during which it has performed better financially for its shareholders than *any* of

Reality Check *Why Be Ethical? Because the Law Requires It*

Today, business executives have many reasons to be concerned with the ethical standards of their organizations. Perhaps the most straightforward reason is that the law requires it, often as a minimum. In 2002, the U.S. Congress passed the Sarbanes-Oxley Act to address the wave of corporate and accounting scandals. Section 406 of that law, "Code of Ethics for Senior Financial Officers," requires that corporations have a Code of Ethics "applicable to its principal financial officer and comptroller or principal accounting officer, or persons performing similar functions." The Code must include standards that promote:

1. Honest and ethical conduct, including the ethical handling of actual or apparent conflicts of interest between personal and professional relationships.
2. Full, fair, accurate, timely, and understandable disclosure in the periodic reports required to be filed by the issuer.
3. Compliance with applicable governmental rules and regulations.

*Note that you will see "Reality Checks" throughout each chapter in the text. Slightly different from Decision Points, these boxed additions offer practical applications of the concepts discussed during that chapter segment or examples of the ways in which the concepts are implemented in "real" business decision making.

its top five competitors, returning 400 percent from 2002 to 2007, at a time when the S&P returned only 13 percent, and over 900 percent in the past ten years.[7]

The Reality Check, "Why Be Ethical? Because the Law Requires It" describes some legal requirements that have been created since the Enron fiasco. Beyond these specific legal obligations, organizational sustainability is reliant on ethical decisions in myriad ways. Unethical behavior not only creates legal risks for a business, it creates financial and marketing risks as well. Managing these risks requires managers and executives to remain vigilant about their company's ethics. It is now clearer than ever that a company can lose in the marketplace, go out of business, and its employees go to jail if no one is paying attention to the ethical standards of the firm.

Moreover, given the declining average life expectancy of firms,[8] maintaining an ethical advantage becomes a vital distinction between successful and unsuccessful firms. A firm's ethical reputation can provide a competitive edge in the marketplace with customers, suppliers, and employees. On the positive side, managing ethically can also pay significant dividends in organizational structure and efficiency. Trust, loyalty, commitment, creativity, and initiative are just some of the organizational benefits that are more likely to flourish within ethically stable and credible organizations (see the Reality Check, "Why Be Good?"). Research demonstrates that 94 percent of workers consider a firm's ethics critically important in their choice of employers. In fact, 82 percent of employees say that they would prefer a position at lower pay in a firm with ethical business practices compared to a higher paying job at a company with questionable ethics. Further, one-third of U.S. workers have walked off of a job on the basis of their ethics.[9] Alternatively, the consumer boycotts of such well-known firms

Reality Check *Why Be Good?*

The Institute for Business, Technology and Ethics suggests the following "Nine Good Reasons" to run a business ethically:

1. Litigation/indictment avoidance
2. Regulatory freedom
3. Public acceptance
4. Investor confidence
5. Supplier/partner trust
6. Customer loyalty
7. Employee performance
8. Personal pride
9. It is the right thing to do

Source: Institute for Business, Technology and Ethics, *Ethix*, no. 22 (March/April 2002), p. 11.

as Nike, McDonald's, Home Depot, Fisher-Price and Wal-Mart, mentioned previously, give even the most skeptical business leader reason to pay attention to ethics.

For business students, the need to study ethics should be as clear as the need to study the other subfields of business education. As discussed above, without this background, students simply will be unprepared for a career in contemporary business. But even for students who do not anticipate a career in business management or business administration, familiarity with business ethics is just as crucial. After all, it was not only the managers at Enron who suffered because of their ethical lapses. Our lives as employees, as consumers, and as citizens are affected by decisions made within business institutions; therefore, everyone has good reasons for being concerned with the ethics of those decision makers.

Moreover, as leaders and as emerging leaders, we need to explore how to manage the ethical behavior of others so that we can impact their decisions and encourage them to make ethical, or more ethical, decisions. Certainly, unethical behavior continues to permeate organizations today at all levels; and business decision makers—at all levels—must be equipped with the tools, the knowledge, and the skills to confront that behavior and to respond to it summarily. Just imagine the impact in terms of role modeling of this single statement by Prince Bandar Bin Sultan, in connection with allegations that he received secret and personal "commissions" of approximately $240 million each for the past ten years in connection with a defense contract between the British government and Saudi arms manufacturer, BAE Systems:

> *[T]he way I answer the corruption charges is this. In the last 30 years, . . . we have implemented a development program that was approximately, close to $400 billion worth. You could not have done all of that for less than, let's say, $350 billion. Now, if you tell me that building this whole country and spending $350 billion out of $400 billion, that we had misused or got corrupted with $50 billion, I'll tell you, 'Yes.' But I'll take that any time.*

> *But more important, who are you to tell me this? I mean, I see every time all the scandals here, or in England, or in Europe. What I'm trying to tell you is, so what? We did not invent corruption. This happened since Adam and Eve. I mean, Adam and Eve were in heaven and they had hanky-panky and they had to go down to earth. So I mean this is- this is human nature. But we are not as bad as you think!*[10]

In that case, British Prime Minister Tony Blair had originally allowed the fraud investigation to be dropped. He offered the following statement, in an effort to explain his reasons for the decision. "This investigation, if it had gone ahead, would have involved the most serious allegations in investigations being made into the Saudi royal family. My job is to give advice as to whether that is a sensible thing in circumstances where I don't believe the investigation incidentally would have led anywhere except to the complete wreckage of a vital strategic relationship for our country. . . . Quite apart from the fact that we would have lost thousands, thousands of British jobs."[11]

Some observers may look to the choices made in late 2008 and 2009 by American International Group (AIG), the world's largest insurer, as another example of poor role modeling. One can easily see the impact of those decisions on reputation. In September, 2008, AIG was on the brink of bankruptcy. There was a realistic fear that if the company went under the stability of the U.S. markets may have been in serious jeopardy. Over a five-month period, the U.S. government bailed out AIG to the tune of $152.2 billion (funded by U.S. tax dollars) in order to keep the company afloat, since AIG arguably was "too big to fail."

While that consequence alone was unfortunate, it certainly was not unethical. However, in decisions that damaged the reputations of many involved, among other charges, one month after AIG received the first round of bailout money, its executives headed to California for a weeklong retreat at an extremely luxurious hotel, with the company covering the nearly half a million dollar tab *with the bailout money.* Six months later, these same executives rewarded themselves with bonuses totaling over $100 million. Although then-President Obama (some say belatedly) derided the executives for their legally-awarded bonuses, many of the bonuses were paid nevertheless because they had been promised through employee contracts before AIG had received any bailout money for the purposes of "retaining talent."[12]

While it did not reach full congressional hearing, the House even prepared a bill that would impose a 90 percent tax on the bonuses paid to executives by AIG and other companies that were getting assistance from the government of more than $5 million. Instead, the House passed The Grayson-Himes Pay for Performance Act in April 2009, "to amend the executive compensation provisions of the Emergency Economic Stabilization Act of 2008 to prohibit unreasonable and excessive compensation and compensation not based on performance standards."[13] This bill would ban future "unreasonable and excessive" compensation at companies receiving federal bailout money. Treasury secretary Timothy Geithner would have the power to define what constitutes reasonable compensation and to review how companies give their bonuses.

The case for business ethics is clear and persuasive. Business must take ethics into account and integrate ethics into its organizational structure. Students need to study business ethics. But what does this mean? What is "*ethics,*" and what is the objective of a class in business ethics?

Business Ethics as Ethical Decision Making

As the title of this book suggests, our approach to business ethics will emphasize **ethical decision making.** No book can magically create ethically responsible people or change behavior in any direct way. But students can learn and practice responsible and accountable ways of thinking and deliberating. We assume that decisions that follow from a process of thoughtful and conscientious reasoning will be more responsible and ethical. In other words, *responsible decision making and deliberation will result in more responsible behavior.*

So what is the point of a business ethics course? On one hand, "ethics" refers to an academic discipline with a centuries-old history; we might expect knowledge about this history to be among the primary goals of a class in ethics. Thus, in an ethics course, students might be expected to learn about the great ethicists of history such as Aristotle, John Stuart Mill, and Immanuel Kant. As in many other courses, this approach to ethics would focus on the *informational content* of the class.

2 OBJECTIVE

Yet, according to some observers, ethical theories and the history of ethics is beside the point. These stakeholders, including some businesses looking to hire college graduates, business students and even some teachers themselves, expect an ethics class to address ethical *behavior,* not just information and knowledge about ethics. After all, what good is an ethics class if it does not help prevent future Enrons? For our purposes, **ethics** refers not only to an academic discipline, but to that arena of human life studied by this academic discipline, namely, *how human beings should properly live their lives.* An ethics course will not change your capacity to think, but it could stimulate your choices of what to think about.

A caution about influencing behavior within a classroom is appropriate here. Part of the hesitation about teaching ethics involves the potential for abuse; expecting teachers to influence behavior could be viewed as permission for teachers to impose their own views on students. To the contrary, many believe that teachers should remain value-neutral in the classroom and respect a student's own views. Another part of this concern is that the line between motivating students and manipulating students is a narrow one. There are many ways to influence someone's behavior, including threats, guilt, pressure, bullying, and intimidation. Some of the executives involved in the worst of the recent corporate scandals were very good at using some of these methods to motivate the people who worked for them. Presumably, none of these approaches belong in a college classroom, and certainly not in an ethical classroom.

But not all forms of influencing behavior raise such concerns. There is a major difference between manipulating someone and persuading someone, between threatening (unethical) and reasoning (more likely ethical). This textbook resolves the tension between knowledge and behavior by emphasizing ethical judgment, ethical deliberation, and ethical decision making. In line with the Aristotelian notion that "we are what we repeatedly do," we agree with those who believe that an ethics class should strive to produce more ethical *behavior* among the students who enroll. But we believe that the only academically and ethically legitimate way to achieve this objective is through careful and reasoned decision making. Our fundamental assumption is that a process of rational decision making, a process that involves careful thought and deliberation, can and will result in behavior that is more reasonable, accountable, and ethical.

Perhaps this view is not surprising after all. Consider any course within a business school curriculum. Few would dispute that a management course aims to create better managers. We would judge as a failure any finance or accounting course that denied a connection between the course material and financial or accounting practice. Every course in a business school assumes a connection between what is taught in the classroom and appropriate business behavior. Classes in management, accounting, finance, and marketing all aim to influence students' behavior. We assume that the knowledge and reasoning skills learned in the classroom will lead to better decision making and, therefore, better behavior within a business context. A business ethics class follows this same approach.

While few teachers think that it is our role to *tell* students the right answers and to *proclaim* what students ought to think and how they ought to live, still fewer think that there should be no connection between knowledge and behavior. Our role should not be to preach ethical dogma to a passive audience, but instead to treat students as active learners and to engage them in an active process of thinking, questioning, and deliberating. Taking Socrates as our model, philosophical ethics rejects the view that passive obedience to authority or the simple acceptance of customary norms is an adequate ethical perspective. Teaching ethics must, in this view, challenge students to *think for themselves.*

It is this autonomy of thought that encouraged us to include the reading by Binyavanga Wainaina, "How to Write about Africa." Wainaina's article is stunning in its ability to force us to look at the way in which we *normally* discuss developing countries, as well as its refusal to offer direction as to how we *should* discuss these subjects. Nowhere in this reading are you going to find the "right" answer. The article instead accentuates the stereotypes or, at least, generalizations that we commonly use and leaves it to the reader to create a more ethical alternative. The decision-making model that will be presented in the next chapter will offer guidance on the process of ethical analysis, deliberation, and reasoning that should provide some assistance in this type of independent and accountable decision making.

Business Ethics as Personal Integrity and Social Responsibility

Another element of our environment that impacts our ethical decision making and behavior involves the influence of social circumstances. An individual may have carefully thought through a situation and decided what is right, and then may be motivated to act accordingly. But the corporate or social context surrounding the individual may create serious barriers to such behavior. As individuals, we need to recognize that our social environment will greatly influence the range of options that are open to us and can significantly influence our behavior. People who are otherwise quite decent can, under the wrong circumstances, engage in unethical behavior while less ethically-motivated individuals can, in the right circumstances, do the "right thing." Business leaders, therefore, have a responsibility for the business environment that they create; we shall later refer to this environment as the "corporate culture." The environment can, therefore, strongly encourage or discourage ethical behavior. Ethical business leadership is precisely this skill: to create the circumstances within which good people are able to do good, and bad people are prevented from doing bad.

Again, the Enron case provides an example. Sherron Watkins, an Enron vice president, seemed to understand fully the corruption and deception that was occurring within the company; and she took some small steps to address the problems within the Enron environment. But when it became clear that her boss might use her concerns against her, she backed off. The same circumstances were involved in connection with some of the Arthur Andersen auditors. When some individuals raised concerns about Enron's accounting practices, their supervisors pointed out that the $100 million annual revenues generated by the Enron account provided good reason to back off. The "Sherron Watkins" Decision Point exemplifies the culture present at Enron during the heat of its downfall.

3 OBJECTIVE

At its most basic level, ethics is concerned with how we act and how we live our lives. Ethics involves what is perhaps the most monumental question any human being can ask: *How should we live?* Ethics is, in this sense, *practical,* having to do with how we act, choose, behave, and do things. Philosophers often emphasize that ethics is **normative,** which means that it deals with our reasoning about how we *should* act. Social sciences, such as psychology and sociology, also examine human decision making and actions; but these sciences are **descriptive** rather than normative. When we say that they are descriptive, we refer to the fact that they provide an account of how and why people *do* act the way they do—they describe; as a normative discipline, ethics seeks an account of how and why people *should* act a certain way, rather than how they *do* act.

How should we live? This fundamental question of ethics can be interpreted in two ways. "We" can mean each one of us individually, or it might mean all of us collectively. In the first sense, this is a question about how I should live my life, how I should act, what I should do, and what kind of person I should be. This meaning of ethics is based on our value structures, defined by our moral systems; and, therefore, it is sometimes referred to as **morality.** It is the aspect of ethics

Decision Point — *Sherron Watkins*

Following is a portion of a memo that Sherron Watkins, an Enron vice president, sent to CEO Kenneth Lay as the Enron scandal began to unfold. As a result of this memo, Watkins became infamous as the Enron "whistleblower."

> Has Enron become a risky place to work? For those of us who didn't get rich over the last few years, can we afford to stay? Skilling's [former Enron CEO Jeffrey Skilling] abrupt departure will raise suspicions of accounting improprieties and valuation issues. . . . The spotlight will be on us, the market just can't accept that Skilling is leaving his dream job. . . . It sure looks to the layman on the street that we are hiding losses in a related company and will compensate that company with Enron stock in the future. . . .
>
> I am incredibly nervous that we will implode in a wave of accounting scandals. My eight years of Enron work history will be worth nothing on my résumé, the business world will consider the past successes as nothing but an elaborate accounting hoax. Skilling is resigning now for "personal reasons" but I would think he wasn't having fun, looked down the road and knew this stuff was unfixable and would rather abandon ship now than resign in shame in two years.
>
> Is there a way our accounting gurus can unwind these deals now? I have thought and thought about a way to do this, but I keep bumping into one big problem—we booked the Condor and Raptor deals in 1999 and 2000, we enjoyed wonderfully high stock price, many executives sold stock, we then try and reverse or fix the deals in 2001, and it's a bit like robbing the bank in one year and trying to pay it back two years later. Nice try, but investors were hurt, they bought at $70 and $80 a share looking for $120 a share and now they're at $38 or worse. We are under too much scrutiny and there are probably one or two disgruntled "redeployed" employees who know enough about the "funny" accounting to get us in trouble. . . . I realize that we have had a lot of smart people looking at this and a lot of accountants including AA & Co. [Arthur Andersen] have blessed the accounting treatment. None of that will protect Enron if these transactions are ever disclosed in the bright light of day. (Please review the late 90's problems of Waste Management (news/quote)—where AA paid $130 million plus in litigation re questionable accounting practices.) . . .
>
> I firmly believe that executive management of the company must . . . decide one of two courses of action: 1. The probability of discovery is low enough and the estimated damage too great; therefore we find a way to quietly and quickly reverse, unwind, write down these positions/transactions. 2. The probability of discovery is too great, the estimated damages to the company too great; therefore, we must quantify, develop damage containment plans and disclose. . . . I have heard one manager-level employee from the principal investments group say, "I know it would be devastating to all of us, but I wish we would get caught. We're such a crooked company." These people know and see a lot.[14]

After the collapse of Enron, Watkins was featured on the cover of *Time* magazine and honored as a corporate whistleblower, despite the fact that she never shared these concerns with anyone other than Kenneth Lay. Yet, it surely took a great deal of courage within the Enron culture even to voice (write) what she wrote above, especially since no one else dared to mention it. How do we reach a judgment about Watkins' actions in this situation?

(*continued*)

(*concluded*)

- What facts would you want to know before making a judgment about Watkins?
- What ethical issues does this situation raise?
- Besides Kenneth Lay, who else might have had an interest in hearing from Watkins? Who else might have had a right to be informed? Did Watkins have a responsibility to anyone other than Lay?
- Other than her informing Lay, what other alternatives might have been open to Watkins?
- What might the consequences of each of these alternatives have been?
- From this section of the memo, how would you characterize Watkins' motivation? What factors seem to have motivated her to act?
- If you were Ken Lay and had received the memo, what options for next steps might you have perceived? Why might you have chosen one option over another?
- Do you think Watkins should have taken her concerns beyond Kenneth Lay to outside legal authorities?

that we refer to by the phrase **"personal integrity."** There will be many times within a business setting where an individual will need to step back and ask: What should I do? How should I act? If morals refer to the underlying values on which our decisions are based, ethics refers to the applications of those morals to the decisions themselves. So, an individual could have a moral value of honesty, which, when applied to her or his decisions, results in a refusal to lie on an expense report. We shall return to this distinction in just a moment.

In the second sense, "How should we live?" refers to how we live together in a community. This is a question about how a society and social institutions, such as corporations, ought to be structured and about how we ought to live together. This area is sometimes referred to as **social ethics** and it raises questions of justice, public policy, law, civic virtues, organizational structure, and political philosophy. In this sense, business ethics is concerned with how business institutions ought to be structured, about whether they have a responsibility to the greater society (corporate social responsibility or CSR), and about making decisions that will impact many people other than the individual decision maker. This aspect of business ethics asks us to examine business institutions from a social rather than from an individual perspective. We refer to this broader social aspect of ethics as decision making for social responsibility.

In essence, managerial decision making will always involve both of these aspects of ethics. Each decision that a business manager makes involves not only a personal decision, but also a decision on behalf of, and in the name of, an organization that exists within a particular social, legal, and political environment. Thus, our book's title makes reference to both aspects of business ethics. Within a business setting, individuals will constantly be asked to make decisions affecting both their own personal integrity and their social responsibilities.

Decision Point *Management and Ethics*

Imagine that you are examining this chapter's opening scenario in one of your classes on Organizational Behavior or Managerial Finance. What advice would you offer to Cemex? What judgment would you make about this case from a financial perspective? After offering your analysis and recommendations, reflect on your own thinking and describe what values underlie those recommendations.

- What facts would help you make your decision?
- Does the scenario raise values that are particular to managers?
- What stakeholders should be involved in your advice?
- What values do you rely on in offering your advice?

Expressed in terms of how we should live, the major reason to study ethics becomes clear. Whether we explicitly *examine* these questions, each and every one of us *answers* them every day through our behaviors in the course of living our lives. Whatever decisions business managers make, they will have taken a stand on ethical issues, at least implicitly. The actions each one of us takes and the lives we lead give very practical and unavoidable answers to fundamental ethical questions. We therefore make a very real choice as to whether we answer them deliberately or unconsciously. Philosophical ethics merely asks us to step back from these implicit everyday decisions to examine and evaluate them. Thus, Socrates gave the philosophical answer to why you should study ethics over 2000 years ago: "The unexamined life is not worth living."

To distinguish ethics from other practical decisions faced within business, consider two approaches to the Malden Mills scenario in the Decision Point, "Loyalty after a Crisis: Should Aaron Feuerstein Rebuild and Pay His Employees in the Meantime." This case could just as well be examined in a management, human resources, or organizational behavior class as in an ethics class. The more social-scientific approach common in management or business administration classes would examine the situation and the decision by exploring the factors that led to one decision rather than another or by asking why the manager acted in the way that he did.

A second approach to Malden Mills, from the perspective of ethics, steps back from the facts of the situation to ask what *should* the manager do, what *rights and responsibilities* are involved? What advice *ought* Feuerstein's tax accountant or human resource manager offer? What *good* will come from this situation? Is Feuerstein being *fair, just, virtuous, kind, loyal, trustworthy?* This normative approach to business is at the center of business ethics. Ethical decision making involves the basic categories, concepts, and language of ethics: *shoulds, oughts, rights* and *responsibilities, goodness, fairness, justice, virtue, kindness, loyalty, trustworthiness,* and *honesty.* For a much more detailed examination of Aaron Feuerstein's decision surrounding Malden Mills, consider Penelope Washbourne's reading, "An Ethical Hero or a Failed Businessman? The Malden Mills Case Revisited"

Decision Point *Loyalty after a Crisis: Should Aaron Feuerstein Rebuild and Pay His Employees in the Meantime?*

During the early evening hours of December 11, 1995, a fire broke out in a textile mill in Lawrence, Massachusetts. By morning, the fire had destroyed most of Malden Mills, the manufacturer of Polartec fabric. The fire seemed a disaster to the company, its employees, its customers, and the surrounding communities.

Malden Mills was a family-owned business, founded in 1906 and run by the founder's grandson Aaron Feuerstein. Polartec is a high-quality fabric well known for its use in the outdoor apparel featured by such popular companies as L.L. Bean, Lands' End, REI, J. Crew, and Eddie Bauer. The disaster promised many headaches for Malden Mills and for the numerous businesses that depended on its products.

Unfortunately, the fire also was a disaster for an entire community. The towns surrounding the Malden Mills plant had originally been home to textile manufacturing. The industry effectively had collapsed during the middle decades of the twentieth century when outdated factories and increasing labor costs led many companies to abandon the area and relocate, first to the nonunionized South, and later to foreign countries such as Mexico and Taiwan. As happened in many northern manufacturing towns, the loss of major industries, along with their jobs and tax base, began a long period of economic decline from which many have never recovered. Malden Mills was the last major textile manufacturer in town, and with 2,400 employees it supplied the economic lifeblood for the surrounding communities. With both its payroll and taxes, Malden Mills contributed approximately $100 million a year into the local economy.

As CEO and President, Aaron Feuerstein faced some major decisions. He could have used the fire as an opportunity to follow his local competitors and relocate to a more economically attractive area. He certainly could have found a location with lower taxes and cheaper labor and, thus, maximizing his earning potential. He could have simply taken the insurance money and decided not to reopen at all. Instead, as the fire was still smoldering, Feuerstein pledged to rebuild his plant at the same location and keep the jobs in the local community. But even more surprising, he promised to continue paying his employees and to extend their medical coverage until they could come back to work.

- What do you believe motivated Feuerstein? What do you think of Feuerstein's decision? What would you have done had you been in his position?
- What facts would be helpful as you make your judgments about Feuerstein?
- How many different values are involved in this situation? How would you describe Feuerstein, just knowing this story? How would you describe his actions after the fire? Can you describe the man and his actions without using ethical or evaluative words?
- Whose interests should Feuerstein consider in making this decision? How many different people were affected by the fire and the decision?
- What other options were available for Feuerstein? How would these alternatives have affected the other people involved?
- Were Feuerstein's actions charitable, or was this something he had a duty or obligation to do? What is the difference between acts of charity and obligatory acts?

To say that ethics is a *normative* discipline is to say that it deals with **norms:** those standards of appropriate and proper (or "normal") behavior. Norms establish the guidelines or standards for determining what we should do, how we should act, what type of person we should be. Another way of expressing this point is to say that norms appeal to certain values that would be promoted or attained by acting in a certain way. Normative disciplines presuppose some underlying values.

4 OBJECTIVE

To say that ethics is a normative discipline is not to say that all normative disciplines involve the study or discipline of ethics. After all, business management and business administration are also normative, are they not? Are there not norms for business managers that presuppose a set of business values? One could add accounting and auditing to this list, as well as economics, finance, politics, and the law. Each of these disciplines appeals to a set of values to establish the norms of appropriate behavior within each field.

These examples suggest that there are many different types of norms and values. Returning to our distinction between values and ethics, we can think of **values** as the underlying beliefs that cause us to act or to decide one way rather than another. Thus, the value that I place on an education *leads me to make the decision* to study rather than play video games. I believe that education is more worthy, or valuable, than playing games. I make the decision to spend my money on groceries rather than on a vacation because I value food more than relaxation. A company's core values, for example, are those beliefs and principles that provide the ultimate guide to its decision making.

Understood in this way, many different types of values can be recognized: financial, religious, legal, historical, nutritional, political, scientific, and aesthetic. Individuals can have their own personal values and, importantly, institutions also have values. Talk of a corporation's "culture" is a way of saying that a corporation has a set of identifiable values that establish the expectations for what is "normal" within that firm. These norms guide employees, implicitly more often than not, to behave in ways that the firm values and finds worthy. One important implication of this guidance, of course, is that an individual's or a corporation's set of values may lead to either *ethical* or *unethical* result. The corporate culture at Enron, for example, seems to have been committed to pushing the envelope of legality as far as possible in order to get away with as much as possible in pursuit of as much money as possible. Values? Yes. Ethical values? No.

One way to distinguish these various types of values is in terms of the ends they serve. Financial values serve monetary ends; religious values serve spiritual ends; aesthetic values serve the end of beauty; legal values serve law, order, and justice, and so forth. Different types of values are distinguished by the various ends served by those acts and choices. How are ethical values to be distinguished from these other types of values? What ends do ethics serve?

Values, in general, were earlier described as those beliefs that incline us to act or choose in one way rather than another. Consider again the harms attributed to the ethical failures at Enron. Thousands of innocent people were hurt by the decisions made by some individuals seeking their own financial and egotistical aggrandizement. This example reveals two important elements of **ethical values.**

First, ethical values serve the ends of human well-being. Acts and decisions that seek to promote human welfare are acts and decisions based on ethical values. Controversy may arise when we try to define human well-being; but we can start with some general observations. Happiness certainly is a part of it, as are respect, dignity, integrity, and meaning. Freedom and autonomy surely seem to be necessary elements of human well-being, as are companionship and health.

Second, the well-being promoted by ethical values is not a personal and selfish well-being. After all, the Enron scandal resulted from many individuals seeking to promote their own well-being. Ethics requires that the promotion of human well-being be done impartially. From the perspective of ethics, no one person's welfare is more worthy than any other's. Ethical acts and choices should be acceptable and reasonable from all relevant points of view. Thus, we can offer an initial characterization of ethics and ethical values. *Ethical values are those beliefs and principles that impartially promote human well-being.*

Ethics and the Law

5 OBJECTIVE

Any discussion of norms and standards of proper behavior would be incomplete without considering the law. Deciding what one *should do* in business situations often requires reflection on what the law requires, expects, or permits. The law provides an important guide to ethical decision making, and this text will integrate legal considerations throughout. But legal norms and ethical norms are not identical, nor do they always agree. Some ethical requirements, such as treating one's employees with respect, are not legally required, though they may be ethically warranted. Conversely, some actions that may be legally permitted, such as firing an employee for no reason, would fail many ethical standards.

A commonly accepted view, perhaps more common prior to the scandals of recent years than after, holds that a business fulfills its social responsibility simply by obeying the law. From this perspective, an ethically responsible business decision is merely one that complies with the law; there is no responsibility to do anything further. Individual businesses may decide to go beyond the legal minimum, such as when a business supports the local arts, but these choices are voluntary. A good deal of management literature on corporate social responsibility centers on this approach, contending that ethics requires obedience to the law; anything beyond that is a matter of corporate philanthropy and charity, something praiseworthy and allowed, but not required.

Over the last decade, many corporations have established ethics programs and have hired ethics officers who are charged with managing corporate ethics programs. Ethics officers do a great deal of good and effective work; but it is fair to say that much of their work focuses on compliance issues. Of course, the environment varies considerably company to company and industry to industry (see Reality Check, "Bribe Payers Index"). The Sarbanes-Oxley Act created a dramatic and vast new layer of legal compliance issues. But is compliance with the law all that is required to behave ethically? Though we will address this issue in greater detail in chapter 5, let us briefly explore at this point several persuasive reasons why legal compliance is insufficient, in order to move forward to our discussion of ethics as perhaps a more effective guidepost for decision making. See also Reality Check, "Ethics: Essential to Governance."

1. Holding that obedience to the law is sufficient to fulfill one's ethical duties begs the question of whether the law, itself, is ethical. Dramatic examples from history, including Nazi Germany and apartheid in South Africa, demonstrate that one's ethical responsibility may run counter to the law. On a more practical level, this question can have significant implications in a global economy in which businesses operate in countries with legal systems different from those of their home country. For instance, some countries permit discrimination on the basis of gender; but businesses that choose to adopt such practices remain ethically accountable to their stakeholders for those decisions. From the perspective of ethics, a business does not forgo its ethical responsibilities based on obedience to the law.
2. Societies that value individual freedom will be reluctant to legally require more than just an ethical minimum. Such liberal societies will seek legally to prohibit the most serious ethical harms; although they will not legally require acts of charity, common decency, and personal integrity that may otherwise constitute the social fabric of a developed culture. The law can be an efficient mechanism to prevent serious harms; but it is not very effective at promoting "goods." Even if it were, the cost in human freedom of legally requiring such things as personal integrity would be extremely high. What would a society be like if it legally required parents to love their children, or even had a law that prohibited lying under all circumstances?
3. On a more practical level, telling business that its ethical responsibilities end with obedience to the law is just inviting more legal regulation. Consider the difficulty of trying to create laws to cover each and every possible business challenge; the task would require such specificity that the number of regulated areas would become unmanageable. Additionally, it was the failure of personal ethics among such companies as Enron and WorldCom, after all, that led to the creation of the Sarbanes-Oxley Act and many other legal reforms. If business restricts its ethical responsibilities to obedience to the law, it should not be surprised to find a new wave of government regulations that require what were formerly voluntary actions.
4. The law cannot possibly anticipate every new dilemma that businesses might face; so, often, there may not be a regulation for the particular dilemma that confronts a business leader. For example, when workplace e-mail was in its infancy, laws regarding who actually owned the e-mail transmissions (the employee or the employer) were not yet in place. As a result, one had no choice but to rely on the ethical decision-making processes of those in power to respect the appropriate boundaries of employee privacy while also adequately managing the workplace (see chapter 7 for a more complete discussion of the legal implications of workplace monitoring). When new quandaries arise, one must be able to rely on ethics since the law might not yet—or might never—provide a solution.

Reality Check *Bribe Payers Index*

Transparency International 2008 Bribe Payers Index (BPI)
The Business Sector Corruption Scorecard
In which business sectors do companies have the highest propensity to bribe government officials?

	Sector	**Score**
0.1	Public works contracts & construction	5.2
▲	Real estate & property development	5.7
worst	Oil & gas	5.9
	Heavy manufacturing	6.0
	Mining	6.0
	Pharmaceutical & medical care	6.2
	Utilities	6.3
	Civilian aerospace	6.4
	Power generation & transmission	6.4
	Forestry	6.5
	Telecommunications & equipment	6.6
	Transportation & storage	6.6
	Arms and defence	6.7
	Hotels, Restaurant & Leisure	6.7
	Agriculture	6.9
	Light manufacturing	6.9
best	Information technology (computers & software)	7.0
▼	Fisheries	7.1
10.0	Banking & finance	7.1

The *Bribe Payers Survey* was carried out on Transparency International's behalf by Gallup International

NOTES:

The countries and territories included in the index are leading international or regional exporting nations, whose combined global exports of goods and services and outflows of foreign direct investment represented 75 percent of the world total in 2006[15]. Australia, Brazil, India and South Africa were included due to their position as major regional trading powers.

The 2008 BPI is derived from a survey of senior business executives in 26 countries: Argentina, Brazil, Chile, Czech Republic, Egypt, France, Germany, Ghana, Hungary, India, Indonesia, Japan, Malaysia, Mexico, Morocco, Nigeria, Pakistan, Philippines, Poland, Russian Federation, Senegal, Singapore, South Africa, South Korea, United Kingdom and the United States.

These countries were selected on the basis of their trade and Foreign Direct Investment (FDI)

(*continued*)

flows, using data from United Nations Conference on Trade and Development (UNCTAD). The combined global imports of goods and services and inflows of foreign direct investment of the 26 countries represented 54 percent of the world total in 2006.

The 2008 *Bribe Payers Index* is based on responses to a survey of senior business executives, the 2008 *Bribe Payers Survey,* designed and commissioned by Transparency International. The *Bribe Payers Survey* covered a wide range of questions about the nature, scope and impact of bribery and corruption. Highlights from the survey can be found in an accompanying report to the release of the 2008 BPI: *Transparency International Bribe Payers Index 2008: Overview Report:* http://www.transparency.org/policy_research/surveys_indices/bpi

The *Bribe Payers Survey* was carried out on Transparency International's behalf by Gallup International between 5 August and 29 October 2008. Gallup International was responsible for the overall implementation of the survey and the data quality control process. It relied on a network of partner institutes to carry out the survey locally.

A total of 19 sectors have been evaluated in the *Bribe Payers Survey.* For the sectoral rankings on public sector bribery and on state capture, respondents were asked their views on up to five sectors with which they had business relationships. As with the BPI, these sectoral rankings therefore draw on the informed perceptions of senior business executives.

Transparency International is funded by various governmental agencies, international foundations and corporations. Ernst & Young, the Federal Ministry of Economic Cooperation and Development in Germany and the Norwegian Agency for Development Cooperation (NORAD) provided financial support for the *Bribe Payers Survey* and the 2008 BPI. In addition, since 2006, Transparency International's corruption measurement instruments have been supported by Ernst & Young. TI does not endorse a company's policies by accepting its financial support, and does not involve any of its supporters in the management of its projects. For details on Transparency International's sources of funding, please see http://www.transparency.org/support_us

A detailed analysis of the methodologies used to develop the BPI can be found in *Transparency International 2008 Bribe Payers Index: Overview Report:* http://www.transparency.org/policy_research/surveys_indices/bpi

United Nations Conference on Trade and Development (UNCTAD) "Handbook of Statistics 2008". http://www.unctad.org/Templates/Page.asp?intItemID=1890&lang=1

This survey company was selected by TI through a competitive public tendering process.

United Nations Conference on Trade and Development (UNCTAD) "Handbook of Statistics 2008". http://www.unctad.org/Templates/Page.asp?intItemID=1890&lang=1

Posted 12/11/2008. Reprinted with permission.

5. Finally, the perspective that compliance is enough relies on a misleading understanding of law. To say that all a business needs to do is obey the law suggests that laws are clear-cut, unambiguous rules that can be easily applied. This rule model of law is very common; but it is not quite accurate. If the law was clear and unambiguous, there would not be much of a role for lawyers and courts.

6 OBJECTIVE

Consider one law that has had a significant impact on business decision making: the Americans with Disabilities Act (ADA). This law requires employers to make reasonable accommodations for employees with disabilities. But what counts as a disability and what would be considered a "reasonable" accommodation? Over the years, claims have been made that relevant disabilities include obesity, depression, dyslexia, arthritis, hearing loss, high blood pressure, facial

Reality Check *Ethics: Essential to Governance*

In 2003, Deloitte polled 5,000 directors of the top 4,000 publicly-traded companies and reported that 98 percent believed that an ethics and compliance program was an *essential* part of corporate governance. Over 80 percent had developed formal codes of ethics beyond those required by Sarbanes-Oxley, and over 90 percent included statements concerning the company's obligations to employees, shareholders, suppliers, customers, and the community at large in their corporate code of ethics.

Clearly, ethics has gone mainstream. Further, corporate leaders have come to recognize that their responsibilities are much wider than previously thought. In practice, if not yet in theory, corporate America has adopted the stakeholder model of corporate social responsibility. Contemporary business now takes seriously its ethical responsibilities to a variety of stakeholders other than its shareholders.

That being said, does the authoring and distribution of a formal code of ethics directly translate into improvements in ethical decision making and corporate culture? In this same survey, fewer than 75 percent of responding companies which have a formal code said they formally checked adherence and fewer than 68 percent provided training on employee responsibilities contained in their code of ethics. Corporate leaders have obviously come to recognize that their responsibilities are much wider than previously thought. Quantifying the benefit of the resulting ethically-driven initiatives and driving continuous improvement represents the next step.

Further, a survey published in 2008 by Deloitte presents a curious detail. Notwithstanding the evident attention paid to ethics *stateside* by these organizations, less than one-third of firms polled are increasing internal controls to abate violations in connection with foreign corruption charges. The Foreign Corrupt Practices Act makes it a federal criminal offense for any company or individual doing business in the United States to offer, pay, or authorize a bribe to a foreign government official to gain some form of business advantage.

"As more U.S. companies seek to expand into developing foreign markets—many of which have spotty reputations for corruption—the need for effective anti-corruption programs and controls to prevent and detect potential violations is critical," warns Ed Rial, leader of Deloitte's FCPA Consulting practice. Rial recommends the following practices to prevent and detect FCPA violations:

- **Find out where payments are going.** Payments are typically routed through third parties or "front" organizations created by the funds' ultimate recipients.
- **Be wary of acquisition or partnership targets** that do not have effective anti-corruption compliance programs. Even if the target is not subject to the FCPA, anti-corruption programs are staples of good corporate governance and a strong ethical culture.
- **Do not rely on off-the-shelf FCPA products alone.** Multi-national companies may benefit from a tailored system to identify areas of risk and monitor them through consistent testing of controls and procedures.
- **Do not assume that some industries are safer than others.** While the defense and energy industries have a higher perceived risk of corruption, cases have been brought against companies in all sectors.

Sources: Mistretta, L. "Deloitte Poll: Less Than One-Third Of Companies Are Increasing Internal Controls To Prevent FCPA Violations," *Press Release* (Apr. 17, 2008) http://www.deloitte.com/dtt/press_release/0,1014,sid%253D2281%2526cid%253D202074,00.html; "Business Ethics and Compliance in the Sarbanes-Oxley Era," A Survey by Deloitte and *Corporate Board Member* Magazine, July 2003 (www.deloitte.com/dtt/cda/doc/content/ethicsCompliance_f.pdf).

scars, and the fear of heights. Whether such conditions are covered under the ADA depends on a number of factors, including the severity of the illness and the effect it has on the employee's ability to work, among others. Imagine that you are a corporate human resource manager and an employee asks you to reasonably accommodate his allergy. How would you decide whether allergies constitute a disability under the ADA?

In fact, the legal answer remains ambiguous. The law offers general rules that find some clarity through cases decided by the courts. Most of the laws that concern business are based on past cases that establish legal precedents. Each precedent applies general rules to the specific circumstances of an individual case. In most business situations, asking "Is this legal?" is really asking "Are these circumstances similar enough to past cases that the conclusions reached in those cases will also apply here?" Since there will always be some differences between cases, the question will always remain somewhat open. Thus, there is no unambiguous answer for the conscientious business manager who wishes only to obey the law. There are few situations where a decision maker can simply find the applicable rule, apply it to the situation, and deduce an answer from it.

Without trying to disparage the profession, but merely to demonstrate the above ambiguity (especially since one of the authors has a legal background!), it is worth remembering that many of the people involved in the wave of recent corporate scandals were lawyers. In the Enron case, for example, corporate attorneys and accountants were encouraged to "push the envelope" of what was legal. Especially in civil law (as opposed to criminal law), where much of the law is established by past precedent, as described above, there is always room for ambiguity in applying the law. Further, in civil law there is a real sense that one has not done anything illegal unless and until a court decides that one has violated a law. This means that if no one files a lawsuit to challenge an action it is *perceived as* legal.

If moral behavior were simply following rules, we could program a computer to be moral.

Samuel P. Ginder

As some theories of corporate social responsibility suggest, if a corporate manager is told that she has a responsibility to maximize profits within the law, a competent manager will go to her corporate attorneys and tax accountants to ask what the law allows. A responsible attorney or accountant will advise how far she can reasonably go before it would obviously be illegal. In this situation, the question is whether a manager has a *responsibility* to "push the envelope" of legality in pursuit of profits.

Most of the cases of corporate scandal mentioned at the start of this chapter involved attorneys and accountants who advised their clients or bosses that what they were doing could be defended in court. The off-book partnerships that were at the heart of the collapse of Enron and Arthur Andersen were designed with the advice of attorneys who thought that, if challenged, they had at least a reasonable chance of winning in court. In the business environment, this strategy falls within the purview of organizational **risk assessment,** defined as "a process . . . to identify potential events that may affect the entity, and manage risk to be within its risk appetite, to provide reasonable assurance regarding the achievement of entity objectives."[16] Accordingly, the decision to "push the envelope" becomes a balance of risk assessment, cost-benefit analysis, and ethics—what is the corporation willing to do, *willing to risk?* Using this model, decision makers might include in their assessment before taking action:

- the likelihood of being challenged in court
- the likelihood of losing the case
- the likelihood of settling for financial damages
- a comparison of those costs
- the financial benefits of taking the action
- the ethical implication of the options available

After action is taken, the responsibility of decision makers is not relieved, of course. The Conference Board suggests that the ongoing assessment and review process might have a greater focus on the final element the ethical implications—because it could involve:

- independent monitoring of whistleblowing or help-line information systems;
- issuing risk assessment reports;
- benchmarking for future activities; and
- modifying programs based on experience.[17]

Because the law is ambiguous, since in many cases it simply is not clear what the law requires, there is little certainty with regard to many of the above factors. Therefore, business managers will often face decisions that will challenge their ethical judgments. To suggest otherwise simply presents a false picture of corporate reality. Thus, even those business people who are committed to strictly obeying the law will be confronted on a regular basis by the fundamental ethical questions: What should I do? How should I live?

As suggested previously, whether we step back and explicitly ask these questions, each of us implicitly answers them every time we make a decision about how to act. Responsible decision making requires that we *do* step back and reflect upon them, and then consciously choose the values by which we make decisions. No doubt, this is a daunting task, even for experienced, seasoned leaders. Fortunately, we are not alone in meeting this challenge. The history of ethics includes the history of how some of the most insightful human beings have sought to answer these questions. Before turning to the range of ethical challenges awaiting each of us in the world of business, we will review some of the major traditions in ethics. Chapter 3 provides an introductory survey of several major ethical traditions that have much to offer in business settings.

Ethics as Practical Reason

7 OBJECTIVE

In a previous section, ethics was described as *practical* and *normative,* having to do with our actions, choices, decisions, and *reasoning* about how we should act. Ethics is therefore a vital element of **practical reasoning**—reasoning about what we should do—and is distinguished from **theoretical reasoning,** which is reasoning about what we should *believe.* This book's perspective on ethical decision making is squarely within this understanding of ethics' role as a part of practical reason.

Recall the Malden Mills case from an earlier Decision Point, "Loyalty after a Crisis." On the surface it provides a clear, if extreme, example of a business leader who was willing to make significant financial sacrifices for the well-being of his employees and community. Aaron Feuerstein could have made many other decisions that would have been financially beneficial, although at a great costs to employees and the surrounding towns. To many people, he was a true hero.

Yet, the case eventually became more complex. One important fact is that Malden Mills was privately owned. Had Feuerstein been CEO of a publicly-traded corporation, his responsibilities would have been significantly different. Because of this fact, some observers describe Feuerstein's decisions as a simple case of personal generosity, but not a helpful model for other corporate executives. As it was, Malden Mills was unable to recover financially from the losses associated with both the fire and Feuerstein's decisions and eventually entered bankruptcy. Critics claim that this fact demonstrates the real costs of such generosity.

Theoretical reason is the pursuit of truth, which is the highest standard for what we should believe. According to this tradition, science is the great arbiter of truth. Science provides the methods and procedures for determining what is true. Thus, the scientific method can be thought of as the answer to the fundamental questions of theoretical reason: What should we believe? So the question arises, is there a comparable methodology or procedure for deciding what we should do and how we should act?

The simple answer is that there is no single methodology that can in every situation provide one clear and unequivocal answer to that question. But there are guidelines that can provide direction and criteria for decisions that are more or less reasonable and responsible. We suggest that the traditions and theories of philosophical ethics can be thought of in just this way. Over thousands of years of thinking about the fundamental questions of how human beings should live, philosophers have developed and refined a variety of approaches to these ethical questions. These traditions, or what are often referred to as ethical theories, explain and defend various norms, standards, values, and principles that contribute to responsible ethical decision making. Ethical theories are patterns of thinking, or methodologies, to help us decide what to do.

The following chapter will introduce a model for making ethically responsible decisions. This can be considered as a model of practical reasoning in the sense that, if you walk through these steps in making a decision about what to do, you

Opening Decision Point Revisited

The Meaning of "Good"

In order to meet the needs of its multiple stakeholders, Cemex had a number of barriers to overcome, some of which are enumerated in the opening scenario. But it persevered, and in an effort both to *do good* by those who were most in need and *do well* by its stockholders, employees, other customers and clients, it developed a program called "*Patrimonio Hoy*" ("Patrimony Today" referring to a Mexican cultural tradition of creating something of value that will be passed on to future generations).[18]

The goals of *Patrimonio Hoy* are threefold:

1. To help people to save until they can buy the appropriate amount of cement;
2. To help them to store it until they are ready to build; and
3. To celebrate the homeowner's accomplishment and contribution to community development in a very public way.

Building on the *tanda* concept, Cemex established groups of three, instead of larger *tandas* so that each member could receive funding more quickly and often. After only two weeks of membership, each participant would receive an installment of cement and supplies on credit, and then a new shipment once every ten weeks for a total of 78 weeks. *Patrimonio Hoy* offers optional storage plus advice from professional builders, engineers, and architects!

How does Cemex know that the members will continue to participate and remain "good" on their money due? For those living in poverty, with very little else, "you depend on your name, your social capital." Cemex, too, had to prove that it would make "good" on its commitments, since corruption by large corporations was not unheard of by those living in poverty. Therefore, all of its processes were completely transparent; it encouraged members to make and enforce their own *tanda* rules and even to be the ones to promote the program.

Perhaps one of the essential elements was the social recognition. It was Cemex that ensured that each family's accomplishments were published in each community's newspaper. It also paid for celebrations for the highest contributors, the fastest builders, the best promoters, and for the housewarming parties in each finished home.

Has Cemex done "good" by these clients, and by everyone else with a stake in its decisions? It has served 205,000 Mexican families through *Patrimonio Hoy* and has expanded the program to include Colombia, Venezuela, Nicaragua, and Costa Rica. It was self-funding after four years and, now, a previously completely overlooked market is one that is growing at a hearty pace. You decide.

would certainly be making a reasonable decision. In addition, the ethical traditions and theories that we describe in Chapter 3 will help flesh out and elaborate upon this decision procedure. Other approaches are possible, and this approach will not guarantee one single and absolute answer to every decision. But this is a helpful beginning in the development of responsible, reasonable, and ethical decision making.

Questions, Projects, and Exercises

1. Other than ethical values, what values might a business manager use in reaching decisions? Are there classes in your college curriculum, other than ethics, which advise you about proper and correct ways to act and decide?
2. Why might legal rules be insufficient for fulfilling one's ethical responsibilities? Can you think of cases in which a business person has done something legally right, but ethically wrong? What about the opposite—are there situations in which a business person might have acted in a way that was legally wrong but ethically right?
3. What might be some benefits and costs of acting unethically in business? Distinguish between benefits and harms to the individual and benefits and harms to the firm.
4. Review the distinction between personal morality and matters of social ethics. Can you think of cases in which some decisions would be valuable as a matter of social policy, but bad as a matter of personal ethics? Something good as a matter of personal ethics and bad as a matter of social policy?
5. As described in this chapter, the Americans with Disabilities Act requires firms to make reasonable accommodations for employees with disabilities. Consider such conditions as obesity, depression, dyslexia, arthritis, hearing loss, high blood pressure, facial scars, and the fear of heights. Imagine that you are a business manager and an employee comes to you asking that accommodations be made for these conditions. Under what circumstances might these conditions be serious enough impairments to deserve legal protection under the ADA? What factors would you consider in answering this question? After making these decisions, reflect on whether your decision was more a legal or ethical decision.
6. Do an Internet search on Malden Mills and research the present status of the business and Aaron Feuerstein's ownership. How much of a difference would it make if Malden Mills was a publicly traded corporation rather than privately owned? Can any lessons be drawn from the present situation?
7. Construct a list of all the people who were adversely affected by the collapse of Enron. Who, among these people, would you say had their rights violated? What responsibilities, if any, did the managers of Enron have to each of these constituencies?
8. What difference, if any, exists between ethical reasons and reasons of self-interest? If a business performs a socially beneficial act in order to receive good publicity, or if it creates an ethical culture as a business strategy, has the business acted in a less than ethically praiseworthy way?
9. During the recession of 2008–2009, many reputable companies suffered bankruptcies while others struggled to survive. Of those that did remain, some opted to reduce the size of their work forces significantly. In a business environment during those times, consider a company that has been doing fairly well, posting profits every quarter and showing a sustainable growth expectation for the future;however, the general ill-ease in the market has caused the company's stock price to fall. In response to this problem, the CEO decides to lay off a fraction of his employees, hoping to cut costs and to improve the bottom line. This action raises investor confidence and, consequently, the stock price goes up. What is your impression of the CEO's decision? Was there any kind of ethical lapse in laying off the employees; or was it a practical decision necessary for the survival of the company?
10. Every year, *Ethisphere Magazine* publishes a list of the world's most ethical companies. Go to their Web site; find and evaluate their rating methodology and criteria; and engage in an assessment (i.e. provide suggestions for any modifications you might make or a more or less comprehensive list, and so on).

Key Terms

After reading this chapter, you should have a clear understanding of the following Key Terms. The page numbers refer to the point at which they were discussed in the chapter. For a complete definition, please see the Glossary.

descriptive ethics, *p. 13*
ethical values, *p. 18*
ethics, *p. 11*
morality, *p. 13*
normative ethics, *p. 13*
norms, *p. 18*
personal integrity, *p. 15*
practical reasoning, *p. 26*
risk assessment, *p. 25*
stakeholders, *p. 7*
social ethics, *p. 15*
theoretical reasoning, *p. 26*
values, *p. 18*

End Notes

1. "Decision Points" appear throughout each chapter in the text. These challenges are designed to integrate the concepts discussed during that particular segment of the chapter and then to suggest questions or further dilemmas to encourage the reader to explore the challenge from a stakeholder perspective and using the ethical decision-making process. This process will be further described in chapter 2. "Opening" Decision Points introduce one of the main themes of the chapters and a conclusion is offered at the end of each chapter.
2. K. Herbst, "Enabling the Poor to Build Housing: Pursuing Profit and Social Development Together" (September 2002), www.changemakers.net (accessed April 13, 2010).
3. G. Santayana, (1905) *Reason in Common Sense,* v. 1, The Life of Reason.
4. L. Saad, "Nurses Shine, Bankers Slump in Ethics Ratings," *Gallup Poll* (Nov. 24, 2008), http://www.gallup.com/poll/112264/Nurses-Shine-While-Bankers-Slump-Ethics-Ratings.aspx (accessed April 13, 2010).
5. Ethics Resource Center, *Ethicstat* (Nov. 2008); S. Allen, "The New ROE: Return On Ethics," *Forbes* (July 21, 2009), http://www.forbes.com/2009/07/21/business-culture-corporate-citizenship-leadership-ethics.html (accessed April 13, 2010).
6. Whole Foods Market IP, LLP, "Declaration of Independence" (2009), http://www.wholefoodsmarket.com/company/declaration.php (accessed July 9, 2009). *See also,* Knowledge @ Wharton, "Building Companies That Leave the World a Better Place" (Feb. 28, 2007), p. 2, *excerpting* R. Sisodia, J. Sheth, and D. Wolfe, Firms of Endearment: How World-Class Companies Profit from Passion and Purpose (Philadelphia, PA: Wharton Business School Publishing 2007), Ch. 6.
7. Knowledge @ Wharton, "Building Companies That Leave the World a Better Place" (Feb. 28, 2007), p. 2, *excerpting* R. Sisodia, J. Sheth, and D. Wolfe, Firms of Endearment: How World-Class Companies Profit from Passion and Purpose (Philadelphia, PA: Wharton Business School Publishing 2007), Ch. 6.
8. Knowledge @ Wharton, "Building Companies That Leave the World a Better Place" (Feb. 28, 2007), p. 1, *excerpting* R. Sisodia, J. Sheth, and D. Wolfe, Firms of Endearment: How World-Class Companies Profit from Passion and Purpose (Philadelphia, PA: Wharton Business School Publishing 2007), Ch. 6.
9. LRN, *Ethics Study: Employee Engagement* (2007), www.lrn.com (accessed April 13, 2010).
10. L. Bergman, and O. Zill de Granados, "Black Money," *Frontline* (April 7, 2009), http://www.pbs.org/wgbh/pages/frontline/blackmoney/etc/script.html (accessed July 17, 2009).

11. K. Sullivan, "Saudi Reportedly Got $2 Billion for British Arms Deal," *The Washington Post* (June 8, 2007), p. A15, http://www.washingtonpost.com/wp-dyn/content/article/2007/06/07/AR2007060701301.html (accessed July 18, 2009).
12. D. Goldman, and T. Luhby, "AIG: The bailout that won't quit - Feb. 27, 2009," *Business, financial, personal finance news - CNNMoney.com* (Feb. 27, 2009), http://money.cnn.com/2009/02/27/news/companies/aig_bailout/ (accessed April 13, 2010); R. Reich, "The real scandal of AIG," Salon.com (Mar. 16, 2009), http://www.salon.com/opinion/feature/2009/03/16/reich_aig/; B. Ross, and T. Shine, "After Bailout, AIG Execs Head to California Resort," *Online news, breaking news, feature stories and more - ABC News* (Oct. 7, 2008), http://abcnews.go.com/Blotter/Story?id=5973452 (accessed April 13, 2010); E. Strott, "Why AIG matters," *MSN Money* (Sept. 16, 2008), http://articles.moneycentral.msn.com/Investing/Dispatch/why-aig-matters.aspx (accessed April 13, 2010).
13. http://www.opencongress.org/bill/111-h1664/show (accessed April 13, 2010).
14. United States Dept. of Justice, Enron Trial Exhibits and Releases, 009811, "Letter directed to 'Mr. Lay'" (March 15, 2006), http://www.justice.gov/enron/exhibit/03-15/BBC-0001/Images/9811.001.PDF (accessed April 13, 2010).
15. Committee of Sponsoring Organizations (COSO) of the Treadway Commission, "Executive Summary," *Enterprise Risk Management—Integrated Framework* (Sept. 2004), p. 2.
16. R. Berenbeim, The Conference Board, *Universal Conduct: An Ethics and Compliance Benchmarking Survey,* Research Report R-1393-06-RR (2006).
17. Data retrieved from ChangeMakers, "Cementing Family Futures" (April 17, 2009), www.changemakers.net (accessed July 16, 2009).

Readings

Reading 1-1

Value Shift

Lynn Sharp Paine

Business has changed dramatically in the past few decades. Advances in technology, increasing globalization, heightened competition, shifting demographics—these have all been documented and written about extensively. Far less notice has been given to another, more subtle, change—one that is just as remarkable as these more visible developments. What I have in mind is the attention being paid to values in many companies today.

When I began doing research and teaching about business ethics in the early 1980s, skepticism about this subject was pervasive. Many people, in business and in academia, saw it as either trivial or altogether irrelevant. Some saw it as a joke. A few were even hostile. The whole enterprise, said critics, was misguided and based on a naïve view of the business world. Indeed, many had learned in their college economics courses that the market is amoral.

Back then, accepted wisdom held that "business ethics" was a contradiction in terms. People joked that an MBA course on this topic would be the shortest course in the curriculum. At that time, bookstores offered up volumes with titles like *The Complete Book of Wall Street Ethics* consisting entirely of blank pages. The most generous view was that business ethics had something to do with corporate philanthropy, a topic that might interest executives *after* their companies became financially successful. But even then, it was only a frill—an indulgence for the wealthy or eccentric.

Today, attitudes are different. Though far from universally embraced—witness the scandals of 2001 and 2002—ethics is increasingly viewed as an important corporate concern. What is our purpose? What do we believe in? What principles should guide our behavior? What do we owe one another and the people we deal with—our employees, our customers, our investors, our communities? Such classic questions of ethics are being taken seriously in many companies around the world, and not just by older executives in large, established firms. Managers of recently privatized firms in transitional economies, and even some far-sighted high-technology entrepreneurs, are also asking these questions.

Ethics, or what has sometimes been called "moral science," has been defined in many ways—"the science of values," "the study of norms," "the science of right conduct," "the science of obligation," "the general inquiry into what is good." In all these guises, the subject matter of ethics has made its way onto management's agenda. In fact, a succession of definitions have come to the forefront as a narrow focus on norms of right and wrong has evolved into a much broader interest in organizational values and culture. Increasingly, we hear that values, far from being irrelevant, are a critical success factor in today's business world.

The growing interest in values has manifested itself in a variety of ways. In recent years, many managers have launched ethics programs, values initiatives, and cultural change programs in their companies. Some have created corporate ethics offices or board-level ethics committees. Some have set up special task forces to address issues such as conflicts of interest, corruption, or electronic data privacy. Others have introduced educational programs to heighten ethical awareness and help employees integrate ethical considerations into their decision processes. Many have devoted time to defining or revising their company's business principles, corporate values, or codes of conduct. Still others have carried out systematic surveys to profile their company's values and chart their evolution over time.

A survey of U.S. employees conducted in late 1999 and early 2000 found that ethics guidelines and training were widespread. About 79 percent of the respondents said their company had a set of written ethics guidelines, and 55 percent said their company offered some type of ethics training, up from 33 percent in 1994. Among those employed by organizations with more than 500 members, the proportion was 68 percent.

Another study—this one of 124 companies in 22 countries—found that corporate boards were becoming more active in setting their companies' ethical standards. More than three-quarters (78 percent) were involved in 1999, compared to 41 percent in 1991 and 21 percent in 1987. Yet another study found that more than 80 percent of the *Forbes* 500 companies that had adopted values statements, codes of conduct, or corporate credos had created or revised these documents in the 1990s.

During this period, membership in the Ethics Officer Association, the professional organization of corporate ethics officers, grew dramatically. At the beginning of 2002, this group had 780 members, up from 12 at its founding 10 years earlier. In 2002, the association's roster included ethics officers from more than half the *Fortune* 100.

More companies have also undertaken efforts to strengthen their reputations or become more responsive to the needs and interests of their various constituencies. The list of initiatives seems endless. Among the most prominent have been initiatives on diversity, quality, customer service, health and safety, the environment, legal compliance, professionalism, corporate culture, stakeholder engagement, reputation management, corporate identity, cross-cultural management, work–family balance, sexual harassment, privacy, spirituality, corporate citizenship, cause-related marketing, supplier conduct, community involvement, and human rights. A few companies have even begun to track and report publicly on their performance in some of these areas. For a sampling of these initiatives, see Reading figure 1.1.

To aid in these efforts, many companies have turned to consultants and advisors, whose numbers have increased accordingly. A few years ago, *BusinessWeek* reported that ethics consulting had become a billion-dollar business. Though perhaps somewhat exaggerated, the estimate covered only a few segments of the industry, mainly misconduct prevention and investigation, and did not include corporate culture and values consulting or consulting focused in areas such as diversity, the environment, or reputation management. Nor did it include the public relations and crisis management consultants who are increasingly called on to help companies handle values-revealing crises and controversies such as product recalls, scandals, labor disputes, and environmental disasters. Thirty or 40 years ago, such consultants were a rare breed, and many of these consulting areas did not exist at all. Today, dozens of firms—perhaps hundreds, if we count law firms and the numerous consultants specializing in specific issue areas—offer companies expertise in handling these matters. Guidance from nonprofits is also widely available.

What's Going On?

A thoughtful observer might well ask "What's going on?" Why the upsurge of interest in ethics and values? Why have companies become more attentive to their stakeholders and more concerned about the norms that guide their own behavior? In the course of my teaching, research, and consulting over the past two decades, I have interacted with executives and managers from many parts of the world. In discussing these questions with them, I have learned that their motivating concerns are varied:

- An Argentine executive sees ethics as integral to transforming his company into a "world-class organization."
- A group of Thai executives wants to protect their company's reputation for integrity and social responsibility from erosion in the face of intensified competition.
- A U.S. executive believes that high ethical standards are correlated with better financial performance.
- An Indian software company executive sees his company's ethical stance as important for building customer trust and also for attracting and retaining the best employees and software professionals.
- A Chinese executive believes that establishing the right value system and serving society are key components in building a global brand.
- The executives of a U.S. company see their efforts as essential to building a decentralized organization and entrepreneurial culture around the world.
- Two Nigerian entrepreneurs want their company to become a "role model" for Nigerian society.
- A Swiss executive believes the market will increasingly demand "social compatibility."
- An Italian executive wants to make sure his company stays clear of the scandals that have embroiled others.

READING FIGURE 1.1 Values in Transition

CORPORATE INITIATIVES—A SAMPLER		
COMPREHENSIVE (APPLYING TO ALL ACTIVITIES AND FUNCTIONS)	*Internally Oriented:*	Ethics programs Compliance programs Mission and values initiatives Business principles initiatives Business practices initiatives Culture-building initiatives Cross-cultural management programs Crisis prevention and readiness
	Externally Oriented:	Reputation management programs Corporate identity initiatives Corporate brand-building initiatives Stakeholder engagement activities Societal alignment initiatives Nonfinancial-performance reporting initiatives
FOCUSED (APPLYING TO PARTICULAR ISSUES OR CONSTITUENCIES)	*Employee Oriented:*	Diversity initiatives Sexual harassment programs Work–family initiatives Workplace environment initiatives
	Customer Oriented:	Product and service quality initiatives Customer service initiatives Product safety initiatives Cause-related marketing
	Supplier Oriented:	Supplier conduct initiatives
	Investor Oriented:	Corporate governance initiatives
	Community Oriented:	Environmental initiatives Corporate citizenship initiatives Community involvement initiatives Strategic philanthropy
	Issue Oriented:	Electronic privacy Human rights initiatives Anticorruption programes Biotechnology issues

- A U.S. executive believes that a focus on ethics and values is necessary to allow his company to decentralize responsibility while pursuing aggressive financial goals.
- A U.S. executive answers succinctly and pragmatically, "*60 Minutes*."

These responses suggest that the turn to values is not a simple phenomenon. Individual executives have their own particular reasons for tackling this difficult and sprawling subject. Even within a single company, the reasons often differ and tend to change over time. A company may launch an ethics initiative in the aftermath of a scandal for purposes of damage control or as part of a legal settlement. Later on, when the initiative is no longer necessary for these reasons, a new rationale may emerge.

This was the pattern at defense contractor Martin Marietta (now Lockheed Martin), which in the mid-1980s became one of the first U.S. companies to establish what would later come to be called an "ethics program." At the time, the entire defense industry was facing harsh criticism for practices collectively referred to as "fraud, waste, and abuse," and Congress was considering new legislation to curb these excesses. The immediate catalyst for Martin Marietta's program, however, was the threat of being barred from government contracting because of improper billing practices in one of its subsidiaries.

According to Tom Young, the company president in 1992, the ethics program began as damage control. "When we went into this program," he explained, "we didn't anticipate the changes it would bring about. . . . Back then, people would have said, 'Do you really need an ethics program to be ethical?' Ethics was something personal, and you either had it or you didn't. Now that's all changed. People recognize the value." By 1992, the ethics effort was no longer legally required, but the program was continued nonetheless. However, by then it had ceased to be a damage control measure and was justified in terms of its business benefits: problem avoidance, cost containment, improved constituency relationships, enhanced work life, and increased competitiveness.

A similar evolution in thinking is reported by Chumpol NaLamlieng, CEO of Thailand's Siam Cement Group. Although Siam Cement's emphasis on ethics originated in a business philosophy rather than as a program of damage control, Chumpol recalls the feeling he had as an MBA student—that "ethics was something to avoid lawsuits and trouble with the public, not something you considered a way of business and self-conduct." Today, he says, "We understand corporate culture and environment and see that good ethics leads to a better company."

Siam Cement, one of the first Thai companies to publish a code of conduct, put its core values into writing in 1987 so they "would be more than just words in the air," as one executive explains. In 1994, shortly after the company was named Asia's "most ethical" in a survey conducted by *Asian Business* magazine, Chumpol called for a thorough review of the published code. The newly appointed CEO wanted to make sure that the document remained an accurate statement of the company's philosophy and also to better understand whether the espoused values were a help or hindrance in the more competitive environment of the 1990s. In 1995, the company reissued the code in a more elaborate form but with its core principles intact. The review had revealed that while adhering to the code did in some cases put the company at a competitive disadvantage, it was on balance a plus. For example, it helped attract strong partners and employees and also positioned the company, whose largest shareholder was the Thai monarchy's investment arm, as a leader in the country.

A very different evolution in thinking is reported by Azim Premji, chairman of Wipro Ltd., one of India's leading exporters of software services and, at the height of the software boom in 2000, the country's largest company in terms of market capitalization. Wipro's reputation for high ethical standards reflects a legacy that began with Premji's father, M.H. Hasham Premji, who founded the company in 1945 to make vegetable oil. The elder Premji's value system was based on little more than personal conviction—his sense of the right way to do things. Certainly it did not come from a careful calculation of business costs and benefits. In fact, his son noted, "It made no commercial sense at the time."

When his father died in 1966, Azim Premji left Stanford University where he was an undergraduate to assume responsibility for the then-family-owned enterprise. As he sought to expand into new lines of business, Premji found himself repeatedly having to explain why the company was so insistent on honesty when it was patently contrary to financial interest. Over time, however, he began to realize that the core values emphasized by his father actually made for good business policy. They imposed a useful discipline on the company's activities while also helping it attract quality employees, minimize transaction costs, and build a good reputation in the marketplace. In 1998, as part of an effort to position Wipro as a leading supplier of software services to global corporations, the company undertook an intensive self-examination and market research exercise. The result was a reaffirmation and rearticulation of the core values and an effort to link them more closely with the company's identity in the marketplace.

Managers' reasons for turning to values often reflect their company's stage of development. Executives of large, well-established companies typically talk about *protecting* their company's reputation or its brand, whereas entrepreneurs are understandably more likely to talk about *building* a reputation or *establishing* a brand. For skeptics who wonder whether a struggling start-up can afford to worry about values, Scott Cook, the founder of software maker Intuit, has a compelling answer. In his view, seeding a company's culture with the right values is "the most powerful thing you can do." "Ultimately," says Cook, "[the culture] will become more important to the success or failure of your company than you are. The culture you establish will guide and teach all your people in all their decisions."

In addition to company size and developmental stage, societal factors have also played a role in some managers' turn to values. For example, executives in the United States are more likely than those who operate principally in emerging markets to cite reasons related to the law or the media. This is not surprising, considering the strength of these two institutions in American society and their relative weakness in many emerging-markets countries. Since many ethical standards are upheld and reinforced through the legal system, the linkage between ethics and law is a natural one for U.S. executives. In other cases, executives offer reasons that mirror high-profile issues facing their industries or countries at a given time—issues such as labor shortages, demographic change, corruption, environmental problems, and unemployment. Antonio Mosquera, for example, launched a values initiative at Merck Sharp & Dohme Argentina as part of a general improvement program he set in motion after being named managing director in 1995. Mosquera emphasized, however, that promoting corporate ethics was a particular priority for him because corruption was a significant issue in the broader society.

Despite the many ways executives explain their interest in values, we can see in their comments several recurring themes. Seen broadly, their rationales tend to cluster into four main areas:

- Reasons relating to *risk management*
- Reasons relating to *organizational functioning*
- Reasons relating to *market positioning*
- Reasons relating to *civic positioning*

A fifth theme, somewhat less salient but nevertheless quite important for reasons we will come back to later, has to do with the idea simply of "a better way." For some, the rationale lies not in some further benefit or consequence they are seeking to bring about but rather in the inherent worth of the behavior they are trying to encourage. In other words, the value of the behavior resides principally in the behavior itself. For these executives, it is just *better*—full stop—for companies to be honest, trustworthy, innovative, fair, responsible, or good citizens. No further explanation is necessary any more than further explanation is required to justify the pursuit of self-interest or why more money is better than less.

Source: From *Value Shift,* by Lynn Sharp Paine, Copyright © 2004, The McGraw-Hill Companies. Reproduced by permission of the publisher.

Reading **1-2**

An Ethical Hero or a Failed Businessman? *The Malden Mills Case Revisited*

Penelope Washbourne

Introduction

At the annual meeting of the Society for Business Ethics in Boston in 1997 the guest speaker was Aaron Feuerstein, the acclaimed CEO of Malden Mills, who brought tears to the eyes of skeptical academics with his tales of the mill fire in 1995 and his generous actions towards his employees. I had written a case about him during the winter of 1996 and suggested him as a guest speaker for the annual meeting. After the meeting, I was given a guided tour of the gleaming rebuilt factory in Lawrence, Mass., and was duly impressed by the state of the art manufacturing technology used to make that cozy fleece, Polartec, which is made from recycled plastic. Aaron Feuerstein's star continued to shine in the business press, and even in 2004, as a hero who paid his employees for a number of months after the fire destroyed their jobs.

As many noted then and now, here was a true man of virtue, an ethical giant in a business world of massive layoffs such as those at AT&T and Sunbeam, and when compared with colossal failures in leadership in many huge corporations.

I taught this case over the years, with video clips from the national media, in my business ethics courses and was subsequently told by students that the case had made a powerful impression on them. Maybe it was the pictures of those desperately anxious mill workers with their tears and gratitude responding to Feuerstein's announcement after the fire that he was going to continue to pay his workers for another month. "You're a saint" said one. Or maybe it was Feuerstein's own tears that affected my students?

The case touched a deep nerve: here was a business man who put the care of his workers above the bottom line. My goal in writing and teaching about this case was to demonstrate that it is better to teach business ethics with examples of ethical leadership than to continue to focus on, as most of our case books do, the multiple failures in moral leadership in corporate life. Even formerly exemplary companies can fall under an ethical cloud.

Subsequently, though I read that Malden Mills had gone bankrupt, since the tenth year anniversary of the fire was in 2005, I decided to take another look at what the effect had been on the local community of Aaron Feuerstein's actions after the fire. My reading of the events that have taken place since the fire raises an important dilemma for teaching this tale of ethical virtue. What has been the aftermath? It would be nice to say that the gleaming new mill saved the jobs in the community and that Aaron Feuerstein is still in charge of his grandfather's firm, well loved by his workers and local politicians for preserving the one remaining industry in an area of high unemployment.

It would be nice to say that not only is virtue its own reward, but also that it is indeed rewarded by the world. For Aaron Feuerstein and his family firm, unfortunately this is not the case. The actual story is more complex than that, as is often the case in real life.

To describe it briefly: Aaron borrowed money to rebuild the mill, beyond the money he would finally receive from the insurance company. He built a large facility, counting on the expansion of his Polartec fleece lines and the continuation of his brand of upholstery fabrics. His debt was more than his final insurance settlement, the upholstery business proved a failure and he decided to get out of it, cheap competition and an unseasonably warm winter cut into his Polartec sales and he had to declare bankruptcy in 2001. The firm remained under bankruptcy protection until 2003, but Aaron lost control of the company and GE Capital, the main creditor with 16.6 percent, became its largest shareholder, with a dominant influence on the new board. In July 2004 the board hired a new executive. A new manufacturing operation has been opened in China. Jobs in Lawrence and nearby New Hampshire have declined. In the meantime, Aaron and his son Daniel with a group of investors and a commitment to keep jobs in the local communities, attempted to buy back the firm. Their offers were rejected.

How indeed will I teach this case now? Were Aaron's actions after the fire virtuous or reckless? Did his hope for the future and his commitment to the local community blind him to the economic realities of the industry at the time and cause him to overbuild, and so put the whole company in jeopardy? From a utilitarian perspective, did he do the right thing? What was the long-term effect of his actions on the community?

I decided that I had to get close to the source and elected to spend a few days in Lawrence, Massachusetts, and I was able to interview Aaron Feuerstein in his home in Boston. When I interviewed Aaron in November 2004, he said he felt he had failed.

Lawrence, Massachusetts

In fall 2004, the main impression of Lawrence as a community to a visitor unfamiliar with depressed mill towns in New England was decay. The massive empty mill buildings along the Merrimack River have forlorn signs for "Space Available," as if the next high-tech boom was going to transform this now virtual ghost town into a thriving business community. Along the main street with its closed businesses, even the Goodwill center was shuttered. The one remaining open facility was a large Headstart center with its brightly colored plastic play structures. The impression was that this must be a city that is heavily funded with federal grant monies for low income families.

Though large trash receptacles ready for collection lined the narrow residential streets the day I was there, they did not contain the abandoned sofas and junk in the empty lots. The local community newspaper, printed in Spanish and English, spoke of the challenge of trash as a neighborhood problem. The mayor wanted to put awnings over the shops in the main streets, to attract business downtown. Among the nail salons and the few ethnic food establishments, one set of buildings, and one alone, remained a viable concern, Malden Mills Inc. Located next to the Arlington section of town, one of the poorest neighborhoods, the mill is the only sizable employer in Lawrence, Massachusetts.

Five hundred of its employees live in a five mile radius of the mill and many walk to work. It would be fair to say that the economic well-being of Lawrence and its nearby community in New Hamphire, depressed as they are, is intimately connected to the well-being of the one remaining manufacturing facility paying union wages at an average rate in 2004 of $12.50 an hour, with benefits. The unemployment rate in Lawrence has remained at two and a half to three times the state average for the last 20 years , between 10 and 15 percent since 1983. The academic standings of the local schools are the lowest in the state.

My trip to Lawrence answered my question: Why did Aaron Feuerstein feel and still feel today such a fierce loyalty and sense of obligation to the community of Lawrence and its neighboring towns? What did it mean to those communities that he decided to rebuild the mill and committed to pay his employees for several months after the fire? As he told me, the tears of the workers after the fire were not tears of gratitude towards him, but recognition that without the mill there was nothing left for them, their future, or their community.

The 72,000 People of Lawrence and Their History

This city calls itself the "city of immigrants." It claims that 45 different nationalities and ethnicities have lived in Lawrence. It was founded as a mill town in 1842 to establish woolen and cotton mills and to exploit the new technology of water power along the swift-flowing rivers. The large labor pool required for the factories was imported, and consisted largely of women and immigrants, who lived in dormitories and boarding houses. At its peak, between 1890 and 1915, there were 90,000 residents in Lawrence.

Lawrence was the site of the famous "Bread and Roses" strike in 1912 when after nine weeks of a strike for better conditions during a harsh winter, the company bosses brought the state militia out to attempt to force the 30,000 strikers into submission and prevent them from shipping their children out to relatives and sympathetic families in other communities.

Thus, over the years, Lawrence became known for being in the forefront of the struggle for workers' rights and for the right to organize unions. Now earlier generations of Scots and Irish and Eastern European immigrants have been been replaced by Puerto Ricans and first-generation immigrants from Central America. Their mill jobs allow them the ability to function in their native languages, a rare option in high-paying employment where knowledge of English is often a necessity.

Though most of Lawrence's jobs have disappeared as the mills finally closed after World War II, Aaron Feuerstein's commitment to continuing his operation in this immigrant, unionized town is unique. It stems from a recognition of the value of his own family's history and his grandfather's legacy. As a Hungarian Jewish immigrant in New York City at the turn of the century, his grandfather sold dry goods and eventually moved to Massachusetts and began the family firm in 1907. Aaron remembers his roots and the history of earlier generations of immigrant labor who formed the economic engine that brought succeeding generations to a better way of life. His antipathy to shipping jobs South and to offshoring manufacturing jobs at the expense of domestic workers comes from a profound respect for the skills of those who worked hard to build a future for their families in this country.

Though Aaron had indeed laid off workers due to business conditions, nevertheless he believes we owe these workers in this community an opportunity to perform on the job, for themselves and the community. This is a relationship of mutual respect and obligation that has been carried through three generations of Feuersteins towards their union workers and their communities in Massachusetts and New Hampshire. Aaron spoke proudly of never having had a strike over the years and of having tough but fair negotiations with the unions during his tenure in the company.

Knowing of Aaron's commitment to keep jobs in the local community, the union leadership had hoped that the Feuersteins would be successful in their efforts to regain control of the company. Since the advent of the new company management, the union threatened a strike last fall in November 2004, but finally settled on a new contract.

Aaron had resurrected himself once before when he went bankrupt in the 1980s. His technological innovations captured a new market in fleece material which he branded under the name of Polartec for garments for outdoor enthusiasts. His workers had come through for him in that difficult time. Once again he believed he could resurrect his company from the ashes. Could he do it again?

Aaron's sense of failure, at this point in his life (he was 80 in 2005), paternalistic though it may sound, may have to do with failing to live up to the legacy of the family firm that had been handed to him, failing the very community he had pledged to support with good jobs, and failing to protect them from the cost-cutting strategies in which wages are just an expense.

The Business Strategy and Hope for Lawrence

When fleece was invented it filled a wonderful need in the market for garments that did not become wet with moisture and perspiration, as cotton did, but were wickable, allowing the person to stay warm. Aaron's strategy was to pursue research and development and create high-end, high-quality products that could be recognized as a brand: "Polartec." Since its first invention the number of different weights, colors, and features has exploded, with windproof features and even designs for children's outerwear. Aaron believed that Malden Mills could stay ahead of increasing competition of offshore manufacturers and the "commodification" of the industry by staying ahead of the innovation curve. Fleece was soon everywhere, not just in high-quality jackets for climbers and winter sports enthusiasts, but in regular articles of clothing for adults and children, as well as blankets and throws.

After the fire, even though one of his main customers, Lands' End, initially showed support and featured the story of the mill's fire and Aaron's actions towards his employees in its spring 1996 catalogue, Aaron eventually lost major customers, including Lands' End, which sought other suppliers. Along with the interruption in supply, apparently the Polartec brand did not have the power in the general market, except in specialized high-end products, to withstand the flood of cheaper goods coming from Asia.

After the fire another of his product lines, jacquard upholstery velvet, proved to be unsuccessful in earning a brand identity. Furniture manufacturers were unwilling to pay the premium for a branded fabric and in 1998, Aaron got out of that business. It represented about 50 percent of the company's business at the time of the fire, and its production lines were hard hit by the fire and took longer to resume operation than the polarfleece lines.

One business strategy implemented after the fire by one of the company's former executives, Cesar Aguilar, who spent an uncomfortable weekend in wet clothing as part of his military reserve training, is beginning to pay off for the company and for the community, however. Malden Mills is supplying warm winter clothing to the troops in Afghanistan and Iraq as well as conducting research into new lightweight electronic high-tech fabrics that soldiers can wear next to their skin and that can monitor their vital signs and be of assistance in determining injuries. Another innovation is a next-to-skin fabric that would prevent the growth of bacteria and odor for soldiers who are out in the field. The U.S. military approved $21 million for Polartec garments for 2005, a portion of which goes to the garment manufacturer. That figure includes $1.5 million for research.

The military contracts offer a ray of hope for the company. Not only must all products made for the U.S. Armed Services be made in the United States, but the innovations in new products designed for military use can be developed into commercial applications in the future. In addition, according to a company spokesman the military business is not seasonal, which makes it easier to balance the workload. The military contract currently represents about 20 percent of Malden Mills' business.

What Went Wrong?

After a traumatic event such as the fire, one's decision-making capacity is impaired. I know this from personal experience, having escaped from the Oakland Hills fire in 1991 where almost 3,000 homes were destroyed and 24 people ultimately died. I think my interest in this case certainly was influenced by having had this common experience. After a fire, "post-traumatic distress" is an important factor. Aaron even witnessed his factory burning down. In the aftermath of the fire, the shock and sense of loss are enormous, and yet major decisions that have a long-term impact must be made immediately. Relations with family and friends are strained. In Aaron's case, he had a huge sense of responsibility for the injured workers, several of whom were badly burned, though luckily none died, and for those who risked their lives to save parts of the buildings that were not so heavily engulfed. In addition, the fire happened just before Christmas. Though some members of his board, which included members of his own family who worked in the company, opposed it, Feuerstein generously offered to pay his idled workers for the following month, even though he was not required to do so. He said he did not do it for the publicity, but because he was firmly convinced it was the right thing to do. But in hindsight, was it the right thing to do?

Feuerstein renewed his pledge to his 1,500 employees for another three months. As the news spread of his actions he received about $1 million in donations, from small to large checks from all around the country. By the end of a month some of his operations were up and running again as they shifted equipment undamaged by the fire to other locations. Some of the manufacturing facilities for Polartec had been spared.

Was Feuerstein's generosity to his employees a costly decision that ultimately put his company in jeopardy? It cost about $15 million. One view is that by itself it may not have been a foolhardy decision, given the growing business he was in. Sales of Polartec had been growing by 50 percent anually at the time of the fire. Aaron also knew that if his business was going to have a chance to rebuild, he was going to have to rely heavily on his workers to put in an extraordinary effort to get him up and running again.

After three months the remaining workers who were still out of work were supported by unemployment and special funds from the gifts that had been donated.

The outpouring of support, both financial and in the public arena, surprised Feuerstein. He was a private man, an owner of a small family firm, little known outside of New England, and now all of a sudden he was in front of the cameras, making statements about the state of American business. He was invited to sit behind Hillary Clinton at President Clinton's State of the Union Address in January 1996. The names of Malden Mills and Aaron Feuerstein were in all the press and created a flood of goodwill for the company.

He was lauded not only for paying his workers after the fire, but for his immediate commitment to rebuild the factory in the same location. As he said so frequently in interviews after the fire, he and his father had not moved the operation to the South as many other mills did in search of cheaper labor in the 1950s and 1960s, so why would he abandon Lawrence now? He continues to believe that highly skilled labor can produce the best quality products, which in turn can differentiate a company from its competition, and that there is still a place for manufacturing in this country. This commitment earned him enormous political support from the local politicians, the governor, Senators Kennedy and Kerry, and New Hampshire representatives.

The Decision to Rebuild

At issue seems to be not the fact of rebuilding in Lawrence, but the manner in which Aaron Feuerstein proceeded on this project.

Aaron knew that he was "fully insured." What he did not know, what no claimant after a loss knows, is what the actual payout amount will be. He would not know that for many months of negotiations with the insurer. At the point of a claim, the relationship with the insurer turns from one of being, as it were, "in good hands" to one that is adversarial in nature.

The insurer tries to keep the settlement as low as possible and the claimant wants to replace the buildings that burned. The insurer AGI was a tough negotiator, settling well after the newly rebuilt factory had been completed in 1997. The final insurance settlement was about $300 million, covering only 75 percent of the $400 million in rebuilding costs that Feuerstein had borrowed to put his factory in operation.

Was Aaron's decision to rebuild in the immediate aftermath of the fire one of an emotion-driven "survival instinct"? The firm's famous clock tower had been saved during the fire. How could Aaron not see that as a symbol of the firm's commitment to rise from the ashes? Was the idea of renting or renovating facilities, or scaling down the size, never seriously considered? Was the promise of all that cash that would allow him to replace aging equipment with brand new machines, to build a new state of the art facility to deal with the overbearing heat in summer and accommodate the new computerized methodologies, a license to spend more than he should?

Even within the context of rebuilding it was clear that Aaron thought big and wanted the best. There was dispute among the members of the board and with his own son about the scale of the rebuilding. The insurance coverage did not specify that the buildings had to be rebuilt at all or require a minimal square footage, but Aaron opted for the best. He replaced almost all of the space that had been lost, anticipating that his Polartec sales would continue to grow, even though his son was advising him to scale back the square footage. He later admitted that maybe his building plans had been overly extravagant, even to the point of buying new equipment, whereas before the fire he would have bought used. While the mill was being rebuilt, he had leased space for some of his operations in neighboring towns, but now it was he who was to have excess space as the business turned down.

What was Aaron's failure? Did he fail to anticipate the great gap between his rebuilding costs and his final insurance settlement? Did he fail to anticipate that in spite of great attention and support on one level from all the media, months of interruption of his supply would enable his competitors to gain an edge and win customers? Was his attention so focused on recovery from the fire and its aftermath, the insurance claims, and the lawsuits against the company from injured employees, that he failed to see the business risks? Was he imprudent or unlucky that a warm winter depressed fleece sales just at the time his upholstery line was floundering? Was Aaron Feuerstein trying to singlehandedly buck the inexorable pressure on the costs of manufacturing and prices that eventually led the new board after the bankruptcy to a partnership with a mill in China? In 2004 this outsourced production was at about 10 percent of production, but that figure is likely to rise due to the expiration of the textile tariffs with China in January 2005.

The Legacy

Under the special arrangements of the bankruptcy settlement, Aaron and his sons had an opportunity to bid on the firm for another year, but their bids were rejected by the current owners. His group of financial investors, along with the Import-Export Bank, which had guaranteed a loan, had plans to develop the excess mill space into mixed income housing units and retain jobs in the local area. Though Aaron at 79 had surgery on his heart in July 2004, his determination to regain control over the company remained undimmed. He feared it would become another commodity company and the original vision of investing in innovative products that require a highly skilled workforce would be lost. He did not want to run the mill as CEO, but he wanted to resurrect the legacy of the family firm, committed to the goal of continuing to provide high-quality, well-paying jobs to the people of Massachusetts and New Hampshire.

If it were dependent solely on the force of his personality, it would have happened. Aaron is an obstinate man. The local politicians were supporting him, hoping that he could be given the chance to preserve the jobs in the local area.

Since Aaron failed to regain control of the family firm, has he failed? He believes that he has. But as a former journalist at the *Boston Globe* assures him, "You have won, Aaron, no matter what happens!" His ethical legacy is independent of whether or not his family regains control of Malden Mills.

Though his enterprise may have failed, he rebuilt the mill in Lawrence and gave the community hope that there is a future for their families. The new owners currently repeat their commitment to the community, though they state that more jobs will probably be offshored in the future.

What Aaron did was indeed an example of virtue ethics since it was in his character to be concerned for his employees. Examples of his prior support for them, such as giving assistance to help buy a house or send a child to college, were recounted by workers after the fire. However, what Aaron did in paying his workers after the fire was more a demonstration of Carol Gilligan's "Ethic of Care," shaped by the importance of preserving relationships. When faced with the decision of what he could do for his workers he asked himself the question, not what was his duty to do, but what was the most loving thing to do?

This act has called American business leaders to consider again the employment relationship between an enterprise and its workers, not as being exclusively an economic one, but also a personal and communal one. Aaron Feuerstein's acts, which put his workers' needs above his own economic self-interest, were grounded in his religious convictions as an orthodox Jew. He believes he has a responsibility to them as individuals and to the common good. He had the unique chance to show that rather than pursuing the course of the moral minimum, he chose the moral maximum. As he said to me, *"At the end of the day, at the Final Judgment, will it be enough to say, 'I have been the CEO of a company and made a lot of money?' After your basic needs are met, what is the point of all that activity, if not to do some good? . . . on Judgment Day what do you amount to?"*

In the retail outlet at Malden Mills among the colorful bolts of cloth and remnants are two images that caught my attention. One was a portrait of Aaron Feuerstein made out of different colored cotton spools, a diffuse image made by an employee.

The other was a wall hanging embroidered by children at a synagogue school as a gift in thanks to Aaron for his support of them. What is his legacy? He is clearly loved.

Aaron is a unique businessman: He lives modestly and his heavily thumbed Bible sits on his table beside his two volumes of Shakespeare's comedies and tragedies.

He reads them frequently.

Is this a tragic tale? Maybe, but for Shakespeare's best tragic heroes, their defeat at the hands of fate is not the end. The truth of their life lives on.

Reading 1-3

How to Write about Africa

Binyavanga Wainaina

Always use the word 'Africa' or 'Darkness' or 'Safari' in your title. Subtitles may include the words 'Zanzibar', 'Masai', 'Zulu', 'Zambezi', 'Congo', 'Nile', 'Big', 'Sky', 'Shadow', 'Drum', 'Sun' or 'Bygone'. Also useful are words such as 'Guerrillas', 'Timeless', 'Primordial' and 'Tribal'. Note that 'People' means Africans who are not black, while 'The People' means black Africans.

Never have a picture of a well-adjusted African on the cover of your book, or in it, unless that African has won the Nobel Prize. An AK-47, prominent ribs, naked breasts: use these. If you must include an African, make sure you get one in Masai or Zulu or Dogon dress.

In your text, treat Africa as if it were one country. It is hot and dusty with rolling grasslands and huge herds of animals and tall, thin people who are starving. Or it is hot and steamy with very short people who eat primates. Don't get bogged down with precise descriptions. Africa is big: fifty-four countries, 900 million people who are too busy starving and dying and warring and emigrating to read your book. The continent is full of deserts, jungles, highlands, savannahs and many other things, but your reader doesn't care about all that, so keep your descriptions romantic and evocative and unparticular.

Make sure you show how Africans have music and rhythm deep in their souls, and eat things no other humans eat. Do not mention rice and beef and wheat; monkey-brain is an African's cuisine of choice, along with goat, snake, worms and grubs and all manner of game meat. Make sure you show that you are able to eat such food without flinching, and describe how you learn to enjoy it—because you care.

Taboo subjects: ordinary domestic scenes, love between Africans (unless a death is involved), references to African writers or intellectuals, mention of school-going children who are not suffering from yaws or Ebola fever or female genital mutilation.

Throughout the book, adopt a *sotto* voice, in conspiracy with the reader, and a sad *I-expected-so-much* tone. Establish early on that your liberalism is impeccable, and mention near the beginning how much you love Africa, how you fell in love with the place and can't live without her. Africa is the only continent you can love—take advantage of this. If you are a man, thrust yourself into her warm virgin forests. If you are a woman, treat Africa as a man who wears a bush jacket and disappears off into the sunset. Africa is to be pitied, worshipped or dominated. Whichever angle you take, be sure to leave the strong impression that without your intervention and your important book, Africa is doomed.

Your African characters may include naked warriors, loyal servants, diviners and seers, ancient wise men living in hermitic splendour. Or corrupt politicians, inept polygamous travel-guides, and prostitutes you have slept with. The Loyal Servant always behaves like a seven-year-old and needs a firm hand; he is scared of snakes, good with children, and always involving you in his complex domestic dramas. The Ancient Wise Man always comes from a noble tribe (not the money-grubbing tribes like the Gikuyu, the Igbo or the Shona). He has rheumy eyes and is close to the Earth. The Modern African is a fat man who steals and works in the visa office, refusing to give work permits to qualified Westerners who really care about Africa. He is an enemy of development, always using his government job to make it difficult for pragmatic and good-hearted expats to set up NGOs or Legal Conservation Areas. Or he is an Oxford-educated intellectual turned serial-killing politician in a Savile Row suit. He is a cannibal who likes Cristal champagne, and his mother is a rich witch-doctor who really runs the country.

Among your characters you must always include The Starving African, who wanders the refugee camp nearly naked, and waits for the benevolence of the West. Her children have flies on their eyelids and pot bellies, and her breasts are flat and empty. She must look utterly helpless. She can have no past, no history; such diversions ruin the dramatic moment. Moans are good. She must never say anything about herself in the dialogue except to speak of her (unspeakable) suffering. Also be sure to include a warm and motherly woman who has a rolling laugh and who is concerned for your well-being. Just call her Mama. Her children are all delinquent. These characters should buzz around your main hero, making him look good. Your hero can teach them, bathe them, feed them; he carries lots of babies and has seen Death. Your hero is you (if reportage), or a beautiful, tragic international celebrity/aristocrat who now cares for animals (if fiction).

Bad Western characters may include children of Tory cabinet ministers, Afrikaners, employees of the World Bank. When talking about exploitation by foreigners mention the Chinese and Indian traders. Blame the West for Africa's situation. But do not be too specific.

Broad brushstrokes throughout are good. Avoid having the African characters laugh, or struggle to educate their kids, or just make do in mundane circumstances. Have them illuminate something about Europe or America in Africa. African characters should be colourful, exotic, larger than life—but empty inside, with no dialogue, no conflicts or resolutions in their stories, no depth or quirks to confuse the cause.

Describe, in detail, naked breasts (young, old, conservative, recently raped, big, small) or mutilated genitals, or enhanced genitals. Or any kind of genitals. And dead bodies. Or, better, naked dead bodies. And especially rotting naked dead bodies. Remember, any work you submit in which people look filthy and miserable will be referred to as the 'real Africa', and you want that on your dust jacket. Do not feel queasy about this: you are trying to help them to get aid from the West. The biggest taboo in writing about Africa is to describe or show dead or suffering white people.

Animals, on the other hand, must be treated as well rounded, complex characters. They speak (or grunt while tossing their manes proudly) and have names, ambitions and desires. They also have family values: *see how lions teach their children?* Elephants are caring, and are good feminists or dignified patriarchs. So are gorillas. Never, ever say anything negative about an elephant or a gorilla. Elephants may attack people's property, destroy their crops, and even kill them. Always take the side of the elephant. Big cats have public-school accents. Hyenas are fair game and have vaguely Middle Eastern accents. Any short Africans who live in the jungle or desert may be portrayed with good humour (unless they are in conflict with an elephant or chimpanzee or gorilla, in which case they are pure evil).

After celebrity activists and aid workers, conservationists are Africa's most important people. Do not offend them. You need them to invite you to their 30,000-acre game ranch or 'conservation area', and this is the only way you will get to interview the celebrity activist. Often a book cover with a heroic-looking conservationist on it works magic for sales. Anybody white, tanned and wearing khaki who once had a pet antelope or a farm is a conservationist, one who is preserving Africa's rich heritage. When interviewing him or her, do not ask how much funding they have; do not ask how much money they make off their game. Never ask how much they pay their employees.

Readers will be put off if you don't mention the light in Africa. And sunsets, the African sunset is a must. It is always big and red. There is always a big sky. Wide empty spaces and game are critical—Africa is the Land of Wide Empty Spaces. When writing about the plight of flora and fauna, make sure you mention that Africa is overpopulated. When your main character is in a desert or jungle living with indigenous peoples (anybody short) it is okay to mention that Africa has been severely depopulated by Aids and War (use caps).

You'll also need a nightclub called Tropicana, where mercenaries, evil nouveau riche Africans and prostitutes and guerrillas and expats hang out.

Always end your book with Nelson Mandela saying something about rainbows or renaissances. Because you care.

Source: Reprinted with permission of the author, from Granta, V. 92 (Winter 2005), p. 1.

Chapter 2

Ethical Decision Making: Personal and Professional Contexts

This above all: to thine own self be true, and it must follow, as the night the day, Thou canst not then be false to any man.

Shakespeare

To be nothing but yourself, in a world which is doing its best to make you everybody else, means to fight the hardest battle which any human being can fight, and never to stop fighting.

e.e. cummings

Personal freedom cannot grow beyond personal responsibility. The more people learn to be fully accountable for their lives, the more freedom each of us can enjoy and the more fulfilling all of our lives will be.

Reed Konsler

Remember always that you not only have the right to be an individual, you have an obligation to be one.

Eleanor Roosevelt

Do not believe in anything simply because you have heard it. Do not believe in anything simply because it is spoken and rumored by many. Do not believe

Opening Decision Point *What Would You Do?*

Imagine that you are the first person to arrive for your business ethics class. As you sit down at your desk, you notice an iPod on the floor underneath the adjacent seat. You pick it up and turn it on. It works just fine, and it even has some of your favorite music listed. Looking around, you realize that you are still the only person in the room and that no one will know if you keep it.

Not being able to decide immediately, and seeing that other students are beginning to enter the room, you place the iPod down on the floor next to your own backpack and books. As the class begins, you realize that you have the full class period to decide what to do.

- What would you think about as you sat there trying to decide what to do?
- What would you do?

Now let us change the scenario. Instead of being the person who finds the iPod, imagine that you are a friend who sits next to that person. As class begins, your friend leans over, tells you what happened, and asks for advice.

The lesson for today's business ethics class is chapter 2 of your textbook, *Business Ethics: Decision Making for Personal Integrity and Social Justice.*

Finally, imagine that you are a student representative on the judicial board of your school. This student decides to keep the iPod and is later accused of stealing. How would you make your decision?

- What are the key facts that you should consider before making a decision, as either the person who discovered the iPod, the friend, or the judicial board member?
- Is this an ethical issue? What exactly are the ethical aspects involved in your decision?
- Who else is involved, or should be involved, in this decision? Who has a stake in the outcome?
- What alternatives are available to you? What are the consequences of each alternative?
- How would each of your alternatives affect the other people you have identified as having a stake in the outcome?
- Where might you look for additional guidance to assist you in resolving this particular dilemma?

in anything simply because it is found written in your religious books. Do not believe in anything merely on the authority of your teachers and elders. Do not believe in traditions because they have been handed down for many generations. But after observation and analysis, when you find that anything agrees with reason and is conducive to the good and benefit of one and all, then accept it and live up to it.

Buddha

Chapter Objectives

After reading this chapter, you will be able to:

1. Describe a process for ethically responsible decision making.
2. Apply this model to ethical decision points.
3. Explain the reasons why "good" people might engage in unethical behavior.
4. Explore the impact of managerial roles on the nature of our decision making.

Introduction

Chapter 1 introduced our approach to business ethics as a form of practical reasoning, a process for decision making in business. Putting ethics into practice requires not simply decision making, but *accountable* decision making. Chapter 1 also suggested that, even if a person does not consciously think about a decision, her or his own actions will involve making a choice and taking a stand. If you find a lost iPod, you cannot avoid making an ethical decision, whether by act or omission. Whatever you do—or do not do—with the iPod, you will have made a choice that will be evaluated in ethical terms and have ethical implications.

The previous chapter provided a general context for thinking about business ethics; in the current chapter, we begin to bring this topic to a more practical level by examining ethical decision making as it occurs in everyday life and within business contexts. We will examine various elements involved in individual decision making and apply those concepts to the decisions individuals make every day in business. This chapter also examines various ways in which ethical decision making can go wrong, as well as the ways in which effective business leaders can model the most effective ethical decision making.

A Decision-Making Process for Ethics

Let us consider an initial sketch of an **ethical decision-making process.** How would you decide what to do in the iPod case? First, you might wonder how the iPod ended up under the desk. Was it lost? Perhaps someone intentionally discarded the iPod. Would that fact make a significant difference in the ethical judgment that you would make? Or, suppose the person who discovered the iPod actually saw it fall from another student's backpack. Would that make a difference in your judgment about that person?

1 OBJECTIVE

The first step in making decisions that are ethically responsible is to *determine the facts* of the situation. Making an honest effort to understand the situation, to distinguish facts from mere opinion, is essential. **Perceptual differences** surrounding how individuals experience and understand situations can explain many ethical disagreements. Knowing the facts and carefully reviewing the circumstances can go a long way towards resolving disagreements at an early stage. For example, disagreements about Aaron Feuerstein's responsibilities at Malden Mills, discussed in a Decision Point in chapter 1, might depend on the facts about local unemployment rates. One person might think that his decision does not pose a significant ethical question because that person perceives that the employees involved could always get other jobs. Someone else might hold the opposite view because they have a perception of high unemployment rates, which will mean that few employees will, in fact, be able to find other jobs.

Let us turn to the iPod case. What facts would be useful to know before making a decision? Suppose you already owned an iPod. Would that make a difference? Suppose you knew who sat at the desk in the previous class. Imagine that, in fact, the iPod had been in a place not easily seen and you had observed it there over the course of several days. Suppose the iPod did not work and, instead of being discovered underneath a seat, you found it in a wastebasket. How would your decision change as any of these facts changed? Can you imagine a situation in which what looks like an ethical disagreement turns out to be a disagreement over the facts? Considering another technology-based area of challenge, would a situation that involved sharing copyrighted music files over email be an ethical disagreement or a disagreement over the facts?

Given the general importance of determining the facts, there is a role for science (and theoretical reason) in any study of ethics. An ethical judgment made in light of a diligent determination of the facts is a more reasonable ethical judgment that one made without regard for the facts. A person who acts in a way that is based upon a careful consideration of the facts has acted in a more ethically responsible way than a person who acts without deliberation. The sciences, and perhaps especially the social sciences, can help us determine the facts surrounding our decisions. For a business example, consider what facts might be relevant for making a decision regarding child labor. Consider how the social sciences of anthropology and economics, for example, might help us understand the facts surrounding employing children in the workplace within a foreign country. Applying this strategy to a business operation would encourage business decision makers to seek out perhaps alternative or somewhat less traditional methods of gathering facts to ensure that she or he has compiled all of the necessary data in processing the most ethical decision.

A second step in responsible ethical decision making requires the ability to recognize a decision or issue as an ethical decision or ethical issue. It is easy to be led astray by a failure to recognize that there is an ethical component to some decisions. *Identifying the ethical issues involved* is the next step in making responsible decisions. Certainly, the first and second steps might arise in reverse order, depending on the circumstances. At times, you have a selection of facts that give rise to a particular ethical dilemma or issue. However, just as likely, there may also be times when you are presented with an issue from the start, say, when a colleague asks you for guidance with a challenging ethical predicament. The issue identification, therefore, becomes the first step, while fact gathering is a necessary step number two.

In the iPod case, imagine that the student claims that he simply discovered a lost item and kept it. He denies that this is even an ethical issue at all because, after all, he did not *steal* the iPod. What is the difference between stealing and finding a lost item? Similarly, in many business situations, what appears to be an ethical issue for one person will be perceived as a simple financial decision by others. How does one determine that a question raises an ethical issue at all? When does a *business* decision become an *ethical* decision?

First, of course, we need to recognize that "business" or "economic" decisions and ethical decisions are not mutually exclusive. Just because a decision is made on economic grounds does not mean that it does not involve ethical considerations, as well. Being sensitive to ethical issues is a vital characteristic that needs to be cultivated in ethically responsible people. Beyond sensitivity, we also need to ask how our decisions will impact the well-being of the people involved—what are the implications for stakeholders?

Consider how ethics and economics intersect in connection with executive compensation, for example. In the beginning of 2009, a number of publicly held corporations opted to permit shareholders to offer advisory votes on the amount of executive compensation. Though Congress considered mandating this shareholder involvement,[1] Intel was one firm that made the decision to preempt legislative action by implementing non-binding shareholder guidance on its own. In the face of senior executives walking away from corporate disasters with so-called golden parachutes, Intel did not want to make front-page news with more of the same. Imagine how its choice played out, after other firms, such as Merrill Lynch took as much as an $8.4 billion write-down of securities backed by subprime mortgages while ensuring a comfortable landing for its outgoing CEO, Stan O'Neal, who went home happy with a $250 million bonus. As you may recall, chapter 1 described ethical values as concerned with the *impartial* promotion of human well-being. To the degree that a decision affects the well-being—the happiness, health, dignity, integrity, freedom, respect—of the people involved, it is a decision with ethical implications. Shall we also consider then the environment, animals, future generations? There are often ethical implications for these entities, as well. In the end, it is almost impossible to conceive of a decision we might make that does not have at least some impact on the well-being of another. Accordingly, one could suggest that practically all of our decisions have ethical implications.

In business contexts, it can be easy to become so involved in the financial aspects of decisions that one loses sight of the ethical aspects. Perhaps the Merrill Lynch board did not realize how the above CEO bonus might appear under troubling circumstances at the time it created the compensation package. Some writers have called this inability to recognize ethical issues **normative myopia,** or shortsightedness about values.[2] Normative myopia does not occur

Reality Check *Is There an Ethics of Writing Papers?*

Perhaps the most common ethical issue that students and teachers confront involves plagiarism. In fact, 36 percent of high school students in a 2008 survey of almost 30,000 students in the United States said that they used the internet to plagiarize an assignment.[4] From the academic perspective, there is no more serious offense than plagiarizing the work of others. Yet, many students seem honestly surprised to learn that what they believed was research is interpreted as unethical behavior by their teachers.[5]

Many students rely on Internet sources while writing their school papers. It is very easy to "cut and paste" sections of an online source into one's own writing assignment. On one particular Web site, users can post a question with which they are struggling and identify the amount they are willing to pay for an answer. "Tutors" then write up a custom lesson that answers the questions posted in order to receive payment. The Web site claims it does not help the student cheat; instead, it is simply offering an online tutoring service. It contends that all users, both students and tutors, must agree to the Web site's academic honesty policy in order to use the Web site's services.

No doubt, some of this is intentional cheating, such as when a student downloads or purchases an entire paper or answer from a "tutor" or other Internet source. But, in many cases, students seem honestly perplexed that their teacher treats an unattributed "cut and paste" passage as cheating. Few teachers have escaped situations in which they have had to explain to a student why this practice is unethical.

Such cases are not rare. People often make bad ethical decisions because they fail to understand that there is an ethical issue involved. Typically, they have not thought through the implications of their decision and have not stepped back from their situation to reflect on their choice and to consider their decision from other points of view. Often, they are simply too involved in the immediate situation to think about such things. We can think of such condition as "normative myopia" or "inattentional blindness."

THE GLOBAL PERSPECTIVE

A 2008 survey commissioned by the *Wall Street Journal* of almost 20,000 people from 19 countries predictably found that the acceptability of business practices depends in part of local culture.[6] However, the study also found that, overall, there is a growing concern about cheating in general—in many areas of our personal and professional lives. The increase is blamed, in part, on enhanced competition and greater inequalities. It is also laid at the feet of those who choose not to report these unethical or inappropriate practices to those who might be able to stop them; the study pointed to more opportunities to cheat without suffering the consequences.

Points of note:[7]

- When it comes to cheating, in business deals, on taxes, or on the playing field, people often point a finger at Italy. European survey respondents (10 percent) most commonly named Italy as the country that cheats the most in business. Italians themselves (40 percent) also said they were the worst nationality when it comes to honesty in business.
- Across the 19 countries included in the poll, 55 percent of respondents said cheating in business deals was more common than 10 years ago, while only 7 percent said it was less common.
- Hungary led that category, with 74 percent of respondents saying cheating was more common in business than it was a decade ago, while only 3 percent said it was less frequent. At the other end of the spectrum, the Czech Republic (37 percent), Netherlands (42 percent), Spain (42 percent), and Russia (44 percent) were among the countries where fewer people believed an increase in cheating existed than those who perceived it to have decreased.
- The Swedish (19 percent) and Dutch (12 percent) respondents who admitted to cheating on their taxes showed a remarkable level of honesty about their dishonest ways.
- Forty-eight percent of respondents around the world said cheating on taxes was more common today than 10 years ago, while 10 percent of respondents said it was less common.

Reality Check *Bounded Ethicality*

Bounded ethicality is exacerbated by the demands of executive life, which causes an overreliance on intuition rather than on intentional deliberation.

Max Bazerman, "Why We Aren't as Ethical as We Think We Are"

Which means that:

- More time for reflection = less likely to engage in inappropriate behavior (*intentional deliberation*)
- No time for reflection = we do things we might regret! (*overreliance on intuition*)

Source: Adapted from Gallup Management Journal, "Evaluating your business ethics" (June 12, 2008), http://gmj.gallup.com/content/107527/Evaluating-Your-Business-Ethics.aspx#1.

only in business. (See the Reality Check, "Is There an Ethics of Writing Papers?") Bazerman and Chugh similarly warn of **inattentional blindness**, which they suggest results from focusing failures.[3] If we happen to focus—or if we are told specifically to pay attention to a particular element of a decision or event—we are likely to miss all of the surrounding details, no matter how obvious. These focusing failures then result in a moment where we ask ourselves, "How could I have missed that?" You may recall speaking on a cell phone while driving and perhaps missing a highway turn-off by mistake.

The problem is that when we focus on the wrong thing, or fail to focus, Bazerman and Chugh warn that we may fail to see key information that will lead us to success or prevent unethical behavior; we may fail to use the information because we do not know it is relevant; or we may be aware, but we might fail to contribute it to the group. Any of these breakdowns can have disastrous or dangerous consequences. (See Reality Check, "Bounded Ethicality.")

Bazerman and Chugh identify a third means by which ethical issues might go unnoticed: **change blindness**. This omission occurs when decision makers fail to notice gradual changes over time. They offer the example of the Arthur Andersen auditors who did not notice how low Enron had fallen in terms of its unethical decisions. One of the means by which to protect against these decision risks is to ensure that decision makers seek input from others in their decision processes. The researchers report that group input—*any* other input—is almost always a positive factor since individuals collectively can possess and utilize more information than any single person.

The third step involved in ethical decision making involves one of its more critical elements. We are asked to *identify and to consider all of the people affected by a decision, the people often called stakeholders.* "Stakeholders," in this general sense, include all of the groups and/or individuals affected by a decision, policy or operation of a firm or individual. (See Figure 2.1.) Examining issues from a variety of perspectives other than one's own, and other than what local conventions suggest, helps make one's decisions more reasonable, accountable,

FIGURE 2.1
Stakeholder Map

Source: Patricia Werhane © 2009, reprinted with permission.

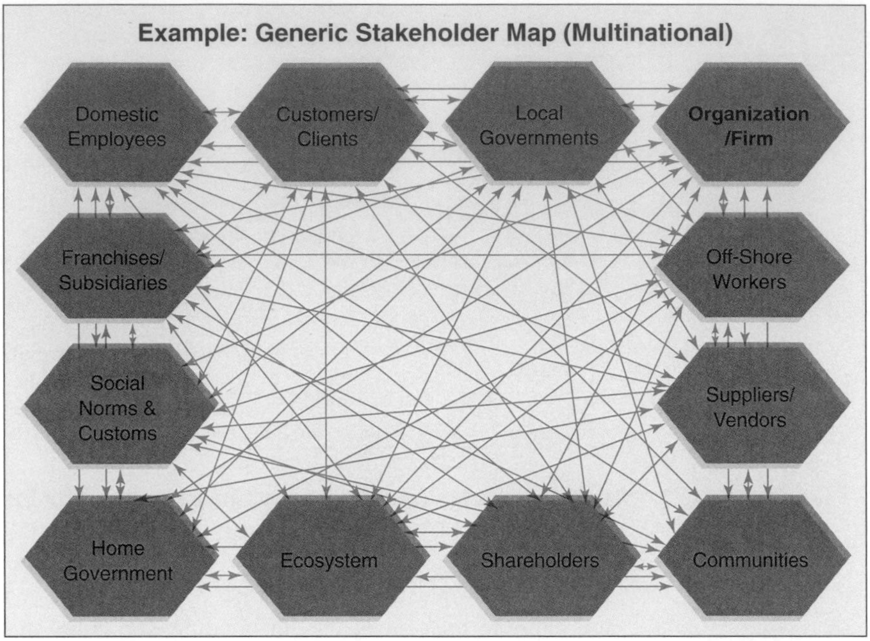

and responsible. And, to the contrary, thinking and reasoning from a narrow and personal point of view virtually guarantees that we will not fully understand the situation. Making decisions from a narrow and personal point of view likewise ensures that we are liable to make a decision that does not give due consideration to other persons and perspectives.

One helpful exercise for considering the effects of a decision on others is to shift one's role. Rather than being in the position of the person who discovers the iPod, what would you think of this case if you were the person who lost it? How does that impact your thinking? What would your judgment be if you were the friend who was asked for advice? A long tradition in philosophical ethics argues that a key test of ethical legitimacy is whether a decision would be acceptable from the point of view of all parties involved. If you could accept a decision as legitimate, no matter whose point of view you take, that decision is likely to be fair, impartial, and ethical. If you acknowledge that you would not accept the legitimacy of keeping the iPod if you were the person who lost it rather than the person who found it, then that is a strong indication that the decision to keep it is not a fair or ethical one.

As an example, global mining and extraction company BHP Billiton conducts a comprehensive stakeholder exploration process and then posts the results of this analysis on the Internet in order to demonstrate a commitment to transparency to its stakeholders.[8] It defines its key stakeholders as "people who are adversely

Reality Check *With Friends like These . . .*

Is Aaron Feuerstein a model for every business leader? Unfortunately, the Malden Mills case did not have a completely happy ending. Initially, all went well. Malden Mills was able to rebuild its factory and reopen sections within a year. Employees came back to work and the community seemed to recover. But Malden Mills could not fully recover. Insurance covered only three-fourths of the $400 million cost of rebuilding and by 2001 Malden Mills filed for bankruptcy protection. During the summer of 2004, Malden Mills emerged from bankruptcy; but, its board of directors was now controlled by its creditors, led by GE Commercial Finance Division.

The new board replaced Aaron Feuerstein as CEO and board chairman, although he retained the right to buy back the controlling interest if he could raise sufficient financing. In October 2004, the board rejected Feuerstein's offer to buy back the company. In response to the company's contract offer that included cuts in health care benefits, the union representing the remaining 1,000 workers at Malden Mills voted to authorize a strike in December 2004, the first in company history.

Are strong ethical values and ethically praiseworthy decisions good for business? The only reasonable answer might be that sometimes they are and sometimes they are not.

or positively impacted by our operations, those who have an interest in what we do, or those who have an influence on what we do"; and then it requires all of its locations to identify their key stakeholders and to consider their expectations and concerns for all operational activities across the life cycle of operations. "Sites are also required to specifically consider any minority groups (such as indigenous groups) and any social and cultural factors that may be critical to stakeholder engagement."[9] In an effort to describe in detail its engagement process, a portion of spreadsheet that outlines BHP Billiton's thought process is included in Exhibit 2.1. Both the readings, "Managing for Stakeholders" by R. Edward Freeman and "What Stakeholder Theory Is Not" by Robert Phillips, et al., elaborate on stakeholder theory with additional examples, benefits, and some cautions to its analysis.

Consider Aaron Feuerstein's decisions on the night of his factory fire, as described in the Decision Point in chapter 1. In his position, some people might think first of how the fire would affect their own personal well-being. The financial status of the owner and his family was seriously threatened by the fire; but a decision that considered only the owner's point of view would not be a responsible decision. The fire also had a great impact on the lives of employees, thousands of whom were about to lose their only source of income. In addition, the fire would have serious consequences for the wider community, a community already harmed by business relocations and vulnerable to any further economic downturn. Customers were also vulnerable to harms caused by the loss of the exclusive supplier of an important product. In the case of every stakeholder, the harms were undeserved. That is, no one had done anything wrong; no one was at fault; yet, all stood to suffer serious harms. The Reality Check, "With Friends like These . . . ," explores later implications.

The fact that many decisions will involve the interests of multiple stakeholders also helps us to understand a major challenge to ethical decision making. The very fact that there are many perspectives and interests at stake means that ethical decisions often involve dilemmas. Each alternative will impose costs on some stakeholders and offer benefits to others. Making a decision that benefits one group often means that other stakeholders will be denied benefits.

Once we have examined the facts, identified the ethical issues involved, and identified the stakeholders, we need to *consider the available alternatives.* Creativity in identifying options—also called **"moral imagination"**—is one element that distinguishes good people who make ethically responsible decisions from good people who do not.[10] It is important not only to consider the obvious options with regard to a particular dilemma, but also the much more subtle ones that might not be evident at first blush. When reviewing the Malden Mills circumstances, ask yourself how many people would have even thought about paying employees while the factory was being rebuilt. Aaron Feuerstein utilized moral imagination in doing so.

EXHIBIT 2.1

BHP Billiton's Stakeholder Relationships

STAKEHOLDER	WHO ARE THEY?	INTERESTS AND CONCERNS	ENGAGEMENT METHODS
Business Partners	Our business partners include those organisations with which we have joint ventures.	Business partners are generally interested in being assured that suitable governance mechanisms are in place to ensure financial returns are delivered while mitigating non-financial risks sufficiently.	• We communicate with our business partners and regularly share knowledge and programs through joint venture boards and operating committees. • We seek to ensure that the conduct of our business partners reflects our own commitment to the Universal Declaration of Human Rights and our Guide to Business Conduct. • Joint Venture Partners have participated in our HSEC audit programs. • Annual financial and sustainability reports.

Source: http://www.bhpbilliton.com/bbContentRepository/docs/ourStakeholders2008.pdf © BHP Billiton. Reprinted with permission.

Consider, too, the less dramatic case of discovering a lost iPod. One person might decide to keep it because she judges that the chances of discovering the true owner are slim and that, if she does not keep it, the next person to discover it will make that decision. Another person might be able to think of some alternatives beyond those choices. For example, she could return early for the next class to see who is sitting at the desk, or she could find out who teaches the previous class and ask that teacher for help in identifying the owner. Moral imagination might be something as simple as checking in a lost and found department. How would the school community be changed if students went out of their way to return lost items rather than keeping them for their own use?

The next step in the decision-making process is to *compare and weigh the alternatives*—create a mental spreadsheet that evaluates the impact of each alternative you have devised on each stakeholder you defined. Perhaps the most helpful way to accomplish this task is to try to place oneself in the other person's position, as discussed above. Understanding a situation from another's point of view, making an effort to "walk a mile in their shoes," contributes significantly to responsible ethical decision making. Weighing the alternatives will involve predicting the likely, the foreseeable, and the possible consequences to all the relevant stakeholders. A critical element of this evaluation will be the consideration of ways to mitigate, minimize, or compensate for any possible harmful consequences or to increase and promote beneficial consequences.

Ethicists sometimes ask the decision maker to consider whether he would feel proud or ashamed if *The Wall Street Journal* (or whatever is your relevant daily newspaper) printed this decision as a front page article, or whether he could explain it to a 10-year-old child so the child thinks it is the right decision, or whether it will stand the test of time. Note that, in the iPod case, the student was described as looking around to see if anyone else noticed his discovery. Would your behavior change if other people knew about it? The point of this exercise is to recognize that a fully responsible and ethical decision should be explainable, defensible and justifiable to the entire range of stakeholders involved. Typically, it is the irresponsible decisions that we wish to keep hidden. (See Reality Check, "The Ultimate Recognition of Impact on Stakeholders.")

But consequences or justifications are not the only means for comparing alternatives. Some alternatives might concern matters of principles, rights or duties that override consequences. Aaron Feuerstein believed that the long-term loyalty of his employees created a special duty not to abandon them in times of crisis. Within business settings, individuals may often have specific duties associated with their position. A purchasing manager for a large retail store has a duty associated with her role that directs her to avoid conflicts of interest in dealing with suppliers. Are duties associated with company rules, professional codes of conduct, business roles, or legal duties involved? Perhaps guidance is available in

Reality Check *The Ultimate Recognition of Impact on Stakeholders*

Excerpt from transcript of Bernard Madoff's statement to the court during his sentencing, as provided by the court (June 29, 2009):[11]

> Your Honor, for many years up until my arrest on December 11, 2008, I operated a Ponzi scheme through the investment advisory side of my business . . . I am actually grateful for this first opportunity to publicly speak about my crimes, for which I am so deeply sorry and ashamed. As I engaged in my fraud, I knew what I was doing was wrong, indeed criminal.
>
> When I began the Ponzi scheme I believed it would end shortly and I would be able to extricate myself and my clients from the scheme. However, this proved difficult, and ultimately impossible, and as the years went by I realized that my arrest and this day would inevitably come.
>
> I am painfully aware that I have deeply hurt many, many people, including the members of my family, my closest friends, business associates and the thousands of clients who gave me their money.
>
> I cannot adequately express how sorry I am for what I have done. I am here today to accept responsibility for my crimes by pleading guilty and, with this plea allocution, explain the means by which I carried out and concealed my fraud . . .

Source: Associated Press, http://www.google.com/hostednews/ap/article/ALeqM5hTuZNL7UWWzyen2zkeWJTvnlov_AD96SM6500

specific circumstances from these sources or others (see Reality Check, "Seeking Guidance?")

One additional factor in comparing and weighing alternatives requires consideration of the effects of a decision on one's own integrity, virtue, and character. Understanding one's own character and values should play a role in decision making. By all accounts, Aaron Feuerstein was a deeply religious and moral man who, in many ways, could not have acted differently than he did. A responsible person will ask: "What type of person would make this decision? What kind of habits would I be developing by deciding in one way rather than another? What type of corporate culture am I creating and encouraging? How would I, or my family, describe a person who decides in this way? Is this a decision that I am willing to defend in public?" Such questions truly go to the heart of ethical business leadership. An honest person might not even think about retaining the iPod; keeping it for oneself is simply not an option for such a person.

Once you have explored the above variables, it is time to *make a decision.* However, the process is not yet complete. To be accountable in our decision making, it is not sufficient to deliberate over this process, only to later throw up our hands once the decision is made: "It's out of my hands now!" Instead, we have the ability as humans to learn from our experiences. That ability creates a responsibility to then evaluate the implications of our decisions, to *monitor and learn from the outcomes,* and to modify our actions accordingly when

Reality Check *Seeking Guidance?*

Each time you are honest and conduct yourself with honesty, a success force will drive you toward greater success. Each time you lie, even with a little white lie, there are strong forces pushing you toward failure.

Joseph Sugarman

I believe that every right implies a responsibility; every opportunity, an obligation; every possession, a duty.

John D. Rockefeller Jr.

Men of integrity, by their existence, rekindle the belief that as a people we can live above the level of moral squalor. We need that belief; a cynical community is a corrupt community.

John W. Gardner

There is nothing noble about being superior to some other man. The true nobility is in being superior to your previous self.

Hindu Proverb

I hope that my achievements in life shall be these—that I will have fought for what was right and fair, that I will have risked for that which mattered, and that I will have given help to those who were in need, that I will have left the earth a better place for what I've done and who I've been.

C. Hoppe

faced with similar challenges in the future. The Decision Point, "Applying the Decision-Making Model," gives us a chance to put this decision-making process into practice.

The reading by Bowen McCoy, "Parable of the Sadhu," demonstrates this deliberative process. McCoy reviews his decision making after the fact and evaluates the implications of his decision, recognizing the responsibility that each participant had for the outcome. While the top of a mountain might seem quite a distance from the comfort within which you might be reading this text, McCoy suggests that the time to first consider what we might do, when and where to take a stand, is not really the top of that mountain but right here in this comfort zone. The group may have overlooked creative options, not spent the time necessary to consider all stakeholders, or failed in other ways. Instead, it is much more effective to have the time and space in which to consider these questions now, before we are faced with them, than when they become urgent and we must engage in "thin air thinking," not the best environment for our high quality decision making.

2 OBJECTIVE

The ethical traditions and theories that we describe in the next chapter will help us flesh out and elaborate upon this decision process. Other approaches to ethically responsible decision making are possible; and this approach will not guarantee one single and absolute answer to every decision. But, it is a helpful beginning in the development of responsible and ethical decision making. (See Figure 2.2.)

Decision Point *Applying the Decision-Making Model*

Let us give it a try: Should Richard Grasso give back any of the $139.5 million he received in his final year as chairman of the New York Stock Exchange?

Consider how one might begin to use this model to deliberate about an ethical issue in business. Richard Grasso is the former chairman of the New York Stock Exchange. During his last year as chairman, he received total compensation of $140 million and was slated to receive approximately another $48 million in retirement benefits. This compensation package was determined by the employment contract he had signed with the NYSE board of directors. Mr. Grasso resigned in the face of public criticism of this pay package and, at least initially, agreed to forgo the final $48 million. What is your judgment about this situation?

What facts might be relevant? Presumably you would want to know what work he had done to earn this salary. What were his responsibilities? You might also want to know who decided that he should receive so much money and under what circumstances this decision was made.

As it turned out, the board of directors for the NYSE approved the compensation package, but some of those responsible for setting his pay, including the director of the NYSE human resources department who made the pay recommendation to the board's compensation committee, were friends of Grasso. He had appointed them to their positions and he played a role is determining their own pay. The facts also are that the NYSE is a nonprofit organization, which functions to regulate publicly traded companies. The companies being regulated by the NYSE ultimately were the very same companies that were paying Grasso.

What ethical issues does this case raise? At first glance, concerns over conflicts of interest, deception, fraud, misallocation of funds, and theft, as well as such personal ethical questions as greed and arrogance, come to mind.

If one thinks that the only people involved in this case are the NYSE board as the employer, and Mr. Grasso as employee, one might be tempted to conclude that this was a private business matter between an employer and an employee. But the *stakeholders* involved here include not only members of the board and other employees, but quite literally every company whose securities are traded on the NYSE and every investor who relies on the integrity of the NYSE to oversee and regulate the sale of securities. Because so much of the stock exchange's work must depend on investor confidence and trust in the system and because this case worked to undermine that confidence and trust, many other people have something at stake in its outcome.

The *available options* will depend on who the decision maker is. Ultimately, the New York State Attorney General sued both the NYSE and Richard Grasso to recover some of the money paid as salary. As an individual investor, one might not have much of an option in responding to this event. But as citizens, we have other options.

FIGURE 2.2
An Ethical Decision-Making Process

Determine the facts

- Identify the ethical issues involved
- Identify stakeholders and consider the situation from their point of view
- Consider the available alternatives—also called "moral imagination"
- Consider how a decision affects stakeholders, comparing and weighing the alternatives, based on:
  - Consequences
  - Duties, rights, principles
  - Implications for personal integrity and character
- Make a decision
- Monitor and learn from the outcomes

When Ethical Decision Making Goes Wrong: Why Do "Good" People Engage in "Bad" Acts?

To say that each individual has the capability to follow a similar decision-making process or possesses the capacity to make autonomous decisions is not to say that every individual always does so. There are many ways in which responsible decision making can go wrong and many ways in which people fail to act in accordance with the ethical judgments they make. Sometimes, of course, people can simply choose to do something unethical. We should not underestimate the real possibility of immoral choices and unethical behavior.

But, at other times, well-intentioned people fail to make ethical choices. What factors determine which companies or individuals engage in ethical behavior and which do not? Why do people we consider to be "good" do "bad" things? This does not mean that these unethical decisions or acts are excusable, but that the individuals who engage in the unethical behavior may have done so for a variety of reasons. As it turns out, there are many stumbling blocks to responsible decision making and behavior. (See reading by Dennis Moberg, "When Good People Do Bad Things at Work.")

3 OBJECTIVE

Some stumbling blocks to responsible action are cognitive or intellectual. As the model of ethical decision making outlined above suggests, a certain type of ignorance can account for bad ethical choices. Sometimes that *ignorance* can be almost willful and intentional. After you discover a lost iPod, you might rationalize to yourself that no one will ever know, no one is really going to be hurt, an owner who is so careless deserves to lose the iPod. You might try to justify the decision by telling yourself that you are only doing what anyone else would do in this circumstance. You might even choose not to think about it and try to put any guilty feelings out of your mind.

Another cognitive barrier is that we sometimes only *consider limited alternatives.* When faced with a situation that suggests two clear alternative resolutions, we often consider only those two clear paths, missing the fact that other alternatives might be possible. Upon discovering a lost iPod, you might conclude that if you do not take it, someone else will. Because the original owner will lose out in both cases, it is better that you benefit from the loss than if someone else benefits. Responsible decision making would require that we discipline ourselves to explore additional methods of resolution.

We also generally feel most comfortable with *simplified decision rules.* Having a simple rule to follow can be reassuring to many decision makers. For example, assume you are a business manager who needs to terminate a worker in order to cut costs. Of course, your first thought may be to uncover alternative means by which to cut costs instead of firing someone, but assume for the moment that cutting the workforce is the only viable possibility. It may be easiest and most comfortable to terminate the last person you hired, explaining, "I can't help it; it must be done, last in/first out, I have no choice. . . ." Or, in the iPod case, "finders keepers, losers weepers" might be an attractive rule to follow. Using a simple decision rule might appear to relieve us of accountability for the decision (you did not "make" the decision; the rule required the decision to be made), even if it may not be the best possible decision.

We also often select the alternative that satisfies *minimum decision criteria,* otherwise known as "satisficing." We select the option that suffices, the one that people can live with, even if it might not be the best. Imagine a committee at work that needs to make a decision. They spend hours arriving at a result and finally reach agreement. At that point it is unlikely that someone will stand up and say, "Whoa, wait a minute, let's spend another couple of hours and figure out a *better* answer!" The very fact that a decision was reached by consensus can convince everyone involved that is must be the most reasonable decision.

Other stumbling blocks are less intellectual or cognitive than they are a question of motivation and willpower. As author John Grisham explained in his book *Rainmaker,* "Every (lawyer), at least once in every case, feels himself crossing a line he doesn't really mean to cross. It just happens." Sometimes it is simply *easier to do the wrong thing.* After all, who wants to go through all the trouble of finding the lost and found office and walking across campus to return the iPod? Consider how you would answer the questions asked in the Reality Check, "The Ethics of Cheating."

Unfortunately, we do not always draw the lines for appropriate behavior in advance, and even when we do, they are not always crystal clear. As Grisham suggests, it is often easy to do a little thing that crosses the line, and the next time it is easier, and the next easier still. One day, you find yourself much further over your ethical line than you thought you would ever be.

People also sometimes make decisions they later regret because they *lack the courage* to do otherwise. It is not always easy to make the right decision; you might lose income, your job, or other valuable components of your life. Sherron Watkins was only one of many Enron employees who explained their reluctance to push their concerns by reference to the culture of intimidation and fear that characterized upper management at Enron. Courage is also necessary when

Reality Check *The Ethics of Cheating*

A 2008 survey of more than 29,000 American high school students revealed that 30 percent had stolen from a store in the previous year, 64 percent had cheated on a test and, as mentioned earlier in the chapter, 36 percent said they plagiarized using the Web. Perhaps even more shocking are the following responses: 93 percent of these youth reported that they were "satisfied" with their personal ethics, and 77 percent said that "when it comes to doing what is right, I am better than most people I know."[12]

As appalling—or disturbing—as those statistics might be, students fare worse when they are categorized by academic discipline. Research has demonstrated that *business* undergraduate students are *the most likely* to have cheated on a test, when compared with prelaw students and the general population.[13] In response to a statement claiming that *not* cheating is the best way to get ahead in the long run, business students claimed, "You snooze, you lose."[14] Does this mean that, perhaps, there is a failure in ethics in the business arena because the people who go into business already cheat? Or is it that business students are aware that the business arena demands this type of unethical conduct so they prepare themselves for it from the start? Competitiveness might blur the border between ethical and unethical. Either way, as our parents have told us, simply because an environment is replete with a certain type of behavior does not mean that we must follow suit, nor does it relieve us of our responsibility for actions in that environment (thus the common parental question, "If Janie jumps off a bridge, are you going to follow?").

responding to significant *peer pressure*. Though we might have believed that we could leave this behind in high school or college, unfortunately, we are subject to it throughout our lives. We tend to give in to peer pressure in our professional environments, both because we want to "fit in" and to achieve success in our organizations, and also because our *actual* thinking is influenced by our peers. We feel as if our disagreement means that we might be wrong. Accordingly, we either change our minds to fit our environments, or we simply listen only for the evidence that supports this new way of thinking until our minds slowly change on their own.

Of course, the usual suspects for explaining unethical conduct are still very much apparent in the scandals that make the front pages every day. The enormous amounts of corporate executive compensation, lack of oversight of corporate executive decisions, significant distance between decision makers and those they impact, financial challenges, and a set of ethical values that has not yet caught up to technological advances—all of these factors can create an environment rife with ethical challenges and unethical decisions. We can benefit from unethical acts, from gaining something as simple as an iPod, to something as significant as a salary package of $180 million. Temptation is often all around us and any person can succumb to it. The questions that are most difficult to answer are often those that are most important to answer in defining who we are. Give it a try in the Decision Point, "The Value of Values."

Making ethically responsible decisions throughout one's life is perhaps the most serious challenge we all face. The easiest thing to do would be to remain

Decision Point *The Value of Values*

All around us there is a breakdown of values . . . It is not just the overpowering greed that pervades our business life. It is the fact that we are not willing to sacrifice for the ethics and values we profess. For an ethics is not an ethics and a value is not a value without some sacrifice to it. Something given up, something not taken. Something not gained.

Jerome Kohlberg, Jr., addressing investors at his retirement from his private equity firm, Kohlberg, Kravis, Roberts & Co. (May 18, 1987)

What values are most important to you? What are you willing to sacrifice to maintain your own values? What is important? What are your priorities?

Questions to Ask Yourself:

- Are there any values that you would quit a job over?
- What would you be willing to die for?
- What do you stand for, personally and professionally?
- Is it not important to consider the answers to these questions *before* you are actually faced with a decision?

passive and simply conform to social and cultural expectations, to "go with the flow." But such passivity is exactly the sort of unexamined life that Socrates claimed was not worth living. To live a meaningful human life, we must step back and reflect on our decisions, assuming the responsibility of autonomous beings.

Before leaving this discussion it is worth reflecting on those people who do not succumb to temptations and who may not even deliberate in the face of an ethical dilemma. In the following chapter, we will describe an ethical tradition that emphasizes ethical character and virtues. For many people, finding a lost iPod would not raise much of a dilemma at all. Many people would not have to deliberate about what to do or go through a decision-making process before acting. Many people have developed a certain type of character, a set of ethical habits, that will encourage them, without deliberation, to act ethically. For every Richard Grasso, there are many business executives who could, *but do not,* take exorbitant salaries, scheme to manipulate stock options, and otherwise seek to enrich themselves. For example, Colleen Brown, the CEO of Fischer Communications, took a voluntary pay cut of ten percent in 2008 in order to help the company survive during its difficult economic times.[15] Similarly, when CEO Jim Owens realized that Caterpillar customers were experiencing a "continued deterioration of conditions," he cut executive pay in 2009 by fifty percent, reduced senior management base salaries and implemented a hiring freeze in order to ensure Caterpiller's sustainability.[16] Developing such habits, inclinations, and character is an important aspect of living an ethical life. (See Reality Check earlier in the chapter, "Bounded Ethicality.")

Ethical Decision Making in Managerial Roles

At several points already in this text we have acknowledged that individual decision making can be greatly influenced by the social context in which it occurs. Social circumstances can make it easier or more difficult to act in accordance with one's own judgment. Within business, an organization's context sometimes makes it difficult for even the best-intentioned person to act ethically, or it can make it difficult for a dishonest person to act unethically. Responsibility for the circumstances that can encourage ethical behavior and can discourage unethical behavior falls predominantly to the business management and executive team. Chapter 4 will examine this issue in more detail as we introduce the concepts of corporate culture and ethical leadership; but, it is helpful to begin to explore this topic here.

The decision-making model introduced in this chapter develops from the point of view of an individual who finds herself in a particular situation. Personal integrity lies at the heart of such individual decision making: What kind of person am I or do I aspire to be? What are my values? What do I stand for? Every individual also fills a variety of social roles, and these roles carry with them a range of expectations, responsibilities, and duties. Within a business setting, individuals must consider the ethical implications of both **personal and professional decision making**. Some of our roles are social: friend, son or daughter, spouse, citizen, neighbor. Some are institutional: manager, teacher, student-body president. Among the major roles and responsibilities that we will examine in this text are those associated with specific professions: attorneys, accountants, auditors, financial analysts, and others. Decision making in these contexts raises broader questions of social responsibilities and social justice.

4 OBJECTIVE

Consider how different roles might impact your judgment about the discovery of the iPod. Your judgment about the iPod might differ greatly if you knew that your friend had lost it, or if you were a teacher in the class, or if you were a member of the campus judicial board. Our judgment about Richard Grasso might change when we learn that his professional responsibility included oversight of a regulatory body that governed the very companies that were paying his salary.

In a business context, individuals fill roles of employees, managers, senior executives, and board members. Managers, executives, and board members have the ability to create and shape the organizational context in which all employees make decisions. They, therefore, have a responsibility to promote organizational arrangements that encourage ethical behavior and discourage unethical behavior.

The following three chapters develop these topics. Chapter 3 will provide an overview of how some major ethical traditions might offer guidance both to individual decision makers and to those who create and shape social organizations. Chapter 4 will examine topics of corporate culture, ethical organizations, and ethical leadership. Chapter 5 examines corporate social responsibility, the ends towards which ethical organizations and ethical leaders should aim.

Opening Decision Point Revisited

What Would You Do?

Applying our decision-making model to the iPod case, we would first try to determine the facts. Knowing that the iPod functioned perfectly would be good evidence for concluding that it was left behind accidentally rather than intentionally discarded. Knowing the actual cost of the iPod would also be evidence that it is something likely to be highly valued and not something easily abandoned. The cost, as well as your own understanding of private property, makes it clear that this situation raises ethical issues of rights, happiness, personal integrity, and honesty.

Most obviously, this would seem to involve two major stakeholders: the true owner and yourself. But, upon reflection, you can understand that whatever decision you make will have broader implications. People will talk about the stolen iPod or the iPod that had been returned; and these ramifications could encourage or diminish a campus culture of trust and honesty.

Imagining yourself in the position of the student who lost the iPod or of the student who might sit in judgment at a campus judicial hearing can provide a perspective otherwise easily missed if you think only of yourself. Imagining the results of keeping the iPod and then having that fact discovered and publicized is another helpful step. How would you try to justify that decision to others? Considering the number of hours someone might have to work at an on-campus job in order to earn enough money to buy another iPod introduces another important perspective. Finally, a concern with personal integrity would encourage you to reflect on the type of person who keeps another's property and to ask yourself if this is who you really are and want to be.

Given all these steps, it would be difficult to imagine that one could justify a decision to keep the iPod.

Questions, Projects, and Exercises

1. Consider your own personal values and explain where they originated. Can you pinpoint their derivation? To what degree have you chosen your own values? To what degree are your own values products of your family, your religious or cultural background, or your age? Does it matter where values originate?
2. Identify an activity that is outside of your "zone of comfort"; in other words, do something that you might not otherwise do, experience something that you might not otherwise experience, because the activity would otherwise be something with which you would be uncomfortable. This activity does not need to be something enormous or intimidating; but instead it could be something as basic as being the first to apologize after an argument, or agreeing to dress up for a masquerade party when you might not usually feel comfortable doing so. You might offer to cook dinner for a friend, when that would normally be an uncomfortable arrangement; or you might ask a question in class, or offer to lead a presentation, if those are things that make you uncomfortable.

It is important that you consider your expectations (i.e., how do you think you will feel, what do you think it will be like?) *before* engaging in this activity, and write them down. Then, after the experience, complete the assignment by writing a description of the actual experience and indicating whether the reality matched your expectations, considering in particular your original perceptions and expectations and whether they were accurate. How closely can we trust our perceptions and pre-judgments about our expectations of experiences? How true is our "gut instinct?"

3. What issue, challenge, or idea do you care about most in the world? Share it in a brief essay, then convince your reader why it is so important that she or he should also care about that issue to the same extent. It may be effective to use the theories discussed in prior chapters to persuade your reader of the value of your argument.
4. Your CEO recognizes you as having extraordinary skills in decision making and communications, so she asks for guidance on how to best communicate her plans for an imminent reduction in force. What are some of the key strategies you will suggest she employ in reaching such a decision and making the announcement?
5. Describe the qualities you believe are necessary in an "ethical leader." Provide support for your contentions and explain why a leader should display these qualities in order to be considered "ethical" from your perspective. Then identify someone you believe embodies these qualities in her or his leadership and provide examples. Finally, provide an example of someone who you believe does not possess these qualities and describe that person's leadership.
6. How can your global firm best ensure that it is taking into account the perceptual differences that may exist as a result of diverse cultures, religions, ethnicities, and other factors when creating a worldwide marketing plan?
7. Describe an event or decision that you would judge to be clearly unethical. Can you imagine any circumstances in which it would be ethical? Can you imagine a situation in which you yourself would do something unethical?
8. As a class exercise, write a brief account of any unethical or ethically questionable experience you have witnessed in a work context. Read and discuss the examples in class, keeping the authors anonymous. Consider how the organization allowed or encouraged such behavior and what might have been done to prevent it.
9. Lisa is trying to raise funds to support the creation of a free clinic in a poor neighborhood in her hometown. She has been trying very hard, but she has not been able to raise enough money to get the clinic up and running. One day, she gets a huge check from a high profile business executive whom she met at a fund raiser. She is ecstatic and finally sees her dream taking shape. However, after a few days, the person who gave Lisa the money is arrested for fraud, money laundering, and tax evasion. What should Lisa do? Should she still keep the money and look the other way? Does the source of the money matter or does the end justify the means?
10. Bernard Madoff ran a Ponzi Scheme for nearly two decades. Many have questioned how he got away with it for such a long time. Explain the role that normative myopia might have played in the duration of his scheme. Using the Internet, conduct research in connection with the Madoff scandal, and determine the key factors that you believe may have helped him to have coordinated this scheme so successfully.

Key Terms

After reading this chapter, you should have a clear understanding of the following Key Terms. The page numbers refer to the point at which they were discussed in the chapter. For a more complete definition, please see the Glossary.

bounded ethicality, *p. 51*
change blindness, *p. 51*
ethical decision-making process, *p. 47*
inattentional blindness, *p. 51*
moral imagination, *p. 54*
normative myopia, *p. 49*
perceptual differences, *p. 47*
personal and professional decision making, *p. 63*

End Notes

1. H.R. 1257, Shareholder Vote on Executive Compensation Act, 110th Cong., 2007–2008, (Apr. 20, 2007), http://www.govtrack.us/congress/bill.xpd?bill=h110-1257 (accessed April 5, 2010).
2. The concept of normative myopia as applied to business executives can be found in Diane Swanson, "Toward an Integrative Theory of Business and Society," *Academy of Management Review,* 24, no. 3 (July 1999): 506–521.
3. D. Chugh and M. Bazerman, "Bounded Awareness: What You Fail to See Can Hurt You," *Mind & Society,* v. 6 (2007), p. 1.
4. D. Crary/*Associated Press,* "Nationwide Survey Finds High Levels of Cheating, Stealing by High School Students," *ABC News* (Nov. 30, 2008), http://abcnews.go.com/US/WireStory?id=6361818&page=1 (accessed April 5, 2010).
5. For just one Web site of many that compiles definitions of violations of academic integrity, as well as strategics to maintain academic integrity, see http://academicintegrity.depaul.edu.
6. A. Cohen, "Who Cheats? Our Survey on Deceit," *Wall Street Journal* (June 27, 2008), http://online.wsj.com/article/SB121448862810107085.html (accessed July 7, 2009).
7. A. Cohen, "Who Cheats? Our Survey on Deceit," *Wall Street Journal* (June 27, 2008), http://online.wsj.com/article/SB121448862810107085.html (accessed July 7, 2009).
8. See, *e.g.* http://www.bhpbilliton.com/bbContentRepository/docs/ourStakeholders 2008.pdf (accessed April 5, 2010).
9. http://www.bhpbilliton.com/bb/sustainableDevelopment/ourStakeholders.jsp (accessed April 5, 2010).
10. For a far more in-depth analysis of moral imagination, please see Patricia H. Werhane, *Moral Imagination and Management Decision-Making* (New York: Oxford University Press, 1999).
11. http://www.nytimes.com/2009/06/30/business/30bernietext.html (accessed July 11, 2009).
12. Crary, D./*Associated Press,* "Nationwide Survey Finds High Levels of Cheating, Stealing by High School Students," *ABC News* (Nov. 30, 2008), http://abcnews.go.com/US/WireStory?id=6361818&page=1 (accessed April 5, 2010).
13. Rick Tetzeli, "Business Students Cheat Most," *Fortune,* July 1, 1991, p. 14. See also James Stearns and Shaheen Borna, "A Comparison of the Ethics of Convicted Felons and Graduate Business Students: Implications for Business Practice and Business Ethics Education," *Teaching Business Ethics* 2 (1998), pp. 175–195. This research found that MBA students were more likely to cheat than convicted felons.
14. Stearns and Borna, "A Comparison of the Ethics of Convicted Felons and Graduate Business Student," p. 18.

15. "Fisher Communications CEO Will Take 10% Pay Cut," *Seattle Times* (Dec. 16, 2008), http://seattletimes.nwsource.com/html/businesstechnology/2008528477_webfisherco16.html (accessed April 5, 2010).

16. L. Hill, "Caterpillar Cuts Executive Salaries, Launches Voluntary Retrenchment Plan," *Mining Weekly* (Dec. 22, 2008), http://www.miningweekly.com/article.php?a_id5150024 (accessed April 5, 2010).

Readings

Reading 2-1

The Parable of the Sadhu

Bowen H. McCoy

Last year, as the first participant in the new six-month sabbatical program that Morgan Stanley has adopted, I enjoyed a rare opportunity to collect my thoughts as well as do some traveling. I spent the first three months in Nepal, walking 600 miles through 200 villages in the Himalayas and climbing some 120,000 vertical feet. My sole Western companion on the trip was an anthropologist who shed light on the cultural patterns of the villages that we passed through.

During the Nepal hike, something occurred that has had a powerful impact on my thinking about corporate ethics. Although some might argue that the experience has no relevance to business, it was a situation in which a basic ethical dilemma suddenly intruded into the lives of a group of individuals. How the group responded holds a lesson for all organizations, no matter how defined.

The Sadhu

The Nepal experience was more rugged than I had anticipated. Most commercial treks last two or three weeks and cover a quarter of the distance we traveled.

My friend Stephen, the anthropologist, and I were halfway through the 60-day Himalayan part of the trip when we reached the high point, an 18,000-foot pass over a crest that we'd have to traverse to reach the village of Muklinath, an ancient holy place for pilgrims.

Six years earlier, I had suffered pulmonary edema, an acute form of altitude sickness, at 16,500 feet in the vicinity of Everest base camp, so we were understandably concerned about what would happen at 18,000 feet. Moreover, the Himalayas were having their wettest spring in 20 years, hip-deep powder and ice had already driven us off one ridge. If we failed to cross the pass, I feared that the last half of our once-in-a-lifetime trip would be ruined.

The night before we would try the pass, we camped in a hut at 14,500 feet. In the photos taken at that camp, my face appears wan. The last village we'd passed through was a sturdy two-day walk below us, and I was tired.

During the late afternoon, four backpackers from New Zealand joined us, and we spent most of the night awake, anticipating the climb. Below, we could see the fires of two other parties, which turned out to be two Swiss couples and a Japanese hiking club.

To get over the steep part of the climb before the sun melted the steps cut in the ice, we departed at 3:30 A.M. The New Zealanders left first, followed by Stephen and myself, our porters and Sherpas, and then the Swiss. The Japanese lingered in their camp. The sky was clear, and we were confident that no spring storm would erupt that day to close the pass.

At 15,500 feet, it looked to me as if Stephen were shuffling and staggering a bit, which are symptoms of altitude sickness. (The initial stage of altitude sickness brings a headache and nausea. As the condition worsens, a climber may encounter difficult breathing, disorientation, aphasia, and paralysis.) I felt strong—my adrenaline was flowing—but I was very concerned about my ultimate ability to get across. A couple of our porters were also suffering from the height, and Pasang, our Sherpa sirdar (leader), was worried.

Just after daybreak, while we rested at 15,500 feet, one of the New Zealanders, who had gone ahead, came staggering down toward us with a body slung across his shoulders. He dumped the almost naked, barefoot body of an Indian holy man, a sadhu, at my feet. He had found the pilgrim lying on the ice, shivering and suffering from hypothermia. I cradled the sadhu's head and laid him out on the rocks. The New Zealander was angry. He wanted to get across the pass before the bright sun melted the snow. He said, "Look, I've done what I can. You have porters and Sherpa guides. You care for him. We're going on!" He turned and went back up the mountain to join his friends.

I took a carotid pulse and found that the sadhu was still alive. We figured he had probably visited the holy shrines at Muklinath and was on his way home. It was fruitless to question why he had chosen this desperately high route instead of the safe, heavily traveled caravan route through the Kali Gandaki gorge. Or why he was shoeless and almost naked, or how long he had been lying in the pass. The answers weren't going to solve our problem.

Stephen and the four Swiss began stripping off their outer clothing and opening their packs. The sadhu was soon clothed from head to foot. He was not able to walk, but he was very much alive. I looked down the mountain and spotted the Japanese climbers, marching up with a horse.

Without a great deal of thought, I told Stephen and Pasang that I was concerned about withstanding the heights to come and wanted to get over the pass. I took off after several of our porters who had gone ahead.

On the steep part of the ascent where, if the ice steps had given way, I would have slid down about 3,000 feet, I felt vertigo. I stopped for a breather, allowing the Swiss to catch up with me. I inquired about the sadhu and Stephen. They said that the sadhu was fine and that Stephen was just behind them. I set off again for the summit.

Stephen arrived at the summit an hour after I did. Still exhilarated by victory, I ran down the slope to congratulate him. He was suffering from altitude sickness—walking 15 steps, then stopping, walking 15 steps, then stopping. Pasang accompanied him all the way up. When I reached them, Stephen glared at me and said: "How do you feel about contributing to the death of a fellow man?"

I did not completely comprehend what he meant. "Is the sadhu dead?" I inquired.

"No," replied Stephen, "but he surely will be!"

After I had gone, followed not long after by the Swiss, Stephen had remained with the sadhu. When the Japanese had arrived, Stephen had asked to use their horse to transport the sadhu down to the hut. They had refused. He had then asked Pasang to have a group of our porters carry the sadhu. Pasang had resisted the idea, saying that the porters would have to exert all their energy to get themselves over the pass. He believed they could not carry a man down 1,000 feet to the hut, reclimb the slope, and get across safely before the snow melted. Pasang had pressed Stephen not to delay any longer.

The Sherpas had carried the sadhu down to a rock in the sun at about 15,000 feet and pointed out the hut another 500 feet below. The Japanese had given him food and drink. When they had last seen him, he was listlessly throwing rocks at the Japanese party's dog, which had frightened him.

We do not know if the sadhu lived or died.

For many of the following days and evenings, Stephen and I discussed and debated our behavior toward the sadhu. Stephen is a committed Quaker with deep moral vision. He said, "I feel that what happened with the sadhu is a good example of the breakdown between the individual ethic and the corporate ethic. No one person was willing to assume ultimate responsibility for the sadhu. Each was willing to do his bit just so long as it was not too inconvenient. When it got to be a bother, everyone just passed the buck to someone else and took off. Jesus was relevant to a more individualistic stage of society, but how do we interpret his teaching today in a world filled with large, impersonal organizations and groups?"

I defended the larger group, saying, "Look, we all cared. We all gave aid and comfort. Everyone did his bit. The New Zealander carried him down below the snow line. I took his pulse and suggested we treat him for hypothermia. You and the Swiss gave him clothing and got him warmed up. The Japanese gave him food and water. The Sherpas carried him down to the sun and pointed out the easy trail toward the hut. He was well enough to throw rocks at a dog. What more could we do?"

"You have just described the typical affluent Westerner's response to a problem. Throwing money—in this case, food and sweaters—at it, but not solving the fundamentals!" Stephen retorted.

"What would satisfy you?" I said. "Here we are, a group of New Zealanders, Swiss, Americans, and Japanese who have never met before and who are at the apex of one of the most powerful experiences of our lives. Some years the pass is so bad no one gets over it. What right does an almost naked pilgrim who chooses the wrong trail have to disrupt our lives? Even the Sherpas had no interest in risking the trip to help him beyond a certain point."

Stephen calmly rebutted, "I wonder what the Sherpas would have done if the sadhu had been a well-dressed Nepali, or what the Japanese would have done if the sadhu had been a well-dressed Asian, or what you would have done, Buzz, if the sadhu had been a well-dressed Western woman?"

"Where, in your opinion," I asked, "is the limit of our responsibility in a situation like this? We had our own well-being to worry about. Our Sherpa guides were unwilling to jeopardize us or the porters for the sadhu. No one else on the mountain was willing to commit himself beyond certain self-imposed limits."

Stephen said, "As individual Christians or people with a Western ethical tradition, we can fulfill our obligations in such a situation only if one, the sadhu dies in our care; two, the sadhu demonstrates to us that he can undertake the two-day walk down to the village; or three, we carry the sadhu for two days down to the village and persuade someone there to care for him."

"Leaving the sadhu in the sun with food and clothing—where he demonstrated hand-eye coordination by throwing a rock at a dog—comes close to fulfilling items one and two," I answered. "And it wouldn't have made sense to take him to the village where the people appeared to be far less caring than the Sherpas, so the third condition is impractical. Are you really saying that, no matter what the implications, we should, at the drop of a hat, have changed our entire plan?"

The Individual versus the Group Ethic

Despite my arguments, I felt and continue to feel guilt about the sadhu. I had literally walked through a classic moral dilemma without fully thinking through the consequences. My excuses for my actions include a high adrenaline flow, a superordinate goal, and a once-in-a-lifetime opportunity—common factors in corporate situations, especially stressful ones.

Real moral dilemmas are ambiguous, and many of us hike right through them, unaware that they exist. When, usually after the fact, someone makes an issue of one, we tend to resent his or her bringing it up. Often, when the full import of what we have done (or not done) hits us, we dig into a defensive position from which it is very difficult to emerge. In rare circumstances, we may contemplate what we have done from inside a prison.

Had we mountaineers been free of stress caused by the effort and the high altitude, we might have treated the sadhu differently. Yet isn't stress the real test of personal and corporate values? The instant decisions that executives make under pressure reveal the most about personal and corporate character.

Among the many questions that occur to me when I ponder my experience with the sadhu are: What are the practical limits of moral imagination and vision? Is there a collective or institutional ethic that differs from the ethics of the individual? At what level of effort or commitment can one discharge one's ethical responsibilities?

Not every ethical dilemma has a right solution. Reasonable people often disagree; otherwise there would be no dilemma. In a business context, however, it is essential that managers agree on a process for dealing with dilemmas.

Our experience with the sadhu offers an interesting parallel to business situations. An immediate response was mandatory. Failure to act was a decision in itself. Up on the mountain we could not resign and submit our résumés to a headhunter. In contrast to philosophy, business involves action and implementation—getting things done. Managers must come up with answers based on what they see and what they allow to influence their decision-making processes. On the mountain, none of us but Stephen realized the true dimensions of the situation we were facing.

One of our problems was that as a group we had no process for developing a consensus. We had no sense of purpose or plan. The difficulties of dealing with the sadhu were so complex that no one person could handle them. Because the group did not have a set of preconditions that could guide its action to an acceptable resolution, we reacted instinctively as individuals. The cross-cultural nature of the group added a further layer of complexity. We had no leader with whom we could all identify and in whose purpose we believed. Only Stephen was willing to take charge, but he could not gain adequate support from the group to care for the sadhu.

Some organizations do have values that transcend the personal values of their managers. Such values, which go beyond profitability, are usually revealed when the organization is under stress. People throughout the organization generally accept its values, which, because they are not presented as a rigid list of commandments, may be somewhat ambiguous. The stories people tell, rather than printed materials, transmit the organization's conceptions of what is proper behavior.

For 20 years, I have been exposed at senior levels to a variety of corporations and organizations. It is amazing how quickly an outsider can sense the tone and style of an organization and, with that, the degree of tolerated openness and freedom to challenge management.

Organizations that do not have a heritage of mutually accepted, shared values tend to become unhinged during stress, with each individual bailing out for himself or herself. In the great takeover battles we have witnessed during past years, companies that had strong cultures drew the wagons around them and fought it out, while other companies saw executives—supported by golden parachutes—bail out of the struggles.

Because corporations and their members are interdependent, for the corporation to be strong the members need to share a preconceived notion of correct behavior, a "business ethic," and think of it as a positive force, not a constraint.

As an investment banker, I am continually warned by well-meaning lawyers, clients, and associates to be wary of conflicts of interest. Yet if I were to run away from every difficult situation, I wouldn't be an effective investment banker. I have to feel my way through conflicts. An effective manager can't run from risk either; he or she has to confront risk. To feel "safe" in doing that, managers need the guidelines of an agreed-upon process and set of values within the organization.

After my three months in Nepal, I spent three months as an executive-in-residence at both the Stanford Business School and the University of California at Berkeley's Center for Ethics and Social Policy of the Graduate Theological Union. Those six months away from my job gave me time to assimilate 20 years of business experience. My thoughts turned often to the meaning of the leadership role in any large organization. Students at the seminary thought of themselves as antibusiness. But when I questioned them, they agreed that they distrusted all large organizations, including the church. They perceived all large organizations as impersonal and opposed to individual values and needs. Yet we all know of organizations in which people's values and beliefs are respected and their expressions encouraged. What makes the difference? Can we identify the difference and, as a result, manage more effectively?

The word *ethics* turns off many and confuses more. Yet the notions of shared values and an agreed-upon process for dealing with adversity and change—what many people mean when they talk about corporate culture seem to be at the heart of the ethical issue. People who are in touch with their own core beliefs and the beliefs of others and who are sustained by them can be more comfortable living on the cutting edge. At times, taking a tough line or a decisive stand in a muddle of ambiguity is the only ethical thing to do. If a manager is indecisive about a problem and spends time trying to figure out the "good" thing to do, the enterprise may be lost.

Business ethics, then, has to do with the authenticity and integrity of the enterprise. To be ethical is to follow the business as well as the cultural goals of the corporation, its owners, its employees, and its customers. Those who cannot serve the corporate vision are not authentic businesspeople and, therefore, are not ethical in the business sense.

At this stage of my own business experience, I have a strong interest in organizational behavior. Sociologists are keenly studying what they call corporate stories, legends, and heroes as a way organizations have of transmitting value systems. Corporations such as Arco have even hired consultants to perform an audit of their corporate culture. In a company, a leader is a person who understands, interprets, and manages the corporate value system. Effective managers, therefore, are action-oriented people who resolve conflict, are tolerant of ambiguity, stress, and change, and have a strong sense of purpose for themselves and their organizations.

If all this is true, I wonder about the role of the professional manager who moves from company to company. How can he or she quickly absorb the values and culture of different organizations? Or is there, indeed, an art of management that is totally transportable? Assuming that such fungible managers do exist, is it proper for them to manipulate the values of others?

What would have happened had Stephen and I carried the sadhu for two days back to the village and become involved with the villagers in his care? In four trips to Nepal, my most interesting experience occurred in 1975 when I lived in a Sherpa home in the Khumbu for five days while recovering from altitude sickness. The high point of Stephen's trip was an invitation to participate in a family funeral ceremony in Manang. Neither experience had to do with climbing the high passes of the Himalayas. Why were we so reluctant to try the lower path, the ambiguous trail? Perhaps because we did not have a leader who could reveal the greater purpose of the trip to us.

Why didn't Stephen, with his moral vision, opt to take the sadhu under his personal care? The answer is partly because Stephen was hard-stressed physically himself and partly because, without some support system that encompassed our involuntary and episodic community on the mountain, it was beyond his individual capacity to do so.

I see the current interest in corporate culture and corporate value systems as a positive response to pessimism such as Stephen's about the decline of the role of the individual in large organizations. Individuals who operate from a thoughtful set of personal values provide the foundation for a corporate culture. A corporate tradition that encourages freedom of inquiry, supports personal values, and reinforces a focused sense of direction can fulfill the need to combine individuality with the prosperity and success of the group. Without such corporate support, the individual is lost.

That is the lesson of the sadhu. In a complex corporate situation, the individual requires and deserves the support of the group. When people cannot find such support in their organizations, they don't know how to act. If such support is forthcoming, a person has a stake in the success of the group and can add much to the process of establishing and maintaining a corporate culture. Management's challenge is to be sensitive to individual needs, to shape them, and to direct and focus them for the benefit of the group as a whole.

For each of us the sadhu lives. Should we stop what we are doing and comfort him; or should we keep trudging up toward the high pass? Should I pause to help the derelict I pass on the street each night as I walk by the Yale Club en route to Grand Central Station? Am I his brother? What is the nature of our responsibility if we consider ourselves to be ethical persons? Perhaps it is to change the values of the group so that it can, with all its resources, take the other road.

When Do We Take a Stand?

I wrote about my experiences purposely to present an ambiguous situation. I never found out if the sadhu lived or died. I can attest, though, that the sadhu lives on in his story. He lives in the ethics classes I teach each year at business schools and churches. He lives in the classrooms of numerous business schools, where professors have taught the case to tens of thousands of students. He lives in several casebooks on ethics and on an educational video. And he lives in organizations such as the American Red Cross and AT&T, which use his story in their ethics training.

As I reflect on the sadhu now, 15 years after the fact, I first have to wonder, What actually happened on that Himalayan slope? When I first wrote about the event, I reported the experience in as much detail as I could remember, but I shaped it to the needs of a good classroom discussion. After years of reading my story, viewing it on video, and hearing others discuss it, I'm not sure I myself know what actually occurred on the mountainside that day!

I've also heard a wide variety of responses to the story. The sadhu, for example, may not have wanted our help at all—he may have been intentionally bringing on his own death as a way to holiness. Why had he taken the dangerous way over the pass instead of the caravan route through the gorge? Hindu businesspeople have told me that in trying to assist the sadhu, we were being typically arrogant Westerners imposing our cultural values on the world.

I've learned that each year along the pass, a few Nepali porters are left to freeze to death outside the tents of the unthinking tourists who hired them. A few years ago, a French group even left one of their own, a young French woman, to die there. The difficult pass seems to demonstrate a perverse version of Gresham's law of currency: The bad practices of previous travelers have driven out the values that new travelers might have followed if they were at home. Perhaps that helps to explain why our porters behaved as they did and why it was so difficult for Stephen or anyone else to establish a different approach on the spot.

Our Sherpa sirdar, Pasang, was focused on his responsibility for bringing us up the mountain safe and sound. (His livelihood and status in the Sherpa ethnic group depended on our safe return.) We were weak, our party was split, the porters were well on their way to the top with all our gear and food, and a storm would have separated us irrevocably from our logistical base.

The fact was, we had no plan for dealing with the contingency of the sadhu. There was nothing we could do to unite our multicultural group in the little time we had. An ethical dilemma had come upon us unexpectedly, an element of drama that may explain why the sadhu's story has continued to attract students.

I am often asked for help in teaching the story. I usually advise keeping the details as ambiguous as possible. A true ethical dilemma requires a decision between two hard choices. In the case of the sadhu, we had to decide how much to sacrifice ourselves to take care of a stranger. And given the constraints of our trek, we had to make a group decision, not an individual one. If a large majority of students in a class ends up thinking I'm a bad person because of my decision on the mountain, the instructor may not have given the case its due. The same is true if the majority sees no problem with the choices we made.

Any class's response depends on its setting, whether it's a business school, a church, or a corporation. I've found that younger students are more likely to see the issue as black-and-white, whereas older ones tend to see shades of gray. Some have seen a conflict between the different ethical approaches that we followed at the time. Stephen felt he had to do everything he could to save the sadhu's life, in accordance with his Christian ethic of compassion. I had a utilitarian response: Do the greatest good for the greatest number. Give a burst of aid to minimize the sadhu's exposure, then continue on our way.

The basic question of the case remains, When do we take a stand? When do we allow a "sadhu" to intrude into our daily lives? Few of us can afford the time or effort to take care of every needy person we encounter. How much must we give of ourselves? And how do we prepare our organizations and institutions so they will respond appropriately in a crisis? How do we influence them if we do not agree with their points of view?

We cannot quit our jobs over every ethical dilemma, but if we continually ignore our sense of values, who do we become? As a journalist asked at a recent conference on ethics, "Which ditch are we willing to die in?" For each of us, the answer is a bit different. How we act in response to that question defines better than anything else who we are, just as, in a collective sense, our acts define our institutions. In effect, the sadhu is always there, ready to remind us of the tensions between our own goals and the claims of strangers.

Source: Reprinted by permission of Harvard Business Review. "The Parable of the Sadhu," and "When Do We Take a Stand?" both by Bowen H. McCoy, May–June, 1977.

Reading 2-2

Managing for Stakeholders[1]

R. Edward Freeman

I. Introduction

The purpose of this essay is to outline an emerging view of business that we shall call "managing for stakeholders".[2] This view has emerged over the past thirty years from a group of scholars in a diverse set of disciplines, from finance to philosophy.[3] The basic idea is that businesses, and the executives who manage them, actually do and should create value for customers, suppliers, employees, communities, and financiers (or shareholders). And, that we need to pay careful attention to how these relationships are managed and how value gets created for these stakeholders. We contrast this idea with the dominant model of business activity; namely, that businesses are to be managed solely for the benefit of shareholders. Any other benefits (or harms) that are created are incidental.[4]

Simple ideas create complex questions, and we proceed as follows. In the next section we examine why the dominant story or model of business that is deeply embedded in our culture is no longer workable. It is resistant to change, not consistent with the law, and for the most part, simply ignores matters of ethics. Each of these flaws is fatal in business world of the 21st Century.

We then proceed to define the basic ideas of "managing for stakeholders" and why it solves some of the problems of the dominant model. In particular we pay attention to how using 'stakeholder' as a basic unit of analysis makes it more difficult to ignore matters of ethics. We argue that the primary responsibility of the executive is to create as much value for stakeholders as possible, and that no stakeholder interest is viable in isolation of the other stakeholders. We sketch three primary arguments from ethical theory for adopting "managing for stakeholders." We conclude by outlining a fourth "pragmatist argument" that suggests we see managing for stakeholders as a new narrative about business that lets us improve the way we currently create value for each other. Capitalism is on this view a system of social cooperation and collaboration, rather than primarily a system of competition.

II. The Dominant Story: Managerial Capitalism with Shareholders at the Center

The modern business corporation has emerged during the 20th Century as one of the most important innovations in human history. Yet the changes that we are now experiencing call for its reinvention. Before we suggest what this revision, "managing for stakeholders" or "stakeholder capitalism," is, first we need to understand how the dominant story came to be told.

Somewhere in the past, organizations were quite simple and "doing business" consisted of buying raw materials from suppliers, converting it to products, and selling it to customers. For the most part owner-entrepreneurs founded such simple businesses and worked at the business along with members of their families. The development of new production processes, such as the assembly line, meant that jobs could be specialized and more work could be accomplished. New technologies and sources of power became readily available. These and other social and political forces combined to require larger amounts of capital, well beyond the scope of most individual owner-manager-employees. Additionally, "workers" or non-family members began to dominate the firm and were the rule rather than the exception.

Ownership of the business became more dispersed, as capital was raised from banks, stockholders, and other institutions. Indeed, the management of the firm became separated from the ownership of the firm. And, in order to be successful, the top managers of the business had to simultaneously satisfy the owners, the employees and their unions, suppliers and customers. This system of organization of businesses along the lines set forth here was known as managerial capitalism or laissez faire capitalism, or more recently, shareholder capitalism.[5]

As businesses grew, managers developed a means of control via the divisionalized firm. Led by Alfred Sloan at General Motors, the divisionalized firm with a central headquarters staff was widely adapted.[6] The dominant model for managerial authority was the military and civil service bureaucracy. By creating rational structures and processes, the orderly progress of business growth could be well-managed.

Thus, managerialism, hierarchy, stability, and predictability all evolved together, in the United States and Europe, to form the most powerful economic system in the history of humanity. The rise of bureaucracy and managerialism was so strong, that the economist Joseph Schumpeter predicted that it would wipe out the creative force of capitalism, stifling innovation in its drive for predictability and stability.

During the last 50 years this "Managerial Model" has put "shareholders" at the center of the firm as the most important group for managers to worry about. This mindset has dealt with the increasing complexity of the business world by focusing more intensely on "shareholders" and "creating value for shareholders." It has become common wisdom to "increase shareholder value", and many companies have instituted complex incentive compensation plans aimed at aligning the interests of executives with the interests of shareholders. These incentive plans are often tied to the price of a company's stock which is affected by many factors not the least of which is the expectations of Wall Street analysts about earnings per share each quarter. Meeting Wall Street targets, and forming a stable and predictable base of quarter over quarter increases in earnings per share has become the standard for measuring company performance. Indeed all of the recent scandals at Enron, Worldcom, Tyco, Arthur Anderson and others are in part due to executives trying to increase shareholder value, sometimes in opposition to accounting rules and law. Unfortunately, the world has changed so that the stability and predictability required by the shareholder approach can no longer be assured.

The Dominant Model Is Resistant to Change

The Managerial View of business with shareholders at the center is inherently resistant to change. It puts shareholders' interests over and above the interests of customers, suppliers, employees, and others, as if these interests must conflict with each other. It understands a business as an essentially hierarchical organization fastened together with authority to act in the shareholders' interests. Executives often speak in the language of hierarchy as "working for shareholders", "shareholders are the boss", and "you have to do what the shareholders want". On this interpretation, change should occur only when the shareholders are unhappy, and as long as executives can produce a series of incrementally better financial results there is no problem. According to this view the only change that counts is change oriented toward shareholder value. If customers are unhappy, if accounting rules have been compromised, if product quality is bad, if environmental disaster looms, even if competitive forces threaten, the only interesting questions are whether and how these forces for change affect shareholder value, measured by the price of the stock every day. Unfortunately in today's world there is just too much uncertainty and complexity to rely on such a single criterion. Business in the 21st Century is global and multi-faceted, and shareholder value may not capture that dynamism. Or, if it does, as the theory suggests it must eventually, it will be too late for executives to do anything about it. The dominant story may work for how things turn out in the long run on Wall Street, but managers have to act with an eye to Main Street as well, to anticipate change to try and take advantage of the dynamism of business.[7]

The Dominant Model Is Not Consistent with the Law

In actual fact the clarity of putting shareholders' interests first, above that of customers, suppliers, employees, and communities, flies in the face of the reality the law. The law has evolved to put constraints on the kinds of tradeoffs that can be made. In fact the law of corporations gives a less clear answer to the question of in whose interest and for whose benefit the corporation should be governed. The law has evolved over the years to give *de facto* standing to the claims of groups other than stockholders. It has in effect, required that the claims of customers, suppliers, local communities, and employees be taken into consideration.

For instance, the doctrine of "privity of contract," as articulated in *Winterbottom v. Wright* in 1842, has been eroded by recent developments in products liability law. *Greenman v Yuba Power* gives the manufacturer strict liability for damage caused by its products, even though the seller has exercised all possible care in the preparation and sale of the product and the consumer has not bought the product from nor entered into any contractual arrangement with the manufacturer. *Caveat emptor* has been replaced in large part, with *caveat venditor*. The Consumer Product Safety Commission has the power to enact product recalls, essentially leading to an increase in the number of voluntary product recalls by companies seeking to mitigate legal damage awards. Some industries are required to provide information to customers about a product's ingredients, whether or not the customers want and are willing to pay for this information. Thus, companies must take the interests of customers into account, by law.

A similar story can be told about the evolution of the law forcing management to take the interests of employees into account. The National Labor Relations Act gave employees the right to unionize and to bargain in good faith. It set up the National Labor Relations Board to enforce these rights with management. The Equal Pay Act of 1963 and Title VII of the Civil Rights Act of 1964 constrain management from discrimination in hiring practices; these have been followed with the Age Discrimination in Employment Act of 1967, and recent extensions affecting people with disabilities. The emergence of a body of administrative case law arising from labor-management disputes and the historic settling of discrimination claims with large employers have caused the emergence of a body of management practice that is consistent with the legal guarantee of the rights of employees.

The law has also evolved to try and protect the interests of local communities. The Clean Air Act and Clean Water Act, and various amendments to these classic pieces of legislation, have constrained management from "spoiling the commons". In an historic case, *Marsh v. Alabama,* the Supreme Court ruled that a company-owned town was subject to the provisions of the U.S. Constitution, thereby guaranteeing the rights of local citizens and negating the "property rights" of the firm. Current issues center around protecting local businesses, forcing companies to pay the health care costs of their employees, increases in minimum wages, environmental standards, and the effects of business development on the lives of local community members. These issues fill the local political landscapes and executives and their companies must take account of them.

Some may argue that the constraints of the law, at least in the U.S., have become increasingly irrelevant in a world where business is global in nature. However, globalization simply makes this argument stronger. The laws that are relevant to business have evolved differently around the world, but they have evolved nonetheless to take into account the interests of groups other than just shareholders. Each state in India has a different set of regulations that affect how a company can do business. In China the law has evolved to give business some property rights but it is far from exclusive. And, in most of the European Union, laws around "civil society" and the role of "employees" are much more complex than even U.S. law.

"Laissez faire capitalism" is simply a myth. The idea that business is about "maximizing value for stockholders regardless of the consequences to others" is one that has outlived its usefulness. The dominant model simply does not describe how business operates. Another way to see this is that if executives always have to qualify "maximize shareholder value" with exceptions of law, or even good practice, then the dominant story isn't very useful anymore. There are just too many exceptions. The dominant story could be saved by arguing that it describes a normative view about how business should operate, despite how actual businesses have evolved.[8] So we need to look more closely at some of the conceptual and normative problems that the dominant model raises.

The Dominant Model Is Not Consistent with Basic Ethics

Previously we have argued that most theories of business rely on separating "business" decisions from "ethical" decisions.[9] This is seen most clearly in the popular joke about "business ethics as an oxymoron". More formally we might suggest that we define:

The Separation Fallacy

It is useful to believe that sentences like, "x is a business decision" have no ethical content or any implicit ethical point of view. And, it is useful to believe that sentences like "x is an ethical decision, the best thing to do all things considered" have no content or implicit view about value creation and trade (business).

This fallacy underlies much of the dominant story about business, as well as in other areas in society. There are two implications of rejecting the Separation Fallacy. The first is that almost any business decision has some ethical content. To see that this true one need only ask whether the following questions make sense for virtually any business decision.

The Open Question Argument

1. If this decision is made for whom is value created and destroyed?
2. Who is harmed and/or benefited by this decision?
3. Whose rights are enabled and whose values are realized by this decision (and whose are not)?
4. What kind of person will I (we) become if we make this decision?

Since these questions are always open for most business decisions, it is reasonable to give up the Separation Fallacy, which would have us believe that these questions aren't relevant for making business decisions, or that they could never be answered. We need a theory about business that builds in answers to the "Open Question Argument" above. One such answer would be "Only value to shareholders counts", but such an answer would have to be enmeshed in the language of ethics as well as business. Milton Friedman, unlike most of his expositors, may actually give such a morally rich answer. He claims that the responsibility of the executive is to make profits subject to law and ethical custom. Depending on how "law and ethical custom" is interpreted, the key difference with the stakeholder approach may well be that we disagree about how the world works. In order to create value we believe that it is better to focus on integrating business and ethics within a complex set of stakeholder relationships rather than treating ethics as a side constraint on making profits. In short we need a theory that has as its basis what we might call:

The Integration Thesis

Most business decisions or sentences about business have some ethical content, or implicit ethical view. Most ethical decisions or sentences about ethics have some business content or implicit view about business.[10]

One of the most pressing challenges facing business scholars is to tell compelling narratives that have the Integration Thesis at its heart. This is essentially the task that a group of scholars, "business ethicists" and "stakeholder theorists", have begun over the last 30 years. We need to go back to the very basics of ethics. Ethics is about the rules, principles, consequences, matters of character, etc. that we use to live together. These ideas give us a set of open questions that we are constantly searching for better ways to answer in reasonable complete ways.[11] One might define "ethics" as a conversation about how we can reason together and solve our differences, recognize where our interests are joined and need development, so that we can all flourish without resorting to coercion and violence. Some may disagree with such a definition, and we do not intend to privilege definitions, but such a pragmatist approach to ethics entails that we reason and talk together to try and create a better world for all of us.

If our critiques of the dominant model are correct then we need to start over by re-conceptualizing the very language that we use to understand how business operates. We want to suggest that something like the following principle is implicit in most reasonably comprehensive views about ethics.

The Responsibility Principle[12]

Most people, most of the time, want to, actually do, and should accept responsibility for the effects of their actions on others.

Clearly the Responsibility Principle is incompatible with the Separation Fallacy. If business is separated from ethics, there is no question of moral responsibility for business decisions; hence, the joke is that 'business ethics' is an oxymoron. More clearly still, without something like the Responsibility Principle it is difficult to see how ethics gets off the ground. "Responsibility" may well be a difficult and multi-faceted idea. There are surely many different ways to understand it. But, if we are not willing to accept the responsibility for our own actions (as limited as that may be due to complicated issues of causality and the like), then ethics, understood as how we reason together so we can all flourish, is likely an exercise in bad faith.

If we want to give up the separation fallacy and adopt the integration thesis, if the open question argument makes sense, and if something like the responsibility thesis is necessary, then we need a new model for business. And, this new story must be able to explain how value creation at once deals with economics and ethics, and how it takes account of all of the effects of business action on others. Such a model exists, and has been developing over the last 30 years by management researchers and ethics scholars, and there are many businesses who have adopted this "stakeholder framework" for their businesses.

III. Managing for Stakeholders

The basic idea of "managing for stakeholders" is quite simple. Business can be understood as a set of relationships among groups which have a stake in the activities that make up the business. Business is about how customers, suppliers, employees, financiers (stockholders, bondholders, banks, etc.), communities and managers interact and create value. To understand a business is to know how these relationships work. And, the executive's or entrepreneur's job is to manage and shape these relationships, hence the title, "managing for stakeholders".

Reading figure 2.1 depicts the idea of "managing for stakeholders" in a variation of the classic "wheel and spoke" diagram.[13] However, it is important to note that the stakeholder idea is perfectly

READING FIGURE 2.1

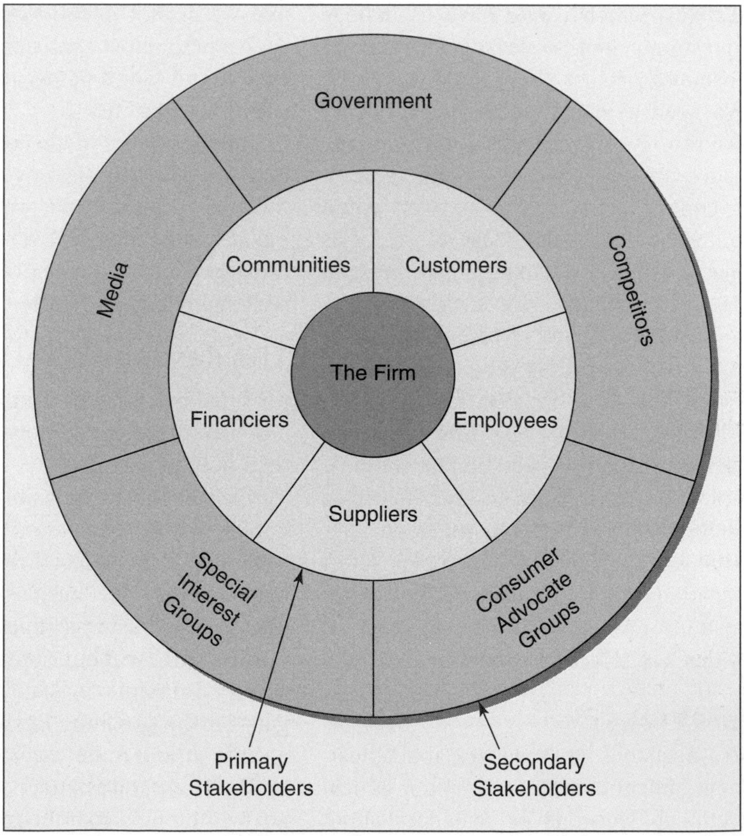

general. Corporations are not the center of the universe, and there are many possible pictures. One might put customers in the center to signal that a company puts customers as the key priority. Another might put employees in the center and link them to customers and shareholders. We prefer the generic diagram because it suggests, pictorially, that "managing for stakeholders" is a theory about management and business; hence, managers and companies in the center. But, there is no larger metaphysical claim here.

Stakeholders and Stakes

Owners or financiers (a better term) clearly have a financial stake in the business in the form of stocks, bonds, and so on, and they expect some kind of financial return from them. Of course, the stakes of financiers will differ by type of owner, preferences for money, moral preferences, and so on, as well as by type of firm. The shareholders of Google may well want returns as well as be supportive of Google's articulated purpose of "Do No Evil". To the extent that it makes sense to talk about the financiers "owning the firm", they have a concomitant responsibility for the uses of their property.

Employees have their jobs and usually their livelihood at stake; they often have specialized skills for which there is usually no perfectly elastic market. In return for their labor, they expect security, wages, benefits and meaningful work. Often, employees are expected to participate in the decision making of the organization, and if the employees are management or senior executives we see them as shouldering a great deal of responsibility for the conduct of the organization as a whole. And, employees are sometimes financiers as well, since many companies have stock ownership plans, and loyal employees who believe in the future of their companies often voluntarily invest. One way to think about the employee relationship is in terms of contracts. Customers and suppliers exchange resources for the products and services of the firm and in return receive the benefits of the products and services. As with financiers and employees, the customer and supplier relationships are enmeshed in ethics. Companies make promises to customers via their advertising, and when products or services don't deliver on these promises then management has a responsibility to rectify the situation. It is also important to have suppliers who are committed to making a company better. If suppliers find a better, faster, and cheaper way of making critical parts or services, then both supplier and company can win. Of course, some suppliers simply compete on price, but even so, there is a moral element of fairness and transparency to the supplier relationship.

Finally, the local community grants the firm the right to build facilities, and in turn, it benefits from the tax base and economic and social contributions of the firm. Companies have a real impact on communities, and being located in a welcoming community helps a company create value for its other stakeholders. In return for the provision of local services, companies are expected to be good citizens, as is any individual person. It should not expose the community to unreasonable hazards in the form of pollution, toxic waste, etc. It should keep whatever commitments it makes to the community, and operate in a transparent manner as far as possible. Of course, companies don't have perfect knowledge, but when management discovers some danger or runs afoul of new competition, it is expected to inform and work with local communities to mitigate any negative effects, as far as possible.

While any business must consist of financiers, customers, suppliers, employees, and communities, it is possible to think about other stakeholders as well. We can define "stakeholder" in a number of ways. First of all we could define the term fairly narrowly to capture the idea that any business, large or small, is about creating value for "those groups without whose support, the business would cease to be viable". The inner circle of Reading figure 2.1 depicts this view. Almost every business is concerned at some level with relationships among financiers, customers, suppliers, employees, and communities. We might call these groups "primary" or "definitional". However, it should be noted that as a business starts up, sometimes one particular stakeholder is more important than another. In a new business start up, sometimes there are no suppliers, and paying lots of attention to one or two key customers, as well as to the venture capitalist (financier) is the right approach.

There is also a somewhat broader definition that captures the idea that if a group or individual can affect a business, then the executives must take that group into consideration in thinking about how to create value. Or, a stakeholder is any group or individual that can affect or be affected by the realization of an organization's purpose. At a minimum some groups affect primary stakeholders and we might see these as stakeholders in the outer ring of Reading figure 2.1 and call them "secondary" or "instrumental".

There are other definitions that have emerged during the last 30 years, some based on risks and rewards, some based on mutuality of interests. And, the debate over finding the one "true definition" of 'stakeholder' is not likely to end. We prefer a more pragmatist approach of being clear of the purpose of using any of the proposed definitions. Business is a fascinating field of study. There are very few principles and definitions that apply to all businesses all over the world. Furthermore, there are many different ways to run a successful business, or if you like, many different flavors of "managing for stakeholders". We see limited usefulness in trying to define one model of business, either based on the shareholder or stakeholder view that works for all businesses everywhere. We see much value to be gained in examining how the stakes work in the value creation process, and the role of the executive.

IV. The Responsibility of the Executive in Managing for Stakeholders

Executives play a special role in the activity of the business enterprise. On the one hand, they have a stake like every other employee in terms of an actual or implied employment contract. And, that stake is linked to the stakes of financiers, customers, suppliers, communities, and other employees. In addition, executives are expected to look after the health of the overall enterprise, to keep the varied stakes moving in roughly the same direction, and to keep them in balance.[14] No stakeholder stands alone in the process of value creation. The stakes of each stakeholder group are multi-faceted, and inherently connected to each other. How could a bondholder recognize any returns without management paying attention to the stakes of customers or employees? How could customers get the products and services they need without employees and suppliers? How could employees have a decent place to live without communities? Many thinkers see the dominant problem of "managing for stakeholders" as how to solve the priority problem, or "which stakeholders are more important," or "how do we make tradeoffs among stakeholders". We see this as a secondary issue.

First and foremost, we need to see stakeholder interests as joint, as inherently tied together. Seeing stakeholder interests as "joint" rather than opposed is difficult. It is not always easy to find a way to accommodate all stakeholder interests. It is easier to trade off one versus another. Why not delay spending on new products for customers in order to keep earnings a bit higher? Why not cut employee medical benefits in order to invest in a new inventory control system?

Managing for stakeholders suggests that executives try to reframe the questions. How can we invest in new products and create higher earnings? How can we be sure our employees are healthy and happy and are able to work creatively so that we can capture the benefits of new information technology such as inventory control systems? In a recent book reflecting on his experience as CEO of Medtronic, Bill George summarized the managing for stakeholders mindset:[15]

> Serving all your stakeholders is the best way to produce long term results and create a growing; prosperous company . . . Let me be very clear about this: there is no conflict between serving all your stakeholders and providing excellent returns for shareholders. In the long term it is impossible to have one without the other. However, serving all these stakeholder groups requires discipline, vision, and committed leadership.

The primary responsibility of the executive is to create as much value as possible for stakeholders.[16] Where stakeholder interests conflict, the executive must find a way to rethink the problems so that these interests can go together, so that even more value can be created for each. If tradeoffs have to be made, as often happens in the real world, then the executive must figure out how to make the tradeoffs, and immediately begin improving the tradeoffs for all sides. Managing for stakeholders is about creating as much value as possible for stakeholders, without resorting to tradeoffs.

We believe that this task is more easily accomplished when a business has a sense of purpose. Furthermore, there are few limits on the kinds of purpose that can drive a business. Wal-Mart may stand for "everyday low price". Merck can stand for "alleviating human suffering". The point is that if an entrepreneur or an executive can find a purpose that speaks to the hearts and minds of key stakeholders, it is more likely that there will be sustained success.

Purpose is complex and inspirational. The Grameen Bank wants to eliminate poverty. Fannie Mae wants to make housing affordable to every income level in society. Tastings (a local restaurant) wants to bring the taste of really good food and wine to lots of people in the community. And, all of these organizations have to generate profits, or else they cannot pursue their purposes. Capitalism works because we can pursue our purpose with others. When we coalesce around a big idea, or a joint purpose evolves from our day to day activities with each other, then great things can happen. To create value for stakeholders, executives must understand that business is fully situated in the realm of humanity. Businesses are human institutions populated by real live complex human beings. Stakeholders have names and faces and children. They are not mere placeholders for social roles. As such, matters of ethics are routine when one takes a managing for stakeholders approach. Of course this should go without saying, but a part of the dominant story about business is that business people are only in it for their own narrowly defined self interest. One main assumption of the managerial view with shareholders at the center is that shareholders only care about returns, and therefore their agents, managers, should only care about returns. However, this does not fit either our experiences or our aspirations. In the words of one CEO, "The only assets I manage go up and down the elevators everyday".

Most human beings are complicated. Most of us do what we do because we are self-interested and interested in others. Business works in part because of our urge to create things with others and for others. Working on a team, or creating a new product or delivery mechanism that makes customers lives better or happier or more pleasurable all can be contributing factors to why we go to work each day. And, this is not to deny the economic incentive of getting a pay check. The assumption of narrow self-interest is extremely limiting, and can be self-reinforcing—people can begin to act in a narrow self-interested way if they believe that is what is expected of them, as some of the scandals such as Enron, have shown. We need to be open to a more complex psychology—one any parent finds familiar as they have shepherded the growth and development of their children.

V. Some Arguments for Managing for Stakeholders

Once you say stakeholders are persons then the ideas of ethics are automatically applicable. However you interpret the idea of "stakeholders", you must pay attention to the effects of your actions on others. And, something like the Responsibility Principle suggests that this is a cornerstone of any adequate ethical theory. There are at least three main arguments for adopting a managing for stakeholders approach. Philosophers will see these as connected to the three main approaches to ethical theory that have developed historically. We shall briefly set forth sketches of these arguments, and then suggest that there is a more powerful fourth argument.[17]

The Argument from Consequences

A number of theorists have argued that the main reason that the dominant model of managing for shareholders is a good idea is that it leads to the best consequences for all. Typically these arguments invoke Adam Smith's idea of the invisible hand, whereby each business actor pursues her own self interest and the greatest good of all actually emerges. The problem with this argument is that we now know with modern general equilibrium economics that the argument only works under very specialized conditions that seldom describe the real world. And further, we know that if the economic conditions get very close to those needed to produce the greatest good, there is no guarantee that the greatest good will actually result.

Managing for stakeholders may actually produce better consequences for all stakeholders because it recognizes that stakeholder interests are joint. If one stakeholder pursues its interests at the expense of all the others, then the others will either withdraw their support, or look to create another network of stakeholder value creation. This is not to say that there are not times when one stakeholder will benefit at the expense of others, but if this happens continuously over time, then in a relatively free society, stakeholders will either: (1) exit to form a new stakeholder network that satisfies their needs; (2) use the political process to constrain the offending stakeholder; or, (3) invent some other form of activity to satisfy their particular needs.[18]

Alternatively, if we think about stakeholders engaged in a series of bargains among themselves, then we would expect that as individual stakeholders recognized their joint interests, and made good decisions based on these interests, better consequences would result, than if they each narrowly pursued their individual self interests.[19]

Now it may be objected that such an approach ignores "social consequences" or "consequences to society", and hence, that we need a concept of "corporate social responsibility" to mitigate these effects. This objection is a vestigial limb of the dominant model. Since the only effects, on that view, were economic effects, then we need to think about "social consequences" or "corporate social responsibility". However, if stakeholder relationships are understood to be fully embedded in morality, then there is no need for an idea like corporate social responsibility. We can replace it with "corporate stakeholder responsibility" which is a dominant feature of managing for stakeholders.

The Argument from Rights

The dominant story gives property rights in the corporation exclusively to shareholders, and the natural question arises about the rights of other stakeholders who are affected. One way to understand managing for stakeholders is that it takes this question of rights, seriously. If you believe that rights make sense, and further that if one person has a right to X then all persons have a right to X, it is just much easier to think about these issues using a stakeholder approach. For instance, while shareholders may well have property rights, these rights are not absolute, and should not be seen as such. Shareholders may not use their property to abridge the rights of others. For instance, shareholders and their agents, managers, may not use corporate property to violate the right to life of others. One way to understand managing for stakeholders is that it assumes that stakeholders have some rights. Now it is notoriously difficult to parse the idea of "rights". But, if executives take managing for stakeholders seriously, they will automatically think about what is owed to customers, suppliers, employees, financiers and communities, in virtue of their stake, and in virtue of their basic humanity.

The Argument from Character

One of the strongest arguments for managing for stakeholders is that it asks executives and entrepreneurs to consider the question of what kind of company they want to create and build. The answer to this question will be in large part an issue of character. Aspiration matters. The business virtues of efficiency, fairness, respect, integrity, keeping commitments, and others are all critical in being successful at creating value for stakeholders. These virtues are simply absent when we think only about the dominant model and its sole reliance on a narrow economic logic.

If we frame the central question of management as "how do we create value for shareholders" then the only virtue that emerges is one of loyalty to the interests of shareholders. However if we frame the central question more broadly as "how do we create and sustain the creation of value for stakeholders" or "how do we get stakeholder interests all going in the same direction," then it is easy to see how many of the other virtues are relevant. Taking a stakeholder approach helps people decide how companies can contribute to their well-being and kinds of lives they want to lead. By making ethics explicit and building it into the basic way we think about business, we avoid a situation of bad faith and self deception.

The Pragmatist's Argument

The previous three arguments point out important reasons for adopting a new story about business. Pragmatists want to know how we can live better, how we can create both ourselves and our communities in way where values such as freedom and solidarity are present in our everyday lives to the maximal extent. While it is sometimes useful to think about consequences, rights, and character in isolation, in reality our lives are richer if we can have a conversation about how to live together better. There is a long tradition of pragmatist ethics dating to philosophers such as William James and John Dewey. More recently philosopher Richard Rorty has expressed the pragmatist ideal:[20]

> . . . pragmatists . . . hope instead that human beings will come to enjoy more money, more free time, and greater social equality, and also that they will develop more empathy, more ability to put themselves in the shoes of others. We hope that human beings will behave more decently toward one another as their standard of living improves.

By building into the very conceptual framework we use to think about business a concern with freedom, equality, consequences, decency, shared purpose, and paying attention to all of the effects of how we create value for each other, we can make business a human institution, and perhaps remake it in a way that sustains us.

For the pragmatist, business (and capitalism) has evolved as a social practice; and important one that we use to create value and trade with each other. On this view, first and foremost, business is about collaboration. Of course, in a free society, stakeholders are free to form competing networks. But, the fuel for capitalism is our desire to create something of value, and to create it for ourselves and others. The spirit of capitalism is the spirit of individual achievement together with the spirit of accomplishing great tasks in collaboration with others. Managing for stakeholders makes this plain so that we can get about the business of creating better selves and better communities.

End Notes

1. The ideas in this paper have had a long development time. The ideas here have been reworked from: R. Edward Freeman, *Strategic Management: A Stakeholder Approach* [Boston: Pitman, 1984]; R. Edward Freeman, "A Stakeholder Theory of the Modern Corporation, in T. Beauchamp and N. Bowie (eds.) *Ethical Theory and Business* [Englewood cliffs: Prentice Hall, 7th edition, 2005], also in earlier editions coauthored with William Evan; Andrew Wicks, R. Edward Freeman, Patricia Werhane, and Kirsten Martin, *Business Ethics: A Managerial Approach,* [Englewood Cliffs: Prentice Hall, forthcoming in 2008];

and, R. Edward Freeman, Jeffrey Harrison, and Andrew Wicks, *Managing for Stakeholders,* [New Haven: Yale University Press, forthcoming in 2007]. I am grateful to editors and coauthors for permission to rework these ideas here.

2. It has been called a variety of things from "stakeholder management", "stakeholder capitalism", "a stakeholder theory of the modern corporation", etc. Our reasons for choosing "managing for stakeholders" will become clearer as we proceed. Many others have worked on these ideas, and should not be held accountable for the rather idiosyncratic view outlined here.
3. For a stylized history of the idea see R. Edward Freeman, "The Development of Stakeholder Theory: An Idiosyncratic Approach," in K. Smith and M. Hitt, (eds.) *Great Minds in Management,* Oxford: Oxford University Press, 2005.
4. One doesn't manage "for" these benefits (and harms).
5. The difference between managerial and shareholder capitalism is large. However, the existence of agency theory lets us treat the two identically for our purposes here. Both agree on the view that the modern firm is characterized by the separation of decision making and residual risk bearing. The resulting agency problem is the subject of a vast literature.
6. Alfred Chandler's brilliant book, Strategy and Structure, Boston: MIT Press, 1970. chronicles the rise of the divisionalized corporation. For a not so flattering account of General Motors during the same time period see Peter Drucker's classic work, *The Concept of the Corporation.* New York: Transaction Publishers, Reprint Edition, 1993.
7. Executives can take little comfort in the nostrum that in the long run things work out and the most efficient companies survive. Some market theorists suggest that finance theory acts like "universal acid" cutting through every possible management decision, whether or not, actual managers are aware of it. Perhaps the real difference between the dominant model and the "managing for stakeholders" model proposed here is that they are simply "about" different things. The dominant model is about the strict and narrow economic logic of markets, and the "managing for stakeholders" model is about how human beings create value for each other.
8. Often the flavor of the response of finance theorists sounds like this. The world would be better off if, despite all of the imperfections, executives tried to maximize shareholder value. It is difficult to see how any rational being could accept such a view in the face of the recent scandals, where it could be argued that the worst offenders were the most ideologically pure, and the result was the actual destruction of shareholder value (see *Breaking the Short Term Cycle,* Charlottesville, VA: Business Roundtable Institute for Corporate Ethics/CFA Center for Financial Market Integrity, 2006). Perhaps we have a version of Aristotle's idea that happiness is not a result of trying to be happy, or Mill's idea that it does not maximize utility to try and maximize utility. Collins and Porras have suggested that even if executives want to maximize shareholder value, they should focus on purpose instead, that trying to maximize shareholder value does not lead to maximum value (see J. Collins and J. Porras, *Built To Last,* New York: Harper Collins, 2002).
9. See R. Edward Freeman, "The Politics of Stakeholder Theory: Some Future Directions," *Business Ethics Quarterly,* 4, 409–422.
10. The second part of the integration thesis is left for another occasion. Philosophers who

read this essay may note the radical departure from standard accounts of political philosophy. Suppose we began the inquiry into political philosophy with the question of "how is value creation and trade sustainable over time" and suppose that the traditional beginning question, "how is the state justified" was a subsidiary one. We might discover or create some very different answers from the standard accounts of most political theory. See R. Edward Freeman and Robert Phillips, "Stakeholder Theory: A Libertarian Defense", *Business Ethics Quarterly,* Vol. 12, No. 3, 2002, pp. 331ff.

11. Here we roughly follow the logic of John Rawls in *Political Liberalism,* (New York: Columbia University Press, 1995).
12. There are many statements of this principle. Our argument is that whatever the particular conception of responsibility there is some underlying concept that is captured like our willingness or our need, to justify our lives to others. Note the answer that the dominant view of business must give to questions about responsibility. "Executives are responsible only for the effects of their actions on shareholders, or only in so far as their actions create or destroy shareholder value."
13. The spirit of this diagram is from R. Phillips, *Stakeholder Theory and Organizational Ethics* (San Francisco: Berret-Koehler Publishers, 2003).
14. In earlier versions of this essay in this volume we suggested that the notion of a fiduciary duty to stockholders be extended to "fiduciary duty to stakeholders". We believe that such a move cannot be defended without doing damage to the notion of "fiduciary." The idea of having a special duty to either one or a few stakeholders is not helpful.
15. Bill George, *Authentic Leadership,* San Francisco: Jossey Bass, Inc., 2004.
16. This is at least as clear as the directive given by the dominant model: Create as much value as possible for shareholders.
17. Some philosophers have argued that the stakeholder approach is in need of a "normative justification." To the extent that this phrase has any meaning, we take it as a call to connect the logic of managing for stakeholders with more traditional ethical theory. As pragmatists we eschew the "descriptive vs. normative vs. instrumental" distinction that so many business thinkers (and stakeholder theorists) have adopted. Managing for stakeholders is inherently a narrative or story that is at once: *descriptive* of how some businesses do act; *aspirational* and *normative* about how they could and should act; *instrumental* in terms of what means lead to what ends; and *managerial* in that it must be coherent on all of these dimensions and actually guide executive action.
18. See S. Venkataraman, "Stakeholder Value Equilibration and the Entrepreneurial Process," *Ethics and Entrepreneurship,* The Ruffin Series, 3: 45–57, 2002; S. R. Velamuri, "Entrepreneurship, Altruism, and the Good Society", *Ethics and Entrepreneurship,* The Ruffin Series, 3: 125–143, 2002; and, T. Harting, S. Harmeling, and S. Venkataraman, "Innovative Stakeholder Relations: When "Ethics pays" (and When it Doesn't)" *Business Ethics Quarterly,* 16: 43–68, 2006.
19. Sometimes there are tradeoffs and situations that economists would call "prisoner's dilemma" but these are not the paradigmatic cases, or if they are, we seem to solve them routinely, as Russell Hardin has suggested in Morality within the Limits of Reason, Chicago: University of Chicago Press, 1998.
20. E. Mendieta (ed.) *Take Care of Freedom and Truth Will Take Care of Itself: Interviews with Richard Rorty* (Stanford: Stanford University Press, 2006) p. 68.

Reading **2-3**

What Stakeholder Theory Is Not

Robert Phillips, Ed Freeman, and Andrew Wicks

At its current stage of theoretical development, stakeholder theory may be undermined from at least two directions: critical distortions and friendly misinterpretations. Some have sought to critique the theory based upon their own stylized conception of the theory and its implications. Though not always without some textual evidence for such characterizations, we argue that many of these distortions represent straw-person versions of the theory. At the least, the critical misinterpretations do not represent the strongest, most defensible variation of stakeholder theory.

Critical Distortions

Stakeholder Theory Is an Excuse for Managerial Opportunism

The shareholder wealth maximization imperative is frequently motivated by so-called agency problems: hazards arising from the separation of risk bearing and decision-making (also known as ownership and control, respectively). The concern is that without this moral imperative, managers would enrich themselves at the expense of the organization and the recipients of its residual cash flows, the shareholders . . .

Rather than morally superior, therefore, stakeholder theory is actually immoral inasmuch as it ignores this agency relationship or so goes the argument.[1] This criticism is, however, the result of the over-extended metaphor of agency theory in economics. If managers are agents or fiduciaries at all, it is to the *organization* and not to the shareowners. Clark (1995) writes:

> To an experienced corporate lawyer who has studied primary legal materials, the assertion that corporate managers are agents of investors, whether debt holders or stockholders, will seem odd or loose. The lawyer would make the following points. (1) corporate officers like the president and treasurer are agents of the corporation itself; (2) the board of directors is the ultimate decision-making body of the corporation (and in a sense is the group most appropriately identified with 'the corporation'); (3) directors are not agents of the corporation but are *sui generis;* (4) neither officers nor directors are agents of the stockholder; but (5) both officers and directors are 'fiduciaries' with respect to the corporation and its stockholders.

The corporation is not coextensive with the shareholders. It is an entity unto itself. It may enter into contracts and own property (including its own stock[2] or that of other corporations). It has standing in a court of law. Limited liability assures that shareowners are not, in general, personally liable for the debts of the organization (cf., Sollar, 2001). Top managers are agent for the corporation and this is not merely a shorthand way of saying that they are agents for the shareholders. The corporation is meaningfully distinct.[3] The same goes for other limited liability entities such limited liability partnerships to the extent that it is the partnership that has legal standing separate from that of the partners themselves and the partners enjoy immunity from personal responsibility for the actions and debts of the organization.

Some have suggested that stakeholder theory provides unscrupulous managers with a ready excuse to act in their own self-interest thus resurrecting the agency problem that the shareholder wealth maximization imperative was designed to overcome. Opportunistic managers can more easily act in their own self-interest by claiming that the action actually benefits some stakeholder group or other. (Jensen 2000, Marcoux 2000, Sternberg 2000). "All but the most egregious self-serving managerial behavior will doubtless serve the interest of some stakeholder constituencies and work against the interests of others" (Marcoux 2000: 97) and by appealing to the interests of those who benefit, the manager is able to justify the self-serving behavior. Hence, stakeholder theory "effectively destroys business accountability . . . because a business that is accountable to all, is actually accountable to none" (Sternberg 2000: 510).

The first response to this criticism is to point out that no small measure of managerial opportunism has occurred in the name of shareholder wealth maximization. In addition to the debacles at Enron and WorldCom, one need only consider the now dethroned king of shareholder wealth Al Dunlap for an illustration.[4] Dunlap grossly mismanaged at least two companies to his own significant financial gain. And every move he made was in the name of shareholder wealth. Dunlap agreed to pay $15 million to settle a lawsuit brought by the shareholders of Sunbeam Coproration.[5] There is little reason to believe that stakeholder theory will provide any more or less justification for the opportunistic manager.

This criticism of stakeholder theory is a version of the evil genie argument. Managerial opportunism is a problem, but it is no more a problem for stakeholder theory than the alternatives. Indeed, there may be some reason to believe stakeholder theory is more resistant to managerial self-dealing. In their discussion of "stakeholder-agency" theory Hill and Jones (1992) argue that managers' interest in organizational growth (citing remuneration, power, job security and status as motivating this interest) pins contrary not only to the interest of stockholders, but also contrary to the interests of stakeholders. They write, "Obviously, the claims of different groups may conflict . . . However, on a more general level, each group can be seen as having a stake in the continued existence of the firm." (1992: 145). Stakeholder theory, therefore, does not advocate the service of two masters. Rather, managers serve the interest of one master—the organization.

Stakeholder Theory Cannot Provide a Specific Objective Function for the Corporation

Another common critique concerns the "radical under-determinism" of stakeholder theory. That is, "in rejecting the maximization of long term owner value as the purpose of business, and requiring business instead simply to 'balance' the interests of all stakeholders, stakeholder theory discards the objective basis for evaluating business action" (Sternberg 2000: 51) and the theory fails to be "illuminatingly action-guiding" (Marcoux 2000).

In one sense, this critique is accurate. Stakeholder theory does fail to provide an algorithm for day-to-day managerial decision-making. This is due to the level of abstraction at which the discussion is taking place. Stakeholder theory provides method by which stakeholder obligations are derived and an admonition that managers must account for the interests of these stakeholders when making decisions. It is impossible to say *a priori* what these interests will be and how they may be accounted for due to the myriad ways that an organization might be arranged. Hence, it is impossible for such a theory to dictate specific action in the abstract.

However, this is another example of an evil genie criticism. The same critique may be leveled at the conventional shareholder-centered view. That is, the managerial dictate to maximize shareholder wealth stands mute when queried, How? This is because there are innumerable ways to do so.[6] Indeed, this indeterminacy and the impossibility of a one right way to mange is the reason for the business judgment rule discussed above and the courts hesitance to pierce the corporate veil.

Ostensible critics of stakeholder theory, including Jensen and Sternberg, eagerly embrace an instrumental variation of stakeholder management as a means to "maximize the total market value of the firm" or "maximize long-term owner value," respectively. In his critique of stakeholder theory, Jensen concedes that, "value maximizing says nothing about how to create a superior vision or strategy"

(2000: 49), though "Maximizing the total market value of the firm-that is the sum of the market values of the equity, debt and any other contingent claims outstanding on the firm—is one objective function that will resolve the tradeoff problem among multiple constituencies." (Jensen 2000: 42).

Perhaps taking the organization's objective function to be the maximization of total market value (or profits or wealth) does make *ex post* measurement of success more determinate than optimizing the well-being of multiple stakeholders." Distributing the value thus created is a simpler matter for "shareholder theory" than for stakeholder theory as well. Shareholder theory could, thus, be considered superior in light of the fact of hounded rationality and the limits on human cognitive capacity. There is no reason to believe, however, that stakeholder management would be any easier or the theory more determinate ex ante when undertaken for instrumental rather than normative reasons. Moreover, every ex post decision provides the *ex ante* circumstances for the next set of decisions. Even considering value maximization as a scorekeeping device (Jensen 2002) is problematic when the score for the current game determines how subsequent games are played and coached.

As for the argument form simplicity, Albert Einstein is quotes as advising, "Make things as simple as possible-but no simpler." The theory and practice of management certainly can be simplified—consider bookstore shelves packed with books on how to manage in a minute. Simplicity, however, is not the lone criterion of usefulness. There is no reason to believe that stakeholder management would be any easier or the theory more determinate when undertaken for instrumental rather than normative reasons.

The belief that maximizing "the total market value of the firm" or "long-term owner value" is more determinate than the balancing of stakeholder interests may itself prove dangerous due to what we may term the delusion of determinacy. That is, under conditions of uncertainty and bounded rationality, managers may be led to believe that the standard objective function dictates action in a way that is more specific than stakeholder theory. It does not—and the belief that it does gives managers an unfounded sense of confidence in their decisions. Managerial wisdom and judgment are replaced with a false sense of mathematical precision . . .

Stakeholder Management Means That All Stakeholders Must Be Treated Equally

It is commonly asserted that stakeholder theory implies that all stakeholders must be treated equally irrespective of the fact that some obviously contribute more than others to the organization (Gioia 1999; Marcoux 2000; Sternberg 2000: cf. Jones and Wicks 1999b). Prescriptions for equality have been inferred from discussions of "balancing" stakeholder interests and are in direct conflict with the advice of some experts on organizational design and reward systems (e.g. Nadler and Tushman 1997).

Marcoux is among those who make this criticism in his analysis of the concept of balance in stakeholder theory. He begins by outlining three potential interpretations of balance (or equity) on a stakeholder account.

> Egalitarianism—Distribution based on something like Rawls's difference principle (Rawls 1971).[7]
>
> Equalitarianism—Equal share for all stakeholders
>
> Pareto-Consequentialism—making at least one better without diminishing anyone

Marcoux's arguments against these three candidates are largely sound. However, he misses one of the more obvious—and indeed strongest—interpretations of balance among organizational stakeholders: meritocracy.[8] On the most defensible conception of stakeholder theory, benefits are distributed based on relative contribution to the organization. This interpretation is suggested in a quotation from the Sloan Colloquy. They write, "Corporations should attempt to distribute the benefits of their activities as equitably as possible among stakeholders, *in light of their respective contributions, costs, and risks.*"[9] Inasmuch as this quote was used early in the paper to exemplify the centrality of balance to stakeholder theory, it is surprising that Marcoux fails to appeal to it in his won interpretations of balance.

Similarly, Sternberg argues that "in maintaining that all stakeholders are of equal importance to a business and that business ought to be answerable equally to them all, stakeholder theory confounds business with government." (2000: 50). She cites no author, however, who argues for such equality of importance or managerial answerability. This is, again, suggestive of a straw-person argument. A meritocratic interpretation of stakeholder balance overcomes the objection that a stakeholder-based firm using either the egalitarian or equalitarian interpretation would be unable to obtain equity or any other manner of financing. Certainly equity financing is centrally important to organizations and, as such, providers of this capital would garner a substantial portion of the economic benefits of the firm as well as receive a great deal of managerial attention in organizational decision-making. On the conception of stakeholder theory proffered here, shareholders would get a fair return on their investment without managerial concern that is exclusive of other groups to whom an obligation is due.[10] Still less does the stakeholder theory is a theory of organizational strategy and ethics and NOT a theory of the whole political economy.

This meritocratic hierarchy isn't the only criterion by which stakeholders may be arranged. Phillips (2001) has suggested that stakeholders may usefully be separated in to normative and derivative stakeholders. Normative stakeholders are those to whom the organization has a direct moral obligation to attend to their well-being. They provide the answer to seminal stakeholder query. For whose benefit ought the firm he managed. Typically normative stakeholders are those most frequently cited in stakeholder discussions such as financiers, employees, customers, suppliers and local communities.

Alternatively, derivative stakeholders are those groups or individuals who can either harm or benefit the organization, but to whom the organization has no direct moral obligation as stakeholder.[11] This latter group might include such groups as competitors, activists, terrorists, and the media.[12] The organization is not managed for the benefit of derivative stakeholders, but to the extent that they may influence the organization or its normative stakeholders, managers are obliged to account for them in their decision-making. Far from strict equality, therefore, there are a number of more convincing ways that stakeholder theory may distinguish between and among constituency groups . . .

Friendly Misinterpretations

Stakeholder Theory Is a Comprehensive Moral Doctrine

In his discussion of the idea of an overlapping consensus, Rawls (1993) distinguishes between his own theory and what he terms comprehensive moral doctrines. A comprehensive moral doctrine is one that is able to cover the entirety of the moral universe without reference to any other theory. All moral questions can be answered from within a comprehensive moral doctrine. Rawls claims that not only does his conception not depend on a single religious, national, cultural or moral theory for is foundation, but that it is consistent with a "reasonable pluralism" of such doctrines. One need not convert from her preferred doctrine in order to accept justice as fairness. All reasonable moral doctrines already accept it from within their own conception.

Moreover, not only stakeholder theory not a comprehensive moral doctrine, but it is yet another step removed even from Rawls's own theory. Stakeholder theory is a theory of organizational ethics. As described by Phillips and Margolis (1999), theories of organizational ethics are distinct from moral and political theories due to the difference in the subject matter of the various disciplines. Contrary to the assumptions of political theory; organizations are, to use Rawls (1993) terms, voluntary associations rather than a part of the basic structure of society. Further, interaction within and among organizations create moral obligations over and above those duties that arise due simply to one's status as a human being or citizen of a nation.

Stakeholder theory is not intended to provide an answer to all moral questions. Stakeholder-based obligations do not even take precedence in all moral questions in an organizational context. Violations of the human rights of a constituency group by commercial organizations and the gratuitous destruction of the natural environment are morally wrong, but such judgments rely on concepts outside of stakeholder theory as herein delimited (Orts and Strudler 2002; Phillips and Reichart 2000). Stakeholder theory shares this delimitation with its supposed rival theory of shareholder wealth maximization—at least as elaborated by Friedman (1971). Friedman's defense of shareholder wealth maximization is a moral one based on the property rights of shareholders. Noteworthy for our purposes, Friedman's admonition includes the condition that shareholder wealth maximization must take place within the constraints of law and morality. This suggests that there is another level of analysis operative in Friedman's system. So too is the case with stakeholder theory.

Conclusion

This paper attempts to add clarity to stakeholder theory by addressing a number of straw-person objections posed by critics of the theory as well is a few friendly overextensions and distortions averred by stakeholder theory advocates. We do not presume to dictate the research agenda of other scholars. However, we believe that it is important to avoid talking past the many intelligent and thoughtful opponents of stakeholder theory as well as avoid "preaching to the choir' by offering extensions that will only convince one who already advocates some version of the theory. By clearing away some of the most common misconceptions of stakeholder theory, we suggest that we are in a better position to see both the power and the limitations of this approach.

End Notes

1. Even should our arguments about agency and stakeholder theory prove unconvincing, we are not the first to address the issue; previous accounts include Quinn and Jones (1995), Jones (1995), and the articles in Howie and Freeman (1992).
2. We might test the proposition that shareholders won the corporation through a thought experiment: Who would own the corporation if it bought back all of its own stock?
3. See also Orts (1997)
4. Albert J. Dunlap, *Mean Business,* (New York: Simon & Schuster). John A. Byrne. Chainsow (New York: HarperBusiness)
5. Former Sunbeam Chief Exec Settles Shareholder Lawsuit for $15M. *Down Jones Newswire.* January 14, 2002.
6. There are also multiple means of measurement (e.g., accounting profits, firm value, dividends, long and short term market value for shares). Thanks to an anonymous reviewer for pointing out this out.
7. Rawls's Difference Principle says that social institutions should be arranged such that nay inequalities in the distribution of social goods must redound to the benefit of the least well off.
8. Paul Glezen has also suggested "balance" may be insightfully interpreted in the sense meant when discussing balance in wine. We do not pursue this interpretation, but merely point it out as an interesting variation.
9. Sloan Stakeholder Colloquy, 1999, "Clarkson Principles." The Sloan Stakeholder Colloquy was a broad and important effort to promote and organize research on issues surrounding stakeholder theory.
10. Notably, when profits are discussed among the visionary companies of Collins and Porras (1994), it is not in terms of maximization, but "reasonable" (Cord). 'fair' (Johnson vs. Johnson), "adequate" (Motorola), and "attractive" (Marriott).

11. The organization may have other duties or obligations to non-stakeholders, such as the duty to not cause harm to, lie to, or steal from them. These duties exist prior to and separate from stakeholder obligations and are not considered when establishing stakeholder status. See Phillips 1997.
12. These lists of typical stakeholders are only for the purpose of generic example. Which specific groups are what sort of stakeholder, or indeed which are stakeholders at all, cannot be determined in the abstract. This can only be determined by reference to actual organizations in actual relationships with other groups.

References

Note: References have been removed from publication here, but are available on the book website at www.mhhe.com/busethics2e.

Reading 2-4

When Good People Do Bad Things at Work: *Rote Behavior, Distractions, and Moral Exclusion Stymie Ethical Behavior on the Job*

Dennis J. Moberg

The news is full of the exploits of corporate villains. We read about how officials at Lincoln Savings and Loan bilked thousands out of their customers' retirement nest eggs. There are stories of the lies Brown and Williamson Tobacco executives told about the addictive nature of cigarettes and the company's subsequent campaign to destroy whistle-blower Jeffrey Wigant. Also in the news are the top managers at Time Warner who looked the other way rather than forgo millions from the sale of rap music with lyrics that advocated violence directed at women and the police. Such acts are hard to forgive. Scoundrels such as these seem either incredibly weak or dangerously flawed.

Yet not all corporate misdeeds are committed by bad people. In fact, a significant number of unethical acts in business are the likely result of foibles and failings rather than selfishness and greed. Put in certain kinds of situations, good people inadvertently do bad things.

For those of us concerned about ethical actions and not just good intentions, the problem is clear. We must identify the situational factors that keep people from doing their best and eliminate them whenever we can.

Problem No. 1: Scripts

One factor is something psychologists call scripts. This term refers to the procedures that experience tells us to use in specific situations. When we brush our teeth or congratulate a friend on the arrival of a new grandchild, we probably use scripts.

Unlike other forms of experience, scripts are stored in memory in a mechanical or rote fashion. When we encounter a very familiar situation, rather than actively think about it, we reserve our mental energy for other purposes and behave as though we are cruising on automatic pilot.

In a classic psychological experiment, people approached someone at an office machine making copies and asked, "May I please make just one copy because . . ." The person at the machine generally complied with this request, but the really interesting finding was that the likelihood of compliance was totally independent of the reasons stated. In fact, superfluous reasons such as "because I need to make a copy" were just as successful as good reasons such as "because my boss told me she needed these right away." Apparently, we have all experienced this situation so often that we don't give the reasons our full attention, not to mention our careful consideration.

One ethical lapse clearly attributable to scripts was Ford Motor Co.'s failure to recall the Pinto in the 1970s. The Pinto was an automobile with an undetected design flaw that made the gas tank burst into flames on impact, resulting in the death and disfigurement of scores of victims. Dennis Gioia, the Ford recall coordinator at the time, reviewed hundreds of accident reports to detect whether a design flaw was implicated. Later, he recalled,

> When I was dealing with the first trickling-in of field reports that might have suggested a significant problem with the Pinto, the reports were essentially similar to many others that I was dealing with (and dismissing) all the time. . . . I was making this kind of decision automatically every day. I had trained myself to respond to prototypical cues, and these didn't fit the relevant prototype for crisis cases.

Situations like this occur frequently in the work world. Repetitive jobs requiring vigilance to prevent ethical lapses can be found in quality control, customer service, and manufacturing. In this respect, consider what happened when a nurse with a script that called for literal obedience to a doctor's written orders misread the directions to place ear drops in a patient's right ear as "place in Rear." Good people can inadvertently do very bad things.

Scripts may also be at work when we come face to face with those who are suffering. In situations where we observe the pain of those in need, scripts permit us to steel ourselves against feelings of empathy. Most of us have been approached by the homeless on the street, exposed to horrific images on the television news, and asked for donations on behalf of the victims of natural disasters.

According to research at the University of Kansas, scripts allow people to avoid responsibility for the suffering of others in situations when providing help appears costly. In work contexts, this might explain why businesspeople do not always respond philanthropically to documented cases of human suffering. What appears to be calculated indifference may actually not be calculated at all.

Whenever there is repetition, there are likely to be scripts. Accordingly, the best way to eliminate the potential of scripts to result in unethical behavior is to keep people out of highly repetitive situations. Technology can and has been used to eliminate highly routine tasks, but job rotation is also an option. For example, the *Daily Oklahoman* newspaper of Oklahoma City cross-trains most of its editors and schedules them to switch roles often. This helps keep the editors mentally sharp.

One editor who often switches roles from night to night commented: "You're fresh when you come to a particular job. Like last night I did inside [design], and it was a long and torturous night because of the large paper. But then again I turn around and do something thoroughly different tonight, so I don't feel like I'm trudging back to the same old rut again."

Daily Oklahoman News Editor Ed Sargent thinks editing quality has improved because those who switch roles are exposed to the different approaches their colleagues take to the job. "Every editor has different opinions, obviously, about what's a big error and what's a little error," he said. Although the original intent of the role switching was to distribute stress more evenly, a side effect is that the paper is probably less prone to ethical lapses.

Problem No. 2: Distractions

Scripts are cognitive shortcuts that take the place of careful thinking. A similar human tendency is our mindless treatment of distractions. Think for a moment about the last time you drove to a very important meeting. Once there, were you able to recall any details of your journey? Most of us cannot, which demonstrates that when concentrating on completing an involving task, we don't deal well with distractions.

This inattention to what is happening on the periphery can get us into trouble with our spouses and significant others, and it can also result in ethical lapses. In one very telling experiment, divinity students were told that they had to deliver a lecture from prepared notes in a classroom across campus. Half the students were told they had to hurry to be on time, and the other half were told they had more than ample time.

On the way, the students came across a person in distress (actually an actor), who sat slumped motionless in a doorway, coughing and groaning. Shockingly, only 16 of the 40 divinity students stopped to help, most of them from the group that had ample time. To those in a hurry, the man was a distraction, a threat to their focus on giving a lecture. Ironically enough, half of them had been asked to discuss the parable of "The Good Samaritan."

Mindlessness about distractions at work is most pronounced when employees, with limited means of gaining perspective, are encouraged to be focused and driven. The best way to combat this tendency is for senior managers to model the virtue of temperance. If the president of a company is a workaholic, it is difficult to convince employees to be open to problems on the outskirts of their commitments. In contrast, an organizational culture that facilitates work–family balance or encourages employee involvement in the community may move experiences that should not be seen as mere distractions onto the center stage of consciousness.

Problem No. 3: Moral Exclusion

A final problem that brings out the worst in good people is the very human tendency to morally exclude certain persons. This occurs when individuals or groups are perceived as outside the boundary in which moral values and considerations of fairness apply. The most striking example occurs during warfare when the citizens of a country readily perceive their enemies in demonic terms. Yet, this tendency to discount the moral standing of others results in us discounting all kinds of people, some of them as close as coworkers and valued customers.

Greater awareness and extensive training have reduced some of the exclusion women and people of color have historically experienced. More work needs to be done in this area, as well as in other equally insidious forms of exclusion.

One way such exclusion shows up is in our use of pronouns. If *we* are in marketing and *they* are in production, the chances are that the distance may be great enough for us to be morally indifferent to what happens to them. Similarly, if we use stereotypic terms like *bean counter* or sneer when we say *management,* then it is clear that people in these categories don't count.

Not surprisingly, one way to expand the scope of justice is to promote direct contact with individuals who have been morally excluded. One company that applied this notion in an intriguing way is Eisai, a Japanese pharmaceutical firm. In the late 1980s, Haruo Naito had recently become CEO, and his closest advisers expressed concern that his managers and employees lacked an understanding of the end users of Eisai's products.

Hearing this, Naito decided to shift the focus of attention from the customers of his company's products—doctors and pharmacists—to *their* customers—patients and their families. Eisai managers, he decided, needed to identify better with end users and then infuse the insights from this sense of inclusion throughout the organization. This was a revolutionary idea for this company of 4,500 employees, but Naito believed his employees needed a more vivid reason to care deeply about their work.

"It's not enough to tell employees that if they do something, the company will grow this much or their salary will increase this much. That's just not enough incentive," says Naito. "You have to show them how what they are doing is connected to society, or exactly how it will help a patient." Accordingly, Naito decided to send 100 managers to a seven-day seminar: three days of nursing-home training and four days of medical care observation.

These managers were then sent to diverse regions throughout Japan, where they had to deal with different people, many of whom were in critical condition. They met patients with both physical and emotional problems; some of the patients they came in contact with died during their internships.

This pilot program grew to include more than 1,000 Eisai employees. Pretty soon, even laboratory support personnel had to leave their benches and desks and meet regularly with pharmacists and hospital people.

"Getting them out of the office was a way to activate human relationships," says Naito. Another way was to institute hotlines, which have generated product ideas. As a consequence, many new Eisai drugs were produced, including some that have promise in dealing with Alzheimer's disease. Clearly, moral inclusion was stimulated at Eisai, at least insofar as the end users of its products are concerned.

Failing to Bother

Jesuit scholar James F. Keenan reminds us that "sinners in the New Testament are known not for what they did, but for what they failed to do—for failing to bother." We are all prone to this failure, but not necessarily because we are sinners. Repetition, distractions, and our natural tendency to exclude those unfamiliar to us cloud our best thinking and forestall the expression of our virtues. We owe it to ourselves to resist these pernicious influences, and we owe it to those in our work communities to help them to do the same.

Source: *Issues in Ethics* 10, no. 2 (Fall 1999), Markkula Center for Applied Ethics, (http://www.scu.edu/ethics/publications/iie/v10n2/peopleatwork.html). Reprinted by permission of the author.

Chapter 3

Philosophical Ethics and Business

Opening Decision Point

Executive Compensation: Needed Incentives, Justly Deserved, or Just Distasteful?

Perhaps no part of the financial market collapse of late 2008, and the government bailout that followed, caused as much public outcry as did the financial bonuses and compensation paid to senior executives of failed companies. American International Group (AIG) became the target of much of this criticism. Persuaded that AIG was "too big to fail," by March 2009 the U.S. federal government had committed $180 billion dollars to rescue AIG from bankruptcy. In early March of 2009, AIG announced that it was paying $165 million in bonuses to 400 top executives in its financial division, the very unit that was at the heart of the company's collapse.

AIG cited two major factors in the defense of these bonuses: they were owed as a result of contracts that had been negotiated and signed before the collapse, and they were needed to provide an incentive to retain the most talented employees at a time when they were most needed.

Critics claimed that the bonuses were an example of corporate greed run amok. They argued that contractual obligations should have been overridden and renegotiated at the point of bankruptcy. They also dismissed the effectiveness of the incentive argument since this supposed "talent" was responsible for the failed business strategy that led to AIG's troubles in the first place.

As part of the government bailout of AIG, Edward M. Liddy, an associate of Secretary of the Treasury Henry Paulson, was named CEO of AIG in September of 2008. Former CEO Martin Sullivan resigned earlier in the summer as AIG's financial troubles intensified, but he did not retire without first securing a $47 million severance package. In comparison, Liddy himself accepted a salary of $1, although his contract held out the possibility of future bonuses.

In testimony before the U.S. Congress soon after being named CEO, Liddy was asked to explain the expense of a recent AIG-sponsored retreat for AIG salespeople. The retreat cost AIG over $400,000 and was, in Liddy's words, a "standard practice within the industry." Six months later, when news broke about the $165 million bonus payments, Liddy—suggesting that the executives consider doing "the right thing" by returning the bonuses—described them as "distasteful."

Within months of taking office, the Obama administration took steps to limit executive compensation at firms that accepted significant government bailout money, including the retirement packages of the former CEOs of Citigroup, General Motors, and Bank of America. Announcing this action, Treasury Secretary Timothy Geithner observed that "this financial crisis had many significant causes, but executive compensation practices were a contributing factor."

- How would you describe the bonuses paid to AIG executives in March of 2009? Is it an ethical issue at all? Why or why not?
- Are there any facts that you would want to know before making a judgment?
- What alternatives to paying the bonuses would have been available to Edward Liddy?

(continued)

(*concluded*)

- Do you agree that AIG had an obligation to pay the bonuses? How strong is the duty to fulfill a contract, even one requiring payment of such bonuses? When should a contract be overridden by other concerns?
- Do you think the employees deserved the bonuses?
- How would you judge whether or not the bonuses were effective incentives?
- Do you agree with Liddy that they were "distasteful"? Is this judgment a matter of personal opinion and taste, or is it instead a reasonable and objective judgment?
- Who are the stakeholders in the decision to pay bonuses to AIG executives? How do their interests affect the contract between AIG and its employees?
- During the presidential debates in October 2008, then-candidate Barack Obama said that "the Treasury should demand that money back and those executives should be fired." Do you agree?
- Is executive compensation purely a private matter between an employer and employee, or should it be a matter of public concern and government policy?

Chapter Objectives

After reading this chapter, you will be able to:

1. Explain the ethical theory of utilitarianism.
2. Describe how utilitarian thinking underlies economic and business decision making.
3. Explain how the free market is thought to serve the utilitarian goal of maximizing the overall good.
4. Explain some challenges to utilitarian decision making.
5. Explain principle-based, or deontological ethical theories.
6. Explain the concept of human rights and how they are relevant to business.
7. Distinguish moral rights from legal rights.
8. Explain several challenges to deontological ethics.
9. Describe and explain virtue based theories of ethical character.

Introduction: Ethical Theories and Traditions

Consider the reasons that you or others offered to defend or criticize the payment of large bonuses to AIG executives. Upon reflection, these reasons fall into three general categories. Some reasons appeal to the *consequences* of paying the bonuses: they either will, or will not, provide incentives for producing good work and beneficial future consequences. Other reasons appeal to certain *principles:* one should not break a contractual promise, even if it has unpopular results; one should never benefit from serious harms that have been caused by one's own actions. Other reasons cite matters of *personal character:* accepting bonuses is greedy, or distasteful. Paying the bonuses that were due in the face of public criticism was courageous and had to be done as a matter of integrity.

As it turns out, the three major traditions of ethical theory that we shall rely on in this text are represented by these three categories. This should be no surprise since ethical traditions in philosophy reflect common ways to think and reason about how we should live, what we should do. Ethics of consequences, ethics of principles, and ethics of personal character are the traditions that will be introduced in this chapter.

Chapters 1 and 2 introduced ethics as a form of practical reasoning in support of decision making about how we should live our lives. Ethics involves what is perhaps the most significant question any human being can ask: How *should* I live my life? But, of course, this question is not new; every major philosophical, cultural, political, and religious tradition in human history has grappled with it. In light of this, it would be imprudent to ignore these traditions as we begin to examine ethical issues in business.

Nevertheless, many students think that discussions of ethical theories and philosophical ethics are too abstract to be of much help in business. Discussion of ethical "theories" often seems to be too *theoretical* to be of much relevance to business. Throughout this chapter, we hope to suggest a more accessible understanding of ethical theories, one that will shed some light on the practical and pragmatic application of these theories to actual problems faced by business people. (For an examination of the pragmatic application, see the reading by Norman Bowie at the end of this chapter, "It Seems Right in Theory but Does It Work in Practice?")

An ethical theory is nothing more than an attempt to provide a systematic answer to the fundamental ethical question: How should human beings live their lives? In many ways, this is a simple question that we ask, at least implicitly, every day. What am I going to do today, and why? Ethics can be understood as the practice of examining these decisions and thinking about answers to that question: Why?

Ethical theories attempt to answer the question of how we should live, but they also give *reasons* to support their answers. Ethics seeks to provide a rational justification for *why* we should act and decide in a particular prescribed way. Anyone can offer prescriptions for what you should do and how you should act, but a *philosophical* and reasoned ethics must answer the "Why?" question as well.

Many people and cultures across the world would answer this "why" question in religious terms and base their normative judgments on religious foundations. "You ought to live your life in a certain way because God commands it." The biggest practical problem with this approach, of course, is that people differ widely about their religious beliefs. If ethics is based on religion, and if different cultures have widely divergent religious beliefs, then it would seem that ethics cannot escape the predicament of relativism. (See the Decision Point "Who Is to Say What Is Right or Wrong" for more on ethical relativism.)

Unlike religious ethics which explains human well-being in religious terms, philosophical ethics provides justifications that must be applicable to all people regardless of their religious starting points. The justifications of philosophical ethics connect the "oughts" and "shoulds" of ethics to an underlying account of

Decision Point *Who Is to Say What Is Right or Wrong?*

Are you an ethical relativist? **Ethical relativism** holds that ethical values are relative to particular people, cultures, or times. Relativism denies that there are can be any rationally justified or objective ethical judgments. When there are ethical disagreements between people or cultures, the ethical relativist concludes that there is not way to resolve that dispute and prove one side is right or more reasonable than the other.

Consider Edward Liddy's description of the AIG bonuses as "distasteful." Ordinarily, we think of matters of taste as personal, subjective things. You enjoy spicy Indian food, while I prefer simple Midwestern meat and potatoes. It is all a matter of personal taste. Liddy may have found the bonuses distasteful, but others find them well-deserved. Ethical relativists believe that ethical values are much like tastes in food; it all depends on, or it is all relative to, one's own background, culture, and personal opinions.

Do you believe that there is no way to decide what is ethically right or wrong? Imagine a teacher returns an assignment to you with a grade of "F." When you ask for an explanation, you are told that, frankly, the teacher does not believe that people "like you" (e.g., men, Christians, African Americans) are capable of doing good work in this field (e.g., science, engineering, math, finance). When you object that this is unfair and wrong, the teacher offers a relativist explanation. "Fairness is a matter of personal opinion," the professor explains. "Who determines what is fair or unfair?" you ask. Your teacher claims that his view of what is fair is as valid as any other. Because everyone is entitled to their own personal opinion, he is entitled to fail you since, in his personal opinion, you do not deserve to succeed.

- Would you accept this explanation and be content with your failing grade? If not, how would you defend your own, opposing view?
- Are there any relevant facts on which you would rely to support your claim?
- What values are involved in this dispute?
- What alternatives are available to you?
- Besides you and your teacher, are there any other stakeholders—people who are or should be involved in this situation?
- What reasons would you offer to the dean in an appeal to have the grade changed?
- What consequences would this professor's practice have on education?
- If reasoning and logical persuasion do not work, how else could this dispute be resolved?

human well-being. Thus, for example, "you should contribute to disaster relief because it will reduce human suffering" is a philosophical justification for an ethical judgment, whereas "you should contribute to disaster relief because God commands it, or because it will bring you heavenly rewards" are religious rather than philosophical justifications. (For a discussion on the application of relativism, oughts and shoulds to the particular concept of bribery, see the reading "Ethical Dimensions of Decision-Making in the Developing World: The Case of Bribery in Mauritus" by Geetanee Napal at the end of this chapter.)

Finally, ethical theories are not comprised of one single principle or framework. Ethical theories evolved over time and have been refined and developed by many different thinkers. The insights of an ethical theory prove to be lasting because they truly do pick out some important elements of human experience. To emphasize this fact, this chapter will refer to these theories more commonly as ethical "traditions."

This chapter will introduce three ethical traditions that have proven influential in the development of business ethics and that have a very practical relevance in evaluating ethical issues in contemporary business. **Utilitarianism** is an ethical tradition that directs us to decide based on overall *consequences* of our acts. **Deontological ethics** direct us to act on the basis of moral *principles* such as respecting human rights. **Virtue ethics** directs us to consider the *moral character* of individuals and how various character traits can contribute to, or obstruct, a happy and meaningful human life. The Caux Round Table (CRT) Principles for Responsible Business, included at the end of this chapter, provide an interesting blend of utilitarian, deontological, and virtue-based guidelines for business.

Utilitarianism: Making Decisions Based on Ethical Consequences

1 OBJECTIVE

The first ethical tradition that we shall examine, utilitarianism, has its roots in eighteenth and nineteenth century social and political philosophy, but its core idea is just as relevant in the twenty-first century. Utilitarianism's fundamental insight is that we should decide what to do by considering the *consequences* of our actions. In this sense, utilitarianism has been called a **consequentialist** approach to ethics and social policy: we should act in ways that produce better consequences than the alternatives we are considering. Much more needs to be said to turn this simple insight into an adequate ethical theory. The first, and most obvious, question is: What is meant by "better consequences"?

The most cogent answer to this question can be given in terms of the ethical values described in the previous chapters. "Better consequences" are those that promote human well-being: the happiness, health, dignity, integrity, freedom, respect of all the people affected. If these elements are basic human values, then an action which promotes more of them than the alternative action does is more reasonable from an ethical point of view. A decision that promotes the greatest amount of these values for the greatest number of people is the most reasonable decision from an ethical point of view.

Utilitarianism is commonly identified with the principle of "maximize the overall good" or, in a slightly different version, of producing "the greatest good for the greatest number." The ultimate ethical goal, according to utilitarians, is to produce the best consequences for all parties affected by the decisions. Decisions that accomplish this goal are the right decisions to make ethically; those that do not are ethically wrong.

The emphasis on the overall good, and upon producing the greatest good for the greatest number, make utilitarianism a social philosophy that opposes policies that aim to benefit only a small social, economic, or political minority. In this way, utilitarianism provides strong support for democratic institutions and policies. Government and all social institutions exist for the well-being of all, not to further the interests of the monarch, the nobility, or some small group of the elite. Likewise, the economy and economic institutions exist to provide the highest standard of living for the greatest number of people, not to create wealth for a few.

As another business-related example, consider the case of child labor, discussed in further detail in chapter 6. Utilitarian thinking would advise us to consider all the likely consequences of a practice of employing young children in factories. Obviously, there are some problematic consequences: children suffer physical and psychological harms, they are denied opportunities for education, their low pay is not enough to escape a life of poverty, and so forth. Many of the human values previously described are diminished by child labor. But these consequences must be compared to the consequences of alternative decisions. What are the consequences if children in poor regions are denied factory jobs? These children would still be denied opportunities for education; they are in worse poverty; and they have less money for food and family support. In many cases, the only alternatives for obtaining any income available to young children who are prohibited from joining the workforce might include crime, drugs, or prostitution. Further, we should consider not only the consequences to the children themselves, but to the entire society. Child labor can have beneficial results for bringing foreign investment and money into a poor country. In the opinion of some observers, allowing children to work for pennies a day under sweatshop conditions produces better overall consequences than the available alternatives. Thus, one might argue on utilitarian grounds that such labor practices are ethically permissible because they produce better overall consequences than the alternatives.

This example highlights several important aspects of utilitarian reasoning. Because utilitarians decide on the basis of consequences, and because the consequences of our actions will depend on the specific facts of each situation, utilitarians tend to be very pragmatic thinkers. No act is ever absolutely right or wrong in all cases in every situation; it will always depend on the consequences. For example, lying is neither right nor wrong in itself, according to utilitarians. There might be situations in which lying will produce greater overall good than telling the truth. In such a situation, it would be ethically justified to tell a lie.

Also, utilitarian reasoning usually supplies some support for competing available alternatives, e.g., ban child labor as harmful to the overall good or allow child labor as contributing to the overall good. Deciding on the ethical legitimacy of alternative decisions requires that we make judgments about the likely consequences of our actions. How do we do this? Within the utilitarian tradition, there is a strong inclination to turn to social science for help in making such predictions. After all, social science studies the causes and consequences of individual

Reality Check *Is Utilitarianism Egoistic?*

While the imperative to maximize pleasure or happiness sounds selfish and egoistic, utilitarianism differs from **egoism** in important ways. Egoism is also a consequentialist theory, but it focuses on the happiness of the individual. In other words, instead of determining the "greatest good for the greatest number," egoism seeks "the greatest good for me!"

Utilitarianism judges actions by their consequences for the general and overall good. Consistent with the utilitarian commitment to democratic equality, however, the general good must take into consideration the well-being of each and every individual affected by the action. In this way utilitarianism serves the ultimate goal of ethics: the impartial promotion of human well-being. It is impartial because it considers the consequences for everyone, not just for the individual. People who act in ways to maximize only their own happiness or the happiness of their company are not utilitarians, they are egoists.

and social actions. Who is better situated than a social scientist to help us predict the social consequences of our decisions? Consider the fields to which one might turn in order to determine the likely consequences of child labor. Economics, anthropology, political science, sociology, public policy, psychology, and medical and health sciences are some of the fields that could help determine the likely consequences of such practices in a particular culture.

In general, the utilitarian position is that happiness is the ultimate good, the only thing that is and can be valued for its own sake. Happiness is the best and most reasonable interpretation of human well-being. (Does it sound absurd to you to claim that unhappiness is good and happiness is bad?) The goal of ethics, both individually and as a matter of public policy, should be to maximize the overall happiness. (See Reality Check, "Is Utilitarianism Egoistic?")

Utilitarianism and Business

2 OBJECTIVE

We previously claimed that studying ethical theories had a practical relevance for business ethics. In fact, perhaps utilitarianism's greatest contribution to philosophical thought has come through its influence in economics. With roots in Adam Smith, the ethics which underlie much of twentieth century economics—essentially what we think of as the free market—is decidedly utilitarian. In this way, utilitarianism continues to have a very strong impact on business and business ethics.

Utilitarianism answers the fundamental questions of ethics—What should we do?—by reference to a rule: maximize the overall good. But another question remains to be answered: *How* do we achieve this goal? What is the best means for attaining the utilitarian goal of maximizing the overall good? Two answers prove especially relevant in business and business ethics.

3 OBJECTIVE

One movement within utilitarian thinking invokes the tradition of Adam Smith and claims that free and competitive markets are the best means for attaining utilitarian goals. This version would promote policies that deregulate private industry, protect property rights, allow for free exchanges, and encourage competition. In

Reality Check *Utilitarian Experts in Practice*

Consider how the Federal Reserve Board sets interest rates. There is an established goal, a public policy "good," that the Federal Reserve takes to be the greatest good for the country. (This goal is something like the highest sustainable rate of economic growth compatible with minimal inflation.) The Fed examines the relevant economic data and makes a judgment about the present and future state of the economy. If economic activity seems to be slowing down, the Fed might decide to lower interest rates as a means for stimulating economic growth. If the economy seems to be growing too fast and the inflation rate is increasing, they might choose to raise interest rates. Lowering or raising interest rates, in and of itself, is neither good nor bad; the rightness of the act depends on the consequences. The role of public servants is to use their expertise to judge the likely consequences and make the decision that is most likely to produce the best result.

such situations decisions of rationally self-interested individuals will result, as if lead by "an invisible hand" in Adam Smith's terms, to the maximum satisfaction of individual happiness.

In classic free market economics, economic activity aims to satisfy consumer demand. People are made happy—human welfare or well-being increases—when they get what they desire. Overall human happiness is increased therefore when the overall satisfaction of consumer demand increases. The law of supply and demand tells us that economies should, and healthy economies do, produce (supply) those goods and services that consumers most want (demand). Since scarcity and competition prevent everyone from getting all that they want, the goal of free market economics is to optimally satisfy, i.e., maximize, the satisfaction of wants (happiness). Free markets accomplish this goal most efficiently, according to defenders, by allowing individuals to decide for themselves what they most want and then bargain for these goods in a free and competitive marketplace. This process will, over time and under the right conditions, guarantee the optimal satisfaction of wants, which this tradition equates with maximizing overall happiness.

Given this utilitarian goal, current free market economics advises us that the most efficient means to attain that goal is to structure our economy according to the principles of free market capitalism. This requires that business managers, in turn, should seek to maximize profits. This idea is central to one common perspective on corporate social responsibility. By pursuing profits, business ensures that scarce resources are going to those who most value them and thereby ensures that resources will provide optimal satisfaction. Thus, competitive markets are seen as the most efficient means to the utilitarian end of maximizing happiness.

A second influential version of utilitarian policy turns to policy experts who can predict the outcome of various policies and carry out policies that will attain utilitarian ends. Because utilitarian reasoning determines what to do on the basis of consequences, reasonable judgments must take into account the likely consequences of our actions. But predicting consequences of human action can be studied and improved by careful observation. Experts in predicting such consequences, usually trained in the social sciences such as economics, political science, and public policy, are familiar with the specifics of how society works and they therefore are in a position to determine which policy will maximize the overall good. (See Reality Check, "Utilitarian Experts in Practice.")

This approach to public policy underlies one theory of the entire administrative and bureaucratic side of government and organizations. From this view, the legislative body (from Congress to local city councils) establishes the public goals that we assume will maximize overall happiness. The administrative side (presidents, governors, mayors) executes (administers) policies to fulfill these goals. The people working within the administration know how the social and political system works and use this knowledge to carry out the mandate of the legislature. The government is filled with such people, typically trained in such fields as economics, law, social science, public policy, and political science. This utilitarian approach, for example, would be sympathetic with government regulation of business on the grounds that such regulation will ensure that business activities do contribute to the overall good.

The dispute between these two versions of utilitarian policy, what we might call the "administrative" and the "market" versions of utilitarianism, characterize many disputes in business ethics. One clear example concerns regulation of unsafe or risky products. (Similar disputes involve worker health and safety, environmental protection, regulation of advertising, and almost every other example of government regulation of business.) One side argues that questions of safety and risk should be determined by experts who then establish standards that business is required to meet. Government regulators (for example, the Consumer Products Safety Commission) are then charged with enforcing safety standards in the marketplace. (See Decision Point, "Should Financial Markets Face Greater Government Regulation?")

The other side argues that the best judges of acceptable risk and safety are consumers themselves. A free and competitive consumer market will insure that people will get the level of safety that they want. Individuals calculate for themselves what risks they wish to take and what trade-offs they are willing to make in order to attain safety. Consumers willing to take risks likely will pay less for their products than consumers who demand safer and less risky products. The very basic economic concept of efficiency can be understood as a placeholder for the utilitarian goal of maximum overall happiness. Thus, market-based solutions will prove best at optimally satisfying these various and competing interests and will thereby serve the overall good.

Challenges to Utilitarian Ethics

4 OBJECTIVE

While the utilitarian tradition contributes much to responsible ethical decision making, it is not without problems. A review of some general challenges to utilitarianism can guide us in evaluating later applications of utilitarian decision making.

Decision Point *Should Financial Markets Face Greater Government Regulation?*

In the aftermath of the financial meltdown of 2008–09, many people believe that a lack of regulation and oversight by government agencies such as the Federal Reserve Bank and the Securities and Exchange Commission (SEC) played a major role in causing the crisis. From this perspective, the financial crisis was hastened by more than two decades of U.S. public policy that moved away from regulation in the name of less government, fewer regulations, and a more free economy.

Critics argue that a deregulated market allowed a wide range of suspect financial practices that are associated with some of the largest business failures in world history. Weak or nonexistent government regulation failed to protect the economy from the "off-book partnerships" made famous by Enron; the sub-prime mortgages that led to the collapse of three of the largest investment banks in the world, Lehman Brothers, Bear Stearns, and Merrill Lynch; and credit default swaps that were central to the problems of AIG. Of equal importance, failure to police mergers and acquisitions by enforcing anti-trust regulations created a number of firms that were judged to be "to big to fail," leading to huge government bailouts. Indeed, many critics claim that the deep recession of 2008–09 was directly related to the failure of unregulated markets in such fields as finance, real-estate, and the auto industry.

Defenders and critics of deregulation agree that a healthy and efficient economy is the best means for maximizing the overall social good. They disagree on whether a healthy economy is one that leaves the market free of government regulation, or one in which government regulators play an active role. Given that this issue isn't a simple matter of regulations or not, but involves a range of options along a continuum of less-to-more regulation, do you generally support more or less government regulation of economic markets?

- What facts are relevant in answering this question? Does it depend on the type of regulation or the industry being regulated?
- How would you decide if a regulation is successful? A failure?
- What values support a policy of deregulation? What values count against it?
- Other than the industry regulated, who are some other stakeholders that might be affected by government regulation?
- What might serve as an alternative to government regulations? Can professional codes and standards play a role?

A first set of problems concerns the need for utilitarian reasoning to count, measure, compare, and quantify consequences. If utilitarianism advises that we make decisions by comparing the consequences of alternative actions, then we must have a method for making such comparisons. In practice, however, some comparisons and measurements are very difficult.

For example, in principle, utilitarianism tells us that the interests of all stakeholders who will be affected by a decision ought to be included in calculating the consequences of a decision. But there simply is no consensus among utilitarians on how to measure and determine the overall good. Many business ethics issues highlight how difficult this could be. Consider the consequences of using nonrenewable energy sources and burning fossil fuels for energy. Imagine trying to calculate the consequences of a decision to invest in construction of a nuclear power plant whose wastes remain toxic for tens of thousands of years. Consider how difficult it would be to calculate all the consequences of the decision faced by members of Congress to provide hundreds of billions of dollars to bailout companies that are "too big to fail."

A second challenge goes directly to the core of utilitarianism. The essence of utilitarianism is its reliance on consequences. Ethical and unethical acts are determined by their consequences. In short, the end justifies the means. But this seems to deny one of the earliest ethical principles that many of have learned: the end does not always justify the means.

This challenge can be explained in terms of ethical principles. When we say that the ends do not justify the means what we are saying is that there are certain decisions we should make or certain rules we should follow no matter what the consequences. Put another way, we have certain duties or responsibilities that we ought to obey even when doing so does not produce a net increase in overall happiness. Examples of such duties are those required by such principles as justice, loyalty, and respect, as well as the responsibilities which flow from our roles as a parent, spouse, friend, citizen, or professional.

Several examples can be used to explain why this is a serious criticism of utilitarian reasoning. Since utilitarianism focuses on the overall consequences, utilitarianism seems willing to sacrifice the good of individuals for the greater overall good. So, for example, it might turn out that the overall happiness would be increased if children were held as slave labor. Utilitarians would object to child labor, not as a matter of principle, but only if and to the degree that it detracts from the overall good. If it turns out that slavery and child labor increases the net overall happiness, utilitarianism would have to support these practices. In the judgment of many people, such a decision would violate fundamental ethical principles of justice, equality, and respect.

The ethical tradition that we will turn to in the next section argues that individuals possess certain basic rights that should not be violated even if doing so would increase the overall social happiness. Rights function to protect individuals from being sacrificed for the greater overall happiness. Thus, for example, it is often argued that child labor is ethically wrong in principle even if it contributes to the overall social good because it violates the rights of young children.

A similar example cites those principles that arise from commitments that we all make and the duties that flow from them. For example, as a parent we love our children and have certain duties to them. Violating such commitments and duties would require individuals to sacrifice their own integrity for the common good.

Such commitments and duties play a large role in business life. Contracts and promises are exactly the commitments that one ought to honor, even if the consequences turn out to be unfavorable. The defense of bonuses to AIG executives that cited the contractual duty to pay them is an example of this type of reasoning. The duties that one takes on as part of a professional role function in a similar way. Arthur Andersen's auditors should not have violated their professional duties simply to produce greater overall beneficial consequences. Lawyers have a duty not to help their clients find ways to violate the law, even if they are offered a high salary to do so. Teachers should not violate their professional duties by failing students whom they do not like. Aaron Feuerstein might claim that despite bad overall consequences, he had to remain loyal to his employees as a matter of principle. We will consider similar themes professional commitments and duties when later chapters examine the role of professional responsibilities within business institutions.

Nevertheless, utilitarian ethics does contribute to responsible decision making in several important ways. First, and most obviously, we are reminded of the significance of consequences. Responsible decision making requires that we consider the consequences of our acts. But, the shortcomings of utilitarian reasoning must also be kept in mind. It is difficult to know everyone who will be affected by our decisions and how they are impacted. Utilitarian reasoning demands rigorous work to calculate all the beneficial and harmful consequences of our actions. Perhaps more importantly, utilitarian reasoning does not exhaust the range of ethical concerns. Consequences are only a part of the ethical landscape. Responsible ethical decision making also involves matters of duties, principles, and personal integrity. We turn to such factors in the following sections.

Deontology: An Ethics of Rights and Duties

5 OBJECTIVE

Making decisions based upon the consequences certainly should be a part of responsible ethical decisions making. But this approach must be supplemented with the recognition that some decisions should be a matter of principle, not consequences. In other words, the ends do not always justify the means. But how do we know what principles we should follow and how do we decide when a principle should trump beneficial consequences? Principle-based, or "deontological" ethical theories, work out the details of such questions.

The language of "deontology" and "deontological ethics" is very abstract and is likely to strike many students as so much academic gobbledygook. But the idea behind this approach is commonsensical. Ethical principles can simply be thought of as a type of rule, and this approach to ethics tells us that there are some rules that we ought to follow even if doing so prevents good consequences from happening or even if it results in some bad consequences. Rules or principles (e.g., "obey the law," "keep your promises," "uphold your contracts") create **duties** that bind us to act or decide in certain ways. For example, there is an ethical rule prohibiting slave labor, even if this practice would have beneficial economic consequences for society.

What rules should we follow? Legal rules, obviously, are one major set of rules that we ought to follow. We have a duty to pay our taxes, even if the money might be more efficiently spent on our children's college education. We ought to stop at a red light, even if no cars are coming and I could get to my destination that much sooner. I ought not to steal my neighbor's property, even if he will never miss it and I will gain many benefits form it. Decision making within a business context will involve many situations in which one ought to obey legal rules even when the consequences, economic and otherwise, seem to be undesirable.

Other rules are derived from various institutions in which we participate, or from various social roles that we fill. As a teacher, I ought to read each student's research paper carefully and diligently, even if they will never know the difference and their final grade will not be affected. In my role as teacher and university faculty member, I have taken on certain responsibilities that cannot be abandoned whenever it is convenient for me to do so. As the referee in a sporting event, I have the duty to enforce the rules fairly, even when it would be easier not to do so. Similar rule-based duties follow from our roles as friends (do not gossip about your friends), family-members (do your chores at home), students (do not plagiarize), church member (contribute to the church's upkeep), citizens (vote), and good neighbors (do not operate your lawn mower before 8 A.M.).

There will be very many occasions in which such role-based duties arise in business. As an employee, one takes on a certain role that creates duties. Every business will have a set of rules that employees are expected to follow. Sometimes these rules are explicitly states in a code of conduct, other times in employee handbooks, still others are simply stated by managers. (See Reality Check, "Ethical Principles and the United Nations Global Compact.") Likewise, as a business manager, there are many rules one ought to follow in respect to stockholders, employees, suppliers, and other stakeholders.

Perhaps the most dramatic example of role-based duties concerns the work of professionals within business. Lawyers, accountants, auditors, financial analysts, bankers have important roles to play within political and economic institutions. Many of these roles, often described as "gatekeeper functions," insure the integrity and proper functioning of the economic, legal, or financial system. Chapter 2 introduced the idea of professional responsibilities within the workplace and this theme will be developed further in chapter 10.

The Enron and Arthur Andersen case provides a helpful example for understanding professional duties. While examining Enron's financial reports, the auditors at Arthur Andersen knew that diligent application of strict auditing standards required one decision, but that the consequences of this diligent application would be harmful to Arthur Andersen's business interests. A fair analysis of this aspect of the Enron–Arthur Andersen scandal would point out that Andersen's auditors failed their ethical duties precisely because they did not follow the rules governing their professional responsibilities and allowed beneficial consequences to override their professional principles. (See Reality Check, "Ethical Rules as a Check on Misguided Consequences.")

So far we have mentioned legal rules, organizational rules, role-based rules, and professional rules. We can think of these rules as part of a social agreement, or social contract, which functions to organize and ease relations between

Reality Check *Ethical Principles and the United Nations Global Compact*

Ethical principles and duties can often be found in corporate and professional codes of conduct. One example of such a code that has had worldwide impact is the U.N. Global Compact's code. The United Nations launched the U.N. Global Compact in 2000 as a means to encourage businesses throughout the world to commit to ethical business practices. Businesses joining the Global Compact commit to following ten fundamental ethical principles in the areas of human rights, labor, the environment, and anti-corruption. The United Nations describes its principles as follows:

> The Global Compact asks companies to embrace,support and enact, within their sphere of influence, a set of core values in the areas of human rights, labour standards, the environment, and anti-corruption.

Human Rights

Principle 1: Businesses should support and respect the protection of internationally proclaimed human rights; and

Principle 2: make sure that they are not complicit in human rights abuses.

Labour Standards

Principle 3: Businesses should uphold the freedom of association and the effective recognition of the right to collective bargaining;

Principle 4: the elimination of all forms of forced and compulsory labour;

Principle 5: the effective abolition of child labour; and

Principle 6: the elimination of discrimination in respect of employment and occupation.

Environment

Principle 7: Businesses should support a precautionary approach to environmental challenges;

Principle 8: undertake initiatives to promote greater environmental responsibility, and

Principle 9: encourage the development and diffusion of environmentally friendly technologies.

Anti-Corruption

Principle 10: Businesses should work against corruption in all its forms, including extortion and bribery.

Since its founding in 2000, over 5,200 businesses in 130 countries have joined the Global Compact and committed to these principles. Included in this list are such well-known U.S. firms as Accenture, Alcoa, Campbell Soup, Coca-Cola, Deloitte Touche, Ford Motor Co., Gap, General Mills, Hewlett-Packard, Intel, JC Penny, KPMG, Levi Strauss, Merck, Microsoft, PepsiCo, Starbucks, Sun Microsystems, Dow Chemical, and Timberland.

Source: United National Global Compact, "The Ten Principles," http://unglobalcompact.org/AboutTheGC/TheTenPrinciples/index.html

individuals. No group could function if members were free at all times to decide for themselves what to do and how to act. By definition, any cooperative activity requires cooperation, i.e., requires rules that each member follows.

In the view of many philosophers, fundamental ethical duties must bind us in a stricter way than the way we are bound by contracts or by professional duties. You should not be able to "quit" ethical duties and walk away from them in quite the way that one can dissolve a contract or walk away from professional duties by quitting the profession. In the language of many philosophers, ethical duties should be **"categorical" imperatives** rather than hypothetical. Hypothetical duties would be like professional code of conduct that binds you *only if* you are a member of the profession. Categorical duties do not contain this "if" clause.

Reality Check *Ethical Rules as a Check on Misguided Consequences*

The Enron and Arthur Anderson case demonstrates one of the major vulnerabilities of the consequentialist approach. Utilitarians would rightfully point out that Andersen's auditors did not make decisions according to strict utilitarian ethical principles. The auditors calculated the consequences, but only those to their own firm and their own well-being. Had they truly calculated the *overall* consequences of their decisions, as utilitarianism requires, Andersen's auditors may very well have made the right ethical decision. Instead, they thought only about the $100 million of business generated by Enron and decided to allow this influence to override their principles. But, this shows the difficulty in calculating consequences. Because it is so difficult to know all of the consequences of our actions, it will always be tempting to consider only the consequences to ourselves and our associates. To avoid the slide from utilitarian overall consequences to more solely individualistic, egoistic (and non-ethical) consequences, deontological ethics advises us to follow the rules, regardless of consequences.

I *should* or *must* (an imperative) obey a fundamental ethical rule *no matter what* (a categorical).

Human Rights and Duties

6 OBJECTIVE

Are there *any* such fundamental duties? Are there any rules we should follow, decisions we should make, no matter what the consequences? The foremost advocate of this tradition in ethics, the eighteenth century German philosopher Immanuel Kant, argued that, at bottom, there is essentially one fundamental moral duty, one categorical imperative: respect the dignity of each individual human being. A more simple way to say this is to say that every individual human being has a **human right** to be treated with respect.

Kant claimed that this duty to respect human dignity could be expressed in several ways. One version directs us to act according to those rules that could be universally agreed to by all people. (This is the first form of the famous "Kantian categorical imperative.") Another, less abstract version, requires us to treat each person as an end in themselves and never only as means to our own ends. In other words, our fundamental duty is to treat people as subjects capable of living their own lives and not as mere objects that exist for our purposes. To use the familiar subject/object categories from grammar, humans are subjects because they make decisions and perform actions rather than being objects that are acted upon. Humans have their own ends and purposes and therefore should not be treated simply as a means to the ends of others.

Since every person has this same fundamental duty towards others, each of us can be said to have fundamental human rights: the right to be treated with respect, to expect that others will treat us as an end and never as a means only, and to be treated as an autonomous person. I have the right to pursue my own autonomously chosen ends as long as I do not in turn treat other people as means to my ends and this right applies equally to each and every individual.

Such human rights, or moral rights, have played a central role in the development of modern democratic political systems. The U.S. Declaration of Independence speaks of "inalienable rights" that cannot be taken away by government. Following World War II, the United Nations created the U.N.'s Declaration of Human Rights as a means for holding all governments to fundamental standards of ethics. The reading "Business and Human Rights: A Not-So-New Framework for Corporate Responsibility" by Christine Bader and John Morrison, which follows this chapter, examines how the United Nations' Declaration of Human Rights might also provide a framework for understanding business' social responsibilities.

To return to an earlier example, this deontological or Kantian tradition in ethics would object to child labor because such practices violate our duty to treat children with respect. We violate the rights of children when we treat them as mere means to the ends of production and economic growth. We are treating them merely as means because, as children, they have not rationally and freely chosen their own ends. We are simply using them as tools or objects. Thus, even if child labor produced beneficial consequences, it would be ethically wrong because it violates a fundamental human right.

In this way, the concept of a human or moral right is central to the principle-based ethical tradition. The inherent dignity of each individual means that we cannot do whatever we choose to another person. Human rights protect individuals from being treated in ways that would violate their dignity and that would treat them as mere objects or means. Rights imply that some acts and some decisions are "off-limits." Accordingly, our fundamental moral duty (the "categorical imperative") is to respect the fundamental human rights of others. Our rights establish limits on the decisions and authority of others.

Consider how rights function relative to the utilitarian goal of maximizing the overall good. Suppose that you owned a local business and your local government decided that your property would make a great location for a city park. Imagine that you are the only person who disagrees. On utilitarian grounds, it might seem that your land would best serve the overall good by being used for a park. However, your property rights prevent the community from taking your land (at least without just compensation) to serve the public. A similar issue happens with the music and video downloads and file sharing. Some would argue on utilitarian grounds that the greatest happiness would be promoted by allowing unlimited free file-sharing of music and video files. Clearly, more people would get more of what they want and happiness would be optimized under such a scheme. But the owners of these files, those individuals and companies who have property rights over them, would claim that their rights should not be violated simply to produce greater overall consequences. For another example about conflicting rights, see the Decision Point, "Eminent Domain for the Public Good."

In summary, we can say that human rights are meant to offer protection of certain central human interests, prohibiting the sacrifice of these interests merely to provide a net increase in the overall happiness. The standard account of human rights offered through the Western ethical tradition connects basic human rights

Decision Point

Eminent Domain for the Public Good

Should the government be able to take private property as a means to increase the local tax base? In the summer of 2005, the U.S. Supreme Court decided that the city of New London, Connecticut, could legally exercise eminent domain by seizing private property as part of a plan to redevelop a waterfront area. The city argued that the private homes and property in the area would be better used if it were developed by private businesses as part of a more upscale residential and commercial project. The increased property values would create an increased tax base leading to increased public revenues and thereby providing greater good for a greater number of people. Citizens in the area who were to lose their homes argued that their rights were being violated. The Court, in *Kelso vs. New London,* concluded that their constitutional and legal rights were not violated. How would you have decided if you were on the Supreme Court and do you perceive a violation of ethical rights?

- What facts would you need to have in order to make a decision in this case?
- Other than the legal rights involved, what ethical values are involved in this case?
- Besides the homeowners, the city government, and the developers are there any other stakeholders who should be involved in this case?
- How do you think that the city decided that the beneficial consequences of this policy would outweigh the harmful consequences?
- What duties do city government officials have to individual homeowners and to the city as a whole ?

to some theory of a basic human nature. The Kantian tradition claims that our fundamental human rights, and the duties that follow from them, are derived from our nature as free and rational beings. Humans do not act only out of instinct and conditioning; they make free choices about how they live their lives, about their own ends. In this sense, humans are said to have a fundamental human right of **autonomy,** or *"self-rule."*

From these origins, we can see how two related rights have emerged as fundamental within philosophical ethics. If autonomy, or self-rule, is a fundamental characteristic of human nature, then the freedom to make our own choices deserves special protection as a basic right. But, since all humans possess this fundamental characteristic, equal treatment and equal consideration must also be fundamental rights. They are, according to much of this tradition, "natural rights" that are more fundamental and persistent than the legal rights created by governments and social contracts. (See the Reality Check, "Are Fundamental Human Rights Universally Accepted?")

Christine Bader has served as the Advisor to the U.N. Special Representative of the Secretary-General for business and human rights, and John Morrison has

Reality Check *Are Fundamental Human Rights Universally Accepted?*

In 1948, the United Nations adopted a Universal Declaration of Human Rights. Since that time, this Declaration has been translated into more than 300 languages and dialects. The Declaration contains thirty articles outlining basic human rights. In part, the declaration includes the following:

PREAMBLE

Recognition of the inherent dignity and of the equal and inalienable rights of all members of the human family is the foundation of freedom, justice and peace in the world.

Article 1.
All human beings are born free and equal in dignity and rights. They are endowed with reason and conscience and should act towards one another in a spirit of brotherhood.

Article 2.
Everyone is entitled to all the rights and freedoms set forth in this Declaration, without distinction of any kind, such as race, colour, sex, language, religion, political or other opinion, national or social origin, property, birth or other status.

Article 3.
Everyone has the right to life, liberty and security of person.

Article 4.
No one shall be held in slavery or servitude; slavery and the slave trade shall be prohibited in all their forms.

Article 5
No one shall be subjected to torture or to cruel, inhuman or degrading treatment or punishment.

Article 9.
No one shall be subjected to arbitrary arrest, detention or exile.

Article 10.
Everyone is entitled in full equality to a fair and public hearing by an independent and impartial tribunal, in the determination of his rights and obligations and of any criminal charge against him.

Article 18.
Everyone has the right to freedom of thought, conscience and religion; this right includes freedom to change his religion or belief, and freedom, either alone or in community with others and in public or private, to manifest his religion or belief in teaching, practice, worship and observance.

Article 19.
Everyone has the right to freedom of opinion and expression; this right includes freedom to hold opinions without interference and to seek, receive and impart information and ideas through any media and regardless of frontiers.

Article 23.
(1) Everyone has the right to work, to free choice of employment, to just and favourable conditions of work and to protection against unemployment.
(2) Everyone, without any discrimination, has the right to equal pay for equal work.
(3) Everyone who works has the right to just and favourable remuneration ensuring for himself and his family an existence worthy of human dignity, and supplemented, if necessary, by other means of social protection.
(4) Everyone has the right to form and to join trade unions for the protection of his interests.

Article 25.
(1) Everyone has the right to a standard of living adequate for the health and well-being of himself and of his family, including food, clothing, housing and medical care and necessary social services, and the right to security in the event of unemployment, sickness, disability, widowhood, old age or other lack of livelihood in circumstances beyond his control.

Article 26.
(1) Everyone has the right to education.

been the Executive Director of the Institute for Human Rights and Business. Together, they have drafted a discussion, included at the end of this chapter that advocates for these fundamental human rights as an appropriate underlying framework for business' role in society, no matter what region or sector. Since there remains a gap in governance between what businesses are permitted to do according to the laws of the countries in which they operate and "permitted" to do according to a recognition of the fundamental rights discussed above, Bader and Morrison explain the U.N. Special Representative's framework for multinational corporations of "Protect, Respect, and Remedy." Consider the realistic corporate application of the rights protected under the U.N.'s Declaration of Human Rights (see Reality Check, "Are Fundamental Human Rights Universally Accepted?") under that framework (see the reading at the end of the chapter).

Moral Rights and Legal Rights

7 OBJECTIVE

It will be helpful at this point to distinguish between **moral rights** and legal rights. To illustrate this distinction, let us take employee rights as an example. Three senses of employee rights are common in business. First, there are those *legal* rights granted to employees on the basis of legislation or judicial rulings. Thus, employees have a right to a minimum wage, equal opportunity, to bargain collectively as part of a union, to be free from sexual harassment, and so forth. Second, employee rights might refer to those goods that employees are entitled to on the basis of contractual agreements with employers. In this sense, a particular employee might have a right a specific health care package, a certain number of paid holidays, pension funds, and the like. Finally, employee rights might refer to those moral entitlements to which employees have a claim independently of any particular legal or contractual factors. Such rights would originate with the respect owed to them as human beings.

To expand on this understanding, consider how legal and contractual rights interact. In general, both parties to an employment agreement bargain over the conditions of work. Employers offer certain wages, benefits, and working conditions and in return seek worker productivity. Employees offer skills and abilities and seek wages and benefits in return. Thus, employment rights emerge from contractual promises. However, certain goods are legally exempt from such negotiation. An employer cannot make a willingness to submit to sexual harassment or acceptance of a wage below the minimum established by law a part of the employment agreement. In effect, legal rights exempt certain interests from the employment contract. Such legal rights set the basic legal framework in which business operates. They are established by the legal system in which business operates and, in this sense, are part of the price of doing business. Consider your own perspective on this question in the Decision Point: "Do Employees Have Moral Rights?"

So, too, human rights lie outside of the bargaining that occurs between employers and employees. Unlike the minimum wage, moral rights are established

Decision Point *Do Employees Have Moral Rights?*

Employees certainly have legal rights, such as the right to be paid a minimum wage, to enjoy equal opportunity in the workplace, and to be free from sexual harassment. Many employees also have contractual rights, such as the right to an employer contribution to a retirement plan, health care, or certain number of vacation and sick days. But do employees really have rights against their employer that are not specified in the law or in the employment contract? Do employers have duties to their employees other than what is required by law and the employment contract? If every human has a right to health care, do employers have a moral duty to provide health insurance for every employee? Do employers have a duty to provide a just wage? Do employers have a duty to respect an employee's right to privacy?

and justified by moral, rather than legal, considerations. Moral rights establish the basic moral framework for legal environment itself, and more specifically for any contracts that are negotiated within business. Thus, as described in the United States Declaration of Independence, governments and laws are created in order to secure more fundamental natural moral rights. The rights outlined above in the excerpt from the United Nations fit this conception of fundamental moral rights.

Challenges to an Ethics of Rights and Duties

8 OBJECTIVE

So what rights do we have and what does that mean for the duties of others? In the U.S. Declaration of Independence, Thomas Jefferson claimed that we have "inalienable rights" to life, liberty, and the pursuit of happiness. Jefferson was influenced by the British philosopher John Locke, who spoke of "natural rights" to life, health, liberty, and possessions. The U.N. Universal Declaration of Human Rights (see the reality check) lists more than 26 human rights that are universal.

Acknowledging this diversity of rights makes it easy to understand the two biggest challenges to this ethical tradition. There appears to be much disagreement about what rights truly are basic human rights and, given the multiplicity of rights, it is unclear how to apply this approach to practical situations, especially in cases where rights seemingly conflict.

Take, for example, a possible right to health care. During debates over health care reform in the U.S. Congress in 2009, many claimed that humans have a right to health care. Other societies would seem to agree in that many countries have instituted national health plans to provide citizens with at least minimal health care. The U.N. Declaration would seem to agree, claiming that humans have a right "to a standard of living adequate for the health and well-being" and that this right includes medical care. But many disagree and point out that such a right would carry significant costs for others. If every human has a right to health care, who has the duty to provide it and at what costs? Does this mean that doctors and nurses can be required to provide free medical care? Does this right entail a right to the best treatment possible? To elective surgeries? To wellness care or nursing homes? To cosmetic surgery?

Critics charge that unless there is a specific person or institution that has a duty to provide the goods identified as "rights," talk of rights amounts to little more than a wish list of things that people want. What are identified as "rights" often are nothing more than good things that most people desire. But, if every human truly does have a right to a standard of living adequate for all the goods mentioned in Article 25 of the U.N. Declaration, who has the duty to provide them?

More relevant to business is the Declaration's Article 23 that everyone has a "right to work and free choice of employment." What would this mean to a business? Is it helpful to say that an employee's human rights are violated if they are laid-off during a recession? Who has the duty to provide jobs to every unemployed person? This same Article refers to a "right to just and favourable remuneration." But what is a just wage and who gets to decide?

The first major challenge to an ethics based on rights is that there is no agreement about the scope and range of such rights. Which good things qualify as rights, and which are merely things that people want? Critics charge that there is no way to answer this. Yet, unless there is some clear way to distinguish the two, the list of rights will only grow to unreasonable lengths and the corresponding duties will unreasonably burden everyone.

A second challenge also points to practical problems in applying a theory of rights to real-life situations. With a long list of human rights, all of which are claimed to be basic and fundamental, we need a practical guide to decide what to do when rights come into conflict. For example, how would we decide between one individual's right to medical care and the physician's right to just remuneration of her work? Suppose the person needing medical care could not afford to pay a just fee for the care?

Perhaps the most important such conflict in a business setting would occur when an employer's rights to property come into conflict with an employee's alleged rights to work, just wages, and health care. While the U.N. Declaration does not mention a right to property as a basic human right, many philosophers in the Western tradition agree with John Locke and include it among our natural rights. Granting economic rights to employee would seem to create numerous conflicts with the property rights of employers. Critics point out that the ethical tradition of rights and duties has been unable to provide a persuasive and systematic account for how such conflicts are to be resolved.

Virtue Ethics: Making Decisions Based on Integrity and Character

9 OBJECTIVE

For the most part, utilitarian and deontological approaches to ethics focus on rules that we might follow in deciding what we should do, both as individuals and as citizens. These approaches conceive of practical reason in terms of

Reality Check *Virtues in Practice*

The language of virtues and vices may seem old-fashioned or quaint for modern readers, but this was a dominant perspective on ethics in the western world for centuries. If you develop a list of adjectives that describe a person's character, you will find that the language of virtues and vices is not as outdated as it may seem.

The ancient Greeks identified four primary virtues: courage, moderation, wisdom, and justice. Early Christians described the three cardinal virtues of faith, hope, and charity. Boys Scouts pledge to be trustworthy, loyal, helpful, friendly, courteous, kind, obedient, cheerful, thrifty, brave, clean, and reverent.

According to ancient and medieval philosophers, the virtues represented a balanced mean, the "golden mean," between two extremes, both of which would be considered vices. Thus, for example, a brave person finds the balance between too little courage, which is cowardice, and too much courage, which would be reckless and foolhardy.

The virtues are those character traits or habits that would produce a good, happy, and meaningful life. Practicing such virtues and habits and acting in accord with one's own character is to live a life of integrity.

deciding how to act and what to do. Chapter 1 pointed out, however, that ethics also involves questions about the type of person one should become. Virtue ethics is a tradition within philosophical ethics that seeks a full and detailed description of those character traits, or virtues, that would constitute a good and full human life.

Virtues can be understood as those character traits that would constitute a good and meaningful human life. Being friendly and cheerful, having integrity, being honest, forthright and truthful, having modest wants, and being tolerant are some of the characteristics of a good and meaningful human life. (For additional qualities, see the Reality Check, "Virtues in Practice.") One can see virtue ethics at play in everyday situations:we describe someone's behavior as being out of character or describe someone as being a person of integrity. Perhaps the best place to see the ethics of virtue is in the goal of every good parent who hopes to raise happy and decent children.

To understand how virtue ethics differs from utilitarian and deontological approaches, consider the problem of egoism. As mentioned previously, egoism is a view which holds that people act only out of a self-interest. Many economists, for example, assume that all individuals always act out of self-interest; indeed, many assume that rationality itself should be defined in terms of acting out of self-interest. The biggest challenge posed by egoism and, according to some, the biggest challenge to ethics is the apparent gap between self-interest and altruism, or between motivation that is "self-regarding" and motivation that is "other-regarding." Ethics requires us, at least at times, to act for the well-being of others. Yet, some would claim that this is not possible. Humans only act from self-interested motives.

An ethics of virtue shifts the focus from questions about what a person should *do,* to a focus on who that person *is.* This shift requires not only a different view of ethics but, at least as important, a different view of ourselves. Implicit in this

Reality Check *Is Selfishness a Virtue?*

Does ethics demand that we sacrifice our own interests for others? If so, is this reasonable? Is it even possible?

The tension between ethics and self-interest has been central to philosophical ethics since at least the time of Socrates and Plato. Ethical responsibilities certainly seem to require that we sometimes restrict our own actions out of consideration for the interest of other people. Yet, some thinkers have concluded that such a requirement is unreasonable and unrealistic. It is unreasonable because it would be too much to ask people to act against their own self-interest; and it would be unrealistic because, in fact, it is simply part of human nature to be selfish.

Twentieth-century philosopher Ayn Rand argued that selfishness is a virtue. Rand denied that altruism, acting for the interests of others, was an ethical virtue. Altruism too easily makes people predisposed to sacrifice for others and ignores their own basic interests. Instead, she argued that ethically responsible people stand up for their own interests and should be motivated by a concern with their own interests. From this perspective, selfishness is a virtue; people who act out of a concern for their own interests will live more fulfilling and happy human lives.

This philosophical starting point has led many thinkers, including Rand herself, to adopt a political and social philosophy of libertarianism. This is the view that the fundamental right of individuals is the right to liberty, understood as the right to be free from interference by others. Libertarianism also provides philosophical support for free market capitalism and is often the ethical view implicit in the thinking of people in business. Free markets are the economic system that best serve the libertarian goal of protecting individual rights of liberty.

But even Rand recognized that selfishness in this philosophical sense was not the same as what is commonly understood as selfish behavior. Simply doing whatever one wants will not necessarily work for one's own self-interest. The behavior of the stereotypical selfish and self-centered person who is antagonistic to others is not likely to lead to a happy, secure, and meaningful life. Rand recognized that self-interest, properly understood, may sometimes demand that we restrict and regulate our own desires. Further, since the virtue of selfishness applies equally to all people, our own self-interest is limited by the equal rights of others.

Thus, Rand's version of libertarianism is not as extreme as it might first appear. No ethical tradition expects people to live a life of total self-sacrifice and self-denial. But even those who might be described as ethical egoists concede that rational self-interest does create ethical limits to our own actions and that narrowly selfish people are unethical.

distinction is the recognition that our identity as individuals is constituted in part by our wants, beliefs, values, and attitudes. A person's **character**—those dispositions, relationships, attitudes, values, and beliefs that popularly might be called a "personality"—is not some feature that remains independent of that person's identity. Character is not like a suit of clothes that you step into and out of at will. Rather, the self is identical to a person's most fundamental and enduring dispositions, attitudes, values, and beliefs.

Note how this shift changes the nature of justification in ethics. If, as seems true for many people, an ethical justification of some act requires that it be tied to self-interest, we should not be surprised to find that this justification often fails. Ethical controversies often involve a conflict between self-interest and ethical values. Why should I do the ethical thing if it would require me to give up a lot of money? For a personality that does not already include a disposition to be modest, the only avenue open for justification would involve showing how the disposition serves some other interest of that person. Why should an executive turn down a multi-million dollar bonus? The only way to answer this question appears to be to show how it would be in his self-interest to do so. But, this is at times unlikely. (See Reality Check, "Is Selfishness a Virtue?")

On the other hand, for the person already characterized by modest and unaffected desires, the question of justifying smaller salaries is less relevant. If I am the type of person who had moderate and restrained desires for money, then there is no temptation to be unethical for the sake of a large bonus. For many people, the "self" of self-interest is a caring, modest, unaffected, altruistic self. For these people, there simply is no conflict between *self*-interest and altruism.

The degree to which we are capable of acting for the well-being of others therefore seems to depend on a variety of factors such as our desires, our beliefs, our dispositions, and our values; in short, it depends on our character or the type of person we are. If people are caring, empathetic, charitable, and sympathetic, then the challenge of selfishness and egoism is simply not a factor in their decision making.

Virtue ethics emphasizes the more affective side of our character. Virtue ethics recognizes that our motivations—our interests, wants, desires—are not the sorts of things that each one of us chooses anew each morning. Instead, human beings act in and from character. By adulthood, these character traits typically are deeply ingrained and conditioned within us. Given that our character plays such a deciding role in our behavior, and given the realization that our character can been shaped by factors that are controllable (by conscious individual decisions, by how we are raised, by the social institutions in which we live, work, and learn), virtue ethics seeks to understand how those traits are formed and which traits bolster and which undermine a meaningful, worthwhile, and satisfying human life.

Virtue ethics can offer us a more fully textured understanding of life within business. Rather than simply describing people as good or bad, right or wrong, an ethics of virtue encourages a fuller description. For example, we might describe Aaron Feurestein as heroic and courageous. He is a man of integrity, who sympathizes with employees and cares about their well-being. Other executives might be described as greedy or ruthless, proud or competitive. Faced with a difficult dilemma, we might ask what a person with integrity would do? What an honest person would say? Do I have the courage of my convictions? In other words, you might consider someone you believe to be virtuous and ask yourself what that person would do in this situation. What would a virtuous person do?

Besides connecting the virtues to a conception of a fuller human life, virtue ethics also reminds us to examine how character traits are formed and conditioned. By the time we are adults, much of our character is formed by such factors as our parents, schools, church, friends, and society. But powerful social institutions such as business and especially our own places of employment and our particular social roles within them (e.g., manager, professional, and trainee) have a profound influence on shaping our character. Consider an accounting firm

Reality Check *Can Virtue Be Taught?*

Plato's famous dialogue the *Meno* opens with the title character asking Socrates this basic question: Can virtue be taught? If ethics involves developing the right sort of character traits and habits, as the virtue theorist holds, then the acquisition of those traits becomes a fundamental question for ethics. Can we teach people to *be* honest, trustworthy, loyal, courteous, moderate, respectful, and compassionate?

Meno initially cast the question in terms of two alternatives: either virtue is taught or it is acquired naturally. In modern terms, this is the question of nurture or nature, environment or genetics. Socrates' answer is more complicated. Virtue cannot simply be taught by others, nor is it acquired automatically through nature. Each individual has the natural potential to become virtuous, and learning from one's surroundings is a part of this process. But, ultimately, virtues must be developed by each individual through a complex process of personal reflection, reasoning, practice, and observation, as well as social reinforcement and conditioning. Virtues are habits, and acquiring any habit is a subtle and complex process.

Parents confront this question every day. I know my children will lead happier and more meaningful lives if they are honest, respectful, cheerful, moderate and not greedy, envious, gloomy, arrogant, or selfish. Yet simply telling my children to be honest and to avoid greed is insufficient; nor can I remain passive and assume that these traits will develop naturally. Instilling these character traits and habits is a long-term process that develops over time.

Business institutions also have come to recognize that character formation is both difficult and unavoidable. Employees come to business with certain character traits and habits, and these can get shaped and reinforced in the workplace. Hire a person with the wrong character traits, and there will be trouble ahead. Designing a workplace, creating a corporate culture, to reinforce virtues and discourage vice is one of the greatest challenges for an ethical business.

that hires a group of trainees fully expecting that fewer than half will be retained and where only a very small group will make partner. That corporate environment encourages motivations and behavior very different from a firm that hires fewer people but gives them all a greater chance at long-term success. A company that sets unrealistic sales goals will find it creates a different sales force than one that understands sales more as customer service. Virtue ethics reminds us to look to the actual practices we find in the business world and ask what types of people are being created by these practices. Many individual moral dilemmas that arise within business ethics can best be understood as arising from a tension between the type of person we seek to be and the type of person business expects us to be. (See Reality Check, "Can Virtue Be Taught?")

Consider an example described by someone who is conducting empirical studies of the values found within marketing firms and advertising agencies. This person reported that, on several occasions, advertising agents told her that they would never allow their own children to watch the very television shows and advertisements that their own firms were producing. By their own admission, the ads for such shows aim to manipulate children into buying, or getting their parents to buy, products that had little or no real value. In some cases, the ads promoted beer drinking and the advertisers themselves admitted, as their "dirty little secret," that they were intended to target the teenage market. Further, their own research evidenced the success of their ads in increasing sales.

Independent of the ethical questions we might ask about advertising aimed at children, a virtue ethics approach would look at the type of person who is so able to disassociate oneself and one's own values from one's work, and the social institutions and practices that encourage it. What kind of person is willing to subject others' children to marketing practices that they are unwilling to accept for their own children? Such a person seems to lack even the most elementary form of personal integrity. What kind of institution encourages people to treat children in ways that they willingly admit are indecent? What kind of person does one become working in such an institution?

A Decision-Making Model for Business Ethics Revisited

This chapter provided a detailed introductory survey of ethical theory. While some of these topics might appear esoteric and too abstract for a business ethics class, they have a very practical aim. Understanding the philosophical basis of ethics will enable you to become more aware of ethical issues, better able to recognize the impact of your decisions, and more likely to make better informed and more reasonable decisions. In addition, the theories allow us to better and more articulately explain why we have made or wish to make a particular decision. While a statement such as "we should engage in this practice because it is right" might seem a bit vague or unpersuasive, an alternate explanation such as "we should engage in this practice because more people will be better off than harmed if we do so" could be tremendously effective and convincing. When a decision leader asks you why you support or oppose a specific proposal, your response now has comprehensive substance behind it and will therefore be more sophisticated, credible and influential.

These ethical theories and traditions also provide important ways in which to develop the decision-making model introduced in chapter 2. These ethical theories, after all, provide systematic and sophisticated ways to think and reason about ethical questions. We now can offer a more detailed version of our decision-making model, one in which ethical theories are integrated into an explicit decision procedure. The decision-making process introduced here aims, above all else, to help you make ethically responsible business decisions. To summarize, we review that decision-making process in more detail below. (See the following Reality check, "Nash's 12 Questions" for an alternative decision-making model.)

1. **Determine the facts.** Gather all of the relevant facts. It is critical at this stage that we do not unintentionally bias our later decision by gathering only those facts in support of one particular outcome.
2. **Identify the ethical issues involved.** What is the ethical dimension? What is the ethical issue? Often we do not even notice the ethical dilemma. Avoid normative myopia.
3. **Identify stakeholders.** Who will be affected by this decision? What are their relationships, their priorities to me, and what is their power over my decision

Reality Check *Nash's 12 Questions*

There is nothing magical about the decision-making model that we introduce here. This is simply one way to frame the many factors involved in responsible decision making. There are other models that can work just as well. One such model, proposed by philosopher Laura Nash, suggests asking oneself 12 questions prior to reaching a decision in an ethical dilemma:

1. Have you defined the problem accurately?
2. How would you define the problem if you stood on the other side of the fence?
3. How did the situation occur in the first place?
4. Who was involved in the situation in the first place?
5. What is your intention in making this decision?
6. How does this intention compare with likely results?
7. Who could your decision or action injure?
8. Can you engage the affected parties in a discussion of the problem before you make your decision?
9. Are you confident that your decision will be as valid over a long period as it seems now?
10. Could you disclose without qualms your decision or action to your boss, your CEO, the board of directors, your family, or society as a whole?
11. What is the symbolic potential of your action if understood?
12. Under what conditions would you allow exceptions to your stand?[1]

or results? Who has a stake in the outcome? Do not limit your inquiry only to those stakeholders to whom you believe you owe a duty; sometimes a duty arises as a result of the impact. For instance, you might not necessarily first consider your competitors as stakeholders; however, once you understand the impact of your decision on those competitors, an ethical duty may arise

4. **Consider the available alternatives.** Exercise "moral imagination." Are there creative ways to resolve conflicts? Explore not only the obvious choices, but also those that are less obvious and that require some creative thinking or moral imagination to create.
5. **Consider how a decision affects stakeholders.** Take the point of view of other people involved. How is each stakeholder affected by my decision? Compare and weigh the alternatives: ethical theories and traditions can help here.
   a. Consequences
      i. beneficial and harmful consequences
   b. Duties, rights, principles
      i. What does the law say?
      ii. Are there professional duties involved?
      iii. Which principles are most obligatory?
      iv. How are people being treated?
   c. Implications for personal integrity and character
      i. What type of person am I becoming through this decision?
      ii. What are my own principles and purposes?
      iii. Can I live with public disclosure of this decision?

Opening Decision Point Revisited

Executive Compensation

In early June 2009, the U.S. Treasury Department appointed Kenneth Feinberg to oversee compensation packages that are offered to executives at firms that received significant government bailout money. The companies included AIG, CitiGroup, Bank of America, and General Motors. In making the announcement, Treasury Secretary Timothy Geithner said "The financial crisis had many significant causes, but executive compensation practices were a contributing factor. Incentives for short-term gains overwhelmed the checks and balances meant to mitigate against the risk of excessive leverage."

Feinberg was immediately dubbed the first ever "compensation czar" and critics saw this appointment as a first step towards government wage controls. Defenders saw this as long-overdue and a necessary step to bring fairness to executive compensation and hoped that this practice would extend beyond only those firms receiving government funding.

- What consequences, good and bad, short- and long-term, can you reasonably foresee from this appointment?
- What principles might be cited to defend this position? What principles might it violate?
- What would be the virtues necessary for someone to be a good compensation czar? What vices would make such a person bad in this position?
- Should government set a "maximum wage" limit in the way that it sets a minimum wage?

6. **Guidance.** Can you discuss the case with relevant others; can you gather additional opinions or perspectives? Are their any guidelines, codes, or other external sources that might shed light on the dilemma?
7. **Assessment.** Have you built in mechanisms for assessment of your decision and possible modifications? Are they necessary? Make sure that you learn from each decision and move forward with that increased knowledge; you may face similar decisions in the future or find it necessary to make changes to your current situation.

Questions, Projects, and Exercises

1. Using the distinction between theoretical reason and practical reason introduced in chapter 1, identify which of your other business courses have practical goals. Which courses aim to help student learn how to make responsible decisions about what they should do and how they should act? Can you identify the values that are either implicitly or explicitly taught in these classes?
2. What makes a decision or issue *ethical?* How would you explain the differences between ethical/non-ethical, and ethical/unethical?

3. What ethical issues or dilemmas have you ever experienced in the workplace? How were they resolved? Are there any ethical issues or dilemmas presently being discussed at your school?
4. Are there some ethical values or principles that you believe are relative to one's own culture, religion, or personal opinion? Are there some that you believe are not? What makes them different?
5. Do an Internet search on international human rights and/or fundamental moral rights. Can you make the argument that any moral rights are universally acknowledged?
6. Why might the political goal of economic growth be considered a utilitarian goal?
7. Some political philosophers understand the ethical foundations of legislatures to be utilitarian, while the ethical foundation of the judiciary is deontological. How would you explain this distinction?
8. Do people have a right to do whatever they want? If not, in what sense can people have a right to liberty or personal freedom?
9. The right of private property is often described as a "bundle" of rights. What rights are involved in ownership of property?
10. Relying on the description of virtue ethics, how would you describe Aaron Feuerstein's character? What type of person would make the decision he made?
11. Can such character traits as honesty, loyalty, trustworthiness, compassion, and humility be taught? Do people learn to be selfish, greedy, aggressive, or do these traits come naturally?
12. Do professionals such as accountants and lawyers have duties and obligations that other people do not? From where would such duties come?

Key Terms

After reading this chapter, you should have a clear understanding of the following Key Terms. The page numbers refer to the point at which they were discussed in the chapter. For a more complete definition, please see the Glossary.

End Note

1. Laura Nash, "Ethics without the Sermon," *Harvard Business Review,* 56, no. 6 (1981): 80–81.

Readings

Reading 3-1: "Business and Human Rights: A Not-So-New Framework for Corporate Responsibility," by Christine Bader and John Morrison, *p. 125*

Reading 3-2: "The Caux Principles for Responsible Business," Caux Round Table, *p. 130*

Reading 3-1

Business and Human Rights: *A Not-So-New Framework for Corporate Responsibility*

Christine Bader and John Morrison

Using human rights to understand, guide, and regulate business is a relatively recent phenomenon, one that at first might seem counterintuitive. The modern international human rights system is based on the Universal Declaration of Human Rights (UDHR), which was agreed to in 1948 by the world's governments to hold each other to account after the atrocities of World War II. The UDHR says nothing about companies;[1] nor do the International Covenants that followed to provide more detail on what the UDHR intended. For business to embrace human rights would seem to contradict the notion, most famously articulated by Milton Friedman, that "there is one and only one social responsibility of business: to use its resources and engage in activities designed to increase its profits so long as it stays within the rules of the game, which is to say, engages in open and free competition without deception or fraud."[2]

However, human rights are a compelling proposition for the globalising economy. While corporate social responsibility (CSR)—a term used to capture any form of corporate engagement on social issues—is increasingly popular, it is culturally relative: There are no universal CSR principles, beyond what a particular company operating in a particular area decides for itself.

Human rights, however, as embodied in the UDHR, is the single statement of societal values for all people of the world, irrespective of nationality, religion, gender or ethnicity. A global set of principles is of great utility for companies that transcend national borders and strive for legitimacy in the global marketplace.

This article recounts the recent history of business and human rights, with particular attention to two initiatives: a United Nations (UN) mandate on business and human rights and the Business Leaders Initiative on Human Rights (BLIHR). It asserts that human rights provide the right framework for considering business's role in society, no matter what region or sector.

In the 1990s, apparel and footwear companies (notably, Nike and the clothing line by U.S. television celebrity Kathie Lee Gifford) came under fire for having their products made in factories in the developing world where workers were paid poorly, subject to terrible working conditions, and sometimes physically abused. At the same time, companies in the oil, gas, and mining sectors were accused of supporting human rights abuses committed by the governments of the countries in which they were operating. Ken Saro-Wiwa was a Nigerian activist executed after leading protests against the environmental damage that Shell's operations allegedly caused in his country; some observers believe that Shell could have prevented the execution by arguing that Saro-Wiwa was entitled to his freedom of speech. A few years later, BP (formerly British Petroleum) was accused of supporting a rogue, violent element of the Colombian military that was perpetrating abuses in the name of protecting company facilities.

By the end of the decade, the companies under fire and some of their peers came together with human rights groups and other interested parties to develop codes of conduct for their respective industries. Some of these multi-stakeholder initiatives, most notably the Fair Labor Association and the Voluntary Principles on Security & Human Rights, still exist today and continue to attract new members.[3]

In the first decade of the new century, human rights discussions spread into other business sectors. In 2003 a number of banks, under fire for funding projects with adverse human rights impacts, launched the Equator Principles, a set of social and environmental standards that the banks agreed to adhere to for certain kinds of loans.[4]

In 2004, Yahoo! complied with a request from the Chinese government to hand over information about one of its users, journalist Shi Tao—which enabled authorities to find and jail him. In 2006, Google launched Google.cn, its search engine supported by servers in China—and in doing so agreed to censor search results. Those companies followed suit of the aforementioned industries by entering into multi-stakeholder discussions on a code of conduct, resulting in the establishment of the Global Network Initiative in 2008.[5]

Virtually all businesses can impact human rights. These impacts can of course be positive: The jobs that companies provide can lead to stronger realization of a great range of rights, including the right to work, right to an adequate standard of living and right to own property. As people achieve greater economic freedom, they are poised to demand and achieve greater fulfillment of other rights, such as the right to education and the right to participate in cultural life and in government.

But as the aforementioned examples show, business can also infringe on human rights. So what should company responsibilities be with respect to human rights?

There have been attempts to saddle companies with all of the same responsibilities as governments. This is not appropriate: Governments are held accountable by their constituents, for example through elections. In contrast, company executives answer to their directors and shareholders—who are likely to be far removed from the people who their business is affecting. What recourse is available for victims of corporate-related abuse? They can try to sue the company—that is, if they can afford a lawyer, if there is a court that will accept both the case and the company as being in its jurisdiction. Or they can try to mount a public campaign to try to embarrass the company into behaving differently—but that's rarely effective for redressing actual harm.

During his term as UN Secretary-General, Kofi Annan often expressed belief in the power of business to be a force for good. He established the UN Global Compact, an initiative in which companies commit to implementing ten principles upholding social and environmental standards; he made it clear that business has a role to play in the achievement of the Millennium Development Goals, eight ambitious targets for reducing global poverty by 2015.[6]

In 2005, Annan appointed Harvard professor John Ruggie to be UN Special Representative of the Secretary-General for business and human rights. Ruggie was charged with bringing clarity to what had become quite a polarized debate: Some campaigning organizations wanted an international treaty on corporate responsibility; some business interests were adamant that no new standards were necessary; and most governments were largely disengaged.

Ruggie's first task was to better understand the problem he was meant to address: What human rights abuses have been linked to corporations: in what industries, in what countries, and what rights have been at stake? What have the UN treaty bodies, the divisions of the UN whose job it is to interpret human rights conventions, said about corporations? What jurisprudence is there about business and human rights? What rights do companies themselves recognize and how, through their own policies and practices? What is the cause of this rapid growth in alleged corporate-related abuses?[7]

Over the past few decades, companies have globalized while governments are confined by state borders. A computer hardware company with headquarters in the U.S. could be importing iron from South America to make equipment assembled in east Asia that will be shipped to European consumers who call helpdesks in south Asia. One product—and yet, if the iron ore mine is using forced labour, or the manufacturing facility bans independent trade unions, it is likely that no one will be penalized. U.S. courts would consider the mine and assembly operations distinct legal entities, subject only to local courts; the South American country might be reluctant to pursue charges for fear of tainting its reputation as an attractive place for foreign investment; and some governments restrict union activity.

This misalignment between global companies and national legal systems leads to governance gaps that enable human rights abuses to take place. Indeed, Ruggie's research and reports from others showed that the worst cases of corporate-related human rights harm occur disproportionately in low income countries; in countries that often had just emerged from or still were in conflict; and in countries where the rule of law was weak and levels of corruption high—in otherwise, where governance was likely to be the weakest.

Eventually it became clear to Ruggie, through extensive global consultations and research, that what was needed was an overarching framework for business and human rights, based on some fundamental principles that everyone agreed, upon and within which principles and specific guidance could be further developed. Ruggie presented that framework to the UN Human Rights Council in 2008, with the title of "Protect, Respect, Remedy".

The first pillar of the framework, "Protect", emphasizes the duty of governments to protect against human rights abuses by third parties, including business. International law clearly states that governments have a duty to protect people within their territory or jurisdiction against human rights abuses by non-State actors, including by business. States must take all necessary steps to protect against such abuse, including preventing, investigating, and punishing the abuse, and provide access to redress when abuses occur.

The second pillar of the framework, "Respect", affirms the corporate responsibility to respect human rights: in other words, not to infringe on the rights of others, and to demonstrate that respect through ongoing human rights due diligence. The responsibility to respect is not a Ruggie invention: It is recognized by organizations like the International Labor Organization, the Organization of Economic Cooperation and Development, and the world's largest employer groups such as the International Chamber of Commerce and the International Organisation of Employers.[8] Companies increasingly recognize their responsibility to respect through their own public statements and by joining initiatives such as the Global Compact.

The third pillar of the framework, "Remedy", underscores the need for more effective access to remedies for victims of corporate-related abuse. Even with the best intentions by governments and companies, disputes over corporate impact on human rights are likely to occur, and as mentioned earlier, people seeking redress currently have few good options. In addition, effective grievance mechanisms can not only help solve issues when they arise, but can also provide feedback to a company that shows where it might need to change practices—and most importantly, catch problems before they escalate to abuses.

The Human Rights Council unanimously endorsed the "Protect, Respect, Remedy" framework, making it the first substantive policy statement on business and human rights by a UN body, and extended Ruggie's mandate so that he can develop more specific recommendations within each pillar. But one group of leading multinational companies had already begun exploring what the responsibility to respect means for them.

Following the 2002 World Summit on Sustainable Development in Johannesburg, a small group of people including Anita and Gordon Roddick, co-founders of The Body Shop International plc, the cosmetics company known for its activist stances against animal testing and for fair trade, realized that there was no equivalent to the Business Leaders Initiative on Climate Change for social issues. In May 2003, the Business Leaders Initiative on Human Rights (BLIHR)[9] was founded by seven companies: ABB, Barclays, MTV Europe, National Grid, Novartis Foundation for Sustainable Development, Novo Nordisk and The Body Shop International. Mary Robinson, former President of Ireland and UN High Commissioner for Human Rights, became BLIHR's Honorary Chair.[10]

During 2004, Hewlett-Packard Company, StatoilHydro and Gap Inc. joined the initiative. In 2006, Alcan Inc., AREVA, Ericsson and General Electric joined; and in August 2007, The Coca-Cola Company brought the total number of BLIHR companies to thirteen.

BLIHR's primary purpose was to find practical ways of implementing the Universal Declaration of Human Rights and to inspire other businesses to do the same. With that two-pronged mission, BLIHR's work evolved into two streams: a toolbox of practical materials to aid the integration of human rights into business; and a soapbox, by which BLIHR members would promote greater awareness of human rights with other companies in their respective industries and beyond.

During its first three years, BLIHR worked to understand how human rights can be applied in specific companies, and what sorts of tools and information might be needed to do so. In 2006, BLIHR produced a guide for integrating human rights into business, based on standard business management systems, in partnership with the Global Compact and the UN High Commissioner for Human Rights. Central to this guide and the BLIHR toolbox is a matrix enabling business to map their existing policy and practice against the Universal Declaration of Human Rights and associated covenants.

BLIHR's work is part of a flurry of activity in recent years by a wide variety of organizations that have developed materials and programs to improve business's impact on human rights. These initiatives generally fall into one of three categories:

1. Principles: A number of organizations have developed general principles, sometimes for a particular industry or topic, meant to enable companies to state their commitment to human rights at a very high level as a first step. Examples include the UN Global Compact and the UN Principles for Responsible Investment.[11]
2. Procedures: Some initiatives have gone to the next level of granularity by developing more specific tools to help companies manage human rights. This includes guidance on assessing human rights impacts, for example from the Danish Institute for Human Rights's Human Rights and Business Project.[12]
3. Monitoring and Reporting: Some organizations have focused on assessing and reporting on these processes once they're in place. Most prominent in this area has been the Global Reporting Initiative.[13]

BLIHR companies tested many of these tools and participated in many related initiatives, and in doing so demonstrated that embracing human rights can result in better management of risk to their business and the people their business affects; more informed decision-making; and stronger relationships with stakeholders. BLIHR concluded in 2009 as it was never meant to be a permanent initiative, but as one of its founding members put it, a "strong shot of coffee". Members of the BLIHR community are continuing to evangelize for business and human rights, within their industries and more broadly.

Some skeptics of the business and human rights movement claim that it is solely a Western phenomenon. However, there are several indications that countries outside of North America and Europe are viewing business through a human rights lens:

- South Africa's post-apartheid constitution explicitly holds companies accountable for the full range of civil, political, economic, social and cultural rights. National human rights institutions in Kenya, Malawi, Zambia, Uganda and Ghana are increasingly turning their attention to business, and companies in Darfur are being scrutinized over whether they are exacerbating conflict there.
- In India, a growing number of domestically-owned companies expanding abroad are increasingly engaged in human rights as they seek to find a more objective framework for applying traditional Indian values in other cultures. The Global Business Initiative on Human Rights[14] (part of BLIHR's legacy) and Partners In Change co-hosted a meeting of 40 Indian companies in New Delhi in November

2009 where human rights was seen as a key facet of operating internationally.

- The Chinese government passed new laws in 2007 strengthening labor rights, and has been outspoken in promoting CSR with its companies. The Shenzen Stock Exchange encourages companies to release social responsibility reports along with their annual reports.[15]

Both the business community and the human rights community have a vested interest in universalism. Companies that operate globally often lament the inconsistency of laws, standards, and enforcement across jurisdictions. The expectation that companies respect human rights is a universal norm, espoused by citizens all over the world. The global financial crisis that began in 2008 demonstrated that universal frameworks are necessary—and that human rights and business are inextricably linked.

The UN "Protect, Respect, Remedy" framework is one step towards strengthening global governance. There has already been considerable uptake of the framework by both companies and governments, as the BLIHR companies began to demonstrate.

It is important not to overstate success to date: Only a few hundred companies—of the hundreds of thousands of multinationals, never mind small to medium-sized enterprises—have human rights policies. Few management education programs train future business leaders on human rights, and indeed few corporations proactively seek human rights expertise—until disaster strikes.

However, it is clear that human rights are an enduring framework with powerful application to the role of business in society—all over the world. The next few years will see continued application of the framework, and hopefully continuous improvement in our understanding and management of business's impacts on society.

End Notes

1. The UDHR does, however, call on "all organs of society" in its preamble, which is often interpreted to include business. However, this is a moral statement and not one with legal effect.
2. Friedman, M., "The Social Responsibility of Business is to Increase its Profits," *The New York Times Magazine* (September 13, 1970).
3. See Fair Labor Association, http://fairlabor.org/ and International Business Leaders Forum, Business for Social Responsibility, "Voluntary Principles on Security and Human Rights," http://voluntaryprinciples.org/ (accessed November 10, 2009).
4. Equator Principles, http://www.equator-principles.com/ (accessed November 10, 2009).
5. Global Network Initiative (2008), http://globalnetworkinitiative.org/ (accessed November 10, 2009).
6. See United Nations Global Compact, http://www.unglobalcompact.org/ and United Nations Millennium Development Goals, http://www.un.org/millenniumgoals/ (accessed November 10, 2009).
7. All materials related to John Ruggie's mandate are archived at the Business & Human Rights Resource Centre web portal, http://www.business-humanrights.org/ (accessed November 7, 2009).
8. See, e.g., "Joint initial views of the International Organisation of Employers (IOE), the International Chamber of Commerce (ICC) and the Business and Industry Advisory Committee to the OECD (BIAC) to the Eighth Session of the Human Rights Council on the Third report of the Special Representative of the UN Secretary-General on Business and Human Rights" (May 2008), http://www.business-humanrights.org/SpecialRepPortal/Home/ReportstoUNHumanRightsCouncil/2008 (accessed November 7, 2009).
9. www.blihr.org
10. Business Leaders Initiative on Human Rights, http://blihr.org/ (accessed November 10, 2009).
11. Principles for Responsible Investment, http://www.unpri.org/ (accessed November 10, 2009).

12. Danish Institute for Human Rights, http://www.humanrights.dk/business (accessed November 10, 2009).
13. Global Reporting Initiative, http://www.globalreporting.org/Home (accessed November 10, 2009).
14. www.global-business-initiative.org.
15. For this and other examples, see Ruggie's Corporate Law project, described at http://www.business-humanrights.org/SpecialRepPortal/Home/Materialsbytopic/Corporatelaw/CorporateLawTools (accessed November 7, 2009).

Reading **3-2**

The Caux Principles for Responsible Business[1]

The Caux Round Table (March 2009)

Introduction

The Caux Round Table (CRT) Principles for Responsible Business set forth ethical norms for acceptable businesses behavior.

Trust and confidence sustain free markets and ethical business practices provide the basis for such trust and confidence. But lapses in business integrity, whether among the few or the many, compromise such trust and hence the ability of business to serve humanity's needs.

Events like the 2009 global financial crisis have highlighted the necessity of sound ethical practices across the business world. Such failures of governance and ethics cannot be tolerated as they seriously tarnish the positive contributions of responsible business to higher standards of living and the empowerment of individuals around the world.

The self-interested pursuit of profit, with no concern for other stakeholders, will ultimately lead to business failure and, at times, to counterproductive regulation. Consequently, business leaders must always assert ethical leadership so as to protect the foundations of sustainable prosperity.

It is equally clear that if capitalism is to be respected, and so sustain itself for global prosperity, it must be both responsible and moral. Business therefore needs a moral compass in addition to its practical reliance on measures of profit and loss.

The CRT Principles

The Caux Round Table's approach to responsible business consists of seven core principles as detailed below. The principles recognize that while laws and market forces are necessary, they are insufficient guides for responsible business conduct.

The principles are rooted in three ethical foundations for responsible business and for a fair and functioning society more generally, namely: responsible stewardship; living and working for mutual advantage; and the respect and protection of human dignity.

The principles also have a risk management foundation—because good ethics is good risk management. And they balance the interests of business with the aspirations of society to ensure sustainable and mutual prosperity for all.

The CRT Principles for Responsible Business are supported by more detailed Stakeholder Management Guidelines covering each key dimension of business success: customers, employees, shareholders, suppliers, competitors, and communities.

Principle 1–Respect Stakeholders Beyond Shareholders

- A responsible business acknowledges its duty to contribute value to society through the wealth and employment it creates and the products and services it provides to consumers.

- A responsible business maintains its economic health and viability not just for shareholders, but also for other stakeholders.
- A responsible business respects the interests of, and acts with honesty and fairness towards, its customers, employees, suppliers, competitors, and the broader community.

Principle 2–Contribute to Economic, Social and Environmental Development

- A responsible business recognizes that business cannot sustainably prosper in societies that are failing or lacking in economic development.
- A responsible business therefore contributes to the economic, social and environmental development of the communities in which it operates, in order to sustain its essential 'operating' capital—financial, social, environmental, and all forms of goodwill.
- A responsible business enhances society through effective and prudent use of resources, free and fair competition, and innovation in technology and business practices.

Principle 3–Respect the Letter and the Spirit of the Law

- A responsible business recognizes that some business behaviors, although legal, can nevertheless have adverse consequences for stakeholders.
- A responsible business therefore adheres to the spirit and intent behind the law, as well as the letter of the law, which requires conduct that goes beyond minimum legal obligations.
- A responsible business always operates with candor, truthfulness, and transparency, and keeps its promises.

Principle 4–Respect Rules and Conventions

- A responsible business respects the local cultures and traditions in the communities in which it operates, consistent with fundamental principles of fairness and equality.
- A responsible business, everywhere it operates, respects all applicable national and international laws, regulations and conventions, while trading fairly and competitively.

Principle 5–Support Responsible Globalisation

- A responsible business, as a participant in the global marketplace, supports open and fair multilateral trade.
- A responsible business supports reform of domestic rules and regulations where they unreasonably hinder global commerce.

Principle 6–Respect the Environment

- A responsible business protects and, where possible, improves the environment, and avoids wasteful use of resources.
- A responsible business ensures that its operations comply with best environmental management practices consistent with meeting the needs of today without compromising the needs of future generations.

Principle 7–Avoid Illicit Activities

- A responsible business does not participate in, or condone, corrupt practices, bribery, money laundering, or other illicit activities.
- A responsible business does not participate in or facilitate transactions linked to or supporting terrorist activities, drug trafficking or any other illicit activity.
- A responsible business actively supports the reduction and prevention of all such illegal and illicit activities.

End Note

1. The Caux Round Table, http://www.cauxroundtable.org/index.cfm?&menuid=8 (March 2009).

Reading **3-3**

Ethical Dimensions of Decision-Making in the Developing World: *The Case of Bribery in Mauritius*

Geetanee Napal

Introduction

The developing world faces the problem of corruption, bribery being the most common form of corruption. To some people, the practice of bribery provides an easy way out and is viewed as acceptable (Select Committee on Fraud and Corruption, 2001), as distinct from being accepted as an inevitable practice, with a feeling of resignation. This paper is based on the results of a survey run in Mauritius, a developing nation, the objective of which was to determine how ethical dimensions (moral, cultural and duty) impact on decision making in a developing nation and draw general conclusions for the developing world.

In designing the survey, emphasis was laid on ethical issues likely to be encountered in the business sector in a developing nation that is, direct corruption in the form of bribery. For analytical purposes, a multi-dimensional ethics scale was used to assess the impact of moral, cultural and duty factors on the ethical perceptions of business people. Respondents were asked to rate the action likely to be adopted in specific hypothetical ethical dilemmas, using each of the normative philosophy scales developed by Reidenbach and Robin (1988) and consisting of three major dimensions that is, a moral equity dimension, a contractualism dimension and a relativism dimension (Kujala, 2001).

The paper starts with a discussion of the relevant literature, followed by a brief description of the research environment and an overview of the survey findings.

Corruption in Business

Corruption constitutes a serious problem for many countries around the globe. A corrupt setting is referred to as a system characterised by flawed governance, corruptible individuals and authoritarian regimes (Segal, 1999). Various authors acknowledge the presence of corruption in all types of society, in both developed and developing countries including France, Italy, Belgium, The Netherlands, America, Russia, Japan, Hong Kong, Singapore, Malaysia, China, India, Korea (Brown and Cloke, 2006; Leisinger, 1999; Matland, 1998; O'Donnell, 1997; Ng, 2006; Priem et al. 1998; Rabe, 1999; Scanlan, 2004; Toye and Moore, 1998). In certain contexts corruption is culturally accepted and is encouraged by the traditional offering of gifts or bribes to officials. Corruption can take the form of abuse of authority and manipulation of resources. In some places, such acts take place on a large scale amongst powerful political leaders and business executives. There is the perception that ruling parties hold monopoly power and there is no political will to fight corruption in developing nations. Amongst the factors that account for corruption are low wages, abuse of power and problems caused by colonialism. Where corruption prevails resources are misallocated, authorities are undermined and both public and private sector development tend to suffer.

Common forms of corruption include bribery and extortion. Extortion can take the form of either gifts or favours as a condition to the execution of public duty or the abuse of public funds for one's own benefit. Bribery is the act of accepting gifts or favours offered, the objective being to induce the person to give special consideration to the interests of the donor. Some cultures condone the act of bribery as long as it brings in opportunities. Bribery involves "the payment or remuneration of an agent of some organisation to do things that are inconsistent with the purpose of his or her position or office. Good examples of such act include paying a judge to be partial to your case, paying a policeman to forego giving you a speeding ticket, or paying a buyer to use your company's services" (Adams and Maine, 1998: 49). The concept of bribery has for long dominated the world of business. Bribery is a form of corruption and constitutes a key issue that business executives often face in the context of global ethics. To some cultures however, giving presents and gratifications to government officers is an indispensable courtesy and a normal way of doing business. As such, bribery is not always considered as an offence.

Cross-Cultural Issues

Unethical practices and corruption in business predominate in various sectors of developing economies. These act as barriers to development and limit the potential to offer an acceptable quality of life to the people of these countries. Corruption takes the form of bribes and illegal payments in the context of trade, aid and investment flows between countries. It can entail preferential access to trading opportunities, favouritism in the processing of investment proposals and kickbacks derived from the abuse of international procurement procedures with serious economic repercussions.

In India for example, corruption has taken such a wide dimension that it has become an industry; 'like an industry it seeks to create a public demand' (Alatas, 1999, p. 57). Opportunities to corrupt exist in various sectors of the Indian economy, including the education sector. The admission to university represents a good example: while eighty percent admission to the tertiary education institution is on merit, the remaining twenty percent is officially reserved for citizens who have represented the state. On the job market, young and ambitious candidates offer money and get appointed. It is common habit for politicians and influential people to place their friends or relations in advertised jobs and get 'rewarded' for such practices.

Similarly in China, people have little faith in social justice and the fairness of society. In an opinion poll, 64.3 percent of respondents held that an honest person would always be at a disadvantage. In 1995, President Jiang Zemin's anti-corruption campaign targeted 'the very top of the party and its commercial princes'. China experienced numerous major corruption scandals, which gave the Chinese population the impression, that some of the government and the Communist party were under the influence of "an all-powerful syndicate of free-booting racketeers" (Van Kemenade, 1998, p. 20). China was in close competition with Indonesia for the first place as the most corrupt country in Asia (Transparency International Corruption Index 1995, Germany). On a scale of one to ten, ten corresponding to high levels of corruption, China's score exceeded eight. In some cases, corrupt individuals got promoted to senior positions for purely political reasons (Van Kemenade, 1998). This trend characterises the developing world in general. In Africa for example, corruption is viewed as part of the culture.

It is common practice for government officials to negotiate for bribes prior to awarding licences or signing loan agreements or authorizing development projects (National Integrity Systems, Transparency International, Country Study Report, Zambia, 2003). In some African states, investigations on corruption are viewed as harassment of the people. Employees of institutions like the Police Service, the Judiciary, the Revenue Authority or the Passports Office expect bribes to do their work and to overlook regulations or to influence a judgement in favour of the donor of the bribe. As a result, the quality of service rendered is lowered and citizens lose confidence in national institutions. The major causes of corruption include wide discretionary powers vested in public officials, poor conditions of service in the public service, weak systems of internal control, the absence of a code of conduct in the public sector, weak enforcement of anti-corruption legislation, socio-cultural norms associated with an individualistic culture that favours loyalty to one's friends and family members and unethical political leadership.

Is It Right to Bribe?

Donaldson and Werhane (1996) question the practice of bribery: "Is it morally right to pay a bribe to gain business?" If specific norms permit bribery in a particular country, then the practice of bribery is culturally or traditionally acceptable in that country. It is a fact that in some contexts, the laws of relativism condone bribery (De George, 1999). Sometimes personal values tend to supersede corporate values when one is involved in ethical dilemmas (Badaracco and Webb, 1995).

Bribery is subject to varying interpretations worldwide. Bribe payers may defend themselves by associating their actions with utilitarian principles, namely that "the good outweighs the bad" (De George, 1999: 73). If one were to base oneself on deontology to question the 'ethics' behind bribery, the outcome would be different as the objective is to consider the act of bribery itself. Deontology focuses on one's duty or obligation to explore the motives behind particular alternatives.

Bribery is a common feature of business as there is a perception that it has a positive impact through the 'grease effect', i.e. bribing a bureaucrat as a means to bypass red tape and act as an incentive to make civil servants more productive (Leff, 1964). A similar argument was put forward recently by Blackburn et al. (2006) namely that corruption could be growth-enhancing if it helps circumvent heavy and unnecessary regulations in the bureaucratic process. Laczniak and Murphy (1993) focus on situations where the payment of bribes may be of direct benefit to businesses, in the context of international trade. This gives bribe-payers access to profitable contracts over competitors. There is evidence that large bribes are paid in order to get access to foreign contracts or to avail of tax incentives. However, some authors are of the opinion that the use of bribes as speed-money in a bureaucratic setting is self-defeating (Kauffman and Wei, 2000). In fact, there is little evidence of positive effects of corruption in countries with red tape (Ades and di Tella, 1997). Can one justify having recourse to bribes as a means to overcoming institutional rigidities that stand in the way of progress?

Business conducted through unethical procedures remains a dangerous practice (Rossbacher, 2006). After all, the costs associated with corruption have to be borne by the State. Corruption alters the composition of government expenditure thereby hindering productive activities and negatively impacting on economic and social development (Tanzi and Davoodi, 1998; Mauro, 1998; Gupta et al, 2001). The results of empirical studies show that corruption reduces the effectiveness of aid-funded projects and further weakens political support for and within donor countries (Brautigam, 1992; Harriss-White and White, 1996). Even petty corruption, as judged by sums of money changing hands, contributes to a pervasive syndrome of problems that keeps developing nations poor (Galtung, 1997; Hancock, 1989; Khan, 1996). Unethical conduct usually starts in a mild form but spreads quite fast, eventually leading to systemic corruption (Leisinger, 1999). Often, nothing is done to stop this unhealthy pattern of behaviour so that it progressively becomes entrenched in the system. In the long run, it gets more difficult to eliminate this culture of corruption. As this trend is pursued, corruption impairs the rule of law and weakens the foundation on which economic growth depends, thereby undermining development.

Corrupt economies tend to lose out on the world market. The stability of a corrupt regime only consolidates and intensifies corruption. Any government who becomes the ally of corruption would only convert such stability into an obstructive and destructive force inimical to economic growth and development. In some places, corrupt financial or economic practices of extensive dimension are culturally accepted (Tanzi, 1998; Alatas, 1999; Chakraborty, 1997). Business enterprises themselves with some highly honourable exceptions, often consider corrupt practices to be part of the normal business process (Rossbacher, 2006).

Many developing nations illustrate the type of corruption referred to as the abuse of trust in the interest of personal and private gain. On the one hand there are corruptible individuals and on the other, there are socially powerless people who, by their condition, are tempted to 'seek opportunities' by having recourse to illicit activities. This explains the culture of bribery that characterises some societies. The Mauritian experience shows that corruption can take the form of abuse of authority, manipulation of resources, both in the public and private sectors (Ribouet, 2007; Thanay, 2007). In addition to instances of petty corruption, large-scale corruption prevails in specific sectors. Officials involved in development projects, procurement and the privatisation of state-owned enterprises, amongst other activities are often involved in grand corruption. People are more likely to be punished for petty corruption while no sanction is imposed on the socially powerful found guilty of grand corruption. It is a fact that corruption is associated on the one hand with government and politics and on the other, with business and the way businesses and states interact.

The following sections give an overview of the research setting, methodology and the survey conducted amongst Mauritian employees of the service sector namely from consultancy businesses, the financial services sector and the hospitality industry. The hypothetical situations presented to participants refer to clear cases of corruption, with different degrees of ethical consequence.

Research Setting

Mauritius is a developing island nation in the Indian Ocean, independent in its government since 1968. Originally claimed by the Dutch, its history includes 100 years of French rule, followed by a century of British rule. Relative to land area, it is one of the most densely populated countries on earth—has a population of more than 1.2 million people—and has one of the most diverse populations on the globe, with residents of Indian, Chinese, European and African descent in the country. Over the decades, many other subcultures have emerged including Franco-Mauritian, Anglo-Mauritian, Hindu, Muslim and Creole subcultures.

According to the latest household budget survey, the average annual income in this nation is 122,000 rupees, equivalent to less than $4,100 US or £2,800 per year. Consequently, there is a tendency to associate corruption with low income although recent corruption scandals proved the contrary. The evidence shows that high-level officials seek financial security through illicit transactions and this is confirmed by the findings of the Select Committee on Fraud and Corruption, 2001. Anti-corruption strategies formulated by the previous regime, upon winning the 2000 elections, included the introduction of anti-corruption legislation and the creation of a totally independent and empowered institution to fight corruption. In spite of these initiatives however, Mauritius has been unable to control corruption. The current regime, in their electoral campaign that preceded the general elections of 2005, strongly emphasized their intention to combat corruption, but again there has been no concrete action. It is quite common for political people to focus on how endangering corruption is, but they only do so as Opposition members. Efforts to develop the economy have sometimes been obstructed by piecemeal approaches that have jeopardized national integrity through an increase in corrupt practices associated with a lack of transparency and accountability. The country has a history of corruption and has recently faced a number of high-profile cases of corruption, in both the public and private sectors. Mauritius has consistently scored between 4.1 and 5.0 out of 10 on the Corruption Perceptions Index of Transparency International from 1998 to 2007 (on a scale of 0–10, 0 being most corrupt and 10 being cleanest). Yet, every government denies the validity of the Corruption Perceptions Index, stating that it is based on perceptions and therefore does not reflect reality.

What seem to predominate in Mauritius are socio-cultural norms related to the individualistic culture that favours loyalty to one's close relations and unethical political leadership. The weakness of pressure groups, inclusive of the media in developing nations means that business people do not feel compelled to observe or respect standards of ethics as is the case in first-world countries, hence the prevalence of corruption.

Methodology

Scenarios representing acts of bribery were presented to the sample population. Respondents were asked to rate the action likely to be adopted, using the normative philosophy scales developed by Reidenbach and Robin (1988). Based on a content analysis of five theories of ethics namely, justice, deontology, relativism, utilitarianism and egoism an eight-item multidimensional ethics scale (*fair, just, moral, acceptability to family, cultural acceptability, traditional acceptability, violates an unspoken promise and violates an unwritten contract*) was developed. These eight items were condensed into three dimensions that is, moral equity, contractualism and relativism dimensions (Kujala, 2001).

Summary of Survey Findings

The scenarios constituting the survey can be described as follows: Scenario 1 involves corruption on a small scale while Scenario 3 presents a more serious issue where the objective is to evade the payment of a licence. On the other hand, Scenario 2 carries even more significant ethical consequences as a convicted individual uses his power to bribe the judiciary to rule in his favour.

Petty corruption in the form of a speed-up gratuity can take the form of either gifts or favours as a condition to the execution of public duty. In Scenario 1, the bribe payer offers a speed-up gratuity to local authorities to get a building permit or to empower the authorities and hasten procedures. Participants drew a distinction between moral (fair, just, acceptable to family) and cultural dimensions (culturally acceptable, traditionally acceptable), hence condemning the act of bribe offer, considered as an illicit activity. Results show that the cultural acceptability of offering a bribe as a speed-up gratuity is a powerful predictor of whether or not people would rate such act as ethical.

Scenario 2 refers to an accused party who decides to bribe the best judges to give him a 'fair' trial. There is an allegation of criminal behaviour against an individual who corrupts the judiciary to avoid punishment. If he succeeds in his attempt to 'clear' his name, he would constitute an exception to the basic rule that condemns crime. If participants perceive the accused person as innocent, they may consider the act of bribe offer as an initiative undertaken to do justice to the latter. The moral issue here is the act of bribing the judiciary. Respondents view bribery at such a level as widely practised and accepted. The notion of bribery was associated with culture, implying that the cultural acceptability of bribing the judiciary is a powerful predictor of whether people would evaluate such a choice as 'ethical'.

Scenario 3 presents another instance of bribery. It involves the evasion of payment of a municipality licence. In many countries, such act is considered as a criminal offence leading to heavy fines and imprisonment. On the other hand however, some people may regard the practice of bribery as justifiable if they believe that paying a larger sum in the form of licence constitutes a 'waste of money'. The results indicate that the cultural acceptability of offering bribery to evade the payment of a licence is a powerful predictor of whether people would consider such act as right.

In earlier studies conducted in the United States of America, participants gave priority to duty concepts as they evaluated the ethicality of the scenarios. In the present study, the relativistic scales were rated as more significant than the duty/contractualism scales as respondents evaluated each scenario. Participants were all from the business sector, which could explain the association of moral factors with relativistic ones. Had we sampled a population of students following a 'Business Ethics' course or young graduates for instance, the outcome might have been different. In this case, participants might have clearly distinguished between notions of morality and culture, rather than demonstrate a strong reliance on cultural factors. One could also expect greater reliance on duty factors in explaining ethical perceptions.

Conclusion

The results give evidence of a strong cultural factor that explained the responses to the scenarios and confirm that moral evaluations are specific to situations. While earlier studies emphasized the idea of implicit contract and promise as being inherent in the evaluation of an ethical problem, this theory does not hold in the case of a developing nation. In two of the scenarios (Scenarios 1 and 3), participants made a clear distinction between the moral and relativistic scales. This is probably because the hypothetical situations involved more serious unethical conduct like the payment of bribery or tax evasion. The consequences associated with bribery are more serious that is, they carry higher risks. From the findings of Scenario 2, we conclude that although bribery constitutes an unethical practice, in that particular case it has been condoned culturally. The survey findings relate closely to what the existing literature states that is, the laws of relativism condone bribery in some contexts (De George, 1999; Donaldson and Werhane, 1996).

One of the most significant findings of this study is the importance of the relativistic factor in explaining ethical judgments. This result has never emerged in earlier applications of the R & R scale in the United States of America. Although universal rules condemn tax evasion, bribery, crime and unethical conduct in general, our results give evidence that developing countries interpret universal rules differently. This confirms that the model of ethical decision making in a developing nation is different from the one used in the developed world. It can be said that these survey results emphasise the strength of the cultural/relativistic dimension on ethical thinking in a developing country, reflecting the state of emerging economies with an individualistic culture.

Reference

Note: Notes and references removed for publication here, but are available on the book website at www.mhhe.com/busethics2e.

Reading 3-4

It Seems Right in Theory but Does It Work in Practice?[1]

Norman E. Bowie

It is not uncommon for business people, including business executives, to find the conclusions of an ethical theory as it applies to a case in business to be persuasive, but nonetheless not accept the conclusions because to do so would be impractical from a business point of view. Thus it might be right in theory but it is not practical in business. There are three great traditions in ethical theory, the virtue theory of Aristotle, the duty theory of Immanuel Kant, and the utilitarianism of Jeremy Bentham and John Stuart Mill. In recent times these traditions have been supplemented by other theories such as feminist ethics. It seems to me that if ethical theory is to serve as a foundation for business ethics, it must be the case that these traditional theories are not only persuasive as theories but also can be applied practically to actual business practice. In this essay, I will try to show how the fundamental principles of Kant's ethical theory are both theoretically persuasive and practical in a business context.

Before proceeding it is important to note that the question I am addressing is not strictly an ethical question. After all under our starting assumption business people have already agreed that as a matter of ethical theory, they are persuaded by the answer the ethical theory gives to the case at hand. They just don't think that doing what the ethical theory requires is possible in a business context. What the business person seems to want is for an answer that is both ethically justified and prudent from a business perspective. For Kant showing that something is ethically required is sufficient since morality always trumps prudence. Although Kantians may accept the moral answer as definitive for action, business people will not. If acting morally undermines my business, why should I be moral? That is the question that a business person is like to ask.

Framing the issue as ethics vs. business is an example of what R. Edward Freeman calls "the separation thesis." By the separation thesis he means the thesis that ethical concerns and business concerns are in two separate realms. Freeman argues that business and ethics are always intertwined in business activity. A manager should strive to make business decisions that are both ethically sound and sound in business terms. In what follows I will show how Kant's theory enables managers to make decisions that are sound from both an ethical and a business point of view.

Business Decisions Should Not Be Self Defeating

Kant's fundamental moral principle is the categorical imperative. Kant's moral imperative is categorical because it always holds—there are no "ifs, and, or buts." The classic statement of the categorical imperative is "One must always act on that maxim that one can will to be a universal law." What does Kant mean here? An illustration regarding stealing should help. Why is stealing even when one is in difficult financial circumstances wrong? Suppose one is in difficult financial circumstances and is tempted to steal? If one should decide to steal what is the principle (maxim) for such an action? It must be that "it is morally permissible for me to steal when I am in financial difficulty." Kant now requires that on the basis of rational consistency we must make my maxim "it is ok for me to steal when I am in financial difficulty" into a universal principle, "it is morally permissible for any person in financial difficulty to steal." After all what applies in one case must apply in all similar cases. However, the universal maxim that would permit stealing is self-defeating. An important point of a system of property rights is that it assumes that property rights are morally protected even if others might need the property more. To accept a maxim that permits stealing is to undermine the very system of property rights—the very property rights that the thief must presuppose in order to be a thief.

If this seems too abstract consider the rule of lining up. Suppose one is in a hurry and wonders if it would be morally permissible to cut in line? The maxim for that action would be "it is morally permissible to cut in line when one is in a hurry." However, the universal version of that maxim is that "It is morally permissible for anyone to cut in line when he or she is in a hurry." But that maxim is self-defeating. If anyone could cut in line when he or she was in a hurry, the very notion of lining up would make no sense. A similar argument shows that lying or the breaking of contracts is wrong.

Kant's reasoning shows why free riding is wrong. A free rider benefits when others follow the rule, but the free rider does not. If everyone behaved as the free rider (if the free riding maxim were made universal), there could be no free riding because you would no longer have the rule. Universal free riding on a rule makes the rule nugatory. Put it another way, the free rider is not making a contribution to the institution that relies on the contributions of those participating in the institution—a contribution the free rider agreed to make when he or she participated in the institution. Now if a maxim permitting free riding were universalized, the institution itself would be undermined.

Kant's reasoning here is highly practical in business. After the collapse of the communist economic system in Russia, one of the tasks Russia had was to establish a stock market. However, the companies that were listed on the stock market did not give out accurate financial information. In other words these companies were not transparent and there was no regulatory apparatus in place to make them transparent. But a stock market can only exist if there is a reasonable amount of transparency regarding the financials of the listed companies. Thus the initial attempts at a stock market fell short; the stock market in Russia only came into existence when a number of companies were able to establish themselves as truth tellers about their financial condition.

Poland had a similar difficulty in establishing a national banking system. The first attempt to establish a national bank failed because people did not pay back their loans. If enough people fail to pay their loans, the bank cannot stay in business.

Kant's reasoning is also relevant when one examines the string of financial scandals in the United States culminating in the subprime lending crisis of 2007–2008. The categorical imperative shows why breaking a promise is wrong. If a maxim that permitted promise breaking were made universal, then promises would have no point. A promise breaker can only succeed if most people keep their promises. If anyone could break his or her promise whenever it was convenient, then no one would make promises. The breaking of contracts is also wrong for the same reason.

Financial market work best when there is maximum transparency. The greater the amount of knowledge, the easier it is to assign risk. Increasing transparency makes markets more efficient. Thus participants in the financial markets support rules that increase transparency. What contributed to the Enron debacle was the fact that off balance sheet entities were created that hid Enron's risks. Once the risks came to light, Enron collapsed very quickly. Something similar happened in the subprime mortgage crisis. Mortgages with varying degrees of risk were bundled together in ways that made in very difficult to determine the underlying value of the assets behind the mortgages. Once the housing market turned and prices began to fall, investors began to worry about the risk but were unable to determine what their risks were. What amounted to a run on the bank occurred with the firm Bear Stearns. It was widely rumored that Lehman Brothers and even Merrill Lynch might go under. Only action by the Federal Reserve provided sufficient capital to prevent a financial collapse. Nonetheless financial institutions lost hundreds of billions of dollars. Financial markets require transparency. Universalizing actions that undermine transparency undermine financial markets. When a tipping point is reached, financial markets freeze up and cease to function. Participants in markets are morally required to support transparency.

Both academics and practitioners concerned with corporate strategy have discovered the role of trust as a significant element of competitive advantage. Let us define a trusting relationship as one where those in the relationship will not take undue advantage of opportunistic situations. In business, relationships built on trust provide competitive advantage in two basic ways. First, within a firm, trusting relationships make the firm more efficient. For example, when there is trust between employers and employees, there is less monitoring, some behavior may not need to be monitored at all and there is less need for detailed information. The relation between an employer and an employee can be a mentoring relationship rather than simply a monitored relationship. As a result teamwork is more easily achieved. All of this creates a competitive advantage for those companies that pursue enlightened human resource management based on trust.

Another way of illustrating the competitive advantage of trust relationships is to look at a common management problem. With a commission system, sales people are given incentives to sell as much of a product as they can without regard to the ability of the manufacturing unit of the business to manufacture the product in a timely manner. If a manager wants to build a cooperative relation between sales and manufacturing, then he or she must think carefully about the use of commissions as a way to reward sales. Yet another illustration is provided by a long standing tradition in American business to separate the design process from manufacturing. Thus engineers create prototypes that are then given to manufacturing to produce. However, since there was no communication between design and manufacturing, inevitably there are "bugs" that need to be worked out. Working out the bugs is an unnecessary transaction cost that could be greatly mitigated or even avoided if engineering and manufacturing worked together through both the design and the manufacturing stage. The Japanese auto manufacturers learned this early and the efficiencies that resulted helped Japan seize extensive market share at the expense of American automobile manufacturers.

It may seem that these arguments are purely consequentialist. They are consequentialist but not purely so. Consider the following argument that shows the power of Kant's categorical imperative here.

1. A business that fails to be competitive will go out of business.
2. A person or group of persons who start a business and invest in it, do not want it to go out of business.
3. Building relationships of trust are necessary if the business is to be competitive.
4. Therefore intentional actions that fail to develop these trust relationships involve the business people in self-defeating actions. The actors both want the business to survive and by consciously failing to take the actions necessary for it to survive, they show that they do not want it to survive and that is surely self-defeating behavior.

Thus Kant's categorical imperative shows that trusting relationships are required on both utilitarian grounds and on Kantian grounds as well.

Business Decisions Should Not Violate the Humanity of a Person

Kant's ethical theory involves more than a formal test that ethical decisions should not be self-defeating. After all suppose that treating employees simply as a cost and thus as interchangeable with capital and machinery gave business a competitive advantage. Using an argument similar to the one I used for trusting relationships I could show that such treatment of people would be morally required. But, according to Kant, treating employees in that way would be immoral.

Kant has a second formulation of the categorical imperative which says, "Act so that you treat humanity, whether in your own person or in that of another, always as an end and never as a means merely." To act in accord with this formulation of the categorical imperative, one must treat persons with respect. Why? Because persons have a dignity that Kant said was beyond price. That is why Kant would not permit employers to treat employees as if they were simply on a par with capital or machinery—as if they were mere factors of production.

Kant argued that only human beings were free and that as a result of being free, they could act rationally by which Kant meant that could act according to laws of their own making. As free and rational creatures, they could also be held responsible for their actions. Since persons can be held responsible, they can be held subject to moral law. It is the fact that persons are free, rational, responsible beings capable of acting morally that gives them the dignity that is beyond price.

Kant believed that each of us recognizes that we have dignity that is entitled to respect. Indeed in contemporary society, failure to respect a person can easily result in the disrespected person acting angrily or even violently against those who show disrespect. Since each of us feels entitled to respect and is justified in this feeling, then as a matter of logic each of us must respect those who are like us, namely we must respect other persons. Since the obligation of respect is a matter of consistency, the first and second formulations of the categorical imperative are linked.

The obligation to respect persons has direct application to business and business ethics. Management actions that coerce people or deceive them do not treat employees with respect. Coercion is a direct denial of autonomy and deception also robs a person of his or her freedom since alternatives that would be available to a person are kept off the table. The courts have recognized that coercion is a serious violation of ethics. In the classic case of Henningsen vs. Bloomfield Motors the court voided standardized warranties that limited liability in the light of injury from defective automobiles. The court said, "The warranty before us is a standardized form designed for mass use. It is imposed on the automobile consumer. He takes it or leaves it. No bargaining is engaged in with respect to it."

The court must have reasoned that the take it or leave it alternative is analogous to the demand of the armed robber, "your money or your life." Although there is a choice here, it is a coerced choice.

Certain business practices support respecting the humanity of a person. Open book management is a technique that in effect turns everyone in the business into a chief finance officer (CFO). Under this technique all employees receive all the numbers that are relevant to the business. In this way they understand the business and are better able to act for the longer term success of the business. Open book management has a number of devotees and is increasingly adopted. Open book management in conjunction with other enlightened management practices empowers employees and empowerment is one way of showing that the employee is respected. Another way to show respect for employees is to provide them with meaningful work. Empowerment is one of the characteristics of meaningful work. A complete list of the characteristics of meaningful work is beyond the scope of this essay, but suffice it to say, if employees believed their work was meaningful, some popular phrases or references would not be so ubiquitous. There would not be as many references to TGIF or to Monday as blue Monday or Wednesday as hump day (half way to TGIF). Empowered employees who believe they are making a contribution to the public good through their work are highly motivated and contribute mightily to the success of the business enterprise. What is right in ethical theory in this case contributes to successful business practice.

Business Should Be Seen as a Moral as well as an Economic Community

If employees deserve a kind of respect that capital and machinery does not, then what should a business look like from the point of view of a Kantian? Kant's third formulation of the categorical imperative helps us understand what such a business should look like. Kant says that we should act as if we were a member of an ideal kingdom of ends in which we were both subject and sovereign at the same time. Substitute "moral organization" for "ideal kingdom of ends." How should such an organization be run? Well if the rules for running the organization are to be morally justified, they would have to be rules that everyone in the organization could accept. In that way each person would be both subject and sovereign with respect to the rules.

Kant's ideas here are a moral challenge to hierarchical theories of management—a challenge to a management philosophy that says to the employee, "Yours is not to question why, but simply do or die." Kant's moral theory is also a challenge to the pervasive doctrine of employment at will—a doctrine which says that you can be fired for any reason, good, bad, or morally unjustifiable reason. For Kant unjustifiable actions cannot be moral actions. What Kant's third formulation requires is that employees have a say in the organization's rules and procedures. The work of psychologists has shown that Kant's moral demands are sound from a practical point of view. Some of the pioneering work here has been done by Chris Argyris one of the most consistent critics of hierarchical management. Employees who are given a say are more highly motivated employees and highly motivated employees contribute to the bottom line of the business. Also teamwork and cooperation, which are so highly valued in today's organization, require that members of the organization have voice in how the organization is run and in the decisions it makes.

Also a Kantian who views the organization from the perspective of an ideal kingdom of ends will not treat the organization as a mere instrument for their own personal use. If the individuals in an organization view it purely instrumentally, these individuals are predisposed to behave in ways that harm organizational integrity. The insight of the contemporary Kantian John Rawls that organizations are social unions constituted by certain norms is useful here. Organizations are not mere instruments for achieving individual goals. To develop this notion of a social union, Rawls contrasts two views of how human society is held together: In the private view human beings form social institutions after calculating that it would be advantageous to do so; in the social view human beings form social institutions because they share final ends and value common institutions and activities as intrinsically good. In a social union, cooperation is a key element of success because each individual in a social union knows that he cannot achieve his interests within the group by himself. The cooperation of others is necessary as it provides stability to the organization, enables it to endure, and enables individuals both to realize their potential and to see the qualities of others that lead to organizational success. Rawls's notion of a social union has much in common with Kant's ideal kingdom of ends.

This analysis can be applied directly to the issue of excessive executive compensation and to the endless chain of corporate scandals from 2001 to the 2007–2008 sub-prime mess. Many have reacted to the recent wave of corporate scandals by saying that executives are overly greedy: a character flaw. But why have some executives become greedy? The explanation is in the distinction between viewing an organization as merely an instrument to satisfying one's individual needs and seeing an organization as a social union. If the organization is seen as a means to personal enrichment and not seen as a cooperative enterprise of all those in the organization, it should come as no surprise that the executives of such an organization feel entitled to the rewards. Psychological theorists have shown that people tend to take credit when things go well and blame bad luck or circumstances beyond one's control when things go badly. Thus a CEO takes all the credit when an organization performs well but blames the general economy or other factors when things go poorly. This human tendency is predictable when executives look at organizations instrumentally.

Conclusion

This essay provides a brief tour through Kantian ethical theory and shows how it is both theoretically sound and practical. At least with Kantian ethics there need be no divergence between good theory and sound practice.

End Note

1. The ideas in the essay are adapted from my book *Business Ethics: A Kantian Perspective,* Blackwell Publishers 1999.

Chapter 4

The Corporate Culture—Impact and Implications

Our plans miscarry because they have no aim. When a person does not know what harbor he [or she] is making for, no wind is the right wind.

Seneca

There is nothing more difficult to carry out, nor more doubtful of success, nor more dangerous to handle, than to initiate a new order of things.

Machiavelli

Opening Decision Point *Creating an Ethics Program*

Imagine that you work in the Human Resources department of your company. Your CEO has asked the HR department to develop an ethics program for the firm, and you have been assigned responsibility for creating it. You have been asked to report back to your CEO in two weeks with a draft version of a code of ethics for the company, a summary of other elements that the ethics program will include, and a proposal for how you will be able to assess whether the program is working. Your CEO also asks that you come prepared to explain to her what role she can play in promoting ethics and in insuring the success of the ethics program.

In beginning your research, you discover that there are a number of potentially desirable and somewhat overlapping outcomes of effective ethics programs:

1. Discovery of unethical/illegal behavior and reducing meltdowns, resulting in avoidance or reduction of fines/criminal charges (applies to several below).
2. Generation of awareness of ethical and legal issues.
3. Provision of a resource for guidance and advice.
4. Accurate reports of wrongdoing.
5. Greater customer loyalty, resulting in increased sales and better reputation.
6. Incorporation of values in decision processes.
7. Development of greater employee commitment and loyalty to the organization, resulting in higher productivity.
8. Satisfaction of external and internal stakeholder needs (all resulting in more effective financial performance).

Play the role of this HR person in several different types of businesses: a fast-food restaurant, an automobile dealership, a retail store selling consumer electronics, a government agency, and a large international corporation.[1]

- List the issues you think should be addressed in a code of ethics.
- Other than a code of ethics, what other elements would you include in an ethics program?
- How will you define "success"? Are there any facts that you will need to gather to make this judgment?
- How would you measure success along the way? How will you measure whether your ethics program is "working" before you reach any end objective?
- Who will you define as your primary stakeholders?
- What are the interests of your stakeholders in your program and what are the impacts of your program on each stakeholder? How might the measurement of the program's success influence the type of people attracted to the firm or people who are most motivated within your organization?
- How will you answer the CEO's questions about her own role in promoting ethics?

Chapter Objectives

After reading this chapter, you will be able to:

1. Define corporate culture.
2. Explain how corporate culture impacts ethical decision making.
3. Discuss the differences between a compliance-based culture and a values-based culture.
4. Discuss the role of corporate leadership in establishing the culture.
5. Explain the difference between effective leaders and ethical leaders.
6. Discuss the role of mission statements and codes in creating an ethical corporate culture.
7. Explain how various reporting mechanisms such as ethics hotlines and ombudsmen can help integrate ethics within a firm.
8. Discuss the role of assessing, monitoring, and auditing the culture and ethics program.
9. Explain how culture can be enforced via governmental regulation.

What Is Corporate Culture?

This chapter examines the ways in which corporations develop ethical cultures, cultures in which individuals are encouraged and supported in making ethically responsible decisions. The decision-making model of ethics that we have introduced in the opening chapters emphasizes the responsibility of individuals for the decisions they make in business. These decisions impact one's own personal integrity and also have consequences for many stakeholders with whom business organizations interact.

But, personal decision making does not exist in a vacuum. Decision making within a firm is influenced, limited, shaped and, in some cases, virtually determined by the corporate culture of the firm. Individuals can be helped—or hindered—in making the "right" or "wrong" decision (according to their own values) by the expectations, values, and structure of the organization in which they live and work. This chapter surveys some of the major issues surrounding the development, influence, and management of a corporate culture, as well as the role of business leaders in creating, enhancing, and preserving cultures that support ethical behavior.

Even in this age of decentralized corporations and other institutions, there remains a sense of culture in organizations. This is especially true in small local firms, but it is just as true of major global corporations such as Google or BP. Despite the fact that corporations have many locations, with diverse employee groups and management styles, an individual working for a large global firm in one country will share various aspects of her or his working culture with someone working for the same firm halfway around the world. This is not to say that their working environments cannot be wholly different in many regards; the corporate culture, however, survives the distance and differences.

FIGURE 4.1

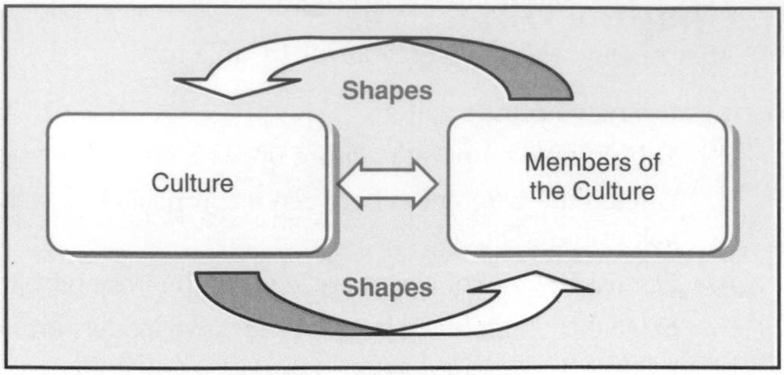

1 OBJECTIVE

What do we mean by *corporate culture?* Every organization has a **culture** fashioned by a shared pattern of beliefs, expectations, and meanings that influence and guide the thinking and behaviors of the members of that organization. While culture shapes the people who are members of the organization, it is also shaped by the people who comprise that organization (See Figure 4.1.) Consider how your own company, organization or school, dormitory, or fraternity/sorority differs from a similar one. Is there a "type" of person stereotypical of your organization, dormitory, or fraternity/sorority? Are there unspoken but still influential standards and expectations that shape students at your school? How would you be different if you had chosen a different institution, joined a different fraternity or sorority or had participated in a different organization? (See Reality Check, "Built to Last.")

Businesses also have unspoken yet influential standards and expectations. IBM was once famous for a culture in which highly starched white shirts and ties (it was a very male culture) were part of the required dress code. Many software and technologies companies have reputations for cultures of informality and playfulness. Some companies have a straight nine-to-five work schedule; others expect employees to work long hours and on weekends. A person who joins the second type of firm with a "nine-to-five attitude," intending to leave as the clock strikes five, might not "fit" and is likely not to last long. The same might hold true for a firm's values. If you join a firm with a culture that supports other values than those with which you are comfortable, there will be values conflicts—for better or worse.

No culture, in business or elsewhere, is static. Cultures change; but modifying culture—indeed, having any impact on it at all—is a bit like moving an iceberg. The iceberg is always moving and if you ignore it the iceberg will continue to float with whatever currents hold sway at the moment. One person cannot alter its course alone; but strong leaders—sometimes from within, but often at the top—can have a significant impact on a culture. A strong business leader can certainly have a significant impact on a corporate culture.

A firm's culture can be its sustaining value, offering it direction and stability during challenging times or it can prevent a firm from responding to challenges in creative and timely ways. For example, some point to Toyota's culture—embodied in "the 14 principles of the Toyota Way"—as the basis for its high quality and consistent customer satisfaction.[2] Others suggest that the "Toyoto Way" prevented

Reality Check *Built to Last*

Does a corporate culture matter? James Collins and Jerry Porras, authors of the best-selling book *Built to Last: Successful Habits of Visionary Companies,* researched dozens of very successful companies looking for common practices that might explain their success. These companies not only outperformed their competitors in financial terms; they have outperformed their competition financially *over the long term.* On average, the companies Collins and Porras studied were more than 100 years old. Among their key findings was the fact that the truly exceptional and sustainable companies all placed great emphasis on a set of core values. These core values are described as the "essential and enduring tenets" that help to define the company and are "not to be compromised for financial gain or short-term expediency."[3]

Collins and Porras cite numerous examples of core values that were articulated and promoted by the founders and CEOs of such companies as IBM, Johnson & Johnson, Hewlett Packard, Procter & Gamble, Wal-Mart, Merck, Motorola, Sony, Walt Disney, General Electric, and Philip Morris. Some companies made "a commitment to customers" their core value, while others focused on employees, their products, innovation, or even risk-taking. The common theme was that core values and a clear corporate purpose, which together are described as the organization's core ideology, were essential elements of sustainable and financially successful companies.

Discussing a corporation's "culture" is a way of saying that a corporation has a set of identifiable values. All of the companies that Collins and Porras described are known for having strong corporate cultures and a clear set of values. In more recent research, Harvard professors Jim Heskett and Earl Sasser, along with coauthor Joe Wheeler, strongly support the conclusions reached by Collins and Porras. In their 2008 book, *The Ownership Quotient,* they connect strong, adaptive cultures to the valuable corporate outcomes of innovation, productivity, and a sense of ownership among employees and customers. By analyzing traits that the authors found common to these organizations, we can learn much about what sustains them.

1. Leadership is critical in codifying and maintaining an organizational purpose, values, and vision. Leaders must set the example by living the elements of culture.
2. Like anything worthwhile, culture is something in which you invest.
3. Employees at all levels in an organization notice and validate the elements of culture.
4. Organizations with clearly codified cultures enjoy labor cost advantages.
5. Organizations with clearly codified and enforced cultures enjoy great employee and customer loyalty.
6. An operating strategy based on a strong, effective culture is selective of prospective customers.
7. The result of these cultural elements is "the best serving the best."
8. This self-reinforcing source of operating leverage must be managed carefully to make sure that it does not result in the development of dogmatic cults with little capacity for change.
9. Organizations with strong and adaptive cultures foster effective succession in the leadership ranks.
10. Cultures can sour.[4]

the company from responding to reports of unintended acceleration in many of its vehicles in a responsible, swift, effective, and transparent way.

"Since Toyota's founding we have adhered to the core principle of contributing to society through the practice of manufacturing high-quality products and services. Our business practices and activities based on this core principle created

Reality Check *Walk This Way: The Toyota Way*

The 14 Principles of the Toyota Way constitute Toyota's system of continuous improvement in production and management.

1. Base your management decisions on a long-term philosophy, even at the expense of short-term financial goals.
2. Create a continuous process flow to bring problems to the surface.
3. Use "pull" systems to avoid overproduction.
4. Level out the workload (*heijunka*). (Work like the tortoise, not the hare.)
5. Build a culture of stopping to fix problems, to get quality right the first time.
6. Standardized tasks and processes are the foundation for continuous improvement and employee empowerment.
7. Use visual control so no problems are hidden.
8. Use only reliable, thoroughly tested technology that serves your people and processes.
9. Grow leaders who thoroughly understand the work, live the philosophy, and teach it to others.
10. Develop exceptional people and teams who follow your company's philosophy.
11. Respect your extended network of partners and suppliers by challenging them and helping them improve.
12. Go and see for yourself to thoroughly understand the situation (*genchi genbutsu*).
13. Make decisions slowly by consensus, thoroughly considering all options; implement decisions rapidly (*nemawashi*).
14. Become a learning organization through relentless reflection (*hansei*) and continuous improvement (*kaizen*).

Source: Liker, J., "An Executive Summary of the Culture Behind TPS" (Oct. 29, 2003) http://www.si.umich.edu/ICOS/Liker04.pdf.

values, beliefs and business methods that over the years have become a source of competitive advantage. These are the managerial values and business methods that are known collectively as the Toyota Way," explains Fujio Cho, then-President, Toyota (from the *Toyota Way* document, 2001).

The stability that a corporate culture provides can be a benefit at one time can be a barrier to success at another. Review the 14 Principles of the Toyota Way in the accompanying Reality Check, "Walk This Way: The Toyota Way" and reflect on which might have contributed to a culture of high quality products and which might have contributed to a culture of defensiveness, secrecy, and denial.

Defining the specific culture within an organization is not an easy task since it is partially based on each participant's perception of the culture. In fact, perception may actually impact the culture in a circular way—a culture exists, we perceive it to be a certain type of culture, we respond to the culture on the basis of our perception, and we thereby impact others' experience of the culture. Several of the elements that are easiest to perceive, such as attitudes and behaviors, are only a small fraction of the elements that comprise the culture. In addition, culture is present in and can be determined by exploring any of the following, among others:

- Tempo of work
- The organization's approach to humor
- Methods of problem solving
- The competitive environment

FIGURE 4.2

Source: Illustration copyright © Nancy Margulies, St. Louis, MO. Reprinted with permission of the artist.

- Incentives
- Individual autonomy
- Hierarchical structure

Even with this list of cultural elements, it can be difficult for individuals in a firm to identify the specific characteristics of the culture within which they work. That phenomenon is best illustrated by the cartoon in Figure 4.2. Culture becomes so much a part of the environment that participants do not even notice its existence. Consider the culture you experience within your family. Often, it is only when you first move away from your family (when you go off to college, for example), that you can even recognize that your family has its own culture. As you delve into the quirky particularities of your family's relationships, choices, preferences, communication styles, even gift-giving practices, you will notice that each family has a culture that is distinct and self-perpetuating. It is the same with business.

Culture and Ethics

How, exactly, does the notion of culture connect with ethics? More specifically, what role does corporate culture play in business ethics? We can answer these questions by reflecting on several topics introduced previously.

2 OBJECTIVE

In chapter 1, we considered the law's limitations in ensuring ethical compliance. For example, U.S. law requires business to make reasonable accommodations for employees with disabilities. But the law can be ambiguous in determining whether a business should make a reasonable accommodation for an employee with allergies, depression, dyslexia, arthritis, hearing loss, or high blood pressure. In situations where the law provides an incomplete answer for ethical decision making, the business culture is likely to be the determining factor in the decision. Ethical businesses must find ways to encourage, to shape, and to allow ethically responsible decisions.

Each of the factors in the decision-making model we introduced in chapter 2, from fact gathering through moral imagination to assessment, can be supported or discouraged by the environment in which the decision is made. An ethical environment, or culture, would be one in which employees are empowered and expected to act in ethically responsible ways, even when the law does not require it. Later in this chapter, we will examine types of cultures and various ways in which a corporation can create or maintain a culture that encourages ethical action. But to understand that cultures can influence some types of behaviors and discourage others, consider as an example two organizational approaches to the relief efforts following hurricane Katrina in September 2005.

On one hand, the Federal Emergency Management Agency (FEMA) was charged with overall responsibility for the government's response to the hurricane. FEMA was created in 1979 when several governmental agencies, ranging from fire prevention, to insurance, to civil defense, were merged into one larger agency. FEMA itself was later subsumed into the federal Department of Homeland Security. By all accounts at the time of the hurricane, FEMA was a bureaucratic, hierarchical organization. Established rules and procedures were to be followed when making decisions. Many decisions required approval from people in authority. At one point, emergency personnel were delayed in reaching the hurricane area for days because FEMA rules required that they first attend mandatory training sessions on preventing sexual harassment in the workplace—unquestionably important, of course, but perhaps they could have taken place after this particular *emergency* situation.

Despite years of preparation and planning, the magnitude of the hurricane and resultant flooding overwhelmed FEMA's ability to respond. When the situation did not fit plans and the rules no longer applied, FEMA's bureaucracy seemed incapable of acting. Temporary homes and supplies, despite being stored nearby, were not moved into the area for months after the storm because those in authority had not yet given approval. Decisions were made and later retracted. Days after the hurricane, while television reports showed thousands of people stranded at the New Orleans convention center, FEMA director Michael Brown claimed that he had learned of these survivors only from a reporter's question. Apparently, no one had told the FEMA director of the problem; therefore, he could not make a decision, and thousands of people went without help. The organization seemed unable to move information up to decision makers, and lower-level managers lacked authority to decide for themselves.

Analyzed according to the theories from chapter 3, the culture lacked ethical justification as well. Explored from a utilitarian perspective, it certainly was not a culture that revolved around the consequences of its decision-making process. While the ultimate decision might have incorporated this type of consideration, the culture itself did not place great weight on the impact of its process on its stakeholders. Human well-being, especially the health and dignity of the people affected by the tragedy, was not given the highest priority. Given this omission, one might look at whether some overarching universal principle or right was protected by the hierarchical decision-making process enforced during the time following the hurricane. Surely, FEMA would point to its strict adherence to the law; but those who might have otherwise made decisions in a more autonomous manner would have pointed instead to the "higher" values of health and human dignity.

In comparison, the United States Coast Guard is an organization with similar responsibilities for search and rescue during emergency situations. In fact, FEMA director Brown was eventually removed from his position and replaced by a Coast Guard admiral. The Coast Guard has a reputation for being a less bureaucratic organization. The unofficial motto is to "rescue first, and get permission later," reflecting a far more utilitarian perspective to its mission. The Coast Guard empowers frontline individuals to solve problems without waiting for superiors to make decisions or to give directions. Imagine how the same person working in either of these organizations would approach a decision—and who that person might perceive to be her or his primary stakeholders—and you will have some idea of the importance of organizational culture.

It is fair to say that FEMA and the Coast Guard are two very similar organizations with similar missions, rules, and legal regulations; but they have significantly different cultures. The decisions made throughout both organizations reflect the culture of each. The attitudes, expectations, and habits encouraged and reinforced in the two agencies reflect the differences of culture.

The notion of expectations and habits is linked closely to a topic raised in our discussion of the philosophical foundations of ethics. Chapter 3 introduced the ethics of virtue and described the virtues as character traits and habits. The cultivation of habits, including the cultivation of ethical virtue, is greatly shaped by the culture in which one lives. When we talk about decision making, it is easy to think in terms of a rational, deliberative process in which a person consciously deliberates about and weighs each alternative before acting. But the virtue ethics tradition reminds us that our decisions and our actions are very often less deliberate than that. We are as likely to act out of habit and based on character as we are to act after careful deliberations. So the question of where we get our habits and character is all-important.

Part of the answer surely is that we can choose to develop some habits rather than others. But, it is also clear that our habits are shaped and formed by education and training—by culture. This education takes place in every social environment, ranging from our families and religions, to entire societies and cultures. It also takes place in the workplace, where individuals quickly learn behaviors that are appropriate and expected through those which get rewarded and promoted. Intentionally or not, business institutions provide an environment in which habits are formed and virtues, or vices, are created.

The effect of this workplace culture on decision making cannot be overemphasized. The Ethics Resource Center reports that the "strength of the enterprise-wide ethics culture is the *single factor with the greatest impact* on misconduct."[5] Since strong cultures have been shown to dramatically decrease misconduct, increase the likelihood of reporting, and reduce retaliation against employees who report, this impact becomes a leadership imperative.[6] It is not difficult to see, therefore, that an ethical culture can have a direct and practical impact on the bottom line. Research supports this impact; when looking at stock performance from 1998 to 2006, the 100 companies on Fortune's Best Places to Work list have outperformed the Standard & Poor's 500 by more than eight percentage points.[7] If attended to and supported, a strong ethical culture can serve as a deterrent to stakeholder damage and improve bottom line sustainability. If ignored, the culture

FIGURE 4.3

Source: Adapted from Rushworth Kidder, Institute for Global Ethics, "Overcoming Ethical Nonchalance in the Boardroom," *Ethics Newsline* 7, no. 22 (June 1, 2004): 1.

If Ignored . . .
Additional Costly Examples

- ***(During One Two-Week Period)***
- **Lucent Technologies:**
  - Settled a class-action suit for misleading investors ($517 million) and was then fined for obstructing the probe ($25 million).
- **Pfizer:**
  - Found guilty of aggressively marketing one of its drugs to doctors for "off-label" use in unapproved ways ($430 million).
- **Citigroup:**
  - Liable for loan abuses to low-income and high-risk borrowers ($70 million), one week after it settled a class-action suit for biasing its brokerage advice in urging investors to buy WorldCom stock ($2.65 billion).
- **NEC:**
  - Fined for fraud under its contract to provide Internet access to the nation's poor schools ($20.7 million).

could instead reinforce a perception that "anything goes," and "any way to a better bottom line is acceptable," destroying long-term sustainability. See, also, how the devastating impact is not limited to a single industry or type of business, as is demonstrated by Figure 4.3. Responsibility for creating and sustaining such ethical corporate cultures rests on business leaders. In fact, Ralph Larsen sets the leadership example by affirming that at Johnson & Johnson its "credo is all about personal responsibility."

Collins and Porras' book *Built to Last: Successful Habits of Visionary Companies* explains the power of a corporate culture to shape the individuals who work within it. While it may be true that individuals can shape an organization, and perhaps charismatic leaders can do this especially well, it is equally true, if not more so, that organizations shape individuals. Imagine spending a 20-, 30-, or even 40-year career in the same organization. The person you become, your attitudes, values, expectations, mind-set, and habits, will be significantly determined by the culture of the organization in which you work.

Compliance and Value-Based Cultures

3 OBJECTIVE

In the 1990s, a distinction came to be recognized in types of corporate culture: some firms were classified as **compliance-based cultures** (the traditional approach) while others were considered to be integrity-based or **values-based cultures.** These latter cultures are perceived to be more flexible and far-sighted corporate environments. The distinction between compliance-based and values-based cultures perhaps is most evident in accounting and auditing situations; but it can also be used more generally to understand wider corporate cultures. See Table 4.1

TABLE 4.1
The Evolution of Compliance Programs into Values-Based Programs

Source: Paul Lindow and Jill Race, "Beyond Traditional Audit Techniques," *Journal of Accountancy Online* (July 2002), http://www.aicpa.org/PUBS/JOFA/jul2002/lindow.htm.

Traditional	Progressive (Best Practices)
Audit focus	Business focus
Transaction-based	Process-based
Financial account focus	Customer focus
Compliance objective	Risk identification, process improvement objective
Policies and procedures focus	Risk management focus
Multiyear audit coverage	Continual risk-reassessment coverage
Policy adherence	Change facilitator
Budgeted cost center	Accountability for performance improvement results
Career auditors	Opportunities for other management positions
Methodology: Focus on policies, transactions, and compliance	Methodology: Focus on goals, strategies, and risk management processes

for an analysis of the differences between the traditional, compliance-based culture and the more progressive-style cultures that have evolved.

As the name suggests, a compliance-based culture emphasizes obedience to the rules as the primary responsibility of ethics. A compliance-based culture will empower legal counsel and audit offices to mandate and to monitor compliance with the law and with internal codes. A values-based culture is one that reinforces a particular set of *values* rather than a particular set of *rules*. Certainly, these firms may have codes of conduct; but those codes are predicated on a statement of values and it is presumed that the code includes mere examples of the values' application. Integrating these values into the firm's culture encourages a decision-making process that uses the values as underlying principles to guide employee decisions rather than as hard-and-fast rules.

The argument in favor of a values-based culture is that a compliance culture is only as strong and as precise as the rules with which workers are expected to comply. A firm can only have a certain number of rules and the rules can never unambiguously apply to every conceivable situation. A values-based culture recognizes that where a rule does not apply the firm must rely on the personal integrity of its workforce when decisions need to be made. (See Reality Check, "Compliance versus Values.")

This is not to say that values-based organizations do not include a compliance structure. In fact, an Ethics Resource Center study found that "strict compliance and audit programs are often springboards for implementing more comprehensive programs addressing ethical values. When this occurs, compliance goals typically do not diminish. Rather a focus on ethical values adds important priorities and incentives."[8]

The goals of a traditional compliance-oriented program may include meeting legal and regulatory requirements, minimizing risks of litigation and indictment, and improving accountability mechanisms. The goals of a more evolved and inclusive ethics program may entail a broader and more expansive application

Reality Check *Compliance versus Values*

The master said, govern the people by regulations, keep order among them by chastisements, and they will flee from you, and lose all self-respect. Govern them by moral force, keep order among them by ritual, and they will keep their self-respect and come to you of their own accord.

The Analects of Confucius

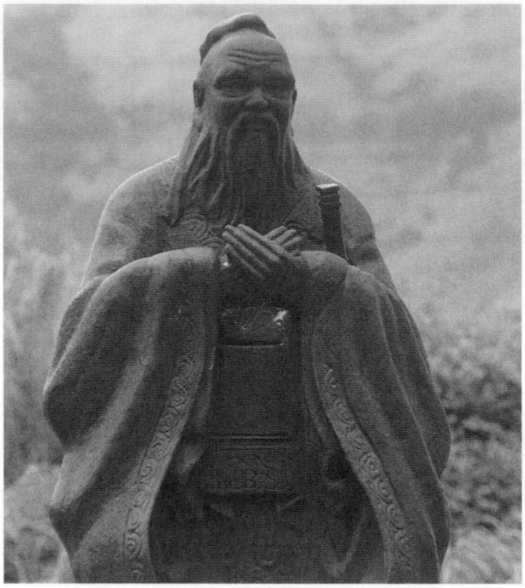

to the firm, including maintaining brand and reputation, recruiting and retaining desirable employees, helping to unify a firm's global operations, creating a better working environment for employees, and doing the right thing in addition to doing things right. You should notice the more comprehensive implications of the latter list for the firm, its sustainability, and its long-term bottom line.

If a firm were to decide that it prefers the benefits and structure of a values-based orientation to its ethics program, the next question is how to integrate ethics into the compliance environment to most effectively prevent these common dilemmas and to create a "culture" of ethics. That question is addressed in the next section.

Ethical Leadership and Corporate Culture

If the goal of corporate culture is to cultivate values, expectations, beliefs, and patterns of behavior that best and most effectively support ethical decision making, it becomes the primary responsibility of corporate leadership to steward this effort. Leaders are charged with this duty in part because stakeholders throughout the organization are guided to a large extent by the "tone at the top." This is not at all to relieve leaders throughout an organization from their responsibilities as role models, but instead to suggest the pinnacle position that the executive leader plays in setting the direction of the culture. In fact, neither can be successful independent of the other; there must be a consistent *tone* throughout the firm. For an articulate and forceful statement of how to set this tone and maintain it, see the reading "Leadership in a Values-Based Organization: The Sears Lectureship

Reality Check *The Eliot Spitzer Mirror Test for Leaders*

Do not do anything that would require you to have to issue this statement to the press:

> From those to whom much is given, much is expected. I have been given much: the love of my family, the faith and trust of the people of New York and the chance to lead this state. I am deeply sorry that I did not live up to what was expected of me.
>
> *Eliot Spitzer, apologizing to the citizens of the State of New York, after he had violated his own "Mr. Clean" laws against prostitution*[9]

in Business Ethics at Bentley College—Thursday, February 7, 2002" by Ralph Larsen, past Chairman and CEO of Johnson & Johnson. Larsen explains, "Being bound together around the values . . . around our credo . . . being bound together around values is like the trim tab for leadership at Johnson & Johnson."

Merck's CEO, Raymond Gilmartin, further elaborates, "In thought, word, and deed, a company's leaders must clearly and unambiguously both advocate and model ethical behavior."[10] If a leader is perceived to be shirking her or his duties, misusing corporate assets, misrepresenting the firm's capabilities, or engaging in other inappropriate behavior, stakeholders receive the message that this type of behavior is not only acceptable, but perhaps expected and certainly the way to get ahead in that organization! It is that type of leader who might benefit from the test articulated in the Reality Check, "The Eliot Spitzer Mirror Test for Leaders."

Instead, if a leader is clearly placing her or his own ethical behavior above any other consideration, stakeholders are guided to follow that role model and to emulate that priority scheme. Ethical leaders say "no" to conduct that would be inconsistent with their organization's and their own personal values. If they demonstrate this courage, they are sending the message that this is the way to succeed in this culture. They also expect others to say no to them. Clearly, one of a leader's primary responsibilities, therefore, is to be a role model by setting a good example, by keeping promises and commitments, by maintaining their own standards, and by supporting others in doing so. See the Reality Check, "The Impact of Ethical Leadership."

4 OBJECTIVE

Beyond personal behavior, leadership sets the tone through other mechanisms such as the dedication of resources. Ethical business leaders not only talk about ethics and act ethically on a personal level, but they also allocate corporate resources to support and to promote ethical behavior. There is a long-standing credo of management: "budgeting is all about values." More common versions are "put your money where your mouth is" and "walk the talk."

For example, when **ethics officers** were first introduced to the corporate structure in the early 1990s, the extent to which they were supported financially indicated their relevance and influence within the organization. Ethics was not a priority if the general counsel served as the ethics officer in her "spare time," and no additional resources were allocated to that activity. Ehtics holds a different position in the firm if a highly skilled individual is hired into an exclusive position as ethics officer and is given a staff and a budget to support the work required.

Reality Check *The Impact of Ethical Leadership*

Leadership support for ethical behavior has a significantly higher impact on favorable ethics-related outcomes than does **any** training method.[11]

Ethics-Related Outcomes	**Impact of Organizational Support Compared to the Impact of Training Methods**
Employees:	*Organizational support had:*
Observing less misconduct	Over 10 times the effect of the training method with the most impact
Feeling less pressure	8.5 times the effect of the training method with the most impact
Trusting others to keep commitments	5 times the effect of the training method with the most impact
Positive attitudes toward organization	4 times the effect of the training method with the most impact
Reporting misconduct	1.5 times the effect of the training method with the most impact
Ability to apply training	1.1 times the effect of the training method with the most impact

Similarly, if a firm mandates ethical decision making from its workers through the implementation of a code of conduct, extending the same standard for its vendors, suppliers, and other contractors, then trains all of these stakeholders with regard to these expectations, and refers to the code and this process on a regular basis, these efforts demonstrate how seriously the firm takes the code.

A 2008 study by KPMG demonstrated that 86 percent of the *Fortune Global 200* have a business code of ethics, with the number of codes represented by that group doubling over the past 10 years.[12] KPMG found that one of the top three reasons for this increase was to create a shared company culture. One way in which leaders create that shared culture was explored in a study of the nature of ethical leadership that emphasized the importance of being *perceived* as a people-oriented leader, as well as the importance of leaders engaging in *visible ethical action*. Beyond people-orientation, traits that were important also included receptivity, listening and openness, in addition to the more traditionally considered traits of integrity, honesty, and trustworthiness. Finally, being perceived as having a broad ethical awareness, showing concern for multiple stakeholders (a responsibility *to* stakeholders, rather than *for* them, as Ralph Larsen emphasizes), and using ethical decision processes are also important.[13] Those perceived as ethical leaders do many of the things "traditional leaders" do (e.g., reinforce the conduct they are looking for, create standards for behavior, and so on), but they do that within the context of an ethics agenda. People perceive that the ethical leader's goal is not simply job performance, but performance that is consistent with a set of ethical values and principles. Finally, ethical leaders demonstrate caring for people (employees and external stakeholders) in the process.

Reality Check *Perception of Leadership Qualities*

The Pew Research Center conducted a survey of 2,250 adults in the United States and asked them whether the following leadership qualities were more true for men or women.[14] As you can see, women bested the men in five of eight categories, and tied them in two others. The only trait where men demonstrated strength over women was decisiveness. Some might contend that even this result is the consequence of a purportedly female style of decision making that is more collaborative and consensus-oriented, arguably an effective leadership style.

Leadership Traits: Women Rule!
% saying this trait is more true of...

■ Men □ Women

Trait	Men	Women
Honest	20	50
Intelligent	14	38
Hardworking	28	28
Decisive	44	33
Ambitious	34	34
Compassionate	5	80
Outgoing	28	47
Creative	11	62

Note: Traits listed in order of the public's ranking of their importance to leadership. "Equally true" and "don't know" responses are not shown.

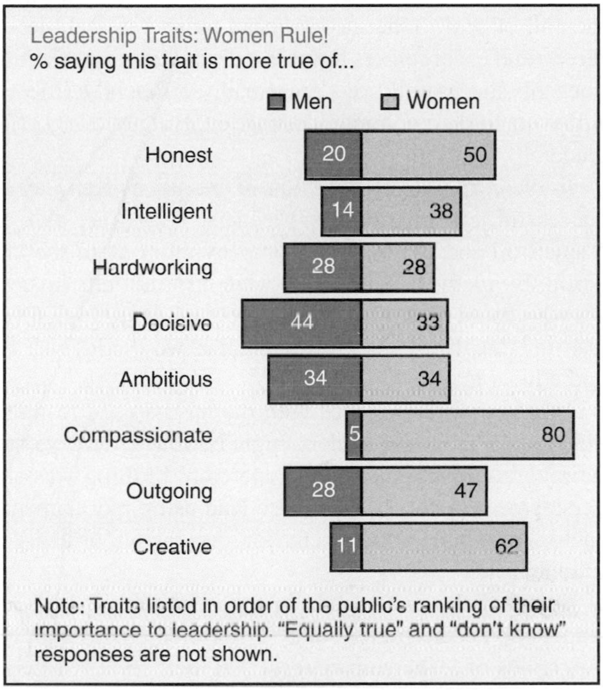

Source: http://pewsocialtrends.org/pubs/708/gender-leadership

However, as mentioned above, all of these traits and behaviors must be visible. If an executive is "quietly ethical" within the confines of the top management team, but more distant employees do not know about her or his ethical stance, they are not likely to be perceived as an ethical leader. Traits and behaviors must be socially visible and understood in order to be noticed and influence perceptions.[15] Take a look at the importance of that visibility in the Reality Check, "Perception of Leadership Qualities." People notice when an executive walks the talk and acts on concerns for the common good, society as a whole, and long-term business prospects. Executives are expected to be focused on the financial bottom line and the short-term demands of stock analysts, but it is noteworthy when they focus on these broader and longer-term concerns.

Effective Leadership and Ethical, Effective Leadership

As we have discussed, being perceived as a leader plays an important role in a leader's ability to create and transform an ethical corporate culture. Key executives have the capability of transforming a business culture, for better or for worse. If the corporate culture has a significant impact on ethical decision making within the firm, leaders have the responsibility for shaping that environment so that ethical decision making can flourish. But what is the difference between the effective leader and the *ethical,* effective leader?

5 OBJECTIVE

This distinction is clearly critical since there are many effective leaders; are they all ethical? What do we mean by an "ethical" leader? Since leaders guide, direct, and escort others towards a destination, an effective leader is someone who does this successfully and, presumably, efficiently. Effective leaders are able to get followers to their common destination. But not every effective leader is an ethical leader.

In the corporate context, Enron executives Ken Lay and Jeffrey Skilling were successful, effective business leaders. They were able to transform Enron from a small oil and gas pipeline company into one of the largest corporations in the world. By many accounts, they were inspirational, imaginative, and creative leaders who could motivate their staff to attain very high levels of success. They were also unethical leaders. How, then, can we distinguish between effective leaders and ethical leaders?

One key difference lies with the means used to motivate others and achieve one's goals. Effective leaders might be able to achieve their goals through threats, intimidation, harassment, and coercion. Skilling was said to be a very difficult person to work for. One can also lead using more amenable interpersonal means such as modeling ethical behavior, persuasion, or using the impact of one's institutional role.

Some of the discussions in the literature on leadership suggest that ethical leadership is determined solely by the *methods* used in leading. Promoters of certain styles of leadership suggest that their style is a superior style of leadership. Consequently, they tend to identify a method of leading with "true" leadership in an ethical sense. Along this line of thinking, for example, Robert Greenleaf's "Servant Leadership" suggests that the best leaders are individuals who lead by the example of serving others, in a non-hierarchical style. Other discussions similarly suggest that "transformative" or "transactional" leaders employ methods that empower subordinates to take the initiative and to solve problems for themselves, and that this constitutes the best in ethical leadership.

Certainly, ethically appropriate methods of leadership are central to becoming an ethical leader. Creating a corporate culture in which employees are empowered and expected to make ethically responsible decisions is a necessary part of being an ethical business leader. But, while some means may be ethically more appropriate than others (e.g., persuasion rather than coercion), it is not the method alone that establishes a leader as ethical. The other element of ethical leadership involves the *end* or *objective* towards which the leader leads. Recalling our discussion of ethical theory from chapter 3, this distinction should sound reminiscent of the emphasis on means in the deontological theory of universalism or the focus on ends or results in teleological utilitarianism. Ethical leadership seems to embody both elements. If we judge a leader solely by the results produced—the utilitarian greatest good for the greatest number—we may ignore the mistreatment of workers that was necessary to achieve that end. Alternatively, if we look only to the working conditions protected by universalism, we may not appropriately account for a failure to produce a marketable product or one sufficient to reap a profit necessary to support the working conditions provided in a sustainable manner.

Similarly, in the business context, productivity, efficiency, and profitability are minimal goals in order to be sustainable. A business executive who leads a firm into bankruptcy is unlikely to qualify as an effective or successful leader. An executive who transforms a business into a productive, efficient, and profitable business, to the contrary, likely will be judged as a successful business leader. One who succeeds in a manner that respects subordinates and/or empowers them to become creative and successful in themselves is, at least at first glance, both an effective and ethical leader. But is profitability and efficiency accomplished through ethical means alone enough to make a business leader an ethical leader?

Imagine a business leader who empowers her or his subordinates, respects their autonomy by consulting and listening, but who leads a business that publishes child pornography or pollutes the environment or sells weapons to radical organizations. Would the *method* of leading, alone, determine the ethical standing of such a leader? Beyond the goal of profitability, other socially responsible goals might be necessary before we conclude that the leader is fully ethical. Chapter 5 will pick up on this theme as we examine corporate social responsibility.

Building a Values-Based Corporate Culture

Recall the iceberg example we discussed earlier; we explained that modifying culture alone seems about as tough as moving an iceberg. Each individual in an organization has an impact on the corporate culture, although no one individual can build or change the culture alone. Culture derives from leadership, integration, assessment, and monitoring.

Mission Statements, Credos, Codes of Conduct, and Statements of Values

One of the key manifestations of ethical leadership is the articulation of values for the organization. Of course, this articulation may evolve after an inclusive process of values identification; it need not simply mimic the particular values of one chief executive. However, it is that leader's responsibility to ensure that the firm is guided by some set of organizing principles that can guide employees in their decision-making processes. But do codes make a difference? Consider the Reality Check, "Do Codes Make a Difference," which seeks to respond to that question by exploring Johnson & Johnson's experience as one of the first firm's to have a code.[16]

Reality Check *Do Codes Make a Difference?*

As a result of its quick and effective handling of its experience with tainted Tylenol in both 1982 and 1986, Johnson & Johnson has often been viewed as one of the most admired firms in the world. J&J had sales of $61.9 billion in 2009, representing its 77th year of consecutive sales increases. It has had 26 consecutive years of earnings increases and 47 consecutive years of dividend increases. Its market value in April 2010 was more than $179 billion, up from $38 billion in 1991, evidence that a firm that lives according to its strong values and a culture that supports those values can not only survive but sustain a profit over the long term.[17] CEO Ralph Larsen credits these successes directly to the J&J Credo: "it's the glue that holds our decentralized company together . . . For us, the credo is our expression of managing the multiple bottom lines of products, people, planet and profits. It's the way we conceptualize our total impact on society."[18]

The Johnson & Johnson Credo and History

At Johnson & Johnson there is no mission statement that hangs on the wall. Instead, for more than 60 years, a simple, one-page document—Our Credo—has guided our actions in fulfilling our responsibilities to our customers, our employees, the community and our stockholders. Our worldwide Family of Companies shares this value system in 36 languages spreading across Africa, Asia/Pacific, Eastern Europe, Europe, Latin America, Middle East and North America.

Our Credo History[19]

General Robert Wood Johnson, who guided Johnson & Johnson from a small, family-owned business to a worldwide enterprise, had a very perceptive view of a corporation's responsibilities beyond the manufacturing and marketing of products.

As early as 1935, in a pamphlet titled TRY REALITY, he urged his fellow industrialists to embrace what he termed "a new industrial philosophy." Johnson defined this as the corporation's responsibility to customers, employees, the community and stockholders.

But it was not until eight years later, in 1943, that Johnson wrote and first published the Johnson & Johnson Credo, a one-page document outlining these responsibilities in greater detail. Johnson saw to it that the Credo was embraced by his company, and he urged his management to apply it as part of their everyday business philosophy.

The Credo, seen by business leaders and the media as being farsighted, received wide public attention and acclaim. Putting customers first and stockholders last was a refreshing approach to the management of a business. But it should be noted that Johnson was a practical minded businessman. He believed that by putting the customer first the business would be well served, and it was.

The Corporation has drawn heavily on the strength of the Credo for guidance through the years, and at no time was this more evident than during the TYLENOL® crises of 1982 and 1986, when the McNeil Consumer & Specialty Pharmaceuticals product was adulterated with cyanide and used as a murder weapon. With Johnson & Johnson's good name and reputation at stake, company managers and employees made countless decisions that were inspired by the philosophy embodied in the Credo. The company's reputation was preserved and the TYLENOL® acetaminophen business was regained.

Today the Credo lives on in Johnson & Johnson stronger than ever. Company employees now participate in a periodic survey and evaluation of just how well the company performs its Credo responsibilities. These assessments are then fed back to the senior management, and where there are shortcomings, corrective action is promptly taken.

(*continued*)

Over the years, some of the language of the Credo has been updated and new areas recognize the environment and the balance between work and family have been added. But the spirit of the document remains the same today as when it was first written.

When Robert Wood Johnson wrote and then institutionalized the Credo within Johnson & Johnson, he never suggested that it guaranteed perfection. But its principles have become a constant goal, as well as a source of inspiration, for all who are part of the Johnson & Johnson Family of Companies.

More than 60 years after it was first introduced, the Credo continues to guide the destiny of the world's largest and most diversified health care company.

Our Credo

We believe our first responsibility is to the doctors, nurses and patients, to mothers and fathers and all others who use our products and services. In meeting their needs everything we do must be of high quality. We must constantly strive to reduce our costs in order to maintain reasonable prices. Customers' orders must be serviced promptly and accurately. Our suppliers and distributors must have an opportunity to make a fair profit.

We are responsible to our employees, the men and women who work with us throughout the world. Everyone must be considered as an individual. We must respect their dignity and recognize their merit. They must have a sense of security in their jobs. Compensation must be fair and adequate, and working conditions clean, orderly and safe. We must be mindful of ways to help our employees fulfill their family responsibilities. Employees must feel free to make suggestions and complaints. There must be equal opportunity for employment, development and advancement for those qualified. We must provide competent management, and their actions must be just and ethical.

We are responsible to the communities in which we live and work and to the world community as well. We must be good citizens—support good works and charities and bear our fair share of taxes. We must encourage civic improvements and better health and education. We must maintain in good order the property we are privileged to use, protecting the environment and natural resources.

Our final responsibility is to our stockholders. Business must make a sound profit. We must experiment with new ideas. Research must be carried on, innovative programs developed and mistakes paid for. New equipment must be purchased, new facilities provided and new products launched. Reserves must be created to provide for adverse times. When we operate according to these principles, the stockholders should realize a fair return.[20]

6 OBJECTIVE

Before impacting the culture through a **code of conduct** or statement of values, a firm must first *determine its mission* so that decision makers have direction when determining dilemmas. In the absence of other values, the only value is profit—at any cost. Consequently, without additional guidance from the top, a firm is sending a clear message that a worker should do whatever it takes to reap profits. A code of conduct, therefore, may more specifically delineate this foundation both for internal stakeholders, such as employees, and for external stakeholders, such as customers. In so doing, the code has the potential to both enhance corporate reputation and to provide concrete guidance for internal decision making, thus creating a built-in risk management system.

The vision can be inspiring—indeed it *should be* inspiring. For instance, when David Packard passed away, Bill Hewlett, his business partner in creating HP, commented, "as far as the company is concerned, the greatest thing he left behind him was a code of ethics known as 'the HP Way.'"[21] Similarly, Jim Collins, author of *Built to Last* and *Good to Great,* explains, "Contrary to business school doctrine, we did not find 'maximizing shareholder wealth' or 'profit maximization' as the dominant driving force or primary objective through the history of most of the visionary companies. They have tended to produce a cluster of objectives, of which money is only one—and not necessarily the primary one."[22] By establishing (especially through a participatory process) the core tenets on which a company is built, corporate leadership is effectively laying down the law with regard to the basis and objectives for all future decisions. In fact, the **mission statement** or corporate credo serves as an articulation of the fundamental principles at the heart of the organization and those that should guide all decisions, without abridgment.[23] From a universalist perspective, while many decisions might be made with the end in mind (utilitarian), none should ever breach the underlying mission as an *ultimate dictate.*

Developing the Mission and Code

The 1990s brought a proliferation of corporate codes of conduct and mission statements as part of the corporate response to the Federal Sentencing Guidelines for Organizations (see later in this chapter), and a 2002 survey found that 75 percent of these mention the word *ethics.*[24] The success of these codes depends in large part on the process by which they are conceived and written, as well as their implementation. As with the construction of a personal code or mission, it is critical to first ask yourself what you stand for or what the company stands for. Why does the firm exist? What are its purposes? How will it implement these objectives? Once you make these determinations, how will you share them and encourage a commitment to them among your colleagues and subordinates? (See Table 4.2.)

The second step in the development of guiding principles for the firm is the articulation of a *clear vision* regarding the firm's direction. Why have a code? Bobby Kipp, PricewaterhouseCoopers' global ethics leader, explains: "We felt it was important for all our clients, our people and other stakeholders to understand exactly what we stand for and how they can expect us to conduct ourselves . . . The code doesn't change the basic nature of the business we undertake, but instead it articulates the way we strive to conduct ourselves. The code shows how we apply our values to our daily business practices."[25]

The third step in this process is to identify *clear steps* as to how this cultural shift will occur. You have a code, but you cannot simply "print, post and pray," as Ethics Resource Center past-President Stuart Gilman has referred to Enron's experience. Do you just post a sign on the wall that says, "Let's make more money!" Of course not. You need to have processes and procedures in place that support and then sustain that vision. Put in a different way, "a world-class code is no guarantee of world-class conduct," cautions four other scholars in a *Harvard Business Review* article on benchmarking codes. "A code is only a tool,

TABLE 4.2
Ethics Code Guidelines

Source: Ethics Resource Center, "Code Construction and Content," http://www.ethics.org/printable_code_outline.html. Reprinted with permission of Ethics Resource Center.

The Ethics Resource Center provides the following guidelines for writing an ethics code:

1. Be clear about the objectives the code is intended to accomplish.
2. Get support and ideas for the code from all levels of the organization.
3. Be aware of the latest developments in the laws and regulations that affect your industry.
4. Write as simply and clearly as possible. Avoid legal jargon and empty generalities.
5. Respond to real-life questions and situations.
6. Provide resources for further information and guidance.
7. In all its forms, make it user-friendly because ultimately a code fails if it is not used.[26]

and like any tool, it can be used well or poorly—or left on the shelf to be admired or to rust."[27]

Finally, to have an effective code that will successfully impact culture, there must be a belief throughout the organization that this culture is actually possible and achievable. If conflicts remain that will prevent certain components from being realized, or if key leadership is not on board, no one will have faith in the changes articulated. See Table 4.2 for Ethics Resource Center guidelines on writing an effective ethics code.

It should be noted that, while many organizations have individual codes of conduct, industries and/or professions might also publish codes of conduct that apply to firms or people who do business in those arenas. While adherence to some codes is prerequisite to participation in a profession, such as the legal community's Code of Professional Responsibility, many codes are produced by professional associations and are voluntary in nature. For example, certified public accountants, the defense industry, the direct marketing industry, and some faculty associations all have codes.[28] One might presume that implementation would be effective in all areas based on the industry-wide approach; however, research shows that it is only successful if there is an extremely cooperative approach, uniform, verifiable performance indicators, a credible verification system, elements of broader societal concerns, and if the code's scope and claims are substantiated.[29]

Culture Integration: Ethics Hotlines, Ombudspersons, and Reporting

7 OBJECTIVE

Recalling Gilman's warning not to "print, post and pray," many business firms must have mechanisms in place that allow employees to come forward with questions, concerns, and information about unethical behavior. Integrating an ethical culture throughout a firm and providing means for enforcement is vitally critical both to the success of any cultural shift and to the impact on all stakeholders. Integration can take a number of different forms, depending both on the organizational culture and the ultimate goals of the process.

One of the most determinative elements of integration is communication because without it there is no clarity of purpose, priorities, or process.

Decision Point *Short Term versus Long Term*

You are a corporate vice president of one of the largest units in your organization. Unfortunately, you have noticed over the past few years that your unit has developed a singular focus on profits, since employees' performance appraisals and resulting compensation increases are based in significant part on "making the numbers." Though the unit has done well in this regard, you have noticed that people have been known to cut corners, to treat others less respectfully than you would like, and to generally disregard other values in favor of the bottom line. While this might be beneficial to the firm in the short run, you have grave concerns about the long-term sustainability of this approach.

- What are the ethical issues involved in striving to define or impact the culture of a unit?
- How might you go about defining the culture of your unit so that employees might be able to understand your concerns?
- What will be the most effective means by which to alter this culture?
- What stakeholders would be involved in your suggestion in response to the previous question? How might the different stakeholder groups be impacted by your decision on this process?
- How can you act in order to ensure the most positive results? How will you measure those results or determine your success? Will you measure inputs or outcomes, responsibilities, and rights?

Communication of culture must be incorporated into the firm's vocabulary, habits, and attitudes to become an essential element in the corporate life, decision making, and determination of success. In the end, the Ethics & Policy Integration Centre contends that communication patterns describe the organization far better than organization charts! The Decision Point, "Short Term versus Long Term" challenges you to create some of those integrative mechanisms, while the Reality Check, "Examples of Culture Integration" demonstrates how two firms have imaginatively responded to this very challenge.

To explore the effectiveness of a corporation's integration process, consider whether incentives are in the right place to encourage ethical decision making and whether ethical behavior is evaluated during a worker's performance review. It is difficult to reward people for doing the right thing, such as correctly filing an expense report, but as the Lockheed Martin Chairman's Award shows, incentives such as appropriate honors and positive appraisals are possible. Are employees comfortable raising questions relating to unethical behavior? Are multiple and varied reporting mechanisms in place? Do employees believe their reports will be free from retaliation? What can be done to ensure that employees who violate the company code are disciplined appropriately, even if they are good performers?

How does communication about ethical matters occur? The fact of the matter is that reporting ethically suspect behavior is a difficult thing to do. Childhood memories of "tattletales" or "snitches," along with a general social prohibition against informing on others, create barriers to reporting unethical behavior.

Reality Check *Examples of Culture Integration*

- Lockheed Martin offers its Chairman's Award, which is bestowed on the employee who most fully represents the spirit of the culture. In addition, the company coordinates an ethics film festival that encourages workers—on their own time and without financial assistance—to create short videos on ethics at the firm.
- DuPont strives to reinforce the message in a slightly different way. The firm has decided to publicize compliance transgressions (omitting the names to protect privacy) and the results of discipline. Though this "tell all" method might have its lawyers quaking in their seats, DuPont believes that, without it, workers have no idea what behavior is acceptable or unacceptable.

More ominously, individuals often pay a real cost when they report on unethical behavior (such as retaliation), especially if workplace superiors are involved in the report of wrongdoing.

Whistleblowing is one of the classic issues in business ethics. Whistleblowing involves the disclosure of unethical or illegal activities to someone who is in a position to take action to prevent or punish the wrongdoing. Whistleblowing can expose and end unethical activities. But it can also seem disloyal; it can harm the business; and, sometimes, it can exact significant costs on the whistleblower.

Whistleblowing can occur internally, as when Sherron Watkins reported her concerns to Ken Lay regarding Enron (see chapter 1). It can occur externally, as when Jeffrey Wigand (portrayed in the movie *The Insider*), reported to *60 Minutes* about Brown & Williamson's activities in not only concealing and knowingly misleading the public about the harmful effects of cigarettes, but also in using additives that increased the potential for harm. Whistleblowing can also occur externally when employees report wrongdoing to legal authorities, as when rocket engineer Roger Boisjoly reported the activities of his employer Morton Thiokol, along with NASA, prior to the launch of the space shuttle *Challenger.*

Because whistleblowing to external groups, such as the press and the legal authorities, can be so harmful to both the whistleblower and to the firm itself, internal mechanisms for reporting wrongdoing are preferable for all concerned. But the internal mechanisms must be effective, must allow confidentiality, if not anonymity, and must strive to protect the rights of the accused party. In addition to or as part of ethics and compliance officers' responsibilities, many firms have created ethics ombudsman and internal or external ethics hotlines. These mechanisms allow employees to report wrongdoing and to create mechanisms for follow-up and enforcement.

While these responses might seem evident, reasonable, and commonplace, many organizations do not have them in place for a variety of reasons. In addition, even when they are in place, people who observe threats to the organization opt not to report the threat or possible wrongdoing. Consider the *Columbia* space shuttle disaster, which is reviewed by the Columbia Accident Investigation

Board in the reading, "Assessment and Plan for Organizational Culture Change at NASA." On Feb. 1, 2003, the *Columbia* space shuttle lost a piece of its insulating foam while the shuttle reentered the earth's atmosphere. The damage resulted in the death of seven astronauts, one of NASA's most serious tragedies. The foam had dislodged during the original launch, which then damaged one of the shuttle's wings, which caused the accident a few weeks later on re-entry. When the foam dislodged, no one could actually assess the true extent of the damage. No one could "see around the corner," so to speak. The engineers could see the foam strike the wing but, because of a poor angle of sight and the fact that foam strikes had not caused major accidents in the past, senior managers downplayed the threat.

Was this an operations failure, a failure in judgment, pressure from above to complete the shuttle mission, the cavalier, cowboy culture of NASA to keep moving forward *at any cost? Columbia's* engineers worked in a data-driven culture. No one made a move without data to support it; unless there was data to prove that the vehicle was unsafe with the current "proven" technology, they could not justify the extra cost of scheduling a moon walk to investigate.

Is this a crisis of culture or a failure in a whistleblowing system? Some analysts consider it instead a "natural, albeit unfortunate, pattern of behavior . . . a prime example of an ambiguous threat—a signal that may or may not portend future harm."[30]

One of the challenges with reporting systems is that they do not make the values of the organization clear, what is or is not accepted within its culture. Therefore, while massive threats might give rise to quite evident responses, "the most dangerous situations arise when a warning sign is ambiguous and the event's potential for causing a company harm is unclear. In these cases, managers tend to actively ignore or discount the risk and take a wait-and-see attitude."[31] There are methods by which firms might actively curtail these negative influences. For instance, leaders should *model* the act of reporting wrongdoing, in an obvious manner, so that everyone throughout the organization can see that reporting is the highest priority—not covering up malfeasance. Leaders can explain the process of decision making that led to their conclusion. While "crisis management" teams or plans are often unsuccessful (since they are so seldom used, there is no habit formed at all), *practicing* reports is a valuable exercise. Running drills or rehearsals of challenging events will allow for much greater comfort and generate a level of expectation among workers that might not otherwise exist. In addition, a culture that allows sufficient time for reflection in order to reach responsible decisions is most likely to encourage consideration of appropriate implications. Finally, the most effective way to ensure clarity and thereby ensure a successful reporting scheme is to consistently and continuously communicate the organization's values and expectations to all stakeholders, and to reinforce these values through the firm's compensation and reward structure. See the reading, "Whistleblowing Today: Critical Issues Facing Business Leadership" by Wim Vandekerckhove to learn of the various approaches to the issue taken by different countries.

Beyond the question of cultural differences in reporting sensitivities and processes, a firm must consider the bare logistical questions in global implementation of its code of conduct and ethics and compliance program. How will the code and accompanying program align with local standards of practice, laws, and customs? Will there be just one version of the code for world operations, or multiple versions for each local base of operations, and not simply in the local language but modified in order to be sensitive to these local standards and customs? How 'deep' will your code reach into your supply chain? The codes of some firms apply only to their employee base while others apply to all vendors, suppliers, and other contracting parties. Must you consult with (or even seek approval from) labor representatives, unions and/or works councils prior to implementing the code or program in any of the countries in which you operate? Finally, be aware that the standard acknowledgement form that many employees are asked to sign upon receipt of a code of conduct in the United States may be presumed to be coerced in other environments, given the unequal bargaining positions of the parties. While you might opt to dispense with that requirement, how will you serve the purpose of demonstrating acceptance and understanding?

Assessing and Monitoring the Corporate Culture: Audits

8 OBJECTIVE

Unfortunately, if one does not measure something, people often perceive a decline in its importance. The same result occurs with regard to culture. If we cannot or do not measure, assess, or monitor culture, it is difficult to encourage others throughout the organization to pay attention to it. The contrary is true, however; monitoring and an ongoing ethics audit allow organizations to uncover silent vulnerabilities that could pose challenges later to the firm, thus serving as a vital element in risk assessment and prevention. By engaging in an ongoing assessment, organizations are better able to spot these areas before other stakeholders (both internal and external) spot them.

Beyond uncovering vulnerabilities, an effective monitoring process may include other significantly positive objectives. These may include an evaluation of appropriate resource allocation, whether the program is keeping pace with organizational growth, whether all of the program's positive results are being accurately measured and reported, whether the firm's compensation structure is adequately rewarding ethical behavior, and whether the "tone at the top" is being disseminated effectively.

Identifying positive results might be a familiar process. But, how do you detect a potentially damaging or ethically challenged corporate culture—sometimes referred to as a "toxic" culture? The first clear sign would be a lack of any generally accepted fundamental values for the organization, as discussed above. In addition, warning signs can occur in the various component areas of the organization. How does the firm treat its customers, suppliers, clients, and workers? The management of its internal and external relationships is critical evidence of its values. How does the firm manage its finances? Of course, a firm can be in a state of financial disaster without engaging in even one unethical act (and vice versa); but the manner in which it manages and communicates its financial environment is telling.

Reality Check *Warning Signs!*

PricewaterhouseCoopers (PwC) offers a list of early warning signs of an *ethically troubled organization* that sometimes, though not always, indicate areas of concern regarding fraud, conflicts of interest, ineffective controls, imbalance of power, inappropriate pressure, or other areas:

1. An inability to generate positive cash flows despite positive earnings and growth.
2. Unusual pressure to achieve accounting-based financial objectives.
3. Compensation tied closely or only to financial results.
4. Debt covenants that have been violated (or are close to being so).
5. Increased liabilities with no apparent source of funding.
6. Off-balance sheet transactions.
7. Complex or creative structures.
8. Ratios/trends that buck expectations or industry trends.
9. Large returns or revenue credits after the close of the period.
10. A large number of nonstandard adjusting entries.
11. A history of unreliable accounting estimates.
12. Numerous related-party transactions.
13. Transactions with no or questionable business purposes.

In addition, PwC suggests the following *organizational warning signals:*

1. An unusually complex organizational structure; numerous entities with unclear purpose.
2. Insufficient management depth in key positions, especially positions that manage risks.
3. Rapid growth or downsizing that places stress on organizational resources.
4. Resignations of management or board members for reasons other than retirement, health, or conflict of interest.
5. A member of the board or senior management who was possibly involved in or aware of financial manipulation that resulted in restatement is still connected with the organization.
6. An understaffed finance/accounting staff.
7. Undersized or understaffed internal audit department.
8. No audit committee or ineffective committee.
9. Management conveys a lifestyle beyond their financial means.
10. The scope of internal audit seems too narrow.
11. Failure to address weaknesses in controls or process.

On the other hand, the Institute for Business, Technology and Ethics cites the following eight traits of a *healthy organization culture:*

1. Openness and humility from top to bottom of the organization.
2. An environment of accountability and personal responsibility.
3. Freedom from risk taking within appropriate limits.
4. A fierce commitment to "doing it right."
5. A willingness to tolerate and learn from mistakes.
6. Unquestioned integrity and consistency.
7. A pursuit of collaboration, integration, and holistic thinking.
8. Courage and persistence in the face of difficulty.

Consulting firm LRN suggests myriad options by which to measure the impact of efforts to change a culture. The first is to determine whether employee perception of the culture or working conditions has changed. Surveys of employee job satisfaction in general or about specific elements of the culture may return interesting data, though sometimes employees will tell the firm what they believe the organization wishes to hear. Alternatively, leaders may opt for an audit by an independent organization in order to determine the employee perception or to assess the firm's vulnerabilities or risks. The external auditor will also be able to provide information relating to benchmarking data in connection with the firm's code, training program, or other education or integration components, as well as the evaluation of those programs if they are offered. Data surrounding the help line or hotline is also noteworthy in terms of both the quantity and quality of the calls and responses. As with any element of the working environment, any feedback or other communication from employees, whether at the beginning of employment, throughout or subsequent to employment, should be gathered and analyzed for valuable input regarding the culture.[32] Information is available everywhere—take a look at the "Warning Signs!" Reality Check. For an extensive set of recommended questions to guide a strategic monitoring audit, see the reading, "Does the Company Get It—20 Questions to Ask Regarding Compliance, Ethics, and Risk Management" by OCEG at the end of the chapter.

Mandating and Enforcing Culture: The Federal Sentencing Guidelines for Organizations

9 OBJECTIVE

When internal mechanisms for creating ethical corporate cultures prove inadequate, the business community can expect governmental regulation to fill the void. The **United States Sentencing Commission** (USSC), an independent agency in the United States Judiciary, was created in 1984 to regulate sentencing policy in the federal court system. Prior to that time, differences in sentencing, arbitrary punishments, and crime control had been enormous issues before Congress. By using the USSC to mandate sentencing procedures and make recommendations for terms, Congress has been able to incorporate the original purposes of sentencing in federal court procedures, bringing some of these challenges and variations under control.

Beginning in 1987, the USSC prescribed mandatory **Federal Sentencing Guidelines for Organizations** that apply to individual and organizational defendants in the federal system, bringing some amount of uniformity and fairness to the system. (See Figure 4.4.) These prescriptions, based on the severity of the offense, assign most federal crimes to one of 43 "offense levels." Each offender also is placed into a criminal history category based upon the extent and recency of past misconduct. The court then inputs this information into a sentencing grid and determines the offender's sentence guideline range (ranges are either in six-month intervals or 25 percent of the sentence, whichever is greater), and is subject to adjustments.

In its October 2004 decision in *U.S. v. Booker,* however, the Supreme Court separated the "mandatory" element of the guidelines from their advisory role, holding that their mandatory nature violated the Sixth Amendment right to a jury trial. Accordingly, though no longer mandatory, a sentencing court is still required

FIGURE 4.4
Sources of Culture

Review: Culture Derives from Leadership, Integration, and Assessment/Monitoring

1. **Leadership** (and maintenance) of the control environment
   - Through high-level commitment and management responsibility, leaders set the standard and the tone
2. **Control activities, information, and communication**
   - Statements, policies, operating procedures, communications and training
   - Constant/consistent integration into business practices
3. **Review, assessment, ongoing monitoring**
   - Monitoring, evaluation, historical accountability

to consider guideline ranges. The court is also permitted to individually tailor a sentence in light of other statutory concerns. You can imagine that this modification from mandatory to "required to consider" has not come without a bit of confusion. "Judges are still generally following the guidelines with new cases. But figuring out what to do with all the cases that have been sentenced under the old guidelines is the closest thing to chaos you can describe," says law professor Douglas Berman.[33]

The relevance of these guidelines to our exploration of ethics and, in particular, to our discussion of the proactive corporate efforts to create an ethical workplace is that the USSC strived to use the guidelines to create both a legal *and an ethical* corporate environment. This effort was supported by the Sarbanes-Oxley Act, which subsequently directed the USSC to consider and to review its guidelines for fraud relating to securities and accounting, as well as to obstruction of justice, and specifically asked for severe and aggressive deterrents in sentencing recommendations. Further, the Sarbanes-Oxley Act required public companies to establish a code of conduct for top executives and, if they did not have one, to explain why it did not exist. Several stock exchanges followed suit and also required codes of business conduct and ethics from its publicly held companies.

In recognition of the significant impact of corporate culture on ethical decision making, the USSC updated the guidelines in 2004 to include references not only to compliance programs but also to "ethics and compliance" programs and, further, required that organizations promote "an organizational culture that encourages ethical conduct and commitment to compliance with the law." The revision also includes a requirement that organizations assess areas of risk for ethics and compliance, and periodically measure the effectiveness of their programs. In addition, the criteria for an effective program, which used to be outlined just in the guidelines' commentary, are now found in a separate specific guideline.

The guidelines seek to encourage corporations to create or maintain effective ethics and compliance programs. Those companies that can demonstrate that they have these programs, but find themselves in court as a result of a bad apple or two, either will not be penalized or the recommended penalty will be reduced (called a "mitigated" penalty). On the other hand, firms that do not have effective ethics and compliance systems will be sentenced to an additional term of probation and ordered to develop a program during that time (called an "aggravated" penalty).

The USSC notes that organizations shall "exercise due diligence to prevent and detect criminal conduct; and otherwise promote an organizational culture that encourages ethical conduct and a commitment to compliance with the law." The guidelines identify those specific acts of an organization that can serve as due diligence in preventing crime and the *minimal* requirements for an effective compliance and ethics program. These include the following actions:[34]

1. **Standards and Procedures.** The organization shall establish standards and procedures to prevent and detect criminal conduct.
2. **Responsibility of Board and other Executives; Adequate Resources and Authority.**
   - (A) The organization's board shall be knowledgeable about the compliance and ethics program and shall exercise reasonable oversight with respect to its implementation and effectiveness.
   - (B) High-level personnel must be assigned to have responsibility for the program and must then ensure its effectiveness.
   - (C) Specific individual(s) within the organization shall be delegated day-to-day operational responsibility for the program and shall report periodically to these high-level personnel on the effectiveness of the compliance and ethics program. They shall also be given adequate resources, appropriate authority, and direct access to the governing authority.
3. **Preclusion from Authority: Prior Misconduct.** The organization shall avoid placing people in charge of the program who have previously engaged in illegal activities or other conduct inconsistent with an effective compliance and ethics program.
4. **Communication and Training.** The organization shall communicate its standards and procedures to all members of the organization through training or other means appropriate to such individuals' respective roles and responsibilities.
5. **Monitoring, Evaluation, Reporting Processes.** The organization shall take reasonable steps:
   - (A) to ensure that the organization's compliance and ethics program is followed, including monitoring and auditing to detect criminal conduct;
   - (B) to evaluate periodically the effectiveness of the organization's compliance and ethics program; and

Reality Check *The Global Culture for Corporations: Compliance and Ethics Issues to Consider*

GUIDANCE FROM *ETHISPHERE:*

Brazil

1. **CORRUPTION** According to a business survey conducted in 2005 by PriceWaterhouseCoopers, 70 percent of firms in Brazil report having spent at least 3 percent of revenues on bribes. Most of these bribes are to expedite procedures, special treatment, or access to traditional transactions.

   DEAL WITH IT Given recent history, Brazilian business people have become sensitive to corruption and how it impacts Brazil's future growth and investment opportunities. Federal agents are also increasingly effective in policing illegal business behavior. You will, therefore, likely encounter understanding when you make the case for compliance. Transparency in any business relationship or activity, however, such as accounting practices that allow for the review of resource use, provides the best assurance. In dealing with any political contributions, be sure to follow the stipulations established by the Internal Revenue Service and be prepared for a potential audit at any time.

2. **DIRTY MONEY** In 2000, a report by CPI accused more than 800 Brazilians, including politicians and influential business figures, of drug trafficking. Poor record keeping and accounting practices can cover illegal activities such as drug trafficking and money laundering. Imprecise records can also facilitate tax evasion and other misuse of resources.

   DEAL WITH IT Do not engage in business transactions with individuals that have roles in unidentified businesses, government or public offices. Keep all records as clear and organized as possible and keep an electronic or hard copy of any relevant monetary transactions. Also, keep updated records of employees and suppliers and request copies of official identification whenever you formalize any type of working relationship. There are certified credit check services, like those offered by Serasa, that allow financial and tax due diligence of business partners.

3. **GÉRSON'S LAW** In the 1970s, Gérson, a famous soccer player, appeared in a cigarette advertising campaign saying, "Take advantage of every situation to get ahead." Sometimes called Gérson's law, this mentality is used from time to time to justify unethical behavior. While in decline, the attitude persists in certain regions, especially outside of international business centers.

   DEAL WITH IT Ethics and compliance training will increase your employee's understanding of what is appropriate behavior as well as the risks that unethical action poses for company. With agents outside your company, it is important to evaluate a potential partner's commitment to ethical practice prior to formalizing a relationship.

Jordan

1. **PRICE HAGGLING** Foreigners often complain about the wide price ranges that exist in the formal and informal economies. Haggling and bargaining are techniques often necessary in Jordanian business settings, something which can create discomfort or foster distrust among those unaccustomed to the practice.

   DEAL WITH IT This specific practice is embedded in the cultural traditions of the nation. Although there is no single simple solution for it, formal processes such as tenders and foreign aid contract requirements can force competitors to be more transparent in terms of costs and prices. It can also be helpful to recognize that the bargaining process is an opportunity to understand the business style of your potential partners and to establish mutually understood relationships with them.

2. **WOMEN IN PROFESSIONS** The role of women in Jordanian society has been evolving at a slow pace and some social preconceptions can inhibit the work of women managers. In addition, lack of equal opportunity employment laws and some specific norms, like those that prohibit nighttime

(*continued*)

employment, can be constraining for female workers.

DEAL WITH IT The Jordan Constitution presents men and women as equal and this should be used as the basis for employment opportunities. Equal access to education is broadening the professions that are practiced by women. When confronting conservative attitudes to female employment you should advise the participants that Jordan's policies consider this discrimination.

3. **RELIGIOUS DISCRIMINATION** According to the constitution Islam is the state religion. Christianity is also recognized as a religion and therefore its practice is allowed. However, the Government does not recognize the Druze or Baha'i faiths as religions, but nonetheless allows the practice of these faiths. Baha'is have been known to face both official and social discrimination, such as prohibitions from registering schools or places of worship.

   DEAL WITH IT Although some religions and churches might not be recognized, there is usually a tolerant attitude toward them. In order to avoid discrimination issues at work, it is best not to encourage any religious practice (such as praying hours) and ensure the respect of workers individual preferences.

South Africa

1. **WORKPLACE INEQUALITY AND DISCRIMINATION** A notable difference between the South African and U.S. workplaces is the inherent imbalance of the workforce, particularly at the management and executive level. Concerns for discriminatory practices are unique in this developing country in that there are not only issues with discrimination based on gender, race and religion, but other measures such as age, sexual orientation, HIV/AIDS status and disability.

   DEAL WITH IT Be sure that your company's Code of Conduct and HR policies account for the unique obstacles when hiring in SA—each should contain detailed and frank discussions of the equal opportunities for employment offered by a firm. Measures should be taken to see that hiring practices are not only nondiscriminatory, but transparent and well documented so as to protect your organization from potential liability.

2. **BRIBERY** Transparency International ranked South Africa as the sixth country in the world most likely to bribe. More and more, South African companies not only see bribery as an accepted practice when conducting business in the region, but a necessary component for success.

   DEAL WITH IT Companies should be proactive in trying to mitigate the risks presented. Objectively research the South African market and where your company is likely to encounter bribery issues—the more you understand this issue, the better you can prepare employees to avoid it. A robust compliance program with a focus on corruption is more likely to win leniency from regulators in the event of malfeasance. Finally, insist on conducting periodic audits—this extends to potential partners, subcontractors and agents. Although this won't be common practice for your local counterparts, and you may encounter some resistance, it's a vital step to ensure that your organization isn't committing—knowingly or unknowingly—Foreign Corrupt Practices Act violations that could cost millions.

3. **CORRUPTION** The factor that has contributed the most to corruption growth in South Africa? Corruption and illegal practices that go unchecked, unregulated and unpunished. This happens for many reasons, mostly having to do with inadequate control policies and legislation and insufficient resources to form a unified effort against corruption. It's a commonly held belief in South Africa that corruption efforts have taken a back seat to other pressing issues like poverty, HIV/AIDS, inequalities and high unemployment.

   DEAL WITH IT Companies engaging in business in South Africa will, for the time being, have to be proactive in not only ensuring that they have vigorous internal control policies in place that define and outline penalties for corruption in addition to

(*continued*)

providing adequate reporting mechanisms, but also to conduct due diligence when selecting and auditing partners and vendors.

Source: F. Arreola and G. Unruh, "Global Compliance: Brazil," *Ethisphere* (September 20, 2008), http://ethisphere.com/global-compliance-brazil/; F. Arreola and G. Unruh, "Global Compliance: Jordan," *Ethisphere* (May 13, 2009), http://ethisphere.com/global-compliance-jordan/; E. Russell, "Global Compliance: South Africa," *Ethisphere* (March 25, 2008), http://ethisphere.com/global-compliance-south-africa/. Reprinted with permission from *Ethisphere*. http://www.ethisphere.com.

(C) to have and publicize a system, which may include mechanisms that allow for anonymity or confidentiality, whereby the organization's employees and agents may report or seek guidance regarding potential or actual criminal conduct without fear of retaliation.

6. **Incentive and Disciplinary Structures.** The organization's compliance and ethics program shall be promoted and enforced consistently throughout the organization through
   (A) appropriate incentives to perform in accordance with the compliance and ethics program; and
   (B) appropriate disciplinary measures for engaging in criminal conduct and for failing to take reasonable steps to prevent or detect criminal conduct.
7. **Response and Modification Mechanisms.** After criminal conduct has been detected, the organization shall take reasonable steps to respond appropriately to the criminal conduct and to prevent further similar criminal conduct, including making any necessary modifications to the organization's compliance and ethics program.

In connection with item number one on the list, imagine the challenges faced by companies seeking to ensure compliance in a variety of distinct cultures throughout the world. The Reality Check, "The Global Culture for Corporations: Compliance and Ethics Issues to Consider," explores some of those obstacles with regard to three countries. These three were chosen simply to provide a window into the array of issues for which companies need to be prepared today.

Item number two, mandates that the organization's governing body (usually, a board of directors) has the duty to act prudently, to be knowledgeable about the content and operation of the compliance and ethics program, and must undergo ongoing and consistent training. The content could include instruction surrounding the nature of board fiduciary duties, personal liability, stock exchange regulations, insider trading, confidentiality, intellectual property, and business secrets. The Conference Board, who was responsible for research regarding the frequency of board training, found it noteworthy that "accounting literacy" was not mentioned by executives among issues that should be included. Its research did reveal, however, that more than two-thirds of boards spend two hours or less *per year* on ethics and compliance training.[35]

Decision Point *Legal Pressure to Violate Confidentiality*

Protecting confidentiality is one of the most effective tools in creating a corporate culture in which illegal and unethical behavior can be uncovered. Corporate ethics officers, ombudsman, and ethics hotlines typically guarantee that any reports of illegal or unethical behavior will be held in strictest confidence. Ethics officers promise anonymity to whistleblowers, and those who report wrongdoing trust that this promise of confidentiality will be upheld.

However, Federal Sentencing Guidelines can create real ethical dilemmas for corporations that promise anonymity and confidentiality. The guidelines call for significantly reduced punishment for firms that immediately report potential wrongdoing to government authorities. Failure to report evidence of wrongdoing can mean the difference between a significant penalty and exoneration. Of course, failure to promise confidentiality can also be evidence of an ineffective ethics and compliance system, itself a potential risk for receiving stiffer legal penalties.

- Should ethics officers guarantee confidentiality to those who report wrongdoing, and should they violate that confidence to protect the firm from prosecution?
- What facts would you want to know before making this decision?
- Can you imagine any creative way out of this dilemma?
- To whom does the ethics officer owe duties? Who are the stakeholders?
- What are the likely consequences of either decision? What fundamental rights or principles are involved?

Though these steps are likely to lead to an effective program, "[such a program] is more than checking off the items on a list. This concept of 'due diligence' is a restless standard, as flexible as changing events reflected in the day's headlines and as creative as the minds of potential wrongdoers."[36] For instance, the guidelines require an investigation in response to a report of wrongdoing; but they also seem to require more than that. A firm must learn from its mistakes and take steps to prevent recurrences such as follow-up investigation and program enhancements. The USSC also mandates consideration of the size of the organization, the number and nature of its business risks, and the prior history of the organization; mitigating factors such as self-reporting of violations, cooperation with authorities, and acceptance of responsibility; and aggravating factors such as its involvement in or tolerance of criminal activity, a violation of a prior order, or its obstruction of justice. These standards are to be judged against applicable industry standards; however, this requires that each firm benchmark against comparable companies. Consider the challenges involved in developing an airtight system and process in the Decision Point, "Legal Pressure to Violate Confidentiality."

Opening Decision Point Revisited *Creating an Ethics Program*

You have developed and implemented an ethics program. But how do you know whether the ethics program is "working"? How will you define "success"? Who do you define as your primary stakeholders? What are their interests in your program and what are the impacts of your program on each stakeholder? How could you modify your program to ensure even greater success?

This Decision Point asks you to define the "success" of an ethics program, an extraordinary challenge even for those in this business for many years. One way to look at the inquiry would be to consider the measures by which you might be willing to be evaluated, since this is your project. Overall, you will need to explore whether there are pressures in your environment that encourage worker misconduct. You will need to consider whether there are systematic problems that encourage bad decisions. Have you identified all the major legal, ethical, and reputational risks that your organization faces, and have you determined the means by which to remediate those risks?

Because you will encourage the performance that you plan to measure, it is important to determine whether you will be most concerned with the end results or consequences or with the protection of particular values articulated by your program or codes. If you measure outcomes alone, you will have a singular focus on the achievement of those outcomes by decision makers. If you measure the protection of rights alone, you may be failing to consider the long-range implications of decisions in terms of their costs and benefits to the firm.

In a 1997 survey of members of the Ethics Officers Association, 47 percent of ethics officers reported that the guidelines were an influential determinant of their firm's commitment to ethics.[37] Another USSC study showed that the guidelines influenced 44.5 percent of these officers to enhance their existing compliance programs.[38]

To provide some context to this exploration, consider which offenses are most likely to lead to a fine for an organization. In 2001, the USSC received information on 238 organizations sentenced under chapter 8 (a 21.7 percent decrease from the previous year). The sentenced organizations had pled guilty in 92.4 percent of the cases. Of the fines and restitution imposed, 30 percent were issued for cases of fraud, with antitrust offenses and import/export violations the next most common crimes at 6.7 percent each. Of those violations not included in the fine list, violations of environmental laws with regard to water topped the list at 13 percent. The mean restitution imposed was $4 million and the mean fine was $2 million.[39]

Questions, Projects, and Exercises

1. To help understand an organizational culture, think about some organization to which you belong. Does your company, school, or fraternity/sorority have its own culture? How would you describe it? How does it influence individual decision making and action? Would you be a different person had you attended a different school or joined a different fraternity/sorority? How would you go about changing your organization's culture?
2. Consider how you evaluate whether a firm is "one of the good guys" or not. What are some of the factors you use to make this determination? Do you actually know the facts behind each of those elements, or has your judgment been shaped by the firm's reputation? Identify one firm you believe to be decent or ethical and make a note of the basis for that conclusion. Next identify a second firm that you do not believe to be ethical or that you think has questionable values and write down the basis for that alternate conclusion. Now, using the Internet and other relevant sources, explore the firms' cultures and decisions, checking the results of your research against your original impressions of the firms. Try to evaluate the cultures and decisions of each firm as if you had no idea whether they were ethical. Were your impressions accurate or do they need to be modified slightly?
3. You will need to draft a memorandum to your chief executive identifying the value of a triple bottom line approach, which would represent an enormous shift from the firm's current orientation. What are the three key points that you could make and how would you best support this argument?
4. Now that you have an understanding of corporate culture and the variables that impact it, how would you characterize an ethically effective culture, one that would effectively lead to a profitable and valuable long-term sustainability for the firm?
5. One element that surely impacts a firm's culture is its employee population. While a corporate culture can shape an employee's attitudes and habits, it will do so more easily if people who have already developed those attitudes and habits are hired in the first place. How would you develop a recruitment and selection process that would most successfully allow you to hire the best workers for your particular culture? Should you get rid of employees who do not share the corporate culture? If so, how would you do that?
6. What are some of the greatest benefits and hazardous costs of compliance-based cultures?
7. Assume you have a number of suppliers for your global apparel business. You have in place a code of conduct both for your workplace and for your suppliers. Each time you visit a particular supplier, even on unannounced visits, it seems as if that supplier is in compliance with your code. However, you have received communications from that supplier's employees that there are violations. What should you do?
8. You are aware of inappropriate behavior and violations of your firm's code of conduct throughout your operation. In an effort to support a collegial and supportive atmosphere, however, you do not encourage co-workers to report on their peers. Unfortunately, you believe that you must make a shift in that policy and institute a mandatory reporting structure. How would you design the structure and how would you implement the new program in such as way that the collegiality that exists is not destroyed?
9. *Wasta* is the term used in the United Arab Emirates (UAE) for favoritism. In the UAE, it is a highly valued element of the culture. In fact, while nepotism might be kept under wraps or discussed in hushed tones in an American firm, *Wasta* is more likely to be

worn on one's sleeve among UAE professionals. It is precisely who-you-know that often dictates the position you might get in many companies or how fast you might get approved for certain processes. If you were assigned to build and then lead a team based in the UAE that would be comprised of both UAE nationals (called "Emiratis") as well as U.S. ex-pats, how might you most effectively respond to this culture of historical and embedded preferential treatment, reflecting the local realities, while at the same time respecting your own or your home country's value structure, *if different?*

10. A large U.S.-based corporation has decided to develop a mission statement and then conduct training on a new ethics program. It engages you to assist in these endeavors. What activities would you need to conduct in order to complete this project? What are some of the concerns you should be sure to consider?
11. Put yourself in the position of someone who is establishing an organization from the ground up. What type of leader would you want to be? How would you create that image or perception? Do you create a mission statement for the firm and/or a code of conduct? What process would you use to do so? Would you create an ethics and/or compliance program and how would you then integrate the mission statement and program throughout your organization? What do you anticipate might be your successes and challenges?
12. With regard to employee recognition in the work place, what effects would a program like "employee of the month" have on the corporate culture, and what factors might lead you to recommend it as a motivational program for your company?
13. Identify an industry in which you would like to work, and choose a company for whom you would like to work, ideally. Use the company's Web site to learn about their core values and culture in order to find your best fit and then explain your choice. Next, identify a company at which you would not like to work based on its core values and culture. Explain your reasons.

Key Terms

After reading this chapter, you should have a clear understanding of the following Key Terms. The page numbers refer to the point at which they were discussed in the chapter. For a more complete definition, please see the Glossary.

code of conduct, *p. 161*
compliance-based culture, *p. 152*
culture, *p. 146*
ethics officers, *p. 155*
Federal Sentencing Guidelines for Organizations, *p. 169*
mission statement, *p. 162*
United States Sentencing Commission, *p. 169*
values-based culture, *p. 152*
whistleblowing, *p. 165*

End Notes

1. Adapted from EPIC, "Measuring Organizational Integrity and the Bottom Line Results One Can Expect," http://www.epic-online.net/quest_7.html (accessed April 4, 2010).
2. J. Liker, *Toyota Culture: The Heart and Soul of the Toyota Way* (Burr Ridge, IL: McGraw-Hill, 2007).
3. J. Collins and J. Porras, *Built to Last: Successful Habits of Visionary Companies* (New York: HarperCollins, 1994), p. 73.
4. Adapted from J. Heskett, E. Sasser, and J. Wheeler, *The Ownership Quotient: Putting the Service Profit Chain to Work for Unbeatable Competitive Advantage* (Boston: Harvard Business Publishing, 2008).
5. Ethics Resource Center, *National Business Ethics Survey* (2007).
6. *Id.*

7. J. Marquez, "Kindness Pays, or Does It?" *Workforce Management* (June 25, 2007), p. 40–49
8. J. Joseph, *Integrating Ethics and Compliance Programs* (Washington, DC: Ethics Resource Center, 2001), p. 9.
9. "Spitzer Resigns after Sex Scandal, Pressure," National Public Radio (Mar. 12, 2008), http://www.npr.org/templates/story/story.php?storyId=88134976 (accessed April 4, 2010).
10. R. Gilmartin, "Ethics and the Corporate Culture," *Raytheon Lectureship in Business Ethics* (November 10, 2003).
11. Ethics Resource Center, "Reducing Perceived Pressure to Behave Unethically: The Roles of Leaders and Co-Workers" (2008), http://www.ethics.org (accessed April 4, 2010).
12. KPMG, *Business Codes of the Global 200* (2008), http://www.kpmg.com/SiteCollectionDocuments/BusinessCodes_ofthe_Global200.pdf (accessed April 4, 2010).
13. L. Trevino, M. Brown, and L. Hartman, "A Qualitative Investigation of Perceived Executive Ethical Leadership: Perceptions from Inside and Outside the Executive Suite," *Human Relations* 56, no. 1 (January 2003): 5–37.
14. Pew Research Center, "Men or Women: Who's the Better Leader?" (Aug. 25, 2008), http://pewsocialtrends.org/pubs/708/gender-leadership (accessed July 9, 2009).
15. L. Trevino, M. Brown, and L. Hartman, "A Qualitative Investigation of Perceived Executive Ethical Leadership: Perceptions from Inside and Outside the Executive Suite," *Human Relations* 56, no. 1 (January 2003): 5–37.
16. www.jnj.com/our_company/our_credo_history/index.htm (accessed April 4, 2010).
17. Johnson & Johnson, "Investor Fact Sheet" (2009) http://files.shareholder.com/downloads/JNJ/887702064x0x359569/33FDBE7F-89FC-461D-9236-C47F29782B37/2008_Investor_Fact_Sheet.pdf (accessed April 8, 2010); "Johnson & Johnson At a Glance," *Forbes* (April 8, 2010), http://finapps.forbes.com/finapps/jsp/finance/compinfo/CIAtAGlance.jsp?tkr=JNJ (accessed April 8, 2010).
18. R. Larsen, "Leadership in a Values-Based Organization," *Sears Lectureship in Business Ethics, Bentley College* (February 7, 2002).
19. www.jnj.com/our_company/our_credo_history/index.htm (accessed April 4, 2010).
20. Courtesy of Johnson & Johnson, http://www.jnj.com/our_company/our_credo_history/index.htm and http://www.jnj.com/our_company/our_credo/index.htm (accessed April 4, 2010).
21 J. Collins and J. Porras, "Building Your Company's Vision," *Harvard Business Review* (September/October 1996).
22. M. Satin, "We Need to Alter the Culture at Places Like Enron—Not Just Pass More Laws," *Radical Middle Newsletter* (March/April 2002), http://www.radicalmiddle/com (accessed April 4, 2010).
23. For an exception analysis of the distinction between four types of ethics statements—values statements, corporate credos, codes of ethics and Internet privacy policies—*see* P. E. Murphy, "Developing, Communicating and Promoting Corporate Ethics Statements: A Longitudinal Analysis," *Journal of Business Ethics* 62 (2005):183–189.
24. American Management Association, *2002 Corporate Values Survey,* American Management Association Report (2002).
25. PricewaterhouseCoopers, "Why Have a Code?" http://www.pwc.com/extweb/newcoatwork.nsf/docid/BCC554487E1C3BC680256C2B003115D5 (accessed April 4, 2010).
26. Ethics Resource Center, "Code Construction and Content," http://www.ethics.org/printable_code_outline.html (accessed April 4, 2010).

27. L.S. Paine, R. Deshpande, J.D. Margolis, and K.E. Bettcher, "Up to Code: Does Your Company's Conduct Meet World-Class Standards?" *Harvard Business Review* (December 2005).
28. American Institute of Certified Public Accountants, http://www.aicpa.org/About/code/index.html; the Defense Industry Initiative on Business Ethics and Conduct, http://www.defenseethics.org/; the Direct Marketing Association, http://www.the-dma.org/nonprofitfederation/EthicsGuidelines103007.pdf; the Academy of Management, http://www.aomonline.org/aom.asp?ID=181 (accessed April 4, 2010).
29. N. B. Kurland, "The Defense Industry Initiative: Ethics, Self-Regulation, and Accountability," *Journal of Business Ethics,* v. 12, no. 2 (1993): 137–145; J. D. Neill, O. S. Stovall, and D. L. Jinkerson, "A Critical Analysis of the Accounting Industry's Voluntary Code of Conduct," *Journal of Business Ethics* 59, no. 1-2 (2005): 101–108; A. Prakash, "Responsible Care: An Assessment," *Business & Society,* 39 (2000): 183–209.
30. M. Roberto, R. Bohmer, and A. Edmondson, "Facing Ambiguous Threats," *Harvard Business Review* (Nov. 2006), 106–113, http://hbr.org/2006/11/facing-ambiguous-threats/ar/1 (accessed April 4, 2010).
31. Id.
32. LRN, *The Impact of Codes of Conduct on Corporate Culture* (Los Angeles, CA: LRN, 2006).
33. K. Axtman, "Cases Test New Flexibility of Sentencing Guidelines," *Christian Science Monitor* (February 18, 2005).
34. USSC, *Guidelines Manual,* sec. 8B2.1, "Effective Compliance and Ethics Program" (2005), http://www.ussc.gov/2005guid/8b2_1.htm (accessed July 7, 2009).
35. R.E. Berenbeim, "How Prepared Are Companies for the Revised Sentencing Guidelines?" The Conference Board, *Executive Action* A-0139-05-EA (March 2005).
36. J. Murphy, "Lost Words of the Sentencing Guidelines," *Ethikos* (November/ December 2002), p. 5.
37. Ethics Officer Association, 1997 Member Survey (2000), p. 9.
38. USSC, "Corporate Crime in America: Strengthening the 'Good Citizen' Corporation" (1995), pp. 123–191.
39. Data is from the United States Sentencing Commission, Office of Policy Analysis, 2001 Datafile, OPAFYOI.

Readings

Reading 4-1

Leadership in a Values-Based Organization: *The Sears Lectureship in Business Ethics at Bentley College—Thursday, February 7, 2002*

Ralph S. Larsen, Former Chairman of the Board and Chief Executive Officer, Johnson & Johnson

Thank you for that kind introduction. I am very pleased to be here representing the more than 100,000 people of Johnson & Johnson, people who work so hard each day, not only building our business, but doing it in the right way.

I'm honored to be a part of this lecture series, and so, the first reason I'm here is because you asked. The second reason is that the older I get, the more I like hanging around with people younger than I am, people on the threshold of their careers. You keep us young and nimble. You have a way of distilling and challenging our thought processes. You remind us of what it's all about.

Last year I spoke with a young lady who was serving as a fellow in our corporate communications department. This is a program we have with the Rutgers School of Communications. These master's students work for us as interns for one or two years as they complete their program. I was struck by her story, and I wanted to share it with you today.

Well, somehow our company made an impression on this young girl in India, thousands and thousands of miles away from the headquarters where she ultimately worked. When she came to us she brought with her the expectation that we would be as community-oriented, thoughtful, values-oriented, and as upstanding as she had seen on the outside. She also came with the full expectation that she would find an environment where she could express her values and feel encouraged to do the right thing.

Now, I share Sandhya's story with you because I think it's just terrific that a young person can be touched and motivated by our company's values. And I think it's even more encouraging that this motivation meant that she sought out a job with us. You, too, might have some preconceptions about the kinds of organizations you want to join, and if you do end up someplace with a strong set of core values, I can give you a glimpse of what to expect once you get there.

Obviously, I can speak only from my personal experience which is almost exclusively in Johnson & Johnson. As chairman and CEO for the past 13 years, I have had the best job in corporate America—of that I am sure. The reason is that leading a company like Johnson & Johnson, with a strong foundation built on values and a heritage based on ethical principles, is very special. There are certain boundaries in place: things you simply don't do, well-accepted management practices that just won't work, changes that just won't stick, parts of our history that simply won't give way to certain new ideas.

* * * *

In his renowned book, *The Fifth Discipline*, Peter Senge uses something called a "trim tab" to explain certain theories of leverage within a system. In this case, how do you get something really big, like an oil tanker ship, to change course? Well, you move the rudder, of course. But the rudder itself is so big that there's water pressure keeping it where it is. So, there is this very small piece (a rudder for the rudder if you will) called a trim tab that compresses the water around the rudder. That action makes it easier for the rudder to move through the water. Easier, therefore, for the rudder to change the direction of the ship. You don't see the trim tab. You probably never even knew it was there, but it makes an incredible difference to the navigation of the ship.

Being bound together around the values . . . around our credo . . . being bound together around values is like the trim tab for leadership at Johnson & Johnson. What I mean is that because it is a deep point of leverage, it makes a huge difference. It's the point of leverage that makes leadership not only possible but also meaningful and enjoyable. Johnson & Johnson's strong values have been instrumental in our charting a course that has proved successful, and for that I am very thankful.

- Sales last year were $33 billion, almost triple what they were a decade ago, representing our 69th consecutive year of sales increases.
- We've had 17 consecutive years of double-digit earnings increases.
- And we've had 39 consecutive years of dividend increases.
- And our shareowners have done very well. The market value of Johnson & Johnson ended last year at more than $180 billion, up from approximately $38 billion ten years ago.

At Johnson & Johnson, it's the glue that holds our decentralized company together. It's called our credo, and it is a 60 year-old deceptively simple one-page document. Our credo grew out of General Robert Wood Johnson's (the patriarch of our company) very simple, yet very profound, management philosophy. In essence, it says that our first responsibility is to our customers, to give them high-quality products at fair prices. Our second responsibility is to our employees, to treat them with dignity and respect and pay them fairly. Our third responsibility is to the communities in which we operate, to be good corporate citizens and protect the environment. And then, it says that our final responsibility is to our shareholders, to give them a fair return.

In the final analysis, the Credo is built on the notion that if you do a good job in fulfilling the first three responsibilities, then the shareholder will come out all right. That is exactly what has happened over all these years, and that is what we continue to strive for today.

* * * *

Clearly, as the chief executive officer, I am ultimately accountable for everything that happens, both good and bad. But more than anything else, I am responsible for the tone at the top. To run a good and decent company with good and decent people. I work hard at setting the right tone. I spend a tremendous amount of time developing and selecting credo-based leaders and ensuring that we have the proper systems and controls in place.

But with more than 100,000 people throughout our family of companies, I must rely on all of our company leaders and their teams to do the right thing and work with me to instill credo values throughout their organizations. They share with me the challenge of being responsible for making sure we operate in accordance with our credo values in all that we do.

* * * *

Now, it has occurred to me that I am making all this sound kind of simple. It is not. In a highly competitive, financially driven world with the tyranny of quarterly earnings and with multiple constituencies, actually living the credo in a meaningful way is a constant challenge. At the end of the day, our credo is all about personal responsibility.

As you read through it, each of the four responsibilities outlined starts with the preposition "to" and that is very important. Said another way, our credo isn't about us being responsible for something. A school child is responsible for her backpack. An assembly line worker is responsible for placing a product in a package. But when you are responsible to, you are responsible "to a person" or "to a group of people." And that's what our credo says . . . we are responsible to our customers, mothers and fathers, doctors and nurses; responsible to employees; responsible to people in communities. This is an intrinsically subjective area precisely because it's personal. It's about owing part of yourself to others. It's a serious responsibility.

I'm no linguist, and so I don't know where the root of the two uses of a particular word in French come together, but I am struck that the word to be physically burdened with lots of luggage, chargé, is the same word used to describe a person who has taken on a responsibility. It's part of a title to indicate you're in charge. The idea is simple; when you're in charge, you are responsible. And this responsibility weighs heavily, particularly when you have to balance the interests of different people, all people you are responsible to.

* * * *

During my tenure at Johnson & Johnson, I've spent more time on people issues than anything else by far. People decisions are the ones that keep me awake at night. Let me give you an example.

Several years ago, we made the decision to close approximately 50 small plants around the world. It involved laying-off several thousand people, many in communities and countries in which I knew the people would have a very tough time finding comparable employment. We had never done anything like that before.

I worried about my responsibility to the men, women, and their families who would lose their jobs. But our operating costs at these small plants were way out of line, and we were becoming less and less competitive. So yes, I was responsible to our employees in those plants, but I was also responsible to the patients who needed our products to keep them affordable. And I was responsible to all of our other employees around the world to keep the company healthy and growing. The harsh reality was that a great many more would be hurt down the road if I failed to act and we became less and less competitive.

In addition to our employees, I was also responsible to the tens of thousands of stockholders (individuals, retired folks, pension plans, and mutual funds) who owned our stock. The facts were clear . . . I knew what had to be done, and we did it as thoughtfully and sensitively as possible. But the decision was hard, because it was personal.

At a deeper level, what became crystal clear was that competing on a global basis with Olympic-class companies had changed the ground rules forever. This new world meant that we could no longer guarantee that if you came to work every day and did your job well, you could count on being employed with us for life. That's the way it used to be, but that was a responsibility that we could no longer fulfill. Rather, we had to focus on making people employable for life. And that's where we put our resources, at lifelong development of skill sets that could be used in many different companies and industries.

The bright side to all of this is that being responsible to people has a tendency to become mutual. If I am responsible to you, you are more likely to be responsible to me, and that means I have colleagues I can trust. People are committed to people, not just to paychecks. There's a sense that we are all in it together. In our case, we're all working to get life-saving and life-enhancing products to people who need them. Improving the quality of life and healing and curing disease is our heritage and mission. Being bound together in one purpose makes us able to achieve incredible heights, not only as a group, but as individuals.

* * * *

We don't hire people into Johnson & Johnson and "credo-ize" them. They come to us with good values, and then we try to create an environment in which those values can be lived out. I don't think it's just luck, for example, that the companies known to offer great service are also those who reach out to communities, who are cited as good corporate citizens. I think all of these things stem from a place where people feel that responsibility to other people is part of their job. Where it's not just OK but expected that people take care of people—expected that leaders take care of people. Where values are indeed encouraged and respected.

I'm not saying that having core values guarantees success in every market condition. That's too simplistic, and we all know that's not true. Companies with great reputations run into problems all the time . . . look at HP, or Kodak, or Xerox, and the list goes on. But the point is that the folks at these companies have worked hard to do the right thing over many years. They continue to make huge efforts in innovation to keep up with and even overtake their fast-moving market.

But sometimes changing conditions are such that companies hit hard times, a rough patch, and they will have to sort it out and chart their course. We study other companies intensely . . . the high-flying ones and the ones going through tough times in tough industries. We particularly focus on their record of innovation. What are they doing that's new and innovative, and can we apply it to our company? The point is we are willing to learn from anyone, and we find that companies are more than willing to share ideas.

Is it harder to lead innovation in a company where there is such a strong heritage . . . a certain way of doing things based on a set of core values? Well it might be, and I'll be the first to admit that our values, while touching a place in people's hearts, make them feel more comfortable and safe in a shared sense of purpose. But there is a difference between feeling secure and being complacent.

Many pundits argue that to be truly innovative you must shake things up . . . create a sense of urgency. Make people see that they can't possibly continue in their old ways—threaten them, get their attention by scaring them to death. I suppose that's one way of doing it, but I don't agree with it.

It may take more time on the front end, but we've found that we get incredible results by taking the time to explain the challenges to our people and by working with them and letting them come up with the options and solutions. We try to create a sense of safe harbor where people can experiment and innovate and take intelligent risks. A climate where it's OK if you fail. The important thing is that you keep trying, striving to improve. It's your track record over time that we evaluate you on.

* * * *

You see there are two ways to get to the top of the mountain. Gear up and climb straight up the face, or take a more circuitous route, gaining a little bit of altitude as you cross the mountain sideways looping back and forth. There are people born to be rock climbers, and I, my friends, am not one of them.

I have the good fortune to lead a company that tends to take the longer route. True, we might not be as exciting to watch as a rock climber, but we deliver results day in and day out, year in and year out, decade in and decade out.

* * * *

Leaders can make values a priority that gets measured and rewarded. We can work hard at making sure that the company's values are well expressed, well-understood, explicit and visible in all that we do, in all of our programs, policies, products. But the most important thing is to set the proper personal example, the tone at the top.

Our values need to be visible to people like Sandhya, young people who will become the next generation of leaders. The leaders who will wrestle with increasingly complex problems in a complicated world. A world in which often there is no clear answer and where you are not sure of what the "right" thing to do is. Leaders with good judgment who know how to preserve important values and hold fast to them, while at the same time knowing when and how fast to change to meet the challenges of a new world.

If this all sounds interesting to you as you pursue your career, I would urge you to join a company rich in values. There are no perfect people, and there are no perfect companies. We all have our weaknesses and warts. But make sure the company you join has a set of core values that you are comfortable with, that you are proud of, and which will bring out the very best in you.

Thank you very much.

Reading **4-2**

Whistleblowing Today: *Critical Issues Facing Business Leadership*

Wim Vandekerckhove

Introduction

Whistleblowing is the deliberate, non-obligatory act of disclosure, by an individual with privileged access to data or information of an organization, about a non-trivial illegality or other wrongdoing under the control of that organization, to an entity who has the power to rectify the wrongdoing. The growing number of whistleblowing policies implemented by organizations and enacted by governments has made the question of whether that entity is internal or external to the organization less of an issue. Whistleblowing policies may protect whistleblowers from retaliation under certain conditions and these conditions may be stipulated in the whistleblowing policy. More precisely, whistleblowing policies specify who can make a protected disclosure (actor), what disclosures can be made (subject), and to whom the disclosure should be made (recipient).

The protection of whistleblowers against organizational retaliation became an issue in the early 1970's as a protest against the ethos of the 'organization man,' which demanded absolute loyalty of the employee to the employer. Whistleblower activism denounced organizational closure and advocated that public interest should at all times take priority over an organization's interest in secrecy. A lot has changed since the early 1970's. Managers and auditors now start to recognize the value of procedures that allow concerns to be raised inside the organization rather than force responsible employees to go outside. And governments increasingly prescribe whistleblowing policies through legislation. Today, there are whistleblowing laws not only in the US, but also very important ones in Australia, the UK, South Africa, New Zealand, Japan, Belgium, Roumania and Norway. Legal proposals are being discussed in the Netherlands, Canada, Ireland, India. In many more countries, discussions of legislation are underway (see Vandekerckhove 2006 for a discussion of these).

Research into the psychological profile of whistleblowers and the sociological characteristics of organisations where whistleblowing occurs (see Miceli and Near 1992 and Miethe 1999) has had an impact on whistleblowing advocacy. It has certainly helped to clarify some misunderstandings about whistleblowers and has led to greater acceptance by management of protection and internal procedures.

Nevertheless, some issues remain unsettled and this article discusses some of those issues. For example, while most whistleblowing policies require disclosures to be made in good faith, it remains troublesome to defend this requirement. As whistleblowing policies are implemented globally, the question of the extent to which cultural differences are restraining factors is an important yet unresolved issue. Another issue is whether whistleblowing can be conceived as a duty rather than just a right. Finally, whilst most internal procedures have been set up to receive anonymous disclosures, Europe seems to be heading a different direction by preferring confidential disclosures to anonymous ones. The reasons for that distinction are quite convincing, the responsibilities however are bigger as well.

Current Issues

Motive

Whether or not the whistleblower's motive ought to be taken into consideration before offering protection remains an unresolved issue. Most policies explicitly mention 'good intention' or 'genuine whistleblower' as a precondition for protection against retaliation.

One reason that it is featured might be to counter the standard argument against protection, namely that disgruntled employees abuse whistleblowing procedures by telling lies about their colleagues or line manager, only motivated by personal gain. Another reason might be the portrayal of whistleblowers in the media as moral heroes. Important, however, is that there is also a downside to mentioning motive as a condition for protection. Jubb (1999) left motive out of his definition of whistleblowing because motives may be mixed, misrepresented and very difficult, if not impossible, to decipher. Whilst the quality of a whistleblowing procedure or regulation can be measured by the clarity and lack of ambiguity of the conditions imposed on the protection, the introduction of a proper motive as a condition increases the arbitrariness of the protection. Who is to judge the whistleblower's motive? It makes raising concern much more risky for potential whistleblowers.

Moreover, the relevance of the whistleblower's motive is not that obvious, given the finality of whistleblower protection, namely to further the public interest. Indeed, as the report from the OECD work group on whistleblowing argued: 'as the purpose of a whistleblowing framework is to deter corruption rather than to encourage external disclosures, [labour representatives] were not persuaded that the motive or honesty of the whistleblower should be a critical factor in any new regime' (OECD 2000, 9).

The only whistleblowing policy that explicitly taps into personal gain motivated whistleblowing is the False Claims Act in the US, which offers rewards for information. The act establishes that anyone who sues in the name of the US government in relation to fraud also sues for herself. Basically, the idea is that the person or organization filing the lawsuit gets a percentage of the money the government is able to recover. Although the idea was raised during the parliamentary discussion in the Netherlands[1] and by the UK Home Office,[2] the False Claims Act provisions have not been taken over in any whistleblowing regulation so far. To reward personal gain motivated whistleblowing seems to be a US idiosyncrasy.

Collectivism vs. Individualism

This brings us to a next issue regarding whistleblowing, namely whether or not cultural differences are of any explanatory relevance. Here, a distinction must be made between possible differences in attitudes towards whistleblowing on the one side and differences in whistleblowing schemes on the other. Current research (Thomas and Miller 2005; Park et al 2005) seems to suggest that people from cultures where collectivism is more important than individualism are more likely to blow the whistle. However, whether they actually do is not known and also depends on organizational and regulatory features.

When we look at whistleblowing schemes and legislation, the story is somewhat different. Intuitively, one would expect national culture to matter a great deal as to how whistleblower protection is advocated. Not only do whistleblowing policies affect an organization's autonomy with regard to the wider society, protecting whistleblowers is also a serious intervention in how people relate to one another within organizations. Therefore, one could argue that certain 'good reasons' for protecting whistleblowers might work in one region of the world, but not in another.

Contrary to that intuition, Vandekerckhove (2006) concludes that the efficiency, accountability and corporate governance underpin whistleblowing schemes regardless of national cultures. It is as if these arguments constitute a semantic 'fit' above national cultures. This is no surprise if we acknowledge that describing and designing organizations and the relations between organizations and society through the concepts of flexibility, decentralization, governance, network and stakeholder, has become a global way of doing so. It appears as if this particular discourse on and from organizations has become more pervasive than national culture.

Hence, instead of emphasizing cultural differences, it might be more accurate to say that in those countries where organizations are increasingly described and problematized in terms of flexibility, decentralization, governance, network and stakeholder, whistleblowing policies appear as a necessity and hence are being enacted into legislation.

This is the case in Australia, where the antipathy towards 'dobbing' or betraying 'mateship' has precluded federal whistleblowing legislation covering the private sector, until HIH, Australia's second largest general insurer, collapsed in 2001. The HIH collapse could have been avoided, if only early warnings from an insider and several others to the Australian Prudential Regulatory Authority (APRA) asking to inspect HIH would have been followed up on. All of a sudden, the culture of 'mateship' was no longer convincing. Restoring investor trust acquired an urgency that was able to convince beyond the importance of 'mates'. In September 2002, federal government issues a policy proposal paper setting out ideas for protecting private sector whistleblowers.

In October 2003, a draft bill was released and by June 2004, the CLERP Act (Corporate Law Economic Reform Program) was a fact. The point I am trying to illustrate is that certain situations are perceived as necessities and can as such wipe away cultural arguments. In the case of Australia, the 'cultural' argument that seemed to have blocked private sector whistleblower protection for ten years, got washed away by one crisis. And all of a sudden, it is that same Australian private sector which is urging whistleblower protection to be legislated.

Another example is Japan where whistleblowing legislation was enacted in June 2004. For a country with one of the strongest corporatist cultures in the world, this sounds weird. Organizational loyalty in the old sense, the belief that illegality or malpractice should be overlooked or ignored for the sake of the corporation, is still very strong, but Japanese corporate culture is nevertheless showing cracks. Lifetime employment is fading, workforce reductions are taking place, and a lot of corporations have stopped offering low-price accommodation to their workers. Also the last ten years, notions such as 'accountability', 'freedom of information', 'governance', 'business ethics' have been taken up in the language (Miki 2004). Thus, it is not national culture that seems most relevant, but rather the extent to which the conceptual hegemony of globalization is cracking up that national culture that is important.

Right and Duty

Whistleblowing legislation has up till now only recognized the *right* to blow the whistle. Some exceptions are important, however. Specific 'gatekeeper' functions have been assigned the duty to report malpractice.

Recently, Boatright (2007) defined gatekeepers as intermediary parties—accountants, lawyers, and bankers—whose cooperation is necessary for business organizations to function and who by withholding cooperation are able to prevent significant misconduct. Boatright (2007: 620) notes that, although it is clear that an intermediary has a moral responsibility "not to knowingly provide substantial assistance to a client's wrongdoing," it is far less clear to what extent an intermediary is morally *obligated* to determine whether a client is committing some wrong. In other words, gatekeepers should not participate or facilitate wrongdoing; but what should they do to avoid such liability? And to what cost?

Tsahuridu and Vandekerckhove (2007) examine the boundaries between the right and the duty to blow the whistle. They submit that, if it is correct that internal whistleblowing procedures can be seen as institutional mechanisms supporting moral autonomy, then the successful implementation of such procedures theoretically annuls the distinction between right and duty. There then remains no excuse for not raising a concern. Hence, knowing about a malpractice but not speaking up makes one complicit to that malpractice.

All this might seem very academic humbug to the practitioner, were it not that some developments make this kind of work necessary. For example, the Sarbanes-Oxley Act does impose some liability on gatekeepers and Hassink et al (2007) comment that the majority of the European organizational whistleblowing policies adopted a tone that was at least moderately authoritative, with codes speaking of a requirement or duty to report violations, and employees who 'must', 'should' or 'are expected to' report these. More importantly, Hassink et al. (2007) found that in 30 percent of the policies reviewed, "it was made clear that failing to report a violation (remaining silent about a breach or concealing information about one) is a violation in itself." And although French and Belgian governmental privacy commissions have issued statements that whistleblowing schemes may not impose mandatory reporting on employees and that therefore, use of the reporting scheme must be optional, the whistleblowing policy of the European Commission, implemented after the Cresson crisis, maintains a mandatory disclosure procedure.[3]

Anonymous or Confidential

A fourth issue is whether whistleblowers should be allowed to make anonymous disclosures. It is sometimes argued that anonymity is the best protection. It is also the easiest way to solicit information without having a duty to protect those disclosing the information. In this sense, it should be no surprise that nearly all commercially operated 'hotlines' are anonymous whistleblowing schemes. By definition, anonymous whistleblowers cannot be protected, for the simple fact that we don't know who it is that we should be protecting. Also, anonymous reports are harder to investigate because there is no way to obtain additional information from the whistleblower. Finally, anonymous reporting facilities might increase the risk of slanderous reporting. A good alternative to anonymous reporting is confidential reporting. In such a scheme, the recipient knows the identity of the whistleblower but keeps it confidential from management or other parties.

Just recently, policy makers in Europe gave a clear signal that confidential schemes are to be preferred to anonymous ones. The provisions of the Sarbanes-Oxley Act enacted in the US in 2002 had also implications for oversees corporations that were traded on the US stock market. More precisely, these corporations had to comply with Section 301 of the Act, which stipulates that 'Each audit committee shall establish procedures for [. . .] the confidential, anonymous submission by employees [. . .] of concern regarding questionable accounting or auditing matters.' In Germany and France, labour unions had argued that some whistleblowing schemes set up by corporations were unlawful. Court rulings confirmed this, by stating that whistleblowing schemes were not compatible with the European Directive on privacy (Directive 95/46/EC). Of course this caused a huge dilemma for some major European companies. Meanwhile, there is an advice paper from the Article 29 Working Party (approved in February 2006), which states that confidential reporting is to be preferred to anonymous reporting. Also, the French CNIL (Commission nationale de l'informatique en des libertés) issued a 'guideline document' in November 2005, in which it finds the encouragement of anonymous reporting unacceptable and suggests restrictive handling of anonymous reporting. This position was followed by the Belgian Privacy Commission early 2006. If the guidelines from these authorities are followed up on, then it might very well be that the European whistleblowing scheme will differ from that elsewhere in the world.

How to Mitigate Ethical Risks in Whistleblowing

The discourse on organisations that became dominant from the 1990's on—and that is based on procedural normative concepts like 'decentralisation', 'flexibility', 'network', 'corporate governance', 'integrity', 'trust', 'stakeholder'—implicates the necessity of gathering information outside of the hierarchical line about the production process. As a result, internal audits, board-disclosure and internal whistleblowing procedures are increasingly put forward as important corporate governance mechanisms.

Although this reformulated whistleblowing argument has been successful in the sense that significant progress was made on whistleblowing legislation worldwide, this reformulation—internal whistleblowing as a corporate governance mechanism—also entails new ethical risks. Although internal whistleblowing is justified within the dominant organisational discourse—gathering information in this way is necessary in order to guarantee efficiency, risk management and good governance—these justifications entail particular modalities of implementation that ethically are not unproblematic. These ethical risks include the following:

- Over-responsibilisation of the individual employee—institutionalisation of the employee into the guardian of organisational legitimacy,
- Fading of the distinction between the right and the duty of an employee to report suspected wrongdoing,
- A shift from whistleblower protection as a means to hold organisations accountable for social responsibilities, to whistleblowing procedures as a mean to hold employees accountable for their performance and engagement. Characteristic for this shift is: absence of unions as recipients in internal whistleblowing procedures, restriction of subjects allowed to report on, the omission of external recipients in procedures communicated to employees, restriction of persons who can be recognised as whistleblowers to current employees,
- Neglect of the necessity to protect internal whistleblowers against retaliation as a result of merely focussing on gathering information. Characteristic of this neglect is the preference of anonymous procedures above confidential procedures.

What these risks boil down to is that, instead of providing organisational support for the moral autonomy of employees, internal whistleblowing procedures make employees liable both when they raise concern—for example when internal procedures are so complex the employee is bound to make mistakes—as well as when they remain silent while knowing what was going wrong.

Mitigating these risks is an important task for managers and policy makers if the full potential of whistleblowing policies for the well-being of business and society is to be realized. Two areas of attention that can help to mitigate these ethical risks are first the significant distinction between concern and allegation; and second the importance of independent advice.

When making an allegation, one is convinced that there is wrongdoing. Allegations also include naming someone who is causing the wrongdoing—a colleague, a manager or 'the' organisation. Hence someone is being accused. If whistleblowing takes the form of an allegation and someone is being accused, all kinds of defence strategies are unlocked and there is a big chance that the messenger will get shot while the attention shifts from the alleged wrongdoing to the personal row which whistleblowing has then become. When whistleblowing takes the form of an allegation, there is no way back. If the whistleblower was mistaken, false accusations have been made and a counter charge for defamation is likely to follow. It is obvious that no one benefits from this.

In contrast to those circumstances, raising a concern is articulating a worry. No proof is needed and no accusation is made. Rather, raising a concern is an invitation to look into the matter—'I am not sure but something might be going wrong'. Raising a concern is much less charged than making an allegation. Moreover, concerns allow for a way back as it might be very reasonable for someone to have that particular concern in a given situation. Hence, if organisations could implement their internal whistleblowing policy in such a way that it invites employees to raise concerns rather than forces them to make allegations, much of the watchdog atmosphere and explosive rows around whistleblowing can be avoided. The difficulty is how to do this. Much has to do with building trust between employees and management. Hence it must be clear that it takes time for an organisation to realise a concern-raising-and-allegation-avoiding culture. What certainly helps this culture come about is clearly communicating to employees that raising concern is encouraged by management and is preferred to making allegations.

This brings us to the second area of attention when mitigating ethical risks, namely the importance of independent advice. Consulting a lawyer prior to raising a concern informs a potential whistleblower on his rights and duties. It gives them a clear image on where they stand. This is completely safe for the organisation—unless it intends to retaliate against the whistleblower—as the lawyer is bounded by confidentiality. It must be clear that getting legal advice should not be confounded with making a disclosure, or contacting a whistleblower organisation or self-help group. It must also be clear that external legal advice augments trust because the person giving the advice is in no way tied to the organisation. An exception to this is Public Concern at Work, a UK charity that is dedicated to offer free legal advice to potential whistleblowers. The charity also advises public authorities and policy makers in the UK and because it has done exemplary work also in the rest of the world. Some business organisations in the UK explicitly state in their internal whistleblowing policy that employees can get legal advice from Public Concern at Work. The charity nevertheless retains its independence because of its reputation built by its role as the forerunner of whistleblowing policy in Europe. No parallel to that organisation exists in any other European country. Perhaps in the US, the GAP (Government Accountability Project) comes close, and in South Africa the ODAC (Open Democracy Advice Centre) might come close.

The Whistleblowing Paradox

Despite all the research into whistleblowing, all the whistleblowing legislation out there, and all the good reasons for organisations to take their whistleblowers seriously, internal (let alone external) whistleblowing remains a difficult and at times a messy issue. Why? Perhaps I can best describe it with the following paradox. The kind of organisations that are able to implement internal whistleblowing procedures in a satisfactory way—they actually work and employees trust them—are the kind of organisations that strictly speaking do not need them, because they already have the organisational culture in which people do and are encouraged to raise concern. On the other hand, the kind of organisations that really need internal procedures—because things are going terribly wrong and no one dares to speak out—are not capable of zimplementing them so that they will actually work, because no one trusts anything management does.

Hence the difficulty lies in changing an organisation that is incapable of making internal whistleblowing procedures work into an organisation that does not need them. Perhaps the best way to bring about that change is to start implementing one. Not just out of the blue but with knowledge of the research on whistleblowing, of the good reasons for doing so, while learning from others' experience in doing so and while carefully mitigating the ethical risks involved.

End Notes

1. The discussion took place in 2004 in 'De Tweede Kamer', which is the name for parliament in the Netherlands. During that discussion, Marijnissen from the Socialist Party tabled a list of suggestions from his party towards a better and more effective fight against fraud. One of his suggestions was to offer whistleblowers, besides protection through labour law, a substantial reward. The same was suggested by Halsema–from Green Left–who called for a 'whistleblower fund' from which whistleblowers could be paid a financial reward if they come up with hard evidence on big fraud cases. (see Handelingen Tweede Kamer (2004: 3660-3710 and the notes on pages 3735–37).
2. Also, in 2007, the UK Home Office started a debate on whether citizens and employees who blow the whistle should be rewarded with a percentage of the penalties or damages paid by the wrongdoer. The debate had been initiated in the context of a Home Office review of how the Assets Recovery Agency could meet its targets of recovering £250 million a year.

Public Concern at Work rejected this idea in its response to the Home Office consultation (PCAW 2007).

3. Art 22a of the Staff Regulations of Officials of the European Communities, see OLAF (2005).

References

Note: Notes and references removed for publication here, but are available on the book website at www.mhhe.com/busethics2e.

Reading 4-3

Assessment and Plan for Organizational Culture Change at NASA

The *Columbia* Accident Investigation Board

Editors' note: Following the accident that destroyed the Space Shuttle *Columbia* in 2003, the National Aeronautics and Space Administration (NASA) appointed the *Columbia* Accident Investigation Board (CAIB) to investigate the causes of the accident. The loss of *Columbia* came eighteen years after the Space Shuttle *Challenger* exploded during take-off. The CAIB report identified the organizational culture at NASA as having "as much to do with the accident as the External Tank foam." Following the CAIB report, NASA hired an outside consulting firm, Behavioral Science Technology (BST), to recommend changes in the organization. This reading is taken from the BST report of their investigation. As was the case following the *Challenger* disaster, responsibility for the accident was attributed as much to the culture and practices of NASA as it was to physical or mechanical causes.

Executive Summary

On February 1, 2003, the Space Shuttle *Columbia* and its crew of seven were lost during return to Earth. A group of distinguished experts was appointed to comprise the *Columbia* Accident Investigation Board (CAIB), and this group spent six months conducting a thorough investigation of the cause of the accident. The CAIB found that NASA's history and culture contributed as much to the *Columbia* accident as any technical failure.

As a result of the CAIB and related activities, NASA established the objective of completely transforming its organizational and safety culture. BST was selected to assist NASA in the development and implementation of a plan for changing the safety climate and culture Agency wide. The scope of this effort is to develop and deploy an organizational culture change initiative within NASA, with an emphasis on safety climate and culture.

The first task assigned to BST was to conduct an assessment of the current status and develop an implementation plan, both to be completed within 30 days. This report summarizes the assessment findings and the recommended implementation plan.

This assessment concluded that there are many positive aspects to the NASA culture. The NASA culture reflects a long legacy of technical excellence, a spirit of teamwork and pride, and a can-do approach to task achievement. In particular, culture attributes related to work group functioning at the peer level are among the strongest we have seen. These characteristics are consistent with NASA's rating in the 2003 Office of Personnel Management Survey at the top of the Best Places to Work in the Federal Government.

Despite these positive attributes, there are some important needs for improvement. The present NASA culture does not yet fully reflect the Agency's espoused core values of Safety, People, Excellence, and Integrity. The culture reflects an organization in transition, with many ongoing initiatives and lack of a clear sense at working levels of "how it all fits together."

- **Safety** is something to which NASA personnel are strongly committed in concept, but NASA has not yet created a culture that is fully supportive of safety. Open communication is not yet the norm and people do not feel fully comfortable raising safety concerns to management.
- **People** do not feel respected or appreciated by the organization. As a result, the strong commitment people feel to their technical work does not transfer to a strong commitment to the organization.
- **Excellence** is a treasured value when it comes to technical work, but is not seen by many NASA personnel as an imperative for other aspects of the organization's functioning (such as management skills, supporting administrative functions, and creating an environment that encourages excellence in communications.)
- **Integrity** is generally understood and manifested in people's work. However, there appear to be pockets where the management chain has (possibly unintentionally) sent signals that the raising of issues is not welcome. This is inconsistent with an organization that truly values integrity.

There is an opportunity and need to become an organization whose espoused values are fully integrated into its culture—an organization that "lives the values" by fostering cultural integrity. We recommend an initiative with that as its theme.

The recommended initiative should address working through existing leaders to instill behaviors consistent with the Agency's values and the desired culture, while also establishing the foundation for developing future leaders who will sustain that culture and individual contributors who reflect the desired culture in their actions. A long-term (three year) plan is identified with a specific series of actions identified in the first five months to launch this effort.

BST's first efforts were to understand the current culture and climate at NASA in order to identify focus areas for improvement. We approached this task with the belief that there was much that was positive about NASA's culture. Our challenge was to build from positive aspects of the existing culture, strengthening the culture and at the same time addressing the issue raised in the CAIB report.

By culture we mean the shared values and beliefs of an organization—commonly described as "the way we do things here." The culture can also be thought of as the shared norms for the behavior in the organization, often motivated by unstated assumptions.

Where organizational culture comprises unstated assumptions that govern how we do things within an organization, climate describes the prevailing influences on a particular area of functioning (such as safety) at a particular time. Thus, the culture is something that is more deeply embedded and long-term, taking longer to change and influencing organizational performance across many areas of functioning. Climate, on the other hand, changes faster and more immediately reflects the attention of leadership.

Culture influences behavior in that the group's shared norms and beliefs will influence what people do. However, leaders' behavior is an important influence on culture. Through the examples they set, the messages they send, and the consequences they provide, leaders influence the behaviors of others, as well as their beliefs about what is acceptable and what is valuable to the organization.

The CAIB had produced a detailed report on the causes of the *Columbia* accident, and explicitly addressed "organizational causes" as the critical contributor. Specifically, the CAIB identified the following organizational cause of the *Columbia* accident:

> "The organizational causes of this accident are rooted in the Space Shuttle Program's history and culture, including the original compromises that were required to gain approval for the Shuttle Program, subsequent years of resource constraints, fluctuating priorities, schedule pressures, mischaracterizations of the Shuttle as operational rather than developmental, and lack of an agreed national vision. Cultural traits and organizational practices detrimental to safety and reliability were allowed to develop, including: reliance on past success as

a substitute for sound engineering practices (such as testing to understand why systems were not performing in accordance with requirements/specifications); organizational barriers which prevented effective communication of critical safety information and stifled professional differences of opinion; lack of integrated management across program elements; and the evolution of an informal chain of command and decision making processes that operated outside the organization's rules. In the Board's view, NASA's organizational culture and structure had as much to do with this accident as the External Tank foam. Organizational culture refers to the values, norms, beliefs, and practices that govern how an institution functions. At the most basic level, organizational culture defines the assumptions that employees make as they carry out their work. It is a powerful force that can persist through reorganizations and the reassignment of key personnel."

Source: The full *Columbia* Accident Investigation Board report is available at http://caib.nasa.gov/.

Reading 4-4

Does the Company Get It?—20 Questions to Ask Regarding Compliance, Ethics, and Risk Management[1]

OCEG

This OCEG questionnaire has been designed as a tool that can be used to determine whether a company has an effective process and culture in place to control and mitigate compliance and ethics related risks.

Questions 1 through 3 address organizational culture to determine if a company is taking the formal steps necessary to address the subject of compliance and ethics—and whether management, the Board of Directors and the employees really believe that compliance and ethics are an integral part of the company's corporate culture. A stakeholder should evaluate whether the company has seriously considered all of the enterprise risks of non-compliance or unethical conduct, has established its own goals and objectives, and has communicated its behavioral expectations effectively throughout the organization.

Questions 4 and 5 consider scope and strategy of the compliance and ethics program, assessing how thoroughly it can address potential risks. Most important is the integration of that process with overall enterprise risk management. The Securities & Exchange Commission expects compliance and ethics issues to be considered even when fast-paced decisions must be made. Stakeholders in publicly traded companies must be able to determine whether the compliance and ethics program is sufficiently broad in scope and well enough planned to address this need.

Questions 6 through 8 identify the structure and resources dedicated to the ethics and compliance program, judging the seriousness of commitment to effective management of the program. It is the audit committee's responsibility to ensure that a structural process is in place that encourages both top-down communication and bottom up feedback, and that issues are dealt with quickly and completely. If the proper resources are not funded and in place to prevent the audit committee from becoming a "choke point," the program will be judged a failure, and the blame for inadequately addressing enterprise risk will be placed on upper management.

Questions 9 through 14 evaluate management of policies and training, and further address program adequacy by looking at the mechanics of the processes in place. These questions evaluate how Codes of Conduct and other policies are distributed, tracked and kept up to date, and under what circumstances they can be waived or overridden. They also address how employees and other stakeholders are trained to understand and apply established policies and procedures, and how information is communicated to them.

Questions 15 through 18 focus on internal enforcement, assessing whether the company appropriately and consistently deals with violations of established policies and procedures. If individuals are allowed to ignore, disobey or even mock the objectives and requirements of the compliance and ethics program, stakeholders can conclude that management is not fully committed to ensuring ethical conduct.

Questions 19 and 20 assess evaluation and continual improvement efforts in the compliance and ethics program. Without processes to judge program elements and implement necessary improvements, any compliance and ethics program will have difficulty staying efficient, effective and up to date. Well-developed routine monitoring and periodic assessment processes, with clear paths for communication of recommended changes, may be the best sign of a mature and effective management system.

Culture

1. What does your organization say about compliance, ethics, and values in its formal mission and vision statement?

Why Ask This Question?

Review of the formal mission and vision statement gives the investor some insight into the organization's compliance and ethics values and commitments. An investor should look at the scope of this statement to see if the organization addresses some or all of the following constituencies: employees, customers, suppliers, shareholders, and the community/society at large.

Potential Answers

- There is a separate formal compliance and ethics mission and vision statement.
- There is no formal mission and vision statement but there is a general Code of Conduct.
- Mission and vision for compliance and ethics is part of the overall organizational mission and vision statement.

Red Flags

- The absence of a formal statement may indicate that management is not taking a necessary first step regarding compliance and ethics management. In addition, this may violate Sarbanes-Oxley provisions and listing requirements (if publicly traded).
- A boiler plate or unspecific mission statement indicates lack of thought, and possibly commitment, to an effective compliance and ethics function.

2. How does your Board, and management, set the "tone at the top" and communicate compliance and ethics values, mission, and vision?

Why Ask This Question?

An organization that can articulate the formal and informal processes that it uses to communicate mission, vision, and values exhibits a clear understanding of the need for leadership in compliance and ethics and the benefit of strong communication of Board and management commitment.

Potential Answers

- Distribute a Code of Conduct.
- Email all employees regularly.
- Communicate responsibilities in annual/quarterly meeting.
- Discussion of mission, vision and values in staff meetings and at presentations by leadership.

Red Flags

- If top leadership does not periodically or continuously communicate the values, mission, and vision (which represent the expectations of the organization), employees and other stakeholders may believe the formal statements lack credibility and executive backing.
- Passive or canned communications are often ignored by employees. More active forms of

communicating expectations (e.g., inclusion of compliance and ethics criteria in performance reviews and compensation structures/decisions) send a clearer message.

3. How do you know if your employees and other stakeholders are "convinced" that the organization is serious about its compliance and ethics responsibilities?

Why Ask This Question?

When an organization can answer this question, indicating that its leadership and management at least tries to measure stakeholder beliefs, it evidences a strong commitment to follow through and support for its values, mission and vision. In addition, the answer to this question will help to measure whether the communications are understood and whether or not the actual mission, vision and values are embraced by employees.

Potential Answers

- Annual survey.
- Focus groups or interviews.
- Collect data during annual reviews.
- Exit interviews.
- Informal conversations.

Red Flags

- No effort is made to collect or determine employee and other stakeholder perceptions—This may indicate management is passively or affirmatively ignorant of the perceptions on the "shop floor." It may also mean that leadership views its job as done when a mission statement is issued.
- Company says it is "too expensive" to poll employees—There are inexpensive means of polling employee perceptions. Leadership and management should have some interest in knowing if their message is heard and believed.
- Company says it doubts the value of poll results in determining true employee beliefs—This may indicate that even the leadership does not believe that its mission and values are taken seriously, and that it knows that "practice" does not follow the company's stated "principles."

Scope/Strategy

4. What is the scope of your compliance and ethics program and how does it integrate with your overall business strategy?

Why Ask This Question?

If an organization understands its domestic risks, but has little understanding of its international risks, problems may arise. Similarly, the company may deal with compliance and ethics risks in functional "Domains" of Financial Assurance, Employment, Environmental, etc. with little coordination between them, and may effectively address certain areas of concern but fail to address others. Coordination of the compliance and ethics function with larger business strategy and goals is also essential.

Potential Answers

- We address compliance and ethics globally/locally.
- We address compliance and ethics issues in each function separately.
- Reactive or proactive consideration of business strategy in development or management of compliance and ethics functions.

Red Flags

- Inability to articulate a meaningful program—This may indicate a well developed and managed program does not exist, or that management is unaware of the program's operations. In either case, severe legal risk exists.
- Inability to articulate relationship between program and larger business strategy—this may indicate low level consideration by management to compliance and ethics functions.

5. How do you assess compliance and ethics risks and how does this process integrate with enterprise risk management (ERM)?

Why Ask This Question?

The more detailed and routine the risk assessment process, the more likely it is effective. In addition, understanding of ERM (e.g., COSO ERM) and integration with enterprise-wide analysis of risk may indicate a higher level of leadership and management concern for compliance and ethics functions.

Potential Answers

- Compliance and ethics risks are considered as part of our quarterly/annual risk management process.
- We deal with compliance and ethics risks in our compliance department (or legal office). They tell us what we need to do.

Red Flags

- Inability to articulate how legal and ethical risks are considered as part of ERM—This may indicate that management does not fully consider and analyze where legal and ethical risks are present. It may also indicate that legal and ethical risk management is not appropriately funded.
- Inability to understand ERM—This may indicate management does not have a comprehensive understanding of risks that may impede the organization from reaching its objectives.

Structure/Resources

6. What position in the organization provides oversight and leadership in the compliance/ethics function and where does this position fall in the organizational chart?

Why Ask This Question?

It is vital to know where responsibility for the compliance and ethics function falls in order to determine the level of influence and independence held by the person or people in such management positions. The identification of a chief compliance/ethics officer, the chain of authority this person (or people) reports within, the level of access to the Board, and which Board committee has oversight all serve as indicators of the strength and value attributed to the compliance and ethics function. In addition, it is valuable to know if compliance and ethics responsibilities are separated within the entity or combined. If separated, it is vital to learn how they coordinate.

Potential Answers

- Full-time chief compliance and ethics officer/Part-time chief compliance and ethics officer.
- Chief ethics officer and separate lower level compliance managers within functional areas.
- Reports to the CEO/general counsel/dotted-line to the audit committee, etc.

Red Flags

- Independence is questionable—Without sufficient independence, the chief compliance and ethics officer may not be objective when viewing the activities of senior executives.
- Lack of senior level oversight—Federal Sentencing Guidelines indicate that a sufficiently senior level executive should provide program oversight.
- Lack of adequate coordination between "ethics" and "compliance" management.

7. What is the organizational structure of your compliance and ethics management team?

Why Ask This Question?

Different organizational structures are appropriate for different organizations and the answer to this question allows analysis of the appropriateness of structure and the actual commitment of resources to compliance and ethics.

Potential Answers

- Centralized vs. Decentralized. Dedicated Team vs. Shared or "Virtual" Team where compliance and ethics management responsibilities are part of other job roles.

Red Flags

- Structure does not match larger organization—An investor should be careful to note if the structure makes sense given the nature of the organization. For example, a centralized team of

3 people is probably inconsistent with a global conglomerate of 50,000 employees.

- A team that relies solely on part-time managers with other duties may not have adequately dedicated resources

8. How are resources allocated for compliance and ethics management activities, both routinely and to address significant issues that arise?

Why Ask This Question?

How an organization determines to spend money and time on compliance and ethics matters is a good indication of the seriousness with which it takes these commitments and obligations.

Potential Answers

- Unified budget.
- Part of several department budgets.
- Funds identified for potential issues that risk analysis indicates may arise in a given budget cycle.

Red Flags

- No budget or unclear articulation of the budget may indicate the organization has seriously underfunded compliance and ethics management activities.
- Disconnected budget—If the budget is not directed by the chief compliance and ethics officer, it may indicate that there is a lack of coordinated strategy.
- Short term budget determinations without long range budgets to address anticipated future needs may indicate lack of adequate planning and analysis.

Policies

9. What does your Code of Conduct address and who receives it?

Why Ask This Question?

SOX and the Exchanges require a Code of Conduct for publicly traded companies. Beyond these requirements, a comprehensive Code of Conduct (or collection of policies) addressing all legal and regulatory requirements, expectations of employee/management behavior, ethical business conduct and social responsibility indicates an organization which has evaluated its values and decided how to articulate them.

Potential Answers

- The organization should be able to furnish its Code of Conduct and other policies, and identify the audience to whom they are distributed.
- The leadership and management should know the scope and content of the Code of Conduct and, in general, other policies.

Red Flags

- No Code of Conduct—This is such a widely accepted practice that it should be considered a basic requirement.
- Code is "canned"—If the Code of Conduct looks and feels like a generic policy, it may indicate that the organization has not thoughtfully addressed its unique compliance and ethics risk areas. As well, employees will most likely believe it is simple "window dressing" rather than a real guidepost for conduct.
- A Code of Conduct that does not adequately address all risk areas of the organization or clear ly enunciate company values and expectations for behavior.

10. How do you distribute your Code of Conduct and confirm that employees both receive and understand the Code and other policies?

Why Ask This Question?

This gives insight into whether or not the Code is simply a piece of paper that is signed by each employee and filed for legal purposes—or if some confirmation of "understanding" is sought; a clear indication of leadership's seriousness in demanding compliance with the Code and policies.

Potential Answers

- Distribute paper Code with new hire training and have employees sign it.
- Distribute the Code electronically each year with a multiple choice test.
- Present the Code of Conduct in live or electronic training sessions with opportunity for questions and discussion.

Red Flags

- No confirmation of receipt—This may indicate that, although it exists, the code is not being properly sent to employees.
- Weak confirmation of understanding—In addition to distributing the Code of Conduct, the organization should strive to ensure that the Code is understood by employees and other stakeholders.
- Too expensive—If an organization says that it is cost prohibitive to distribute the Code of Conduct to all employees with confirmation of receipt; it is probably unaware of many low cost and free tools. It also most likely indicates a low level of leadership commitment to the Code.

11. What is your process for updating policies/procedures?

Why Ask This Question?

Evidence of an established process for updating policies and procedures indicates a well managed component of the compliance and ethics program. Absence of such may indicate inadequate resources or lack of commitment to the program.

Potential Answers

- Annual review, quarterly review, etc.
- Notification from trade associations or outside counsel/consultants of changes in law/regulations.

Red Flags

- No process or infrequent updates—This may indicate that the organization is "out of date" with regard to its compliance and ethics risks.
- Sole reliance on periodic and non-routine updates from outside counsel/associations.
- No consideration of changes in organizational activities/locales, etc.

12. Can any requirements established by the Code of Conduct and other policies be waived or overridden and, if so, what is the process for doing so?

Why Ask This Question?

It is not inappropriate to provide for override of Code and policy requirements in certain circumstances, but it is important to know when and how they can be waived, and to ensure that a transparent process for doing so in place.

Potential Answers

- All waivers must be approved by the Board and included in Board minutes.
- There is no formal process, but waiver decisions are made on a case-by-case basis by the Board, or management, or counsel.

Red Flags

- No process or a very loose case-by-case process.
- Lack of transparency/no waivers are disclosed.

Communication and Training

13. How often, and by what methods, does your management communicate the values, mission, and vision of the compliance and ethics program to employees and other stakeholders?

Why Ask This Question?

Having a mission statement is not enough—it is important to know that it is regularly and effectively communicated to employees and stakeholders so that they know the organization's values and believe that the organization's leadership is serious about acting on those values.

Potential Answers

- Annual meeting for employees.
- Annual report for shareholders.

- Each master supplier agreement contains a statement regarding our Code of Conduct.
- Regular and routine reference to the Code of Conduct in all presentations by leadership about the organization's activities, plans and future.
- Regular and routine informal reference to values and mission by all levels of management.

Red Flags

- Lack of formal communication.
- 100% of communication is formal—While formal communications are important, most research confirms that employees gain much from informal communications from senior executives and managers about compliance and ethics responsibilities.

14. Do you provide comprehensive training and conduct performance evaluations for each job role to ensure compliance and ethics responsibilities are understood and followed, and that necessary skills are learned and employed?

Why Ask This Question?

Effective processes for ensuring employees have and use the information and skills needed to ulfill their compliance and ethics responsibilities is a critical component of an effective program. "Policies" do not necessarily equal "Performance."

Potential Answers

- For each role, we have a compliance and ethics curriculum.
- We embed some compliance and ethics training in each of our courses.
- We embed compliance and ethics criteria into our job evaluations.

Red Flags

- No training or claimed "on the job" training.
- New hire "dunk"—When all new employees are "dunked" into the same new hire program, regardless of job role, it may indicate that the organization has not clearly identified compliance and ethics risks as the apply to each job. As well, this may be viewed by DOJ and the courts as a lack of effort on the part of the organization (see Ad Hoc Committee on Federal Sentencing Guidelines for Organizations).
- Training only upon initial hiring—research shows training must be repeated for adequate learning. As well, the Federal Sentencing Guidelines for Organizations appear to head in the direction of increased training (see Ad Hoc Committee on Federal Sentencing Guidelines for Organizations).
- No consideration of compliant or ethical behavior in performance reviews or, even worse, positive evaluation or rewards even in the face of noncompliant behavior.

Issue Management

15. How do employees, agents and other stakeholders raise issues regarding compliance and ethics-related matters?

Why Ask This Question?

Providing effective avenues to raise issues without fear of retribution is a critical component of an effective program. It is important to know how employees and other stakeholders can raise issues and to confirm that they not only know how to do so, but also feel safe and comfortable in doing so or are even encouraged and rewarded.

Potential Answers

- Telephone helpline staffed by internal/external personnel.
- Web-based format.
- Email program.
- In person to supervisor or designated person.

Red Flags

- No help contribution line mechanism for immediate reporting of critical issues.
- No possibility of anonymous reporting.
- Lack of access for stakeholders who are not employees.

- Lack of consistent call-handling or report of issue management.
- Inability to certify that stakeholders are aware of the mechanism—This may indicate that the organization is not in compliance with Sarbanes-Oxley section 301.

16. How do you handle compliance and ethics issues that arise and scrutinize the sources of compliance failures?

Why Ask This Question?

It is not enough that a mechanism exists to report issues—management must have effective and consistent methods for managing and resolving issues and the source of recurrent problems.

Potential Answers

- Consistent process for all issues that can be fully explained and demonstrated.
- Consistent process for issues within a particular Domain (employment, financial, environmental, etc.), but not for all relevant Domains.
- Case by case basis.

Red Flags

- Lack of consistency.
- Lack of independent processing.
- Lack of scrutiny of sources of repeat problems.

17. How consistently, and in what way, have you taken action against violators of the Code and Program?

Why Ask This Question?

This gives insight into whether the organization has put some real "teeth" in the compliance and ethics program by disciplining violators.

Potential Answers

- Each organization should be able to provide examples of past actions taken.

Red Flags

- Termination of employment should be a possible outcome for failing to meet compliance or ethics requirements. Without this potential, employees and other stakeholder may not believe there are "teeth" to the program.
- Lack of consistency—If noncompliant or unethical behavior is tolerated, the program has no credibility.

18. What is the process for determining which issues are escalated to the Board and for informing the Board when issues are resolved?

Why Ask This Question?

This gives insight into the process for escalating and reporting compliance and ethics issues to the Board—and whether or not the Board is actually involved in the process and resolution of issues when appropriate.

Potential Answers

- Quarterly report to the audit committee regarding "significant" financial issues.
- Annual report to the Board regarding "significant" issues in all Domains (financial, employment, environmental, etc.).
- Report to Board, through legal counsel, of material risks presented by issues that arise.
- Board notification and involvement only in financial assurance areas or issues directly related to Board or Senior Management actions.

Red Flags

- No escalation criteria.
- No follow-up by Board.

Evaluation

19. What ongoing processes are in place to monitor the effectiveness of the compliance and ethics program?

Why Ask This Question?

This gives insight into whether the organization monitors efficacy and relative performance of its program against peers. Right now, true benchmarking is difficult due to inconsistent approaches, etc. Initiatives such as OCEG should help to solve this problem.

Potential Answers

- We perform annual internal audit of compliance and ethics controls.
- We perform periodic benchmarking with industry peers.
- We retain outside consultants to perform external audit of controls in some or all functional areas.
- We measure and keep records of compliance and ethics issues over time for use in improving controls.

Red Flags

- No process.
- Process lacks independence.
- Process has no ongoing, day to day component—only widely spaced periodic audits.
- Audits only determine that controls are followed, not that they are effective.

20. Does the organization engage an external law firm or consultant to audit compliance and ethics program elements?

Why Ask This Question?

While some organizations view external audits as a negative policing of employees, there is value in an independent external analysis of the effectiveness of selected controls and level of compliance with those controls. External assessors can also bring new ideas and tools to the attention of management.

Potential Answers

- We use our outside counsel.
- We use our external auditor/some other auditor.
- We use an outside risk management or ethics consultant.

Red Flags

- Process lacks independence.
- Process only judges compliance with selected controls and does not evaluate the appropriateness of the controls or their effectiveness in achieving compliance and ethical behavior.

End Note

1. Open Compliance and Ethics Group (OCEG), *Internal Audit Guide* (May 2006).

Chapter 5

Corporate Social Responsibility

Business has to take account of its responsibilities to society in coming to its decisions, but society has to accept its responsibilities for setting the standards against which those decisions are made.[1]

Sir Adrian Cadbury

By "social responsibility," we mean the intelligent and objective concern for the welfare of society that restrains individual and corporate behavior from ultimately destructive activities, no matter how immediately profitable, and leads in the direction of positive contributions to human betterment, variously as the latter may be defined.[2]

Kenneth R. Andrews

We are not in business to make maximum profit for our shareholders. We are in business . . . to serve society. Profit is our reward for doing it well. If business does not serve society, society will not long tolerate our profits or even our existence.[3]

Kenneth Dayton, former Chairman of the Dayton-Hudson Corporation

You never expect justice from a company, do you? They neither have a soul to lose nor a body to kick.

Sydney Smith, 1771–1845, English writer, clergyman

Opening Decision Point

Social Entrepreneurship: Banking on Poverty

Is it possible to create and run a for-profit business that has the goal of helping the poor as its strategic mission? Combining profitability with a social mission is the insight of **Social Entrepreneurship,** a movement that seeks to address social problems through the creativity and efficiency of market forces. Social Entrepreneurship differs from the work of non-profit groups such as NGOs and corporate foundations in that social entrepreneurs explicitly aim to be profitable.

Social entrepreneurship involves the standard entrepreneurial characteristics of innovation, creativity, and risk-taking, but marshals these skills to address social needs. Entrepreneurs are among the first who identify an untapped market and then are creative in developing a means for meeting this demand and are willing to take the risk that their creation will, in fact, satisfy the demand. For social entrepreneurs, the untapped market is a social and ethical need such as social justice, environmental protection, education, or health care. As Bill Drayton, the founder of Ashoka, a leading support structure for social entrepreneurs, has said, "social entrepreneurs are not content just to give a fish or teach how to fish. They will not rest until they have revolutionized the fishing industry."

One of the best-known Social Entrepreneurs is Muhammad Yunus, founder of the Grameen Bank in Bangladesh. An economist who began his career as a university professor in the United States, Yunus returned to his native Bangladesh in the early 1970s soon after that country gained its independence from Pakistan. Yunus hoped he could contribute to this new country's independence with his expertise in economics. Bangladesh was a desperately poor country struggling with the effects of a harsh famine. Yunus soon came to believe that the people of Bangladesh needed more direct help than what he could offer in a university economics class.

While touring the rural villages one day (the name "Grameen" translates as rural or village in the Bengali language), he met a small group of women who were making bamboo stools that they later sold at local markets. The women explained that they borrowed money from local money-lenders to purchase supplies, sometimes paying as much as 10 percent interest each week. Supplies cost only pennies a day, but after repaying their loans the women earned two cents each day. This amount kept the women and their families in a cycle of poverty, earning just enough to repay debts but never enough to escape debt. After investigating further, Yunus and his students concluded that the entire village was kept in debt by borrowing an amount less than 27 dollars. The idea for the Grameen Bank was born from the recognition that very small amounts of capital, loaned directly to poor people at low rates, could have a tremendous positive impact in helping entire villages escape a cycle of poverty. The Grameen Bank's business model is to lend small amounts of money directly to the poorest people, with no collateral, to help them establish and sustain small businesses.

Grameen's approach to addressing poverty differs widely from that favored by multinational organizations such as the World Bank, which would provide large internationally subsidized loans to governments. The track record of such international loans is mixed. For example, one report claims that, of the $30 billion

(*continued*)

(concluded)

in foreign aid directed to Bangladesh in the last quarter of the twentieth century, only 25 percent was actually spent in Bangladesh. The remaining 75 percent was spent in the donor countries themselves on administrative, equipment, and commodity costs.[4] Because international loans are targeted for huge infrastructure projects, and because the equipment and expertise for such projects exists primarily in the developed world, much of the money ends up in the developed countries. In fact, much of international aid, and especially food aid, come with a requirement that products be purchased from the lending countries. Of the money that actually reached Bangladesh in those years, most of it went to local suppliers, contractors and others among that country's elite.

Microcredit is Grameen's alternative to such enormous international loans. Developed within the last few decades, microcredit policies target loans and financing directly to poor people themselves, enabling the poor to become more self-sufficient. Microcredit extends loans at low interest rates to people for self-employment and entrepreneurial projects that have potential to help people escape poverty and become self-reliant. Traditional lending institutions would not make loans to the poor—the people who most need credit—since poor people are deemed unworthy of credit. They have no resources to use as collateral for a loan. Further, traditional lending institutions judge the amount of money typically involved in microcredit loans, often less than $100, too small to be profitable.

Yunus identified a social need: small loans at interest rates small enough to allow craftswomen to escape a cycle of poverty. He came up with the innovative idea of founding a bank specializing in microfinance. Capital was raised though donations and grants at the start but, as Grameen's success grew, all loans are now capitalized through deposits and interest earned from lending. Grameen Bank is owned by its borrowers, does not require collateral for its loans, and has been profitable in all but three years since its founding in 1976. Today, the Grameen Bank's balance sheet would be the envy of countless traditional banks that have not survived the recent banking and financial crisis. By 2009, Grameen Bank had almost 8 million borrowers, 95 percent of whom are women. It has issued over $8 billion in micro-lending loans and has a repayment rate of 98 percent.

- Is the Grameen bank different from other banks? How is it different or similar? Are the Grameen Bank's stakeholders different from or similar to those of other banks?
- What role does profitability play in your judgment about a firm's choices surrounding social responsibility? Is your perception of a business' ethical standing diminished in any way by its pursuit of profit?
- What are the strengths of Grameen's business model; how have these strengths contributed to its business sustainability? Do you see any challenges or weaknesses?
- In a famous essay on corporate social responsibility, economist Milton Friedman claimed that "[f]ew trends could so thoroughly undermine the very foundations of our free society as the acceptance by corporate officials of a social responsibility other than to make as much money for their stockholders as possible." How would you expect Muhammad Yunus to respond to this claim?

Chapter Objectives

After reading this chapter, you will be able to:

1. Define corporate social responsibility.
2. Describe and evaluate the economic model of corporate social responsibility.
3. Distinguish key components of the term *responsibility.*
4. Describe and evaluate the philanthropic model of corporate social responsibility.
5. Describe and evaluate the social web model of corporate social responsibility.
6. Describe and evaluate the integrative model of corporate social responsibility.
7. Explain the role of reputation management as motivation behind CSR.
8. Evaluate the claims that CSR is "good" for business.

Introduction

This chapter addresses the nature of corporate social responsibility (CSR) and how firms opt to meet and demonstrate their fulfillment of this perceived responsibility. In one sense, no one denies that business has *some* social responsibilities. At a minimum, it is indisputable that business has a social responsibility to obey the law. Economists might also say that business has a social responsibility to produce the goods and services that society demands. If a firm fails to meet society's interests and demands, it will simply fail and go out of business. But, beyond these legal and economic responsibilities, controversies abound. In general terms, we can say that the primary question of CSR is the extent to which business has social responsibilities that go *beyond* producing needed goods and services within the law. There are a range of answers to this question and it will be helpful to distinguish some prominent alternatives along this continuum.

1 OBJECTIVE

Most involved in business would accept the general definition of the term **corporate social responsibility** as referring to the responsibilities that a business has to the society in which it operates. From an economic perspective, a business is an institution that exists to produce goods and services demanded by society and, by engaging in this activity, the business creates jobs and wealth that benefit society further. The law has created a form of business called *corporations,* which limits the liability of individuals for the risks involved in these activities. Legislatures thought that businesses could be more efficient in raising the capital necessary for producing goods, services, jobs, and wealth if individuals were protected, and people would therefore be encouraged to engage in these activities.

2 OBJECTIVE

This narrow view of CSR, what we shall refer to as the **economic model of CSR,** holds that business' sole duty is to fulfill the economic functions businesses were designed to serve. On this narrow view, the social responsibility of business managers is simply to pursue profit within the law. Because profit is an indication that business is efficiently and successfully producing the goods and services that society demands, profit is a direct measure of how well a business firm is meeting society's expectations. Because corporations are created by society and require a stable political and economic infrastructure in which to conduct business, like all other social institutions, they are expected to obey the legal mandates established by the society. This economic model of CSR denies that business has any social responsibilities beyond the economic and legal ends for which it was created.

Though Adam Smith was among the first to articulate a version of this perspective, Milton Friedman's classic 1970 *New York Times* article, "The Social Responsibility of Business Is to Increase Its Profits," is perhaps best known as an argument for this economic model of the social responsibility of business. Contrary to popular belief, Friedman does not ignore ethical responsibility in his analysis; he merely suggests that decision makers are fulfilling their responsibility if they follow their firm's self-interest in pursuing profit. Friedman explains that a corporate executive has a

> responsibility to conduct business in accordance with [his or her employer's] desires, which generally will be to make as much money as possible while conforming to the basic rules of society, *both those embodied in law and those embodied in ethical custom* (emphasis added).

This common view of corporate social responsibility has its roots in the utilitarian tradition and in neoclassical economics (as discussed in the section on utilitarianism in chapter 3). As agents of business owners, the contention is that managers do have social responsibilities—their primary responsibility is to pursue maximum profits for shareholders. By pursuing profits, a business manager will allocate resources to their most efficient uses. Consumers who most value a resource will be willing to pay the most for it; so profit is the measure of optimal allocation of resources. Over time, the pursuit of profit will continuously work towards the optimal satisfaction of consumer demand which, in one interpretation of utilitarianism, is the optimal social good.

Debates concerning CSR start with alternatives to the narrow view expressed by Freidman and others. In what follows, we will categorize these alternatives into three general models. As alternatives to the economic model, we will describe the *philanthropic model,* the *social web model,* and the *integrative model* of CSR. Recognize that these three models are intended to be general categories into which various specific versions of CSR can be fit; others may describe them differently and, certainly, there will be individual businesses that overlap these categories. Nevertheless, these models provide a helpful way to understand debates surrounding corporate social responsibility.

Ethics and Social Responsibility

3 OBJECTIVE

To help us sort through these alternative models of CSR and to better understand the extent of business' social responsibility, let us begin with a general discussion of the potential responsibilities of a business and how they can be understood from an ethical perspective.

The words *responsible* and *responsibility* are used in several different ways. When we say that a business is responsible, we might mean that it is reliable or trustworthy. Thus, we might say that a business is very responsible in providing good customer service. For example, you might recommend a car dealership to a friend by describing them as a responsible, trustworthy business. A second meaning of responsible involves attributing something as a cause for an event or action. For example, poor lending practices were responsible (i.e. the cause) for the collapse of many banks during the 2008 economic crisis; and the location of the gas tank was responsible for fires in the Ford Pinto. A third sense involves attributing liability or accountability for some event or action, creating an obligation to make things right again. To say, for example, that a business is responsible for a polluted river is not only to say that the business caused the pollution, but also that the business is at fault for it and should be held accountable. An unavoidable accident would be a case in which someone was responsible in terms of causing the accident, but did not bear responsibility in terms of being liable or at fault.

Laws regarding product safety and liability involve many of these meanings of being responsible. When a consumer is injured, for example, a first question to ask is whether the product was responsible for the injury, in the sense of having caused the injury. For example, several years ago a controversy developed over the drug Vioxx, produced by Merck. Some evidence suggested that Vioxx was responsible for causing heart attacks in some users. In the debates that followed, two questions required answers. Was Vioxx the cause of the heart attacks, and was Merck at fault, i.e. should it be held legally liable, for the heart attacks? Once the causal question is settled, we might then go on to ask if the manufacturer is responsible in the sense of being at fault and therefore being liable for paying for the damages caused by the product. Both ethics and tort law involve the question of liability or fault for causing harm. (See Figure 5.1, "Responsible and Responsibility.")

It is this last sense of responsibility as accountability that is at the heart of CSR. Corporate social responsibility refers to those actions for which a business can be held accountable. We can think of responsibilities as those things that we ought, or should, do, even if we would rather not. Responsibilities bind,

FIGURE 5.1
Responsible and Responsibility

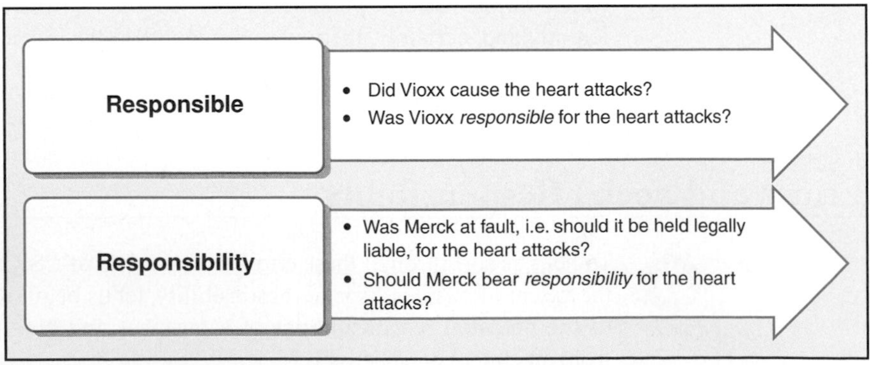
Responsible
• Did Vioxx cause the heart attacks?
• Was Vioxx *responsible* for the heart attacks?
Responsibility
• Was Merck at fault, i.e. should it be held legally liable, for the heart attacks?
• Should Merck bear *responsibility* for the heart attacks?

or compel, or constrain, or require us to act in certain ways. We can be expected to act in order to fulfill our responsibilities; and we will be held accountable if we do not. Thus, to talk about corporate social responsibility is to be concerned with society's interests that should restrict or bind business' behavior. Social responsibility is what a business should or ought to do for the sake of society, even if this comes with an economic cost.

Philosophers often distinguish between three different types of responsibilities in this sense, on a scale from more to less demanding or binding. First, the most demanding responsibility, often called duty or obligation in order to indicate that they oblige us in the strictest sense, is the responsibility not to cause harm to others. Thus, a business ought not to sell a product that causes harm to consumers, even if there would be a profit in doing so. A second, less binding, responsibility is to prevent harm even in those cases where one is not the cause. These so-called "good Samaritan" cases are examples of people acting to prevent harm, even though they have no strict duty or obligation to do so. Finally, there might be responsibilities to do good. Volunteering and charitable work are typical examples of responsibilities in this sense. To call an act volunteer work is precisely to suggest that it is optional; one does not have a duty to do it, but it is still a good thing to do.

Is there a duty not to cause harm? Let us consider how each of these three types of responsibilities might be seen in business. The strongest sense of responsibility is the duty not to cause harm. Even when not explicitly prohibited by law, ethics would demand that we not cause avoidable harm. If a business causes harm to someone and, if that harm could have been avoided by exercising due care or proper planning, then both the law and ethics would say that business should be held liable for violating its responsibilities.

In practice, this ethical requirement is the type of responsibility established by the precedents of tort law. When it is discovered that a product causes harm, then business can appropriately be prevented from marketing that product and can be held liable for harms caused by it. So, in a classic case such as asbestos, businesses are restricted in marketing products that have been proven to cause cancer and other serious medical harms.

Is there a responsibility to prevent harm? But there are also cases in which business is not causing harm, but could easily prevent harm from occurring. A more inclusive understanding of corporate social responsibility would hold that business has a responsibility to prevent harm. Consider, as an example, the actions taken by the pharmaceutical firm Merck with its drug Mectizan. Mectizan is a Merck drug that prevents river blindness, a disease prevalent in tropical nations. River blindness infects between 40 and 100 million people annually, causing severe rashes, itching, and loss of sight. A single tablet of Mectizan administered once a year can relieve the symptoms and prevent the disease from progressing—quite an easy and effective means to prevent a horrendous consequence.

On the surface, Mectizan would not be a very profitable drug to bring to market. The once-a-year dosage limits the demand for the drug among those people who require it. Further, the individuals most at risk for this disease are among the poorest people living in the poorest regions of Africa, Asia, Central America, and South America. However, in 1987, Merck began a program that provides Mectizan free of charge to people at risk for river blindness and pledges to "give it away free, forever." Cooperating with the World Health Organization, UNICEF, and the World Bank, Merck's program has donated more than 1.8 billion doses of Mectizan (by 2007), which have been distributed to 40 million people each year since 1987. The program has also resulted in the development of a health care system, necessary to support and administer the program, in some of the poorest regions of the world. By all accounts, Merck's Mectizan Donation Program has significantly improved the lives of hundreds of millions of the most vulnerable people on earth. Merck's actions were explained by reference to part of its corporate identity statement: "We are in the business of preserving and improving human life."[5]

Clearly Merck was not at all responsible for causing river blindness and, therefore, according to the standard of CSR discussed above, Merck had no social responsibility in this case. But, Merck itself saw the issue differently. Given the company's core business purpose and values, its managers concluded that they did have a social responsibility to prevent a disease easily controlled by their patented drug. Moreover, as we will discuss below, Merck recognized that it was the right thing to do for its business. George Merck, grandson of Merck's founder, explains, "We try never to forget that medicine is for the people. It is not for the profits. The profits follow and, if we have remembered that, they have never failed to appear. The better we have remembered it, the larger they have been."

Is there a responsibility to do good? The third, and perhaps the most wide-ranging, standard of CSR would hold that business has a social responsibility to do good things and to make society a better place. Corporate philanthropy would be the most obvious case in which business takes on a responsibility to do good. Corporate giving programs to support community projects in the arts, education and culture are clear examples. Some corporations have a charitable foundation or office that deals with such philanthropic programs. (See the Reality Check, "Corporate Philanthropy: How Much Do Corporations Give?") Small business owners in every town across America can tell stories of how often they are approached to give donations to support local charitable and cultural activities.

Many of the debates surrounding corporate social responsibility involve the question of whether business really has a responsibility to support these valuable causes. Some people argue that, like all cases of charity, this is something that deserves praise and admiration; but it is not something that every business *ought* to do. Philosophers sometimes distinguish between obligations/duties and responsibilities precisely in order to make this point. A responsible person is charitable; but donating to charity is neither an obligation nor a duty. Others argue that business does have an obligation to support good causes and to "give back" to the community. This sense of responsibility is more akin to a debt of gratitude and thankfulness—something less binding than a legal or contractual obligation perhaps, but more than a simple act of charity. Perhaps a clear way to understand

Reality Check *Corporate Philanthropy: How Much Do Corporations Give?*

In 2005, total charitable giving in the United States was estimated to be more than $260 billion. Individual contributions totalled $199 billion, or more than 75 percent. Corporate giving totalled $13.8 billion, or 5.3 percent of the total, slightly more than the average 5 percent annual giving rate over the past 40 years. Both this increase in corporate giving and the 6.4 percent increase in individual contributions have been attributed to strong economic growth as well as responses to global natural disasters.

Source: Giving USA, "Charitable Giving Rises 6 Percent to More Than $260 Billion in 2005," press release (June 19, 2006), http: //www. aafrc.org/press_releases/trustreleases/0606_PR.pdf.

the distinction is to compare it to your obligation to write a thank-you note to your grandmother for the extraordinary hand-knit sweater that she sent you for your birthday gift. You might not have a legal requirement to send the note, but nevertheless you feel a strong duty to do so. This discussion can help us gain a fuller understanding of the models of CSR described below and in Figure 5.2, "Models of Corporate Social Responsibility."

FIGURE 5.2
Models of Corporate Social Responsibility

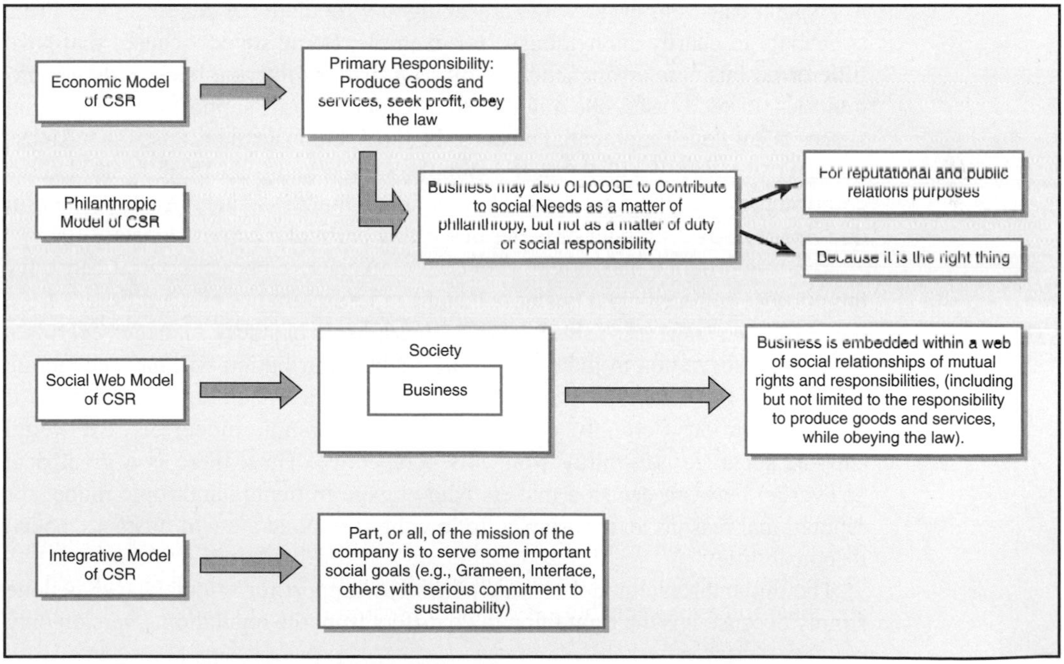

Philanthropic Model of CSR

4 OBJECTIVE

As the name suggests, the **philanthropic** (or philanthropy) **model of CSR** holds that, like individuals, business is free to contribute to social causes as a matter of philanthropy. From this perspective, business has no strict obligation to contribute to social causes; but it can be a good thing when they do so. Just as individuals have no ethical *obligation* to contribute to charity or to do volunteer work in their community, business has no ethical obligations to serve wider social goods. But, just as charity is a good thing and something that we all want to encourage, business should be encouraged to contribute to society in ways that go beyond the narrow obligations of law and economics. This approach is especially common in small, locally-owned businesses where the owners also often play a prominent leadership role within their local community.

Within the philanthropy model, there are occasions in which charity work is done because it brings the firm good public relations, provides a helpful tax deduction, builds good-will and/or a good reputation within the community. (See the Reality Check, "Putting Your Money Where Your Mouth Is?"*)* Many corporate sponsorships in the arts or contributions to community events benefit businesses in this way. Peruse the program you receive when entering a local art gallery, museum, theater, or school event, and you will likely see a list of local businesses who serve as donors or sponsors who have contributed to the event. In these cases, business has engaged in supporting these activities, and they have received some benefit in return.

Of course, there are also those cases in which a business might contribute to a social causes or event without seeking any reputational benefit. Some firms contribute to charity anonymously, for example. Some support causes that have little or no business or financial pay-off as a matter of giving back to their communities. In such cases, one might contend that corporate support for these social causes is not done for potential business benefits, but instead because the business manager or owner decides that it is simply a good and right thing to do. Others could suggest that the contributor has concluded that the society in which the firm does business is a stronger or better one if this particular activity exists.

You might notice that situations where a business supports a social cause for the purpose of receiving a business benefit in return are not much different from the economic view of CSR. In these situations, a business manager exercises managerial discretion in judging that the social contribution will have economic benefits. In these cases, the social contribution is as much an investment as it is a contribution. Certainly, proponents of the economic model of CSR would support social responsibility from this perspective. Thus, there is a great deal of overlap between decision makers who engage in the philanthropic model for reputational reasons and those who follow the economic view of business' social responsibilities.

The philanthropic model in which business support for a social cause is done simply because it is the right thing to do differs from the reputational version only

Reality Check *Putting Your Money Where Your Mouth Is?*

Do you make purchases based on a company's social contributions? Are you more or less likely to buy something if you know that a company supports causes that are (or are not) important to you? Philantropic CSR suggests that businesses contribute to society in the hopes that this will have beneficial reputational pay-offs. Research conducted by MORI in 2003 found that 84 percent of respondents to its survey said that a company's level of social responsibility was a "very important" or "fairly important" factor in their decision to purchase a particular product.

Perhaps more important is whether you believe that companies care about what is important to you. In that same research, MORI found that 47 percent of those questioned believed that companies did not listen to the public or respond to public concerns about social and environmental issues.

Source: MORI, *The Public's Views of Corporate Responsibility 2003* (London, UK: MORI), www.ipsos-mori.com/publications/jld/publics-views-of-corporate-responsibility.pdf, p. 2.

in terms of the underlying motivation. To some, this seems a trivial difference. In one case, the social good is done as a means to economic ends; in the other, it is done as an end in itself. Yet, this different motivation is, in the opinion of others, precisely what makes one action ethically responsible and the other not. From the perspective of the economic model of CSR, only philanthropy done for reputational reasons and financial ends is ethically responsible. Because business managers are the agents of owners, they have no right to use corporate resources except to earn owners greater returns on their investment. From the perspective of the philanthropic model, philanthropy done for financial reasons is not fully ethical and not truly an act of social responsibility.

Social Web Model of CSR

5 OBJECTIVE

A variety of perspectives on CSR would fall under what we call the **social web model of CSR.** They all share in common the view that business exists within a web of social relationships. The social web model views business as a citizen of the society in which it operates and, like all members of a society, business must conform to the normal ethical duties and obligations that we all face. While producing goods and services and creating wealth and profits are among business' responsibilities, they do not trump the other ethical responsibilities that equally bind all members of a society. (See the article, "Does It Pay to Be Good?" by A. J. Vogl at the end of this chapter for a discussion of the business case for this model.)

Philosopher Norman Bowie has defended one version of CSR that would fall within this social web model. Bowie argues that, beyond the economic view's duty to obey the law, business has an equally important ethical duty to respect human rights. Respecting human rights is the "moral minimum" that we expect of every person, whether they are acting as individuals or within corporate institutions. To explain this notion of a "moral minimum," Bowie appeals to the framework for distinguishing responsibilities that was described above and that is derived from the deontological traditional in ethics described in chapter 3.

Bowie identifies his approach as a "Kantian" theory of business ethics. In simple terms, he begins with the distinction between the ethical imperatives to cause no harm, to prevent harm, and to do good. People have a strong ethical duty to cause no harm, and only a *prima facie* duty to prevent harm or to do good. The obligation to cause no harm, in Bowie's view, overrides other ethical considerations. The pursuit of profit legitimately can be constrained by this ethical duty. On the other hand, Bowie accepts the economic view that managers are the agents of stockholder-owners and thus they also have a duty (derived from the contract between them) to further the interests of stockholders. Thus, while it is ethically good for managers to *prevent harm* or *to do good,* their duty to stockholders overrides these concerns. As long as managers comply with the moral minimum and cause no harm, they have a responsibility to maximize profits.

Thus, Bowie would argue that business has a social responsibility to respect the rights of its employees, even when not specified or required by law. Such rights might include the right to safe and healthy workplaces, right to privacy, right to due process. Bowie would also argue that business has an ethical duty to respect the rights of consumers to such things as safe products and truthful advertising, even when not specified in law. But, the contractual duty that managers have to stockholder-owners overrides the responsibility to prevent harm or to do (philanthropic) good.

Example of a Social Web Model: Stakeholder Theory

Perhaps the most influential version of CSR that would fall within the social web model is **stakeholder theory.** Stakeholder theory begins with the recognition that every business decision affects a wide variety of people, benefiting some and imposing costs on others. Think of the cases we have mentioned to this point—Malden Mills, Enron and Arthur Andersen, AIDS drugs in Africa, executive compensation, AIG—and recognize that decisions made by business managers produce far-ranging consequences to a wide variety of people. Remember, as well, the economic lesson about opportunity costs. Every decision involves the imposition of costs, in the sense that every decision also involves opportunities foregone, choices given up. Stakeholder theory recognizes that every business decision imposes costs on someone and mandates that those costs be acknowledged. In other words, any theory of corporate social responsibility must then explain and defend answers to the questions: for whose benefit and at whose costs should the business be managed?

The economic model argues that the firm should be managed for the sole benefit of stockholders. This view is justified by appeal to the rights of owners, the fiduciary duty of managers, and the social benefits that follow from this arrangement. The stakeholder theory argues, on factual, legal, economic, and ethical grounds, that this is an inadequate understanding of business. Let us examine who are the stakeholders, what reasons can be offered to justify the legitimacy of their claims on management, and what are the practical implications of this view for business managers.

R. Edward Freeman has offered a defense of the stakeholder model in his essay "Managing for Stakeholders" that is reprinted at the end of chapter 2. Freeman describes both a narrow and a wider understanding of the concept of a "stakeholder." In a narrow sense, a stakeholder includes anyone who is vital to the survival and success of the corporation. More widely, a stakeholder could be "any group or individual who can affect or be affected by the corporation."

Stakeholder theory argues that the narrow economic model fails both as an accurate descriptive and as a reasonable normative account of business management. As a descriptive account of business, the classical model ignores over a century of legal precedent arising from both case law and legislative enactments. While it might have been true over a century ago that management had an overriding obligation to stockholders, the law now recognizes a wide range of managerial obligations to such stakeholders as consumers, employees, competitors, the environment, and the disabled. Thus, as a matter of law, it is simply false to claim that management can ignore duties to everyone but stockholders.

We also need to recognize that these legal precedents did not simply fall from the sky. It is the considered judgment of the most fundamental institutions of a democratic society, the courts and legislatures, that corporate management must limit their fiduciary duty to stockholders in the name of the rights and interests of various constituencies affected by corporate decisions.

Factual, economic considerations also diminish the plausibility of the economic model. The wide variety of markets failures well-established in economics show that, even when managers pursue profits, there are no guarantees that they will serve the interests of either stockholders or the public. When markets fail to attain their goals, society has no reason to sanction the primacy of the fiduciary obligation to stockholders.

But perhaps the most important argument in favor of the stakeholder theory rests in ethical considerations. The economic model appeals to two fundamental ethical norms for its justification: utilitarian considerations of social well-being and individual rights. On each of these normative accounts, however, due consideration must be given to all affected parties. Essential to any utilitarian theory is the commitment to balance the interests of all concerned and to give to each (arguably, equal) consideration. The stakeholder theory simply acknowledges this fact by requiring management to balance the ethical interests of all affected parties. Sometimes, as the classical model would hold, balancing will require management to maximize stockholder interests; but sometimes not. Utilitarianism requires management to consider the consequences of its decisions for the well-being of all affected groups. Stakeholder theory requires the same.

Likewise, any theory of moral rights is committed to the equal rights for all. In its Kantian formulation, this ethical theory argues that the overriding moral imperative is to treat all people as ends and never as means only. Corporate managers who fail to give due consideration to the rights of employees and other concerned groups in the pursuit of profit are treating these groups as means to the ends of stockholders. This, in the Kantian tradition, is unjust. (Of course, ignoring the interests of stockholders is equally unjust.)

Thus, the stakeholder theory argues that on the very same grounds that are used to justify the classical model, a wider "stakeholder" theory of corporate social responsibility is proven ethically superior. Freeman argues that "the stakeholder theory does not give primacy to one stakeholder group over another, though there will be times when one group will benefit at the expense of others. In general, however, management must keep the relationships among stakeholders in balance."[6]

Firms exist in a web of relationships with many stakeholders and these relationships can create a variety of responsibilities. As we have seen in many of the cases and examples mentioned previously, it may not be possible to satisfy the needs of each and every stakeholder in a situation. But, stakeholder theory also recognizes that some stakeholders have different power and impact on decisions than others; that organizations have distinct missions, priorities and values, affecting the final decisions. Therefore, social responsibility would require decisions to prioritize competing and conflicting responsibilities.

Integrative Model of CSR

6 OBJECTIVE

Most discussions about CSR are framed in terms of a debate: Should business be expected to sacrifice profits for social ends? Much of the CSR literature assumes a tension between the pursuit of profit and social responsibility. But, of course, there have always been organizations that turn this tension around, organizations that pursue social ends as the very core of their mission. Non-profits, such as hospitals, NGOs, foundations, professional organizations, schools, colleges, and government agencies, have social goals at the center of their operations. The knowledge and skills taught in business schools, from management and marketing to human resources and accounting, are just as relevant for non-profits as they are in for-profit organizations. For this reason alone, students in these various sub-disciplines of a business school curriculum should be familiar with non-profit business models.

But there is a growing recognition that some for-profit organizations also have social goals as a central part of the strategic mission of the organization. In two areas in particular, social entrepreneurship and sustainability, we find for-profit firms that do not assume a tension between profit and social responsibility. The Grameen Bank, as described in the Opening Decision Point, is one example of the growing movement of social entrepreneurship. Firms that make environmental sustainability as central to their mission, such as Interface Corporation, are examples of the second area. (See the Reality Check, "Browsing for Social Good.")

Because these firms bring social goals into the core of their business model, and fully integrate economic and social goals, we refer to this as the **integrative model of CSR.** At first glance, firms that adopt the integrative model raise no particular ethical issues. Even advocates of the narrow economic model of CSR such as Milton Friedman, would agree that owners of a firm are free to make the pursuit of social goals a part of their business model. They would just disagree that these social goals should be part of *every* business' mission. (For a clear

Reality Check *Browsing for Social Good*

The popular Web browser Firefox and e-mail program Thunderbird are products of Mozilla Corporation, a for-profit subsidiary of Mozilla Foundation, a non-profit organization. Mozilla Corporation had revenues of more than $75 million in 2007. Mozilla is described on its Web site as follows:

> **What is Mozilla?**
>
> We're a global community of thousands who sincerely believe in the power of technology to enrich people's lives.
>
> We're a public benefit organization dedicated not to making money but to improving the way people everywhere experience the Internet.
>
> And we're an open source software project whose code has been used as a platform for some of the Internet's most innovative projects.
>
> The common thread that runs throughout Mozilla is our belief that, as the most significant social and technological development of our time, the Internet is a public resource that must remain open and accessible to all. With this in mind, our efforts are ultimately driven by our mission of encouraging choice, innovation and opportunity online.
>
> To achieve these goals, we use a highly transparent, extremely collaborative process that brings together thousands of dedicated volunteers around the world with our small staff of employees to coordinate the creation of products like the Firefox Web browser. This process is supported by the Mozilla Corporation, which is a wholly-owned subsidiary of the non-profit Mozilla Foundation.
>
> In the end, the Mozilla community, organization and technology is all focused on a single goal: **making the Internet better for everyone.**

Source: http://www.mozilla.com/en-US/about/whatismozilla.html

articulation of the arguments surrounding each of the CSR models, see the article, "Rethinking the Social Responsibility of Business" reprinted at the end of this chapter.)

Noone is claiming that every business should adopt the principles of social entrepreneurs and devote all their activities to service of social goals. There are clearly other needs that businesses are designed to address. At best, social entrepreneurs demonstrate that profit is not incompatible with doing good, and therefore that one can do good profitably. (See the Reality Check: "Fairness in a Cup of Coffee: Example of the Integrative Model.") On the other hand, there are some who would argue that the ethical responsibilities associated with sustainability are relevant to every business concern. In some ways, sustainability offers a model of CSR that suggests that ethical goals should be at the heart of every corporate mission. There are reasons to think that sustainability promises to be a concept of growing importance in discussions of CSR.

The Implications of Sustainability in the Integrative Model of CSR

Sustainability, and specifically its definition, will be discussed in greater detail in chapter 9; but as a topic within CSR, sustainability holds that a firm's financial

Reality Check *Fairness in a Cup of Coffee: Example of the Integrative Model*

The integrative model of CSR is evidenced in a company called Equal Exchange (www.equalexchange.com), which is a worker-owned and governed business committed to Fair Trade with small-scale coffee, tea, and cocoa farmers. Its "Vision of Fairness to Farmers" explains its model:

A Vision of Fairness to Farmers

Fairness to farmers. A closer connection between people and the farmers we all rely on. This was the essence of the vision that the three Equal Exchange founders—Rink Dickinson, Michael Rozyne, and Jonathan Rosenthal—held in their minds and hearts as they stood together on a metaphorical cliff back in 1986.

The three, who had met each other as managers at a New England food co-op, were part of a movement to transform the relationship between the public and food producers. At the time, however, these efforts didn't extend to farmers outside of the U.S.

The founders decided to meet once a week—and did so for three years—to discuss how best to change the way food is grown, bought, and sold around the world. At the end of this time they had a plan for a new organization called Equal Exchange that would be:

- *A social change organization that would help farmers and their families gain more control over their economic futures.*
- *A group that would educate consumers about trade issues affecting farmers.*
- *A provider of high-quality foods that would nourish the body and the soul.*
- *A company that would be controlled by the people who did the actual work.*
- *A community of dedicated individuals who believed that honesty, respect, and mutual benefit are integral to any worthwhile endeavor.*

No Turning Back

It was a grand vision—with a somewhat shaky grounding in reality. But Rink, Michael, and Jonathan understood that significant change only happens when you're open to taking big risks. So they cried "¡Adelante!" (rough translation from the Spanish: "No turning back!") and took a running leap off the cliff. They left their jobs. They invested their own money. And they turned to their families and friends for start-up funds and let them know there was a good chance they would never see that money again.

The core group of folks believed in their cause and decided to invest. Their checks provided the $100,000 needed to start the new company. With this modest financing in hand, Rink, Michael, and Jonathan headed into the great unknown. At best, the project, which coupled a for-profit business model with a nonprofit mission, was viewed as utopian; at worst it was regarded as foolish. For the first three years Equal Exchange struggled and, like many new ventures, lost money. But the founders hung on and persevered. By the third year they began to break even.

Source: http://www.equalexchange.coop/story

goals must be balanced against, and perhaps even over-ridden by, environmental considerations. Defenders of this approach point out that all economic activity exists within a biosphere that supports all life. They argue that the present model of economics, and especially the macroeconomic goal of economic growth, is already running up against the limits of the biosphere's capacity to sustain life. Fundamental human needs for goods such as clean air, water, nutritious food, and a moderate climate are threatened by the present dominant model of economic activity.

Reality Check *Will Sustainability Reports Replace the Annual Financial Reports?*

Various laws and regulations require corporations to file an annual report that provides a comprehensive accounting of a business' activities in the preceding year. The report is intended to provide shareholders and the public with information about the financial performance of the company in which they have invested. While a variety of information is contained in an annual report, they are primarily financial reports and they will include an auditor's report and summary of revenues and expenses.

Within the last decade, thousands of companies have supplemented this financial annual roport with a **corporate sustainability report**, which provides an overview of the firm's performance on environmental and social issues. In some cases, sustainability reports are replacing financial reporting by integrating assessment of financial, environmental, and social performance into one comprehensive report.

According to the Global Reporting Initiative, a non-profit organization that was instrumental in creating a widely accepted sustainability reporting framework,

> Sustainability reporting is a process for publicly disclosing an organization's economic, environmental, and social performance. Many organizations find that financial reporting alone no longer satisfies the needs of shareholders, customers, communities, and other stakeholders for information about overall organizational performance. The term "sustainability reporting" is synonymous with citizenship reporting, social reporting, triple-bottom line reporting and other terms that encompass the economic, environmental, and social aspects of an organization's performance.

Source: http://www.globalreporting.org

From this perspective, the success of a business must be judged not only against the financial bottom line of profitability, but also against the ecological and social bottoms lines of sustainability. A business or industry that is financially profitable, but that uses resources (for example, fossil fuels) at unsustainable rates and that creates wastes (for example, carbon dioxide) at rates that exceeds the earth's capacity to absorb them, is a business or industry that is failing its fundamental social responsibility. Importantly, a firm that is environmentally unsustainable is also a firm that is, in the long-term, financially unsustainable. (To learn more about how firms are sharing the results of their sustainability efforts, see the Reality Check: "Will Sustainability Reports Replace the Annual Financial Reports?")

The sustainability version of CSR suggests that the long-term financial well-being of every firm is directly tied to questions of how the firm both affects and is affected by the natural environment. A business model that ignores the biophysical and ecological context of its activities is a business model doomed to failure.

Exploring Enlightened Self-Interest: Does "Good Ethics" Mean "Good Business"?

7 OBJECTIVE

In one of the quotations that opened this chapter, the former Chairman of the Dayton-Hudson Corporation, Kenneth Dayton explained that "If business does not serve society, society will not long tolerate our profits or even our existence."

This logic suggests that CSR not only provides benefits to society, but it can also benefit an organization by securing its place within a society. Are there other reasons, self-interested and economic, for a business to engage in socially responsible activities? Can we make a "business case" for CSR, such as the reputational value we discussed above? (See the interview with Timberland CEO Jeff Swartz reprinted at the end of this chapter for a business person's response to this question.)

Perhaps the most obvious answer is the one we touched upon earlier with regard to the impact that CSR can have on a firm's reputation within a community. CSR-related activities can improve profitability by enhancing a company's standing among its stakeholders, including consumers and employees. For example, some evidence suggests that employees who are well treated in their work environments may prove more loyal, more effective and productive in their work. Liz Bankowshi, director of social missions at Ben & Jerry's Homemade Ice Cream Company, claims that 80 to 90 percent of Ben & Jerry's employees work there because "they feel they are part of a greater good."[7] The positive impact on the bottom line, therefore, stems not only from customer preference but also from employee preference.

The problem with a focus on reputation, however, is that social responsibility then can become merely social marketing. That is, a firm may use the image of social responsibility to garner customer support or employee loyalty while the facts do not evidence a true commitment. Paul Hawken, cofounder of Smith & Hawken gardening stores and an advocate of business social responsibility, reminds us that:

> [y]ou see tobacco companies subsidizing the arts, then later you find out that there are internal memos showing that they wanted to specifically target the minorities in the arts because they want to get minorities to smoke. That's not socially responsible. It's using social perception as a way to aggrandize or further one's own interests exclusively.[8]

Of course, the gap between perception and reality can work in the opposite direction as well. Consider Procter & Gamble Co., which was harshly criticized by respondents to a survey seeking to rank firms on the basis of their corporate philanthropy. Respondents contended that P&G did "absolutely nothing to help" after the September 11 tragedy in New York City.[9] However, in truth, P&G provided more than $2.5 million in cash and products, but they simply did not publicize that contribution. The same held true for Honda Motor Co., which donated cash, all-terrain vehicles, and generators for use at the World Trade Center site during the same time period. Perhaps unaware of these efforts, respondents instead believed these companies to lack compassion for their failure to (publicly) support America.

The practice of attending to the "image" of a firm is sometimes referred to as **reputation management.** There is nothing inherently wrong with managing a firm's reputation, and in fact the failure to do so might be a poor business decision; but observers could challenge firms for engaging in CSR activities *solely* for the

Reality Check *Enron as "Most Admired"*

As a firm, would you rather be an unethical firm with a good reputation or an ethical firm with a reputation for injustice? Enron included the following laudatory praises in its 2000 Corporate Responsibility Annual Report. The list drives home the challenges incumbent in any awards mechanism that strives to reward a trait such as "most innovative" or "all-star, most admired" rather than an enduring, measurable element of the corporate environment. On the other hand, awards such as those below can serve as influential motivating factors in corporate financial decisions, so many executives in fields impacted by these honors would prefer they remain.

As Reported in Enron's 2000 Corporate Responsibility Annual Report:

The Most Innovative Company in America
Fortune Magazine for six consecutive years

100 Best Companies to Work for in America
Fortune Magazine for three consecutive years, ranked no. 22 in 2000

All-Star List of Global Most Admired Companies
Fortune Magazine, ranked no. 25 in 2000

100 Fastest Growing Companies
Fortune Magazine, ranked no. 29 in 2000

The report goes on to say:

The principles that guide our behavior are based on our vision and values and include the following:

- Respect
- Integrity
- Communication
- Excellence

In 2001, we will continue to develop a systematic approach toward corporate responsibility, refine our implementation strategy, formalize stakeholder engagement, and strengthen our risk management practices.

Source: 2000 Enron Corporate Responsibility Annual Report (2001), pp. 2–3.

purpose of impacting their reputations. The challenge is based on the fact that reputation management often *works!* Figure 5.3 shows the elements that Harris Interactive considers critical to the construction of a reputation and the resulting benefits that attention to these elements can produce. If a firm creates a good image for itself, it builds a type of trust bank—consumers or other stakeholders seem to give it some slack if they then hear something negative about the firm. Similarly, if a firm has a negative image, that image may stick, regardless of what good the corporation may do. Plato explored this issue when he asked whether one would rather be an unethical person with a good reputation or an ethical person with a reputation for injustice. You may find that, if given the choice between the two, companies are far more likely to survive under the first conception than under the second. On the issue of reputation management and the impact of a variety of stakeholders on a firm's reputation, see the Reality Check, "Will Sustainability Reports Replace the Annual Financial Reports?," the Reality Check, "Enron as 'Most Admired,'" and examine the perspectives of various consumer and advocacy groups in connection with well-known businesses at any of the following Web sites:

- www.bankofamericafraud.org
- www.boycottameritech.com

- www.cokespotlight.org
- www.ihatestarbucks.com
- www.noamazon.com
- www.starbucked.com
- www.walmartsurvivor.com

In some ways, reputation may often be more forceful than reality, as with the P&G and Honda cases mentioned above. Shell Oil has publicized its efforts toward good citizenship in Nigeria; but it has an unfortunate record in terms of the timing of its responsiveness to spills; and its community development projects have created community rifts in areas around oilfields. Similarly, British American Tobacco heavily and consistently promotes its high health and safety standards; but it receives ongoing reports from contract farmers in Brazil and Kenya about ill health as a result of tobacco cultivation. Which image would you expect to be more publicized and, therefore, more likely to remain in stakeholders' consciousness?

A larger question involves the possible correlation between profits and ethics. Is good ethics also good business? One important justification offered for CSR, what is often called *enlightened self-interest,* presumes that it is, or at least it can be. A great deal of research has concentrated on examining this connection. In fact, theorists continue to dispute whether ethical decisions lead to more significant profits than unethical decisions. While we are all familiar with examples of unethical decisions leading to high profits, there is general agreement that, in the long run, ethics pays off. However, it is the measurement of that payoff that is the challenge. In Figure 5.3, Harris Interactive juxtaposes indicators of performance in the CSR arena with those traditionally used in the financial environment to

FIGURE 5.3
The Construction of Corporate Reputation

Source: Copyright © Harris Interactive Research. Reprinted by permission from http://www.harrisinteractive.com/services/reputation.asp.

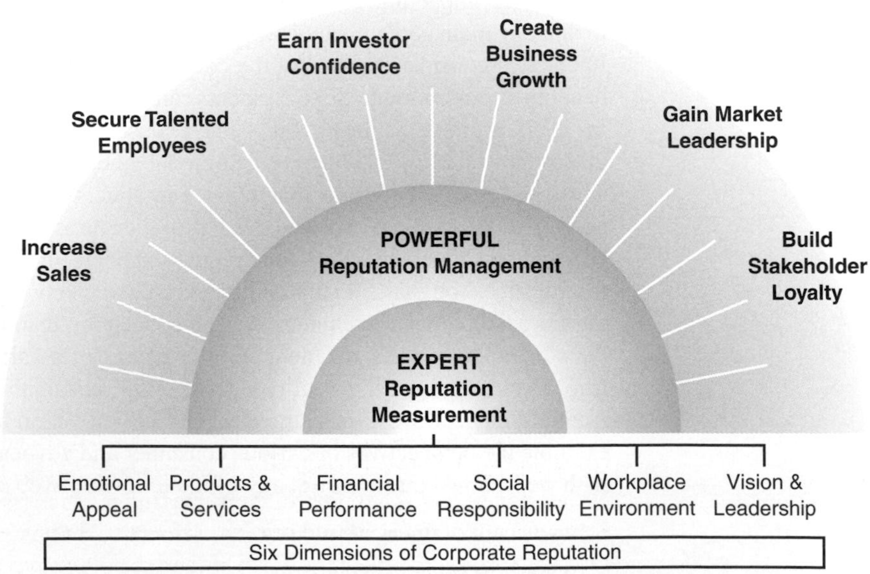

TABLE 5.1
Multiple Bottom-Line Performance Indicators

Ten Measures of Business Success	Ten Dimensions of Corporate Sustainable Development Performance
Financial Performance	**Governance**
1. Shareholder value	1. Ethics, values, and principles
2. Revenue	2. Accountability and transparency
3. Operational efficiency	**General**
4. Access to capital	3. Triple bottom-line commitment
Financial Drivers	**Environment**
5. Customer attraction	4. Environmental process focus
6. Brand value and reputation	5. Environmental product focus
7. Human and intellectual capital	**Socioeconomic**
8. Risk profile	6. Socioeconomic development
9. Innovation	7. Human rights
10. License to operate	8. Workplace conditions
	Stakeholder Engagement
	9. Engaging business partners
	10. Engaging non-business partners

Source: Adapted from Oliver Dudok van Heel, John Elkington, Shelly Fennell, and Franceska van Dijk, *Buried Treasure: Uncovering the Business Case for Corporate Sustainability* (London: SustainAbility, 2001).

provide some guidance in this area. Though executives responsible for organizational measurement and risk assessment might be less familiar with the processes for assessing the elements included on the right side of the chart, those elements are by no means less measurable. Often, however, the long-term value is not as evident or obvious.

8 OBJECTIVE

Though there are many justifications for ethics in business, often the discussion returns to, well, *returns*—is there a business case for a return on investment from ethics? There is evidence that good ethics is good business; yet the dominant thinking is that, if it cannot be measured, it is not important. As a result, efforts have been made to measure the bottom-line impact of ethical decision making.

Measurement is critical since the business case is not without its detractors. David Vogel, a political science professor at Berkeley, contends that, while there is a market for firms with strong CSR missions, it is a niche market and one that therefore caters to only a small group of consumers or investors.[10] He argues that, contrary to a global shift in the business environment, CSR instead should be perceived as just one option for a business strategy that might be appropriate for certain types of firms under certain conditions, such as those with well-known brand names and reputations that are subject to threats by activists. He warns of the exposure a firm might suffer if it then does not live up to its CSR promises.

Reality Check *The Relativity of Reputations*

Note that a reputation is relevant to the variety of a business' stakeholders—not just to its purchasing consumers. A survey conducted in the United Kingdom found that 33 percent of workers in that country are "very likely" to seek new employment during the next year because of their current employer's poor record on corporate social responsibility.[11] Employers are also more likely to seek out new hires with a demonstrated awareness of social and environmental responsibility—in fact, a *Wall Street Journal* survey found that 77 percent of corporate recruiters said it is important in their hiring decisions.[12] Moreover, investors are sinking almost $1.3 billion into socially responsible mutual funds, effectively putting their money where their mouths are.[13]

He also cautions against investing in CSR when consumers are not willing to pay higher prices to support that investment. Though this perspective is persuasive, a review of the scholarly research on the subject suggests the contrary on numerous counts, most predominantly the overall return on investment to the corporation.

Persuasive evidence of impact comes from a recent study titled "Developing Value: The Business Case for Sustainability in Emerging Markets," based on a study produced jointly by SustainAbility, the Ethos Institute, and the International Finance Corporation. (See Table 5.1). The research found that in emerging markets cost savings, productivity improvement, revenue growth, and access to markets were the most important business benefits of sustainability activities. Environmental process improvements and human resource management were the most significant areas of sustainability action. The report concludes that it does pay for businesses in emerging markets to pursue a wider role in environmental and social issues, citing cost reductions, productivity, revenue growth, and market access as areas of greatest return for multinational enterprises (MNEs).

In addition, studies have found that there are a number of expected—and measurable—outcomes to ethics programs in organizations. Some people look to the end results of firms that have placed ethics and social responsibility at the forefront of their activities, while others look to those firms that have been successful and determine the role that ethics might have played. (For additional areas of measurement, see the Reality Checks, "The Relativity of Reputations" and "So They Say.") With regard to the former, consider Johnson & Johnson, known for its quick and effective handling of its experience with tainted Tylenol. As highlighted in a Reality Check in chapter 4, Johnson & Johnson has had more than seven decades of consecutive sales increases, two decades of double-digit earnings increases, and four decades of dividend increases. Each of these quantifiable measurements can perhaps serve as proxies for success, to some extent, or at least would be unlikely to occur in a company permeated by ethical lapses.

Moreover, a landmark study by Professors Stephen Erfle and Michael Frantantuono found that firms that were ranked highest in terms of their records on a variety of social issues (including charitable contributions, community outreach programs, environmental performance, advancement of women, and promotion of

Reality Check *So They Say*

Whether at the World Trade Organization, or at the OECD, or at the United Nations, an irrefutable case can be made that a universal acceptance of the rule of law, the outlawing of corrupt practices, respect for workers' rights, high health and safety standards, sensitivity to the environment, support for education and the protection and nurturing of children are not only justifiable against the criteria of morality and justice. The simple truth is that these are good for business and most business people recognize this.[14]

Thomas d' Aquino, CEO of Canada's Business Council on National Issues

We all pay for poverty and unemployment and illiteracy. If a large percentage of society falls into a disadvantaged class, investors will find it hard to source skilled and alert workers; manufacturers will have a limited market for their products; criminality will scare away foreign investments, and internal migrants to limited areas of opportunities will strain basic services and lead to urban blight. Under these conditions, no country can move forward economically and sustain development. . . . It therefore makes business sense for corporations to complement the efforts of government in contributing to social development.[15]

J. Ayala II

Our findings, both cross-sectional and longitudinal, indicate that there are indeed systematic linkages among community involvement, employee morale, and business performance in business enterprises. To the best of our knowledge, this is the first time that such linkages have been demonstrated empirically. Moreover, the weight of the evidence produced here indicates that community involvement is positively associated with business performance, employee morale is positively associated with business performance, and the interaction of community involvement—external involvement—with employee morale—internal involvement—is even more strongly associated with business performance than is either "involvement" measure alone.[16]

Report of study by UCLA graduate school of business Professor David Lewin and J. M. Sabater (formerly IBM director of corporate community relations) in 1989 and 1991 involving in-depth, statistical research surveys of over 150 U.S.-based companies to determine whether there is a verifiable connection between a company's community involvement and its business performance

minorities) had greater financial performance as well. Financial performance was better in terms of operating income growth, sales-to-assets ratios, sales growth, return on equity, earnings-to-asset growth, return on investment, return on assets, and asset growth.[17] The Reality Check, "So They Say," demonstrates that these perspectives are gaining traction worldwide.

Another study by Murphy and Verschoor reports that the overall financial performance of the 2001 *Business Ethics Magazine* Best Corporate Citizens was significantly better than that of the remaining companies in the S&P 500 index, based on the 2001 *BusinessWeek* ranking of total financial performance.[18] In addition, the researchers found that these same firms had a significantly better reputation among corporate directors, security analysts, and senior executives. The same result was found in a 2001 *Fortune* survey of most admired companies. The UK-based Institute of Business Ethics did a follow-up study to validate these findings and found that, from the perspectives of economic value added, market value added, and the price-earnings ratio, those companies that had a

Opening Decision Point Revisited

Muhammad Yunus insists that the Grameen Bank is *not* a non-profit social organization, but instead is a successful for-profit business. Grameen Bank is 94 percent owned by its borrowers, with the Bangladesh government owning the remaining shares. All profits are put back into the bank to capitalize its operations. While the default rates are extremely low, Grameen keeps the loans on its books and some are years overdue. From its very first loans that targeted poor women, Grameen continues to serve the women of Bangladesh; and approximately 95 percent of its borrowers are women.

By most accounts, Grameen Bank is a success story. It has served the rural poor of Bangladesh, literally the poorest of the world's poor, by providing them with the capital they have needed to begin small businesses and to earn a living. Grameen claims that more than half of its borrowers have been helped out of poverty by micro-lending.

- To what degree do you think that the micro-lending practices of Grameen can be replicated in other places?
- What barriers might prevent this model from being generalized?
- In what ways can Grameen serve as a model for other social entrepreneurs?
- What role, if any, do you think that the prominence of women as Grameen's consumers has played in this success?
- Does Grameen provide lessons for other for-profit businesses? Is there a greater market than normally thought among the world's poor for other corporate products and services?
- In what ways does Grameen Bank differ from other for-profit businesses? Can you think of other for-profits that parallel Grameen in its business model?

code of conduct outperformed those that did not over a five-year period.[19] The higher performance translated into significantly more economic value added, a less volatile price/earnings ratio (making the firm, perhaps, a more secure investment), and 18 percent higher profit/turnover ratios. The research concluded

> This study gives credence to the assertion that "you do business ethically because it pays." However, the most effective driver for maintaining a high level of integrity throughout the business is because it is seen by the board, employees and other stakeholders to be a core value and therefore the right thing to do . . . [A] sustainable business is one which is well managed and which takes business ethics seriously. Leaders of this type of business do not need any assurance that their approach to the way they do business will also enhance their profitability, because they know it to be true.[20]

This chapter sought to answer the question of whether there exists a social responsibility of business. Several sources of that responsibility were proposed. The responsibility may be based in a concept of good corporate citizenship, a social contract, or enlightened self-interest. Notwithstanding its origins, we then explored the challenge of how an inanimate entity like a corporation could actually have a responsibility to others and discussed the extent of that obligation, both in law and ethics.

No matter how one answers the several questions posed by this chapter, however, one thing is certain. It is impossible to engage in business today without encountering and addressing CSR. Despite substantial differences among companies, research demonstrates that almost all companies will confront CSR issues from stakeholders at some point in the near future.[21]

Questions, Projects, and Exercises

1. What is your overall perspective on CSR after reviewing this chapter? If market forces do not encourage responsibility for social causes, should a firm engage in this behavior? Does social responsibility apply only to firms, or do consumers have a responsibility as well to support firms that take socially responsible action and withhold our support from firms that fail to exhibit socially responsible behavior? If we stand by and allow irresponsible actions to take place using profits made on our purchases, do we bear any responsibility?
   - How did you reach your decision? What key facts do you need to know in order to judge a firm's actions or your complicity in them by supporting a firm with your purchases or other choices?
   - How do you determine responsibility? Do you pay attention to these issues in your purchases and other choices?
   - Would you be more likely to support a company by purchasing its products or services if the company (a) donated a portion of the proceeds to a cause that was important to you; (b) paid its workers a "fair" wage (however you would define that concept); or (c) was a good investment for its stockholders? Which consequence is more influential to you? On the contrary, would you refrain from purchasing from a firm that failed in any of those areas?
   - How do the alternatives compare? Do you believe different purchasing decisions by consumers could really make a difference?
2. Which of the four models of CSR is most persuasive to you and why? Which do you believe is most prevalent among companies that engage in CSR efforts?
3. This chapter has asked in several ways whether the social responsibility of the companies you patronize has ever made any difference to your purchasing decisions. Will it make any difference in the future as a result of what you have learned? Consider your last three largest purchases. Go to the Web sites of the companies that manufacture the products you bought and explore those firms' social responsibility efforts. Are they more or less than what you expected? Do your findings make a difference to you in terms of how you feel about these firms, your purchases, and/or the amount of money you spent on these items?
4. One of the leading figures in the Enron debacle was company founder Kenneth Lay, who died in 2006 after his conviction for fraud and conspiracy but before he began serving his sentence. Prior to the events that led to the trial and conviction, Lay was viewed in Houston as one of its "genuine heroes" and Enron was a "shining beacon" according to a professor at Rice University in Houston. The Houston Astros' field was named after Enron when the company gave the Astros a large grant. Enron also gave money to local organizations such as the ballet and national organizations based in

Houston such as United Way. The Lays individually supported Houston's opera and ballet, its Holocaust Museum, the University of Texas cancer center, and other charitable organizations. If you were on the jury, would *any* of this information be relevant to your decision about Mr. Lay's guilt or innocence? If your jury had determined that Mr. Lay was guilty, would *any* of this information be relevant to your decision about the sentence you would then impose? Defend your decision from an ethical perspective.

5. In 2005, Nestlé S.A. CEO Peter Braeck-Letmathe explained, "Companies shouldn't feel obligated to 'give back' to communities because they haven't taken anything away. Companies should only pursue charitable endeavors with the underlying intention of making money. It is not our money we're handing out but our investors'. A company's obligation is simply to create jobs and make products. What the hell have we taken away from society by being a successful company that employs people?"[22] Which model of CSR would the Nestlé CEO advocate, and do you agree with his assessment?
6. Supermodel Kate Moss appeared in photos in a number of tabloid magazines and elsewhere using illegal drugs. Subsequent to the appearance of the photographs, several of her clients, including Chanel, H&M, and Burberry, cancelled their contracts (some only temporarily) with her or determined that they would not renew them when they became eligible for renewal. Other clients opted to retain her services, preferring to "stand by her" during this ordeal. Ms. Moss issued a statement that she had checked herself into a rehabilitation center for assistance with her drug use. Assume that you are the marketing vice president for a major global fashion label that is a client of Ms. Moss at the time of these events. Use the ethical decision-making process to evaluate how to respond to the situation. What is your decision on what to do?
7. What kind of organization would you like to work for? What would be the best? What would be the most realistic? Think about its structure, physical environment, lines of communication, treatment of employees, recruitment and promotion practices, policies towards the community, and so on. Consider also, however, what you lose because of some of these benefits (for example, if the company contributes in the community or offers more benefits for employees, there might be less money for raises).
8. Take another look at the quote earlier in this chapter by Paul Hawken. He seems to be saying that it is not acceptable to use social perception as a way to further one's own interests (exclusively). Now find the Smith & Hawken site on the Web and any additional information you can locate regarding Smith & Hawken or Paul Hawken and CSR. Would you identify Smith & Hawken as a firm interested in CSR? Would you identify Mr. Hawken as an individual interested in CSR or personal social responsibility? Which model of CSR would you suggest that Mr. Hawken supports?
9. Given the significant financial power that a retailer and sponsor like Nike can have in the sports world, does it have any obligation to use that power to do good in connection with its particular industry? A 2006 *New York Times* article[23] suggested that "(m)ore than television packages, more than attendance at the gate, track and field is driven by shoe company dough. Nike could, if it chose, threaten to pull its financial support from the coaches and trainers of athletes who are barred for doping violations. For years, the caretakers of the athletes have also been suspected as the doping pushers. Curiously, Nike hasn't fallen in line with everyone else calling for strict liability among coaches, trainers and athletes." The article instead suggests that Nike does not benefit when a star falls from glory so it tends to shy away from this area of oversight. In fact, it goes so far as to say that "Nike is the doping society's enabler." Can you make the argument that Nike has an obligation to intervene? Or, if you do not agree with an argument for its responsibility to do good, could you instead make an economic argument in favor of intervention?

10. Make a list of the five products on which you have spent the most money over the past three years. Using the Internet, find corporate sustainability reports for the companies that produced those products or that had some responsibility in their production. Are you able to find a sustainability report for each company? What can you determine about the company's sustainability efforts by reviewing these reports? Can you determine anything about their sincerity? Do you perceive that the company is undergoing a fundamental transformation in its efforts to sustainability, or does it seem more a matter of window-dressing (or, in other words, for the *sole* purpose of reputation)?

Key Terms

After reading this chapter, you should have a clear understanding of the following Key Terms. The page numbers refer to the point at which they were discussed in the chapter. For a more complete definition, please see the Glossary.

corporate social responsibility, *p. 206*
corporate sustainability report, *p. 219*
economic model of CSR, *p. 206*
integrative model of CSR, *p. 216*
philanthropic model of CSR, *p. 212*
reputation management, *p. 220*
social entrepreneurship, *p. 204*
social web model of CSR, *p. 213*
stakeholder theory, *p. 214*

End Notes

1. Sir Adrian Cadbury, "Ethical Managers Make Their Own Rules," *Harvard Business Review* (September/October 1987).
2. Kenneth R. Andrews, *The Concept of Corporate Strategy* (Burr Ridge, IL: Irwin,1971), p. 120.
3. Stakeholder Alliance, http://www.stakeholderalliance.org/Buzz.html (accessed April 11, 2010).
4. This data is quoted from Muhammad Yunus, *Banker to the Poor: Micro-lending and the Battle against World Poverty,* (New York: Public Affairs Publishers, 1999), p. 145.
5. "Mission Statement: Our Values," http://www.merck.com/about/mission.html (accessed April 11, 2010)
6. William Evan and R. Edward Freeman, "A Stakeholder Theory of the Modern Corporation: Kantian Capitalism," in *Contemporary Issues in Business Ethics,* 4th ed., ed Joseph R. DesJardins and John McCall (Belmont, CA: Wadsworth Publishing, 2000), p. 89.
7. Joel Makower, *Beyond the Bottom Line* (New York: Simon & Schuster, 1994), p. 68.
8. Makower, *Beyond the Bottom Line,* p. 15.
9. Ronald Alsop, "For a Company, Charitable Works Are Best Carried out Discreetly," *The Wall Street Journal,* January 16, 2002, Marketplace Section, p. 1.
10. David Vogel, *The Market for Virtue: The Potential and Limits of Corporate Social Responsibility* (Washington, DC: Brookings Institution, 2005).
11. The Work Foundation, "The Ethical Employee," http://www.theworkfoundation.com/research/publications/ethical.jsp (2002) (accessed April 11, 2010).
12. Ronald Alsop, "Corporations Still Put Profits First, but Social Concerns Gain Ground," *The Wall Street Journal,* October 30, 2001, p. B12.

13. A. J. Vogl, "Does It Pay to Be Good?" *Across the Board* (January 2003).
14. Quoted in C. Forcese, "Profiting from Misfortune? The Role of Business Corporations in Promoting and Protecting International Human Rights," (MA thesis, Norman Paterson School of International Affairs, Carleton University, Ottawa 1997), referred to in C. Forcese, "Putting Conscience into Commerce: Strategies for Making Human Rights Business as Usual" (Montréal: International Centre for Human Rights and Democratic Development, 1997).
15. J. Ayala II, "Philanthropy Makes Business Sense," *Ayala Foundation Inc. Quarterly* 4, no. 2 (July–September, October–Nov 1995): 3.
16. D. Lewin and J. M. Sabater, "Corporate Philanthropy and Business Performance," *Philanthropy at the Crossroads* (Bloomington: University of Indiana Press, 1996), pp. 105–26.
17. Makower, *Beyond the Bottom Line,* pp. 70–71
18. Curtis Verschoor and Elizabeth Murphy, "The Financial Performance of Large Firms and Those with Global Prominence: How Do the Best Corporations Rate?" *Business & Society Review* 107, no. 3 (2002): pp. 371–80. *See also* Elizabeth Murphy and Curtis Verschoor, "Best Corporate Citizens Have Better Financial Performance," *Strategic Finance* 83, no. 7 (January 2002): p. 20.
19. Simon Webley and Elise More, *Does Business Ethics Pay?* (London: Institute of Business Ethics, 2003), p. 9.
20. Webley and More, *Does Business Ethics Pay?,* p. 33.
21. Margot Lobbezoo, "Social Responsibilities of Business," unpublished manuscript available from the author.
22. Jennifer Heldt Powell, "Nestlé Chief Rejects the Need to 'Give Back' to Communities," *Boston Herald,* March 9, 2005, p. 33, http://www.bc.edu/schools/csom/cga/executives/events/brabeck/ and http://www.babymilkaction.org/press/press22march05.html (accessed April 11, 2010).
23. Selena Roberts, "Coaches like Graham Still Have Their Sponsors," *The New York Times,* August 2, 2006, http://select.nytimes.com/2006/08/02/sports/othersports/02roberts.html?_r=1 (accessed April 11, 2010).

Readings

Reading **5-1**

Rethinking the Social Responsibility of Business: *A* Reason *Debate Featuring Milton Friedman, Whole Foods' John Mackey, and Cypress Semiconductor's T. J. Rodgers*

Thirty-five years ago, Milton Friedman wrote a famous article for *The New York Times Magazine* whose title aptly summed up its main point: "The Social Responsibility of Business Is to Increase Its Profits." The future Nobel laureate in economics had no patience for capitalists who claimed that "business is not concerned 'merely' with profit but also with promoting desirable 'social' ends; that business has a 'social conscience' and takes seriously its responsibilities for providing employment, eliminating discrimination, avoiding pollution and whatever else may be the catchwords of the contemporary crop of reformers."

Friedman, now a senior research fellow at the Hoover Institution and the Paul Snowden Russell Distinguished Service Professor Emeritus of Economics at the University of Chicago, wrote that such people are "preaching pure and unadulterated socialism. Businessmen who talk this way are unwitting puppets of the intellectual forces that have been undermining the basis of a free society these past decades."

John Mackey, the founder and CEO of Whole Foods, is one businessman who disagrees with Friedman. A self-described ardent libertarian whose conversation is peppered with references to Ludwig von Mises and Abraham Maslow, Austrian economics and astrology, Mackey believes Friedman's view is too narrow a description of his and many other businesses' activities. As important, he argues that Friedman's take woefully undersells the humanitarian dimension of capitalism.

In the debate that follows, Mackey lays out his personal vision of the social responsibility of business. Friedman responds, as does T.J. Rodgers, the founder and CEO of Cypress Semiconductor and the chief spokesman of what might be called the tough love school of laissez faire. Dubbed "one of America's toughest bosses" by *Fortune,* Rodgers argues that corporations add far more to society by maximizing "long-term shareholder value" than they do by donating time and money to charity.

Reason offers this exchange as the starting point of a discussion that should be intensely important to all devotees of free minds and free markets.

Putting Customers Ahead of Investors

John Mackey

In 1970 Milton Friedman wrote that "there is one and only one social responsibility of business—to use its resources and engage in activities designed to increase its profits so long as it stays within the rules of the game, which is to say, engages in open and free competition without deception or fraud." That's the orthodox view among free market economists: that the only social responsibility a law-abiding business has is to maximize profits for the shareholders.

I strongly disagree. I'm a businessman and a free market libertarian, but I believe that the enlightened corporation should try to create value for *all* of its constituencies. From an investor's perspective, the purpose of the business is to maximize profits. But that's not the purpose for other stakeholders—for customers, employees, suppliers, and the community. Each of those groups will define the purpose of the business in terms of its own needs and desires, and each perspective is valid and legitimate.

My argument should not be mistaken for a hostility to profit. I believe I know something about creating shareholder value. When I co-founded Whole Foods Market 27 years ago, we began with

$45,000 in capital; we only had $250,000 in sales our first year. During the last 12 months we had sales of more than $4.6 billion, net profits of more than $160 million, and a market capitalization over $8 billion.

But we have not achieved our tremendous increase in shareholder value by making shareholder value the primary purpose of our business. In my marriage, my wife's happiness is an end in itself, not merely a means to my own happiness; love leads me to put my wife's happiness first, but in doing so I also make myself happier. Similarly, the most successful businesses put the customer first, ahead of the investors. In the profit-centered business, customer happiness is merely a means to an end: maximizing profits. In the customer-centered business, customer happiness is an end in itself, and will be pursued with greater interest, passion, and empathy than the profit-centered business is capable of.

Not that we're only concerned with customers. At Whole Foods, we measure our success by how much value we can create for all six of our most important stakeholders: customers, team members (employees), investors, vendors, communities, and the environment. . . .

There is, of course, no magical formula to calculate how much value each stakeholder should receive from the company. It is a dynamic process that evolves with the competitive marketplace. No stakeholder remains satisfied for long. It is the function of company leadership to develop solutions that continually work for the common good.

Many thinking people will readily accept my arguments that caring about customers and employees is good business. But they might draw the line at believing a company has any responsibility to its community and environment. To donate time and capital to philanthropy, they will argue, is to steal from the investors. After all, the corporation's assets legally belong to the investors, don't they? Management has a fiduciary responsibility to maximize shareholder value; therefore, any activities that don't maximize shareholder value are violations of this duty. If you feel altruism towards other people, you should exercise that altruism with your own money, not with the assets of a corporation that doesn't belong to you.

This position sounds reasonable. A company's assets do belong to the investors, and its management does have a duty to manage those assets responsibly. In my view, the argument is not *wrong* so much as it is too narrow.

First, there can be little doubt that a certain amount of corporate philanthropy is simply good business and works for the long-term benefit of the investors. For example: In addition to the many thousands of small donations each Whole Foods store makes each year, we also hold five 5% Days throughout the year. On those days, we donate 5 percent of a store's total sales to a nonprofit organization. While our stores select worthwhile organizations to support, they also tend to focus on groups that have large membership lists, which are contacted and encouraged to shop our store that day to support the organization. This usually brings hundreds of new or lapsed customers into our stores, many of whom then become regular shoppers. So a 5% Day not only allows us to support worthwhile causes, but is an excellent marketing strategy that has benefited Whole Foods investors immensely.

That said, I believe such programs would be completely justifiable even if they produced no profits and no P.R. This is because I believe the entrepreneurs, not the current investors in a company's stock, have the right and responsibility to define the purpose of the company. It is the entrepreneurs who create a company, who bring all the factors of production together and coordinate it into viable business. It is the entrepreneurs who set the company strategy and who negotiate the terms of trade with all of the voluntarily cooperating stakeholders—including the investors. At Whole Foods we "hired" our original investors. They didn't hire us.

We first announced that we would donate 5 percent of the company's net profits to philanthropy when we drafted our mission statement, back in 1985. Our policy has therefore been in place for over 20 years, and it predates our IPO by seven years. All seven of the private investors at the time we created the policy voted for it when they served on our board of directors. When we took in venture capital money back in 1989, none of the venture firms objected to the policy. In addition, in almost 14 years as a publicly traded company, almost no investors have ever raised objections to the policy. How can Whole Foods' philanthropy be "theft" from the current investors if the original owners of the company unanimously approved the policy and all subsequent investors made their investments after the policy was in effect and well publicized?

The shareholders of a public company own their stock voluntarily. If they don't agree with the philosophy of the business, they can always sell their investment, just as the customers and employees can exit their relationships with the company if they don't like the terms of trade. If that is unacceptable to them, they always have the legal right to submit a resolution at our annual shareholders meeting to change the company's philanthropic philosophy. A number of our company policies have been changed over the years through successful shareholder resolutions.

Another objection to the Whole Foods philosophy is where to draw the line. If donating 5 percent of profits is good, wouldn't 10 percent be even better? Why not donate 100 percent of our profits to the betterment of society? But the fact that Whole Foods has responsibilities to our community doesn't mean that we don't have any responsibilities to our investors. It's a question of finding the appropriate balance and trying to create value for all of our stakeholders. Is 5 percent the "right amount" to donate to the community? I don't think there is a right answer to this question, except that I believe 0 percent is too little. It is an arbitrary percentage that the co-founders of the company decided was a reasonable amount and which was approved by the owners of the company at the time we made the decision. Corporate philanthropy is a good thing, but it requires the legitimacy of investor approval. In my experience, most investors understand that it can be beneficial to both the corporation and to the larger society.

That doesn't answer the question of why we give money to the community stakeholder. For that, you should turn to one of the fathers of free-market economics, Adam Smith. *The Wealth of Nations* was a tremendous achievement, but economists would be well served to read Smith's other great book, *The Theory of Moral Sentiments*. There he explains that human nature isn't just about self-interest. It also includes sympathy, empathy, friendship, love, and the desire for social approval. As motives for human behavior, these are at least as important as self-interest. For many people, they are more important.

When we are small children we are egocentric, concerned only about our own needs and desires. As we mature, most people grow beyond this egocentrism and begin to care about others—their families, friends, communities, and countries. Our capacity to love can expand even further: to loving people from different races, religions, and countries—potentially to unlimited love for all people and even for other sentient creatures. This is our potential as human beings, to take joy in the flourishing of people everywhere. Whole Foods gives money to our communities because we care about them and feel a responsibility to help them flourish as well as possible.

The business model that Whole Foods has embraced could represent a new form of capitalism, one that more consciously works for the common good instead of depending solely on the "invisible hand" to generate positive results for society. The "brand" of capitalism is in terrible shape throughout the world, and corporations are widely seen as selfish, greedy, and uncaring. This is both unfortunate and unnecessary, and could be changed if businesses and economists widely adopted the business model that I have outlined here.

To extend our love and care beyond our narrow self-interest is antithetical to neither our human nature nor our financial success. Rather, it leads to the further fulfillment of both. Why do we not encourage this in our theories of business and economics? Why do we restrict our theories to such a pessimistic and crabby view of human nature? What are we afraid of?

Making Philanthropy out of Obscenity

Milton Friedman

By pursuing his own interest [an individual] frequently promotes that of the society more effectually than when he really intends to promote it. I have never known much good done by those who affected to trade for the public good.

Adam Smith, *The Wealth of Nations*

The differences between John Mackey and me regarding the social responsibility of business are for the most part rhetorical. Strip off the camouflage, and it turns out we are in essential agreement. Moreover, his company, Whole Foods Market, behaves in accordance with the principles I spelled out in my 1970 *New York Times Magazine* article.

With respect to his company, it could hardly be otherwise. It has done well in a highly competitive industry. Had it devoted any significant fraction of its resources to exercising a social responsibility unrelated to the bottom line, it would be out of business by now or would have been taken over.

Here is how Mackey himself describes his firm's activities:

1. "The most successful businesses put the customer first, instead of the investors" (which clearly means that this is the way to put the investors first).
2. "There can be little doubt that a certain amount of corporate philanthropy is simply good business and works for the long-term benefit of the investors."

Compare this to what I wrote in 1970:

"Of course, in practice the doctrine of social responsibility is frequently a cloak for actions that are justified on other grounds rather than a reason for those actions.

"To illustrate, it may well be in the long run interest of a corporation that is a major employer in a small community to devote resources to providing amenities to that community or to improving its government . . .

"In each of these . . . cases, there is a strong temptation to rationalize these actions as an exercise of 'social responsibility.' In the present climate of opinion, with its widespread aversion to 'capitalism,' 'profits,' the 'soulless corporation' and so on, this is one way for a corporation to generate goodwill as a by-product of expenditures that are entirely justified in its own self-interest.

"It would be inconsistent of me to call on corporate executives to refrain from this hypocritical window-dressing because it harms the foundations of a free society. That would be to call on them to exercise a 'social responsibility'! If our institutions and the attitudes of the public make it in their self-interest to cloak their actions in this way, I cannot summon much indignation to denounce them."

I believe Mackey's flat statement that "corporate philanthropy is a good thing" is flatly wrong. Consider the decision by the founders of Whole Foods to donate 5 percent of net profits to philanthropy. They were clearly within their rights in doing so. They were spending their own money, using 5 percent of one part of their wealth to establish, thanks to corporate tax provisions, the equivalent of a 501c(3) charitable foundation, though with no mission statement, no separate by-laws, and no provision for deciding on the beneficiaries. But what reason is there to suppose that the stream of profit distributed in this way would do more good for society than investing that stream of profit in the enterprise itself or paying it out as dividends and letting the stockholders dispose of it? The practice makes sense only because of our obscene tax laws, whereby a stockholder can make a larger gift for a given after-tax cost if the corporation makes the gift on his behalf than if he makes the gift directly. That is a good reason for eliminating the corporate tax or for eliminating the deductibility of corporate charity, but it is not a justification for corporate charity.

Whole Foods Market's contribution to society—and as a customer I can testify that it is an important one—is to enhance the pleasure of shopping for food. Whole Foods has no special competence in deciding how charity should be distributed.

Any funds devoted to the latter would surely have contributed more to society if they had been devoted to improving still further the former.

Finally, I shall try to explain why my statement that "the social responsibility of business [is] to increase its profits" and Mackey's statement that "the enlightened corporation should try to create value for all of its constituencies" are equivalent.

Note first that I refer to *social* responsibility, not financial, or accounting, or legal. It is social precisely to allow for the constituencies to which Mackey refers. Maximizing profits is an end from the private point of view; it is a means from the social point of view. A system based on private property and free markets is a sophisticated means of enabling people to cooperate in their economic activities without compulsion; it enables separated knowledge to assure that each resource is used for its most valued use, and is combined with other resources in the most efficient way.

Of course, this is abstract and idealized. The world is not ideal. There are all sorts of deviations from the perfect market—many, if not most, I suspect, due to government interventions. But with all its defects, the current largely free-market, private-property world seems to me vastly preferable to a world in which a large fraction of resources is used and distributed by 501c(3)s and their corporate counterparts.

Put Profits First

T. J. Rodgers

John Mackey's article attacking corporate profit maximization could not have been written by "a free market libertarian," as claimed. Indeed, if the examples he cites had not identified him as the author, one could easily assume the piece was written by Ralph Nader. A more accurate title for his article is "How Business and Profit Making Fit into My Overarching Philosophy of Altruism."

Mackey spouts nonsense about how his company hired his original investors, not vice versa. If Whole Foods ever falls on persistent hard times—perhaps when the Luddites are no longer able to hold back the genetic food revolution using junk science and fear—he will quickly find out who has hired whom, as his investors fire him.

Mackey does make one point that is consistent with, but not supportive of, free market capitalism. He knows that shareholders own his stock voluntarily. If they don't like the policies of his company, they can always vote to change those policies with a shareholder resolution or simply sell the stock and buy that of another company more aligned with their objectives. Thus, he informs his shareholders of his objectives and lets them make a choice on which stock to buy. So far, so good.

It is also simply good business for a company to cater to its customers, train and retain its employees, build long-term positive relationships with its suppliers, and become a good citizen in its community, including performing some philanthropic activity. When Milton Friedman says a company should stay "within the rules of the game" and operate "without deception or fraud," he means it should deal with all its various constituencies properly in order to maximize long-term shareholder value. He does not mean that a company should put every last nickel on the bottom line every quarter, regardless of the long-term consequences.

My company, Cypress Semiconductor, has won the trophy for the Second Harvest Food Bank competition for the most food donated per employee in Silicon Valley for the last 13 consecutive years (1 million pounds of food in 2004). The contest creates competition among our divisions, leading to employee involvement, company food drives, internal social events with admissions "paid for" by food donations, and so forth. It is a big employee morale builder, a way to attract new employees, good P.R. for the company, and a significant benefit to the community—all of which makes Cypress a better place to work and invest in. Indeed, Mackey's own proud example of Whole Foods' community involvement programs also made a profit.

But Mackey's subordination of his profession as a businessman to altruistic ideals shows up as he attempts to negate the empirically demonstrated social benefit of "self-interest" by defining it narrowly as "increasing short-term profits." Why is it that when Whole Foods gives money to a worthy cause, it serves a high moral objective, while a company that provides a good return to small investors—who simply put their money into their own retirement funds or a children's college fund—is somehow selfish? It's the philosophy that is objectionable here, not the specific actions. If Mackey wants to run a hybrid business/charity whose mission is fully disclosed to his shareholders—and if those shareholder-owners want to support that mission—so be it. But I balk at the proposition that a company's "stakeholders" (a term often used by collectivists to justify unreasonable demands) should be allowed to control the property of the shareholders. It seems Mackey's philosophy is more accurately described by Karl Marx: "From each according to his ability" (the shareholders surrender money and assets); "to each according to his needs" (the charities, social interest groups, and environmentalists get what they want). That's not free market capitalism.

Then there is the arrogant proposition that if other corporations would simply emulate the higher corporate life form defined by Whole Foods, the world would be better off. After all, Mackey says corporations are viewed as "selfish, greedy, and uncaring." I, for one, consider free market capitalism to be a high calling, even without the infusion of altruism practiced by Whole Foods.

If one goes beyond the sensationalistic journalism surrounding the Enron-like debacles, one discovers that only about 10 to 20 public corporations have been justifiably accused of serious wrongdoing. That's about 0.1 percent of America's 17,500 public companies. What's the failure rate of the publications that demean business? (Consider the *New York Times* scandal involving manufactured stories.) What's the percentage of U.S. presidents who have been forced or almost forced from office? (It's 10 times higher than the failure rate of corporations.) What percentage of our congressmen has spent time in jail? The fact is that despite some well-publicized failures, most corporations are run with the highest ethical standards—and the public knows it. Public opinion polls demonstrate that fact by routinely ranking businessmen above journalists and politicians in esteem.

I am proud of what the semiconductor industry does—relentlessly cutting the cost of a transistor from $3 in 1960 to *three-millionths* of a dollar today. Mackey would be keeping his business records with hordes of accountants on paper ledgers if our industry didn't exist. He would have to charge his poorest customers more for their food, pay his valued employees less, and cut his philanthropy programs if the semiconductor industry had not focused so relentlessly on increasing its profits, cutting his costs in the process. Of course, if the U.S. semiconductor industry had been less cost-competitive due to its own philanthropy, the food industry simply would have bought cheaper computers made from Japanese and Korean silicon chips (which happened anyway). Layoffs in the nonunion semiconductor industry were actually good news to Whole Foods' unionized grocery store clerks. Where was Mackey's sense of altruism when unemployed semiconductor workers needed it? Of course, that rhetorical question is foolish, since he did exactly the right thing by ruthlessly reducing his recordkeeping costs so as to maximize his profits.

I am proud to be a free market capitalist. And I resent the fact that Mackey's philosophy demeans me as an egocentric child because I have refused on moral grounds to embrace the philosophies of collectivism and altruism that have caused so much human misery, however tempting the sales pitch for them sounds.

Profit Is the Means, Not End

John Mackey

Let me begin my response to Milton Friedman by noting that he is one of my personal heroes. His contributions to economic thought and the fight for freedom are without parallel, and it is an honor to have him critique my article.

Friedman says "the differences between John Mackey and me regarding the social responsibility of business are for the most part rhetorical." But are we essentially in agreement? I don't think so. We are thinking about business in entirely different ways.

Friedman is thinking only in terms of maximizing profits for the investors. If putting customers first helps maximize profits for the investors, then it is acceptable. If some corporate philanthropy creates goodwill and helps a company "cloak" its self-interested goals of maximizing profits, then it is acceptable (although Friedman also believes it is "hypocritical"). In contrast to Friedman, I do not believe maximizing profits for the investors is the only acceptable justification for all corporate actions. The investors are not the only people who matter. Corporations can exist for purposes other than simply maximizing profits.

As for who decides what the purpose of any particular business is, I made an important argument that Friedman doesn't address: "I believe the entrepreneurs, not the current investors in a company's stock, have the right and responsibility to define the purpose of the company." Whole Foods Market was not created solely to maximize profits for its investors, but to create value for all of its stakeholders. I believe there are thousands of other businesses similar to Whole Foods (Medtronic, REI, and Starbucks, for example) that were created by entrepreneurs with goals beyond maximizing profits, and that these goals are neither "hypocritical" nor "cloaking devices" but are intrinsic to the purpose of the business.

I will concede that many other businesses, such as T. J. Rodgers' Cypress Semiconductor, have been created by entrepreneurs whose sole purpose for the business is to maximize profits for their investors. Does Cypress therefore have any social responsibility besides maximizing profits if it follows the laws of society? No, it doesn't. Rodgers apparently created it solely to maximize profits, and therefore all of Friedman's arguments about business social responsibility become completely valid. Business social responsibility should not be coerced; it is a voluntary decision that the entrepreneurial leadership of every company must make on its own. Friedman is right to argue that profit making is intrinsically valuable for society, but I believe he is mistaken that all businesses have only this purpose.

While Friedman believes that taking care of customers, employees, and business philanthropy are means to the end of increasing investor profits, I take the exact opposite view: Making high profits is the means to the end of fulfilling Whole Foods' core business mission. We want to improve the health and well-being of everyone on the planet through higher-quality foods and better nutrition, and we can't fulfill this mission unless we are highly profitable. High profits are necessary to fuel our growth across the United States and the world. Just as people cannot live without eating, so a business cannot live without profits. But most people don't live to eat, and neither must businesses live just to make profits.

Toward the end of his critique Friedman says his statement that "the social responsibility of business [is] to increase its profits" and my statement that "the enlightened corporation should try to create value for all of its constituencies" are "equivalent." He argues that maximizing profits is a private end achieved through social means because it supports a society based on private property and free markets. If our two statements are equivalent, if we really mean the same thing, then I know which statement has the superior "marketing power." Mine does.

Both capitalism and corporations are misunderstood, mistrusted, and disliked around the world because of statements like Friedman's on social responsibility. His comment is used by the enemies of capitalism to argue that capitalism is greedy, selfish, and uncaring. It is right up there with William Vanderbilt's "the public be damned" and former G.M. Chairman Charlie Wilson's declaration that "what's good for the country is good for General Motors, and vice versa." If we are truly interested in spreading capitalism throughout the world (I certainly am), we need to do a better job marketing it. I believe if economists and businesspeople consistently communicated and acted on my message that "the enlightened corporation should try to create value for all of its constituencies," we would see most of the resistance to capitalism disappear.

Friedman also understands that Whole Foods makes an important contribution to society besides simply maximizing profits for our investors, which is to "enhance the pleasure of shopping for food." This is why we put "satisfying and delighting our customers" as a core value whenever we talk about the purpose of our business. Why don't Friedman and other economists consistently teach this idea? Why don't they talk more about all the valuable contributions that business makes in creating value for its customers, for its employees, and for its communities? Why talk only about maximizing profits for the investors? Doing so harms the brand of capitalism.

As for Whole Foods' philanthropy, who does have "special competence" in this area? Does the government? Do individuals? Libertarians generally would agree that most bureaucratic government solutions to social problems cause more harm than good and that government help is seldom the answer. Neither do individuals have any special competence in charity. By Friedman's logic, individuals shouldn't donate any money to help others but should instead keep all their money invested in businesses, where it will create more social value.

The truth is that there is no way to calculate whether money invested in business or money invested in helping to solve social problems will create more value. Businesses exist within real communities and have real effects, both good and bad, on those communities. Like individuals living in communities, businesses make valuable social contributions by providing goods and services and employment. But just as individuals can feel a responsibility to provide some philanthropic support for the communities in which they live, so too can a business. The responsibility of business toward the community is not infinite, but neither is it zero. Each enlightened business must find the proper balance between all of its constituencies: customers, employees, investors, suppliers, and communities.

While I respect Milton Friedman's thoughtful response, I do not feel the same way about T. J. Rodgers' critique. It is obvious to me that Rodgers didn't carefully read my article, think deeply about my arguments, or attempt to craft an intelligent response. Instead he launches various ad hominem attacks on me, my company, and our customers. According to Rodgers, my business philosophy is similar to those of Ralph Nader and Karl Marx; Whole Foods Market and our customers are a bunch of Luddites engaging in junk science and fear mongering; and our unionized grocery clerks don't care about layoffs of workers in Rodgers' own semiconductor industry.

For the record: I don't agree with the philosophies of Ralph Nader or Karl Marx; Whole Foods Market doesn't engage in junk science or fear mongering, and neither do 99 percent of our customers or vendors; and of Whole Foods' 36,000 employees, exactly zero of them belong to unions, and we are in fact sorry about layoffs in his industry.

When Rodgers isn't engaging in ad hominem attacks, he seems to be arguing against a leftist, socialist, and collectivist perspective that may exist in his own mind but does not appear in my article. Contrary to Rodgers' claim, Whole Foods is running not a "hybrid business/charity" but an enormously profitable business that has created tremendous shareholder value.

Of all the food retailers in the *Fortune* 500 (including Wal-Mart), we have the highest profits as a percentage of sales, as well as the highest return on invested capital, sales per square foot, same-store sales, and growth rate. We are currently doubling in size every three and a half years. The bottom line is that Whole Foods stakeholder business philosophy works and has produced tremendous value for all of our stakeholders, including our investors.

In contrast, Cypress Semiconductor has struggled to be profitable for many years now, and their balance sheet shows negative retained earnings of over $408 million. This means that in its entire

23-year history, Cypress has lost far more money for its investors than it has made. Instead of calling my business philosophy Marxist, perhaps it is time for Rodgers to rethink his own.

Rodgers says with passion, "I am proud of what the semiconductor industry does—relentlessly cutting the cost of a transistor from $3 in 1960 to *three-millionths* of a dollar today." Rodgers is entitled to be proud. What a wonderful accomplishment this is, and the semiconductor industry has indeed made all our lives better. Then why not consistently communicate this message as the purpose of his business, instead of talking all the time about maximizing profits and shareholder value? Like medicine, law, and education, business has noble purposes: to provide goods and services that improve its customers' lives, to provide jobs and meaningful work for employees, to create wealth and prosperity for its investors, and to be a responsible and caring citizen.

Businesses such as Whole Foods have multiple stakeholders and therefore have multiple responsibilities. But the fact that we have responsibilities to stakeholders besides investors does not give those other stakeholders any "property rights" in the company, contrary to Rodgers' fears. The investors still own the business, are entitled to the residual profits, and can fire the management if they wish. A doctor has an ethical responsibility to try to heal her patients, but that responsibility doesn't mean her patients are entitled to receive a share of the profits from her practice.

Rodgers probably will never agree with my business philosophy, but it doesn't really matter. The ideas I'm articulating result in a more robust business model than the profit-maximization model that it competes against, because they encourage and tap into more powerful motivations than self-interest alone. These ideas will triumph over time, not by persuading intellectuals and economists through argument but by winning the competitive test of the marketplace. Someday businesses like Whole Foods, which adhere to a stakeholder model of deeper business purpose, will dominate the economic landscape. Wait and see.

Reading 5-2

Does It Pay to Be Good?

A. J. Vogl

Yes, say advocates of corporate citizen, who believe their time has come—finally.

Corporate citizenship: For believers, the words speak of the dawning of a new era of capitalism, when business, government, and citizen groups join forces for the greater good, to jointly tackle such problems as water shortages and air pollution, to do something about the 1.2 billion people who live on less than a dollar a day.

Corporate citizenship: For critics of today's capitalism, the words smack of hypocrisy, big business's cynical response to charges of greed and corruption in high places, intended to mollify those who say corporations have too much power and that they wield it shamelessly. Critics charge that corporate citizenship is a placebo to the enemies of globalization, a public-relations smoke screen, capitalism's last-ditch attempt to preserve itself by co-opting its opposition.

Corporate citizenship: For many, it remains a diffuse concept, but generally it speaks to companies voluntarily adopting a triple bottom line, one that takes into account social, economic, and environmental considerations as well as financial results. Though some associate corporate citizenship with charity and philanthropy, the concept goes further—it embraces a corporate conscience above and beyond profits and markets. David Vidal, who directs research in global corporate citizenship at The Conference Board, comments, "Citizenship is not, as some critics charge, window dressing for the corporation. It deals with primary business relationships that are part of a company's strategic vision, and a good business case can be made for corporate citizenship."

Whether you are a critic or believer, however, there is no question that corporate citizenship—a term that embraces corporate social responsibility (CSR) and sustainability—is no longer a concept fostered by idealists on the fringe. It has entered the mainstream.

No Good Deed Goes Unpunished

As necessary as corporate citizenship may be, it still faces challenges from both inside and outside the corner office. Perhaps the most disheartening of these hurdles is that the most prominent corporate citizens rarely receive rewards commensurate with their prominence. As Hilton and Giles Gibbons, co-authors of the pro-CSR *Good Business: Your World Needs You,* point out, "Curiously, the companies whose hearts are most visibly fixed to their pinstriped sleeves tend to be the ones that attract the most frequent and venomous attacks from anti-business critics." Is this because critics feel that devious agendas lie behind the enlightened policies? Noreena Hertz, a British critic of corporate citizenship, wonders whether Microsoft, by putting computers in schools today, will determine how children learn tomorrow.

Is it that corporations haven't gotten their stories across properly, or that they have—and are still being vilified? The experience of McDonald's in this arena is revealing. In 2002, the fast-food chain published its first social-responsibility report, composed of 46 pages summarizing its efforts in four categories: community, environment, people, and marketplace. The efforts that went into that report were rewarded in some courts of public opinion: In 2000 and 2001 *Financial Times*/PricewaterhouseCoopers surveys of media and NGOs, McDonald's placed 14th among the world's most respected companies for environmental performance.

At the same time, few corporations have been attacked as savagely as McDonald's for its "citizenship." It has been portrayed as an omnivorous monster that destroys local businesses and culture, promotes obesity, treats its employees badly, and despoils the environment. McDonald's goes to great lengths to answer these charges in its social-responsibility report—which was itself widely criticized—but, like Nike, it can't help looking defensive. It will take a great deal more than a report of its good works to diminish the Golden Arches as a symbol of "capitalist imperialism" in the eyes of anti-globalists or to stanch the vitriol on such websites as Mcspotlight.

There's no question that the bar is set exceedingly high in the arena of corporate social involvement. Philip Morris Cos. spends more than $100 million a year, most conspicuously in a series of TV commercials, on measures to discourage underage smoking—and still critics charge that the Philip Morris campaign is a cynical PR stunt that actually encourages kids to smoke. The company has been accused of having "a profound conflict of interest that cannot be overcome."

Another tobacco company, BAT, the world's second-largest, put some members of the social-responsibility establishment in an uncomfortable position when, last July, it became the industry's first company to publish a social-responsibility report. Few knew what to think upon reading the tobacco company's blunt rhetoric—"[T]here is no such thing as a 'safe' cigarette . . . We openly state that, put simply, smoking is a cause of certain serious diseases" and the 18 pages devoted to the risks of smoking. BAT even had its report audited by an independent verifier. All this wasn't nearly enough to satisfy antismoking groups, of course—they continue to view the company with deep suspicion. Would anyone have predicted otherwise?

When accused of being overly suspicious, critics point to one company that, over the last six years, won numerous awards for its environmental, human rights, anti-corruption, anti-bribery, and climate-change policies; a company prominent on "most admired" and "best companies to work for" lists; a company that issued a report on the good deeds that supported its claim to be a top corporate citizen. That company was Enron.

No one would argue that Enron is typical, yet its debacle has tainted other companies. It also raises a difficult question about CSR: What is the link between how a company is managed—corporate governance—and corporate citizenship? Steve Hilton, speaking from London, says that the link is not really understood in the United Kingdom: "People here have not made the connection between the corporate governance, executive-compensation, and accounting-fraud issues in the United States and operational issues that come under the heading of corporate citizenship. I would argue they're all part of the same thing."

So would Transparency International's Frank Vogl, co-founder of the anti-corruption NGO. He believes that CSR has been undermined because it has been disconnected from corporate conduct issues. "Foreign public trust in Corporate America has been diminished," he said, "and there is scant evidence that U.S. business leaders recognize the global impact of the U.S. scandals."

Vogl says that, for most countries in the world, corruption is much more of a social-responsibility issue than either the environment or labor rights. "What U.S. businesspeople see as a facilitating payment may be seen in developing countries as a bribe," he comments, "and I think that provides some insight into why the United States ranks behind 12 other countries on the Transparency International Bribe Payers Index. To me, corporate citizenship means you don't bribe foreign officials. That's the worst kind of hypocrisy."

Will They Be Good in Bad Times?

The specter of hypocrisy raises its head in another quarter as well: Do employees of companies claiming to be good corporate citizens see their employer's citizenship activities as a diversion or cover-up to charges of bad leadership and poor management practices? Certainly, if recent surveys are a guide, top management needs to restore its credibility with employees. In a recent Mercer Human Resource Consulting study, only a third of the 2,600 workers surveyed agreed with the statement, "I can trust management in my organization to always communicate honestly." And a Walker Information survey of employees found that only 49 percent believe their senior leaders to be "people of high personal integrity." If CSR is perceived by employees merely as puffery to make top management look good, it will not get under an organization's cultural skin.

Even if there is a genuine management commitment, corporations have other obligations that may take precedence, begging the question: Will corporations be good citizens in bad times as well as good? The experience of Ford Motor Co. brings the question to earth. In August, Ford issued its third annual corporate-citizenship report. Previous reports had drawn plaudits from environmentalists, but this one, coming at a time when the automaker faced financial difficulties, was attacked by the same environmentalists for failing to set aggressive goals for reducing greenhouse-gas emissions or improving gas mileage. Sierra Club's executive director called it "a giant step in the wrong direction for Ford Motor Co., for American consumers, and for the environment."

Lingering tough economic conditions may impel other companies to take their own "giant steps" backward. An old business saw has it that when times get tough and cuts have to be made, certain budgets are at the top of the list for cutbacks—advertising for one, public relations for another. For companies in which corporate citizenship is seen as an extension of public relations, of "image building" or "reputation management," it may suffer this fate.

Which is as it should be, say some critics. As *The Wall Street Journal* lectured CEO William Ford on its editorial page: "We also hope Mr. Ford has learned from his mistake of ceding the moral and political high ground to environmentalists . . . Businesses needn't apologize for making products that other Americans want to buy. Their first obligation is to their shareholders and employees and that means above all making an honest profit."

Does the "Business Case" Really Have a Case?

But hold on: What about the so-called business case for corporate citizenship—that it contributes to making "an honest profit"? Unfortunately, it's difficult to quantify in cost-benefit terms what that contribution is. Not something to be concerned about, says Simon Zadek, CEO of AccountAbility, a London-based institute that has established CSR verification standards. "It is a fact that the vast majority of day-to-day business decisions are taken without any explicit cost-benefit analysis," he says, pointing to employee training as an example of a corporate expenditure that is difficult to quantify in cost-benefit terms. What he doesn't mention is that, when business is suffering, training is usually among the expenditures to be cut back or eliminated.

Ultimately, Zadek concedes that, in strictly quantifiable terms, one cannot make a cost-benefit case for corporate citizenship. "Although the question 'Does corporate citizenship pay?' is technically right, it is misleading in practice," he says. "Rephrasing the core question as 'In what ways does corporate citizenship contribute to achieving the core business strategy?' is far preferable."

To some hardheaded corporate types, Zadek's reasoning may seem disingenuous, but even the hardheads can't be dismissive—at least publicly. Moreover, they would probably acknowledge that corporate citizenship, in concept and practice, has come too far to be ignored.

In the future, it may well become what Steve Hilton calls a "hygiene factor," a condition of doing business. Hilton's firm, Good Business, consults with firms on citizenship issues. "I think business leaders are coming to realize CSR's potential to go beyond a compliance/risk-management issue into a genuine business tool," he says. "That's been the rhetoric all along, but the reality has been that it's been a slightly marginal issue. With few exceptions, it's been seen as an add-on, without being incorporated into core business decision making."

This is Zadek's point when he argues the case for what he calls "third-generation corporate citizenship." The first generation is defined by cause-related marketing and short-term reputation management.

The second occurs when social and environmental objectives become a core part of long-term business strategy; as an example, he points to automakers competing in the arena of emission controls. The third generation is based on collective action, where corporations join with competitors, NGOs, and government "to change the underlying rules of the game to ensure that business delivers adequate social and environmental results."

Changing the rules means, for one thing, a more level playing field. "In CSR," says AccountAbility COO Mike Peirce, "companies that are leaders might suffer a penalty if there's a big gap between themselves and laggards in the field, so they'd like everybody ticking along at at least a basic level." In other words, a socially responsible company does not want to be penalized financially for being socially responsible. Of course, a cynic might reply that if CSR indeed provides the competitive advantage that its proponents insist it does, then it is the laggards that should suffer the severest financial penalty.

To convince doubters, efforts are being made to schematically quantify corporate social responsibility. In a recent *Harvard Business* Review article titled "The Virtue Matrix: Calculating the Return on Corporate Responsibility," Roger L. Martin makes a point of treating corporate responsibility as a product or service like any other.

According to Martin, who is dean of the University of Toronto's Rotman School of Management, his matrix can help companies sort out such questions as whether a citizenship initiative will erode a company's competitive position.

Even if Martin's formula seems overly clinical, it supports the trend toward closer analysis of what social responsibility means and what it brings to corporations practicing it. But analysis will take you only so far. "[I]t is impossible to prove the direction of the flow of causality," writes Chad Holliday, chairman and CEO of DuPont and co-author of *Walking the Talk: The Business Case for Sustainable Development.* "Does a company become profitable and thus enjoy the luxury of being able to worry about environmental and social issues or does the pursuit of sustainability make a company more profitable?"

But for large public companies, the question of whether it truly pays to be good will be asked less and less; for them, it will be necessary to be good, if only to avoid appearing Neanderthal. That means that corporate social responsibility, itself nothing less than a growth industry today, will become "normalized" into corporate cultures.

Yes, there will be an effort to level the playing field in CSR, but, further, expect citizenship proponents to attempt to raise the field to a higher level by making corporate governance itself the issue. "Unless we make basic structural changes," says Marjorie Kelly, the editor of *Business Ethics* magazine and a frequent critic of CSR, "it'll be nothing but window dressing. The corporate scandals have given a real-world demonstration that business without ethics collapses, and that has given us an extraordinary opportunity to change the way we do business."

Investors Are Listening

For companies in sectors not considered exemplars of corporate citizenship—munitions, pornography, gambling, and tobacco (yes); liquor (probably); and oil (maybe)—there's good news: The market hasn't penalized them for their supposed lack of citizenship. For companies at the opposite end of the spectrum, there's also good news: Investors haven't penalized them for their expenditures on social causes.

On balance, the better news is for the socially responsible companies, who have long labored under the assumption that the investor automatically pays a price for investing in a socially responsible company or mutual fund—the price, of course, being a company or fund that doesn't perform as well as its peers that don't fly the socially responsible banner.

Investors appear to be listening. According to Financial Research Corp., investors added $1.29 billion of new money into socially responsible funds during the first half of 2002, compared to $847.1 million added during all of 2001. Over the year ending July 31, the average mutual fund—including stock, bond, and balanced funds—was down 13 percent, while comparable socially responsible funds were down 19 percent. But advocates point out that different indices—particularly the Domini Social Index, a capitalization-weighted market index of 400 common stocks screened according to social and environmental criteria, and the Citizen's Index, a market-weighted portfolio of common stocks representing ownership in 300 of the most socially responsible U.S. companies—have outperformed the S&P 500 over the last one, three, and five years.

While the $13 billion invested in socially responsible funds (according to Morningstar) comprises only about 2 percent of total fund assets, advocates expect this percentage to climb to 10 percent by 2012, says Barbara Krumsiek, chief executive of the Bethesda, Md.–based Calvert Group, a mutual-fund complex specializing in socially responsible investing. And others' tallies are far higher: The nonprofit Social Investment Forum counts more than $2 trillion in total assets under management in portfolios screened for socially concerned investors, including socially screened mutual funds and separate accounts managed for socially conscious institutions and individual investors.

Plus, recent corporate scandals may have raised many investors' consciousness: In the first half of 2002, socially responsible mutual funds saw their assets increase by 3 percent, while conventional diversified funds lost 9.5 percent in total assets. People may have decided that if their mutual-fund investments were going to lose money, it might as well be for a good cause.

Attacked from All Sides

While many skeptics criticize the ways in which corporate social responsibility is enacted, some take matters a step further by asking if the concept should exist at all. Who would object to the idea of a company doing good, of moving beyond the traditional and literal bottom line, to take a larger view of the reason for its existence? You may be surprised: There are many critics, and they come from various and sometimes unpredictable directions.

First is a group that says corporate social responsibility is flawed at its heart because it's doing the right thing for the wrong reason. The right thing, they believe, is doing the right thing because it is right, as a matter of principle—not because it advances the firm's business interests. The rejoinder, of course, is that if a larger social or environmental good is met, we should not quibble about motivation. As corporate-governance activist Robert A. G. Monks points out: "You can get backing from institutional investors only if you talk a commercial idiom."

Next is a group of dissimilar critics who believe that, in attempting to pursue goals of corporate citizenship, companies are doing things that are none of their business. Paradoxically, these critics come from both the right and the left.

The right feels that the business of business should be business: As Michael Prowse argues in the *Financial Times,* the role of the corporation "is to provide individuals with the means to be socially responsible. Rather than trying to play the role of social worker, senior executives should concentrate on their statutory obligations. We should not expect benevolence of them, but we should demand probity: the socially responsible chief executive is the one who turns a profit without lying, cheating, robbing or defrauding anyone."

The left, on the other hand, feels that corporations are usurping the powers of government, to the detriment of the citizenry and democracy itself. Noreena Hertz, the British academic and broadcaster who wrote *The Silent Takeover: Global Capitalism and the Death of Democracy,* is not only dubious about business taking over responsibilities that she feels properly belong to government—she is skeptical about business's ability to handle them: "[M]anagers of multinationals operating in the third world are often overwhelmed by the social problems they encounter, and understandably find it difficult to know which causes to prioritize . . . Their contributions can be squandered, or diverted through corruption."

And what happens, she asks, when a corporation decides to pull out, if government has allowed private industry to take over its role? Worse still, she worries about situations in which a socially responsible corporation could use its position "to exact a stream of IOUs and quid pro quos, to demand ever more favorable terms and concessions from host governments."

Then there is a group of critics who see corporate citizenship as a diversionary ploy to placate a public outraged at dubious corporate practices. They will concede that Enron, WorldCom, and Tyco are egregious exceptions, but are other companies exemplars of probity? Hardly. Can companies be considered good corporate citizens when they move their headquarters to Bermuda to avoid taxes (and enrich their CEOs in the process)? Can companies like General Electric, Monsanto, Merck, SmithKline Beecham, and Chiquita Brands International claim the moral high ground when they have cut employee benefits in connection with mergers and spin-offs? And what of such companies as Wyeth, Wal-Mart, McKesson, and Merrill Lynch? Can they, ask the critics, be considered high-minded citizens when the top executives accumulate pots of money in their deferred-compensation accounts? This may be why PR eminence grise John Budd says, "For at least the next 18 post-Enron months, I certainly would not counsel any CEO to magically appear publicly as an enlightened champion of social responsibility. The circumstances make it automatic that it would be perceived as spinning."

Last, there is a group of critics that says that simply doing more good than we're doing now is not enough, that we have to rethink the nature of the beast—capitalism itself. Steven Piersanti, president of Berrett-Koehler Publishers, is in the thick of this intellectual contretemps. Last fall, his firm published two books that took divergent views on the issue. The first, *Walking the Talk,* was written by Swiss industrialist Stephan Schmidheiny, along with two colleagues at the World Business Council for Sustainable Development, Chad Holliday of DuPont and Philip Watts of Royal Dutch/Shell. "It advances a reformist view that major changes are needed in our business world," says Piersanti, "but that these changes can best be achieved by reforms within our existing economic structures, institutions, and systems."

The second book, *Alternatives to Economic Globalization: A Better World Is Possible,* presents "an activist view that existing economic structures are insufficient and that new structures, institutions, and systems are needed in the world."

It's likely that doubts about the nature and purpose of corporate citizenship will continue to be raised from all quarters. But with social-responsibility reporting and verification initiatives in place and likely government regulation down the road, there's reason to think that their voices will become more isolated.

Source: *Across the Board,* vol. 40, no. 1 (January/February 2003): pp. 16–23.

Reading 5-3

The Big Interview: Jeff Swartz—"Consumer Trust That's Good for the Sole": *Timberland's Jeff Swartz[1] Explains Why Brands Must Start Engaging Consumers on Social Issues to Rebuild Trust Lost during the Financial Crisis*

John Russell[2]

Good leaders, as a general rule, don't do fear. So it is refreshing to find business chiefs willing to admit that the financial crisis has them spooked. Rather than spreading panic, it shows they are in touch with the rest of us.

Jeff Swartz, president and chief executive of Timberland, is one leader who speaks openly about the harm the financial crisis could do to brands. Reflecting on the anti-capitalist G20 summit protests in London, in April, he says: "It scares the daylights out of people within Timberland."

But although Swartz admits that he is worried by public anger at the financial crisis, he sees the global downturn as a huge opportunity for the company he has been at or near the top of for almost 20 years. He feels the crisis gives brands with a social message the chance to reconnect with disillusioned consumers.

To do so brands will have to overcome the massive social fallout caused by the economic crisis, Swartz says. "The social fabric is frayed at best and torn in many places." He argues that the "vibrations in the system" run much deeper than consumers deciding to shop less. "It's more profound than that. People are asking, 'What's safe? What's the truth?'" The challenge for brands today is to find a message that is relevant for consumers who, as Swartz puts it, are "shaken and stirred and not like James Bond."

Swartz is hoping Timberland can tap into the reserves of social capital it has amassed with consumers over many years to prosper in the current crisis. The company has a strong record of leadership in responsible business, from ethical sourcing to transparent reporting on its social and environmental performance. It now reports quarterly on non-financial matters, for example.

Timberland is reminding customers of this good reputation with a new advertising campaign, running in Europe, which Swartz describes as "edgy." Featuring pictures of a Timberland boot, the ads are headlined: "We build things that last. Maybe we should go into the banking business." Swartz says he "sweated overnight" deciding whether to approve the ads, which mock the finance sector. But he gave them the go-ahead because they speak to consumers' demand for brands they can trust.

Campaign Brand

But it will take more than clever advertising to win over disillusioned consumers. Swartz says he wants Timberland to become an institution people can identify with by campaigning on important social and environmental issues.

"We have just got involved," he says. "For example we are for capping carbon emissions, but not for trading them. Timberland has never had a place in that conversation. We've sat on the side."

Swartz says Timberland decided to get involved in advocacy because its own actions did not seem to make a big enough effort to address global challenges such as climate change.

Swartz believes governments have a key role to play in giving companies incentives to create a low-carbon economy. For example, Timberland's major solar project at its Ontario distribution centre in California—one of the 50 largest solar projects in the world—could not have happened without state subsidies, he says.

But brands are understandably nervous about getting involved in public policy campaigns, Swartz says. "You get into this game and you get your head shot off," he warns. He notes the example of Microsoft when it backed a gay rights bill in Seattle in 2005, only to withdraw its support for the measure after coming under pressure from local church leaders. The company ended up pleasing no one, achieving only a PR disaster for itself.

No wonder many brands prefer simply not to get involved. Swartz says brands in effect end up saying: "We are for profit. Leave us alone and don't break our windows." This is a reference to the way demonstrators attacked bank branches during the G20 protests. Consumers want more than this from brands, he believes.

Engaging Customers

Swartz reckons brave brands that step up to engage customers on social and environmental issues will be rewarded. He says: "Consumers are starting to value brands as social institutions." Swartz is seeing early indications of this, but he stresses that he is yet to see concrete proof of consumers wanting to regard brands in the same way they do NGOs, for example.

Swartz says he saw signs of a shift last year when Timberland experimented with Facebook, the social networking site. The company set up a Facebook group where users could pledge to plant a virtual tree; in return, Timberland pledged to plant a real one.

By the end of the year, Timberland had one million pledges for virtual trees—so many that the brand was struggling to plant real trees fast enough. So Timberland posted what it thought was a tactful message on Facebook explaining that it was falling behind on its side of the deal. The admission got a terrible response. Swartz explains: "We had people in Zimbabwe calling us corporate scumbags—and that was one of the nice ones."

After a day of conference calls to work out how to appease its critics, Swartz did a live Web chat to explain to Facebook users Timberland's side of the story. He says the lesson of this episode was: "Brands must be transparent in a way that we have never been transparent before."

Total transparency does not come easy to brands, Swartz believes. "We are learning how to get naked in front of customers in a socially acceptable fashion, which is not a first instinct for a brand like ours," he says.

For example, Timberland has for three years carried "nutrition labels" on products that show in explicit detail the environmental impact of a product and the child-labour record of the factory that made it.

Swartz says customers want this information, but they also want to be able to compare Timberland with other brands on social and environmental measures. Timberland has offered its label as an example for other brands to use and is working with the Outdoor Industry Association to get such a label adopted. Progress has been slow to date, says Swartz.

As Swartz and Timberland take on their greatest challenge of talking to customers about sustainability, it is easy to forget one of the bread-and-butter issues for a responsible clothing business—managing ethical risks in its supply chain.

After 20 years of hard work, Swartz says Timberland is "almost at the point where we have achieved sustainability in human rights." This does not mean abuses can be eradicated completely from Timberland supplier factories—"there are always problems"—but that its process for dealing with them is running itself and working well, he says.

An effective ethical supply chain programme involves a partnership between the brand, factory owners, factory workers and local NGOs, Swartz says. The goal is to ensure workers go from being "factors in production" to "partners in production."

While sustainability is in sight on the human rights front, Swartz also has ambitious goals to cut the environmental impacts of Timberland shoes, which he notes "are toxic, by definition." His ambition: "We need to make products that endure and last forever." Swartz's goal for Timberland is to "build something that is built so well and styled so powerfully that it will last."

A second green goal is to create products that are completely recyclable and biodegradable. Timberland is not there yet, although Swartz hints that it is getting closer to making products designed so they can be easily taken apart and recycled.

Timberland is already using recycled materials to make its shoes and clothes. In March it announced a deal with Green Rubber, a company that can convert used car tyres back into useable rubber. Timberland is launching two new shoes with soles made from the recycled rubber.

Renewed Vigour

Swartz says that in a recession brands will be more attuned to the opportunities of good environmental stewardship. He says that he is pressing design teams to focus on how to cut the amount of material and number of parts used to make a shoe without compromising its performance. This saves money and resources.

He explains: "At heart, responsible business does not mean being more expensive. You are not responsible in order to save cost, but saving cost is a consequence."

The recession, Swartz says, will not compromise a brand's sustainability efforts. He says the financial mess is a perfect opportunity for brands to make sure they are giving customers what they really want. That means focusing on good products that are built to last, and rebuilding consumer confidence in brands, he says.

Swartz is relishing the challenge. "The crisis is clarifying," he says, comparing the process of re-evaluating Timberland's products to going for a workout on a "crisp autumn morning." He says: "I'm very confident that we are getting in shape like we haven't been in shape for 10 years."

End Notes

1. About Jeff Swartz: Jeff Swartz is grandson of Timberland founder Nathan Swartz and son of current Timberland chairman, Sidney Swartz. The youngest Swartz joined Timberland in 1986 as head of international sales, aged 26. He became chief operating officer in 1991. He moved into his current role of president and chief executive officer in 1998.
2. http://www.ethicalcorp.com/content.asp?contentid=6452

Chapter 6

Ethical Decision Making: Employer Responsibilities and Employee Rights

We can invest all the money on Wall Street in new technologies, but we can't realize the benefits of improved productivity until companies rediscover the value of human loyalty.

Frederick Reichheld, Director, Bain & Co.

There are now more slaves on the planet than at any time in human history. True abolition will elude us until we admit the massive scope of the problem, attack it in all its forms, and empower slaves to help free themselves.

E. Benjamin Skinner, "A World Enslaved"[1]

Opening Decision Point *Abercrombie & Fitch: Image Consciousness?*

In 2003, clothing retailer Abercrombie & Fitch (A&F) was sued by current and past members of its sales force, as well as people who were denied jobs, claiming racial discrimination. The plaintiffs, in a class action lawsuit that grew to include 10,000 claimants, alleged that A&F favored whites in a variety of ways in order to project an image of the "classic American" look. This theme evolved from A&F's origins as the store that clothed both Theodore Roosevelt and Ernest Hemingway. Plaintiffs alleged that people of color were discouraged from applying for positions visible to the public and were instead steered to stockroom jobs. Managers were aware that they were going to be judged on whether their workforce fit the A&F image.

The suit was eventually settled in 2005 for $40 million (you'll find the details in the resolution at the end of this chapter), providing at least some evidence of a lack of diversity in the retailer's operation.

You might find this lack of diversity relevant as you consider some decisions A&F made in 2002, before the lawsuit was filed. A&F opted to produce a line of T-shirts designed to poke fun at particular ethnic groups. One of the shirts advertised the Wong Brothers Laundry Service and had images of two smiling men with bamboo rice-paddy hats, along with a motto, "Two Wongs Can Make it White." Other shirts contained the following statements:

> "Pizza Dojo: Eat in or wok out. You love long time."
>
> "Wok-n-Bowl: Chinese food and bowl."
>
> "Buddha Bash: Get your Buddha on the floor."

Images of the shirts can be viewed at http://www.sfgate.com/cgi-bin/object/article?f=/c/a/2002/04/18/MN109646.DTL&o=0 or at http://www.geocities.com/tarorg/shirts.html.

After protests from Asian-American groups, among others, and negative mail, company spokesman Hampton Carney responded, "We thought everyone would like these T-shirts. We're very, very, very sorry. It's never been our intention to offend anyone. The thought was that everyone would love them, especially the Asian community. We thought they were cheeky, irreverent and funny and everyone would love them. But that has not been the case."

- Do you see a connection between the subject of the lawsuit discussed above and the choices made for the T-shirt line?
- Do you feel that Abercrombie & Fitch did anything wrong in choosing to sell these T-shirts that would justify the protests and negative attention? What are the key facts relevant to your determination?
- What are the ethical issues involved in your decision?
- Who are the stakeholders in this scenario? Are the stakeholders' rights abridged? In what way?
- Even if you answer no to the first question above, evidently certain stakeholders believed that Abercrombie & Fitch acted inappropriately. Other than not selling the shirts at all, is there any other way to have prevented this from happening in the first place? What alternatives were originally available to the

(*continued*)

(*concluded*)

retailer? How would each of these new alternatives have affected each of the stakeholders you have identified?

- As it moves forward from this point, what alternatives now exist for Abercrombie & Fitch to heal relationships with its stakeholders? What recommendations would you offer to Abercrombie & Fitch?

Chapter Objectives

After reading this chapter, you will be able to:

1. Discuss the two distinct perspectives on the ethics of workplace relationships.
2. Explain the concept of due process in the workplace.
3. Define "employment at will" (EAW) and its ethical rationale.
4. Describe the costs of an EAW environment.
5. Explain how due process relates to performance appraisals.
6. Discuss whether it is possible to downsize in an ethical manner.
7. Explain the difference between intrinsic and instrumental value in terms of health and safety.
8. Describe the "acceptable risk" approach to health and safety in the workplace.
9. Describe the nature of an employer's responsibility with regard to employee health and safety and why the market is not the most effective arbiter of this responsibility.
10. Explain the basic arguments for and against regulation of the global labor environment.
11. Describe the argument for a market-based resolution to workplace discrimination.
12. Define diversity as it applies to the workplace.
13. Explain the benefits and challenges of diversity for the workplace.
14. Define affirmative action and explain the three ways in which affirmative action may be legally permissible.
15. Articulate the basic guidelines for affirmative action programs.

Introduction

Ethics in the employment context is perhaps the most universal topic in business ethics since nearly every person will have the experience of being employed. While legislators and the courts have addressed many aspects of the working environment, countless ethical issues remain that these regulatory and judicial bodies have left unresolved. The law provides guidance for thinking about ethical issues in the workplace, but such issues go well beyond legal considerations.

This chapter explores those areas of ethical decision making in the workplace where the law remains relatively fluid and where answers are not easily found by simply calling the company lawyer. Issues may also arise where the law does seem clear but, for one reason or another, it is insufficient to protect the interests of all stakeholders. We will examine various ethical challenges that face the employee, whether that employee is a worker on an assembly line, the manager of a restaurant, or the CEO of a large corporation, and the nature of employer responsibilities. While individual perspectives may change, similar conflicts and stakeholders present themselves across business settings.

As you examine each issue raised in this chapter, consider how you might employ the ethical decision-making process we have discussed to reach the best possible conclusion for the stakeholders involved. Severe time constraints, limited information, and pressure usually accompany these challenging business decisions. Though using the ethical decision-making process may seem cumbersome at the outset, once the process becomes embedded in the professional landscape and culture, its effectiveness and efficiency in resolving these issues will become apparent. In fact, utilizing an ethical decision-making process will avoid later hurdles, thus removing barriers to progress and momentum. Let us consider the issues that exist in the current workplace environment to test the effectiveness of the ethical decision-making process.

Ethical Issues in the Workplace: The Current Environment

We all have decisions to make about how we will treat others in the workplace and how we will ask to be treated. Ethics at work and in human resource management is about our relationships with others and with our organizations. Research demonstrates that companies that place employees at the core of their strategies produce higher long-term returns to shareholders than do industry peers—more than double![2]

The same holds true for interpersonal relationships. Notwithstanding these truths, less than half of U.S. workers feel a strong personal attachment to their organization or believe that the organization deserves their loyalty. Only one in four workers is truly loyal to their place of work. When asked about the greatest influence on their commitment, workers responded that the most important factor is fairness at work, followed by care and concern for employees—all key components of an ethical working environment. These influences play out in practical ways for businesses since research shows that 73 percent of full-time workers encounter ethical lapses in the workplace, with over one-third of these lapses happening at least once per week.[3] The challenge is compounded by the fact that many employees opt not to report these lapses based on a lack of confidence in how management would handle the information.[4]

Reality Check *Protecting Employee Rights through Unions*

In 1960, about one-third of the American workforce was represented by unions. Today, that figure is about 11 percent. Collective bargaining, established to protect the interests of workers, has led to some disappointments. Not surprisingly, federal and state regulations governing work practices have exploded as union membership has declined. The variety of protections is prodigious: anti-discrimination laws, wage and hour laws, worker safety laws, unemployment compensation, workers' compensation, and social security, to name a few.

1 OBJECTIVE

These observations call attention to the fact that there are two very distinct, and sometimes competing, perspectives on the ethics of workplace relationships. On one hand, employers might decide to treat employees well as a means to produce greater workplace harmony and productivity. (This consequentialist approach could be reminiscent of the utilitarian ethics discussed in chapter 3 if couched in terms of the creation of a better workplace for all, though it also raises a question about moral motivation and instrumentalist, self-interested reasons for doing good that is similar to our discussion of corporate social responsibility in chapter 5.) While no one is claiming that employees have some universal right to a "happy" workplace,[5] a comprehensive review of research by Jeffrey Pfeffer suggests that effective firms are characterized by a set of common practices, all of which involve treating employees in humane and respectful ways.[6]

As an example of these concerns, consider the role of emotion in the workplace. Though it is a relatively new area of research, studies suggest that managers can have a significant impact on the emotions of their workers, and this impact can greatly affect productivity and loyalty, as well as perceptions of fairness, care, and concern. Scholars Neal Ashkanasy and Catherine Daus suggest that managers should pay attention to the emotional impact of various jobs within their workplace and model a positive emotional environment.[7]

Rewards and compensation structures can clearly impact the emotions of workers, as can the composition of teams or the power relationships within a workplace. When employees see that a firm values their emotions, as well as exhibits values such as honesty, respect, and trust, they feel less pressure, more valued as employees, and more satisfied with their organizations. Since reporting to external stakeholders has become such a key issue in recent scandals, one might also want to consider whether a more satisfied employee is more or less likely to report misconduct to outside parties.

On the other hand, of course, employers might treat employees well out of a Kantian sense of duty and rights, regardless of the either utilitarian or self-interested productivity consequences. This deontological approach emphasizes the rights and duties of all employees, and treating employees well simply because "it is the right thing to do." Defenders of employee rights argue that rights should protect important employee interests from being constantly subjected to utilitarian and financial calculations. This sense of duty might stem from the law, professional codes of conduct, corporate codes of conduct, or such moral principles as fairness, justice, or human rights on the part of the organization's leadership. (See the Reality Check, "Protecting Employee Rights through Unions.")

Defining the Parameters of the Employment Relationship

The following section will explore the legal and ethical boundaries that will help us define the employment relationship based on some of the principles discussed above. "Employment," *per se,* implicates ethical issues because of the very nature of the relationship it implies. Consider the situation in which an individual agrees to work for another individual. This arrangement raises issues of power, obligation, responsibility, fair treatment, and expectations. In many circumstances, the livelihoods of both parties rely on each other's contributions to the relationship. Though legal requirements might serve to protect some interests, they can only go so far and cover so many bases. We will begin by looking to the ethics underlying the concepts of due process and fairness that help determine what is or is not acceptable behavior in the workplace. We will discover some of the ways in which employers might be able to remain true to these principles, even when specifically challenged by vexing circumstances such as a reduction in force. The relationship is further defined by the application of these principles to working conditions such as health and safety, both in domestic operations and abroad.

Note that the issues in the following sections are predominantly settled from an ethical perspective by their *justification.* In other words, people of goodwill would be likely to agree that an employee has a right to a safe and healthy workplace. Disagreements do remain in discussions surrounding the implementation, interpretation, or extent of that right. In contrast, the second section of this chapter explores several issues that are not perceived as settled from either a legal or ethical point of view. Reasonable minds may differ not only as to whether the means to achieve the ends are justified but whether the ends themselves are just, fair, or ethical. An example of this latter issue would be affirmative action, a thorny matter for courts, managers, and philosophers alike.

Due Process and Just Cause

2 OBJECTIVE

Employment security—getting and keeping a job—is perhaps the most significant aspect of work from the employee's ethical perspective. Fundamental questions of justice arise because employees are subject to considerable harms from a lack of security in their jobs and do not have much power to create security. But should employers' rights and ability to hire, fire, or discipline employees therefore be restricted in order to prevent injustices? Are there any other means by which to protect against unethical behavior or unjust results?

Philosophically, the right of **due process** is the right to be protected against the arbitrary use of authority. In legal contexts, *due process* refers to the procedures that police and courts must follow in exercising their authority over citizens.

Reality Check *Rioting to Support Due Process in France*

As discussed in this chapter, a number of states maintain employment at will for employees. However, this is not the case in some other countries. In France, for instance, French labor laws protect all employees from arbitrary dismissal; employees cannot be fired as long as they maintain a good work record and as long as the firm is economically viable.

During the spring of 2006, protests and riots broke out across France in reaction to a proposed change in these laws. During one weekend alone, hundreds of thousands of protesters clashed with police in cities throughout France.

Ironically, the proposed change in law was itself a response to riots the previous year when unemployed young people, many of them immigrants living in poor neighborhoods, protested the lack of jobs. The French government sought to loosen job protection as a means of encouraging business to hire more young workers. The change would have exempted workers under the age of 25 from the legal job protections during their first two years of employment.

What was intended only as a minor change in a law that, from the U.S. perspective, was already quite radical in protecting worker rights, resulted in massive riots. As a result of these protests, the French government withdrew its proposal.

Few dispute that the state, through its police and courts, has the authority to punish citizens. This authority creates a safe and orderly society in which we all can live, work, and do business. But that authority is not unlimited; it can be exercised only in certain ways and under certain conditions. Due process rights specify these conditions.

Similarly, due process in the workplace acknowledges an employer's authority over employees. Employers can tell employees what to do, and when, and how to do it. They can exercise such control because they retain the ability to discipline or fire an employee who does not comply with their authority. Because of the immense value that work holds for most people, the threat of losing one's job is a powerful motivation to comply. However, basic fairness—implemented through due process—demands that this power be used *justly*. It is the definition of basic fairness that remains the challenge. Review, for instance, the conflicting versions of fairness perceptions in France in 2006 in the Reality Check, "Rioting to Support Due Process in France."

Unfortunately, there is evidence to suggest that this acknowledged authority of employers over employees, or simply managers over subordinates, is not always exercised in a just or fair manner—and it is not only the worker who suffers the consequence. Studies show that anywhere from one-third to two-thirds of employees have suffered some form of "bullying" in the workplace, defined as "the repeated, malicious, health-endangering mistreatment of one employee . . . by one or more employees."[8] The mistreatment need not be physically threatening, of course, but might simply involve a boss who is constantly yelling dictates at workers, or a co-worker who spreads rumors about another in order to sabotage his position.

These behaviors lead not only to emotional abuse but a complete loss of personal dignity, intimidation, and fear. Moreover, others in the workplace suffer vicariously with these same sensations; evidence demonstrates that the employer has significant bottom line expenses from workers' compensation claims based on stress and other emotional stimuli, and there are increased costs related to potential litigation arising from claims of abusive work situations. There is also the indirect impact on employee morale, and certainly the negative effects that occur when one would prefer not to be at the workplace: turnover, absenteeism, poor customer relationships, and acts of sabotage.

The issue of workplace bullying is one that we hear about more and more, especially in economies based on strong service sectors. There have been countless newspaper articles, business journals, academic journals, conferences, and even television news programs devoted to the subject in recent years.[9] It is more predominant in the service sector because that work relies significantly on interpersonal relationships and interaction. "Frequent, ongoing personal interaction between workers often becomes a basic element of a job, especially in work arrangements between supervisors and subordinates. The more people interact, the more likely it is that personalities will clash," says scholar and bullying expert, David Yamada.[10] Add to those interactions the personal threats that people sense from pressures during a downturn in the economy, and one can only imagine the boiling points that might ensure. Yamada tells of a study of an earlier economic slump that found that the environment "ignited explosions of brutality both from innate bullies who thrive on their mistreatment of others and from overburdened bosses who might never have behaved that way in less stressful times."[11]

3 OBJECTIVE

Ironically, while basic fairness may demand that employer power be used justly, the law has not always clearly supported this mandate of justice. Much employment law within the United States instead evolved in a context of a legal doctrine known as **employment at will (EAW)**. Employment at will holds that, in the absence of a particular contractual or other legal obligation that specifies the length or conditions of employment, all employees are employed "at will." This means that, unless an agreement specifies otherwise, employers are free to fire an employee at any time and for any reason. In the words of an early court decision, "all may dismiss their employee at will, be they many or few, for good cause, for no cause, or even for cause morally wrong."[12] In the same manner, an EAW worker may opt to leave a job at any time for any reason, without offering any notice at all; so the freedom is *theoretically* mutual.

The ethical rationale for EAW, both historically and among contemporary defenders, has both utilitarian and deontological elements. EAW was thought to be an important management tool. Total discretion over employment gives managers the ability to make efficient decisions that should contribute to the greater overall good. It was thought that the manager would be in the best position to know what was best for the firm and that the law should not interfere with those decisions. Another basis for EAW was the rights of private property owners to control their property by controlling who works for them.

4 OBJECTIVE

Both legal and ethical analyses of these claims, however, demonstrate that there are good reasons to limit EAW. Even if EAW proved to be an effective management tool (though the reading by Tara Radin and Patricia Werhane,

"Employment-at-Will, Employee Rights, and Future Directions for Employment," tends to erode this view), justice demands that such tools not be used to harm other people. Further, even if private property rights grant managers authority over employees, the right of private property itself is limited by other rights and duties. Also, though the freedom to terminate the relationship is theoretically mutual, the employer is often responsible for the employee's livelihood, while the opposite is unlikely to be true; the differential creates an unbalanced power relationship between the two parties.

Considerations such as these have led many courts and legislatures to create exceptions to the EAW rule (see Table 6.1). Civil rights laws, for example, prohibit firing someone on the basis of membership in certain prohibited classes, such as race, sex, disability, age, national origin, religion, or ethnic background. Labor laws prevent employers from firing someone for union activities. When the employer is the government, constitutional limitations on government authority are extended into the workplace to protect employees.

A crucial element to recognize with these exceptions, however, is the fact that EAW has priority unless the employee can prove that her or his case falls under one of the exceptions. That is, EAW is the default position on which courts will rely until and unless an exception can be demonstrated. The burden of proof lies with the dismissed employee to show that she or he was unjustly or illegally fired. Due process and **just cause**, whether instituted as part of internal corporate policy or through legislation, would reverse this burden of proof and require employers to show cause to justify the dismissal of an employee.

5 OBJECTIVE

Due process issues arise in other employment contexts as well. Employees are constantly supervised and evaluated in the workplace, and such benefits as salary, work conditions, and promotions can also be used to motivate or sanction employees. Thus, being treated fairly in the workplace also involves fairness in such things as promotions, salary, benefits, and so forth. Because such decisions

TABLE 6.1
Exceptions to the Doctrine of Employment at Will

States vary in terms of their recognition of the following exceptions to the doc trine of employment at will. Some states recognize one or more exceptions, while others might recognize none at all. In addition, the definition of these exceptions may vary from state to state.

- Bad faith, malicious or retaliatory termination in violation of *public policy.*
- Termination in breach of the *implied covenant of good faith and fair dealing.*
- Termination in breach of some other *implied contract term,* such as those that might be created by employee handbook provisions (in certain jurisdictions).
- Termination in violation of the doctrine of *promissory estoppel* (where the employee reasonably relied on an employer's promise, to the employee's detriment).
- Other exceptions as determined by *statutes* (such as the Worker Adjustment and Retraining Notification Act [WARN]).

Reality Check *Employing "Employees"*

Since the status of employment at will depends upon the determination of whether someone is employed at all, the definition of "employee" becomes critical. The employment relationship brings with it a plethora of benefits and responsibilities, which means that either party might be in a position to argue in its favor, or against. However, most often, it is the worker who is arguing for employee status.

There are several tests that courts use in order to determine a worker's status as an employee or, to the contrary, an "independent contractor," *e.g.* one who works for another, according to her or his own methods, and who is not under the other's control regarding the physical details of the work. These tests include the common-law test of agency, which focuses on the right of control, the Internal Revenue Service (IRS) 20-factor analysis, and the economic realities analysis. Several courts also use a hybrid approach, using one test that combines factors from other tests.

Under the **common-law agency test,** a persuasive indicator of independent contractor status is the ability to control the manner in which the work is performed. Under the common-law agency approach, the employer need not actually control the work, but must merely *have the right or ability* to control the work for a worker to be classified an employee. In the case of *Estrada v. Federal Express,* the California Court of Appeals evaluated whether Federal Express ground package drivers were employees entitled to reimbursement for work-related expenses. The court applied the common law test and found that they were, in fact, employees. You might be able to begin to understand the magnitude of a decision such as this one when you learn that the fallout was an order by the Internal Revenue Service that Federal Express pay $319 million in back taxes based on the misclassification—and the *Estrada* case only applied to workers over the course of *one single year.*

The second test is the **IRS 20-factor analysis,** a list of 20 factors to which the IRS looks to determine whether someone is an employee or an independent contractor. The IRS compiled this list from the results of judgments of the courts relating to this issue. Finally, under the **economic realities test,** courts consider whether the worker is economically dependent on the business or, as a matter of economic fact, is in business for him- or herself.

Some employers hire individuals as employees rather than independent contractors as a matter of principle. Phyllis Apelbaum, CEO of Arrow Messenger Service in Chicago, explains that her guiding philosophy in terms of her workers is to "hire hard working, friendly messengers; compensate them fairly including benefits and treat them as your greatest asset!" Her employees make a strong contribution to the culture and values of the firm. When Apelbaum considered using independent contractors instead of employees about 15 years ago, she explained, "I wouldn't be able to sleep at night and thought, it'll never work. Well, it has worked for 15 years for other companies. Because of that ethical decision, we have not grown to be the biggest in the city. We've grown nicely, no question about it. But we battle everyday that company that has independent contractors. Because, if you have employees, you've got about a 28 percent bottom number there. So, if the two of us walk in the door, and he charges you a dollar, I'm going to have to charge you $1.28. I'm always fighting that. The ethical decision to go in that direction meant that we had to work harder at our vision to provide better service. Otherwise, why should you be willing to pay 28 cents more? Why? There would be no reason for it."[13]

are typically made on the basis of performance appraisals, due process rights should also extend to this aspect of the workplace. Table 6.2 shows one model for making legally sound performance appraisals.

The ethical questions that remain in this EAW environment, therefore, are whether this atmosphere is one that is most fair and just for all stakeholders, whether it leads to the most effective employment outcomes, and whether it satisfactorily guards the rights and interests of both employers and employees. Relevant inquiries in reaching a conclusion on these matters will include those that comprise our decision-making framework. Consider the key facts relevant to issues of due process and fairness. What are the ethical issues involved in your decision and implementation? Who are the stakeholders involved in your decision? What alternatives are available to you? Might there be a way to safeguard the rights of the stakeholders involved while also protecting the interests of the decision makers? If you are, for instance, striving to serve the autonomy of the employer, could you perhaps serve the due process interests of the employee by offering additional notice of termination or more information about alternatives?

Recall that due process is the right to be protected against the *arbitrary* use of authority. It is your role as decision maker to ensure protection against those arbitrary decisions. Employers should be fair in their implementation of judgments and just in their implementation of process in order to serve the above principles. Once you have conducted a detailed inventory of your personal fundamental values surrounding this vital question in the employment context, compare your conclusions with those reached by Radin and Werhane in the reading, "Employment-at-Will, Employee Rights, and Future Directions for Employment." Is their proposal for a new model of employment, based on employees as *professionals*, realistic and possible?

Downsizing

One of the most emotional issues for both employees and corporate decision makers is the challenge not only of a single termination but letting many employees go when a firm makes a decision to **"downsize."** Terminating workers—whether one or one hundred—is not necessarily an unethical decision. However, the decision itself raises ethical quandaries since alternatives may be available to an organization in financial difficulty. In addition, since a host of negative consequences

TABLE 6.2
Procedural Recommendations for Legally and Ethically Sound Performance Appraisals

Source: S.B. Malos, "Current Legal Issues in Performance Appraisal," in J.W. Smither (ed.), *Performance Appraisal: State-of-the-Art Methods for Performance Management* (San Francisco: Jossey-Bass, 1998), pp. 49–94. Reprinted with permission of the author.

Appraisal procedures should:

1. Be standardized and uniform for all employees within a job group.
2. Be formally communicated to employees.
3. Provide notice of performance deficiencies and opportunities to correct them.
4. Provide access for employees to review appraisal results.
5. Provide formal appeal mechanisms that allow for employee input.
6. Use multiple, diverse, and unbiased raters.
7. Provide written instructions and training for raters.
8. Require thorough and consistent documentation across raters that includes specific examples of performance based on personal knowledge.
9. Establish a system to detect potentially discriminatory effects or abuses of the system overall.

may result, these alternatives may pose a more effective option from the perspective of all stakeholders involved. For example, Leadership IQ, a leadership research and training company, conducted a large-scale survey of over 4,000 workers who remained in over 300 companies that engaged in layoffs. It found that both productivity and quality may suffer as a result of those layoffs.[14] Plus, almost 90 percent of those surviving workers reported that they were less likely to recommend their firm as a good place to work. Large numbers also responded that customer service declined and more errors were made throughout the organizations.

6 OBJECTIVE

Accordingly, the question of whether to resort to widespread terminations based on financial exigency in lieu of other options that may be available does not always lead to a clear answer. Once the decision has been made, are there ways in which an organization can act more ethically in the process of downsizing? How might our earlier discussion of due process and fairness offer some guidance and/or define limitations in a downsizing environment?

In a speech to the Ethics Officers Association, John Challenger suggested that we should consider the following factors in executing that process: planning, timing, notice, impact (on those who will go and those who will stay), and stakeholder perceptions.[15] We can make *better* choices, Challenger argues. In fact, our decision-making model offers significant guidance in a situation such as a downsizing.

First, the decision regarding downsizing should be made by a representative group so that all stakeholder interests can be considered and to earn the trust of those who will be impacted. The facts should be collected and issues should be determined. Since employees should be kept aware of business conditions, the need for a downsizing effort should not come as a great surprise. However, the question of notice is debatable.

It can be argued that a firm should give notice of an intent to downsize as soon as the need is determined, and let those who will be impacted know who will be let go as soon as that list is devised. The Leadership IQ survey discussed above found that productivity and quality were more than two-thirds less likely to suffer when managers exhibited visibility, approachability, and candor.[16] On the other hand, the uncertainty and rumors that are sure to develop between the announcement of downsizing and the decision about who will be terminated may outweigh the benefits gained in early notification. In addition, allowing a worker to remain in a position for a period of time once she or he has been notified of impending termination might not be the best option. Workers may interpret early notice as an effort to get the most out of them before departure rather than an effort to allow them time to come to grips with the loss of their jobs.

These costs and benefits must be weighed in any communication decision and certainly considered in managing and interacting with employees following a layoff. "Managers need to be highly visible to their staff, approachable even when they don't have anything new to say, and candid about the state of things in order to build their trust and credibility. If your company has to conduct a layoff, it is imperative that you train your managers how to both manage that process and deal with the highly debilitating aftermath. Otherwise you will waste any potential cost savings from the layoff on lost productivity, quality problems and service breakdowns," says Mark Murphy, Chairman of Leadership IQ.[17]

Once the stakeholders are identified, it will be vital to enumerate any and all possible options with regard to the downsizing efforts and to catalog the impact of each option on each group of stakeholders. (See the Reality Check, "Is It Really 'Inevitable?'" for a discussion of options.) When a firm decides to downsize, as with any other termination, it is critical to lessen the impact as much as possible and to allow the terminated employees to depart with dignity (for example, unless there is some other reason for the decision, having a security guard follow terminated employees until they leave the building might not be the best option). Above all, during a time when relationships might be strained, it is critical to be honest and forthright and to be sensitive to the experiences of those who will be affected.

From a legal perspective, the decision about whom to include in a downsizing effort must be carefully planned. If the firm's decision is based on some criterion that seems to be neutral on its face, such as seniority, but the plan results in a different impact on one group than another, the decision may be suspect. For example, assume the firm does make termination decisions based on longevity with the organization. Also assume that those workers who are most senior are almost entirely male since women only entered this industry in recent years. If the firm moves forward with this process, the majority of those fired will be women and the majority of those remaining will be men. In this case, the effort may violate Title VII's prohibition against discrimination based on gender because the termination policy has a more significant—and negative—impact on women.

To avoid this result, firms should review both the fairness of their decision-making process and the consequence of that process on those terminated and the resulting composition of the workforce. One of the most effective philosophical theories to employ in downsizing decisions is John Rawls's theory of justice presented in chapter 3. Under his formulation, you would consider what decision you would make—whether to downsize or how to downsize—if you did not know what role you would be playing following the decision. In other words, you might be the corporate executive with the secure position; you might be a terminated employee with years of seniority who was close to retirement; or you might be a worker who survives the termination slips. If you do not know which role you would be playing, Rawls contends that you are more likely to reach a decision that is relatively fairest to all impacted. Consider what facts might shift your decision in one way or another based on this formulation.

Perhaps the most important consideration in the event of a downsizing or layoff is the fact that there are people who will be impacted by the decisions involved, countless stakeholders. In the reading at the end of chapter 4 by Ralph Larsen, past Chairman and CEO, Johnson & Johnson, he explains the angst he experienced when he made a decision to close approximately 50 small plants around the world.

> I was responsible to our employees in those plants, but I was also responsible to the patients who needed our products to keep them affordable. And I was responsible to all of our other employees around the world to keep the company healthy and

Reality Check *Is It Really "Inevitable?"*

As inevitable as downsizing may seem during downturns in the economy, some firms have survived decade after decade without any layoffs. How do they do it? While many firms became quite creative during the economic crisis that began during the second half of 2008, other firms have maintained these innovations for years. For instance, Hypertherm Inc., a manufacturer of metal-cutting equipment, has gone for its entire 40-year history without ever laying off a permanent employee. When the 2008 economic crisis hit, it opted instead to eliminate overtime, cut temporary staff, and delay a facility expansion, citing an ongoing "social contract" with its employees as the root of its strategy.[18]

Another company, Nucor, has not laid off a worker for a period of 20 years. However, it maintains a three-day workweek with an average wage of $8 per hour. When large contracts come in, the company expands to a seven-day workweek and $22 per hour wage. Other firms have entered into agreements with their workers under which the firm promises not to terminate workers for reasons of the economy as long as the workers agree to lower wages or decreased hours during tough periods. For instance, in December 1998, Volkswagen in Brazil was suffering under the collapse of that country's economy and the resulting 25 percent downturn in the Brazilian car market. It avoided terminations at its 20,000-worker plant by moving to a four-day work week.

Other options to stave off terminations can include the obvious decision to freeze hiring, to offer attractive voluntary retirement packages that provide an overall financial benefit to the firm, to reduce hours for all rather than fewer positions, to lower salaries, or to reduce or delay giving raises. Finally, some employers have chosen to cut benefits for which they would normally pay, such as bonuses, employer contributions to retirement plans, training, or education allocations.

growing. The harsh reality was that a great many more would be hurt down the road if I failed to act and we became less and less competitive.

In addition to our employees, I was also responsible to the tens of thousands of stockholders (individuals, retired folks, pension plans, and mutual funds) who owned our stock. The facts were clear. . . I knew what had to be done, and we did it as thoughtfully and sensitively as possible. But the decision was hard, because it was personal.[19]

Health and Safety

The previous sections addressed ethics in the creation or termination of the employment relationship. The following discussion explores one particular responsibility within that relationship—the employer's role in protecting the employees' health and safety while at work. Within the United States and throughout many other countries with developed economies, there is a wide consensus that employees have a fundamental right to a safe and healthy workplace. In some other regions, employees lack even the most basic health and safety protections, such as in working environments that are often termed "sweatshops" (discussed later in this chapter). Even within the United States, this issue becomes quite complicated upon closer examination. Not only is the very extent of an employer's responsibility for workplace health and safety in dispute, there is also significant disagreement concerning the best policies to protect worker health and safety.

How do we measure the intrinsic value of a life, in addition to the instrumental value? Though perhaps an interesting mental exercise in which to engage, it is also a critical component of some business decisions and dilemmas. The following decision, though decades old, continues to teach us the hazards of considering only the instrumental value of a life. Though the instrumental calculation seems to make sense, and presumably it did at the time to those involved, you will see in hindsight that the "human element" seems to be missing.

In 1968, Ford Motor Company made a historic decision regarding the Ford Pinto, which was engineered with a rear gas tank assembly that had a tendency to explode in accidents that involved some rear-end collisions. The company allowed the Pinto to remain on the market after it determined that it would be more costly to engage in a recall effort than to pay out the costs of liability for injuries and deaths incurred. In an infamous memo, Ford's senior management calculated what the company would likely have to pay per life lost. It is noteworthy that these estimates were not Ford's alone but were based instead on figures from the National Highway Traffic Safety Administration.

Expected Costs of Producing the Pinto *with* Fuel Tank Modifications:

- Expected unit sales: 11 million vehicles (includes utility vehicles built on same chassis)
- Modification costs per unit: $11
- **Total Cost: $121 million [11 million vehicles × $11 per unit]**

Expected Costs of Producing the Pinto *without* Fuel Tank Modifications:

- Expected accident results (assuming 2,100 accidents):
  180 burn deaths
  180 serious burn injuries
  2,100 burned out vehicles
- Unit costs of accident results (assuming out of court settlements):
  $200,000 per burn death
  $67,000 per serious injury
  $700 per burned out vehicle
- **Total Costs: $49.53 million** [= (180 deaths × $200k) + (180 injuries × $67k) + (2,100 vehicles × $700 per vehicle)]

Using the figures above, the costs for recalling and modifying the Pinto were $121 million, while the costs for settling cases in which injuries were expected to occur would reach only $50 million.

If you were responsible for deciding whether to engage in the recall, how would you conduct the decision-making process? How would you account for the *intrinsic* as well as the *instrumental* value of a human life? Returning to the question that opened this Decision Point, consider how you would measure your own worth or the value of someone close to you. Who are your stakeholders and what is your value to each of them? How will you measure it—*financially?*

(continued)

(*concluded*)

Would any of the following questions offer you a guidepost?

- How much would your stakeholders suffer if they lost you?
- How much do you currently contribute to society and what would society lose if you were not here?
- How much would society benefit if you continued to survive?

Businesses have reasons to consider these issues, though extraordinarily difficult; how would you prefer that they reach conclusions in these areas?

Like work itself, health and safety are "goods" that are valued both as a means for attaining other valuable ends and as ends in themselves. Whatever else we desire out of life, being healthy and safe makes it much more likely that we will be capable of attaining our ends. In this sense, health and safety have a very high instrumental value since part of their value derives from the fact that we use them to attain other things of value. Insurance therefore seeks to compensate workers for injuries they incur by paying the employees for the wages they lost as a result of being unable to work.

7 OBJECTIVE

Yet health and safety are also valuable in and of themselves. They have intrinsic value in addition to their instrumental value. To understand this distinction, consider how one might respond to the question of how much her or his life is worth. The life of one who dies in a workplace accident has instrumental value that can be measured, in part, by the lost wages that would have been earned had that person lived. But these lost wages do not measure the *intrinsic* value of the life, something that financial compensation simply cannot replace. The Decision Point, "Measuring Our Worth," explores the measurement of intrinsic value.

What is the value of health and what does it mean to be healthy? When is a workplace safe? When is it unsafe? If "healthy" is taken to mean a state of flawless physical and psychological well-being, arguably no one is perfectly healthy. If "safe" means completely free from risk, certainly no workplace is perfectly safe. If health and safety are interpreted as ideals that are impossible to realize, then it would be unreasonable to claim that employees have a right to a healthy and safe workplace.

Health and Safety as Acceptable Risk

8 OBJECTIVE

Employers cannot be responsible for providing an ideally safe and healthy workplace. Instead, discussions in ethics about employee health and safety will tend to focus on the *relative* risks workers face and the level of *acceptable* workplace risk. In this discussion, "risks" can be defined as the probability of harm, and we determine "relative risks" by comparing the probabilities of harm involved in various activities. Therefore, scientists who compile and measure data can determine both risks and relative risks (see Figure 6.1). It is an easy step from these calculations to certain conclusions about acceptable risks. If it can be determined that the probability of harm involved in a specific work activity is equal to or less than the probability of harm of some more common activity, then we can conclude that this activity faces an "acceptable level of risk." From this perspective, *a workplace is safe if the risks are acceptable.*

Imagine if we generalize this conclusion and determine all workplace health and safety standards in this manner. Such an approach would place the responsibility for workplace safety solely on management. A business would hire safety engineers and other experts to determine the risks within their workplace. These experts would know the risk levels that are otherwise accepted throughout the society. These might involve the risks involved in driving a car, eating high-fat food, smoking, jogging, and so forth. Comparing these to the risks faced in the workplace, safety experts could perform a risk assessment and determine the relative risks of work. If the workplace were less risky than other common activities, management could conclude that they have fulfilled their responsibility to provide a healthy and safe workplace.

However, such an approach to workplace health and safety issues has several problems. First, this approach treats employees disrespectfully by ignoring their input as stakeholders. Such paternalistic decision making effectively treats employees like children and makes crucial decisions for them, ignoring their role in the decision-making process. Second, in making this decision, we assume that health and safety are mere preferences that can be traded off against competing values, ignoring the fundamental deontological right an employee might have to a safe and healthy working environment. Third, it assumes an equivalency between workplace risks and other types of risks when there are actually significant differences between them. Unlike many daily risks, the risks faced in the workplace may not be freely chosen, nor are the risks faced in the workplace within the control of workers. Fourth, it disregards the utilitarian concern for the consequences of an unsafe working environment on the social fabric, the resulting product or service created, the morale of the workforce, and the community, as well as other large-scale results of an unhealthy workplace.

FIGURE 6.1 Calculating Acceptable Level of Risk

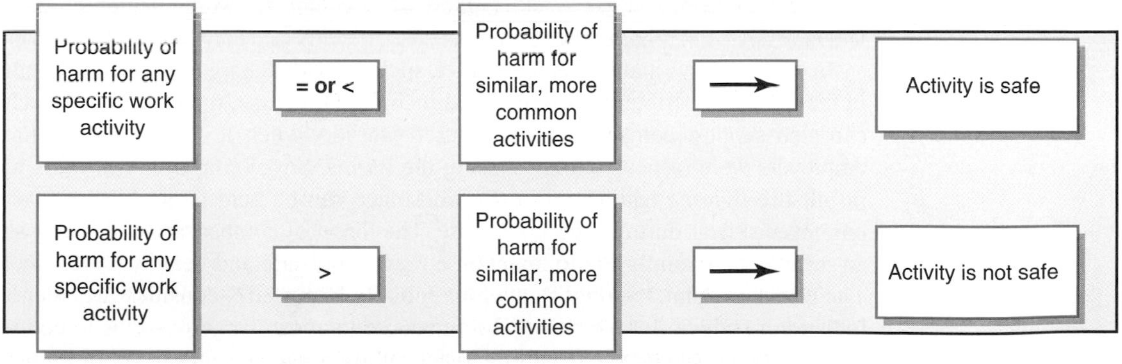

TABLE 6.3
Challenges to the Acceptable Risk Approach to Health and Safety

- Treats employees disrespectfully by ignoring their input as stakeholders.
- Ignores the fundamental deontological right an employee might have to a safe and healthy working environment.
- Assumes an equivalency between workplace risks and other types of risks when there are significant differences between them.
- Improperly places incentives since the risks faced at work could be controlled by others who might stand to benefit by *not* reducing them.

Perhaps most important, unlike some daily risks each of us freely undertakes, the risks faced at work could be controlled by others, particularly by others who might stand to benefit by *not* reducing the risks. For instance, making the workplace safe may pose substantial costs to employers. Relative to the risks one might face by smoking, for example, working in a mill and inhaling cotton dust may not seem as risky. But, in the former case, the smoker chooses to take the risk and could take steps to minimize or eliminate them by her- or himself. In the latter case, the mill worker cannot avoid the risks as long as she or he wants to keep a job. Often someone else can minimize or eliminate these risks; but this other party also has a financial incentive not to do so. In one case, smoking, the decision maker freely chooses to take the risk, knowing that she or he can control it. In the other case, the worker's choices and control are limited. The challenges involved in the acceptable risk approach to workplace health and safety are summarized in Table 6.3. Surely we need another approach.

Health and Safety as Market Controlled

Perhaps we can leave health and safety standards to the market. Defenders of the free market and the classical model of corporate social responsibility would favor individual bargaining between employers and employees as the approach to workplace health and safety. On this account, employees would be free to choose the risks they are willing to face by bargaining with employers. Employees would balance their preferences for risk against their demand for wages and decide how much risk they are willing to take for various wages. Those who demand higher safety standards and healthier conditions presumably would have to settle for lower wages; those willing to take higher risks presumably would demand higher wages.

In a competitive and free labor market, such individual bargaining would result in the optimal distribution of safety and income. Of course, the market approach can also support compensation to injured workers when it can be shown that employers were responsible for causing the harms. So an employer who fails to install fire-fighting equipment in the workplace can be held liable for burns an employee suffers during a workplace fire. The threat of compensation also acts as an incentive for employers to maintain a reasonably safe and healthy workplace. The Decision Point, "Should Dangerous Jobs Be Exported?" considers whether it is therefore ethical for a company to outsource its most dangerous jobs to countries where the labor force is willing to accept low wages for unsafe conditions.

Decision Point *Should Dangerous Jobs Be Exported?*

If one follows the market-based recommendation to allocate workplace risks on the basis of an optimal distribution of risks and benefits, one would conclude that, from a business perspective, dangerous jobs ought to be exported to those areas where wages are low and where workers are more willing to accept risky working conditions. The harms done by dangerous jobs, in terms of forgone earnings, are lower in regions with low wages and lower life expectancies. The benefits of providing jobs in regions with high unemployment would also outweigh the benefits of sending those jobs to regions with low unemployment. (See also the discussion of global labor markets, later in this chapter, and the discussion on exporting toxic wastes in chapter 9.)

- What facts would you want to know before deciding whether the practice of exporting dangerous jobs was fair and responsible?
- What alternatives to exporting dangerous jobs exist for a firm?
- Who are the stakeholders of your decision? What is the impact of each alternative mentioned above on each stakeholder you have identified?
- Should local legal regulations govern the situation?
- What are the consequences of such a decision? What rights and duties are involved? If the consequences are effective and valuable to the majority but fundamental rights are implicated, how will you decide what to do?

9 OBJECTIVE

This free market approach has a number of serious problems. First, labor markets are not perfectly competitive and free. Employees do not have the kinds of free choices that the free market theory would require in order to attain optimal satisfactions—though enlightened self-interest would be a valuable theory to introduce and apply in this environment, it is unrealistic to presume employees always have the choices available to them that make it possible. For example, risky jobs are often also the lowest-paying jobs, and people with the fewest employment choices hold them. Individuals are forced to accept the jobs because they have no choice but to accept; they are not actually "balancing their preferences for risk against their demand for wages" because they do not have options. Second, employees seldom, if ever, possess the kind of complete information efficient markets require. If employees do not know the risks involved in a job, they will not be in a position to freely bargain for appropriate wages and therefore they will not be in a position to effectively protect their rights or ensure the most ethical consequences. This is a particular concern when we recognize that many workplace risks are in no sense obvious. An employee may understand the dangers of heavy machinery or a blast furnace; but few employees can know the toxicity or exposure levels of workplace chemicals or airborne contaminants.

Such market failures can have deadly consequences when they involve workplace health and safety issues. Of course, market defenders argue that, over time:

markets will compensate for such failures, employers will find it difficult to attract workers to dangerous jobs, and employees will learn about the risks of every workplace. But this raises what we have previously described as the "first generation" problem. The means by which the market gathers information is by observing the harms done to the first generation exposed to imperfect market transactions. Thus, workers learn that exposure to lead is dangerous when some female workers exposed to lead suffer miscarriages or when others have children who are born with serious birth defects. We learn that workplace exposure to asbestos or cotton dust is dangerous when workers subsequently die from lung disease. In effect, markets sacrifice the first generation in order to gain information about safety and health risks. These questions of public policy, questions that after all will affect human lives, would never even be asked by an individual facing the choice of working at a risky job. To the degree that these are important questions that ought to be asked, individual bargaining will fail as an ethical public policy approach to worker health and safety. Table 6.4 summarizes the challenges inherent in the free market approach to health and safety.

Health and Safety—Government-Regulated Ethics

In response to such concerns, government regulation of workplace health and safety appears more appropriate from an ethical perspective. Mandatory government standards address most of the problems raised against market strategies. Standards can be set according to the best available scientific knowledge and thus overcome market failures that result from insufficient information. Standards prevent employees from having to face the fundamentally coercive choice between job and safety. Standards also address the first generation problem by focusing on prevention rather than compensation after the fact. Finally, standards are fundamentally a social approach that can address public policy questions ignored by markets.

In 1970, the U.S. Congress established the **Occupational Safety and Health Administration (OSHA)** and charged it with establishing workplace health and safety standards. Since that time, the major debates concerning workplace health and safety have focused on how such public standards ought to be set. The dominant question has concerned the appropriateness of using cost-benefit analysis to set health and safety standards.

When OSHA was first established, regulations were aimed at achieving the safest *feasible* standards. This "feasibility" approach allows OSHA to make tradeoffs between health and economics; but it is prejudiced in favor of health and safety by placing the burden of proof on industry to show that high standards are not economically feasible. Health and safety standards are not required, no

TABLE 6.4
Challenges with the Free Market Approach to Health and Safety

- Labor markets are not perfectly competitive and free.
- Employees seldom, if ever, possess the kind of perfect information markets require.
- We ignore important questions of social justice and public policy if we approach questions solely from the point of view of an individual.

Reality Check *Do Health and Safety Programs Cost Too Much?*

Evidence collected by the Occupational Safety and Health Administration suggests just the opposite: Safety and health programs *add* value and *reduce* costs. Even average companies can reduce injuries 20 to 40 percent by establishing safety and health programs. Several studies have estimated that safety and health programs save $4 to $6 for every dollar invested. Yet, only about 30 percent of U.S. work sites have established these programs. These savings result from a decrease in employee injuries and illnesses, lower workers' compensation costs, decreased medical costs, reduced absenteeism, lower turnover, higher productivity, and increased morale.

Source: Charles N. Jeffress, former assistant secretary for occupational safety and health, U.S. Department of Labor, "Future Directions for OSHA," speech delivered to National Safety Congress, New Orleans, October 19, 1999 (http://www.osha.gov/pls/oshaweb/owadisp.show_document?p table=SPEECHES&p_id=244).

matter the cost; but an industry is required to meet the highest standards attainable within technological and economic reason.

Some critics charge that this approach does not go far enough and unjustly sacrifices employee health and safety. From that perspective, industries that cannot operate without harming the health and safety of its employees should be closed. But the more influential business criticism has argued that these standards go too far. Critics in both industry and government have argued that OSHA should be required to use cost-benefit analysis in establishing such standards. From this perspective, even if a standard is technologically and economically feasible, it would still be unreasonable and unfair if the benefits did not outweigh the costs. These critics argue that OSHA should aim to achieve the optimal, rather than highest feasible, level of safety.

Using cost-benefit analysis to set standards, in effect, returns us to the goals of the market-based, individual bargaining approach. Like that market approach, this use of cost-benefit analysis faces serious ethical challenges. We should note, however, that rejecting cost-benefit analysis in setting standards is not the same as rejecting cost-effective strategies in implementing those standards. A commitment to cost-effectiveness would require that, once the standards are set, we adopt the least expensive and most efficient means available for achieving those standards. Cost-benefit analysis, in contrast, uses economic criteria in setting the standards in the first place. It is cost-benefit, not cost-effectiveness, analysis that is ethically problematic.

The use of cost-benefit analysis in setting workplace health and safety standards commits us to treating worker health and safety as just another commodity, another individual preference, to be traded off against competing commodities. It treats health and safety merely as an instrumental value and denies its intrinsic value. Cost-benefit analysis requires that an economic value be placed on one's life and bodily integrity. Typically, this would follow the model used by the insurance industry (where it is used in wrongful death settlements, for example) in which one's life is valued in terms of one's earning potential. Perhaps the most offensive aspect of this approach is the fact that since, in feasibility analysis,

Decision Point *How Much is Enough?*

Some might argue that even the cost of violating workplace health and safety standards is not sufficiently high to deter unsafe conditions for workers. In one occurrence, OSHA imposed a fine of $8.8 million on Imperial Sugar, the third largest fine in OSHA's history.[20] OSHA had found over one hundred "willful" safety violations at the company's plant in Louisiana. The violations were considered egregious since they were found at this location even *after* the company had experienced an explosion at a Georgia refinery that had killed 13 employees by obvious hazards of which Imperial Sugar was well aware.

If you were on the OSHA Commission to review the amounts of fines imposed, how would you reach a decision as to how much is enough? What factors would you consider?

- Who are the stakeholders involved in your decision?
- What do you foresee will be the impact of your decision on the stakeholders involved?
- How might ethical theory assist you in reaching this particular decision?
- Once you have reached your decision, which constituencies do you anticipate will be most supportive and which will be most against your decision, and why?

health and safety is already traded off against the economic viability of the industry, a shift to cost-benefit analysis entails trading off health and safety against profit margin. (See the Reality Check, "Do Health and Safety Programs Cost Too Much?", as well as the Decision Point, "How Much is Enough?" for an application of cost-benefit analysis.)

The policies that have emerged by consensus within the United States seem to be most defensible. Employees have a legitimate ethical claim on mandatory health and safety standards within the workplace. To say that employees have a right to workplace health and safety implies that they should not be expected to make trade-offs between health and safety standards and job security or wages. Further, recognizing that most mandatory standards reduce rather than eliminate risks, employees should also have the right to be informed about workplace risks. If the risks have been reduced to the lowest feasible level and employees are fully aware of them, then a society that respects its citizens as autonomous decision makers has done its duty.

Global Applications: The Global Workforce and Global Challenges

As you consider the issues of due process, fairness, and health and safety raised thus far in the chapter, note that the law discussed here applies to workers who are employed in the United States. Workers outside of the United States may be subject to some U.S. laws if they work for an American-based organization, though enforcement is scattered. In some cases, workers in other countries are often protected by even more stringent laws than those in the United States. Many countries in the European Union, for example, have strong laws protecting workers' rights to due process and participation. But in many other cases, especially in certain developing countries, workers find themselves subject to conditions that U.S.-based workers would find appalling. While those of us who work in the United States may benefit from battles fought in years past for occupational safety and health, workers in certain Southeast Asian countries, for instance, are simply arguing for at-will bathroom breaks.

10 OBJECTIVE

The response to this stark contrast is not a simple one. Though few people, if any, would argue for the continuation of the circumstances described above, economists and others do not agree about a solution. Some contend that the exploitation of cheap labor allows developing countries to expand export activities and to improve their economics. This economic growth brings more jobs, which will cause the labor market to tighten, which in turn will force companies to improve conditions in order to attract workers (see Figure 6.2). In fact, several commentators argue that encouraging greater global production will create additional opportunities for expansion domestically, providing a positive impact on more stakeholders.[21] Though it is an unpopular sentiment with the general consuming public, many economists argue that the maintenance of **sweatshops** is therefore supported by economic theory. Indeed, even the term *sweatshop* remains open to debate. (See the first end note in the reading by Matthew Zwolinski, "Sweatshops, Choice, and Exploitation.")

The reading by Zwolinski, "Sweatshops, Choice, and Exploitation," explores the issue from a slightly different perspective. He defends the moral legitimacy of sweatshops and responds to the question of whether a worker under these conditions can actually consent to them or be considered to be working "voluntarily" at all. He concludes that a worker actually is able to give consent; therefore,

> there is a strong moral reason for third parties such as consumers and host and home country governments to refrain from acting in ways which are likely to deprive sweatshop workers of their jobs, and both the policies traditionally promoted by anti-sweatshop activists (e.g. increasing the legal regulation of sweatshops, legally prohibiting the sale of sweatshop-produced goods, or subjecting such goods to economic boycott), and some more recent proposals by anti-sweatshop academics (i.e. voluntary self-regulation via industry-wide standards or universal moral norms) are subject to criticism on these grounds.[22]

On the other hand, opponents to this perspective argue that allowing this process to take its course will not necessarily lead to the anticipated result, just as voluntarily improving legal compliance, wages, and working conditions will not inevitably lead to the negative consequences the free market advocates threaten. The reading by T. A. Frank, "Confessions of a Sweatshop Inspector," offers a perspective somewhat in opposition to Zwolinski's. Consider the sign mentioned early in the article, observed in large characters on a factory's wall, "If you don't

FIGURE 6.2
The Case *for* Sweatshops

Source: D. Arnold and L. Hartman, "Worker Rights and Low Wage Industrialization: How to Avoid Sweatshops," *Human Rights Quarterly,* vol. 28, no. 3 (August 2006), pp. 676–700. Reprinted by permission of *Human Rights Quarterly* and its publisher, the Johns Hopkins University Press.

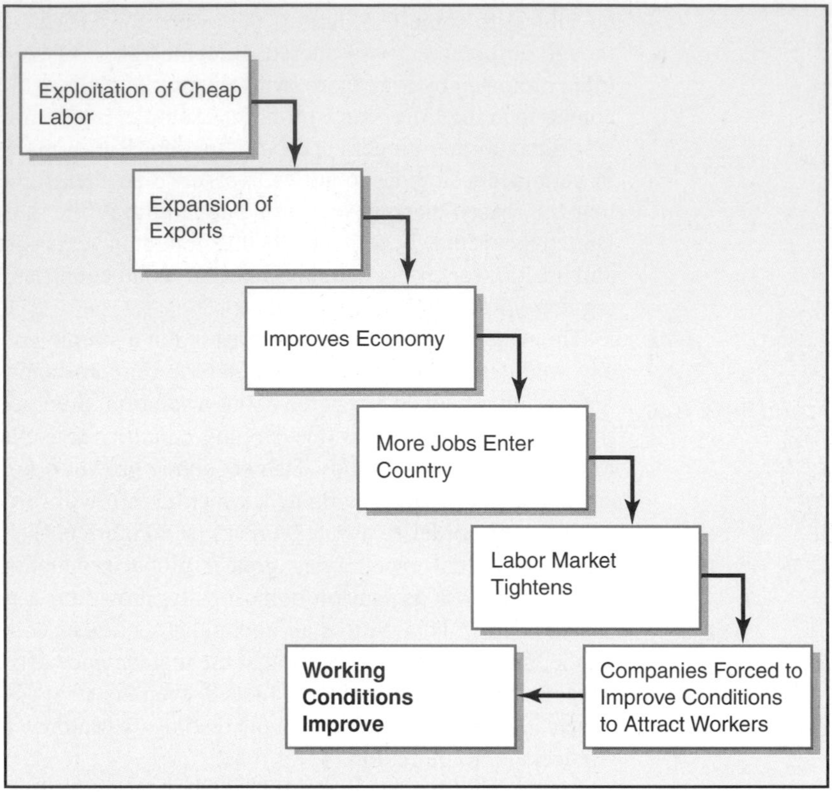

work hard today, look hard for work tomorrow." Frank might take issue with Zwolinski's claim of worker consent to conditions where few alternatives exist. From a unique point of view, Frank shares the experience of inspecting serving as an independent monitor of overseas suppliers to multinational retailers.

One of Frank's key clues to whether a client "cared" about working conditions was the nature of its relationships with its suppliers. "Long-term commitments are what motivate both parties to behave: the supplier wants to preserve the relationship, and the customer wants to preserve its reputation." The case, "Attacking the Roots: Shiraishi Garments Company and an Evolving Thicket of Business Ethics in China," by Bin Jiang and Patrick J. Murphy explores this very question. In that case, Shiraishi Garments Company is a Japanese firm that sources its supply chain from China, where it is confronted with some ethical challenges in connection with working conditions. The CEO senses that he must resolve conflicts between his personal values and professional responsibilities. However, he learns that the development of more meaningful supply chain relationships might just pose some more effective—and ethical—solutions.

As we examine ethical issues in the workplace, a helpful exercise is to consider the global dimension of an ethically responsible workplace. Certainly it is arguable that some minimum standards might apply and multinationals may have some core ethical obligations to employees. But how do we determine what those might be? Should the best employment practices in the United States set the standard for the global economy? That would mean concluding that the standards of one particular country are appropriate for all countries and cultures of the world, not necessarily the optimal conclusion.

Instead, some scholars have argued that Kantian universal principles should govern the employment relationship and that the ethical obligation of respect for persons should guide the employment interactions. "To fully respect a person, one must actively treat his or her humanity as an end, and not merely as a means to an end. This means that it is impermissible to treats persons like disposable tools."[23] Though different ethical theories may yield conflicting responses, it is arguable that a fundamental moral minimum set of standards exists that should be guaranteed to workers in all countries notwithstanding culture, stage of economic development, or availability of resources. Philosophers Arnold and Bowie contend that multinationals "must ensure the physical well-being of employees and refrain from undermining the development of their rational and moral capacities . . . [R]especting workers in global factories requires that factories of multinational corporations (MNCs), including contract factories, adhere to local labor laws, refrain from the use of coercion, provide decent working conditions, and provide wages above the overall poverty line for a 48-hour work week."[24] Others contend the list should also include a minimum age for child labor, nondiscrimination requirements (including the right to equal pay for equal work), and free association including the right to organize and to bargain collectively in contract negotiations.[25]

Even defining a "living wage" is problematic. In a world that cannot seem to agree on the number of people living in poverty,[26] figuring out how much is sufficient to offer a subsistence quality of life represents hurdles. A number of companies have implemented living wage policies in their global operations. For example, the Swedish pharmaceutical company Novartis reports that it pays 100 percent of its global workforce a living wage.[27] Another company, adidas-Salomon, ensures that its contract workers are paid a "fair wage," one that will both meet the needs of workers and provide for discretionary spending; adidas uses a wage setting mechanism with the following objectives:

- Is transparent and has direct input by the workers, ideally through negotiation or collective bargaining, or through alternative legal means, such as a workers council or welfare committee;
- Benchmarks basic pay at a level that is higher than the local minimum wage;
- Acknowledges and rewards workers for productivity gains;
- Includes and takes into account data on general cost of living and workers' needs;
- Is part of a broader and much improved human resource management system;
- Meets in full all legally mandated benefits; and, where practicable,
- Promotes and supports the development of worker cooperatives.[28]

Decision Point *What to Do about Child Labor*

As you explore the question of child labor that follows, consider the many stakeholders involved and the power each one holds (or lack thereof), the options available to the multinational corporations, and the options consumers have in determining from whom they will buy, what rights might be implicated and the consequences of protecting them, and how you would respond if you were a labor advocate seeking to determine the best next steps in the debate.

- What are the key facts relevant to your decision regarding child labor?
- What are the ethical issues involved in child labor? What incentives might be in place that would actively support or pose challenges to your response?
- Who are the stakeholders in connection with child labor?
- What alternative responses might you suggest?
- How would each of your alternatives affect each of the stakeholders you have identified?
- Is there any guidance available from global organizations to assist you in resolving this particular dilemma?

Non-wage benefits are an important and neglected aspect of the debate over global sweatshops. In many instances such benefits can provide an advantage to both the worker and the employer. For example, an MNC factory that provides free health checkups and basic health care services to workers through a factory clinic will typically have a healthier and more productive work force than factories that lack such benefits. Levi Strauss & Company provides medical services to employees, their families, and members of the surrounding communities. The company currently offers medical, dental, and optometry clinics. Beginning in 1999, the company's factories also sponsored vaccination, nutrition, and mental health campaigns. Since public healthcare in the locations where the Levi Strauss factories are located is generally poor, particularly in smaller cities and remote rural areas, companies play a vital role in providing additional assistance. Levi Strauss is not the only company to provide a medical clinic, but one of the few to reach out to the community to explore areas of implementation and integration.[29]

International nongovernmental organizations have also attempted to step into this fray to suggest voluntary standards to which possible signatory countries or organizations could commit. For instance, the International Labour Office has promulgated its Tripartite Declaration of Principles Concerning Multinational Enterprises and Social Policy, which offers guidelines for employment, training, conditions of work and life, and industrial relations. The "Tripartite" part of the title refers to the critical cooperation necessary from governments, employers' and workers' organizations, and the multinational enterprises involved.

As mentioned above, the discussion of legal and ethical expectations and boundaries in this chapter is based on the law in the United States. However, awareness of the limitations of this analysis and sensitivity to the challenges of global implementation are critical in today's multinational business operations. We will revisit the quandary of varying ethical standards as applied to diverse economic and social environments in the next section with regard to the issue of child labor.

The Case of Child Labor

One of the key issues facing business in today's globalized economy is the potential for cultural or legal conflicts in connection with worldwide labor management. Though the issues stir our consciences, their resolution is not so clear. Let us consider, for example, the case of **child labor.** As we begin to understand the circumstances facing children worldwide, we can see that a simple prohibition might not offer us the best possible solution. But what options exist? (For a general inquiry, please see the Decision Point, "What to Do about Child Labor.")

According to International Labour Organization estimates, 250 million children between 5 and 17 years old currently work in developing countries, almost half of them on a full-time basis.[30] "Moreover, some 8.4 million children [a]re engaged in so-called 'unconditional' worst forms of child labor, which include forced and bonded labor, the use of children in armed conflict, trafficking in children and commercial sexual exploitation."[31] Because work takes children out of school, more than half of the child labor force will never be literate.[32] Substandard working conditions have an impact on growth; child employees will be physically smaller than those who did not work as children even into adulthood.[33] By the time child laborers become adults, most will irrevocably be sick or deformed, unlikely to live beyond fifty years old.[34]

Of course, employers in many economically developed countries currently use children as laborers, albeit with restrictions (anyone recall the *eight* in "Jon & Kate + 8?"); so one should carefully review the social and economic structure within which the labor exists. While the easy answer may be to rid all factories of all workers under 18 years of age, that is often not the best answer for the children or the families involved. Prospects for working children in developing countries indeed appear bleak. Children may begin work as young as three years old. They not only may work in unhealthy conditions; they may also live in unhealthy conditions. The labor opportunities that exist almost always require children to work full time, thereby precluding them from obtaining an education.[35] However, if children are not working, their options are not as optimistic as those of children in developed economies. Sophisticated education systems or public schools are not always available. Often children who do not work in the manufacturing industry are forced to work in less hospitable "underground" professions, such as drug dealing or prostitution, simply to earn their own food each day.[36]

Moreover, even if educational alternatives are available in some environments, recommending removal of the child from the workplace completely ignores the financial impact of the child leaving his or her job. The income the youth worker generates may, at the very least, assist in supporting his or her fundamental needs (food, clothing, and shelter); at the most, it may be critical in supporting the entire family.

Decision Point *Gender versus Race*

How would this same story about gender coaching sound if it had to do with one race acting too much like another? Or, how would you feel about the story if it suggested that a certain group of people should "know their place" or people will not want to work with them? What would you think of a program that offered coaching to men on how to be "more like women" because the program suggested that women were put off by boorish, insensitive males?

- What key facts are relevant to the issue of coaching?
- What are the origins of coaching and what challenges have served to create a need for it?
- In addition to the race question raised above, what are some of the other ethical issues that come to mind when you consider this practice?
- Who are the stakeholders involved in this particular issue?
- What alternative responses are available?
- How would each of your alternatives affect each of the stakeholders you have identified?
- Where might you look for additional guidance to assist you in resolving this particular dilemma?

We often do not recognize areas of Western culture that contain or perpetuate covert discrimination. In the article "White Privilege: Unpacking the Invisible Knapsack,"[43] Peggy McIntosh identifies a number of daily conditions a white person in Western society can count on:

- I can go shopping alone most of the time, pretty well assured that I will not be followed or harassed.
- I can open a newspaper or turn on the television and see people of my race represented positively.
- I can do well in a challenging situation without being called a credit to my race.
- I am never asked to speak for all of the people in my racial group.

McIntosh explains that these privileges are like "an invisible weightless knapsack of provisions, maps, passports, codebooks, visas, clothes, tools and blank checks."

U.S. businesses believe they work in a diverse workplace.[44] This is not surprising since the pool of eligible and interested workers is becoming more and more diverse as well. By 2010, only 20 percent of the workforce is comprised of white men under 45.[45] As one might expect, the management composition at firms with diversity programs is significantly more diverse than those at firms that do not have such programs, and 79 percent of senior managers at those firms say that cultivating a more diverse workforce is part of the organization's overall business strategy.

A few European countries have out-paced the United States in terms of diversity efforts and, in particular, in connection with board representation. While the average representation of women on European boards is only 11 percent, Norway

Reality Check *Diversity = $$?*

A groundbreaking study by *Catalyst* in 2004 evidenced a strong link between gender diversity in top management teams and corporate financial performance. The study's authors contend that the link is based on the fact that employers who pay attention to diversity have a larger and more capable applicant pool from whom to choose the best workers. These organizations are also better positioned to respond more effectively to a diverse consumer population. In addition, these firms evidence better decision making, production and other critical success factors.

- The group of companies with the highest representation of women on their top management teams experienced better financial performance than the group of companies with the lowest women's representation.
- In four out of the five industries analyzed, the group of companies with the highest women's representation on their top management teams experienced a higher total return to shareholders than the group of companies with the lowest women's representation.

Source: Catalyst, Inc., "The Bottom Line: Connecting Corporate Performance and Gender Diversity" (2004), http://www.catalyst.org/publication/82/the-bottom-line-connecting-corporate-performance-and-gender-diversity.

(32 percent), Sweden (24 percent), and Finland (19 percent) are well above that average.[46] One reason for Norway's leadership is a federal law that required companies to fill 40 percent of corporate board seats with women by 2008, a target that was met ahead of its date. Failure to comply would result in a complete shutdown of operations.[47] A study by *Catalyst* of the situation of women on boards in the United States shows, to the contrary, that it will take women *seventy years* to reach parity with men in the board rooms of *Fortune* 500 companies at the current rate of change.[48] Firms have begun to take greater and greater notice as *Catalyst's* research does evidence that firms with more women on boards perform better than those with very few, outperforming those in the bottom quartile by 53 percent.[49] The positive impact on the *overall* strategy is not insignificant, as the Reality Check, "Diversity = $$?" further details *Catalyst's* research findings.

13 OBJECTIVE

Diversity has brought benefits to the workplace, but diversity efforts have also created new conflicts. Recall the definition of diversity above: Diversity refers to the presence of differing cultures, languages, ethnicities, races, affinity orientations, genders, religious sects, abilities, social classes, ages, and national origins of the individuals in a firm. When a firm brings together individuals with these (or other) differences—often exposing these individuals to such differences for the first time—areas of tension and anxiety may emerge. In addition, the organization is likely to ask its employees to work together toward common goals, on teams, in supervisory or subordinate roles, and in power relationships, all requests that might lead to conflicts or tension even without additional stressors such as cultural challenges.

Diversity can potentially increase several areas of values tension. Where differences are new or strong, *and* where negative stereotypes previously ruled interactions between particular groups, sensitivity to the potential for conflict is necessary.

Decision Point *Diversity Mentoring Programs*

Chevron Texaco includes case studies in its annual Corporate Responsibility Reports. The following appeared in its 2002 report in a discussion about diversity. As is described on the following page, several years prior, Texaco settled a large discrimination suit and knew it had to make some changes in this area. As you review the statistics above and the case study below, consider these questions:

- What do you believe is Chevron Texaco's motivation?
- Who are its key stakeholders for this particular communication and for the program itself?
- Do you believe the program seems like it is or will be a successful one or, if you might need additional information, what do you believe would be the key components to make this program successful?

DIVERSITY MENTORING PROGRAM

ChevronTexaco Global Lubricants (CTGL) markets more than 3,500 lubricants and coolants around the globe and is ranked among the top three global lubricants companies. CTGL believes that its success depends not just on product quality but also on developing a workforce that mirrors the global diversity of its customers. "Having a diversity of backgrounds and views gives us a unique advantage," says Shariq Yosufzai, president of Global Marketing for Downstream. "The varied perspectives of our colleagues help us better anticipate market challenges and forge better solutions. We must look and think like our customers."

An innovative mentoring process helps CTGL cultivate a diverse management team. Each of the 15 members of the Global Lubricants Leadership Team mentors up to three visibly or globally diverse employees. The goal is to increase the number of diverse candidates for leadership positions around the world, while also providing those leaders continued support to ensure that they succeed, as well as their business.

Another concern involves integrating diverse viewpoints with a preexisting corporate culture. There seems nothing inappropriate about seeking to ensure that workers will support the particular values of a firm, but it might be difficult to do this while also encouraging diversity. Diversity, which might be the source of positive gains for the organization, might also be the source of fundamental differences in values that must be balanced. Some scholars suggest that job applicants be screened with regard to their values, but how can employers do so? Hiring is not an area to be taken lightly, but most firms go with a "gut" instinct about whether or not a job applicant will "fit in." In the same way that you might apply the "can you sleep at night" test to an ethical dilemma after considering all the implications of a decision, you might trust an employment choice to the same test.

It is not discriminatory to refuse to hire someone about whom you simply have a "bad feeling," unless that bad feeling is based on their difference in race or gender. On the other hand, it is vital to be wary of prejudgments based solely on differences in interpretations of culturally based standards. While variance in fundamental standards might justify a sense of a "bad fit" between a potential employer and employee, divergence in culturally based standards such as attire, hair styles, or manner of speaking might instead be treated differently. Efforts at understanding **multiculturalism**, such as acknowledging and promoting diversity through celebration and appreciation of various cultures in the workplace, can serve both to educate and to encourage the benefits linked to diversity efforts.

On the other hand, the cost of ignoring diversity is high, not only in terms of losses of productivity, creativity, and other performance-based measures, but also in terms of legal liability. Texaco experienced what insiders refer to simply as "the crisis" in 1996 when the company was required to pay $175 million to settle a racial discrimination lawsuit. The settlement was based on taped conversations of executives using racist language as well as documented compensation discrimination against minority employees, hundreds of whom were being paid below the minimum salary for their job level.

A firm often reaches its depths before it emerges anew, and Texaco's subsequent numbers tell a much different story. In 2002, minority hires accounted for 46 percent of all new employees, including some key senior executives, and more than 20 percent of promotions, and 34 percent of new hires were women. Texaco pledged to spend at least $1 million with minority and women contractors within five years of the settlement and, of course, diversity training is now mandated for all workers, with management compensation tied to the attainment of success in implementing new initiatives. (See the Decision Point, "Diversity Mentoring Programs," for additional information about Chevron Texaco programs.)

Affirmative Action

Throughout this chapter, we have discussed the means by which to protect employer interests and employee rights. With regard to the latter, we have focused on employee rights to fair treatment and due process in the workplace. A question arises, however, when we consider balancing those rights with competing employee rights, as may occur in the case of **affirmative action**. The question regarding affirmative action is not necessarily whether a person has a right to fair process in connection with employment but instead whether one has a right to the job in the first place. Does one person deserve a position *more* than another person? For instance, efforts to encourage greater diversity may also be seen as a form of **reverse discrimination:** discrimination against those traditionally considered to be in power or the majority, such as white men. A business that intentionally seeks to hire a candidate from an underrepresented group might be seen as discriminating against white males, for example.

The arguments on both sides of this issue have a tendency towards emotional persuasion. Imagine you are hiring a social worker to serve an overwhelmingly African American community that is currently facing issues, among others, of teen pregnancy. Not only might you argue that you want to hire someone who is African American; you might also want a female social worker who might be better able to speak with the teenage women in that community. On the other hand, in front of you is a 40-year-old white male with a master's degree from an extraordinarily valuable program. He has years of experience in the field and in fact has an adopted African American daughter himself. He claims he can handle the job. In fact, he claims he *deserves* the job. Does he? Does it matter whether he deserves it? Does he have a *right* to the job? Assume you still want the younger African American woman you know is next on your interview list. What is the fairest decision? Fair to whom? Fairest to the young women of your community, to the applicants you are interviewing, or to other stakeholders? How should you decide? What will be the consequences of your decision?

Diversity issues raise other less apparent problems. For example, consider a report by the U.S. Commission on Civil Rights that addresses the unique predicament of Asian Americans. The report documents widespread discrimination against Asian Americans, who have long been seen as having escaped the national origin barriers that face other cultures. The report contends that the typical Asian stereotype of being hardworking, intelligent, and successful is actually a detriment to Asian Americans. This stereotype results in the problems of overlooking poor Asians and preventing successful Asian Americans from becoming more successful. It also places undue pressure on young Asian Americans to succeed in school, and it discredits other minorities by arguing that "if Asian Americans can succeed, so can other minorities."[50] In an article highlighting the report, *Fortune* magazine contends that the problem is really that the commission is "being driven crazy by the fact that Asian Americans have been succeeding essentially *without the benefit of affirmative action.* The ultimate problem is not that they may make other minorities look bad—it is that they are making the civil rights bureaucracy look irrelevant."[51] Some theorists argue that formal affirmative action measures have often served to create a greater divide rather than to draw people closer.

14 OBJECTIVE

Let us take a closer look at affirmative action to explore the ethical issues it raises. The term *affirmative action* refers to a policy or a program that tries to respond to instances of past discrimination by implementing proactive measures to ensure equal opportunity today. It may take the form of intentional inclusion of previously excluded groups in employment, education, or other environments.

The use of affirmative action policies in both business and universities has been controversial for decades. (For the latest facts and figures, see the Reality Checks, "Affirmative Action Facts" and "The White Male as Endangered Species.") In its first discussion of affirmative action in employment, the U.S. Supreme Court found that employers could intentionally include minorities (and thereby exclude others) in order to redress past wrongs. However, the holding was not without restrictions, which have caused confusion. Even today, the law is not clear, and we must turn to values systems to provide direction, which we will discuss shortly.

Reality Check *Affirmative Action Facts*

- According to the U.S. Census, 23 percent of the workforce is minority, up from 10.7 percent in 1964.
- In 2003, white women's median weekly earnings were 76 percent those of white men. Black women's earnings were 66 percent of the earnings of white men, and Latina women's earnings were 55 percent of white men's earnings.
- Black women with bachelor's degrees make only $1,545 more per year than white males who have only completed high school.
- In an important longitudinal study of black and white women ages 34 to 44, only one-fifth of the gap between their wages could be explained by education and experience. The study found that while women are segregated into lower-paying jobs, the impact is greater on black women than white women.
- Research indicates that as the percentage of females and the percentage of minorities in a job increases, average pay falls, even when all other factors are held steady.
- Black men with professional degrees receive 79 percent of the salary paid to white men with the same degrees and comparable jobs. Black women earn 60 percent.
- A study conducted by the U.S. Department of Labor found that women and minorities have made more progress breaking through the glass ceiling at smaller companies. Women comprise 25 percent of the managers and corporate officers in smaller establishments, while minorities represent 10 percent. But among *Fortune* 500 companies, women held 18 percent of the managerial jobs, with minorities holding 7 percent.
- The federal Glass Ceiling Commission found that white women made up close to half the workforce, but held only 5 percent of the senior level jobs in corporations. Blacks and other minorities account for less than 3 percent of top jobs (vice president and above).
- Cecelia Conrad, associate professor of economics at Barnard College in New York, examined whether affirmative action plans had hurt worker productivity. She found "no evidence that there has been any decline in productivity due to affirmative action." She also found no evidence of improved productivity due to affirmative action.
- A study of Standard & Poor's 500 companies found firms that broke barriers for women and minorities reported stock market records nearly 2.5 times better than comparable companies that took no action.

Source: D. Bennett-Alexander and L. Hartman, *Employment Law for Business*, 5th ed. (McGraw-Hill/Irwin: Burr Ridge, IL 2005), p. 186.

Affirmative action arises in the workplace in three ways. The first way is through legal requirements. Much of the law relating to affirmative action only applies only to about 20 percent of the workforce; however, those employees of federal contractors with 50 or more employees are subject to Executive Order 11246, which requires affirmative action efforts to ensure equal opportunity. Second, where Executive Order 11246 does not apply, courts may require "judicial affirmative action" in order to remedy a finding of past discrimination. A third form of affirmative action involves voluntary affirmative action plans, which are plans that employers undertake in order to overcome barriers to equal opportunity. These might include training plans and programs, focused recruiting activity,

Reality Check *The White Male as Endangered Species?*

Some white males may feel that they are under siege by the forces of affirmative action and multiculturalism. Still, *Newsweek* argues that being a white man remains a very comfortable role in contemporary America:

But is the white male truly an endangered species, or is he just being a jerk? It's still a statistical piece of cake being a white man, at least in comparison with being anything else. White males make up just 39.2 percent of the population, yet they account for 82.5 percent of the *Forbes* 400 (folks worth at least $265 million), 77 percent of Congress, 92 percent of state governors, 70 percent of tenured college faculty, almost 90 percent of daily-newspaper editors, and 77 percent of TV news directors.

or the elimination of discrimination that might be caused by hiring criteria that exclude a particular group. A demonstrated underrepresentation of a particular group or a finding of past discrimination is required to justify affirmative action efforts under either of these latter two options.

15 OBJECTIVE

After a number of legal opinions, employers are left with some basic guidelines for creating these programs and policies. Consider how the following *legal* constraints to an affirmative action program are in line with deontological and teleological frameworks that also support ethical decision making:

1. The affirmative action efforts or policy may not unnecessarily infringe upon the majority employees' rights or create an absolute bar to their advancement.
2. The affirmative action effort or policy may not set aside any positions for women or minorities and may not be construed as quotas to be met.
3. It should unsettle no legitimate, firmly rooted expectation of employees.
4. It should be only temporary in that it is for the purpose of attaining, not maintaining, a balanced workforce.
5. It should represent a minimal intrusion into the legitimate, settled expectations of other employees.

Opponents to affirmative action contend that the efforts do more harm than good, that affirmative action creates ill will and poor morale among workforces. They argue that it translates into current punishment of past wrongs and therefore is inappropriately placed because those who "pay" for the wrongs are unfairly burdened and should not bear the responsibility for the acts of others. Not only white males make this claim. Ward Connerly, an African American regent of the University of California, discussed affirmative action during a *60 Minutes* interview and stated, "Black Americans are not hobbled by chains any longer. We're free to compete. We're capable of competing. It is an absolute insult to suggest that we can't."

In its first ruling on this issue in more than a decade, the Supreme Court addressed affirmative action again through a case of "reverse discrimination" in 2003. While this particular case involved university admissions, American business was a stakeholder in the case as well. The University of Michigan Law School relied on an admissions policy that took into account the ability of each applicant to contribute to the school's social and intellectual life. As part of this criterion, the school considered the applicant's race, on the assumption that a diverse student body would contribute to the goals of the law school and that a critical mass of minority students was required to accomplish that goal. Thus, although scores from LSAT tests, undergraduate college grades, letters of recommendation, and other traditional factors were primarily used to grant admission, an applicant's race was also a factor. Two white females who were denied admission brought the lawsuit, arguing that admission of minority students with lower grades and test scores violated their rights to equal treatment.

General Motors Corporation filed an *amicus curiae* ("friend of the court") brief in support of the law school's admission policy. By doing so, GM went out of its way at great expense to identify itself as a business stakeholder and argue publicly in support of affirmative action. In its brief, GM claimed that the need to ensure a racially and ethnically diverse student body was a compelling reason to support affirmative action policies. GM claimed that "the future of American business and, in some measure, of the American economy depends on it." In its own business experience, "only a well educated, diverse workforce, comprising people who have learned to work productively and creatively with individuals from a multitude of races and ethnic, religious, and cultural backgrounds, can maintain America's competitiveness in the increasingly diverse and interconnected world economy." Prohibiting affirmative action likely "would reduce racial and ethnic diversity in the pool of employment candidates from which the nation's businesses can draw their future leaders, impeding businesses' own efforts to achieve and obtain the manifold benefits of diversity in the managerial levels of their work forces."[52]

The court seemed to agree.

> [D]iminishing the force of such stereotypes is both a crucial part of the Law School's mission, and one that it cannot accomplish with only token numbers of minority students. Just as growing up in a particular region or having particular professional experiences is likely to affect an individual's views, so too is one's own, unique experience of being a racial minority in a society, like our own, in which race unfortunately still matters. The Law School has determined, based on its experience and expertise, that a "critical mass" of underrepresented minorities is necessary to further its compelling interest in securing the educational benefits of a diverse student body.[53]

Do you believe that a diverse student body contributes to the ability of a school to accomplish its educational mission? Should the law prohibit, allow, or require affirmative action programs? Would General Motors be ethically correct in adopting a similar affirmative action hiring policy? Can you think of cases in which an employee's race or ethnic background would be a qualification—or a disqualification—for employment?

Opening Decision Point Revisited

Abercrombie & Fitch: Image Consciousness?

In the 2003 class action lawsuit against Abercrombie & Fitch, a settlement agreement was reached between A&F and more than 10,000 claimants who were Latino, African American, Asian American, and female applicants and employees of the company. Under the settlement, A&F agreed to pay claims ranging from several hundred dollars to thousands of dollars, depending on the claimant's particular damages and the extent to which they contributed to the prosecution of the case for a total of $50 million, including attorneys' fees. In addition, A&F also is required to institute policies and programs to promote diversity among its workforce and to prevent discrimination based on race or gender.

The following additional elements of the settlement agreement are important because they were included in order to promote diversity in A&F's workforce. Consider whether any of these elements might have helped A&F to avoid the challenging circumstances described at the beginning of this chapter. If it had instituted some of these prior to the T-shirt situation, maybe it would not have found itself in that hot water:

- "Benchmarks" for hiring and promotion of women, Latinos, African Americans, and Asian Americans (goals, rather than quotas).
- A prohibition on targeting fraternities, sororities, or specific colleges for recruitment purposes.
- Advertising available positions in publications that target minorities of both genders.
- A new office of diversity with its own vice president, responsible for reporting to the CEO on Abercrombie's progress toward fair employment practices.
- Hiring 25 recruiters who will focus on and seek women and minority employees.
- Equal Employment Opportunity (EEO) and Diversity Training for all employees with hiring authority.
- Revision of managers' performance evaluations, making progress toward diversity goals a factor in their bonuses and compensation.
- A new internal complaint procedure.
- Marketing materials that will reflect diversity by including members of minority racial and ethnic groups.[54]

Since the time of the settlement and in partial satisfaction of it, A&F has launched a new human resources campaign, "Diversity is who we are." Information about the campaign can be found at A&F's human resources general Web site at http://www.abercrombie.com/anf/hr/jobs/index2.html. The diversity link on the Web site includes photographs of multiracial couples rather than its traditional "American classic" look, images of people of color, and text from the chairman that explains, "*Diversity* and *inclusion* are key to our organization's success. We are determined to have a diverse culture, throughout our organization, that benefits from the perspectives of each individual." Ironically, the main "job opportunities" link on the human resources Web site continues to maintain the standard "American classic" imagery more traditional to A&F's original style.

(*continued*)

(*concluded*)

When one explores the impact of the T-shirt controversy it is interesting to consider both sides of the stakeholder opinions. Though one side expressed emotional pain and derided the perpetuation of historic discrimination, others felt that people have become too thin-skinned and that, as a society, we have moved beyond these issues to a point where poking fun at stereotypes is acceptable, hence A&F's response. One of the values in a diverse workforce is the ability to weigh varying stakeholder perspectives. While one group might consider a marketing campaign to be "poking fun," another might be brutally pained by the mockery. A greater diversity among decision makers certainly does not guarantee that all perspectives are represented, but it does ensure that a broader range of opinions might be considered.

A&F might benefit from a broader range of opinions on a variety of matters. In recent years, it has drawn criticism from Mothers Against Drunk Driving for its "Drinking 101" directions for "creative drinking" in its catalogs aimed at college students and from several family-oriented organizations for its children's thong underwear with the words "eye candy" and "wink wink" printed on the front. With headlines such as "Abercrombie Criticized for Sexy Undies,"[55] perhaps A&F again misjudged its audience. A&F responded that "the underwear for young girls was created with the intent to be lighthearted and cute," and placed any misunderstanding "purely in the eye of the beholder."

Questions, Projects, and Exercises

1. Maya confides in her friend and colleague, Alicia, "My husband Gene is very sick. I haven't shared this with anyone else at work because I didn't want them to think I couldn't manage my responsibilities. He was diagnosed last year with progressive Parkinson's and I thought it would move slowly, and that I could handle everything. Believe me, I am trying to keep everything under control, but our home life is just overwhelming me already. You couldn't imagine how hard this is physically and emotionally—plus there's the added pressure of keeping it under wraps at work. You know they'll start diminishing my role on those larger projects if they knew my attention might be diverted, and Gene and I just can't risk the financial instability that might cause. I really appreciate being able to talk to you. I had to get this off my chest, and I knew I could trust you." Alicia offered her shoulder and told Maya that she could count on her to cover for her, if need be, or to support her in any way she needed. Three weeks later, Alicia and Maya are separately called into the president's office and told that they are both being considered for a more senior-level position. This new position would require a great commitment of both time and energy and would involve taking on a large number of subordinates for mentoring and development. Both women express a strong interest in the position and are told that they will learn of the president's decision within two weeks. What should Alicia do with the information Maya gave her, if anything? Notwithstanding your response to the previous question, if Alicia chooses to inform the president of Maya's current situation, would you consider that action to be wrong, unethical? If you were the president in this current scenario, what could you do to impact the corporate culture in order to ensure that your preferred result in this dilemma occurred in the future?

2. Review the discussion about global labor challenges, explore any additional resources (Web sites or otherwise), and offer your conclusions. In particular, which arguments do you find the most or least persuasive? Are you in favor of greater restrictions and regulations of MNCs and the treatment of their workforces, or would you advocate a more hands-off approach (sometimes described inappropriately as "pro-sweatshops")? Support your conclusions.
3. We can distinguish due process from just cause in the following way: Imagine a company wanted to abandon the arbitrary nature of employment at will and ensure that its employees were treated fairly in any termination decision. Can you imagine how the employment environment in that firm might be different than in other firms? One approach would be to specify the acceptable reasons for terminating an employee. Obvious candidates would include absenteeism, incompetent job performance, theft, fraud, and economic necessity. This approach might also identify unacceptable reasons for dismissal. Such a policy would be identified as a "just cause" practice, since it defines the factors that would justify dismissing an employee for cause. But creating such a list could be a challenge in that one would have to know beforehand all possible reasons for firing someone. As the common law clearly shows, one cannot anticipate all future ways in which something unjust could occur. As a result, a due process policy might be created to complement, or substitute for, a just cause policy. A policy guaranteeing due process, for example, would outline procedures that must be followed before an employee can be dismissed. The process itself is what determines a just dismissal. If an employer followed the process, the decision would be considered just; if the process was violated, then dismissal would be considered unjust. Such procedures might include regular written performance appraisals, prior warnings, documentation, probationary periods, rights to appeal, or response to accusations. Can you imagine other ways in which this hypothetical firm might change standard processes to ensure fairness?
    - What are the key facts relevant to issues of due process and fairness?
    - What are the ethical issues involved in your decision and implementation?
    - Who are the stakeholders involved in your decision?
    - What alternatives are available to you?
    - How would each of your alternatives affect each of the stakeholders you have identified?
    - Where might you look for additional guidance to assist you in resolving this particular dilemma?
4. What is the difference in your mind, and in your common usage, between a perception, a generalization, and a stereotype? Can you give an example of each? After doing so, go to the Web and find dictionary-equivalent definitions of the terms to determine whether your common understanding is the correct one. Are each or all consistently unethical judgments or are they sometimes or always ethically justified in their use and implementation? Under what conditions?
5. A particular research study provides some evidence that those born between 1979 and 1994 are perceived as "impatient, self-serving, disloyal, unable to delay gratification and, in short, feeling that they are entitled to everything without working for it." The study dubs this group the "entitlement generation." Do you know people born during those years? Is this true generally or would you consider the perception instead a stereotype? From where do you think it stems?

6. As a result of rising health care costs and the challenge to contain them, companies are trying to encourage employees to take better care of themselves, and some are even penalizing employees if they do not. One company, AstraZeneca, increased employees' health-insurance premium by $50 a month for each month they failed to complete an online health-risk assessment tool that asked for lifestyle details, then offered recommendations on ways live a more healthy lifestyle. In 2006, an internal Wal-Mart Stores Inc. memo was leaked publicly that suggested that it cut its health care costs by discouraging unhealthy people from applying for jobs. What do you think of businesses' attempts to decrease health care costs by helping employees to become healthier? What are the ethical issues associated with a firm's choice to cut health care costs by eliminating people who are unhealthy? What rights, duties, responsibilities, and consequences does this strategy imply? Do you think people who don't take care of themselves should be responsible for their increased health care costs? How would you feel personally if your past health conditions and current health practices were a part of an employment application?
7. You run a small consulting business that serves a relatively diverse community and have 24 employees in professional positions. You are not subject to Executive Order 11246. You are concerned that, of the employees in professional positions, your workplace has only one African American, no other employees of color, and three women. At this time, your upper-level management—the top six executives and yourself—are all white males. On the other hand, you have 15 support staff (secretaries and other clerical workers), of whom 14 are women and 11 are either African American or Latino.

   You would very much like to better represent the community in which you do business and you believe a diverse workforce has significant business benefits. You therefore decide to institute a program that will increase the numbers of minorities and women in professional positions as soon as possible. Is this permissible? Do you have all the relevant facts you will need to answer this question? What steps will you undertake in your plan to increase these proportions and what pitfalls must you avoid?
8. You are a senior global human resources manager for a large apparel retailer that purchases goods from all over the world. The media have focused a great deal of attention on the conditions of your suppliers' workplaces and, for myriad reasons including a strong commitment to your values-based mission, as well as a concern for your reputation, you are paying close attention to the wages paid to the workers who construct your clothing. Your suppliers in several locations have agreed to talk with you about developing a policy that would apply throughout your operations—now and in the future, wherever you plan to do business—and would impose a minimum wage requirement for all factory workers. You begin to explore some of the resources publicly available to you, such as www.globalexchange.org, www.workersrights.org, www.fairlabor.org, and www.irrc.org, to find out what other firms are doing and what labor advocates recommend in terms of language for policies such as these. You explore Nike's Web site at www.nikebiz.com, http://www.adidas-group.com/en/home/welcome.asp, and others. Now it is time to begin constructing your own policy. What will you include, how specific will you make this policy, how will you determine what will be the "living wage" in each region, and what elements will it contain? Please draft a policy for your company on implementing a living wage worldwide.
9. As a project manager, Kelly is leading a team on an international business trip where she is scheduled to do a presentation on its project and to negotiate a deal. Just a few

days before the trip, Kelly gets a call asking her whether she is willing to let a male member of her team do all the talking because the managers at the company with whom they were planning to do business feel more comfortable dealing with men. Kelly is told that she would still be in charge and that this would never happen again. If this deal works out, it would prove very profitable for the company as well as for Kelly's career. Kelly thinks about the situation in which she finds herself; she has worked very hard on this project and, if the deal is successful, she is bound to get a promotion. On the other hand, she feels discriminated against based on the fact that she is a woman. She has the choice of acting on her principles and calling off the deal, or going ahead with this modification on a "one time basis" and getting a promotion. After contemplating the issue for a while, she decides to go ahead with the deal and let someone else do all the talking. When they get back she is promoted and everybody is happy. What do you think of Kelly's decision? Could this situation be prevented all together? If you were in a similar situation what would you choose to do and why?

10. *Fortune* magazine compiles a "Best Companies to Work For" list every year. Go to their Web site http://money.cnn.com/magazines/fortune/bestcompanies/2009/ and spot trends or similarities, if any, among the listed companies and find policies or programs that you think may help attract employees.

Key Terms

After reading this chapter, you should have a clear understanding of the following Key Terms. The page numbers refer to the point at which they were discussed in the chapter. For a more complete definition, please see the Glossary.

affirmative action, *p. 283*
child labor, *p. 275*
common-law agency test, *p. 258*
diversity, *p. 279*
downsize, *p. 259*
due process, *p. 254*
economic realities test, *p.258*
employment at will (EAW), *p. 256*
IRS 20-factor analysis, *p. 258*
just cause, *p. 257*
multiculturalism, *p. 283*
Occupational Safety and Health Administration (OSHA), *p. 268*
reverse discrimination, *p. 283*
sweatshops, *p. 271*

End Notes

1. E. Benjamin Skinner, "A World Enslaved", *Foreign Policy* (March/April 2008) http://www.foreignpolicy.com/story/cms.php?story_id=4173 (accessed April 16, 2010).
2. A. Edmans, "Does the Stock Market Fully Value Intangibles? Employee Satisfaction and Equity Prices," (Dec. 30, 2008), http://papers.ssrn.com/sol3/papers.cfm?abstract_id=985735 (accessed July 15, 2009); see also Walker Information, "Committed Employees Make Your Business Work," *Employee Relationship Report* (1999) http://www.walkerinfo.com/products/err/ee_study.cfm (accessed April 16, 2010).
3. LRN, "LRN Ethics Study: Workplace Productivity" (2007), p. 2, http://www.ethics.org/files/u5/LRNWorkplaceProductivity.pdf (accessed April 16, 2010).
4. Id.
5. For a curious legal case on this question, see *Sampath v. Concurrent Tech.*, No. 08-2370 (3d Cir. November 14, 2008), http://www.ca3.uscourts.gov/opinarch/082370np.pdf (accessed July 15, 2009), ["Title VII does not 'mandate a happy workplace.'"] and *Jensen v. Potter,* 435 F.3d 444, 451 (3d Cir. 2006), overruled in part on other grounds *by Burlington N. & Santa Fe Ry. Co. v. White,* 548 U.S. 53 (2006).
6. Jeffrey Pfeffer, *The Human Equation: Building Profits by Putting People First* (Boston: Harvard University Press, 1998).

7. Neal Ashkanasy and Catherine Daus, "Emotion in the Workplace," *Academy of Management Executive* 16, no. 1 (2002): 76.

8. G. Namie and R. Namie, *The Bully at Work: What You Can Do to Stop the Hurt and Reclaim Your Dignity on the Job* (Naperville, IL: Sourcebooks, 2003), 3; L. Keashly and K. Jagatic, "U.S. Perspectives on Workplace Bullying," in *Bullying and Emotional Abuse in the Workplace: International Perspectives Research and Practice,* eds. S. Einarsen et al. (London: Taylor & Francis, 2003), 35.

9. T. Parker-Pope, "When the Bully Sits in the Next Cubicle," *New York Times* (March 25, 2008); C. Tuna, "Lawyers and Employers Take the Fight to 'Workplace Bullies'," *Wall Street Journal* (August 4, 2008); S. Fox and L.E. Stallworth, "Racial/Ethnic Bullying: Exploring Links between Bullying and Racism in the US Workplace," *Journal of Vocational Behavior* 66, no. 3 (2005); S. Gardner and P.R. Johnson, "The Leaner, Meaner Workplace: Strategies for Handling Bullies at Work," *Employment Relations Today* (Summer 2001); G. Vega and D. Comer, "Sticks and Stones May Break Your Bones, but Words Can Break Your Spirit: Bullying in the Workplace," *Journal of Business Ethics* 58, nos. 1-3 (2005).

10. D. Yamada, "Workplace Bullying and Ethical Leadership," *Legal Studies Research Paper Series, 08-37* (November14, 2008), http://ssrn.com/abstract=1301554 (accessed July 15, 2009).

11. H. A. Hornstein, *Brutal Bosses and Their Prey: How to Identify and Overcome Abuse in the Workplace* (New York: Riverhead, 1996): 143, cited in D. Yamada, "Workplace Bullying and Ethical Leadership," *Legal Studies Research Paper Series, 08-37* (November 14, 2008), http://ssrn.com/abstract–1301554 (accessed July 15, 2009).

12. *Payne v. Western & A.A.R. Co.*, 81 Tenn. 507 (1884).

13. P. H. Werhane, et al., *Women in Business: The Changing Face of Leadership* (NY: Greenwood Publishing, 2007).

14. Leadership IQ, "Don't Expect Layoff Survivors to Be Grateful," (December 10, 2008), http://www.leadershipiq.com/index.php/news-a-research-/recent-studies/150-layoff?jmid=129346&j=219464243 (accessed July 14, 2009).

15. John A. Challenger, "Downsizing: The Better Ways," *Ethikos* (January/February 2002), p. 7.

16. Leadership IQ, "Don't Expect Layoff Survivors to Be Grateful," (December 10, 2008), http://www.leadershipiq.com/index.php/news-a-research-/recent-studies/150-layoff?jmid=129346&j=219464243 (accessed July 14, 2009).

17. Id.

18. C. Tuna, "Some Firms Cut Costs without Resorting to Layoffs," *Wall Street Journal* (December 15, 2008), http://online.wsj.com/article/SB122929306421405071.html?mod=djem_jiewr_HR (accessed July 14, 2009).

19. Larsen, R.S., "Leadership in a Values-Based Organization," *The Sears Lectureship in Business Ethics at Bentley College* (February 7, 2002).

20. R. Bynum, "OSHA Fines Imperial Sugar $8.7M in Deadly Blast," *ABC News* (July 25, 2008), http://abcnews.go.com/Business/wireStory?id=5449976 (accessed April 16, 2010).

21. Craig Karmin, "Off-shoring Can Generate Jobs in the U.S.," *Wall Street Journal,* March 16, 2004.

22. M. Zwolinski, "Sweatshops, Choice, and Exploitation," *Business Ethics Quarterly* 17, no. 4 (October 2007).

23. D. Arnold and L. Hartman, "Worker Rights and Low Wage Industrialization, How to Avoid Sweatshops," *Human Rights Quarterly* 28, no. 3 (August 2006): 676–700.

24. Denis G. Arnold and Norman E. Bowie, "Sweatshops and Respect for Persons," *Business Ethics Quarterly* 221 (2003): 223–224, cited in D. Arnold and L. Hartman, "Worker Rights."

25. L. Hartman, B. Shaw, and R. Stevenson, "Exploring the Ethics and Economics of Global Labor Standards: A Challenge to Integrated Social Contract Theory," *Business Ethics Quarterly* 13, no. 2 (2003): 193–220.

26. P. Werhane, S. Kelley, L. Hartman, and D. Moberg, *Alleviating Poverty Through Profitable Partnerships: Globalization, Markets and Economic Well-Being* (New York: Routledge/Taylor & Francis, 2009), chapter 1.

27. Klaus Leisinger, *Implementability of the Draft UN Norms in the Pharmaceutical Industry: The Case of Novartis,* presented at Voluntary Codes of Conduct for Multinational Corporations: Promises and Challenges, Baruch College (2004).

28. adidas-Salomon, *A Fair Wage Strategy* (2004), http://www.adidas-salomon.com/en/sustainability/transparency/fair_wage_study/fair_wage_study.asp (accessed April 16, 2010); Chris Manning, *Promoting Fair Wages, Productivity, and Jobs in Garments and Footwear in Indonesia,* http://www.adidas-group.com/en/sustainability/_downloads/fair_wage_study/ManningPositionPaper.pdf (accessed April 16, 2010).

29. T. J. Radin, "Levi Strauss & Co.: Implementation of Global Sourcing and Operating Guidelines in Latin America," in *Rising above Sweatshops,* eds. L.P. Hartman, et al. (New York: Preager Books, 2003), 249.

30. Kebebew Ashagrie, *Statistics on Working Children and Hazardous Child Labor in Brief* (Geneva: ILO, 1998), http://www.ilo.org/public/english/standards/ipec/simpoc/stats/child/stats.htm (accessed July 29, 2006).

31. International Labour Office, *Every Child Counts* (Geneva: International Labour Organization, 2002), http://www.ilo.org/public/english/standards/ipec/simpoc/others/globalest.pdf (accessed July 29, 2006).

32. International Labour Organization, *World Employment Report 1998–1999* (Geneva: International Labour Organization, 1999).

33. World Health Organization, *Children at Work: Special Health Risks, Technical Report Series No. 756* (Geneva: International Labour Organization, 1987); K. Satyanarayan et al., "Effect of Early Childhood Nutrition and Child Labour on Growth and Adult Nutritional Status of Rural Indian Boys around Hyderabad," *Human Nutrition: Clinical Nutrition,* no. 40 C (1986).

34. World Health Organization, *Children at Work, infra,* note 13.

35. See Lammy Betten, *International Labor Law* (1993), p. 316, which notes that child labor legislation may lead to a movement of child labor from the formal to the informal sectors of the economy. See also Ministry of Labour, Manpower and Overseas Pakistanis & SEBCON (Pvt) Ltd., *Qualitative Survey on Child Labour in Pakistan* (Islamabad: International Labour Organization/OPEC, 1996) The ILO study in Pakistan evidences that, among the child labourers interviewed, 72 percent had no access to education at all. Alan R. Myerson, "In Principle, a Case for More 'Sweatshops'," *The New York Times* (June 22, 1997) (online version: http://www.ncpa.org/pd/pdint152.html); "Labor Secretary Herman Speaks Out against Child Labor," *Apparel Industry Magazine* 58, no. 11 (November 1997): 12 [Mohammed Hafizul Islam Chowdhury, an apparel manufacturer from Bangladesh, asks, "Why are Americans against child

labor? It's good in my country because it keeps children off the streets and out of prostitution."]; and Stephen Golub, "Are International Labor Standards Needed to Prevent Social Dumping?"*Finance & Development* (December 1997): 20, 22, http://www.imf.org/external/pubs/ft/fandd/1997/12/pdf/golub.pdf (accessed April 16, 2010).

36. However, some advocacy groups fail to consider all perspectives. For example, the Global Reporting Initiative's discussion on its Child Labour Indicators fails to take into account the impact of the termination of children beyond their removal from the workplace.
37. EEOC, "Sexual Harassment" (2006), http://www.eeoc.gov/types/sexual_harassment.html (accessed April 16, 2010).
38. Richard A. Posner, *Economic Analysis of Law* (New York: Aspen, 2002), 616.
39. Marianne Bertrand and Sendhil Millainathan, "Are Emily and Brendan More Employable than Lakisha and Jamal?" (unpublished paper, University of Chicago, Graduate School of Business, 2002).
40. 42 U.S.C. §§ 2000e-1(b), 12112(c)(1); 29 U.S.C. § 630(f)(1). See also EEOC Enforcement Guidance, N-915.002.
41. *Kern v. Dynalectron Corp.,* 577 F. Supp. 1196, 1200-01 (N.D. Tex. 1983).
42. *Good Morning America,* "Powerfully Nice," abcnews.com. July 16, 2001.
43. Peggy McIntosh, "White Privilege: Unpacking the Invisible Knapsack," *Peace and Freedom* (July/August 1989): 10–12.
44. "Diversity Policies Have Positive Impact on Company Business Performance," *New York Times Company Press Release,* February 13, 2003.
45. Business in the Community, "Workplace," http://www.bitc.org.uk/resources/research/statbank/workplace/index.html (accessed April 16, 2010).
46. http://www.mckinsey.com/careers/women/makingadifference/socialsectorimpact/womenmatter/Mckinsey_women_matter.pdf (accessed April 16, 2010).
47. S. Reier, "In Europe, Women Finding More Seats at the Table," *New York Times,* March 22, 2008, http://www.nytimes.com/2008/03/22/business/worldbusiness/22director.html?_r=1&sq=+ (accessed April 16, 2010).
48. Catalyst, "2005 Catalyst Census of Women Board Directors of the *Fortune* 500" (2006), http://www.catalyst.org/file/9/2005%20wbd.pdf (accessed July 11, 2009)
49. Lois Joy, Ph.D., Director, Research, and Nancy M. Carter, Ph.D., Vice President, Research, at Catalyst Inc., Harvey M. Wagner, Ph.D., and Sriram Narayanan, Ph.D, http://www.catalyst.org/publication/200/the-bottom-line-corporate-performance-and-womens-representation-on-boards
50. Daniel Seligman, "Up from Inscrutable," *Fortune,* April 6, 1992, p. 20.
51. "Up from Inscrutable," *infra,* note 24.
52. General Motors, "Brief of General Motors as *Amicus Curiae* in Support of Defendants" in *Gratz v. Bollinger,* 539 U.S. 244 (2003).
53. *Grutter v. Bollinger* 539 U.S. 306 (2003).
54. The actual consent decree (legal term for a settlement agreement) can be accessed at http://www.afjustice.com/pdf/20050422_consent_decree.pdf (accessed April 16, 2010).
55. *CNN Money* (May 28, 2002), http://money.cnn.com/2002/05/22/news/companies/abercrombie/ (accessed April 16, 2010).

Readings

Reading 6-1

Employment-at-Will, Employee Rights, and Future Directions for Employment

Tara J. Radin and Patricia H. Werhane

Private employment in the United States has traditionally been governed by "employment-at-will" (EAW), which provides for minimal regulation of employment practices. It allows either the employer or the employee to terminate their employment relationship at any time for virtually any reason or for no reason at all. At least 55 percent of all employees and managers in the private sector of the workforce in the United States today are "at-will" employees.

During recent years, the principle and practice of employment-at-will have been under attack. While progress has been made in eroding the practice, the principle still governs the philosophical assumptions underlying employment practices in the United States, and, indeed, EAW has been promulgated as one of the ways to address economic ills in other countries. In what follows, we will briefly review the major critiques of EAW. Given the failure of these arguments to erode the underpinnings of EAW, we shall suggest new avenues for approaching employment issues to achieve the desirable end of employee dignity and respect.

Critiques of EAW

Attacks have been levied against EAW on numerous fronts for generations. While it remains the default rule for the American workplace, a variety of arguments have been made that employees should not be treated "at will." Most of these arguments fall within two broad categories: those that relate to rights and those that relate to fairness.

Rights Talk

The first set of arguments critiquing the principle of EAW is grounded on a commonly held theory of moral rights, that is, the claim that human beings have moral claims to a set of basic rights vis-à-vis their being *human.* This set of arguments makes three points. First, principles governing employment practices that interfere with commonly guaranteed political rights, such as free speech (including legitimate whistleblowing), privacy, due process, and democratic participation, would therefore appear to be questionable principles and practices from a rights perspective. Second, justifiable rights claims are generalizable. It thus follows that, if employers and managers have certain rights, say, to respect, free speech, and choice, employees should also have equal claims to those rights. Third, if property rights are constitutionally guaranteed, it would appear to follow that employees should have some rights to their work contributions, just as managers, as representatives of companies, have rights to exercise property claims.

There are at least three countervailing arguments against these conclusions, however. In the United States, constitutional guarantees apply to interactions between persons or institutions and the state, but they do not extend to the private sector or to the home, except in cases of egregious acts. Claims to employee rights are not, therefore, guaranteed by the Constitution. Second, employment agreements are contractual agreements between consenting adults. Unless a person is forced to work or to perform a particular task, EAW thus protects liberty rights in allowing a person freely to enter into and leave contracts of his or her own choosing. Third, property rights protect companies and their owners, and companies and their managers should be free to hire and fire as they see fit. Indeed, Christopher McMahon, a defender of employee rights, argues that although, as property owners or agents for companies, employers and managers have rights to hire and fire "at will," this does not provide them with moral justification for ignoring other employee rights claims, including, for example, rights to participate in corporate decision making.

Fairness

A second set of arguments against EAW stems from fairness concerns regarding employment-at-will agreements and practices. EAW has, on numerous occasions, seemingly translated into a license for employers and employees to treat one another *amorally,* if not *immorally.* "'Why are you firing me, Mr. Ford?' asked Lee Iacocca, president of Ford Motor Company. Henry, looking at Iacocca, said: 'I just don't like you!'" While EAW demands ostensibly *equal* treatment of both employers and employees, the result is often not inherently *fair* to either. A requirement of "equal" treatment, therefore, is not sufficient. Good employment practices should aim for equality, while, at the same time, allowing for different, though comparable, treatment where relevant differences exist. For example, while it would not necessarily represent a good, or sound, employment practice to demand *equal* pay for all employees and managers, a good practice would be to demand *equal* pay for employees in similar positions doing similar tasks, and *comparable* pay for others, after taking into account relevant differences, such as in experience, position, tenure at the company, and special skills.

Except under conditions of very low unemployment, employers ordinarily stand in a position of power relative to prospective employees, and most employees, at any level, are replaceable with others. At a minimum, though, employees deserve to be given reasons for employment decisions that involve them. Unjustified dismissals are not appropriate in light of employees' considerable investment of time and effort. Employees are human beings, with dignity and emotional attachments, not feeling-less robots. This is not to say that inadequate employees should not be replaced with better performers. but employees at least deserve to find out the reasons underlying employment changes. And if employees are to take charge of their careers, they should receive good reasons for employment decisions and full information. From a management point of view as well, employees should be given *good* reasons for employment decisions, or it appears that management decisions are arbitrary, and this sort of behavior is not in keeping with good management practice. Even if it were possible to defend EAW on the basis of freedom of contracts, in practice, EAW supports inconsistent, even irrational, management behavior by permitting arbitrary, not work-related, treatment of employees—behavior that is not considered a best management practice. Since arbitrary accounting, marketing, and investment practices are not tolerated, arbitrary human resource practices should be considered equally questionable.

We have therefore concluded that due process procedures should be instituted as mandatory procedures in every workplace. On the other side, employers suffer when employees simply walk off jobs without notice. In a much earlier work, Werhane therefore has argued that employees *and* employers have equal rights, rights that would entail reciprocal obligations to inform each other about firing or quitting and to give justifiable reasons for these actions.

Interestingly, due process procedures have become mandatory guarantees for employees in the public sectors of the economy, on the federal, state, and local levels, but not in the private sector. Again, on the basis of the fairness of equal treatment for *all* workers, this appears to be unfair. The inapplicability of constitutional guarantees in the private sector of the economy nevertheless prevails in employment. This is not to suggest that there are no relevant differences between employment in the public and private sector. In fact, there are a number of significant variations, including, but not limited to, salary differentials. Considering the degree of similarity between public and private work, though, it only makes sense that due process be afforded to employees in both sectors.

Erosion of EAW: Law and Public Policy

Despite these and other arguments, there is evidence that the principle, if not the practice, of EAW is alive and well: people are still losing jobs for seemingly arbitrary reasons. Rather than attacking the principle directly, legislatures and courts have created ways to reduce the impact of the practice through narrowly carved-out exceptions, and Congress has chosen to control the scope of EAW through limiting legislation. A wave of federal legislation has also had a significant impact on private employment, beginning with the passage of Title VII of the Civil Rights Act of 1964, which prohibits the discrimination of employees on the basis of "race, color, religion, sex, or national origin." It has been followed by the Age Discrimination in Employment Act, the Pregnancy Discrimination Act, and the employment provisions of the Americans with Disabilities Act. Together, such legislation demonstrates Congress's recognition that there are limits to EAW, and that the default rule cannot, and should not, be used as a license to disregard fundamental rights.

Even greater limiting power lies in the hands of state and local legislatures. Many have sidestepped EAW to recognize employee rights, such as in the area of privacy, by passing statutes on issues ranging from workplace discrimination to drug testing. A few states, such as Colorado, North Dakota, and Nevada, have enacted statutes barring employers from firing employees for legal off-work activity. In 1987, Montana became the first state to pass a comprehensive statute rejecting EAW in favor of "just cause" terminations.[1] Contrary to EAW, the "just cause" standard requires that the reasons offered in termination decisions be defensible.[2] Montana currently stands alone in demanding "just cause" dismissals. Although it is too early to know whether one state's move in this direction signals a trend toward the increasing state challenges to EAW, there is currently no evidence that this is the case.

Courts have also begun to step in and carve out exceptions to EAW as a default rule. Many employers and employees have opted to alter the employment relationship through contractual agreements. Since evidence of such agreements is not always lodged in an explicit arrangement, courts often find it necessary to delve further in order to determine the reasonable assurances and expectations of employers and employees. For example, some courts have held that an employment contract exists, even where it exists only as a result of assumed behavior, through a so-called "implied-in-fact" contract. In *Pugh v. See's Candies, Inc.*, an employee was fired after 32 years of service without explanation. Although no contract existed that specified the duration of employment, the court determined that the implied corporate policy was not to discharge employees without good reasons. The court in *Pugh* determined:

> [T]here were facts in evidence from which the jury could determine the existence of such an implied promise: the duration of appellant's employment, the commendations and promotions he received, the apparent lack of any direct criticism of his work, the assurances he was given, and the employer's acknowledged policies.

Where an employer's behavior and/or policies encourage an employee's reliance upon employment, the employer cannot dismiss that employee without a good reason.

In some states, it can be considered a breach of contract to fire a long-term employee without sufficient cause, under normal economic conditions, even when the implied contract is only a verbal one. In California, for example, the majority of recent implied contract cases have been decided in favor of the employee. Reliance upon employee manuals has also been determined to give rise to reasonable employment expectations. In *Woolley v. Hoffmann-La Roche, Inc.,* the court held that companies are contractually bound by the statements in their employment manuals. In *Woolley,* the employment manual implicitly provided that employees would not be terminated without good cause:

> It is the policy of Hoffmann-La Roche to retain to the extent consistent with company requirements, the services of all employees who perform their duties efficiently and effectively.

The court thus held that an employee at Hoffmann La Roche could not be dismissed without good cause and due process. *Woolley* is but one of many decisions that demonstrate that employers are accountable to employees for what is contained in employment manuals, as if the manual is part of an implicit employment contract.

Courts also have been known to override EAW in order to respond to or deter tortuous behavior. Out of this has arisen the "public policy" exception to EAW. The court has carved out the "public policy" exception to handle situations where employers attempt to prevent their employees from exercising fundamental liberties, such as the rights to vote, to serve on a jury, and to receive state minimum wages. In *Frampton v. Central Indiana Gas Company,* the court found in favor of an employee who was discharged for attempting to collect worker compensation:

> If employers are permitted to penalize employees for filing workmen's compensation claims, a most important public policy will be undermined. The fear of discharge would have a deleterious effect on the exercise of a statutory right. Employees will not file claims for justly deserved compensation . . . [and] the employer is effectively relieved of his obligation . . . Since the Act embraces such a fundamental . . . policy, strict employer adherence is required.

Such decisions clearly demonstrate the court's unwillingness to stand by without doing anything as employers attempt to interfere with fundamental liberties.

The public policy exception is also used in order to discourage fraudulent or wrongful behavior on the part of employers, such as in situations where employees are asked to break a law or to violate state public policies. In *Petermann v. International Brotherhood of Teamsters,* the court confronted a situation where an employee refused to perjure himself to keep his job. The court held that compelling an employee to commit perjury "would encourage criminal conduct . . . and . . . serve to contaminate the honest administration of public affairs." Then, in *Palmateer v. International Harvester Corporation,* the court reinstated an employee who was fired for reporting theft at his plant on the grounds that criminal conduct requires such reporting.

Whistleblower protection is also provided as a result of tort theory. In *Pierce v. Ortho Pharmaceutical Corporation,* the court reinstated a physician who was fired from a company for refusing to seek approval to test a certain drug on human subjects. The court held that safety clearly lies in the interest of public welfare, and that employees are not to be fired for refusing to jeopardize public safety.

Similarly, in *Bowman v. State Bank of Keysville,* a Virginia court asserted its refusal to condone retaliatory discharges. In *Bowman,* a couple of employee-shareholders of a bank voted for a merger at request of the bank's officers. After the vote was counted, the employee-shareholders subsequently retracted their votes and contended that their vote had been coerced. They alleged that the bank officers had warned them that they would lose their jobs if they did not vote in favor of the merger. They were then fired. The court in *Bowman* found in favor of the employee-shareholders. According to the *Bowman* court, "Virginia has not deviated from the common law doctrine of employment-at-will . . . And we do not alter the traditional rule today. Nonetheless, the rule is not absolute." In this way, the *Bowman* court demonstrated that EAW is subject to limitations and exceptions. Even where the EAW doctrine still appears to "thrive," it does so within definite restrictive legal and policy constraints.

Rethinking Employment Relationships

Without attacking or circumventing EAW, it is possible to discern signs of a changing mindset about employment, a mindset that values the competitive advantage of the contributions of good employees and managers. The extensive work of scholars, such as Jeffrey Pfeffer, illustrates this change. Pfeffer, a management professor at Stanford, has argued in a series of books and articles that a "people first" strategy can serve as an economic advantage for companies. In other words, it is not just for the benefit of *employees,* but also for the benefit of *firm employers,* to treat employees with respect. To provide evidence for his point, Pfeffer has studied a number of North American and international companies and amassed a great deal of data that demonstrates that economic success is linked to fair labor practices when employees and managers are considered critical stakeholders for the long-term viability of their companies. According to Pfeffer, the most successful companies—those that have sustained long-term economic profitability and growth—work carefully to engage in employment practices that include selective hiring, employment security, high compensation, decentralization, empowerment and self-managed teams, training, open information, and fair treatment of all of their employees.

From an organizational perspective, contrary to some points of view, it is a mistake to sort out employees, customers, products, services, shareholders, and so on, as if each represented an autonomous set of concerns. For example, a firm cannot do business without people, products, finance and accounting, markets, and a strategy. In times of economic exigency, a merger, or corporate change, it is, therefore, generally *not* to the advantage of a company merely to lop off employees (even if they are the "low hanging [most easily disposable] fruit"), without thinking carefully about their employees *as people,* and recognizing those *people's* contributions to the long-term survival and success of the company. In uncertain times, no company would simply quit doing accounting, and it would be to its peril to quit marketing its products and services. Similarly, to get rid of too many employees would not serve a company's long-term viability very well.

Similarly, Rosebeth Moss Kanter argues that it is in the firm's interest to take care of employees. Kanter contends that it is both desirable and obligatory for companies to give their employees what she calls "employability security": abilities and skills that are transferable to other jobs and other situations in that company or elsewhere so that employees are adaptable in a world of technological and economic change. Today, while some companies engage in layoffs to change employee skills, many managers and companies are training and retraining old workers, giving them new skills. Kanter would argue, with Pfeffer, that it is valuable, in terms of both economics and respect for workers, to have a workforce that is comprised of a collection of highly skilled and employable people who would be desirable assets in a number of employment settings, both within a particular company and among industries.

Linking Pfeffer's and Kanter's findings with a notion of employee rights makes it possible to re-envision the mindset of employment to consider each job applicant, employee, manager, or CEO as a unique individual. In addition, it prompts us to begin to rethink employment, not in terms of employees as merely economic value added, but in terms of employees as *individuals*—unique and particularized *individuals*.

A "Citizen" Metaphor

One way of developing an individualized analysis of employment is through a citizen metaphor. "Citizenship" is a designation that links people to rights and duties relative to their membership in a larger community, such as a political community. There is a growing body of literature addressing this notion of "corporate citizenship." According to Waddock,

> Good corporate citizens live up to clear constructive visions and core values. They treat well the entire range of stakeholders who risk capital in, have an interest in, or are linked to the firm through primary and secondary impacts through developing respectful, mutually beneficial operating practices and by working to maximize sustainability of the natural environment.

Replacing the view that corporations are, or should be, socially responsible, the corporate citizenship model argues that a firm's membership in complex cultural, national, and global communities accords them, like individuals, rights and responsibilities comparable to those accorded to individuals through national citizenship. The belief is that, if corporations are to enjoy operational privileges, they must then honor as well their responsibilities to the communities to which they belong. The model of corporate citizenship is used both to describe corporate relationships with external stakeholders, such as customers, communities, governmental entities, and the environment, and to address corporate responsibilities to internal stakeholders, such as managers and employees.

The citizen metaphor can be applied to managerial-employee relationships as well. This process of portraying employees as citizens is not complicated; it requires, simply, "treating workers like adults." Treating people as adults translates into acknowledging their dignity and respecting their relevant legal and moral rights and duties. Rights and duties connected to "citizenship" reflect the coexistence of people in a common space and help delineate how people can best interact with the fewest conflicts. This space does not have to be a global or semi-global community but could also refer to the context of a firm. Within the firm context, the citizen metaphor links people to one another in such a way that they inevitably take responsibility for working together for the benefit of the firm. At the same time, the metaphor of citizenship requires that each "citizen" has equal rights, and requires that all citizens be treated with respect and dignity. According to such a model, employees thus serve as participants in, and members of, a firm community.

As applied to employment, a citizenship model would take into account productivity and performance, and it would also require rethinking hiring in terms of long-time employment. This would not entail keeping every employee hired, or even guaranteeing lifetime employment. It would, however, at a minimum, require due process for all employment changes, employability training, protection of fundamental rights such as free speech and privacy, and the provision of adequate information to employees about their future and the future of the company. The employability requirement would require employees to serve as good corporate citizens in the broad sense of being able to contribute in a number of areas in the economy, and, if Pfeffer's data is correct, such measures add economic value to shareholders as well. At the same time productivity, loyalty, and good performance would be expected from all employees just as they are expected from citizens in a community.

In sum, if a company's core values were to drive the assumption that each employee is a corporate citizen analogous to a national citizen with similar rights and duties, then the way we would think about employment would change.

Employees and Systems

Systems thinking, a way of looking at business that is becoming increasingly popular, operates similarly to the citizenship model in challenging traditional views of employment. According to systems thinking, employment is a phenomenon embedded in a complex set of interrelationships, between employees and managers or employers, between workers and labor organizations such as unions, and between employment and public policy. It involves customer relationships, human resource policies, and, given pensions plans, often employee/owner relationships with management. Employees are just one of many stakeholders who affect, and are affected by, the companies in which they work. Moreover, companies, and, indeed, industries and the system of commerce, are embedded within a complex structure of laws, regulations, regulatory agencies, public policy, media interaction, and public opinion. And this system—employment—is part of a global economy of exchange, ownership, and trade.

Employees, as "players" in these overlapping sets of systems, are at the same time individuals, members of a company, and factors embroiled in a system of commerce. Their interests are important, but they are not the only interests that must be taken into account. Like the phenomenon of employment, employee rights and responsibilities are embedded in a complex social system of rights and responsibilities. Employee rights claims, thus, are not merely individual manifesto claims to certain privileges, but also entail reciprocal respect for others' rights and responsibilities.

If employment relationships are embedded in a set of systems or subsystems, then it is important—strategically important—for managers and employees to attack employment issues systemically from a fact-finding perspective, from an organizational or social perspective, and from the perspective of the individuals involved, in this case, employees and managers. Conceptualizing employment systemically may help both employees and managers to reconsider their importance in the underlying system of which they are a contributing part. This sort of analysis will neither eliminate nor replace the principle of EAW, but it does represent another step in the process of reconceptualizing employment.

Pfeffer's conclusion, that employees are critical to corporate success, is grounded in a systems approach, which views employees, as well as products, services, and customers, as part of the strategic advantage of the company. By analyzing corporate results, he demonstrates that, without good employees, a company will fail, just as it will fail without customers, and fail if it does not think strategically about its products and services.

In thinking about employment and employees, it is tempting to become preoccupied with managerial/employer responsibilities to employees, as if employees were merely pawns in the system. It is, though, important to note that a systems approach does not preclude individual autonomy. No individual in a free commercial society is defined completely by the set of systems in which he or she participates. Interestingly, a systematic approach actually looks beyond protection of employee rights and emphasizes employee responsibilities as well—to themselves as well as to the firm. As part of the workforce, each of us has claims to certain rights, such as free choice, free speech, rights to strike, rights to work contributions or compensation for those contributions, rights to information, and rights to a safe workplace. As a consequence of claiming such rights, every worker, employee, or manager, in every sector of the economy, has responsibilities as well—responsibilities not merely to employers, but to him- or herself and his or her future, and to manage that future as he or she is able and sees fit.

In other words, systems thinking indicates that employees are, or should be, responsible for their own lives and careers, and they need to take the steps necessary to research and explore mobility options. Thinking about employment systemically and thinking about personal responsibilities as well as responsibilities to others within that system can help employees take charge of their own working lives, professions, and careers.

The view of employment as a system is consistent with the notion of corporate citizenship. The systemic conceptualization of employment gives rise to employee rights and duties that animate the employment system. In other words, the rights employees enjoy, and the duties they must bear, are those that ensure the continued existence of the system. Similarly, through the lens of corporate citizenship, employee rights and duties include those that contribute to the firm. Employees have rights to engage in behavior that allows for their development within the system, or firm, and have duties to enable others to develop as well.

A Professional Model for Employees

Despite developments in eroding EAW through law and public policy, changing mindsets regarding the value of employment and employment practices, the work of Pfeffer, Kanter, and others demonstrating the worth of good employment practices for long-term profitability and success, and the systemic citizen model we propose, the principle of EAW continues to underlie North American management practice, and the language of rights, or employee rights, still evades popular management thinking about employment, at least in the private sectors of the economy. This is most clearly demonstrated by three sets of phenomena. First, there has been a consistent demise of unions and unionism in this country. Since the 1950s, union membership has dropped from about 33 percent of all workers to barely 10 percent today. This demise not only reflects the philosophy of corporations, but it is also the result of a series of public policy initiatives. In addition, it reflects interests of workers, even low-wage workers who toil under strenuous or dangerous conditions, who are nevertheless reluctant to unionize.[3]

Second, despite the enlightened focus on employability and despite an almost full employment economy, layoffs still dominate the ways in which corporations think about employees and employment when making changes in their strategic direction. In 1999 alone, more than a million workers were laid off.[4] Admittedly, given low unemployment, most of these people found new jobs; but this often required relocation and, sometimes, even in this economy, taking less desirable jobs for lower wages. This is particularly true for unskilled workers.

Third, one of the criticisms of Northern Europe's high unemployment and Japan's recent economic difficulties is that these countries have massive legal restrictions on the ability of their companies to engage in flexible employment practices. We are thus exporting our EAW mindset, sometimes as a panacea for economic difficulties that are not always traceable to overemployment. It is important for us to think carefully about the practices we export, particularly considering their questionable success here.

A systems approach, while serving as an obvious description of the complex nature of employment in advanced political economies such as our own, is not internalized in employment thinking today—at least not in the United States. The citizen metaphor requires an expansion of notions of trust and solidarity within firms, and, considering the mobility of the workforce, the ease with which companies can lay off employees and hire new ones, and the preoccupation with short-term bottom lines, it is unlikely that this metaphor will be universally adapted. Given these seemingly contradictory conclusions, then, namely, the persistence of the principle of EAW, the argument that employees have rights and that employees and managers have moral responsibilities to each other, the economic value added of employees to firms, and the questionable adaptability of the citizen metaphor, we are challenged to try to reformulate the notion of employment proactively from an employee perspective—that of the employee as a *professional.*

The popular literature is replete with laments that the "good old days" of alleged employee–employer lifetime employment contracts, company paternalism, and lifetime benefits are under threat of extinction. So, too, are the expectations of loyalty, total commitment, company-first sacrifices, and perhaps, even, obedience and trust. Whether or not there ever were "good old days," such laments could be used to change thinking in a positive way, in that they indicate we have alternatives—the way that we view work is not necessarily the only way. This realization should prompt employees and managers to rethink who they are—to manage their own careers within the free enterprise system and to rejoice in the demise of paternalism such that they no longer can even imagine that a person is dependent upon, or co-dependent upon, a particular employer, training program, or authority. It demands changes in what we have called elsewhere the "boss" mental model, so aptly exploited by Dilbert, and to alter our vision of ourselves from that of "just an employee" to that of an independent worker or manager with commitments to self-development.

While all of this might seem farfetched, particularly for unskilled and uneducated workers, this sort of thinking dates back at least two centuries. As Adam Smith, and later Karl Marx argued, the Industrial Revolution provided the opportunity for workers to become independent of landholder serfdom and free from those to whom they had been previously apprenticed. This occurred because, by providing workers opportunities to choose and change jobs and to be paid for their productivity, people were able to trade their labor without chatteling themselves. This sense of economic independence was never fully realized because, in fact, circumstances often prevent most of us from achieving Smith's ideal "where every man was perfectly free both to choose what occupation he thought proper, and to change it as often as he thought proper."

During and after the Industrial Revolution, one of the great debates about labor was the status of "free labor" versus "wage labor." Free labor was "labor carried out under conditions likely to cultivate the qualities of character that suits citizens to self-government." These conditions included being economically independent, and indeed Thomas Jefferson associated free labor with property ownership and farming. Wage earning was thought by some to be equivalent to slavery since it "denied [workers] economic and political independence essential to republican citizenship." Even the authors of *Rerum Novarum* (1892), the first Papal social encyclical, argue that wage labor should be paid enough to enable each worker to become a property owner and thus gain some degree of independence.

A question remains: How, in the 21st century, is a person to develop this sort of independence and independent thinking about work, when the vast majority of us work for others? A new model of employment is required, and this model requires developing different mindsets about work and working that draw from Smith's and Jefferson's ideas, and, at the same time, take into account the fact that most of us are, and will be, employees.

The model is that of employees as *professionals.* "Profession" refers to "any group of individuals with particular skills who work from a shared knowledge base." A professional is a person who has trained skills in certain areas that position that person as employable in his or her area of expertise. A professional is identified with, and has a commitment to, his or her professional work, and to the ability to be versatile. It is the work and its achievements that are important, even more important, for some professionals, than its monetary reward. Additionally, most professionals belong to independent associations that have their own codes of professional ethics and standards for expertise and certification or licensure.

The responsibilities of a professional are first to his or her expertise, second to his or her profession and the code of that profession, and only third to his or her employer. This is not a model of the "loyal servant," but, rather, of a person who manages him- or herself with employable and retrainable skills that he or she markets, even as he or she may simultaneously be in the employment of others. This is a person who commits to excellence in whatever employment situations he or she encounters, but is not wedded to one employer or one particular job. Further, in some professions, such as law and health care, professionals are encouraged—if not required—to participate in work solely for community benefit.

The professional model is one that has developed primarily in the high tech and dot.com industries, as people with specialized skills have built firms around those skills. While the model has developed within a particular context, it is one that easily could, and should, be emulated elsewhere. The growth of dot.com firms offers an excellent example because through these ventures people have been able to focus on their talents, even as employees have moved from company to company, because employees are valued for their skills rather than their loyalty. Dot.com firms are not models for all employment since they are often narrowly tailored to offering particularized products and services, but they do stand as potential models for a number of companies or divisions within companies.

There are other opportunities for professionalism as well, particularly with regard to contingent workers. For the past 20 years we have witnessed what some label as an alarming trend—the increase in contingent workers—workers who work part-time, or full-time on a contract basis without insurance, pensions, or other benefits. Contingent workers include self-employed, voluntary part-time workers, contract workers and consultants, and home-bound workers. These workers range from dishwashers to professionals and managers. Many have chosen this sort of employment arrangement. Some of these people have benefits independently or through spouses, and they thus appreciate the enhanced flexibility and higher salaries as compared to their full-time counterparts. The problem is that many others resent their "contingency." There are many, who, according to Brockner and Wiesenfeld, see themselves as "peripheral" to the organization, particularly those who are part-time, contract, short-term, or "disposable" workers.

These workers are independent contractors—"free labor"—even though many of them do not revel in that. They are disposable, and some are involuntarily contingent workers, subject to a number of injustices: (1) the involuntary nature of the employment position; (2) the two-tier wage system (a) with unequal compensation, and (b) where many of these workers are psychologically, economically, and socially treated as, and feel themselves to be, second class workers; (3) the fact that women and minorities account for a greater percentage of contingent workers than white males, even taking into account skills, those who opt for part-time and mommy-track employment, and those who cannot speak English or are otherwise disadvantaged. The further decline in union membership and the shift in the composition of the workforce indicate that, by the year 2005, nearly 20 percent of new hires will be white males. This appears to suggest that we will see increased exploitation of new labor and greater utilization of contingent workers.

There is yet another dimension to what might already be considered a gloomy picture. Given the psychological pressures and perception of second class citizenry, involuntary contingent workers in companies tend to be less loyal, less productive, and exhibit lower morale—all of which hurts the long-term productivity and well-being of the company for which they work.

At the same time, contingent workers are not as vulnerable to some of the problems that hinder full-time workers. Contingent workers are less likely to be absent, drink or use drugs on the job, complain, snooze, schmooze, or engage in time-consuming office or work floor politics. Moreover, without the shadow of union protection they are unencumbered by work rules or traditions. They are, therefore, more flexible.

As the number of contingent workers increases, those who choose this path, as well as those who are involuntarily forced into it, should be able to develop a sense of independence, engendered by redefining themselves in relation to their work. This could translate into a rise of professionalism. Because contingent workers are no longer linked to particular companies, it could lead to a shift of loyalty from the company to work and to the profession. In addition, it could lead to the formation of new professional associations—associations, not necessarily industry- or position-specific, which develop guidelines for skills, licensing, and conduct, form employment contracts, develop codes of conduct, and protect members, just as the legal, medical, academic, and, to some extent, the engineering professions do today. These professions, then, could gain leverage with employers, just as unions have done in the past, with leverage translated into equal pay for equal work and professionally provided benefits and pensions.

But what about unskilled low-wage workers? As Barbara Ehrenreich points out in her provocative book, *Nickel and Dimed,* one of the indignities suffered by allegedly "unskilled" work is that their skills are not treated as such. Virtually all work entails some sort of skills—it is just that the "skills" required by this sort of work are not respected by many of us. Another indignity associated with much of low-wage work is that the workers tend not to be respected or treated with dignity, even by their employers. Professionalism of these workers might alleviate this treatment and also help to raise their wages.[5]

Ehrenreich herself recognizes that offering incentives to low-wage workers to take control of their lives and their careers is not easy. Unskilled workers, like many managers today, would have to rethink of themselves as independent contractors with trained or trainable skills that are transferable to a number of job settings, rather than as mere wage earners. By taking their work and productivity contributions seriously, workers with such mindsets would create economic value added for firms and a sense of self-worth. There is little in our backgrounds that assists us in thinking of ourselves as free laborers rather than wage earners. But if George Washington could take scruffy groups of farmers and laborers from thirteen independent colonies each with its own culture and customs, and transform that motley crew into the Revolutionary Army that eventually defeated the British, and if union organizers in the late Nineteenth and early Twentieth Centuries could organize wage laborers to strike, then a revolution of the mental model of employment, from wage earners to free professionals, is not impossible.

Conclusion

We are a country that has thrived on individualism in our political democracy. Although we have made progress in dispelling the public/private division, it will undoubtedly continue to influence the protection of Constitutional rights. We have failed, and probably will continue to fail, to adapt new metaphors that challenge that individualism, such as a systems approach or a citizen metaphor for employment.

This is not where the story ends, though. While EAW remains the default rule for employment in most of the United States, new models are emerging that encourage and motivate both employers and employees to rise above the default rule in order to create a more satisfying workplace, which, at the same time, can boast higher performance.

Hope for a workplace that respects both employers and employees lies in variations of models such as the professional model. Interestingly, the professional model serves as a link between the individualism that cripples other models and the fair employment principles espoused by all of these models. The professional model is a form of, and reinforcement for, individualism. It will be interesting to see how that individualism plays out in the workplace. The model of the worker, the employee, the manager, and the executive as professionals, offers a paradigm for thinking about oneself as *both* independent and part of a political economy. With the pending end of implied job security in every sector of the economy, with global demands on management skills, and with the loss of union representation, this is a model for the future—a model that would circumvent EAW and take us fittingly into a new millennium of global capitalism.

Ironically, recent events surrounding the horrific destruction of the twin towers of the World Trade Center on September 11, 2001, underscore the values that underlie the American workplace, which are about professionals, not robots engaged in routine tasks. Although terrorists attempted to attack capitalism, they were only able to break apart the buildings that housed the tremendous values. As Howard Lutnick, CEO of Cantor Fitzgerald, explained, even in the wake of disaster, his people were anxious to get back to work. They felt a need to be part of something, and that something was work. And Lutnick, like many of the surviving business executives was, and is, struggling to find ways to help support the survivors and the families of those lost—not because they have to, but because they want to do something to assist those who were part of their workplaces.

The time has thus come to look past what our default rule says, in order to pay attention to what the reality is. It no longer makes sense to waste words arguing against EAW. The reality is that, regardless of what the default rule says, there are values embedded in the American workplace that elevate it above that default and point to inherent respect for both employers and employees. It is important for us now to accept EAW for what it is—a mere default—and to move forward by emphasizing models, such as that of professionalism, that help show where the desirable values already exist, and to motivate more employers and employees to adopt similar practices. The firms that not only *survive,* but *succeed,* in the decades to come are going to be those that adopt such models.

Source: *Business Ethics Quarterly* 13, no. 2. ISSN 1052-150X, pp. 113–130. Reprinted by permission.

End Notes

1. In 1991, the Commissioners on Uniform State Laws passed the Model Employment Termination Act, which offers a framework for "just-cause" regimes. State legislatures have looked toward this Act as a model, but no state has yet adopted it.
2. "Just cause" advocates differ as to whether or not they define the standard as demanding merely "fair and honest" reasons or "good" reasons.
3. For example, less than 40 percent of all chicken catchers are unionized, despite the fact that they are exposed to pecking and chicken feather dust all day and work under very dangerous and stressful conditions.
4. According to "Extended Mass Layoffs in the Second Quarter of 2000," USDL 00–266. released September 20, 2000, http://stats.bls.gov/newsrels.htm. 1,099,267 people were separated from their jobs for more than 30 days in 1999, and 971,612 people filed initial claims for unemployment insurance during a consecutive five-week period. During the second quarter of 2000, there were 227,114 separations, and 162,726 initial claimants.
5. As Ehrenreich points out, most people cannot live on a minimum-wage salary so that those working at minimum wage usually have two jobs or a supporting family.

Reading 6-2

Confessions of a Sweatshop Inspector

T. A. Frank[1]

Presidential candidates are calling for tougher labor standards in trade agreements. But can such standards be enforced? Here's what I learned from my old job.

I remember one particularly bad factory in China. It produced outdoor tables, parasols, and gazebos, and the place was a mess. Work floors were so crowded with production materials that I could barely make my way from one end to the other. In one area, where metals were being chemically treated, workers squatted at the edge of steaming pools as if contemplating a sudden, final swim. The dormitories were filthy: the hallways were strewn with garbage—orange peels, tea leaves—and the only way for anyone to bathe was to fill a bucket with cold water. In a country where workers normally suppress their complaints for fear of getting fired, employees at this factory couldn't resist telling us the truth. "We work so hard for so little pay," said one middle-aged woman with undisguised anger. We could only guess how hard—the place kept no time cards. Painted in large characters on the factory walls was a slogan: "If you don't work hard today, look hard for work tomorrow." Inspirational, in a way.

I was there because, six years ago, I had a job at a Los Angeles firm that specialized in the field of "compliance consulting," or "corporate social responsibility monitoring." It's a service that emerged in the mid-1990s after the press started to report on bad factories around the world and companies grew concerned about protecting their reputations. With an increase of protectionist sentiment in the United States, companies that relied on cheap labor abroad were feeling vulnerable to negative publicity. They still are. (See "Disney Taking Heat Over China" in the *Los Angeles Times* this March.)

Today, labor standards are once again in the news. Barack Obama and Hillary Clinton have criticized trade deals such as NAFTA as unfair to American workers, and the new thinking is that trade agreements should include strict labor standards. Obama has cited a recent free trade agreement with Peru as an example of how to go forward. I hope he's right, but let's remember that NAFTA was also hailed, in its day, for including labor protections. Our solutions on paper have proved hard to enforce. Peru attempts to remedy some of the problems of NAFTA, but we're still advancing slowly in the dark.

In the meantime, as governments contemplate such matters on a theoretical level, what's happening on the ground is mostly in the hands of the private sector. Companies police themselves, often using hired outside help. That was the specialty of my company. Visit the Web site of almost any large American retailer or apparel manufacturer and you're likely to see a section devoted to "ethical sourcing" or "our compliance program." (Those are terms for making sure that your suppliers aren't using factories that will land you on the front page of the *New York Times.*) Read on and you'll often see that the company boasts of having a code of conduct that its suppliers must follow—a code of labor standards by which the factories in question will be regularly measured and monitored. Are they to be believed? Well, yes and no. Private monitoring, if done properly, can do a lot of good. But it's a tricky thing.

A simplified story of Nike may be the best way to introduce the origins of the type of work I was in. In the 1960s, Nike (before it was named Nike) based its business on the premise that the company would not manufacture shoes—it would only design and market them. The physical goods would be produced by independent contractors in countries such as Japan or Taiwan, where labor was, at the time, cheap. In short, Nike would be offices, not factories. The idea was innovative and hugely profitable, and countless companies producing everything from sweaters to toys to exercise equipment have since adopted it. It is now standard.

The problem that arose for Nike and many other companies, however, was that the media, starting in the 1990s, began to run stories on terrible labor conditions in factories in Asia. When consumers started to get angry, Nike and many other companies were nonplussed. We're just buying these shoes, they said—it's not our business how Mr. X runs his factory. And they had a point. If, for example, I learned that my dry cleaner was paying his employees less than minimum wage, I might feel bad about it, but I doubt I'd spend hours vetting alternative dry cleaners for labor compliance. I've got too much else to worry about in life, including my shirts. But such musings hardly make for a great press release, and Nike's case included nasty allegations about child labor—twelve-year-old Americans playing with soccer balls sewn by twelve-year-old Pakistanis, that sort of thing. The company's stock value sank.

In this same period, the U.S. Department of Labor, led by Robert Reich, began cracking down on sweatshops within the United States and publicizing the names of firms who were their customers. Because of this, companies such as mine began to offer their services as independent, for-profit monitors of factory labor conditions. We would act as early-warning systems against shady suppliers who mistreated their workers. Based on the reports we provided, our clients could choose either to sever their relations with a given supplier or to pressure them to improve. Business at my old company is still going strong.

In Los Angeles, where small garment shops of, say, thirty employees were the main focus, we usually worked in pairs and did three inspections a day. Outside the country, where the factories were often quite large (several thousand employees) and made anything from toys to gym equipment, we worked alone or in pairs and did one or two a day. The procedures were similar, but the inspections were more thorough abroad. While one of us might tour the work floors to note all the health and safety violations (the gazebo factory, for instance, had no secondary exits, no guarding on machines, no first aid supplies, no eye protection—the list kept going), the other might review permits, employee files, and payroll records to see what shortcomings were apparent on paper alone.

Then we would begin interviewing employees in private, usually twenty or so, hoping to learn from them what our eyes wouldn't tell us. Did the factory confiscate personal documents, such as identity cards, and use them as ransom? (This was most common in the Gulf States, where foreign laborers from places like Bangladesh could find themselves effectively enslaved. But bosses sometimes confiscated national identification documents in China, too.) Were employees free to enter and leave the compound? How many hours a week did they *really* work—regardless of what the time cards might say?

Unfortunately, we missed stuff. All inspections do. And sometimes it was embarrassing. At one follow-up inspection of a factory in Bangkok at which I'd noted some serious but common wage violations, the auditors who followed me found pregnant employees hiding on the roof and Burmese import workers earning criminally low wages. Whoops. On the other hand, sometimes I was the one who uncovered what others had missed. A lot of it had to do with luck. Was the right document visible on the work floor? Did we choose the right employees for interviews—the ones who were willing to confide in outsiders? If we were working through a translator, was his manner of speaking to people soothing?

The major challenge of inspections was simply staying ahead of the factories we monitored. False time cards and payroll records, whole days spent coaching employees on how to lie during interviews, and even renaming certain factory buildings in order to create a smaller Potemkin village—all of these were techniques used by contractors to try to fool us. We were able to detect some of them. A collection of crisp time cards that showed every employee arriving within seconds of the next was easy to spot as having been punched by a single worker standing alone at the time clock. An employee whose recollection of hours worked differed markedly from her time sheet was another indication of shady bookkeeping. But others were hard to defeat. Employee coaching deserves special attention for its crude effectiveness. The following composite dialogue, in which every answer is a lie, is typical of the sort of thing we endured:

Me: How many days a week do you work?

Employee: Five.

Me: Any overtime?

Employee: Almost never. We get time and a half in pay for overtime.

Me: How much do you make per hour?

Employee: I don't know.

Me: How much did you get for your most recent pay period?

Employee: I can't remember.

Me: Rough idea?

Employee: I can't remember.

Me: How do you deal with the fumes from the glue?

Employee: It's no problem. We have masks. *[Note: This was often true—harmful cotton masks that concentrated the fumes.]*

Me: How much do you get paid for Sunday work?

Employee: We don't work on Sundays.

Me: Do you have any sort of worker representative here?

Employee: ?

Me: Someone who represents the workers and talks to your bosses?

Employee: ?

Me: What sort of accidents happen here—you know, people bumping themselves, or cutting themselves?

Employee: No accidents.

Such exchanges, needless to say, rarely produced killer testimony. Sometimes we could work around uncooperative interviewees, or we could get them to stumble over their own answers. However, just talking to employees was no guarantee of anything, no matter how gifted an interrogator you were.

Because any inspection misses something, there were factories that managed to embarrass everyone. In 2000, *BusinessWeek* published an expose about a factory in Guangdong, China, the Chun Si Enterprise Handbag Factory, which made bags for Wal-Mart. Titled "Inside a Chinese Sweatshop: 'A Life of Fines and Beating,'" the article described a nightmarish place in which nine hundred workers were locked in a walled compound all day, and security guards "regularly punched and hit workers for talking back to managers or even for walking too fast." The reporting, by Dexter Roberts and Aaron Bernstein, was superb. Unfortunately, that reporting led to the door of my company, which had been among the auditors monitoring the factory for Wal-Mart. While they had found excessive overtime work and insufficient pay, inspectors had missed the captive workers and physical abuse.

To be sure, the Chun Si Enterprise Handbag Factory episode was a debacle. (I have no inside account of the story, since it took place several years before my arrival.) I suspect, however, that the fault lay with Wal-Mart as much as with the inspectors. I say this because there's a broader point here: Monitoring by itself is meaningless. It only works when the company that's commissioning it has a sincere interest in improving the situation. In the case of Chun Si, inspectors visited five times, according to *BusinessWeek,* and kept finding trouble. Now, anyone in the business knows that when inspections uncover safety violations or wage underpayment more than once or twice—let alone five times—it's a sign that bigger problems are lurking beneath. Companies rarely get bamboozled about this sort of thing unless they want to.

And many prefer to be bamboozled, because it's cheaper. While companies like to boast of having an ethical sourcing program, such programs make it harder to hire the lowest bidder. Because many companies still want to hire the lowest bidder, "ethical sourcing" often becomes a game. The simplest way to play it is by placing an order with a cheap supplier and ending the relationship once the goods have been delivered. In the meantime, inspectors get sent to evaluate the factory—perhaps several times, since they keep finding problems—until the client, seeing no improvement in the labor conditions, severs the bond and moves on to the next low-priced, equally suspect supplier.

For the half-assed company there are also half-assed monitoring firms. These specialize in performing as many brief, understaffed inspections as they can fit in a day in order to maximize their own profits. That gives their clients plausible deniability: problems undiscovered are problems avoided, and any later trouble can be blamed on the compliance monitors. It is a cozy understanding between client, monitoring company, and supplier that manages to benefit everyone but the workers.

While private monitoring can be misused, however, when it's done right it can really produce positive change. I've seen it. When companies make a genuine effort, the results can be impressive: safe factories that pay legal wages. That sounds modest, but it's actually hard to achieve in any country. Just visit a garment shop in Los Angeles.

At my company, I quickly figured out which clients cared. The first test was whether they conducted "pre-sourcing"—inspections of labor conditions before placing an order instead of after. This small step truly separates the top-rung companies from the pack, because to prescreen is to forgo the temptation of hiring the cheapest suppliers. (Those suppliers are the cheapest because they tend to break the rules, so they usually fail the preliminary inspection.) The second test was whether the company had a long-term relationship with its suppliers. Long-term commitments are what motivate both parties to behave: the supplier wants to preserve the relationship, and the customer wants to preserve its reputation. The third test was whether the company requested unannounced inspections as opposed to ones that were arranged in advance. The advantages of this are self-evident. And the final test was whether the company made inspection results public. This was almost never done.

Who, then, were the good actors of the trade? There are a number of them, actually, but here I'll just point out two that often surprise people. The first is Mattel, the same company that was tarnished last summer by a recall of toys that were found to have lead paint on them. Whatever the chemical flaws of their products, Mattel had a reputation among us monitors for earnestness in pressuring its suppliers to improve their labor practices. It also owned and operated a few factories in China—a country with dreadful factories—that were exemplary. These facilities were regularly inspected by independent monitors, and anyone who wants to know what they've found there can visit Mattel's Web site: the reports are public. The second unexpected company is Nike, which long ago took its bad press to heart and remade itself into a role model of how to carry out thoughtful labor monitoring. Nike has become such a leader in the field that its Web site may be the single best resource for those trying to understand the difficult business of international labor standards. Not only does Nike prescreen factories, it also discloses the name and address of every factory it uses and makes public much of its monitoring.

But let's not be confined to praise. You may get the sense that I'm not Wal-Mart's biggest fan. You'd be right. I betray no confidence here, since Wal-Mart wasn't a client of ours while I was at my company. Nevertheless, I still got to visit plenty of its supplier factories. That's because any given factory usually has more than one customer, and during an audit we would always ask the bosses to name their other customers. Wal-Mart was often one of them. And its suppliers were among the worst I saw—dangerous, nasty, and poorly paid even by local (usually Chinese) measures. I noticed that Wal-Mart claimed to require factories to maintain decent labor standards—but why did it seem to think it could find them among the lowest bidders?

Now, I know about good and bad actors mostly because I saw them directly. But ordinary consumers searching on company Web sites—Walmart .com, Nike.com, etc.—can find out almost everything they need to know just sitting at their desks. For instance, just now I learned from Wal-Mart's latest report on sourcing that only 26 percent of its audits are unannounced. By contrast, of the inspections Target conducts, 100 percent are unannounced. That's a revealing difference. And companies that do what Nike does—prescreen, build long-term relationships, disclose producers—make a point of emphasizing that fact, and are relatively transparent. Companies that don't are more guarded. (When in doubt, doubt.)

As for those who feel especially strongly about the issue and kick up a (peaceful) fuss about sweatshops, I think they're doing a valuable thing. Even when they take actions that are sometimes off-base—such as continuing to boycott Nike when its competitors are the bigger problem—the effect is still, overall, good: it scares businesses into taking compliance more seriously. Boycotts, protests, letters to Congress, saber-rattling lawmakers, media exposes—they do have an impact. And just imagine if members of Congress or the executive branch made an effort to praise or shame companies for their records with foreign suppliers and to encourage transparent monitoring in the private sector. I suspect it would do more for international labor standards in months than the most intricate trade agreements could do in years.

I don't pretend that everything monitoring brings about is for the best. An example: Mattel's factories in China are superb, but workers there often earn less than their peers in shadier factories because their employers confine them to shorter workweeks to avoid paying overtime. Another: You may rightly hate the idea of child labor, but firing a fourteen-year-old in Indonesia from a factory job because she is fourteen does nothing but deprive her of income she is understandably desperate to keep. (She'll find worse work elsewhere, most likely, or simply go hungry.) A third: Small village factories may break the rules, but they often operate in a humane and basically sensible way, and I didn't enjoy lecturing their owners about the necessity of American-style time cards and fifteen-minute breaks. But labor standards anywhere have a tendency to create such problems. They're enacted in the hope that the good outweighs the bad.

One final thought: If you're like me, part of you feels that Peru's labor standards are basically Peru's business. It's our job to worry about standards here at home. But that sort of thinking doesn't work well in an era of globalization. We are, like it or not, profoundly affected by the labor standards of our trading partners. If their standards are low, they exert a downward pressure on our own. That's why monitoring and enforcement have such an important role to play. We don't expect developing nations to match us in what their workers earn. (A few dollars a day is a fortune in many nations.) But when a Chinese factory saves money by making its employees breathe hazardous fumes and, by doing so, closes down a U.S. factory that spends money on proper ventilation and masks, that's wrong. It's wrong by any measure. And that's what we can do something about if we try. It's the challenge we face as the walls come down, the dolls, pajamas, and televisions come in, and, increasingly, the future of our workers here is tied to that of workers who are oceans away.

Source: http://www.washingtonmonthly.com/features/2008/0804.frank.html

End Note

1. T. A. Frank, an editor at the *Washington Monthly,* is an Irvine Fellow at the New America Foundation.

Reading **6-3**

Sweatshops, Choice, and Exploitation

Matt Zwolinski

1. Introduction

For the most part, individuals who work in sweatshops choose to do so.[1] They might not *like* working in sweatshops, and they might strongly desire that their circumstances were such that they did not have to do so. Nevertheless, the fact that they choose to work in sweatshops is morally significant. Taken seriously, workers' consent to the conditions of their labor should lead us to abandon certain moral objections to sweatshops, and perhaps even to view them as, on net, a good thing.

This argument, or something like it, is the core of a number of popular and academic defenses of the moral legitimacy of sweatshops. It has been especially influential among economists, who point to the voluntary nature of sweatshop employment as evidence for the claim that Western governments ought not to restrict the importation of goods made by sweatshops (Anderson, 1996, p. 694), or that labor-rights organizations ought not to seek to change the law in countries which host sweatshops in order to establish higher minimum wages or better working conditions (Krugman, 1997; Maitland, 1996), or, finally, that consumer boycotts of sweatshop-produced goods are misguided (Kristof & Wudunn, 2000).

This paper seeks to defend a version of the argument above, while at the same time clarifying its structure and content. The first step is to understand how a worker's consent can have any moral weight at all. How does choice have the power (a 'moral magic,' as some have called it) to transform the moral and legal nature of certain interactions (Hurd, 1996)? I begin the paper in section two by exploring several ways in which choice can be morally transformative. I distinguish between autonomy-exercising and preference-evincing choice, and argue that while the latter has been given the most attention in the mostly consequentialist defenses of sweatshops,[2] the former notion of consent, with its deontological underpinnings, is relevant as well. With this preliminary work accomplished, I then put forward in section three what I take to be the best reconstruction of the argument which seeks to base a moral defense of sweatshops on the consent of their workers. In section four, I explain how this argument undermines various proposals made by anti-sweatshop activists and academics. Sections five and six [not included in this excerpt] are devoted to a critical examination of this argument. I first examine, in section five, whether the morally transformative power of sweatshop workers' consent is undermined by a lack of voluntariness, failure of independence, or exploitation. My conclusion is that, at least in general, it is not. After having completed this discussion of the moral *weight* of consent in section five, I turn to considerations of its moral *force* in section six.[3] If consent makes sweatshop labor morally justifiable, what does that tell us about how businesses, consumers, and governments ought to act? And, perhaps more interestingly, if consent does *not* make sweatshop labor morally justifiable, what does *that* tell us? My position is that there is a large gulf between concluding that the activities of sweatshops are morally evil and concluding that sweatshop labor ought to be legally prohibited, boycotted, regulated, or prohibited by moral norms. To the extent that sweatshops do evil to their workers, they do so in the context of providing their workers with a financial benefit, and workers' eager readiness to consent to the conditions of sweatshop labor shows that they view this benefit as considerable. This fact leads to the ultimate practical conclusion of this paper, which is that there is a strong moral reason for third parties such as consumers and host and home country governments to refrain from acting in ways which are likely to deprive sweatshop workers of their jobs, and that both the policies traditionally promoted by anti-sweatshop activists (e.g. increasing the legal regulation of sweatshops, legally prohibiting the sale of sweatshop-produced goods, or subjecting such goods to economic boycott), and some more recent proposals by anti-sweatshop academics (i.e. voluntary self regulation via industry-wide standards or universal moral norms) are subject to criticism on these grounds.[4]

* * * *

2. The Moral Magic of Choice

An agent's choice, or consent, is transformative insofar as it "alters the normative relations in which others stand with respect to what they may do" (Kleinig, 2001, p. 300). This transformation can affect both the moral and the legal claims and obligations of both the parties involved, and of third parties.[5] Consent to sexual relations, for instance, can render permissible one's partner's otherwise impermissible sexual touching, and render it impermissible for third parties to interfere with the sexual activity to which one has consented. But the moral transformation to which choice gives rise can occur for various reasons. In this section, I will discuss two ways in which choice can be morally transformative, and argue that both are relevant to the case of sweatshop labor.

a. Autonomy-Exercising Choice

One way that choice can be morally transformative is if it is an exercise of an agent's autonomy. Sometimes we view the decisions of others as worthy of our respect because we believe that they reflect the agent's will, or because they stem from desires, goals and projects that are expressive the agent's authentic self.[6] If so, this fact will often provide us with a reason for not interfering with the agent's action even if we think the consequences of her action will be bad for her, and even if we disagree with the reasoning that underlies her decision. I might believe my neighbor's religious practices to be based on an untrue faith, and ultimately detrimental to his financial, emotional, and spiritual well-being. Nonetheless, I am not entitled to compel my neighbor to abandon his religion, and this is not merely because the consequences of my interference would be worse for my neighbor than my doing nothing. Even if I could make him better off by compelling him to abandon his religion, and even if my coercion would have no other ill effects in the world, a respect for my neighbor's autonomy would still require me to abstain from such behavior.[7]

Thus, one way that a worker's choice to accept the conditions of sweatshop labor can be morally transformative is if it is an exercise of autonomy. Such a choice can, I will argue, be morally transformative in certain respects even if it is not a *fully* autonomous one, and even if it does not achieve the full range of moral transformations that such a fully autonomous choice would yield.[8] Specifically, I believe that a worker's autonomous choice to accept conditions of employment establishes a strong claim to freedom from certain sorts of interference by others, even if it fails to render the employment relationship a morally praiseworthy one. But how strong a claim to non-interference does it generate? And against which sorts of interference does it hold?

To take the first question first, it is of course true that not all autonomous choices generate claims to non-interference. But when the subject matter of the choice is of central importance to the agent's identity or core projects, it is plausible to suppose that autonomous choices do generate strong claims to liberty.[9] And it is hard to deny that the choices made by potential sweatshop workers *are* of central importance in just this way. Sweatshop workers do not generally choose to work in order to gain some extra disposable income for luxuries, or simply to take pleasure in the activity of working. They work to survive, or to help their family survive, or so their children can gain an education and escape the misery of poverty that drove them to sweatshops in the first place. Choices such as these involve projects—one's own survival, one's role as a parent or a spouse—that are of central importance to most people's lives. Such choices, when made autonomously, deserve respect.

But what does respect amount to in this context? In the case of religious liberty, we think that the autonomous pursuit of religious practice generates a claim against certain sorts of interference with that practice by others. We might similarly hold, then, that the autonomous acceptance of sweatshop labor generates a claim against interference in carrying out the terms of their agreement, such as the kind that would be involved most obviously in an outright legal prohibition of sweatshop labor. But the idea that autonomous choice generates a claim to noninterference is one which stands in need of closer examination.

The analogy of religious practice is instructive. Note that even in the religious case, not *all* manifestations of religious practice are protected by a claim to non-interference, and not *all* kinds of interference, even those which involve the core aspects of religious practice, are prohibited. A religious believer who desires to murder a nonbeliever because his religion orders him to do so has *no* claim to freedom from interference in pursuit of this project. And even the ordinary religious desire to adhere to a certain structure of beliefs has no claim to freedom from the kind of interference that we classify as "persuasion." I cannot *force* you into abandoning your religious faith, but I can certainly try to talk you out of it.

I do not believe that the above qualifications pose a serious difficulty for the claim that the autonomous choice to accept sweatshop labor is entitled to a claim to non-interference. The reason the religious believer's desire to murder the nonbeliever is not entitled to any such claim is that the activity he wishes to engages in violates the rights of another. But those who worry about sweatshop labor are not typically worried that sweatshop workers are violating anyone else's rights. If anything, they worry that the rights of the sweatshop worker himself are being violated. But the fact that a worker loses some of his rights is a *consequence* of the autonomy of his choice, not an objection to it. One of the things that autonomous choices allow us to do is to waive certain claims that we might have had (in the case of workers, the claim not to be told what to do by others, or the claim to certain kinds of freedom of association, for instance). It is because we think it important to allow people to waive their rights in this way that we find autonomy to be such an important value, and why we believe it proper to respect autonomous choices—at least those which are largely self-regarding—with non-interference.

This is not to say that *all* sorts of interference with a sweatshop worker's choice are impermissible. To take some easy examples, it is of course permissible to use persuasion to try to get a sweatshop worker to not accept conditions of employment that you view as exploitative. And it is likewise permissible to start an ethically run MNE and to compete with the unethical sweatshop for its labor force. There are good reasons, both consequentialist and deontological, for refusing to view these sorts of actions as objectionable violations of workers' autonomy.[10] But it *would* be immoral, I believe, to prevent contracts for sweatshop labor by legislative fiat.[11] To do so would be to violate the autonomy of the workers who would have otherwise chosen to work in such conditions. And what it is immoral to do directly, it is also probably immoral to do indirectly. Laws which have the effect of preventing workers and sweatshops from freely contracting together—such as laws in the host country which raise the price of labor to a prohibitively high rate, or laws in countries that consume sweatshop labor which ban the importation of sweatshop-made goods—are thus also morally suspect.[12]

b. Preference-Evincing Choice

Choices are more than a method of exercising autonomy. Choices also signal information about an agent's preferences. Significantly, this is true even when the choice is made under conditions of less than full autonomy. An agent faced with the gunman's threat of "your money or your life," for instance, still has a choice to make, even if it is only from among a range of options which has been illegitimately restricted by the gunman. And should the agent decide to hand over his wallet, this would tell us that among the two options he faces, as he understands them, he prefers giving his wallet to the gunman to losing his life. This might not be morally transformative in the same *way* as a fully autonomous choice would be, but surely it does *something* to change the moral landscape. Compare the following two cases:

> **Accommodating Kidnapper:** *A* kidnaps *B* and locks her in his basement. When mealtime arrives, *A* asks *B* which of two foods she would prefer to eat, and gives her whichever she requests.
>
> **Curmudgeonly Kidnapper:** *A* kidnaps *B* and locks her in his basement. When mealtime arrives, *A* asks *B* which of two foods she would prefer to eat, and gives her whichever one she does *not* request.

In both versions of the story, *A* illegitimately restricts *B*'s range of options. In neither case is *B*'s choice of meals fully autonomous. Still, it *is* a choice, and it seems clear that *B*'s making it will affect what *A* ought to do. Disregarding *B*'s preferences by giving her the meal that she least prefers is a wrong above and beyond the initial wrong of coercion.[13] By choosing one meal over another, she has conveyed information about her preferences to *A*. And by giving her the meal she least prefers, *A* is knowingly acting in a way likely to make her worse off, and this is wrong.[14] *B*'s choice is thus morally transformative, but in a way different from that described above. Here, the moral transformation occurs as a result of *B*'s choice providing *A* with information about *B*'s preferences. Knowing what somebody prefers often changes what one ought to do. It might not be wrong for me to serve fish to a guest about whom I know nothing. But if my guest tells me that she despises fish, serving it to her anyway would be (*ceteris paribus*) extremely disrespectful. By expressing preferences, choices thus transform the moral landscape.

In the mugging case, the victim's choice to hand over his wallet might not make the mugger's decision to take it a morally praiseworthy one, or even a morally permissible one. In *these* respects, therefore, his choice is *not* morally transformative. But there is another respect in which it is. It is transformative in that it renders impermissible certain attempts by other persons to interfere with his activity. A well-meaning busybody who attempted to prevent the victim from handing over his wallet, believing that death in such circumstances was surely better than dishonor, would be acting wrongly, and what makes the act wrong is that it goes against the victim's choice—whether that choice is fully autonomous or not.

In a similar way, then, a worker's choice to accept sweatshop labor can be morally transformative by signaling information about her preferences. A worker's choice to accept sweatshop labor shows that she prefers that kind of labor to any other alternative. Sweatshop labor might not be the kind of thing for which she has any *intrinsic* desire. But when all things are considered—her poverty, the wages paid by the sweatshop and that paid by alternative sources of employment, etc.—she prefers working there to anything else she might do. And by expressing her preferences, her choice is morally transformative. To attempt to directly remove the option of sweatshop labor (or to act in ways which are likely to indirectly remove that option), while knowing that sweatshop labor is the most preferred option of many workers, is to knowingly act in a way which is likely to cause workers harm. Indeed, given that many potential sweatshop workers seem to express a *strong* preference for sweatshop labor over the alternatives, acting to remove that option is likely to cause them *great* harm.[15] This is, *ceteris paribus,* wrong.

Sweatshop workers' choices can thus be morally transformative in two ways—by being exercises of their autonomy, or by being expressions of their preferences.[16] Note that while both sorts of choice can be morally transformative, they achieve their respective transformations by calling attention to very different sorts of values or considerations. The proper response to an autonomy-exercising choice is one of *respect,* and this respect seems to counsel non-interference with the agent's choice even if we believe the consequences of interfering would be superior for the agent. Preference-evincing choices often give us reason for non-interference as well, but *only because* we think the consequences of doing so will be better in some respect for the agent. The expression of a choice for one thing over another is usually good evidence that one actually prefers that thing over the other, and it is, *ceteris paribus,* better for one to get what one wants.

With this understanding of the morally transformative power of choice in hand, we are now ready to turn to a closer look to the argument with which this paper began—an argument that seeks to base a moral defense of sweatshops on the consent of the workers.

3. The Argument

1. Most sweatshop workers choose to accept the conditions of their employment, even if their choice is made from among a severely constrained set of options.[17]
2. The fact that they choose the conditions of their employment from within constrained set of options is strong evidence that they view it as their most-preferred option (within that set).
3. The fact that they view it as their most-preferred option is strong evidence that we will harm them by taking that option away.
4. It is also plausible that sweatshop workers' choice to accept the conditions of their employment is sufficiently autonomous that taking the option of sweatshop labor away from them would be a violation of their autonomy.
5. All else being equal, it is wrong to harm people or to violate their autonomy.
6. Therefore, all else being equal, it is wrong to take away the option of sweatshop labor from workers who would otherwise choose to engage in it.

I believe this argument (hereafter, "The Argument") captures and clarifies what lies behind many popular defenses of sweatshops. There are three things to note about it. The first is that, unlike popular defenses, The Argument clearly distinguishes two different ways in which workers' choices can serve to establish a claim of non-interference against those who act in ways that make sweatshop labor a non-option—one based in respect for workers' autonomy (1, 4, 5, and 6) and another based in an obligation not to harm (1, 2, 3, 5 and 6). Unlike the standard economic defense of sweatshops, then, The Argument is not purely consequentialist in nature. Appeals to consequences are relevant in The Argument's appeal to the preference-evincing power of choice, which cautions us to avoid harming workers by frustrating their revealed preferences.[18] But The Argument has a deontological foundation as well, which is brought out in its notion of autonomy-exercising choice. Here, The Argument counsels us to refrain from interfering in sweatshop workers' choices, not because that interference would frustrate preference-satisfaction, but because doing so would violate workers' autonomy in their choice of employment.

The second thing to note about The Argument is that, again unlike popular defenses, it is clear regarding the nature of the moral transformation that sweatshop workers' choices effect. Their choice establishes a claim of non-interference against those who might wish to prevent them from engaging in sweatshop labor, or make that labor more difficult to obtain. That is all that is claimed by The Argument. It does not attempt to show that workers' choices render the treatment bestowed on them by their employers morally praiseworthy. It does not even attempt to show that their choice renders such treatment morally *permissible*.[19] And, finally, it does not establish an *insuperable* claim against interference. The Argument shows that harming sweatshop workers or violating their autonomy is wrong, but leaves open the possibility that these wrongs could be justifiable in certain circumstances. The Argument simply shifts the burden of proof on to those who wish to prohibit sweatshop labor to provide such justification.

The final thing to note about The Argument is that its success is extremely sensitive to a wide range of empirical facts. The truth of premise 1, for instance, hinges on whether people *do* in fact choose to work in sweatshops, and fails in cases of genuinely forced labor. The claim that we harm sweatshop workers' by removing what they see as their best option (premise 3) depends on particular facts about the nature of an individual's preferences and their relation to her wellbeing, and the claim that workers' choices are autonomous (premise 4) depends on the particular conditions under which the choice to accept sweatshop labor is made. This sensitivity to empirical facts means that we cannot determine *a priori* whether The Argument is successful. But this is as it should be. Sweatshops are a complicated phenomenon, and while philosophers have an important contribution to make to the conversation about their moral justifiability, it is only a partial contribution. For the complete picture, we need to supplement our moral theorizing with data from (at least) economists, psychologists, and social scientists. In this paper, I will draw on empirical data to support my argument where it is available. Since I am not well positioned to evaluate the soundness of such data, however, I will attempt to clearly signal when I appeal to it, and to indicate the way in which The Argument's success is or is not reliant on its veracity.

4. What Policies Does The Argument Oppose?

The Argument's conclusion is that it is wrong to 'take away' the option of sweatshop labor from those who would otherwise choose to engage in it. But what exactly does it mean to take away the option of sweatshop labor? What sort of policies is The Argument meant to oppose?

a. Bans and Boycotts

The most obvious way in which the option of sweatshop labor can be 'taken away' is a legal ban on sweatshops or, more commonly, on the sale or importation of sweatshop-produced goods. The mechanism by which the former sort of ban removes the option of sweatshop labor is fairly obvious. But bans on the sale or importation of sweatshop goods can, if effective and large enough in scale, achieve the same results. If goods made in sweatshops cannot be sold, then it seems likely that sweatshops will stop producing such goods, and those who were employed in their production will be out of work.[20] Economists and others have therefore criticized such bans as counterproductive in the quest to aid the working poor.[21] As a result, neither sort of ban is defended by many anti-sweatshop scholars writing today, but many activists and politicians persist in their support of such measures.[22] The Argument condemns them.

b. Legal Regulation

Bans on the importation or sale of sweatshop-produced goods take sweatshop jobs away from their workers by making their continued employment no longer economically viable for their employers. The increased legal regulation of sweatshops can accomplish the same effect for the same reason. Legal attempts to ameliorate working conditions in sweatshops by regulating the use of and pay for overtime, minimum wage laws, or workplace safety, for instance, raise the cost which sweatshops must incur to employ their workers. This cost is passed on to the MNE which, in turn, might decide once costs have passed a certain level, to move their operations to another country where labor is more productive or less heavily regulated.[23]

Calls for the increased legal regulation of sweatshops are more common among both activists and academics alike.[24] It is worth noting, though, that calls for the increased enforcement of existing regulations are likely to be indistinguishable in their effects. Many laws in the developing world which ostensibly regulate sweatshop activity are either poorly enforced or completely ignored.[25] Sometimes the lack of enforcement is simply due to insufficient resources on the part of the enforcement agency. But sometimes it is a deliberate choice, since government officials want the tax revenue that MNEs bring to the country and worry that increasing the cost of doing business could lead those MNEs to stay away or leave. Calls for the enforcement of existing regulations do have the advantage over calls for new regulation in that such enforcement will help to promote the rule of law—a key value in both economic development and a healthy democracy.[26] But in terms of their effect on workers' jobs, they are equally bad, and equally opposed by The Argument.

c. Voluntary Self-Regulation

Today, many of the most prominent academic critics of sweatshops focus their energy on calls for voluntary self-regulation on the part of sweatshops. Their hope is that self-regulation can correct the moral failings of sweatshops while at the same time avoiding the unintended harms caused by the more heavy-handed attempts described above.

Nothing in The Argument is opposed to voluntary self-regulation as such. If, as The Argument was specifically formulated to allow, many of the activities of sweatshops are immoral, then they ought to change, and voluntary self-regulation will often be the best way to accomplish this change.

Furthermore, by providing concrete examples of 'positive deviancy'—cases where multinational enterprises have made changes to improve conditions for workers in their supply chain above and beyond those required by market pressures or the law—much of the recent scholarship on self-regulation has provided a valuable model for firms who wish to wish to begin making changes in the right direction.[27]

There are, however, two significant causes for concern over the precise way in which the case for self-regulation has been made in the recent literature. First, to the extent that 'voluntary' self-regulation is to be accomplished by industry-wide standards, the regulation is really only voluntary for the industry as a whole.[28] For any individual firm, compliance is essentially mandatory. Individual firms, then, are in much the same position as they would be under legal regulation, insofar as those who cannot afford to comply with the mandated standard would be forced to cut costs or alter their production in a way that could negatively affect the employment of sweatshop workers. Additionally, industry-wide standards serve as an impediment to the market's discovery process. By establishing *one* standard with which all firms must comply, this sort of approach discourages (and in some cases, prohibits) individual firms from experimenting with their own standards which might be better suited to the particular context in which they are operating.[29]

The second and less well-recognized problem is that by making the case for self-regulation in terms of the *rights* workers have to certain forms of treatment and the *obligations* that MNEs have to ensure such treatment, supporters of 'voluntary' self-regulation end up putting too strong a demand on MNEs for the kind of reform they desire, while paying insufficient attention to ways of helping workers that fall short of their desired goal.

To see this problem more clearly, we can look at the recent work of Denis Arnold. The core philosophical argument of that work claims that workers have rights to freedom and wellbeing,[30] and argues that these rights require MNEs to ensure that certain minimum conditions are met in their supply chain.[31] As an example of the sort of specific obligation to which these general rights to freedom and well-being give rise, Arnold and Hartman state in a recent paper that "respect for the rights of workers to subsistence entails that MNEs and their suppliers have an obligation to ensure that workers do not live under conditions of overall poverty by providing adequate wages for a 48 hour work week to satisfy both basic food needs and basic non-food needs."[32]

Now, it cannot be doubted that it would be a morally praiseworthy thing for MNEs to ensure that their workers are given this level of treatment. But this is not what Arnold is claiming. He is claiming that MNEs have an *obligation* to provide this level of treatment—one that is grounded on workers' *rights*. This is making an extremely strong moral claim. Rights are generally thought to be 'trumps'—considerations which, when brought to bear on a decision, are supposed to override any competing claims.[33] Respecting rights is non-optional.

But notice that while rights as such are non-optional, the right and corresponding obligation that Arnold endorses are conditional in an important way. Workers have a right to certain levels of minimum treatment, and MNEs have an obligation to provide it, *if* MNEs involve those workers in their supply chain. But nothing requires MNEs to do so. Workers have a right to adequate wages *if* MNEs contract with sweatshops to employ them. But MNEs are under no obligation to outsource labor in this way at all. And if the only morally permissible way to engage in such outsourcing is to incur heavy costs by seeing that workers receive the minimum level of wages, safety conditions and so forth demanded by Arnold et al., it is quite possible that many MNEs will choose *not* to do so.

Whether they would or not is, of course, an empirical question the resolution of which is beyond the scope of this paper.[34] But merely noting the possibility highlights an odd feature of the logic of Arnold's position. Arnold is committed to claiming that:

1. It is morally permissible for MNEs not to outsource their labor to workers in the developing world at all.
2. It is not morally permissible for MNEs to outsource labor to workers in the developing world without meeting the minimum conditions set forth by Arnold's account of workers' rights.

But empirically, it seems plausible that

3. Sweatshop labor that falls short of meeting the minimum conditions set forth by Arnold's account of workers' rights can still be a net benefit to workers, relative to their other possible sources of employment.[35]

And clearly,

4. MNEs which do not outsource their labor to workers in the developing world do not benefit those workers at all.[36]

It follows that on Arnold's view,

C1) It is morally permissible for MNEs not to benefit workers at all by not outsourcing their labor to workers in the developing world.

And

C2) It is morally impermissible for MNEs to benefit workers to some extent by outsourcing labor to workers in the developing world without meeting the minimum conditions set forth by Arnold's account of workers' rights.

This means, paradoxically, that according to Arnold's argument MNEs are more morally blameworthy for doing business with a sweatshop that pays less than adequate wages than for doing no business abroad at all, even if workers in the unethical sweatshop would prefer and freely choose their work over the option of no work at all. Indeed, elsewhere in their essay, Arnold and Hartman seem to explicitly embrace this point. They approvingly cite critics (one of whom includes Arnold himself) who argue that "regardless of the kinds of benefits that do or do not accrue from the use of sweatshops, it is simply morally impermissible to subject individuals to extended periods of grueling and mind-numbing labour in conditions that put their health and welfare at risk and which provide them with inadequate compensation" (210-11). But I do not think we should be so quick to declare as irrelevant the benefits that accrue to workers under conditions of labor which fall short of meeting the minimum standards demanded by Arnold. Labor which falls short of a living wage can still help a worker feed their family, educate their children, and generally make their lives better than they would have been without it. This is a morally significant benefit, and one our system of moral norms should at the very least *permit,* if not encourage.

Thus, while The Argument does not condemn voluntary self-regulation as such, it *does* condemn the claim that outsourcing labor to the developing world is only permissible if certain minimum standards are met. For we cannot simply assume that MNEs will continue to outsource labor to the developing world if the only conditions under which they may permissibly do so are ones in which the costs of outsourced labor are significantly higher than they are now.[37] And without this assumption, our system of moral norms ought not to prohibit MNEs from outsourcing labor in a way which falls short of meeting Arnold's standards, for to do so would be to deprive workers of the ability to engage in labor they would freely choose to accept, and thereby frustrate workers' choices and harm the very people we intended to help.

Source: Final Version available in *Business Ethics Quarterly,* vol. 17, no. 4 (October, 2007)

End Notes

1. Definitions of 'sweatshop' vary. Arnold and Hartman (D. Arnold & Hartman, 2006) define a sweatshop as "any workplace in which workers are typically subject to two or more of the following conditions: income for a 48 hour work week less than the overall poverty rate for that country; systematic forced overtime; systematic health and safety risks due to negligence or the willful disregard of employee welfare; coercion; systematic deception that places workers at risk; and underpayment of earnings." Similarly, the U.S. General Accounting Office defines a sweatshop as a business that "regularly violates both wage or child labor and safety or health laws" (U.S. General Accounting Office, 1988). Both of these definitions have merit insofar as they detail the specific kinds of offenses for which sweatshops are generally criticized. But both are, I think, parasitic on a more fundamental *moral* judgment—that a sweatshop is a business that is doing something *wrong.* The boundaries of this moral judgment are fuzzy—sometimes it might take two types of offense

to qualify as a sweatshop, sometimes fewer or more. But when we label something a sweatshop, I believe we are making at least a *prima facie* moral judgment about that entity—that it is behaving in a way that it ought not to behave. See (Zwolinski, 2006). The drawback of this approach is that it runs the risk of skirting the substantive debate over the morality of sweatshops by definition. To avoid this, I propose that we define them as industries which violate labor standards (either host country legal standards or standards defined by international norms) in some of the ways described above in a way which makes their actions *prima facie* wrong. Low wages and psychological coercion appear to be wrongful business practices, but our definition of sweatshop should be open to the possibility that they will be proven not to be so, at least in some cases. For purposes of this essay, I will be interested exclusively in sweatshops in the developing world, and will draw a distinction between sweatshops—which tend to be legally recognized, above-ground businesses, even if some of their specific practices may be illegal or immoral—and the informal sector of the economy, where many of the same practices which occur in sweatshops may occur, but in which enterprises lack the official legal standing that sweatshops have. There are moral debates to be had over the treatment of workers in the informal sector, but the debate over sweatshops has tended to view this sector as an *alternative* to sweatshop labor, and one which does not share the direct connection to questions regarding the responsibilities of MNEs (multi-national enterprises). I therefore limit my discussion in this paper to sweatshops as an aspect of the formal economy.

2. See, for instance, (D. Arnold & Hartman, 2005, pp. 208, 210), where the authors characterize the *laissez-faire* defense of sweatshops as based on consequentialist moral considerations alone. However, while the authors are correct that most of the extant defenses of sweatshops are based on consequentialist moral reasoning, they are surely incorrect in asserting that the *form* of consequentialism at work is necessarily preference-maximizing utilitarianism. A moral theory is consequentialist if it holds that consequences are all that matter in the moral evaluation of an action. But consequentialist theories differ regarding *which* consequences matter and *how* they matter. Rather than seeking to maximize the satisfaction of preferences, for instance, a consequentialist theory might try to maximize the non-violation of rights. See (Nozick, 1974, p. 28), for instance. Or, rather than maximizing some aggregate such as preferences or non-rights violations, a consequentialist theory might weigh the interests of some groups more heavily than others, as do the various forms of prioritarian consequentialist theories. See, for example, (Parfit, 1998) and (Nagel, 1997). I take pains to clarify this distinction now because while the argument in this paper will draw partly on consequentialist considerations, the sort of consequentialism on which it will draw will not be the kind of preference utilitarianism targeted by Arnold and Hartman. See section 3.
3. See (Wertheimer, 1996, p. 28) for a thorough discussion. Briefly, the moral weight of a consideration is the way in which that consideration alters the goodness or badness of a relationship or state of affairs. The moral force of a consideration, on the other hand, is the way in which that consideration affects the reasons agents have for acting one way or another with respect to it.
4. For a clearer statement of the sorts of interference my argument seeks to criticize, see section 4, and the concluding section of this paper.
5. For more on the transformative power of consent, see (Wertheimer, 2003).
6. Characterizations of autonomy vary greatly. Some hold that the autonomy of a desire,

belief, or action depends on its relation to other mental states, such as beliefs or higher-order desires. See, for instance, (Watson, 1975) and (Frankfurt, 1988). Such accounts can be referred to as *coherentist* since, for them, the autonomy of a particular action or mental state is based upon its coherence with other mental states of the agent. A different approach to autonomy makes the autonomy of an action or mental state depend upon its *origin.* Fischer and Ravizza, for instance, hold that actions are autonomous if they are the product of a "reasons-responsive" mechanism (Fischer & Ravizza, 1998). Another division could be drawn between what have been called 'procedural' vs. 'substantive' accounts of autonomy—the difference between the two being that the former holds that autonomy can be assessed independently of the content of an agent's beliefs and desires, by looking at the process by which those beliefs and desires are formed, while the latter does not (See, for a discussion of this distinction, (Mackenzie & Stoljar, 2000). For the purposes of this paper, I wish to remain neutral among these competing conceptions of autonomy. I have attempted to base my argument on the general *concept* of autonomy—that of freedom and self-governance in thought and action—and not on any particular (and controversial) conception. Specifically, the arguments I put forward in section 5.a. are intended to show that failures of autonomy do not undermine the main argument of this paper and should hold regardless of whether one holds a coherentist, originalist, procedural or substantive conception of autonomy.

7. Within limits, of course. If my neighbor's religious practices lead him to be a danger to himself, there may come a point where my interference with those practices becomes justified. The point is not that autonomy is an insuperable barrier to interference, merely that it is a barrier.
8. I will discuss the implications of the non-fully autonomous nature of sweatshop workers' choices in section 5.a.
9. This is, I take it, much of what underlies many arguments for freedom of religion. For an elaboration of this point, and an argument to the effect that there is nothing special about religion *per se* that entitles the practice of it to freedom from interference, see (Nickel, 2005).
10. On the consequentialist side, there are benefits inherent in a system of open market competition and in allowing individuals robust freedom of speech. These benefits might be said to outweigh the harms caused by those who lose their jobs due to market pressure, or those who lose business due to public protests. Deontologically, we might say that individuals have a *right* to free speech or to compete fairly in the market place, but they do not have the right to utilize the coercive apparatus of the state to legally prohibit contracts of which they disapprove. The latter would be a violation of workers' autonomy, but the former would not.
11. Few anti-sweatshop activists actually propose prohibiting sweatshop labor outright. But many propose various forms of regulation (punitive tariffs on sweatshop-made goods, prohibitively expensive regulation of sweatshops, etc.) that are likely to have the consequence of prohibiting workers from entering into mutually beneficial contracts for sweatshop labor. See section 4 of this paper for a more detailed discussion of how the argument of this paper bears on these less (or less-obviously) coercive anti-sweatshop proposals.
12. "Morally suspect," however, (and "immoral" just above), should be read in a *pro tanto* sense. Violating a worker's autonomy is *a wrong,* and this means that it is *the wrong thing to do* if there are no competing considerations to the contrary. It is possible, however, that the wrong of violating sweatshop laborer's autonomy might be less bad than the wrong any other course of action would impose, or that the benefits secured by

wronging sweatshop laborers might be very great. In such cases, violating sweatshop workers' autonomy is arguably not the wrong thing to do, but it is still a wrong nevertheless.

13. Unless, that is, *B* knows something about the conditions of *B*'s choice that we don't know (such as that she *really* wants a ham and cheese sandwich even if her expressed preference is for a bowl of soup). An expression of choice can fail to be morally transformative in various circumstances, and I will discuss some of those circumstances later in this paper. The point here is that the presence of coercion, and hence the absence of full autonomy, is not by itself sufficient to render a choice morally-nontransformative.
14. Unless, again, there is more to the story than I have indicated here. Having one's preferences frustrated is not *always* bad for a person. And knowingly acting in a way likely to make someone worse off is not always wrong. But they are usually, or at least very often, so. This is enough for the purposes of my argument.
15. See, for instance, the quote from Doris Hajewski in section 5.b.
16. The two categories are not mutually exclusive. An autonomy-exercising choice can be preference-evincing, and vice-versa, but it need not be.
17. Many philosophers, myself included, find this severely constrained set of options objectionable. For the purposes of this paper, however, I am treating sweatshops as a somewhat isolated moral phenomenon. That is, I am asking what we should do about sweatshops, while holding most of the other conditions of the world (large inequalities of wealth among nations, severe poverty in the developing world, and a growing system of global capitalism) constant. I hold them constant not because I think they are good things, nor because I think that we ought to do nothing about them, but because this seems to me the only way to make any progress on an issue that is pressing and cannot wait for the resolution of these other problems. Poverty, inequality, and economic development all need to be addressed. My paper seeks to tell us what we should do about sweatshops in the meantime.
18. Note that while this argument relies on considerations that are consequentialist in nature, it does not necessarily rely on a classically utilitarian formulation of consequentialism. My own view, in fact, is that to the extent consequentialist considerations are relevant, they are probably more prioritarian in form than strictly aggregationalist. In other words, we have a duty to promote good consequences, but that duty is especially weighty with regards to the worst-off. This makes the issue of sweatshops especially pressing. Minimum wage laws in a country like the United States might have some of the same unemployment effects as regulations on sweatshops in the developing world. But the people put out of work by regulations in the developing world are in a much worse position both antecedently and subsequent to regulation, and so our moral duty to protect them from harm is both more urgent, and more significant relative to other moral obligations that we might have.
19. The ways in which sweatshops treat their employees might be morally repugnant and absolutely impermissible. But this is not enough to establish that it is morally permissible for third parties to interfere.
20. This is, of course, an empirical claim. It is at least logically possible that sweatshops will respond to boycotts by ceasing to engage in immoral behavior without negatively affecting employment. My argument against boycotts proceeds on the assumption, which I cannot defend here, that the outcome described in the main body of the paper is a significantly likely (though not certain) one.
21. Ian Maitland, for instance, argues in his seminal paper on sweatshops that "attempts to improve on market outcomes" with regard to sweatshop wages, such as boycotts or legal regulation, can yield "unforeseen tragic

consequences" (Maitland, 1996, p. 604). Similarly, Powell (Powell, 2006) argues that "many of the means chosen by [anti-sweatshop] activists will not promote the ends of more ethical treatment of workers."

22. The National Labor Committee, for instance, promotes on the main page of its Web site a bill pending in the U.S. Congress (S. 3485 and H.5635) which would ban the import, export, or sale of sweatshop goods in the United States (National Labor Committee, 2006). See also in this vein, (Bernstein, 2002), which discusses the launching of the Campaign for the Abolition of Sweatshops and Child Labor and quotes Georgetown law professor Robert Stumberg as noting that measures against sweatshops being considered include bans on such imports, forced disclosure of factories where imported goods are made, and bans on government purchases of sweatshop goods." Finally, see the statement of the organization "Scholars Against Sweatshops" (SASL, 2001). This 2001 document signed by over 350 economists and other academics, calls both for the adoption of codes of conduct by universities which would restrict the sorts of apparel companies with which they could do business, and for stricter legal and economic regulations in countries that host sweatshops. In response to those who worry that such restrictive measures might harm the very sweatshop workers they seek to benefit, the authors reassure us "the *aim* of the anti-sweatshop movement is obviously not to induce negative *unintended* consequences such as higher overall unemployment in developing countries" (page 3, emphasis added). For obvious reasons, this seems to miss the point.

23. Again, these are empirical speculations which, though reasonably supported by economic theory, cannot be defended in this paper. See, however, (Sollars & Englander, 2007, pp. 123–129) for an empirically-grounded approach to the unemployment impact of minimum wage increases on sweatshop workers. If my empirical assumptions turn out to be false, then the consequentialist case against the legal regulation of sweatshops is significantly weakened, though one could still argue that the regulations impermissibly interfere in workers' freedom to enter into what they believe to be mutually beneficial contractual arrangements.

24. See, for instance, the references in footnote 22. Additionally, Hartman et al. claim that "because market transactions cannot be relied upon as a basis of avoiding rights violations, the protection of rights must come from the imposition of governmental controls or an effective realignment of consumer choice criteria," (Hartman, Shaw, & Stevenson, 2003, p. 214). Along similar lines, Jan Murray claims that while many anti-sweatshop academics have begun to focus on voluntary corporate self-regulation, it would be "counterproductive to suggest that firms can be seen as the *sole* implementers of the core labor standards, so from both a theoretical and practical perspective it is necessary to see corporate efforts as part of a regulatory continuum" involving both legal regulation, industry-wide standards, and self-regulation by individual firms (Murray, 2003, p. 38, emphasis added).

25. See (D. Arnold & Hartman, 2006), section IV.A for a discussion of this phenomenon with specific examples.

26. See, for instance, (D. G. Arnold & Bowie, 2003) section III, which does not explicitly call for governments to increase their enforcement of existing laws, but does call for MNEs to ensure that their contractors are complying with those laws regardless of enforcement.

27. See, for instance, (D. Arnold & Hartman, 2003) and (D. Arnold, Hartman, & Wokutch, 2003).

28. Such industry-wide standards are often preferred by anti-sweatshop academics for a

variety of reasons having to do with compliance and cost-sharing. See, generally, (D. Arnold, Hartman, & Wokutch, 2003) and, specifically, (D. Arnold & Hartman, 2006, p. 696).

29. See (Powell, 2006, section iv). His point, as I take it, is based on the logic of incentives rather than an inductive survey of empirical data. In Hayekian terms, industry-wide standards have the potential to stifle the market's ability to serve as a 'discovery process,' finding new ways to utilize scarce resources and scattered knowledge to improve human well-being. See (Hayek, 1968).
30. See (D. Arnold, Hartman, & Wokutch, 2003, p. 4) and (D. G. Arnold & Bowie, 2003).
31. (D. Arnold, Hartman, & Wokutch, 2003), chapter 4, but see also (D. G. Arnold & Bowie, 2003), especially sections I and II.
32. (D. Arnold & Hartman, 2005, p. 211).
33. See (Dworkin, 1997).
34. See, however, (Powell, 2006), especially section iv, for a discussion of the economic pressures and unintended harms which voluntary codes of conduct can create. The Argument's objection to voluntary self-regulation is premised on the belief that such regulation will negatively affect sweatshop employees. However, the criticism of Arnold's work which immediately follows does not, as it is based instead upon an internal tension in Arnold's account.
35. See section 5.c of this paper for a defense of this claim in the context of my discussion of the possibility of mutually beneficial exploitation.
36. At least not in the short term. An anonymous reviewer has suggested that MNEs might, by disengaging from immoral economies, spur positive change in the longer-term, in much the way that Western disengagement from South Africa helped bring to an end the system of apartheid. If this were true, it would constitute an important reason for MNEs to refrain from doing business with immoral sweatshops. But 1) it would not necessarily constitute an overriding reason, as one would have to balance the short term harms caused by disengagement with the long term benefits, and it is not obvious that the latter would always trump, and 2) this position would probably only be effective if undertaken by a broad coalition of MNEs, and hence the question remains concerning what individual firms should do now, in the absence of such a coalitional option. Thus while the challenge presented is an important one, it does not detract from the interest of The Argument as presented, and is hence not one that I will further consider in this paper.
37. Sometimes the advocates of voluntary reform write as though this could be assumed. Bowie and Arnold, for instance, write that "our contention is that it is economically feasible for MNEs to voluntarily raise wages in factories in developing economies without causing increases in unemployment. MNEs may choose to raise wages while maintaining existing employment levels. Increased labor costs that are not offset by greater productivity may be passed on to consumers, or, if necessary, absorbed through internal cost cutting measures such as reductions in executive compensation" (D. G. Arnold & Bowie, 2003, p. 239). For a thorough economic critique of this assumption, see (Powell, 2006), especially section iii. As a point of mere logic, however, the fact that some MNEs have managed to raise benefits without (visibly) reducing employment is hardly a good indicator that employment will not be reduced if all MNEs are placed under a moral obligation to raise benefits.

Reference

Note: References removed from publication here, but are available on the book website at www.mhhe.com/busethics2e

Reading 6-4

Attacking the Roots: *Shiraishi Garments Company and an Evolving Thicket of Business Ethics in China*

B. Jiang and P. J. Murphy

1. Introduction

Takashi Shiraishi stared out his office window, watching reflections of a hazy afternoon sun shining on Tokyo Bay. The date was February 9, 2005. Since early the year prior, Shiraishi Garments Co. (SGC) had begun outsourcing its whole production capacity to China in order to dramatically increase its profit margins. As SGC's President, Takashi saw the immediate benefit of such outsourcing to his bottom line. But operations were vastly different in China. Some ethical issues had emerged related to the health and safety of Chinese workers. Some disturbing accidents had occurred in the manufacturing facilities. These events had long concerned Takashi for reasons that were personal. But now the reasons were also becoming business-related. As a consumer products company dealing in clothing and apparel, SGC needed to maintain its positive reputation: business success depended on its brand. Takashi was increasingly certain he was going to have to make a tough strategic management decision to resolve the tradeoff between ethical business operations and being a highly profitable multinational company.

Japanese firms had wrestled with public trust for several years, especially since the Snow Brand milk poisoning episode in 2000. That was when over 13,000 consumers became seriously ill. Cheap labor, albeit domestic, was reported as the reason. Yet, Japanese companies were still moving operations into other countries for more cheap labor, which was also increasing the level of domestic Japanese unemployment. Some of these companies were taking steps to demonstrate concern for international employees with a strong commitment to corporate citizenship. SGC also worked hard to improve labor conditions in its Chinese supply chain. For instance, when local suppliers were reluctant to make the financial investments for first aid training in factories, SGC paid for the initial sessions. Soon thereafter, the Chinese partners saw less time lost due to injuries and began to embrace first aid training. Later, two major suppliers also began to use the same first aid training and noted the same benefits. Although the direct costs were absorbed by SGC's bottom line, Takashi undertook additional similar initiatives, such as the production of a first aid handbook and posters with information about hazardous substances. But it never seemed to be enough. The entire issue was like an evolving thicket of conflicting forces. Takashi realized he was going have to do more than just trim the branches.

2. Finding the Roots

As Takashi gazed at the setting sun, he pondered some more ideas to boost healthier workplace practices. For example, reducing the long working hours and increasing worker compensation throughout its Chinese operations. But such an initiative would seriously affect SGC's bottom line. Quite simply, outputs would reduce drastically because less hours were worked per employee. Although focusing on health and safety might help SGC's reputation, lower revenues did not make business sense, especially in the short term. But accepting the status quo was not necessarily less risky either: SGC's supply chain was showing cracks due to Chinese labor force dynamics. For example, he considered the Chinese workers churning out lady's brassieres for Ginza, the famous shopping district in Tokyo. Those employees were growing miserable while working in factories where security guards kept them behind locked gates and taking a bathroom break for longer than a minute was fineable offense. Employee turnover rates in two of these particular suppliers exceeded 100%. It was becoming impossible to recruit enough employees to maintain production. As a result, SGC orders were increasingly not being filled on time. Takashi found it unbelievable that production demands were so great that a labor shortage was emerging in the world's most populous nation.

Another option, suggested by SGC's Board of Directors, was to withdraw operations from China. SGC could enter other Southeast Asian countries such as Vietnam and Laos, where more cheap labor was available and there was not a growing emphasis on labor conditions. Takashi rejected that option. He was a staunch proponent of the Japanese ideal of Kyosei, which had been embraced by international bodies such as the Caux Roundtable.[1] Just as the Kyosei ideal emphasizes economic and social development, Takashi believed economic survival was not the true goal of SGC. Rather, he wanted SGC to play a role in improving the lives of its customers, shareholders, and employees. In the case of China, therefore, he wanted SGC to contribute to the human rights, welfare, and education of Chinese people.

It was now past dusk. The running lights of cargo ships headed out to sea through the Uraga Channel were visible, and the Tokyo Aqua-line bridge was illuminated. Takashi resolved to make the right strategic decision for SGC before the month of March, in just 19 days. But he did not know where to start. He did not want to lose the competitive advantage of outsourcing to China, and he refused to exploit the labor force. He wanted SGC to maintain the reputation of a company that cared about its employees. This puzzle of how to keep making money in China while emphasizing more ethical business operations was driving him mad. Takashi knew he was not going to solve this puzzle by looking out the window. He vowed to act as quickly as possible. He strode to his desk and picked up the telephone.

3. SGC's Background

Japan has one of the biggest and most sophisticated apparel industries. When it comes to fashion, the Japanese taste in clothing is among the most particular in the world. For centuries, the most cherished possessions of Japanese women have not been silver, gold or any kinds of precious stones. Instead, it has always been the lush rich colors and the perfect fit of their kimonos. Much more than other cultures, clothing signifies worldviews, personal tastes, and sensibilities in Japan. Although many contemporary Japanese live in plain apartments, most have a strong willingness to spend considerable sums of money on fashionable, stylish clothing. This aspect of the market environment underlies SGC's niche. Takashi Shiraishi established SGC in 1978 after watching a news report on television. The oil crisis was hitting the economny hard that year, leading the Japanese government to announce and publicize the "energy suit". The energy suit was a short-sleeved safari outfit designed to allow companies to save expenses on air conditioning. The idea was a total failure however, because although a few ministers wore energy suits for a week or two, nobody would dare to wear one to the office. Takashi's recognized his entrepreneurial opportunity when the news reporter said,

> The businessman puts on the darkest suit he owns, a white shirt, sober tie, and that is what he wears in Japan, no matter what the temperature is outside. The Japanese find this rigidity comforting, as it eliminates the nerve-racking necessity of making choices.

A recent art school graduate, Takashi believed such conservative dressing habits created a real venture opportunity: introducing customization into the drab business attire market. He believed differences in taste, preference, and lifestyle mattered significantly to customers, even to those in the same age demographic. Thus, the purchasing patterns were diversified. He eventually opened a men's clothing shop in a Tokyo department store. Even though the small shop offered products in conservative colors such blue, gray, brown and black, there were other options besides drab suits and neckties. Based on skin color, hair style, and other characteristics, Takashi helped customers select colors, accessories, styles, and shapes for tie knots. He became a master at making customers feel special and important. Such personal attention made all the difference. Customers absolutely enjoyed that SGC took such interest in their appearance.

4. The Growth of SGC

As SGC grew, the clothing designs were transferred to sewing subcontractors in the Tokyo suburbs. SGC usually ordered smaller quantities with more designs whereas other retailers ordered larger quantities and fewer designs. Although it was easier to fill orders for other retailers, the subcontractors were more interested in SGC. As all the retailers wanted low prices and high quality from sewers, business relationships changed frequently because of price wars. Yet, the relation SGC had with its sewing subcontractors remained strong. SGC made detailed reports on defects and also gave advice about how to improve quality and production. SGC shared customer comments and fashion forecasts, too, so subcontractors and suppliers could keep pace with the market.

On average, within two weeks of an order customers would receive customized garments from SGC. The clothes arrived at the customer's home, and sometimes delivery personnel even showed customers how to wear the clothing correctly. Then they would visit the customer ten days later to see if everything was going well. Customers thus felt sense of obligation to SGC, which would always be there should the clothing require service or repair.

The customer-oriented strategy combined with supplier relationship management were successful and good for business. SGC's garments were only 15% higher than ready-made ones, but with SGC consumers were able to choose from more than 10,000 unique style permutations. The SGC brand quickly became synonymous with quality and prestige. During the 1980s, when the Japanese economy was booming, SGC was a medium-sized but prestigious brand. However, by 1991, its annual sales for eleven retail outlets had skyrocketed to exceed 22 billion yen.

5. SGC Tightens Its Belt

As the 1990s progressed, economic globalization and an aging population dramatically changed the Japanese apparel industry. Rather than purchasing completely designed garments, the new generation purchased items from several different shops, mixing them freely to match their flighty sensitivities. Young shoppers displayed a strong tendency to buy clothes at select shops near railway stations and fashion-specific commercial districts rather than conventional department stores, which were more sophisticated but also more traditional. There was also a new casual style trend for male consumers. Perhaps a general disillusionment with the "salary man" lifestyle made a more laid-back attitude seem attractive. Simultaneously, the Japanese economy entered its "ten lost years" once the real estate and stock market bubbles burst in 1990. Japanese

READING TABLE 6.1
Shiraishi Garments Company. Financial Highlights (Yen, in Millions)

March 31 Year-End	2000	2001	2002	2003	2004
Sales	236,225	232,819	221,781	215,822	189,313
Operating income	17,661	14,032	15,275	12,910	12,872
Net income	7,266	6,026	5,049	4,567	4,347

Source: SGC internal documents

consumers lowered spending on clothing by making fewer purchases and preferring lower-priced items. As such, from 1991 to 2004 the percentage of household clothing expenditures decreased every single year.

The Japanese male clothing market was becoming more fashion-oriented but commodity-driven. SGC's customized business attire did not meet this trend well. Since the late 1990s SGC had been struggling with shrinking sales and profit margins, as shown in Reading Table 6.1. At some point, Takashi recognized that he had to cut costs to survive. That point, in 2004, was when Takashi took steps to outsource SGC's sewing operations to Chinese companies.

6. Chinese Allures and Challenges

In 2004 the whole business world was already watching the Chinese economy. The reality of 1.3 billion potential consumers and low labor costs were attractive to American, European, and Japanese companies. Shelves around the world were stacked with low-cost goods churned out by China: the world's workshop and fourth largest economy. Its highest volume products were clothes, toys, and technology appliances (e.g., DVD players). The national minimum wage had increased by 30%. In the poor inland areas, where most migrant laborers come from, more young people could find jobs near their hometowns. As a result, when exporters near the coast had poor working conditions, migrant labors would be less likely to go there for work. Unbeknownst to foreign companies, labor conditions were emerging as an important factor in the national labor market. Once China joined the World Trade Organization (WTO) in 2001, its attractiveness as a manufacturing center increased further. The World Bank then estimated that China would account for half of world textile manufacturing by 2010.

Takashi had conducted his own research in the China as a production solution for his business. Reading Table 6.2 shows Takashi's 2004 data, which revealed that China was not the cheapest place to outsource. However, Takashi believed personally that the criteria for the best place to manufacture were not so straightforward. Right now, the place was China because of low labor costs as well as the tremendous foreign direct investments in its textile and apparel manufacturing industries. Indeed, those industries were growing fast, and the rising productivity of Chinese high-tech sewing facilities were outpacing anything else the world had ever seen. Takashi visited several "supply chain cities" and was utterly impressed that everything needed to manufacture garments existed in a single location. Many Chinese vendors were located within the supply chain cities. Factories were located near textile mills and other suppliers of various components. From a business perspective, then considering the factories, political climate, time, fabric availability, human resources, infrastructure and speed to the Japanese market, Takashi was sure China was preferable to other Asian countries. He wanted to play a role in the positive development of China. From a personal perspective, and based on the historical context of Japanese and Chinese culture in southeast Asia, he saw a particular opportunity with China. His personal interest

READING TABLE 6.2
Hourly Rates for Sewing Laborers in Asian Urban Regions

Country	Rate ($/hr)
Laos	0.04
China (mainland/inner)	0.12
Vietnam	0.12
Sri Lanka	0.14
Bangladesh	0.19
Pakistan	0.23
India	0.25
Indonesia	0.42
China (coastal)	0.48
Japan	10.5

Source: Cal Safety Compliance Corporation (CSCC)

in making contributions to innovation, trust, and world community called for him to embrace an ethical leadership role that might be especially appreciate by Chinese manufacturers.

7. Chinese Manufacturing Practices

Takashi noticed the salary rate in Chinese coastal areas was four times higher than in China western regions. Many labors thus had left rural poverty in the countryside for the new factories along the coast. As the 2004 Chinese New Year approached, Takashi was surprised to see that up to 120 million migrant laborers filled roads and railways to reunite with families in countryside. This large migration helped keep wages low. Migrant laborers were a cheap and compliant work force who had attracted much foreign direct investment and ensured the viability of millions of domestic businesses. However, Chinese prosperity had been achieved through their exploitation. In the Pearl River Delta, for example, one local vendor in SGC's new supply chain told Takashi, "There are many girls with good eyes and strong hands. If we run out of workers who will accept our current wages, we will go deeper into the hinterland and recruit new workers." In that vendor's factory workers were earning basic monthly wages of $37 and worked 16 hours per day, seven days per week. These realities troubled Takashi.

Low wages and poor labor conditions were the dark side of cheap labor costs. Domestic China policy had not yet addressed them effectively as of 2004. Takashi saw that state-owned enterprises, although not productive or profitable, treated workers fairly well. At the same time, private sector companies were exploiting migrant labor, mostly young females. At the very root of the problem was the failure of local government to address the issue. He recounted in his journal, "The local authority's priority is to attract foreign direct investment, and labor law enforcement is a selling point when trying to attract foreign inward investment. But the big problem is that local authorities are flexible in interpreting the law and have scarce resources."

Clothing companies had been a focus of non-governmental organization (NGO) campaigns criticizing low pay, overtime, safety problems and child labor in Chinese supply chains. NGO criticisms could lead to significant damages to a company's reputation. Thus, to operate in China, SGC had to face the problem of labor conditions. Other risks associated with poor labor conditions included quality problems, low productivity, and high employee turnover. Takashi summarized two principal risks associated with operating in China. Reputation, as poor labor conditions created negative publicity damaged the brand value. Also, operational risks were important and stemmed from poor productivity and high employee turnover (due to poor labor conditions).

Foreign companies with factories in China were less exposed to those risks than companies outsourcing production. Control was limited when outsourcing. Companies actual factories in China had implemented occupational health and safety programs. They paid basic wages above the legal minimum. Their social security payments and working hours complied with regulations. Some provided extra benefits, such as housing subsidies and holidays. These factories required a minimum volume of business and had to reinvest continually to update their technology. The overhead costs of an outsourced vendor, on the other hand, were spread over a couple hundred clients. Takashi thought it would take years for a new factory to achieve the best practices, platforms, and intellectual property on par with a third party. So he decided to use Chinese suppliers instead of establishing an SGC factory in China.

8. Potential Suppliers in China

Supplier 1. Located on the outskirts of the city of Wenzhou in Zhejiang province, supplier 1 employed 1,500 laborers. Its number of overtime hours were problematic, as 78% of employees worked at least 132 hours of overtime per month. Most workers arrived at this factory unskilled. Because they were often paid piecemeal, and never for overtime, there was no incentive for the factory to cutback hours. Workers built skills on the job. The factory did not pay for training, carrying hidden costs of low productivity and quality and factory overhead. Although the factory incurred warnings and fines, supplier 1 did not provide any sort of bonus to employees at all. A rule book issued to workers instructed them on every aspect of factory life. The harsh penalty system included fines for any violation of the rules, including (a) arriving late, (b) talking during work, (c) leaving the workplace, or (d) spitting. Supervisors and middle managers spoke rudely and shouted at workers when production goals were not met.

Employees were despondent about the long hours and low pay. The fines and poor quality food exacerbated their unhappiness. Workers reported that there were few ways to communicate at all with managers. Most had no desire to do so. Relationships between workers and supervisors were strained. Employees frequently suspected supervisors of not accurately recording the number of pieces they produced and of extending working hours further than what management had scheduled.

It seemed health and safety management was good. Accidents were recorded by the medical center and minor injuries were dealt with in the first aid room in each production unit. Takashi still had concerns about ergonomic issues such as congested facility layouts, bad lighting, and poor ventilation. Problems also included inappropriate storage and handling of toxic chemicals, improper protection equipment for workers, and the lack of chemical safety training.

Supplier 1 had headaches managing its own suppliers. Low quality and late delivery of raw materials delayed production and squeezed the window of time for jobs and orders. They undertook used purchasing from multiple-source, buying from a list of potential suppliers to avoid getting locked into a sole source.

Supplier 2. A small factory in the city of Dongguan in Guangdong province, employing around 400 workers, sewed garments for SGC and a few other foreign retailers. The managers described relations with foreign purchasers as uncomfortable in terms of tight lead times, late sample approval, and last minute changes to product specifications. All these problems put increased pressure on supplier 2 to deliver orders, which were sometimes not filled. It also led poor communication between merchandisers, factory management, and production.

Insufficient communication about changes to product specification led to more reworking and, therefore, overtime. The reworking time averaged 7% during production and 10% after final inspection. On some production lines with particularly difficult styles, reworking could reach levels of more than 50%. As the piece rate compensation system did not cover reworking, a significant proportion of time was not only utterly unproductive, it was also unpaid. Very few workers knew there was a legal minimum wage. But all were aware they were not compensated for overtime and believed their wages were unfair. Two-way communication between workers and management was poor, so changes in pay or hours were not understood and on occasion resented by workers. There were few effective channels for workers to raise concerns with management, and managers usually did not respond to worker concerns or suggestions. Although the factory levied fines for 18 different kinds of offences, workers did not receive any training. Supplier 2 had other areas of concern. Takaishi saw there were inadequate escape routes and locked or blocked emergency exits. Systems for tracking and improving productivity and quality were poor or nonexistent. There was no formal production line quality control system and no records of reworking rates during the production process. The piecemeal workers were given daily productivity targets and supervisors made daily estimates of how many pieces each worker made. Those records were not kept for more than a few days.

Supplier 2 estimated that 70% of its fabric supplies necessary for production were delivered at least one week late. Worker annual turnover at supplier 2 was extremely high, 140%. Most workers left because of the overtime hours and management had no apparent concern for their well-being.

9. Auditing

Factory auditing by the government was not the best tool for tackling the problem of Chinese labor standards in supply chains but, at the time, it was the only way. Independent auditing is a critical factor that a company can use to maintain its reputation and achieve ethical behavior. But auditing alone, especially if superfical, is not enough to drive positive change. It was easy to audit financial conditions, but difficult to audit a supplier for social conditions related to labor, community, and the environment. Health and safety audits were also difficult. For instance, Takaishi noted one audit checklist item, which stated, "The supplier has a fire alarm." Further questions not considered were, "does it work?" "Do workers know what it is?" "Do workers have the right or the will to use it?" "Would they know what to do in an emergency?" "Can everyone in the factory hear it?"

A black-and-white audit approach could not solve these kinds problems. Even if short timeframes to prepare and improve to pass an audit were granted, the fundamental problem was still poor labor conditions. Post-audit follow-up from the auditors was poor and resulted in few improvements actually being implemented.

Audits even could drive dishonesty, lack of openness, and fraud. Suppliers felt forced to provide the "right" answer or face penalties. Chinese factory managers were becoming skillful faking records and coaching workers to give acceptable responses during interviews. This trend towards concealment was a barrier to improving labor conditions because it wasted time and money without making any change in the workplace.

Whereas workers did not want to work the excessive hours demanded of them, they were willing to work more than the low limits set by Chinese law to increase their pay. They knew that if a factory reduced hours to legal limits as a result of an audit, without some commensurate effort to increase productivity, wages would decrease dramatically.

10. Attacking the Roots

The sun was low and darkness was now descending over the Tokyo Bay's man-made islands. Takashi walked back to the window. His mind was clearer now. He believed that the current approach, dependent on compliance-focused audits, had made little progress in tackling poor labor conditions in SGC's Chinese operations. The days of sweatshop labor might be numbered because the business environment was changing in China. Workers had mobile telephones and word of worker mistreatment spread fast. International purchasers could no longer rely on profits earned by exploiting Chinese workers.

Takashi thought he needed to focus more on continuous improvement and capacity building activity. But a new approach to finding a sustainable solution was needed. If such an approach was impossible, he was prepared to seriously consider getting out of China.

End Note

1. The Caux Round Table Principles were developed in 1994 by business leaders interested in ethical and responsible corporate behavior as a foundation for business worldwide. See www.cauxroundtable.org

Chapter 7

Ethical Decision Making: Technology and Privacy in the Workplace

We must adjust to changing times and still hold to unchanging principles.

Former U.S. President Jimmy Carter

You say you want a revolution? Well, you know, we all want to change the world.

John Lennon and Paul McCartney

Things do not change; we change.

Henry David Thoreau

The CIO "has got this massively more complex job with fewer dollars, less disposable resources to meet that challenge and deliver on expectations to the business. . . . Technology has become the core fabric of how a company operates."

Tom Hogan, Senior Vice President of Software, Hewlett-Packard[1]

Opening Decision Point *"Reasonable" Use of Company Technology*

You have been working since 8:00 A.M. on a very tight deadline for a report due by the end of the day for your manager; and it is now 4:00 p.m. You need to make a doctor's appointment for this Saturday but forgot the telephone number. It will be quicker to look up the number online so you do a quick Google search for it. Of course, it is at that precise moment that your manager walks in and asks whether you might have that report ready yet. You look up and realize that she is frowning at your Google search on the Web. You mumble that it will be ready before the end of the day and she walks away. You close the window, frustrated at being "caught," when you know that your colleagues are constantly playing social games online with their friends during working hours or going on Facebook.

The next day, after you successfully and timely delivered the report, your manager tells you that she has searched through your firm's policies and procedures and notices that there are no rules regarding the use of technology in your work place. Therefore, she would like you to do some research to benchmark the status of these policies in the industry and then propose an appropriate and fair policy for your firm.

- What ethical issues might arise with regard to the development of both the policy and the procedures that you would suggest to enforce them?
- What are the key facts relevant to your decision regarding the practicality of these standards?
- What incentives would actively support or pose challenges to your response above?
- Who are the stakeholders in connection with technology use at your firm?
- What alternative or additional standards might you suggest? Which ethical theories most strongly support which alternatives?
- How would adherence to these standards (or their disregard) affect the stakeholders you have identified?
- Once approved, are there any considerations that you would suggest with regard to the communication of this new policy to the stakeholders?

Chapter Objectives

After reading this chapter, you should be able to:

1. Explain and distinguish the two definitions of privacy.
2. Describe the ethical sources of privacy as a fundamental value.
3. Identify the three legal sources of privacy protection.
4. Discuss the concept of a "reasonable expectation of privacy."
5. Discuss recent development in connection with employee monitoring.
6. Explain the risks involved in a failure to understand the implications of technology and its use.

7. Identify additional ethical challenges posed by technology use.
8. Articulate the manner in which employee monitoring works.
9. Enumerate the reasons why employers choose to monitor employees' work.
10. Discuss the ethics of monitoring as it applies to drug testing.
11. Discuss the ethics of monitoring as it applies to polygraphs, genetic testing, and other forms of surveillance.
12. Explain why monitoring might also pose some costs for the employer and for the employee.
13. Discuss the elements of a monitoring program that might balance the interests of the employee and the employer.
14. Explain the interests of an employer in regulating an employee's activities outside of work.
15. Discuss the implications of September 11, 2001, on privacy rights.

Introduction

In his best-selling book, *The World is Flat,* Thomas Friedman describes the hastening pace of globalization and how significantly the business, economic, and political landscape has changed in just the first decade of the twenty-first century. Friedman employs the image of a "flat world" to convey the idea that neither distance, time, geography, or national boundaries create artificial barriers to business and trade. In fact, nine of the ten forces that Friedman identifies as creating this flat world are the direct result of computer and Internet-related technologies. Even the tenth, the fall of the Berlin Wall and opening of Eastern Europe, is attributed in part to the information revolution that began in the years leading up to the fall of the wall. This is certainly not the first time we have faced the impact of technological changes on our personal privacy (see Reality Check, "Condemned to Repeat").

There can be no doubt that the business world today is global, or that a technological revolution is largely responsible for this fact. Not surprisingly, that technological revolution has brought with it as many challenges as opportunities. Many of these challenges raise ethical questions, particularly as this technology impacts employee and consumer privacy. As you may recall from Figure 1.1 in chapter 1, information threat, loss, or attack is one of the greatest concerns of executives worldwide.[2] In fact, in 2007–2008, between 24 and 31 percent of companies suffered information attack in most of their areas. This chapter will review some of the key ethical issues of technology and privacy, with a particular focus on privacy in the workplace.

Privacy issues in the workplace raise ethical issues involving individual rights as well as those involving utilitarian consequences. Workplace privacy issues evoke an inherent conflict (or some might call it a delicate balance) between what some may consider to be a fundamental right of the employer to protect its interests and the similarly grounded right of the employee to be free from wrongful intrusions into her or his personal affairs. This conflict can arise in the workplace

Reality Check *Condemned to Repeat*

In a 2008 article, Prof. Ariana Levinson cautions:

> 118 years ago Warren & Brandeis proclaimed that **technological change necessitated new protections for the right to privacy.** Today, new protections for the right to privacy are called for once again because, in the American workplace, technological change continues unabated and little privacy is afforded employees from employer monitoring using the technology.

Source: A.R. Levinson, "Industrial Justice: Privacy Protection for the Employed," *Cornell Journal of Law and Public Policy* 18, no. 3 (2009) (posted SSRN September 17, 2008), http://ssrn.com/abstract=1269512.

environment through the regulation of personal activities or personal choices, or through various forms of monitoring. Some forms of monitoring, such as drug testing, may occur after a job offer has been made but even before the individual begins working. Other forms might also occur once the individual begins to work, such as electronic surveillance of e-mail.

Similarly, contrasting utilitarian arguments can be offered on the ethics of monitoring employees. The employer can argue that the only way to manage the workplace effectively and efficiently is to maintain knowledge about and control over all that takes place within it. The employee can simultaneously contend that she or he will be most productive in a supportive environment based on trust, respect, and autonomy. In any case, the question of balance remains—whose rights should prevail or which consequences take precedent?

This chapter will examine technology and its impact on these issues. We will explore the origins of the right to privacy as well as the legal and ethical limitations on that right. We will also explore the means by which employers monitor performance and the ethical issues that arise in connection with these *potential* technological invasions to privacy. We will then connect these issues of technology and privacy to the balance of rights and responsibilities between employers and employees.

Because of the extraordinary breadth of the technology's reach, this chapter could not possibly address all issues under its umbrella. We have therefore sought to limit our coverage in this chapter to issues of technology and privacy *in the workplace* and related arenas. For instance, the intersection between ethics, intellectual property, the law, and technology open far too many doors for the survey anticipated by this text and will therefore not be examined within this overview. Similarly, though a phone company's decision whether to comply with the government's request to turn over phone records certainly raises issues of both technology and privacy, it is not necessarily related to issues of employment, so we will not be examining that decision. However, readers should be aware of these issues and seek to apply the lessons of this chapter to wider issues of privacy and technology in business.

The Right to Privacy

Privacy is a surprisingly vague and disputed value in contemporary society. With the tremendous increase in computer technology in recent decades, calls for greater protection of **privacy rights** have increased. Yet there is widespread confusion concerning the nature, extent, and value of privacy. Some Western countries, for example, do not acknowledge a legal right to privacy as recognized within the United States, while others such as New Zealand and Australia seem far more sophisticated in their centralized and consistent approaches to personal privacy issues. Even within the United States, there is significant disagreement about privacy. The U.S. Constitution, for example, makes no mention of a right to privacy and the major Supreme Court decisions that have relied on a fundamental right to privacy, *Griswold v. Connecticut* and *Roe v. Wade,* remain highly contentious and controversial.

Defining Privacy

1 OBJECTIVE

Two general and connected understandings of privacy can be found in the legal and philosophical literature on this topic: privacy as a *right to be "left alone"* within a personal zone of solitude, and privacy as the *right to control information* about oneself. It is valuable to consider the connection between these two senses of privacy. Certain decisions that we make about how we live our lives, as well as the control of personal information, play a crucial role in defining our own personal identity. Privacy is important because it serves to establish the boundary between individuals and thereby serves to define one's individuality. The right to control certain extremely personal decisions and information helps determine the kind of person we are and the person we become. To the degree that we value the inherent dignity of each individual and the right of each person to be treated with respect, we must recognize that certain personal decisions and information are rightfully the exclusive domain of the individual.

Many people believe that a right to be left alone is much too broad to be recognized as a moral right. It would be difficult for employees, for example, to claim that they should be totally left alone in the workplace. This has led some people to conclude that a better understanding focuses on privacy as involving the *control* of personal information. From this perspective, the clearest case of an invasion of privacy occurs when others come to know personal information about us, as when a stranger reads your e-mail or eavesdrops on a personal conversation. Yet, the claim that a *right* of privacy implies a right to control all personal information might also be too broad. Surely, there are many occasions when others, particularly within an employment context, can legitimately know or need to know even quite personal information about us.

Philosopher George Brenkert has argued that the informational sense of privacy involves a relationship between two parties, A and B, and personal information X about A. Privacy is violated only when B comes to know X, and no relationship exists between A and B that would justify B knowing X. Thus, whether my privacy is violated or not by a disclosure of personal information depends on my relationship with the person or persons who come to know that information. My relationship with my mortgage company, for example, would justify that company's having access to my credit rating, while my relationship with students would not justify their accessing that information. Limiting access of personal information to only those with whom one has a personal relationship is one important way to preserve one's own personal integrity and individuality. It is perhaps that *choice* of limitation or control that is the source of one's sense of privacy. As explained by legal scholar, Jennifer Moore, "maintaining a zone of privacy gives you a degree of control over your role, relationship, and identity, which you would not have if everyone were aware of all available information about you. The choice is part of what makes it possible to be intimate with your friend and to be professional with your employer."[3]

Ethical Sources of a Right to Privacy

2 OBJECTIVE

The right to privacy is founded in the individual's fundamental, universal right to autonomy, in our right to make decisions about our personal existence without restriction. This right is restricted by a social contract in our culture that prevents us from infringing on someone else's right to her or his personal autonomy. Philosopher Patricia Werhane describes this boundary as a **"reciprocal obligation"**; that is, for an individual to expect respect for her or his personal autonomy, that individual has a reciprocal obligation to respect the autonomy of others.[4]

Applied to the workplace, Werhane's concept of reciprocal obligation implies that, while an employee has an obligation to respect the goals and property of the employer, the employer has a reciprocal obligation to respect the rights of the employee as well, including the employee's right to privacy. In other work, Werhane has asserted that a bill of rights for the workplace would therefore include both the right of the employee to privacy and confidentiality, and the right of employers to privacy in terms of confidentiality of trade secrets and so on. This contention is supported throughout traditional philosophical literature. Kant links the moral worth of individuals to "the supreme value of their rational capacities for normative self-determination" and considers privacy a categorical moral imperative.[5]

Ethicists Thomas Donaldson and Thomas Dunfee have developed an approach to ethical analysis that seeks to differentiate between those values that are fundamental across culture and theory **hypernorms** and those values that are determined within **moral free space** and that are not hypernorms. Donaldson and Dunfee propose that we look to the convergence of religious, cultural, and philosophical beliefs around certain core principles as a clue to the identification of hypernorms. Donaldson and Dunfee include as examples of hypernorms freedom of speech, the right to personal freedom, the right to physical movement, and informed consent. Individual privacy is at the core of many of these basic minimal rights and is, in fact, a necessary prerequisite to many of them. Indeed, a key finding of one survey of privacy in 50 countries around the world found the following:

> Privacy is a fundamental human right recognized in all major international treaties and agreements on human rights. Nearly every country in the world recognizes privacy as a fundamental human right in their constitution, either explicitly or implicitly. Most recently drafted constitutions include specific rights to access and control one's personal information.[6]

Accordingly, the value of privacy to civilized society is as great as the value of the various hypernorms to civilized existence. Ultimately, the failure to protect privacy may lead to an inability to protect personal freedom and autonomy. It is important to note here, in particular, that this discussion of privacy foundations might be considered by some to be particularly North American-based in its grounding in the protection of liberty and autonomy. These analysts would suggest that a European foundation would be based in a ground of the protection of human dignity.[7] Notwithstanding this claimed distinction in origin (a discussion which is outside of our scope, though not of our interest), there remains little argument of the vital nature of privacy as means by which to ensure other critical and fundamental hypernorms.

Finally, legal analysis of privacy using **property rights perspective** yields additional insight. "Property" is an individual's life and all non-procreative derivatives of her or his life. Derivatives may include thoughts and ideas, as well as personal information. The concept of property *rights* involves a determination of who maintains control over tangibles and intangibles, including, therefore, personal information. Property rights relating to personal information thus define actions that individuals can take in relation to other individuals regarding their personal information. If one individual has a *right* to her or his personal information, someone else has a commensurate duty to observe that right.

Why do we assume that an individual has the unfettered and exclusive right to her or his personal information? Private property rights depend upon the existence and enforcement of a set of rules that define who has a right to undertake which activities on their own initiative and how the returns from those activities will be allocated. In other words, whether an individual has the exclusive right to her or his personal information depends upon the existence and enforcement of a set of rules giving the individual that right. Do these rules exist in our society, legal or otherwise? In fact, as we will discuss below, the legal rules remain vague. Many legal theorists contend that additional or clearer rules regarding property rights in personal information would lead to an improved and more predictable market for this information, thus ending the arbitrary and unfair intrusions that may exist today as a result of market failures.

Legal Sources of a Right to Privacy

Each employee is a human with private thoughts, private communications, and a private life. These remain as dear to the employee the moment after the employee steps into the workplace or switches on an assigned computer as the moment before. Yet, if the employee needs the job, perhaps to pay the rent, feed her children, maintain a living geographically near to her elderly parents, or even to maintain her status in the community, or her sense of self, then the American employee must, to a large extent, give up her privacy.[8]

As with others areas of lightning-quick advances, the law has not yet caught up with the technology involved in employee privacy. Many recent advances, thus much recent case law, and therefore much of our discussion in this chapter, will focus on employee monitoring, which we will cover in detail shortly. As a result, this is one area where simply obeying the law may fall far short of responsible management practice. While the law might be clear with regard to tapping a worker's telephone, it is less clear in connection with monitoring a worker's e-mail or text messages on a handheld device.

3 OBJECTIVE

Privacy can be legally protected in three ways: by the *constitution* (federal or state), by federal and/or state *statutes,* and by the *common law.* Common law refers to the body of law comprised of the decisions handed down by courts, rather than specified in any particular statutes or regulations.

The Constitution's **Fourth Amendment protection** against an unreasonable search and seizure governs only the public sector workplace because the Constitution applies only to state action. Therefore, unless the employer is the government or other representative of the state, the Constitution generally will not apply.

Statutes also offer little, if any, protection from workplace intrusions. The **Electronic Communications Privacy Act of 1986** (ECPA) prohibits the "interception" or unauthorized access of stored communications. However, courts have ruled that "interception" applies only to messages in transit and not to messages that have actually reached company computers. Therefore, the impact of the EPCA is to punish electronic monitoring only by third parties and not by employers. Moreover, the ECPA allows interception where consent has been granted. Therefore, a firm that secures employee consent to monitoring at the time of hire is immune from ECPA liability. The Reality Check, "Privacy and Technology," provides examples of how these issues might arise in the technology environment.

Some states rely on statutory protections rather than common law. Other states provide state constitutional recognition and protection of privacy rights, including Alabama, Arizona, Florida, Hawaii, Illinois, Louisiana, Montana, South Carolina, and Washington. However, in all states except California, application of this provision to *private* sector organizations is limited, uncertain, or not included at all.

The "invasion of privacy" claim with which most people are familiar is one that developed through case law called **intrusion into seclusion.** This legal violation occurs when someone intentionally intrudes on the private affairs of another when the intrusion would be "highly offensive to a reasonable person." As we begin to live more closely with technology, and the intrusions it allows, we begin to accept more and more intrusions in our lives as reasonable; as privacy invasions become more common, they begin to be closer to what is normal and expected. It may no longer be reasonable to be offended by intrusions into one's

Reality Check *Privacy and Technology*

In an Arizona case, a husband and wife who worked as nurses were fired from a hospital after hospital officials learned that they ran a pornographic Web site when not at work. The couple explained that they engaged in this endeavor in order to save more money for their children's college education. "We thought we could just do this and it really shouldn't be a big deal," said the husband.[9] Though their dismissal attracted the attention of the American Civil Liberties Union for what it considered was at-will gone awry, the nurses had no recourse. In another case, a police officer was docked three days pay when his wife posted nude pictures of herself on the Internet as a surprise to her husband. The pay suspension was justified by the department in that case since police officers could arguably be held to a higher standard of conduct than average citizens.

private life that used to be considered unacceptable. It is important to be aware that, while Georgia was the first jurisdiction whose courts recognized a common law—or court-created—right to privacy, two states, North Dakota and Wyoming, do not recognize any privacy claims generally accepted by the courts.[10]

While no case of employer monitoring has yet reached the U.S. Supreme Court, employer actions have received lower court attention. As early as 1990, Epson America survived a lawsuit filed by a terminated employee who had complained about Epson's practice of reading all employee e-mail.[11] In that case, the court distinguished the practice of *intercepting* an e-mail transmission from storing and reading e-mail transmissions once they had been sent. However, relying on court precedent for protection is a double-edged sword. An employee-plaintiff in one federal action won a case against his employer where the employer had monitored the worker's telephone for a period of 24 hours in order to determine whether the worker was planning a robbery. The court held that the company had gone too far and had insufficient evidence to support its claims.[12] In another action, Northern Telecom settled a claim brought by employees who were allegedly secretly monitored over a 13-year period. In this case, Telecom agreed to pay $50,000 to individual plaintiffs and $125,000 for attorneys' fees.[13]

4 OBJECTIVE

Most recent court decisions with regard to monitoring specifically seem to depend on whether the worker had *notice* that the monitoring might occur. Since the basis for finding an invasion of privacy is often the employee's legitimate and reasonable expectation of privacy, if an employee has actual notice, then there truly is no real expectation of privacy. This conclusion was supported in *K-Mart v. Trotti,* where the court held that search of an employee's company-owned locker was unlawful invasion since the employee used his own lock. However, in a later landmark case, *Smyth v. Pillsbury,* Smyth sued after his manager read his e-mail, even though Pillsbury had a policy saying that e-mails would not be read. The court concluded, "we do not find a **reasonable expectation of privacy** in the contents of e-mail communications voluntarily made by an employee to his supervisor over the company e-mail system, *notwithstanding any assurances that such communications would not be intercepted by management*" (emphasis added). The end result of *Smyth,* then, is to allow for monitoring even when a firm promises not to monitor. Evidence of the impact of this decision is the fact that only one state, Connecticut, requires employers to notify workers when they are being monitored.

Courts have often supported reasonable monitoring of employees in open areas as a method of preventing and addressing employee theft. For example, in *Sacramento County Deputy Sheriff's Ass'n v. County of Sacramento,*[14] a public employer placed a silent video camera in the ceiling overlooking the release office countertop in response to theft of inmate money. The California Court of Appeals determined that the county had engaged in reasonable monitoring because employee privacy expectations were diminished in the jail setting.[15] See Table 7.1 for an overview of how the courts have tended to treat the legality of monitoring from a general perspective.

Global Applications

This somewhat unpredictable regime of privacy protection is all the more problematic to maintain when one considers the implications of the **European Union's Directive on Personal Data Protection.**[16] The directive strives to harmonize all the various means of protecting **personal data** throughout the European Union, where each country originally maintained myriad standards for information gathering and protection. In addition, the directive also prohibits E.U. firms

TABLE 7.1
Legal Status of Employee Monitoring

Telephone calls	Monitoring is permitted in connection with quality control. Notice to the parties on the call is often required by state law, though federal law allows employers to monitor work calls without notice. If the employer realizes that the call is personal, monitoring must cease immediately.
E-mail messages	Under most circumstances, employers may monitor employee e-mails. Even in situations where the employer claims that it will not, it's right to monitor has been upheld. However, where the employee's reasonable expectation of privacy is increased (such as a password-protected account), this may impact the court's decision.
Voice-mail system messages	Though not yet completely settled, the law here appears to be similar to the analysis of e-mail messages.
Internet use	Where the employer has provided the equipment and/or access to the Internet, the employer may track, block, or review Internet use.

Reality Check *New Job Discovered!*

Evidently, the ethical and legal challenges that the issues addressed in this chapter pose are perceived as tremendously complicated and also vital to employers worldwide. As of 2004, there were more than 2,000 "CPOs" (chief privacy officers) in businesses around the world, more than 10 times the estimate three years ago.

Source: Steve Ulfelder, "CPOs on the Rise?" *Computerworld,* March 15, 2004, http://www.computerworld.com/securitytopics/security/story/0,10801,91166,00.html, quoting Alan F. Westin, president of the nonprofit Privacy & American Business.

from transferring personal information to a non-E.U. country unless that country maintains "adequate protections" of its own; in other words, protections equivalent to those the directive guarantees in E.U. countries.[17] Because the United States would not qualify as having adequate protection, the U.S. Department of Commerce negotiated a **Safe Harbor exception** for firms that maintain a certain level of protection of information.[18] If a firm satisfies these requirements, the directive allows the information transfer. If not, both firms can be held liable. (See Table 7.2.)

Given the nature of the legal uncertainty or instability concerning these challenging areas of information gathering, perhaps the only source of an answer is ethics. Yet, "the development of our moral systems has not been able to keep pace with technological and medical developments, leaving us prey individually and societally to a host of dangers."[19] As a court put it in regard to the legitimacy of police use of infrared thermal detection devices aimed at an individual's home without a warrant or notification,

> As technology races with ever increasing speed, our subjective expectations of privacy may be unconsciously altered . . . our legal rights to privacy should reflect thoughtful and purposeful choices rather than simply mirror the current state of the commercial technology industry.[20]

TABLE 7.2 The Safe Harbor Exception

The *Safe Harbor exception* requires that the receiving firm provide the following:

- Clear and conspicuous notice about the personal information collected.
- Choice to opt out of information collection or dissemination.
- Transfer of information to other firms only if they also demonstrate that they maintain the same level of adequate protections.
- Reasonable measures to ensure reliability of the information and protection from disclosure or loss of the information.
- Limitation to information that is relevant to the purpose for which it was gathered; that is, the firm does not access any information that is unrelated to its purposes.
- Access by the subject of the information, who then has the ability to correct any misinformation.
- Mechanisms for ensuring compliance and consequences for noncompliance.

Decision Point *Inquiring Employers Want to Know*

The following information is sometimes requested on standard employment applications, though candidates might consider some of it to be private or personal. Which of the following items about an employee might an employer have a legitimate claim to know, and why?

- A job applicant's social security number
- An applicant's arrest record
- An employee's medical records
- An employee's marital status
- Whether a job applicant smokes
- An employee's political affiliation
- An employee's sexual orientation
- An employee's credit rating

- What facts are relevant to your decisions?
- What would the consequences be of refusing to answer any questions on an employment application?
- Are you basing your decision on particular rights of the employee or the employer?
- Are there people other than the employer and employee who might have a stake in what information is released to employers?

Perhaps the more personalized response of Northrup Grumman Corporation's former ethics officer, Frank Daly, sums it up better: "Can this characteristic of speed drive us and have a negative effect upon how we treat other people? You can't rush love or a soufflé."[21]

What are the implications of this definition or understanding of privacy for businesses and for business ethics analysis? (For one implication, please see the Reality Check, "New Job Discovered!") In general, one would argue that personal information should remain private unless a relationship exists between the business and the individual that legitimates collecting and using personal information about that individual. For example, to determine the range of employee privacy, we would have to specify the nature of the relationship between employer and employee. The nature of the employment relationship will help determine the appropriate boundary between employers and employees and therefore the information that ought to remain rightfully private within the workplace. (See the Decision Point, "Inquiring Employers Want to Know," to consider information reasonably related to the job.) If we adopt something like a contractual model of employment, where the conditions and terms of employment are subject to the mutual and informed consent of both parties, then employee consent would become one major condition on what information employers can collect.

We might summarize our above examination by saying that employee privacy is violated whenever (a) employers infringe upon personal decisions that are not relevant to the employment contract (whether the contract is implied or explicit); or (b) personal information that is not relevant to that contract is collected, stored, or used without the informed consent of the employee. Further, since consent plays a pivotal role in this understanding, the burden of proof rests with the employer to establish the relevancy of personal decisions and information at issue.

Linking the Value of Privacy to the Ethical Implications of Technology

The advent of new technology challenges privacy in ways that we could never before imagine. For example, consider the implications of new technology on employee and employer expectations regarding the use of time; the distinction between work use and personal use of technology; the protection of proprietary information, performance measurement, and privacy interests; or accessibility issues related to the digital divide. Technology allows for in-home offices, raising extraordinary opportunities and challenges, issues of safety, and privacy concerns (there are now almost 34 million U.S. telecommuters[22]). Because each of us is capable of much greater production through the use of technology, technology not only provides benefits but also allows employers to ask more of each employee.

The International Labour Office warns us of the implications of the technology economy:

> More and more, boundaries are dissolving between leisure and working time, the place of work and place of residence, learning and working . . . Wherever categories such as working time, working location, performance at work and jobs become blurred, the result is the deterioration of the foundations of our edifice of agreements, norms, rules, laws, organizational forms, structures and institutions, all of which have a stronger influence on our behavioral patterns and systems of values than we are aware.[23]

New technology, however, does not necessarily impact our value judgments but instead simply provides new ways to gather the information on which to base them. Sorting through these issues is challenging nevertheless. Consider the impact of the attacks of September 11, 2001, on an employer's decision to share personal employee information or customer information with law enforcement. Private firms may be more willing—or less willing—today to share private information than they would have been previously.

Firms often experience, and often find themselves ill prepared for the unanticipated challenges stemming from new technology. Consider the lesson one firm learned about how problems with e-mail use and abuse might extend beyond the end of the employment relationship. After Intel Corporation fired an employee, he began to use e-mail to express some complaints about the company. He repeatedly flooded his former employer's e-mail system with mass communications that the firm's security department was unable to block. Intel took the former employee to court and was successful in blocking any further e-mails on the basis of a legal theory called "trespass to chattels" (a "chattel" refers to an item of personal property as opposed to a piece of real property or real estate). Even after the former employee appealed, claiming that blocking his e-mails violated free speech principles, a California appellate court disagreed and held in favor of Intel.

Do we need "new ethics" for this "new economy"? Perhaps not, since the same values one held under previous circumstances should, if they are true and justified, permeate and relate to later circumstances.[24] However, the perspective one brings to each experience is impacted by the understanding and use of new technology and other advances. As economist Antonio Argandona cautions, there has been a change in values "that may be caused by the opportunities created by the technology."[25] On the other hand, he points to the possibility that new technology may also do much good, including development of depressed regions, increased citizenship participation, defense of human rights, and other potential gains.

Information and Privacy

A business needs to be able to anticipate the perceptions of its stakeholders in order to be able to make the most effective decisions for its long-term sustainability. New technological advancements are often difficult for the public to understand and therefore ripe for challenge. How do you best manage the entrepreneurial passion for forward momentum with stakeholder comfort and security?

The motto at Google, the Internet-based search engine, is the deontological imperative: "don't be evil." Its founders describe that imperative by striving to "define precisely what it means to be a force for good—always do the right, ethical thing. Ultimately, 'don't do evil' seems the easiest way to summarize it."[26] For instance, Google does not allow gun ads, which admittedly upset the gun lobby, so one might expect that Google would be especially sensitive to stakeholder concerns as it develops new technology. Google believed it was providing a value to society when it created an e-mail system called "Gmail." Yet, critics charge that Gmail violates Google's own principles. This free e-mail system provides 7.5 gigabytes of free e-mail storage to anyone in the world—200 times more storage than other free e-mail services. However, there was one catch: Google scans user e-mail in order to target advertisements based on the contents. The company explained, "When people first read about this feature, it sounded alarming, but it isn't. The ads correlate to the message you're reading at the time. We're not keeping your e-mail and mining it or anything like that. . . You should trust whoever is handling your e-mail"[27]

That trust is truly the crux of the issue with the introduction of new technology, isn't it? When consumers rely on technology provided by a business—from e-mail to Internet access and from cell phones to medical labs—they might easily assume that the business will respect their privacy. Most average e-mail users do not understand the technology behind the process. One would like to believe that those responsible for the technology are, themselves, accountable to the user. That would be the ideal.

However, the Electronic Privacy Information Center, a consumer advocacy group, considered Google's marketing plan to be equivalent to a telephone operator who listens in on conversations and then pitches advertisements where relevant. Scanning e-mail violates the two fundamental elements of privacy: the right to be left alone and the right to control information about oneself. Moreover, since the scanning and targeting of advertisements takes place without the user's original knowledge or consent, it violates the ethical foundations of autonomy in the user's right to make decisions about her or his "personal existence." Finally, if one's personal information is respected as property, Google uses individual property without consent.

Google responded that it was not doing anything more than other e-mail services (which also include advertisements) except that its advertising was more relevant to the user's interests. In fact, Google's research showed that people actually followed many of those advertisements and ultimately made purchases. "It's an example of the way we try to do good. It's a high quality product. I like using it. Even if it seems spooky at first, it's useful and it's a good way to support a valuable service," says Google founder Larry Page.[28]

To the contrary, however, by failing to fully comprehend and plan for its stakeholders' perceptions of the program, Google not only breached ethical boundaries but also suffered public backlash. It did not anticipate concerns over privacy or the controversy the program would engender. Critics argued that Google should have consulted with stakeholders, determined the best way to balance their interests, and then considered these interests as they introduced the new program, all of which might have precluded the negative impact on its reputation. The lesson learned is that, notwithstanding even reasonable justification (which remains arguable in this case), people are simply not comfortable with an involuntary loss of control over these personal decisions. Google failed to consider the perspectives of its stakeholders, the impact of its decisions on those stakeholders, and the fundamental values its decision implied. Consider the discomfort evidenced in the Decision Point, "Technology Dilemmas."

Economist Antonio Argandona contends that, if new technology is dependent on and has as its substance information and data, significant moral requirements should be imposed on that information. He suggests the following as necessary elements:

- **Truthfulness and accuracy:** The person providing the information must ensure that it is truthful and accurate, at least to a reasonable degree.
- **Respect for privacy:** The person receiving or accumulating information must take into account the ethical limits of individuals' (and organizations') privacy. This would include issues relating to company secrets, espionage, and intelligence gathering.
- **Respect for property and safety rights:** Areas of potential vulnerability, including network security, sabotage, theft of information and impersonation, are enhanced and must therefore be protected.
- **Accountability:** Technology allows for greater anonymity and distance, requiring a concurrent increased exigency for personal responsibility and accountability.[29]

Questions about using technology for "good" or "evil," from an anonymous Web posting:

> **Management wants me to spy.**
>
> Management wants me to spy on a colleague. I'll be using [a spying program] that is 100% hidden, does screen captures, etc. Is there a document out there that I can have management sign to limit my liability? I want signatures from all management stating that they are authorizing me to spy. Thoughts? I have done this before, but this is the first time that they have asked me to compile data against a user for possible use in court. Thanks.

What are some of the questions or concerns you might bring up in an answer and what would you suggest this individual do to respond to them?

- What are the key facts relevant to your response?
- What is the ethical issue involved in peer spying in the workplace?
- Who are the stakeholders?
- What alternatives would you suggest to this individual, and what alternatives exist for employers who wish to gather information about employees surreptitiously?
- How do the alternatives compare; how do the alternatives affect the stakeholders?

Imagine how firms may respond to this call for responsibility in the development, manufacture, marketing, and service related to new production or other corporate activities. What ethical issues does Argandona's proposal raise, and how will stakeholders be impacted if firms respond positively to this call?

Let us take a look at another example in which consumers were surprised to learn about a business activity that some activists considered a violation of privacy. *Reason* magazine decided to include a customized cover on its June 2004 issue of a satellite picture of the recipient's neighborhood with the individual's home circled.[30] Of course, a magazine will have its recipients' home addresses, but the magazine chose to use the image to illustrate its cover article on the power and importance of databases, illustrating a "we know where you live" mentality. The article focused on the balance between the possible invasions of privacy information that database management affords and the realistic benefits the technology could bring, such as instant credit, customized advertisements, and personalized mortgage offers. Nick Gillespie, *Reason's* editor-in-chief, asks, "what if you received a magazine that only had stories and ads that you were interested in and pertained to you? That would be a magazine everyone would want to read." Is he right? Perhaps. The ethical question is what we are willing to, or what we can be forced to, give up of our personal information, privacy, and autonomy in order to get it.

We have focused mainly on problems that affect the developed world; but let us not forget the less developed world. For millions of individuals and communities, access to computers, information technology, and communications is not something they can take for granted and this creates a literal digital divide. In her reading, "Bridging the Digital Gap in Emerging Economies" Geetanee Napal carefully reports on the ethical issues facing companies with respect to a duty to make telecommunications available on a global basis and to overcome the digital inequality that is belied by the term "global telephony." Perhaps we should be more dubious of a firm which claims to be global. More likely, firms using the term global intend to say "everywhere developed" rather than the implicit and unlimited "everywhere" that the term otherwise categorically claims.

Managing Employees through Monitoring

5 OBJECTIVE

One of the most prevalent forms of information gathering in the workplace, in particular, is monitoring employees' work, and technology has afforded employers enormous abilities to do so effectively at very low costs. If an employer has a rule about the use of technology, how can it ensure that employees are following that rule? For instance, according to a 2009 survey, more than half (54 percent) of firms in the United States have rules prohibiting workers from accessing social networking sites while at work, including Facebook, MySpace, and Twitter.[31] But, unless your supervisor is looking over your shoulder, it would be difficult to check on your access or personal use of technology without some advanced form of online monitoring.

The American Management Association has conducted surveys of mid- to large-sized U.S. firms over the past few years that show an increasing trend with regard to employee **e-mail monitoring.** While its 2003 survey reported that 52 percent of firms monitored e-mail communications, up from 47 percent in 2001, its 2005 survey reported that 55 percent engaged in monitoring (see Figure 7.1). The 2005 survey also found that 42 percent of these firms have a policy that covers its employees' instant message use.[32] An astonishing 41 percent of large companies (those with 20,000 or more workers) actually have people on staff to read the contents of outgoing e-mail.[33] Much of this monitoring is on an occasional basis rather than by regular routine.

The most prevalent subject of monitoring is **Internet use monitoring** (76 percent) followed by e-mail monitoring (55 percent) and videotaping (10 percent).[34] Of firms that monitor, 86 percent notify their workers that they do so. Notably, 14 percent of firms do not notify their workers of e-mail monitoring and 20 percent do not tell them that they are monitoring content of Web sites visited. In actual numbers, estimates regarding the number of workers subject to surveillance are difficult to measure. One estimate contends that the e-mail or Internet use of 14 million U.S. workers is under constant surveillance each day, increasing to 27 million workers around the globe.[35]

FIGURE 7.1
Monitoring Practices of Major U.S. Corporations

Source: Adapted by the authors from data from the American Management Association, 2005 electronic monitoring and surveillance survey (2005).

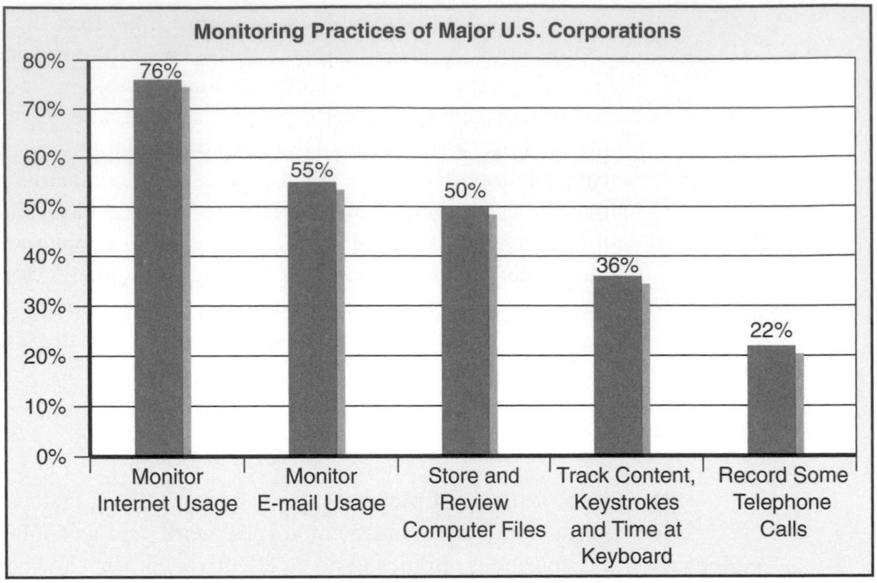

More than 80 percent of mid- to large-sized firms in the United States have Internet access policies. More than 60 percent of these companies have disciplined employees for violations of these policies (with 26 percent reporting that they have terminated an employee for a violation). The leading violations include access to pornography, online chat forums, gaming, investing, or shopping at work.[36]

6 OBJECTIVE

Unfortunately, many of the ethical issues that arise in the area of managing information are not readily visible. When we do not completely understand the technology, we might not understand the ethical implications of our decisions. When that occurs, we are not able to protect our own information effectively because we may not understand the impact on our autonomy, the control of our information, our reciprocal obligations, or even what might be best for our personal existence. For example, do you always consider all the people who might see the e-mails you send? Can your employer read your e-mail? Your first response might be "no, my boss doesn't have my secret password." However, experts tell us that any system is penetrable. Employers have been known to randomly read e-mails to ensure that the system is being used for business purposes. Is this ethical? Does it matter if there is a company policy that systems must only be used for business purposes, or that the employees are given notice that their e-mail will be read?

How do you know that your boss will not forward your disparaging remarks about a colleague directly to that colleague? It can be done with the touch of a key. Are different issues raised by that concern from those that arose with a traditional written letter? People could always send or show your letter to someone. When we mistakenly believe that no one is watching, we may engage in activities that we would otherwise refrain from doing. For instance, you may believe that hitting the "delete" key actually deletes an e-mail message. But it does not always delete that message from the server, so it might be retrieved by your supervisor or have a negative impact in a lawsuit.

These ethical issues may be compounded by the fact that a knowledge gap exists between people who *do* understand the technology and others who are unable to protect themselves precisely because they *do not* understand. You might not expect to be fired for sending out an e-mail—but if you thought about it a bit, you might have known what to expect.

7 OBJECTIVE

Technology allows for access to information that was never before possible. Under previous circumstances, one could usually tell if someone had steamed open a letter over a teapot. Today, you usually cannot discover if someone reads the e-mail you sent yesterday to your best friend. Access can take place unintentionally, as well. In doing a routine background check, a supervisor may unintentionally uncover information of an extremely personal nature that may bear absolutely no relevance to one's work performance. As you will see from the reading, "Medical Ethics for the Newest Practitioners: Health Web Sites—Power and Responsibility in Online Health" by Joshua Newman, the consequences that surround the entering, maintaining, and accessing of personal health data are complex and present potentially huge risks on ethical and legal grounds. Newman reports how such an arbitrary disclosure occurs: because the information, though previously unavailable or too burdensome to uncover, is now freely available and much more easily accessible from a variety of sources.

Moreover, because technology allows us to work from almost anywhere on this planet, we are seldom out of the boundaries of our workplace. For instance, just because you are going to your sister's wedding does not mean that your supervisor cannot reach you. This raises a tough question: *Should* your supervisor try to reach you just because she has the ability to do so? Our total accessibility creates new expectations, and therefore conflicts. How long is reasonable to wait before responding to an e-mail? If someone does not hear from you within 24 hours of sending an e-mail, is it unreasonable for them to resend it? Continuous accessibility blurs the lines between our personal and professional lives. (See Reality Check, "Is Privacy Perception a Factor of Age?")

Another challenge posed by the new technology accessible in the workplace is the facelessness that results from its use. If we have to face someone as we make our decisions, we are more likely to care about the impact of that decision on that person. Conversely, when we do not get to know someone because we do not have to see that person in order to do our business, we often do not take into account the impact of our decisions on him or her. It is merely a name at the other end of an e-mail correspondence, rather than another human being's name. When one puts something in writing, we assume that people mean what they say, and we hold them to it as a precise rendering of their intent. To the contrary, we consider e-mail more akin to conversation, and treat it as such, lobbing notes back and forth, much as we would in a conversation, and permitting the idiosyncrasies that we would allow when speaking. E-mail, in contrast, arose in the personal context as a form of spontaneous, casual, off-the-cuff communication. We do not think in advance and often write quickly without re-reading

Reality Check *Is Privacy Perception a Factor of Age?*

We discussed the definition of privacy at the beginning of this chapter. However, as we have continued through the chapter, you might have thought to yourself that some of the actions that others perceive to be invasive would not seem invasive at all to you. On the other hand, those actions that a court might hold to be reasonable behaviors by an employer might seem completely unreasonable to you, if you were the employee involved. Is the concept of privacy objective, universally defined, or instead is it based on a subjective perception?

Researchers Larry Ponemon and Philip Gordon conducted a national survey in the United States (admittedly, a limitation) that sought to articulate the way in which age affects one's perception of workplace privacy, specifically in connection with technology.[37] Consider the following *key findings* and whether you find your own perceptions aligned with those of your appropriate age group (younger-aged workers (YA) = an employed worker between 18 and 30 years, older-aged workers (OA) = an employed worker who is older than 50 years).

- **E-mail:** Only 38 percent of either group felt that employer monitoring of e-mail that is sent over a work system would be a privacy violation. When the question was changed to ask about online e-mail accounts (such as Gmail or Hotmail), the percentages did not increase significantly (52 percent of YAs and 42 percent of OAs felt that it would be a violation).
- **iPod:** Contrary to e-mail, YAs perceive that their iPods are "almost as an extension of their bodies." Accordingly, 85 percent responded that a ban on iPods in the workplace would constitute a privacy violation. It is interesting to note that this number is *higher* than the number of YAs who felt that unannounced random searches of their iPod would violate their privacy (77 percent). OAs did not feel the same connection to their electronic instruments, with only 68 percent responding that a ban would be a privacy violation and 57 percent finding a random search offensive.
- **Images:** Only 24 percent of YAs thought that it was inappropriate for their employer to use their photograph without their consent, but 41 percent of OAs had the same concern. Ponemon and Gordon believe that this may be due to YAs comfort with the ease of online image distribution.
- **GPS:** YAs were concerned about their employers using GPS location-tracking devices to monitor activities away from the employers' place of business (59 percent), but not to the same extent for OAs, 84 percent of whom expressed concern![38]

before sending. We send things in writing now that we might only have chatted about before.

Given the ease and informality of electronic communications, we also often "say" (write, e-mail, and the like) things to each other that we would never say to someone's face, precisely because we do not have to consider the impact of what we are saying. We are more careless with our communications because they are easier to conduct—just hit a button and they are sent.

To address some of the ethical issues computers present, the Computer Ethics Institute has created "The Ten Commandments of Computer Ethics," which include these imperatives: "Thou shalt not snoop around in other people's computer files; Thou shalt think about the social consequences of the program you are writing or the system you are designing; and Thou shalt always use a computer in

TABLE 7.3
Public Access to Personal Information

Tracing America (www.tracingamerica.com) provides the following personal information at the listed prices:

- Social security numbers, $25
- General all-around background search, $30
- Countywide search for misdemeanors and felonies, $30
- Whether subject has ever spent time in state prison, $25
- Whether subject has ever served time in a federal prison, $50
- National search for outstanding warrants for subject, $50
- Countywide search for any civil filings filed by or against subject, $50
- Subject's driving record for at least three previous years, $30

ways that insure consideration and respect for your fellow humans." Of course, such guidelines have no enforcement mechanism and are little more than suggestions. To see the types of additional information available through other Web services, see Table 7.3.

Why do firms monitor technology usage?

9 OBJECTIVE

A firm chooses to monitor its employees and collect the information discussed above for numerous reasons. Employers need to manage their workplaces to place workers in appropriate positions, to ensure compliance with affirmative action requirements, or to administer workplace benefits. Monitoring also allows the manager to ensure effective, productive performance by preventing the loss of productivity to inappropriate technology use. Research evidences a rise in personal use of technology, with 86 percent of employees admitting sending or receiving personal e-mails at work and 55.1 percent admitting to having received politically incorrect or offensive e-mails at work. Among employers, 62 percent of firms find employees accessing sex sites during the workday.[39] In fact, 10 percent of employees spend more than half the workday on e-mail or surfing nonbusiness sites.[40]

Beyond the management of its human resources, monitoring offers an employer a method by which to protect its others resources. Employers use monitoring to protect proprietary information and to guard against theft, to protect their investment in equipment and bandwidth, and to protect against legal liability (67 percent of firms have been ordered to produce employee e-mail by a court or regulatory body).[41]

In the American Management Association's 2005 survey, employer respondents reported that they engaged in monitoring as a result of their concerns for legal liability. Given the courts' focus in many cases on employer response to claims of sexual harassment or unethical behavior, among other complaints, firms believe they need a way to uncover these inappropriate activities. One-fourth of the largest firms reported firing employees for inappropriate e-mail.[42] (See the Reality Check, "Immoral Mail?" for a quantification regarding "inappropriate" e-mails.) Without monitoring, how would they know what occurs? Moreover, as courts maintain the standard in many cases of whether the employer "knew or should have known" of wrongdoing, the state-of-the-art definition of "should

Reality Check *Immoral Mail?*

A recent study found that 84 percent of those fired because of e-mail activity were accessing sites containing pornography or other inappropriate subject materials.[43] A different survey in the United Kingdom reports that 53 percent of the workers surveyed behave "immorally" in e-mail; 38 percent have used e-mail in the pursuit of political gain within their company, at the expense of others; and 30 percent admit to having sent racist, pornographic, sexist, or otherwise discriminatory e-mails while at work.

Oddly enough, in one case however, the CFO of Mesa Airlines *defended* himself with pornography where he was accused of deleting company information to an ongoing lawsuit from three computers. Instead, he claimed, he was simply trying to delete files of pornography he had downloaded and which he thought might embarrass him. Funny how our concepts of the "lesser evil" shift, depending on the nature of the harm done.

Sources: Institute for Global Ethics, "U.K. Survey Finds Many Workers Are Misusing E-mail," *Newsline* 5, no. 10 (March 11, 2002); Ethisphere, "Mesa Airlines CFO Scrambled to Erase Porn" (September 27, 2007), http://ethisphereblog.com/mesa-airlines-cfo-scrambled-to-erase-porn-not-valuable-evidence/#more-1273 (accessed September 28, 2007).

have known" becomes all the more vital. If most firms use monitoring technology to uncover this wrongdoing, the definition of "*should have* known" will begin to include an expectation of monitoring.

Monitoring Employees through Drug Testing

10 OBJECTIVE

Drug testing is one area in which employers have had a longer history of monitoring employees. The employer has a strong argument in favor of drug or other substance testing based on the law. Since the employer is often responsible for legal violations its employees committed in the course of their job, the employer's interest in retaining control over every aspect of the work environment increases. On the other hand, employees may argue that their drug usage is only relevant if it impacts their job performance. Until it does, the employer should have no basis for testing.

Consider the possibilities of incorrect presumptions in connection with drug testing. For instance, in *Drug Abuse in the Workplace: An Employer's Guide for Prevention,* Mark de Bernardo suggests that possessing crudely wrapped cigarettes, razor blades, or eye droppers; making frequent trips to the bathroom; or dressing inappropriately for the season may be warning signs of drug use.[44] On the other hand, it does not take a great deal of imagination to come up with other, more innocuous alternative possibilities. Yet, an employer may decide to test based on these "signs." Is it ethical to presume someone is guilty based on these signs? Does a person have a fundamental right to be presumed innocent? Or, perhaps, do the risks of that presumption outweigh the individual's rights in this situation and justify greater precautions?

In a study examining the attitudes of college students to drug testing programs, researchers found that "virtually all aspects of drug testing programs are strongly accepted by some individuals and strongly rejected by others." Not surprisingly, the only variable that the researchers found indicative of a student's attitude was whether the student had ever used drugs in the past. Where a student had never used drugs, she or he was more likely to find drug testing programs acceptable.[45] In general, the following factors contribute to greater acceptance and approval by workers: programs that use a task force made up of employees and their supervisors, a completely random program, effective communication of procedures, programs that offer treatment other than termination for first-time offenders, and programs with no distinction between supervisory and other workers.

In the seminal legal case on the issue, *Skinner v. Railway Labor Executives' Ass'n,*[46] the Court addressed the question of whether certain forms of drug and alcohol testing violate the Fourth Amendment. In *Skinner,* the defendant justified testing railway workers based on safety concerns "to prevent accidents and casualties in railroad operations that result from impairment of employees by alcohol or drugs." The court held that "[t]he Government's interest in regulating the conduct of railroad employees to ensure safety, like its supervision of probationers or regulated industries, or its operation of a government office, school, or prison, likewise presents 'special needs' beyond normal law enforcement that may justify departures from the usual warrant and probable cause requirements."

It was clear to the Court that the governmental interest in ensuring the safety of the traveling public and of the employees themselves "plainly justifies prohibiting covered employees from using alcohol or drugs on duty, or while subject to being called for duty." The issue then for the Court was whether, absent a warrant or individualized suspicion, the means by which the defendant monitored compliance with this prohibition justified the privacy intrusion. In reviewing the justification, the Court focused on the fact that permission to dispense with warrants is strongest where "the burden of obtaining a warrant is likely to frustrate the governmental purpose behind the search," and recognized that "alcohol and other drugs are eliminated from the bloodstream at a constant rate and blood and breath samples taken to measure whether these substances were in the bloodstream when a triggering event occurred must be obtained as soon as possible." In addition, the Court noted that the railway workers' expectations of privacy in this industry are diminished given its high scrutiny through regulation to ensure safety. The court therefore concluded that the railway's compelling interests outweighed privacy concerns since the proposed testing "is not an undue infringement on the justifiable expectations of privacy of covered employees."

Where public safety is at risk, there is arguably a compelling public interest claim from a utilitarian perspective that may be sufficiently persuasive to outweigh any one individual's right to privacy or right to control information about oneself. However, what about jobs in which public safety is not at risk? Is it justifiable to test all employees and job applicants? Is the proposed benefit to the employer sufficiently valuable in your perspective to outweigh the employee's fundamental interest in autonomy and privacy? Should a utilitarian viewpoint govern or should deontological principles take priority? Should we consider a distributive justice perspective and the fairest result—does distributive justice apply under these circumstances?

Several major retail employers, including Home Depot, Ikea, and Wal-Mart, have comprehensive drug-testing policies for both job applicants and employees. Many stores also promote their "drug-free" workplace policy as a marketing strategy. With just a few exceptions, such policies are legal throughout the United States. The question is, "Are they ethically appropriate?" The Decision Point, "Limits on Personal Information in Hiring," explores these issues.

Other Forms of Monitoring

Employers are limited in their collection of information through other various forms of testing, such as polygraphs or medical tests. Employers are constrained by a business necessity and relatedness standard or, in the case of polygraphs, by a requirement of reasonable suspicion. With regard to medical information specifically, employers' decisions are not only governed by the Americans with Disabilities Act but also restricted by the **Health Insurance Portability and Accountability Act (HIPAA).** HIPAA stipulates that employers cannot use "protected health information" in making employment decisions without prior consent. Protected health information includes all medical records or other individually identifiable health information.

11 OBJECTIVE

In recent years polygraph and drug testing, physical and electronic surveillance, third-party background checks, and psychological testing have all been used as means to gain information about employees. More recently, electronic monitoring and surveillance are increasingly being used in the workplace. Where might this practice develop in the future? One area that is sure to provide new questions about privacy is genetic testing. Genetic testing and screening, of both employees and consumers, is another new technology that will offer businesses a wealth of information about potential employees and customers. The Genetic Information Non-Discrimination Act of 2009 (GINA) became effective in November 2009 and prohibits discriminatory treatment in employment based on genetic information (disparate impact remains subject to the recommendation of an EEOC commission).

GINA presents interesting questions since it defines "genetic information" in a more broad sense than one might imagine. Under GINA, your genetic information is not merely information about you, but also your family's medical history, including any disease or disorder, or genetic test results of a family member. The term "family member" includes your dependents and relatives all the way to the fourth degree of kinship. In addition, GINA mandates that employers be extremely careful in terms of how they gather and manage employee genetic information as they are subject to similar conditions to the Americans with Disabilities Act.

GINA does provide for exceptions. For instance, an employer can collect genetic information in order to comply with the Family Medical Leave Act or to monitor the biological effects of toxic substances in the workplace. The employer may also gather publicly available genetic information, from public sources such as newspapers. Finally, though GINA contains a strict confidentiality provision,

Decision Point

Limits on Personal Information in Hiring

What limits should be placed on the reasons a job applicant can be denied employment? As we discussed earlier, the law prohibits denying someone a job on the basis of race, religion, ethnicity, gender, or disability. The law generally allows denial of a job on the basis of drug use. Like employment at will, the burden of proof lies with the job applicant to demonstrate that the denial was based on the prohibited categories; otherwise employers need no reason to deny someone a job. Suppose a business wanted to ensure not only a drug-free workplace, but also an alcohol-free workplace. Would a business have the ethical right to deny a job, or dismiss an employee, for drinking alcohol? Courts have been asked to decide the legitimacy of dismissals for cigarette smoking, for political beliefs, and for having an abortion. Which of these do you think is legitimate grounds for dismissal? More than 80 percent of mid- to large-sized firms use these tests or some form of psychological profiling to evaluate potential employees or during orientation.[47] Such tests ask many personal questions, including some that concern a person's sexual life. Would a business have an ethical right to deny employment to someone on the basis of the results of a personality test?

What are some of the questions or concerns you might have while trying to answer the above challenge? What would you suggest a business do to respond to them?

- What are the key facts relevant to your response?
- What are the ethical issues involved in basing hiring decisions on personal information?
- Who are the stakeholders?
- What alternatives would you suggest to business in considering personal information in hiring, and what alternatives exist for employers?
- How do the alternatives compare for business and for the stakeholders?

As a follow-up to the above dilemma, consider the strange culture shift that pre-employment personality tests have created. The *Wall Street Journal* reports that answer keys exist for these tests that they offer.[48] The questions include, "Other people's feelings are their own business?" (rate *strongly agree* to *strongly disagree*); or "You feel nervous when there are demands you cannot meet?" The key offers suggested responses for each question. However, "the producer of the test, called Unicru, says it believes the incidence of cheating is low, because there's no decline in the benefits it brings retailers: lower employee turnover, better safety and improved sales performance." Unicru claims that no key is available since anyone taking the test would need feedback in order to create one. There are purported keys, however, on Facebook and Wikipedia.

- What are the key facts relevant to this particular ethical issue?
- What are the ethical issues involved in basing hiring decisions on the Unicru test?
- Who are the stakeholders involved?
- What alternatives would you suggest to businesses that consider using the Unicru test?
- How do the alternatives compare for business and for the stakeholders?

an employer may release genetic information about an employee under certain specific circumstances:

1. To the employee or member upon request;
2. To an occupational or other health researcher;
3. In response to a court order;
4. To a government official investigating compliance with this Act if the information is relevant to the investigation;
5. In connection with the employee's compliance with the certification provisions of the Family and Medical Leave Act of 1993 or such requirements under state family and medical leave laws; or
6. To a public health agency.[49]

Business Reasons to Limit Monitoring

12 OBJECTIVE

Notwithstanding these persuasive justifications for monitoring in the workplace, employee advocates suggest limitations on monitoring for several reasons. First, there is a concern that monitoring may create a suspicious and hostile workplace. By reducing the level of worker autonomy and respect, as well as workers' right to control their environment, the employer has neglected to consider the key stakeholder critical to business success in many ways—the worker. Another concern demonstrates the problem. Monitoring may arguably constrain effective performance since it can cause increased stress and pressure, negatively impacting performance and having the potential to cause physical disorders such as carpal tunnel syndrome.[50] One study found monitored workers suffered more depression, extreme anxiety, severe fatigue or exhaustion, strain injuries, and neck problems than unmonitored workers. Stress might also result from a situation where workers do not have the opportunity to review and correct misinformation in the data collected. These elements will lead not only to an unhappy, disgruntled worker who perhaps will seek alternative employment but also to lower productivity and performance that will lead to higher costs and fewer returns to the employer. Finally, employees claim that monitoring is an inherent invasion of privacy that violates their fundamental human right to privacy.

Balancing Interests

Therefore, where should the line be drawn between employer and employee rights? Most of us would agree that installing video cameras in the washrooms of the workplace in order to prevent theft may be going a bit too far, but knowing where to draw the line before that might be more difficult. As long as technology exists to allow for privacy invasions, should the employer have the right to use it?

Consider whether monitoring could be made ethical or humane. One suggestion is to give due notice to employees that they will be monitored, plus the opportunity to avoid monitoring in certain situations. For instance, if an employer chooses to monitor random phone calls of its customer service representatives, it could notify the workers that certain calls may be monitored and these calls would be signified by a "beep" on the line during the monitoring. In addition, if workers make a personal call, they may use a non-monitored phone to avoid a wrongful invasion of privacy.

However, such an approach may not solve all the concerns about monitoring. Suppose you are the employer and you want to make sure your service representatives handle calls in a patient, tolerant, and affable manner. By telling the worker which calls you are monitoring, your employees may be sure to be on their best behavior during those calls. This effect of employer monitoring is termed the "Hawthorne Effect": Workers are found to be more productive based on the psychological stimulus of being singled out, which makes them feel more important. In other words, merely knowing one is being studied might make one a better worker. Random, anonymous monitoring may better resolve your concerns (but not those of the worker).

Perhaps the most effective means to achieve monitoring objectives while remaining sensitive to the concerns of employees is to strive towards a balance that respects individual dignity while also holding individuals accountable for their particular roles in the organization. Ann Svendsen, director of the Center for Innovation in Management, studied the link between high-trust stakeholder relationships and business value creation. Svendsen concludes that "trust, a cooperative spirit and shared understanding between a company and its stakeholders, creates greater coherence of action, better knowledge sharing, lower transaction costs, lower turnover rates and organizational stability. In the bigger picture, social capital appears to minimize shareholder risk, promote innovation, enhance reputation and deepen brand loyalty."[51]

13 OBJECTIVE

A monitoring program developed according to the mission of the organization (for example, with integrity), then implemented in a manner that remains accountable to the impacted employees, approaches that balance. Consider the following parameters for a monitoring policy that endeavors to accomplish the goals described above:

- No monitoring in private areas (e.g., restrooms).
- Monitoring limited to within the workplace.
- Employees should have access to information gathered through monitoring.
- No secret monitoring—advance notice required.
- Monitoring should only result in attaining some business interest.
- Employer may only collect job-related information.
- Agreement regarding disclosure of information gained through monitoring.
- Prohibition of discrimination by employers based on off-work activities.

The above parameters allow the employer to effectively and ethically supervise the work employees do, to protect against misuse of resources, and to have an appropriate mechanism by which to evaluate each worker's performance, thus respecting the legitimate business interest of the employer. They are also supported by global organizations such as the International Labour Organization (ILO) (see Table 7.4).

TABLE 7.4
ILO Principles for Protecting Workers' Personal Data

In 1997, the International Labour Organization published a Code of Practice on the Protection of Workers' Personal Data. Though not binding on employers, it serves to help codify ethical standards in connection with the collection and use of employee personal information. The code includes, among others, the following principles:

- 5.1 Personal data should be processed lawfully and fairly, and only for reasons directly relevant to the employment of the worker.
- 5.4 Personal data . . . should not be used to control the behavior of workers.
- 5.6 Personal data collected by electronic monitoring should not be the only factors in evaluating worker performance. . . .
- 5.8 Workers and their representatives should be kept informed of any data collection process, the rules that govern that process, and their rights. . . .
- 5.10 The processing of personal data should not have the effect of unlawfully discriminating in employment or occupation. . . .
- 5.13 Workers may not waive their privacy rights.
- 6.5 An employer should not collect personal data concerning a worker's: sex life; political, religious or other beliefs; or criminal convictions. In exceptional circumstances, an employer may collect personal data concerning those in named areas above, if the data are directly relevant to an employment decision and in conformity with national legislation.
- 6.6 Employers should not collect personal data concerning the worker's membership in a workers' organization or the worker's trade union activities, unless obliged or allowed to do so by law or a collective agreement.

Philosopher William Parent conceives the right to privacy more appropriately as a right to liberty and therefore seeks to determine the potential affront to liberty from the employer's actions. He suggests the following six questions to determine whether those actions are justifiable or have the potential for an invasion of privacy or liberty:

1. For what purpose is the undocumented personal knowledge sought?
2. Is this purpose a legitimate and important one?
3. Is the knowledge sought through invasion of privacy relevant to its justifying purpose?
4. Is invasion of privacy the only or the least offensive means of obtaining the knowledge?
5. What restrictions or procedural restraints have been placed on the privacy-invading techniques?
6. How will the personal knowledge be protected once it has been acquired?[52]

Both of these sets of guidelines may also respect the personal autonomy of the individual worker by providing for personal space within the working environment, by providing notice of where that "personal" space ends, and by allowing access to the information gathered, all designed toward achievement of a personal and professional development objective. The reading, "The Ethical Use of Technology in Business" by Tony Mordini walks us through the ethical decision-making process according to these balancing scenarios in order to demonstrate how they might be applied.

The following section, Regulation of Off-Work Acts, will provide some guidance regarding how far the employer is permitted to go in directing the activities of its workers while they are *not at work*.

Regulation of Off-Work Acts

14 OBJECTIVE

The regulation of an employee's activities when she or he is away from work is an interesting issue, particularly in at-will environments. However, as discussed throughout this chapter, even employers of at-will employees must comply with a variety of statutes in imposing requirements and managing employees. For instance, New York's lifestyle discrimination statute prohibits employment decisions or actions based on four categories of off-duty activity: legal recreational activities, consumption of legal products, political activities, and membership in a union.

Across the nation, there are other less broad protections for off-work acts. A number of states have enacted protections about the consumption or use of legal products off the job, such as cigarettes.[53] These statutes originated from the narrower protection for workers who smoked off-duty. Currently, abstention from smoking cannot be a condition of employment in at least 29 states and the District of Columbia (and those states provide anti-retaliation provisions for employers who violate the prohibition). In fact, instead of simply identifying the right to use lawful products outside of work, Rhode Island goes further by specifically prohibiting an employer from banning the use of tobacco products while not at work.

On the other hand, employers are not prohibited from making employment decisions on the basis of weight, as long as they are not in violation of the American with Disabilities Act (ADA) when they do so. The issue depends on whether the employee's weight is evidence of or results from a disability. If so, the employer must explore whether the worker is otherwise qualified for the position. Under the ADA, the individual is considered "otherwise qualified" if she or he can perform the essential functions of the position with or without reasonable accommodations. If the individual cannot perform the essential functions of the position, the employer is not subject to liability for reaching an adverse employment decision. However, employers should be cautious since the ADA also protects workers who are not disabled but who are *perceived* as being disabled, a category into which someone might fall based on his or her weight.

Laws that protect against discrimination based on marital status exist in just under half of the states. However, though workers might be protected based on marital *status,* they are not necessarily protected against adverse action based on *the identity of the person* they married. For instance, some companies might have an anti-nepotism policy under which an employer refuses to hire or terminates a worker on the basis of the spouse's working at the same firm, or a conflict-of-interest policy under which the employer refuses to hire or terminates a worker whose spouse works at a competing firm.

Since about 40 percent of workers have dated an office colleague, policies, and attitudes on workplace dating have an especially strong potential impact.[54] Though only about 18 percent of workplaces have policies addressing workplace dating and even fewer (9 percent) prohibit it,[55] a New York decision reaffirmed the employer's right to terminate a worker on the basis of romantic involvement. In *McCavitt v. Swiss Reinsurance America Corp.,*[56] the court held that an employee's dating relationship with a fellow officer of the corporation was not a "recreational activity," within the meaning of a New York statute that prohibited employment discrimination for engaging in such recreational activities. The employee argued that, even though his personal relationship with this fellow officer had no repercussions whatever for the professional responsibilities or accomplishments of either, and his employer, Swiss Re, had no written anti-fraternization or anti-nepotism policy, he was passed over for promotion and then discharged from employment largely because of his dating. The court, however, agreed with the employer that termination was permitted since dating was not a recreational activity, and therefore *not* protected from discrimination. While concerns about workplace dating used to surround issues of sexual harassment, they are more likely to involve apprehensions about claims of retaliation after a relationship is over. However, contrary to the court's holding in *McCavitt,* not everyone agrees that the most effective response to the discovery of an illicit relationship is termination of the individual in power. Consider the Decision Point, "To Date or Not to Date."

The majority of states protect against discrimination on the basis of political involvement, though states vary on the type and extent of protection. Finally, lifestyle discrimination may be unlawful if the imposition of the rule treats one protected group differently than another. For instance, if an employer imposes a rule restricting the use of peyote in Native American rituals that take place during off-work hours, the rule may be suspect and may subject the employer to liability. Similarly, the rule may be unlawful if it has a different impact on a protected group than on other groups.

Most statutes or common law decisions, however, provide for employer defenses for those rules that (a) are reasonably and rationally related to the employment activities of a particular employee, (b) constitute a "bona fide occupational requirement," meaning a rule that is reasonably related to that particular position, or (c) are necessary to avoid a conflict of interest or the appearance of conflict of interest.

The question of monitoring and managing employee online communications while the employee is *off work* is relevant to the issues of technology monitoring discussed earlier in this chapter; this question emerges as an astonishingly challenging area of conflict between employers and employees, and one without much legal guidance, demanding sensitive ethical decision making. For instance, consider the question of personal blogs. Though blogs might initially seem an innocent environment in which employees can vent comments during off-work hours regarding their employment situation, imagine the impact of a viral message when

Decision Point *To Date or Not to Date*

The choice to terminate someone for dating a colleague might be considered relatively progressive when compared to the days prior to modern laws in certain countries that manage interpersonal relationships in the workplace (e.g. prohibition of sexual harassment). Yet, one might still be surprised by the reaction of the two authors of a primer on workplace romance, Stephanie Losee and Helaine Olen, who questioned the Red Cross' termination of its former president, Mark Everson, after just six months in the position, after it was found that Mr. Everson had a personal relationship with a subordinate.[57]

Losee and Olen suggest instead something akin to a utilitarian analysis which weighs the man's errors ("People do stupid things at the behest of their hearts," they implore) and the cost of his departure to the Red Cross ("more turmoil at the top is the last thing this worthy charity needs") against the benefits he brought to the organization (he "won raves for the agency's handling of this fall's California wildfires").

Assume you are charged with drafting your organization's policy on workplace dating. In which direction will you tilt with regard to its management of this issue? Utilitarian, such as Losee and Olen, or more in line with the 12 percent of workplaces that simply prohibit workplace dating in order to have a clearer line of demarcation? If you opt for the former, what ethical issues do you anticipate and how do you plan to respond to them since planning ahead will help you to prepare most effectively and ethically? Who are your stakeholders and what options do you have in your responses to those stakeholders in order to best meet each of their interests and rights?

If you opt for a prohibition, how do you plan to enforce it? Are you willing to hire someone who is dating a current employee? Must they stop dating? What problems might arise as a result of your policy, in either direction?

placed on the Web and then allowed to have the exponential impact experienced by some blogs. Since it is estimated that blog readership is in the millions,[58] corporate reputations are at stake and legal consequences can be severe; 26 percent of firms in 2007 were affected by the exposure of sensitive or embarrassing information via the Internet or e-mail.[59] In one situation, a Google employee compared the firm's health plan to Microsoft's, and it did not fare too well. He also blogged about how the company's provision of free food was merely an incentive to work through the dinner hour. The employee was subsequently terminated.

According to ABC News (U.S.), 26 percent of employers access Facebook and other social networking sites during their pre-employment information gathering processes.[60] Since today's youth begin accessing and posting to these sites long before they might anticipate ever being in front of a potential employer, how far back in the past do we really wish to hold our prospective employees responsible? There is a potential here for a responsibility much deeper than that even imposed by the law. For some, this might seem quite reasonable while, for others, it is far beyond reason. Is it ethically justified? From an employee's perspective, they should probably beware. A 2009 poll by

Deloitte reported that 30 percent of firms use social networking as part of their business strategy; so it is clearly on their radar.[61] However, the same survey found that 27 percent of workers do not consider the ethical consequences of comments or videos posted online, and almost 40 percent do not even think about what their employer, prospective employer, clients, or co-workers might say about their online postings.[62]

In addition, while employers are legally prevented from asking candidates about their religion or prior illegal drug use during a job interview, is it ethical for them to seek out that information through online sources when the candidate voluntarily discloses it with no connection with work? For instance, in various individuals' profiles on Facebook, there is posted, "Nothing is more important to me than the values I have learned from being a Seventh Day Adventist." Another person explains that he kicked a drug habit, got out of rehab, and is getting on with his life.[63] The prospective employer could never access this information through the interview so is gathering it in this method any more appropriate? While the laws on this matter vary from country to country (there are far greater limitations on the collection of personal information in Australia, for instance, than in the United States[64]), what ethical values should dictate? Should a single, universal value govern an employer's judgment, or should the employer's behavior also vary from country to country, if it is a global operation?

The Reality Check, "The Employment Relationship Begins Pre-employment," provides an overview of the intersection of the discussions of the prior two sections in its evaluation of privacy, testing, and off-work acts. While our analysis to this point has addressed the regulation of behavior during employment, perhaps it is important to consider your choices before employment and the impact they will have on an employer's later decisions about hiring you. Alternatively, from the employer's perspective, it is important to understand when it is valuable to test prospective employees or why it might be effective to refrain from testing in the hiring process.

Privacy Rights since September 11, 2001

15 OBJECTIVE

The events of September 11, 2001, have had a major impact on privacy within the United States and on the employment environment in particular. The federal government has implemented widespread modifications to its patchwork structure of privacy protections since the terror attacks of September 11, 2001. In particular, proposals for the expansion of surveillance and information gathering authority were submitted and, to the chagrin of some civil rights attorneys and advocates, many were enacted.

The most public and publicized of these modifications was the adoption and implementation of the **Uniting and Strengthening America by Providing Appropriate Tools Required to Intercept and Obstruct Terrorism (USA PATRIOT) Act of 2001**. The USA PATRIOT Act expanded states' rights with regard to Internet surveillance technology, including workplace surveillance, and amended the Electronic Communications Privacy Act. The act also grants access to

Reality Check *The Employment Relationship Begins Pre-employment*

Tara J. Radin and Martin Calkins

Society has traditionally treated the employment relationship as beginning and ending with the start and end dates of the employment appointment. In fact, the relationship begins prior to hiring and ends, often, only with death.

PRE-EMPLOYMENT PRACTICES

The importance of the pre-employment relationship is commonly overlooked. In spite of this, pre-employees (i.e., job candidates) today have few if any legally recognized rights. This is becoming increasingly problematic because of widespread advances in technology and the virtual lack of respect afforded the personal privacy of job-seekers.

A number of companies have recently emerged and are taking advantage of new information-gathering technologies by offering these services to employers in the process of hiring new employees. These companies contract with organizations (and individuals) to gather personal information about potential new hires. They gather any information that is requested about job candidates—from credit histories to their driving records.

While collecting data on people prior to their employment is nothing new, the methods used today lack the transparency of the past and skew the balance of power even more toward the employer and away from the employee. Further, employers do not always ask permission or even inform job candidates that they are doing background checks and are often unwilling to reveal to applicants the specific information that has influenced their hiring decisions.

Firms support this sort of information gathering on the basis that it enables them to make better hiring decisions. Even so, the practice is not without serious drawbacks—even from the perspective of the hiring firms. For one reason, the accuracy of third-party information is not always assured. In addition, there are no guarantees that the data collected is complete. Background checks can result in inaccurate or downright erroneous candidate profiles. While employers assume they are finding out relevant information to enhance their hiring decisions, the reality is that the information they are obtaining might be distorted without their knowledge; instead of eliminating certain risky candidates, they might unknowingly be overlooking "diamonds in the rough."

From the perspective of job applicants, the practice of pre-employment information gathering is particularly insidious. Job candidates are not always given notice that they are being scrutinized and that the material being collected is highly personal. In addition, job candidates are generally not offered the opportunity to provide any sort of rebuttal to the reports generated by information-gathering agencies. This is especially problematic in situations where candidates are rejected on the basis of background checks.

IMPACT OF PRE-EMPLOYMENT PRACTICES

To see how this testing can have a negative impact on the hiring process; take the example of Maria, a fictitious job candidate. Maria applies for a job in marketing for a regional department store. She is asked to take a pre-screening drug test and, through this and the personal information she provides as part of a general background check, the potential employer gains access to Maria's credit report. This report reveals that she has a judgment pending against her. Fearing that Maria is an employment risk, the company decides not to hire her.

While the credit report's data might be accurate, it does not tell the complete story about Maria. It does not indicate, for example, that Maria was the victim of identity fraud. In addition, the report might be inaccurate without her knowledge. While Maria should be aware of the credit information in her report, she has not looked at it in some time and the collecting agency has included some incorrect information. The fact that Maria has an unpaid debt does not provide information inherently relevant to the particular job for which she has applied.

The employer considering Maria's application might rationalize that the background check is necessary to assess her general suitability. Many employers consider this a legitimate purpose and argue that there is a relationship between a candidate's responsibility in handling client affairs and her manner of dealing with personal finances.

(*continued*)

Although such an argument is not without merit, the result seems somewhat excessive. Consider, for example, the relevance of the driving record of a candidate for a bus driver position: it would seem almost counterintuitive not to inquire into that sort of information. There are meaningful differences, however, between this situation and that of Maria. Where work is of a particularly sensitive nature or where the level of the open position is high within a company, background checks directly related to performance might be appropriate when linked to a legitimate business purpose. In addition, the type of company or potential liability for the company could also warrant specific checks. In Maria's situation, none of these circumstances are present.

ARGUMENTS AGAINST EXCESSIVE PRE-EMPLOYMENT TESTING

There are many arguments against pre-employment testing, particularly when used indiscriminately. Excessive pre-employment testing can be attacked on moral grounds. First, it undermines the dignity of the individual by strengthening the notion of the person as a mere factor of production. It effectively enables employers to treat people as a means to achieving profitable ends without regard for the individual as a person valuable in and of him- or herself. In addition, it creates a climate of suspicion that undermines trust and loyalty and encourages duplicity and insincerity. Finally, it affects the character of the companies and individuals who work there. Companies become secretive and manipulative through such information gathering and candidates, in turn, do what they can to conceal information they consider potentially unfavorable to their acceptance or advancement. This sort of behavior is to the detriment of the character of both employers and potential employees.

In addition to these sorts of ethical considerations, there are strong business arguments against excessive use of pre-employment testing. Unfettered collection of personal information disregards property interests associated with that personal information. Hiring practices involving background checks ignore a person's ownership of information about him- or herself. It also erodes the privacy expectations a person has in his or her personal information. Moreover, it creates a bad first impression for potential employees and detracts from general morale. During bad economic times, this might not matter, but when times are good and employment rates are high, potential job candidates are likely to seek out opportunities with employers who do not utilize such intrusive methods. In addition, current employees—those who stay by necessity or choice—will see themselves in a relationship with an employer who does not trust them or respect individual privacy. In other words, the practice used in hiring spills over and effectively becomes the tenor of the overall employment relationship, and this can prove demoralizing to employees and result in an underlying tone of distrust.

RESPONSIBLE USE OF PERSONAL INFORMATION

The availability of abundant information to employers does not mean that they have to use all of it. Ideally, personal information should remain personal and, at the very least, the individual should have the ability to determine who gains access to his or her personal information and to know when someone obtains that information. It is important here to keep in mind that the availability of access is not the same as the moral right to access information or to use that information in a hiring decision.

As employers consider how to use the information they gather, they should consider "legitimate business purpose" as a guiding principle. Where there is a legitimate business purpose (defined generally to be applied to job function, type of company, and so on) and an identifiable direct correlation between that information and the job candidate, it would then seem appropriate for personal information to be solicited.

At the same time and as Maria's situation illustrates, it now becomes incumbent upon individuals to keep better track of their personal information. Now that individuals are aware that credit checks can be performed and used against them, they need to make sure that the credit bureaus have accurate information. In addition, individuals need to be prepared to respond to anomalies that might exist in their personal information. It is no longer an issue of what is right and what is wrong, but what is going to happen. If we know that employers have access to this information, it is for us to determine what we are going to do about it for ourselves.

sensitive data with only a court order rather than a judicial warrant and imposes or enhances civil and criminal penalties for knowingly or intentionally aiding terrorists. In addition, the new disclosure regime increased the sharing of personal information between government agencies in order to ensure the greatest level of protection.

Title II of the act provides for the following enhanced surveillance procedures that have a significant impact on individual privacy and may impact an employer's effort to maintain employee privacy:

- Expands authority to intercept wire, oral, and electronic communications relating to terrorism and to computer fraud and abuse offenses.
- Provides roving surveillance authority under the Foreign Intelligence Surveillance Act of 1978 (FISA) to track individuals. (FISA investigations are not subject to Fourth Amendment standards but are instead governed by the requirement that the search serve "a significant purpose.")
- Allows nationwide seizure of voice-mail messages pursuant to warrants (i.e., without the previously required wiretap order).
- Broadens the types of records that law enforcement may obtain, pursuant to a subpoena, from electronic communications service providers.
- Permits emergency disclosure of customer electronic communications by providers to protect life and limb.
- Provides nationwide service of search warrants for electronic evidence.

These provisions allow the government to monitor anyone on the Internet simply by contending that the information is "relevant" to an ongoing criminal investigation. In addition, the act includes provisions designed to combat money laundering activity or the funding of terrorist or criminal activity through corporate activity or otherwise. All financial institutions must now report suspicious activities in financial transactions and keep records of foreign national employees, while also complying with the anti-discrimination laws discussed throughout this text.

Though some of its surveillance and information sharing provisions were set to expire (or "sunset") in 2005, President George W. Bush reauthorized the act in March 2006, which made permanent or extended many of these authorities. In addition, the USA PATRIOT Act was not the only legislative response. By September 2002, the Office of Management and Budget had recorded 58 new regulations responding to terrorism[65] and both federal and state agencies have passed a number of new pieces of legislation. Not everyone is comfortable with these new protections. Out of concern for the USA PATRIOT Act's newly permitted investigatory provisions, some librarians now warn computer users in their libraries that their computer use could be monitored by law enforcement agencies. *The Washington Post* reports that some librarians are even ensuring privacy by destroying records of sites visited, books checked out, and logs of computer use.[66] The American Civil Liberties Union reports that a number of communities have passed resolutions against the USA PATRIOT Act.[67]

While the Patriot Act has implications for all citizens, it also has direct implications for business since it relies on employers for information gathering,

Opening Decision Point Revisited

"Reasonable" Use of Company Technology

The opening Decision Point asked you to consider what might be involved in the development of a technology use policy for an organization. In order to do so, we first must determine whether we need additional facts before we can reach a judgment. In addition, are we clear on all of the possible ethical issues involved? As mentioned in the chapter, as technology advances, we might not necessarily be prepared for the ethical dilemmas we could face. Would you have considered, for instance, whether an individual or firm is responsible for the end result of what someone ultimately does with technology? If an individual uses technology owned by a firm for an unethical purpose, even without the consent of the firm, might the firm not be accountable for the implications of that unethical conduct, at least under certain circumstances? You have to determine how far you are going to take the responsibility. An effective and valuable starting point from which to answer many of these questions will be your organization's mission statement or other statement of values, policies or procedures.

Have you considered all the stakeholders in connection with computer use? Of course, by now we are used to considering employees, consumers, clients, investors, and even competitors. But have you thought about governments and their interest in protecting or accessing data? What about a data owner? Are there others? Additional research is likely to uncover additional or alternative standards surrounding these issues as well.

What about the question of how you might enforce your policy? Research demonstrates that monitoring may be more acceptable to employees when they perceive that monitoring takes place within an environment of procedural fairness and one designed to ensure privacy.[68] Accordingly, employers should develop concise written policies and procedures regarding the use of company computers, specifically e-mail. The Society for Human Resource Management strongly encourages companies both to adopt policies that address employee privacy and to ensure that employees are notified of such policies. Any e-mail policy should be incorporated in the company policies and procedures manuals, employee handbooks, and instruction aids to ensure that the employee receives consistent information regarding the employer's rights to monitor employee e-mail. Additionally, a company could display a notice each time an employee logs on to a company computer indicating the computers are to be used only for business-related communication or explaining that the employee has no reasonable expectation of privacy in the electronic messages. Employers can also periodically send memos reminding employees of the policy.

Some experts advocate policies that restrict the use of e-mail to business purposes only and that explain that the employer may access the e-mail both in the ordinary course of business and when business reasons necessitate. If the employer faithfully adheres to this policy 100 percent of the time, this process is certainly defensible. However, such a standard is one that is difficult to honor in every case and the employer may be subject to claims of disparate treatment if applied inconsistently. Therefore, a more realistic approach—and one that is generally accepted both in the courts and common practice—suggests that employees limit their use of technology to reasonable personal access that does

(*continued*)

(concluded)

not unnecessarily interfere with their professional responsibilities or otherwise unduly impact the workplace financially or otherwise (referring to bandwidth, time spent online, impact on colleagues, and so on).

Philosopher William Parent conceives the right to privacy more appropriately as a right to liberty and, therefore, seeks to determine the potential affront to liberty from the employer's actions. He suggests the following six questions to determine whether those actions are justifiable or have the potential for an invasion of privacy or liberty, and perhaps they might guide the development of an organizational policy:

1. For what purpose is the undocumented personal knowledge sought?
2. Is this purpose a legitimate and important one?
3. Is the knowledge sought through invasion of privacy relevant to its justifying purpose?
4. Is invasion of privacy the only or the least offensive means of obtaining the knowledge?
5. What restrictions or procedural restraints have been placed on the privacy-invading techniques?
6. How will the personal knowledge be protected once it has been acquired?[69]

Parent's suggestions appear to respect the personal autonomy of the individual worker by providing for personal space within the working environment, by providing notice of where that "personal" space ends, and by allowing access to the information gathered, all designed toward achievement of a personal and professional development objective.

among other requests. Employers have three choices in terms of their response to a governmental request for information. They may opt to voluntarily cooperate with law enforcement by providing confidential employee or customer information upon request and as part of an ongoing investigation. They may instead choose to cooperate by asking for permission to seek employee authorization to release the requested information. Or, finally, they may request to receive a subpoena, search warrant, or FISA order from the federal agency before disclosing an employee's confidential information.[70]

Questions, Projects, and Exercises

1. Marriott Resorts had a formal company party for more than 200 employees. At one point during the party, the company aired a videotape that compiled employees' and their spouses' comments about a household chore they hated. However, as a spoof, the video was edited to make it seem as if they were describing what it was like to have sex with their partner. One employee's wife was very upset by the video and sued Marriott for invasion of privacy. Evaluate her argument, focusing on the ethical arguments for a violation of her rights.
2. Richard Fraser, an at-will independent insurance agent for Nationwide Mutual Insurance Company, was terminated by Nationwide and the parties disagree on the reason

for Fraser's termination. Fraser argues that Nationwide terminated him because he filed complaints regarding Nationwide's allegedly illegal conduct, for criticizing Nationwide to the Nationwide Insurance Independent Contractors Association, and for attempting to obtain the passage of legislation in Pennsylvania to ensure that independent insurance agents could be terminated only for "just cause." Nationwide argues, however, that it terminated Fraser because he was disloyal. Nationwide points out that Fraser drafted a letter to two competitors saying that policy holders were not happy with Nationwide and asking whether the competitors would be interested in acquiring them. (Fraser claims that the letters were drafted only to get Nationwide's attention and were not sent.)

When Nationwide learned about these letters, it claims that it became concerned that Fraser might also be revealing company secrets to its competitors. It therefore searched its main file server—on which all of Fraser's e-mail was lodged—for any e-mail to or from Fraser that showed similar improper behavior. Nationwide's general counsel testified that the e-mail search confirmed Fraser's disloyalty. Therefore, on the basis of the two letters and the e-mail search, Nationwide terminated Fraser's employment agreement. The search of his e-mail gives rise to Fraser's claim for damages under the Electronic Communications Privacy Act of 1986 (ECPA). Do you believe the employer was justified in monitoring the employee's e-mail and then terminating him? What ethical arguments do you believe either side could use in this case?

3. A customer service representative at an electronics store is surfing the Internet using one of the display computers. She accesses a Web site that shows graphic images of a crime scene. A customer in the store who notices the images is offended. Another customer service representative is behind the counter, using the store's computer to access a pornographic site, and starts to laugh. A customer asks him why he is laughing. He turns the computer screen around to show her the images that are causing him amusement. Is there anything wrong with these activities?
4. The term *cybersquatting* refers to the practice of registering a large number of Web site domain names hoping to sell them at huge prices to others who may want the URL or who are prepared to pay to get rid of a potentially confusing domain name. For instance, People for the Ethical Treatment of Animals, which operates www.peta.org, was able to shut down www.peta.com, a pro-hunting Web site that dubbed itself "People Eating Tasty Animals." Cybersquatters often determine possible misspellings or slightly incorrect Web sites with the hopes that the intended Web site will pay them for their new domain. Others might simply hold onto a potentially extremely popular site name based on the expectation that someone will want it. For example, someone paid over $7 million for the address www.business.com. In one case, one day after a partnership was announced that would result in an online bookstore for the Toronto *Globe & Mail* newspaper, with the domain name www.chaptersglobe.com, Richard Morochove, a technology writer, registered the domain chapters-globe.com. When the partnership demanded that he stop using the name, he promptly agreed, as long as he received a percentage of the sales from the Chapters/Globe Web site. The case went to trial. In situations such as these, do you believe the cybersquatter is doing anything wrong? What options might the "intended Web site" owner have?
5. Spam, or spamming, refers to the use of mailing lists to blanket usenets or private e-mail boxes with indiscriminate advertising messages. Some people believe that spamming should be protected as the simple exercise of one's First Amendment right to free speech while others view it as an invasion of privacy or even theft of resources or trespass to property, as Intel argued when a disgruntled ex-employee spammed

more than 35,000 Intel employees with his complaints. In that case, the court agreed, considering his e-mail spamming equivalent to trespassing on Intel's property and recognizing that Intel was forced to spend considerable time and resources to delete the e-mail messages from its system.

It is amusing to note that the source of the term *spam* is generally accepted to be the Monty Python song, "Spam spam spam spam, spam spam spam spam, lovely spam, wonderful spam. . . . " Like the song, spam is an endless repetition of worthless text. Others believe that the term came from the computer group lab at the University of Southern California, which gave it the name because it has many of the same characteristics as the lunchmeat Spam:

- Nobody wants it or ever asks for it.
- No one ever eats it; it is the first item to be pushed to the side when eating the entree.
- Sometimes it is actually tasty, like 1 percent of junk mail that is really useful to some people.[70]

Using stakeholder analysis, make an argument that spamming is either ethical or unethical.

6. Term papers on practically every subject imaginable are available on the Internet. Many of those who post the papers defend their practice in two ways: (1) These papers are posted to assist in research in the same way any other resource is posted on the Web and should simply be cited if used; and (2) these papers are posted in order to encourage faculty to modify paper topics and/or exams and not to simply bring back assignments that have been used countless times in the past. Are you persuaded? Is there anything unethical about this service in general? If so, who should be held accountable, the poster, the ultimate user, or someone else?
7. A college provided its security officers with a locker area in which to store personal items. The security officers occasionally used the area as a dressing room. After incidents of theft from the lockers and reports that the employees were bringing weapons to campus, the college installed a video surveillance camera in the locker area. Did the employees have a reasonable expectation of privacy that was violated by the video surveillance? Explain.
8. You work in the information technology area of a large U.S. corporation. After a rash of mass sexually-explicit e-mails were sent from an inside source to the entire corporate e-mail list, your supervisor asked you to draft a technology usage policy. What are some of the issues you will need to consider?
9. You work as an accountant at large accounting firm where your job leaves you with a lot of down time at the office in between assignments. You spend this time on your office computer developing a program that can make your job even more efficient and it might even be a breakthrough in the industry. This new product could be a huge success and you could make a lot of money. You think of quitting your job and devoting all your time and resources to selling this new product. However, you have developed this product using company equipment and technology, and also used the time you were at work. Do these facts raise any red flags in terms of ethical issues? What should you do?
10. As you learned in this chapter, drug testing in the work place is a somewhat controversial issue in terms of employer responsibilities and employee rights. Using sources from the Web, discuss the pros and cons of these programs.

Key Terms

After reading this chapter, you should have a clear understanding of the following Key Terms. The page numbers refer to the point at which they were discussed in the chapter. For a more complete definition, please see the Glossary.

Electronic Communications Privacy Act of 1986, *p. 340*
e-mail monitoring, *p. 349*
European Union's Directive on Personal Data Protection, *p. 342*
Fourth Amendment protection, *p. 340*
Health Insurance Portability and Accountability Act (HIPAA), *p. 356*
hypernorms, *p. 338*
Internet use monitoring, *p. 349*
intrusion into seclusion, *p. 340*
moral free space, *p. 338*
personal data, *p. 342*
privacy, *p. 335*
privacy rights, *p. 337*
property rights perspective, *p. 339*
reasonable expectation of privacy, *p. 341*
reciprocal obligation, *p. 338*
Safe Harbor exception, *p. 343*
Uniting and Strengthening America by Providing Appropriate Tools Required to Intercept and Obstruct Terrorism (USA PATRIOT) Act of 2001, *p. 364*

End Notes

1. E. Spreling, "The CIO Squeeze," *Forbes* (January 5, 2009), http://www.forbes.com/technology/2009/01/02/cio-squeeze-hogan-tech-cio-cx_es_0105hogan.html?feed=rss_technology&partner=venturebeat.
2. A. Marshall, "Where Business Is Feeling the Heat," in Krielstra, P., Kroll and Economist Intelligence Unit, *Global Fraud Report* (2007/2008).
3. J. Moore, "Your E-mail Trail: Where Ethics Meets Forensics," *Business and Society Review* 114, no. 2 (2009): pp. 273–293, 280.
4. Patricia Werhane, *Persons, Rights, and Corporations* (Englewood Cliffs, NJ: Prentice Hall, 1985), 94.
5. Gerald Doppelt, "Beyond Liberalism and Communitarianism: Towards a Critical Theory of Social Justice," *Philosophy and Social Criticism* 14 (1988): 271, 278.
6. Global Internet Liberty Campaign, "Privacy and Human Rights: An International Survey of Privacy Laws and Practice," (1998), http://www.gilc.org/privacy/survey/exec-summary.html (accessed April 18, 2010).
7. A. Levin and M. J. Nicholson, "Privacy Law in the United States, the EU and Canada: The Allure of the Middle Ground," *Univ. Ohio Law & Tech. Journal* 2 (2005): 357; J. Whitman "The Two Western Cultures of Privacy: Dignity versus Liberty," *Yale Law Journal* 113 (2004): 1151; A. Levin, "Dignity in the Workplace: An Enquiry into the Conceptual Foundation of Workplace Privacy Protection Worldwide," *ALSB Journal of Employment and Labor Law* 11, no. 1 (Winter 2009): 63.
8. A. R. Levinson, "Industrial Justice: Privacy Protection for the Employed," *Cornell Journal of Law and Public Policy* 18, no. 3 (2009) (*posted SSRN* Sept. 17, 2008), 3, http://ssrn.com/abstract=1269512 (accessed July 13, 2009).
9. Mike Brunker, "Cyberporn Nurse: I Feel like Larry Flynt," MSNBC, July 16, 1999.
10. *Lake v. Wal-Mart Stores, Inc.,* 582 N.W.2d 231 (Minn. 1998).
11. No. SCW112749, Cal. Sup. Ct., L.A. Cty., 1989, *appeal denied,* Sup. Ct. Cal., 994 Cal. LEXIS 3670 (6/29/94); James McNair, "When You Use Email at Work, Your Boss May Be Looking In," *Telecom Digest,*icg.stwing.upenn.edu/cis500/reading.062.htm, reprinted from the *Miami Herald* (accessed August 6, 2004).

12. Winn Schwartau, "Who Controls Network Usage Anyway?" *Network World,* May 22, 1995, 71.
13. Bureau of National Affairs, "Northern Telecom Settles with CWA on Monitoring," *Individual Employment Rights,* March 10, 1992, 1.
14. 59 Cal.Rptr.2d 834 (Cal.Ct.App., 1996).
15. See "Ted Clark's Legal Corner: Monitoring Employee Activities: Privacy Tensions in the Public Workplace," *NPLERA Newsletter,* June 1999, http://www.seyfarth.com/practice/labor/articles/II_1393.html (accessed April 18, 2010).
16. Formally known as "Directive 95/46/EC of the European Parliament and of the Council of 24 October 1995 on the Protection of Individuals with Regard to the Processing of Personal Data and on the Free Movement of Such Data, Council Directive 95/46," 1995 O.J. (L281).
17. Council Directive 95/46, 1995 O.J. (L281) at arts, 25–26.
18. Pamela Samuelson, "Data Privacy Law: A Study of United States Data Protection," *California Law Review* 87 no. 3 (May 1999): 751.
19. John Haas, "Thinking Ethically about Technology," The Intercollegiate Review, 5-10, Fall 1992; http://www.mmisi.org/ir/28_01/haas.pdf (accessed April 18, 2010).
20. *State of Washington v. Young,* 123 Wash.2d 173 (1994).
21. Frank Daly, "Reply, Delete . . . or Relate? IT's Human Dimension," Lecture as Verizon Professor in Business Ethics and Technology, Bentley College, March 31, 2004.
22. Dieringer Research Group Inc., "Telework Trendlines, 2009" (Feb. 2009); http://www.worldatwork.org/waw/adimLink?id=31115 (accessed April 18, 2010).
23. U. Klotz, "The Challenges of the New Economy" (October 1999), cited in *World Employment Report 2001: Life at Work in the Information Economy* (Geneva: International Labour Office, 2001), 145.
24. For a similar interpretation, see B. Kracher and C. Corritore, "Is There a Special E-Commerce Ethics?" *Business Ethics Quarterly* 14, no. 1 (2004): 71–94.
25. Antonio Argandona, "The New Economy: Ethical Issues," *Journal of Business Ethics* 44 (2003): 3–22, 26.
26. Google S-1, filed with the Securities and Exchange Commission, http://www.sec.gov/Archives/edgar/data/1288776/000119312504139655/ds1a.htm, appendix B (2004) (accessed April 18, 2010).
27. Google S-1, *infra,* note 17.
28. Google S-1, *infra,* note 17.
29. Antonio Argandoña, "The New Economy: Ethical Issues," *Journal of Business Ethics* 44 (2003): 3–22, 28.
30. David Carr, "Putting 40,000 Readers, One by One, on a Cover," *The New York Times,* April 5, 2004, (http://www.nytimes.com/2004/04/05/business/mediatalk-putting-40000-readers-one-by-one-on-a-cover.html?pagewanted=1 (accessed April 18, 2010).
31. Robert Half Technology, "Whistle—But Don't Tweet—While You Work," *Press Release* (Oct. 6, 2009), http://www.roberthalftechnology.com/PressRoom?id=2531 (accessed April 18, 2010).
32. American Management Association Workplace E-mail and Instant Messaging Survey (2005).
33. Proofpoint, "Proofpoint Releases 2008 Email and Data Loss Prevention Survey, *Press Release* (May 20, 2008), http://www.proofpoint.com/news-and-events/press-releases/pressdetail.php?PressReleaseID=204 (accessed April 18, 2010).

34. Darryl Haralson and Robert W. Ahrens, "Top Methods of Monitoring Employees," USA Today, March 31, 2004, 1. (Original: CSO Magazine Survey of 520 Chief Security Officers and Senior Security Executives, January 2004)
35. American Management Association and epolicy Institute Research, Workplace E-mail and Instant Messaging Survey (May 18, 2005), http://www.epolicyinstitute.com/survey2005Summary.pdf (with login: http://www.amanet.org/research/pdfs/EMS_summary05.pdf) (accessed April 18, 2010). Andrew Schulman, "One-third of U.S. Online Workforce under Internet/Email Surveillance," *Workforce Surveillance Project,* Privacy Foundation, July 9, 2001, http://www.privacyfoundation.org/workplace/business/biz_show.asp?id=70&ac. Schulman reports that, of the 140 million workers in the U.S., 40 million are online. Of that 40 million, 14 million are subject to monitoring (35 percent). Worldwide, 100 million of 3 billion workers are online and 27 million (27 percent) are subject to monitoring (p. 2). See also Linda Rosencrance, "Study: Monitoring of Employee Email, Web Use Escalates," *Computerworld,* July 9, 2001.
36. Vasant Raval, "Ethical Behavior in the Knowledge Economy," *Information Strategy* 16, no. 3 (Spring 2000): 45.
37. Ponemon Institute LLC, "Workplace Survey on the Privacy Age Gap," *The Littler Report* (2008).
38. Adapted from Ponemon Institute LLC, "Workplace Survey on the Privacy Age Gap," *The Littler Report* (2008).
39. Elron Software, "Guide to Internet Usage and Policy" (2001): 7, 17; American Management Association and epolicy Institute Research, Workplace E-mail and Instant Messaging Survey (May 18, 2005), http://www.epolicyinstitute.com/survey2005Summary.pdf (with login: http://www.amanet.org/research/pdfs/EMS_summary05.pdf) (accessed April 18, 2010).
40. American Management Association and epolicy Institute Research, Workplace E-mail and Instant Messaging Survey (May 18, 2005), http://www.epolicyinstitute.com/survey2005Summary.pdf (with login: http://www.amanet.org/research/pdfs/EMS_summary05.pdf) (accessed April 18, 2010). Alan Cohen, "Worker Watchers," *Fortune/CNET Technology Review* (Summer 2001): 70, 76.
41. Bjorn Engelhardt, "Cut costs through email archiving," Business Technology (Sept. 3, 2009), http://businesstechnology.in/tools/expert-articles/2009/09/03/Cut-costs-through-email-archiving.1.html (accessed April 18, 2010).
42. American Management Association and epolicy Institute Research, Workplace E-mail and Instant Messaging Survey (May 18, 2005), http://www.epolicyinstitute.com/survey2005Summary.pdf (with login: http://www.amanet.org/research/pdfs/EMS_summary05.pdf) (accessed April 18, 2010).
43. Wolgemuth, Liz, "5 Ways Your Computer Use Can Get You Fired," U.S. News & World Report (March 11, 2008), http://www.usnews.com/money/careers/articles/2008/03/11/5-ways-your-computer-use-can-get-you-fired.html (accessed April 18, 2010).
44. Mark A. de Bernardo, *Drug Abuse in the Workplace: An Employer's Guide for Prevention,* available from the U.S. Chamber of Commerce, 1615 H Street, NW, Washington, DC 20062.
45. Murphy, K.R., G.C. Thornton, and D.H. Reynolds, "College Students' Attitudes toward Employee Drug Testing Programs," Personnel Psychology, v. 43, no. 3 (2006), http://www3.interscience.wiley.com/journal/119370628/abstract?CRETRY=1&SRETRY=0 (accessed April 18, 2010).

46. 109 S.Ct. 1402 (1989).

47. T. Gutner, "Applicants' Personalities Put to the Test," *Wall Street Journal* (April 24, 2009), http://online.wsj.com/article/SB121969346624670203.html?mod=djem_jiewr_HR (accessed July 6, 2009).

48. V. O'Connell, "Test for Dwindling Retail Jobs Spawns a Culture of Cheating," *Wall Street Journal*, January 7, 2009: A1, http://online.wsj.com/article/SB123129220146959621.html?mod=todays_us_page_one. (accessed April 18, 2010).

49. Genetic Information Nondiscrimination Act of 2008 (HR 493, P.L. No. 110-233), http://www.govtrack.us/congress/bill.xpd?bill=h110-493&tab=summary.

50. W. Herbert and A.K. Tuminaro, "The Impact of Emerging Technologies in the Workplace: Who's Watching the Man (Who's Watching Me)?" *Hofstra Labor and Employment Law Journal* 5 (2009): 355; Bibby, A., "You're Being Followed: Electronic Monitoring and Surveillance in the Workplace" (2006), http://www.andrewbibby.com/pdf/Surveillance-en.pdf (accessed April 18, 2010).

51. A. Svendsen and D. Wheeler, *Measuring the Business Value of Stakeholder Relationships* (*Part 1*) (Toronto CICA, 2001).

52. M. Schulman, "Little Brother Is Watching You," *Issues in Ethics* 9, no. 2 (Spring 1998) http://www.scu.edu/ethics/publications/iie/v9n2/brother.html (accessed April 18, 2010).

53. As of publication, these included Arizona, Connecticut, Washington, DC, Illinois, Indiana, Kentucky, Louisiana, Maine, Mississippi, New Jersey, New Mexico, Oklahoma, Oregon, Rhode Island, South Carolina, South Dakota, Virginia, West Virginia, and Wyoming. See also John Pearce and Dennis Kuhn, "The Legal Limits of Employees' Off-Duty Privacy Rights," *Organizational Dynamics* 32, no. 4 (2003): 372–383.

54. M. Parks, "Workplace Romance," *Society for Human Resource Management, Poll Findings* (January 2006): 6.

55. M. Parks, "Workplace Romance," *Society for Human Resource Management, Poll Findings* (January 2006): 1–2.

56. 37 237 F.3d 166 (2nd Cir. 2001).

57. Losee, S and H. Olen, "For Love or Pink Slips: Why On-The-Job Nookie With The Boss Is A No-No," The Huffington Post (Nov. 28, 2007), http://www.huffingtonpost.com/stephanie-losee-and-helaine-olen/for-love-or-pink-slips-wh_b_74423.html (accessed April 18, 2010).

58. P. Gordon and K. C. Franklin, "Blogging and the Workplace," *Law.com* (August 8, 2006).

59. Id.

60. A. Rupe, "Facebook Faux Pas," *Workforce Management* (March 2007), http://www.workforce.com/archive/feature/24/81/84/index.php.

61. Deloitte LLP, *Social Networking and Reputational Risk in the Workplace* (2009), p. 13.

62. Id., p. 8.

63. Id.

64. G. Bennett, "Australia: You Have Been Poked, High-Fived and Had a Ninja Sent After You—Facebook, Privacy and the Workplace," *Information Law Highlights* (July 25, 2008), http://www.claytonutz.com/.

65. Office of Management and Budget, *Stimulating Smarter Regulation, 2002: Report to Congress on the Costs and Benefits of Regulations and Unfunded Mandates on State,*

Local, and Tribal Entities (Washington, DC: Office of Information and Regulatory Affairs, March 2003), www.whitehouse.gov/omb/inforeg/2002_report_to_congress.pdf.

66. R. Sanchez, "Librarians Make Some Noise over Patriot Act," *Washington Post,* April 10, 2003, A20.
67. ACLU, "List of Communities That Have Passed Resolutions", June 10, 2004, http://www.aclu.org/national-security/list-communities-have-passed-resolutions (accessed April 18, 2010).
68. V. Knapp, "The Impact of the Patriot Act on Employers" (2003), http://www.rothgerber.com/newslettersarticles/le0024.asp (accessed April 18, 2010).
69. L. Reed and B. Freidman, "Workplace Privacy: Employee Relations and Legal Implications of Monitoring Employee E-mail Use," *Employee Responsibilities and Rights Journal* 19, no. 2 (June 2007): 75–83 (accessed April 18, 2010).
70. M. Schulman, "Little Brother Is Watching You," *Issues in Ethics* 9, no. 2 (Spring 1998).
71. http://www.webopedia.com/TERM/s/spam.html (accessed April 18, 2010).

Readings

Reading 7-1

Drug Testing and the Right to Privacy: *Arguing the Ethics of Workplace Drug Testing*

Michael Cranford

In other work, author Cranford argues that drug testing is ethically justified within the terms of the employment agreement, and therefore does not amount to a violation of an employee's right to privacy. In the following article, which is an excerpt from a longer piece, "The Ethics of Privacy," he expands the contention to include an obligation to test in certain employment contexts.

Drug Testing and the Obligation to Prevent Harm

The argument over the ethical justification for drug testing takes a different turn when we consider drug testing, not as an employer's right under the terms of an employment contract, but as a means by which an employer may prevent harms committed by employees who abuse drugs. By "harms" I mean actual or probable dangers to the safety and health of employees (other than the one impaired by drugs) and of persons outside the workplace. At issue are two related arguments, either of which may provide adequate justification for workplace drug testing. The first argument assumes that an employer has a general obligation to prevent harm. This obligation requires an employer to utilize reasonable means to prevent or mitigate potential harms committed in connection with workplace activities. To the extent that drug testing is such a reasonable means, the employer is obligated to test for employee drug abuse.

A primary assumption in this argument is that employees who are drug users pose a threat to the safety and well-being of themselves and others. That alcohol and drug abuse are connected with significant work-related harms is reasonably established, however. For example, the National Transportation Safety Board found that marijuana used by a Conrail engineer was a major contributing factor to the Conrail-Amtrak collision in January 1987, which killed 16 people and injured 170. An earlier study by the Federal Railroad Administration (FRA) determined that between 1969 and 1979 48 major train accidents, 37 deaths, and 80 injuries could be directly connected with alcohol and drug abuse. A similar study concluded that between 1975 and 1983 at least 45 significant train accidents, resulting in 34 fatalities, 66 injuries and over $28 million in property damage, could be directly linked to the errors of alcohol- and drug-impaired employees. Without the benefit of regular post-accident testing, these figures probably amount to less than half of the total drug- or alcohol-related accidents during that period.

The second argument is that employers have not only an obligation to prevent harm, but a responsibility for harms committed by their employees. This responsibility justifies an employer in obtaining information pertaining to employee drug abuse if by acquiring such information the employer can mitigate potential harms. It is this second phase of the argument that has drawn the greatest attention and criticism, though my analysis is ultimately grounded on the corporation's obligation to prevent harm.

Unlike the argument based on performance of contract, drug testing as a means to prevent harm does not entail a devaluation of human beings by considering them as means to purely economic ends. Rather, the purpose of drug testing affirms the essential value and dignity of human beings by subjugating technique and economic efficacy to human safety and well-being. The fact that preventing harms may also be in a company's best economic interests is a conclusion resulting from cost-benefit analysis that has no immediate bearing on a mandatory drug testing program.[1] Drug testing and employee assistance programs themselves place significant financial burdens on corporations that cannot always be rationalized as offsetting accident settlements that only *might* have been paid out.

Responsibility to Drug Test and Questions of Justification

Jennifer Moore addresses the second argument listed, that "because corporations are responsible for harms committed by employees while under the influence of drugs, they are entitled to test for drug use." She invokes Kant's "ought implies can" principle, which states that if a person is obligated to do X then they must have the capacity to do X (i.e., they must be free to do or not do X). In assigning corporations a responsibility for harms caused by employees who abuse drugs, it follows that they must have the capacity to prevent these harms. Specifically, they must have the freedom to test for drug use. Moore then explores the meaning of the statement that corporations are "responsible" for harms committed by employees to determine if drug testing is, in fact, warranted.

Moore's first point is that, whatever is meant by "responsible," it cannot mean *legally* responsible. Legally, the doctrine of *respondeat superior* makes a corporation vicariously liable for an employee's action, regardless of whether or not the corporation was at fault. Legal liability, in this case, does not imply a capacity to have prevented harm. Moore concludes that holding corporations legally liable for harms committed by employees who abuse drugs while at the same time forbidding drug testing is not inconsistent.

Moore seems to think that just because legal liability applies when a corporation cannot prevent harm, a corporation should not attempt to prevent harm to the greatest degree possible, either on the basis of an obligation to beneficence or, in the very least, to minimize its liability. Certainly a corporation can be held liable when it is not at fault, but nothing follows from this with regard to its obligation to public safety when it *is* at fault. To the degree that a corporation *can* be at fault, it should be allowed the ability to prevent harms. Legal liability does imply a justification for drug testing.

Moore then addresses corporate responsibility as a *moral* obligation to prevent harm caused by employees who abuse drugs. The argument goes as follows:

1. If corporations have obligations, they must be capable of carrying them out, on the principle of "ought implies can."
2. Corporations have an obligation to prevent harm from occurring in the course of conducting their business.
3. Drug use by employees is likely to lead to harm.
4. Corporations must be able to take steps to eliminate (or at least reduce) drug use by employees.
5. Drug testing is an effective way to eliminate/reduce employee drug use.
6. Therefore corporations must be permitted to test for drugs.

Moore claims that this conclusion (6) does not follow, since it is not clear that the obligation to prevent harm justifies drug testing:

> Of course this does not necessarily mean that drug testing is *unjustified.* But it does mean that before we can determine whether it is justified, we must ask what is permissible for one person or group of persons to do to another to prevent harm for which they are responsible.

Moore offers a number of examples to show that the obligation to prevent harm cannot justify just any action. In none of her examples, however, does she actually counterpose the act of preventing harm with a right to privacy. For example, her first case is of a hostess who is responsible for a drunken guest leaving her party. Moore argues that she is perhaps allowed to take the guest's car keys away from her, but is not entitled to knock her out and lock her in the bathroom. Moore is relying on the difficulty in discerning between these actions to argue that drug testing is not obviously justified simply because it prevents harm.

While testing impairment by a battery of eye-hand coordination and reflex exercises might detect the most seriously impaired employees at the precise moment of testing, it would not detect employees who remained sober only during the time frame immediately preceding such tests. Such testing is also indeterminate, as anyone can vouch who has successfully passed a field sobriety test while legally intoxicated. Even if some degree of impairment were indicated, the employer is left with no means by which she may evaluate the significance of the employee's failure to pass the test. The difference between an employee who is impaired due to lack of sleep and an employee who is under the influence of an illegal substance is morally significant.[2]

Finally, testing impairment fails to detect habitual users of drugs who, while not noticeably impaired at the precise moment of testing, nonetheless may constitute a significant and ongoing risk. Consequently, testing for impairment is not "just more effective in all ways" than drug testing. Drug testing is not directed at identifying impairment, which (as I have pointed out) is rather difficult to quantify or detect by any means, but at (1) identifying employees who abuse drugs, and (2) deterring habitual users from becoming impaired at the workplace. Toward these ends, drug testing is the most effective and direct means currently available.

In response to Moore, I agree that drug testing is neither necessary nor sufficient for ridding the workplace of drug abuse. Consequently, she is correct in stating that the conclusion to the present argument (6) does not follow. But this is only if we allow her to define what it means for drug testing to be an "effective" way to eliminate or reduce employee drug abuse (5). If by "effective" we understand that drug testing prevents or eliminates harms that would not, in its absence, be prevented or eliminated by some other measure, then it follows that corporations must be permitted to test for drugs. Corporations must be permitted to undertake any reasonable measures for preventing workplace harms when no equally effectual measures are available. I will refer to all such measures as *measures of last resort.* In this understanding of "effective," the conclusion (6) does follow.

But in this case, however, our conclusion (6) is not strong enough. Referring back to our original argument, I asserted that an employer has a general obligation to prevent harm, and that this obligation requires an employer to utilize reasonable means to prevent or mitigate potential harms committed in connection with workplace activities. But if drug testing is necessary in that process as a measure of last resort, then it not only follows that corporations must be permitted to test for drugs, but that corporations are obligated to do so. It is for this reason that a corporation is responsible to take on the "Protector of Harms" role in its relationship with an employee even when such a role is not inherent in the employment contract.

The Kew Gardens Principle and the Obligation to Prevent Harm

There are two elements in my analysis to this point which I have offered without any accompanying substantiation. The first is the claim that an employer has a general obligation to prevent harm. The second is the claim that drug testing is a measure of last resort, as I have defined it. It is only if these assertions are reasonable that it would follow that corporations are obligated to test for drugs.

In defense of both these points I would like to introduce four criteria which together indicate a moral obligation to prevent harm. This combination of features governing difficult cases of assessing moral responsibility has elsewhere been termed the "Kew Gardens Principle."

1. *Need.* A corporation's responsibility to test for drugs, or take any other appropriate measures to reduce the occurrence of harms, is a function of the extent of the harms which may result. In cases where the other three factors are constant, increased need indicates increased responsibility. In reference to his engineering company, Lewis Maltby states that "a single Drexelbrook employee working under the influence of drugs could cause a disaster as tragic as occurred in Bhopal." If true, this would suggest a significant responsibility to prevent such harms.
2. *Proximity.* Proximity is less a function of distance and more a function of awareness. We hold a person blameworthy if she knows of a crisis or a potential crisis and does not do what she can to prevent it. "When we become aware of a wrongdoing or a social injury, we take on obligations that we did not have while ignorant." Greater responsibility exists in situations where one would expect a heightened awareness of need as a consequence of civic duty, duties to one's family, and so on. In other words, we would hold a family member more blameworthy than a stranger for not being aware of a person's critical plight.

   Proximity becomes important in the case of workplace drug abuse because the network of social relationships involved in a daily, cooperative setting, combined with the social and legal perception that an employer is responsible for the activities of her employees, entail a high degree of expectation that the employer not only will learn of a potential harm caused by drug abuse, but *should* learn of it. A corporation delegates its employees to act on its behalf and, in fact, acts only through its employees. This integral and intimate relationship whereby the employees act on behalf of the corporation obligates the corporation to become aware of potential dangers which could result from drug abuse.

While a variety of measures can and have been used that locate and address the problem of workplace drug abuse (such as direct observation of employees, hidden cameras, mandatory educational programs in dealing with drug abuse, and basic dexterity/reflexivity/judgment testing), none of these programs has the same certainty of screening out drug abusers as does drug testing. Direct observation and dexterity tests can be beaten (and are, routinely). While education is an effective counterpreventative, it does not screen out users who are resistant to receiving help—the individuals most likely to place others at risk. On the other hand, it can be argued that drug testing also is falsifiable. If given advance notice of testing, drug users can abstain long enough to pass the test. Or, they can procure a sample of "clean" urine from another individual and substitute it for their own.

At most, these examples argue against regularly scheduled testings—not against random, unannounced testings. These examples also overlook the fact that the time necessary for drug metabolites to become absent from the urine varies from individual to individual and from use to use. Serious and habitual users (who are the most likely to commit harms) would probably be unable to abstain from use long enough even to pass an announced test. And while drug testing is not unfalsifiable, it is more difficult to falsify than other options for testing. Consequently, while not a perfect instrument for the detection of drug abuse, drug testing has an effectiveness and specificity that remain unparalleled.

Since drug testing is the most effective technology currently available to make the employer aware of potential dangers by locating habitual users, and without which many such users will likely not be identified, use of drug testing is obligatory as a measure of last resort. Since no one other than the employer is more aware of the potential for an employee committing work-related harms, a significant moral responsibility to prevent such harms follows.

This responsibility could be mitigated if the employer has a reasonable certainty that an employee (or all employees) does not abuse drugs. Thus, drug testing is not only essential to the employer's obligation to come to know of potential harms, but it reduces a corporation's moral responsibility for harms committed by ruling out drug abuse as a contributing factor.

3. *Capability.* Even if there is a need to which someone has proximity, that person cannot be held morally responsible unless she has the capacity to meet the need. As I have discussed at length, not just any action offered to prevent a harm is necessarily reasonable. What is reasonable is that action which is least intrusive or harmful, most efficient and specific, and with the highest probability of achieving its goals (thus, my principles for what constitutes a reasonable means of coming to know private information). Drug testing, in combination with a counseling and rehabilitation program that relieves employees of hazardous duty, meets these criteria. In most cases, as will be noted below, no other agent has the capability of performing this combination of actions.

4. *Last Resort.* In situations where the other three features are present, one becomes more responsible the less likely it is that someone else will prevent the harm in question. While it is often difficult to assess whether one alone has knowledge of a potential harm, to the degree that one can be certain that one does, and that no one else has the proximity or capacity for intervening, significant responsibility is entailed.

In the case of harms caused by drug abuse, it is rarely the case that an agency outside the workplace will possess the means to either assess the potential for harm (thus need and proximity) or be able to prevent the harm from being realized (by possessing the capacity to locate and remove employees who abuse drugs from hazardous duty). When there is no agency beyond the employer which can effectively prevent harms, the employer becomes the agent of last resort. When there is no method of identifying drug abusers more effective than drug testing, it becomes a method of last resort in the process of preventing drug-related harms in the workplace. Consequently, the criterion of last resort, in connection with the other three features of the Kew Gardens Principle, assign a corporation a high degree of moral responsibility to prevent drug-related harms, and obligate it to make use of reasonable methods for identifying such harms, particularly when more effective methods are unavailable.

The actual degree of responsibility turns on the level of need (criterion #1), however. To the degree that harms are improbable or of little consequence to human life and safety, a corporation's obligation to prevent such harms is diminished. Drug testing is not justified under this argument if the condition it is testing for has little potential to result in any real danger. The difficulty arises in attempting a risk analysis when the effects of impairment remain hypothetical. For example, one might argue that the condition of increased need exists in the case of railroad engineers who control the velocity and breaking of high-speed locomotives. Similarly, a condition of increased need exists in the case of factory workers who operate heavy machinery in a crowded work setting. It is less clear, though, that a condition of increased need arises among clerks at the same railroad, who could potentially create disaster through an error in paper work that goes unnoticed by field operatives. Nor is it clear that a condition of increased need arises in the case of the janitorial staff at a factory, who might perhaps leave a bit too much water on the floor if they were impaired while mopping a hallway. Of these latter examples, the first is improbable, and the last is insignificant (or at least, not significant enough to justify drug testing the entire janitorial staff). While many cases can be cited that are problems in risk assessment, it is critical to note that nothing follows with regard to the obligation to prevent harms in cases that are not problematic. In such cases (like the two listed first), corporations can and should use reasonable means to prevent drug related harms.

Conclusions and Policy Recommendations

It is the position adopted in this paper that (1) a corporation is entitled to drug test its employees to determine employee capacity to perform according to the terms of the employment contract, and (2) a corporation is morally obligated to test employees for drug and alcohol abuse when a condition of impairment would place the safety and health of other human beings at risk. The first of these two justifications, I have argued, quantifies human beings under a measure of efficiency, treating them as means to a purely economic end (i.e., the corporation's profitability). Drug testing does not, in the large majority of cases, benefit the employee's best interests, and is therefore directed at effecting extrinsic goods only (as opposed to respecting the employee's intrinsic value and dignity). This criticism fails in the latter justification, however, since the ultimate end of drug testing *is* the preservation of human life as an intrinsic good. In this case, a corporation is not only entitled to use toxicological testing, but is obligated to do so, to the degree that a critical need to prevent drug-related harms is actually present.

Source: Adapted by permission of the author from his publication, "The Ethics of Privacy: Drug Testing, Surveillance, and Competing Interests in the Workplace" by Cranford, Michael, Ph.D., University of Southern California, 2007, 292 pages; AAT 3291792.

End Notes

1. Though it might have a bearing on a drug testing program that was only enacted for certain projects that were assessed as cost-prohibitive on the basis of potential harms. Consequently, drug testing will only be justified under this argument if it is effected uniformly and mandatorily without regard for such assessments.
2. My point here is best explained by way of an example. Let us say that a young employee dances all night for several nights in a row, and therefore shows up for work impaired due to lack of sleep.

The difference between this individual and someone who is impaired because of substance abuse is at least that the latter admits of an addictive and increasingly significant (and ultimately self-destructive) condition, whereas the former is at worst compulsive, and is therefore unlikely to continue for more than a few nights (even the best of us dancers eventually find ourselves nodding off). There is also the legality of purchasing and using illicit substances, not to mention driving under the influence of illicit substances. Breaking those laws is ethically significant, whereas dancing all night is just dumb—but completely legal.

References

Note: Notes and references removed for publication here, but are available on the book website at www.mhhe.com/busethics2e.

Reading 7-2

Medical Ethics for the Newest Practitioners: *Health Web Sites—Power and Responsibility in Online Health*

Joshua Newman

Over the past several years, Web sites have grown to provide the kinds of online health services that consumers expect in many other fields. Social networks bring people together around health and disease. Many sites serve to guide people through medical care, and finding physicians and hospitals. And direct-to-consumer sites enable the purchase of laboratory tests, medications, and even some forms of treatment. Anyone with an Internet connection now enjoys unprecedented access to the most up-to-date and sophisticated medical information, as well as the means to communicate to a billion people. This has all happened in a relatively short period of time, with virtually no institutional, governmental, or professional regulation.

Medicine, on the other hand, has grown slowly, and has developed a system of ethics. It has been guarded historically by the guild-like professionalism of physicians and civil bodies, after having made, and learned from, terrible and costly mistakes. The Internet puts health provision in the hands of anyone who can browse to or set up a Web site. New risks and responsibilities must be considered in order to maintain the high standards so important to health and prevent harm.

In business and commerce, the phrase *caveat emptor* has been with us for hundreds of years. "Let the buyer beware" guides our stance when confronting used cars, homes, or electronics. Although warrantees and other consumer protections attempt to guard consumers from unscrupulous sellers or shoddy products, sometimes things go wrong. When the product is health the stakes are higher. In contrast to *caveat emptor,* the operative phrase in medicine, which goes back to Hippocrates, has been *primum non nocere,* "first do no harm." When businesses enter the health realm, they have a greater standard to meet. Rather than simply sell their products, they must take into consideration the health and well-being of their customers, much the same way that a physician does.

Online health technology has unique ethical pressures and risks compared to other online activities. Appropriate and lifesaving advice to one person can be deadly to another. Personal health information may expose great vulnerability and address enduring afflictions and conditions. Mistakes in care can cause permanent damage.

The goal of this paper is to elucidate some of the ethical issues that arise with online health technology by looking at five general themes that appear in online health: privacy safeguarding, information integrity, the threat to the doctor-patient relationship, the psychological risks of providing patients with medical information, and disparities of access.

Ethical questions, like the problems that have grown out of the Internet, tend to eschew easy and definite answers. Categorical restriction of online health information or comprehensive official oversight is impractical. The obstacles and costs of building online sites are low enough, and the unlikelihood of regulation make these issues rather in need of self-regulation on the part of the Web sites and culture change in patients and health professionals.

This paper presents some of the potential risks of online health activity so that consumers will enter into online health domains with greater awareness and protection from some of the adversity. Another goal is so that purveyors of online health services will better appreciate their power and appropriately safeguard their sites against the potential to cause harm. Though few business owners can hope to gain the degree of ethical awareness learned by physicians in the face-to-face care for sick and vulnerable patients, hopefully they can approach this ideal. For a long time, people have spoken about the importance of physicians gaining technological proficiency. Perhaps an equally important development will be for online health services to gain ethical proficiency.

In this vein, one of the more important general themes that run through this paper is the idea that as consumers grow in understanding, diagnosing, and treating their own maladies, and purveyors of online health information technology grow in their ability to deliver online health information tools, both will increasingly supplant physicians and other health professionals who used to be the stewards of such domains. Consequently, the degree to which every agent in the health care landscape can learn the highest ethical stances and respect for their power will in part determine the health effects they will achieve.

Privacy

All that may come to my knowledge in the exercise of my profession or in daily commerce with men, which ought not to be spread abroad, I will keep secret and will never reveal.

Hippocrates

Mr. Red suffers from depression and has largely kept it under control. Sometimes his condition flares up and he has a hard time working and taking care of himself. He joins an online social network for people with depression and finds that the support from fellow sufferers is beneficial. It makes him feel a part of a community, and though the online interaction is limited, it allows him to participate and engage other people in ways he finds helpful. When Mr. Red signed up to the Web site he used his personal e-mail address, but now forwards all e-mail through his business address. In a routine audit, his employer sees that Mr. Red is receiving e-mails from the mood disorder Web site. When staffing decisions for an important project come up, knowing that depressed patients sometimes have more missed days of work, and make larger draws on the employee insurance pool, they decide not to give the opportunity to Mr. Red.

Many people identify privacy issues related to personal health information as the most important ethical issue with health information technology. Despite state and federal regulations that attempt to safeguard the storage and transmission of health information, and the general adherence to these laws, several dramatic and widely reported failures to protect the privacy of individuals have sensitized people to the possibility that their information may be released. Noteworthy examples are the unauthorized access to medical records of celebrities and a lost laptop computer from the Veterans Administration that contained tens of millions of people's private information to name just two. Releases of private health information can come from the availability of information in an electronic health system, accidental releases from machines that send or store personal health data, and a number of other ways from billing systems to voice-mail messages. Ironically the value of personal health information requires that it be freely transmissible. Yet to make it transmissible enables misuse and breaches of confidentially.

The nature of personal health information thus makes it both useful and risky. Unintentional release of information can jeopardize employment, insurance, and other relationships. It can cause real harm, as well as upsetting feelings of having our vulnerabilities exposed and privacy violated. Additionally, if people do not feel that their data will be protected, they may not avail themselves of health information technology and its accompanying benefits. As a business issue, those organizations that fail to adequately protect this information will suffer and a useful health service may fail to be utilized amid a lack of confidence.

The theoretical problems with security and privacy have no easy solution. The nature of the problem is such that it is difficult for data to be simultaneously protected and available. Either there will be restrictiveness and a lack of data when it is helpful, or vulnerability of data to unwanted access, and sometimes both. And so we must manage risks as they cannot be ameliorated.

The first level of protection comes from privacy policies and adherence to relevant laws. Yet this modicum of protection should be only the beginning. Web sites that host private health data have an ethical obligation to follow the highest standards of data stewardship. This holds true whether the sites are connected to health providers, in which case they have to follow laws such as HIPAA, or even if they do not formally provide care, in which case they do not currently have any special health information laws to follow. Social networks that enable people to share information do well to warn and monitor for unintended consequences of hosting private information. Sites that collect information of value to advertisers should state clearly their policies of releasing information to marketers and advertisers, and should generally favor privacy and be clear and obvious when they deviate from the standard.

In these ways, by honoring intimate details of people's health, and vigilantly working to avoid the damage that can result from violations of privacy, Web sites can continue to provide and innovate in ways that can help produce and restore health.

Integrity of Information

The search for truth is more precious than its possession.

Albert Einstein

Mr. Brown has high cholesterol. He takes a medication for it because research shows conclusively that lowering cholesterol levels can decrease the risks of cardiovascular disease. He sees online that a prominent pharmaceutical company has come out with a new product to treat high cholesterol. Mr. Brown is conscientious so he does a search on the medication and finds that there are a number of Web sites and blogs that write favorably about the benefits of the new medication. Despite the fact that it costs more than his current treatment, the positive mentions of the medication by a number of sites, from people who have a similar situation as his own, convince him to change medications. Mr. Brown does not realize that the pharmaceutical company has given gifts to the hosts of the blog and shared advice on how to appear prominently in search results. The information he has found may have been biased by the conflict of interest, yet Mr. Brown has no way to know.

Problems of information integrity can arise and cause trouble in different ways. Primarily, they arise because the accuracy and provenance of information is difficult to discern. Anyone can set up a sophisticated Web site whose impressiveness has little correlation to the accuracy and usefulness of the information contained therein. As in the print and real world, conflicts of interest can corrupt online information. False information that might otherwise get revealed through mechanisms of peer review, attribution, and other institutional controls, are nonexistent on blogs and many health-related Web sites. Additionally, in contrast to the copyright notices in every published work, Internet information can go out of date and yet still appear current. The subsequent release of safety notices and medical alerts may never percolate to the more distal Web sites that may nevertheless be considered trusted sources of information. People may act on this incorrect data.

Creators and managers of online health technologies, because they provide this information, need to recognize the responsibility that accompanies their work. They should use common techniques to ensure credibility of information, health and otherwise. They should use and provide references to information sources, especially primary sources, where possible. They should provide dates of the most recent information updates when they present medical information. And they should adopt a system of inventory and scheduled reviews that regularly examine for outdated and potentially harmful information. Furthermore, even bloggers and other informal Web sites that publish information that could be used in the diagnosis and treatment of disease should publish clear conflict of interest statements. In these ways, sites can grow to attain a higher standard of information content and presentation to better serve their users.

All of this may seem a bit excessive to the many who can establish a Web presence full of medical information. After all, it takes about five minutes to set up a blog to discuss health or medicine and appear on the Internet with some authority. The rationale behind implementing the above safeguards is that Web sites have inherent power. Because of the ease of spreading information on the Internet, bad information can be shared swiftly and impact the lives of people who do not have the ability to discern the credibility. And harm can be done.

Fortunately, not every Web site needs to adopt the preceding standards for the market of health information technology to benefit from an ethos of greater credibility. If a critical mass of Web sites maintains the above standards of attribution, dating, updating, and conflict of interest disclosure, their increased credibility will be apparent and superior to those Web sites that do not. As a consequence, consumers of health information technology will have a greater sensitivity to credible information. And those sites that adhere to these standards will show more clearly where the quality resides and through their success, elevate the standard.

Doctor-Patient Relationship

The art of medicine consists in amusing the patient while nature cures the disease.

Voltaire

Ms. White goes to the doctor because she has a cough. Cough is one of the most common complaints in a primary care office. Dr. Gray has few minutes to complete the diagnosis and treatment plan for Ms. White. They have known each other for years and Ms. White is generally healthy. So Dr. Gray comes to the conclusion, using a heuristic in his head that Ms. White is suffering from a virus that is, in fact, the cause of most of the coughs he will see that day. This time, however, he is wrong. Ms. White was cleaning her basement, and breathed in some mold and now has a nasty infection. Dr. Gray makes a misdiagnosis partially because he does not expend the time or attention to ask some questions and ponder the differential diagnosis. Ms. White goes home, and looks up her symptoms on the Internet. She sees that one of the questions on the Web site asks her if she has been cleaning or working in a dark or dirty location. It tells her that she could have aspergillosis, an infection of the aspergillus fungus. She is furious and feels letdown by her doctor. Consequently she vows not to go back to see him. Because of this, she delays an important study, screening exam, or follow-up that impacts her health and well-being.

With the ubiquity of sophisticated and accurate health information on the Internet, many patients can access usable, helpful resources for learning about their health. In this case, the importance of presenting medical information in the context of physician failure is clear. It can benefit the patient. The ethical perspective on this issue, however, is a little more ambiguous than others raised in this paper. Whereas the consequences of some of the other situations related in this paper are clearly negative, one may actually argue for the benefits of highlighting failure in an underperforming physician and in the appropriateness of straining the relationship with an underperforming physician. Maybe one of the goals of health information Web sites should be to shock the health care industry into an honest accounting of their shortcomings. So where then does the ethical issue lie?

Despite the benefits of this knowledge, and the potential for better care, the reality is that patients rarely have the freedom to migrate to another provider so easily, much less to one of higher quality. They just cannot see anyone, anytime, usually due to complex and sometimes limiting policy arrangements. Simply identifying a better physician can be challenging. Furthermore, physicians are important actors in the system and should have the opportunity to improve. Dropping an underperforming physician adds no value to the system.

Patient knowledge of medical diagnosis and treatment has the power to significantly stress the doctor-patient relationship and cause accompanying harm. This relationship has been the touchstone of medical care for millennia. Many people see the qualitative aspects of this relationship as primary to the provision of excellent care. It provides for the significantly high proportion of doctor's visits for non-medical issues, enables the trust necessary for moving forward with difficult treatments and workups, and promotes a caring and therapeutic relationship that can have genuine benefit.

The availability of Internet-based information can erode this relationship.

The Internet has brought unprecedented volume and detail of medical knowledge to anyone with an Internet connection. Gone are the days when a patient must plaintively await the pronouncements of their physician with only a difficult-to-procure second opinion as remedy. Now anyone can browse online and find a number of diagnostic tools that can help hone in on the likely diagnoses. Some of these tools are excellent. They enable patients to enter a large number of symptoms and sift through numerous diagnoses. They can do it at their convenience and for as long as they like. And almost all of these tools are free.

In contrast, most primary care physicians have about 15 minutes to examine, diagnose, and treat a patient. The enormous volume of medical information that a primary care physician needs to know vastly surpasses what any single individual can command. Many physicians learn a great deal and nevertheless manage in this difficult situation by learning repeated pathways for diagnosis and therapy of common conditions. They sometimes run into trouble when an uncommon condition presents, uncommon symptoms overlay a common disease, or new knowledge changes the way a disease should be treated.

From here comes a significant problem. Physicians do make mistakes, and to patients who have placed unwarranted belief in their supremacy, such mistakes can ruin relationships and take patients away from some of the benefits that even their flawed physicians can offer.

Of course no one should excuse physicians who commit errors, or practice with egregious gaps in knowledge. If the information exists, a modern health care system should absolutely deliver the best possible care in every case. However this is a difficult task, despite the best intentions of most physicians.

The potential remedies to address this situation call on patients, physicians, and their sources of information. In general, humility and an honest appraisal of limits and the complexity of the tasks are of prime value to both patients and physicians. A reevaluation of the roles of physicians from being the sole and highest agents in health care needs to yield to a perspective of physicians as members of teams, vulnerable to memory lapses and incomplete knowledge. Patients must be members of these teams, as are online information providers, who need to facilitate understanding of both medical information and the roles of all. As the providers of this information, with profound ability to deliver information, they can help refashion expectations and relationships.

Finding and double-checking information should not be seen as an exercise in "gotcha," and rather should be seen as more of a necessary component in fault tolerance, the industrial engineering principle that guards against adverse consequences from single points of failure. We all need to rethink our views of physicians in this milieu. And through this refashioning we can enlist physicians where they may have been threatened, we can provide increased sophistication of understanding in patients who may feel wronged, and we can, in the process, engineer a more robust system of care where health and outcomes trump egos.

Online providers of health tools have a role to play in all of this by helping to facilitate this new relationship. By giving patients new ways to think about how they manage their health and sharing opportunities to participate, health Web sites can accept the ethical burden of instructing not only about health, but about some of the ways of structuring care relationships. Because some providers are reticent and unfamiliar with these new and popular modes of patient involvement with their own health, online health providers have an opportunity and a duty to address a gap they have a role in enabling.

Anxiety and Psychology of Patients

If you can remedy your suffering, there is no reason to worry. If there is no remedy, there is no reason to worry.

Buddhist saying

Ms. Blue wakes one weekend morning with a stomach discomfort. She feels as if she has not digested her food well, and it seems worse than the other similar feelings she's had. It is true that she had a large dinner last night, and that she's under stress, but it feels worse than it should. So she goes to the Internet and looks up her symptoms. When she puts in her symptoms, she finds that one of the top diagnoses is ovarian cancer. She spends the next several hours researching ovarian cancer, its diagnostic symptoms, epidemiology, poor survival rate, and treatment options. Convinced she has ovarian cancer, she goes to see her physician first thing on Monday morning certain she has ovarian cancer. She demands a CA-125 enzyme assay test, and an ultrasound. When her physician informs her that because of her negative family history, her low risk profile, and the absence of other symptoms a screening assay may be inappropriate, she gets angry, partially as an expression of her anxiety from her presumed diagnosis.

With the proliferation of online health resources, and the high cost and other obstacles to access, patients increasingly take it upon themselves to research, diagnose, and in some cases treat their own illnesses. Overall this is a positive development on the health care landscape. Patients have the best access to their own symptoms, and the greatest investment in their own treatment and health. Yet risks abound.

Problems arise when the subtlety of symptoms or lack of medical experience give rise to the wrong diagnosis and its accompanying effects. Physicians with a great deal of training and access to significant reference resources frequently make wrong diagnoses. Patients, it can be assumed, do so even more often. When people without adequate self-knowledge allow their fears and other issues to run away with themselves, outside of an established care relationship with a health professional, avoidable anxiety and stress can ensue. With the availability and incentive to practice do-it-yourself medicine, sequelae of incorrect treatment or testing can cause lasting harm.

Online health information resources have a complicity in this problem, and purveyors of online health information expose people to the above risks. Almost all of them warn patients, and publish alerts and indemnifications against responsibility for misuse or from negative consequences of the information. And clearly, the obvious remedy, keeping information secret, is not a viable option. In general the availability of information is a positive development, and allows patients to be more aware and active in their own health and care.

No easy solutions exist. Like previous examples, a system of forthrightness and clarity of the risks needs to be made available to patients. Yet this is only one facet of the solution.

Because online health resources enable a new forum for health information delivery outside of the view of professionals, other structures must fill the void and provide protection, especially given the environment into which information is delivered.

Our population, much less our physicians and the larger health system, are not prepared for this group of patients who look up their information. We have paltry systems of public health information, and devote virtually no training to health professionals or health system workers who may be able to address misdiagnoses and anxiety in a proactive way. The problem is worse when we consider that a large number of people seek information online precisely because they cannot access direct care from a practitioner. Thus they are even more vulnerable to misdiagnosis and its accompanying perils.

One innovative solution would be a collaborative network or coalition of online health providers, patient groups, and health professionals to come together on a system of educational interventions that could provide people with tools to better avail themselves of the medical information and avoid pitfalls.

We have, for a long time, provided public health solutions in the form of medicines, vaccines, and disease-specific information. Now that we know that information is one of the strongest contributors to health, we should enable people to better derive health information from online sources in productive ways. We should teach people about symptoms and terminologies. We should educate our population to understand and utilize resources with greater sophistication and proficiency, to know that not all tests should be used as screening, for example. We already provide sophisticated information, images, diagnostic tools, and even therapies directly to consumers. Perhaps we should find ways to convey experience and wisdom as well.

Health and Health Care Disparities

The good we secure for ourselves is precarious and uncertain until it is secured for all of us and incorporated into our common life.

Jane Addams

Mr. and Mrs. Green live off of a fixed income very close to the poverty line. They have a couple of medical conditions for which they need chronic medication. Unfortunately some of their conditions need to be treated with name-brand medications. If they had an Internet connection, they could find out about cost savings programs for these medications, or they could easily order these medications from less expensive pharmacies?. But because they do not have access, they end up paying double what they would have to pay and it adds up to a sizable percentage of their disposable income each month. With an online connection, they could also find out about free clinics, health fairs, and other opportunities to get access. But like a cruel irony, those who most need the benefits that online health services have to offer, are the least able to learn about and avail themselves of the opportunities.

Researchers have documented that those of lower socioeconomic status have worse access to care. They tend to visit physicians less, and when they do, they tend to receive worse care, less aggressive treatment, and less preventive screening. They suffer higher mortality rates and lower life expectancy. Consequently, those who seek to improve health, share a moral consideration to improve access to care for those who are disadvantaged.

Disparities in access to care present an interesting irony in the context of health information technology. Lower socioeconomic groups have the most to gain from increasingly online delivery, yet they tend be least likely to avail themselves of it. Physician density is far lower in poorer neighborhoods. Hospitals are less common, and ancillary services rarely locate in those places where their potential income is less. This, combined with the historically reduced quality of care for these people makes online health information technology especially valuable. In practice, however, poorer people have less comfort with technology, less Internet access, and fewer computers. They have lower levels of self-efficacy, and reduced sophistication, education, and language skills necessary to benefit from online health offerings.

Online health offerings that could bridge the gaps in care can be readily imagined. Many of these innovations would provide the types of routine care and protocols that could be automated and delivered online. For those who have poor access to physicians, many health services functions could be automated. For communities where greater interpersonal and communal interactions are sought, one could imagine call centers or other organized methods of delivery.

Online health businesses can address these issues in two ways. First they should be aware that underprivileged groups have lower access to care and should provide those sorts of health care needs suited to these populations. They should provide tools that promote preventive screening, healthier lifestyle supports, and chronic disease care so direly in need by members of these groups. Secondly, online health providers should consider this lower socioeconomic demographic when fashioning the technology, in order to increase the attractiveness and uptake of online tools to those populations so frequently left out of the calculus.

Web sites that address health and disease should have offerings in Spanish as well as English. There should be visual tools that present multi-ethnic images, icons, and examples. Market tests should incorporate those of minority groups and provide for their needs. In the same ways as we should not discriminate in providing care, our electronic systems should appeal to the broadest range of patients. Rather than being driven by the fact that some users are more valuable than others to advertisers, online health sites should act from the view that all people deserve and need the kinds of health support that technology can offer.

As health care moves increasingly to Internet-based modalities, we will have to find ways to affect the imbalance in access to information technology that can improve the existing disparities. We will also, ironically, have to address exacerbations in disparities caused by the remedies themselves.

Conclusion

The different fields of medicine and health services went through a maturation process over the millennia. They began as ideas, were tried, and ultimately found a mature place in practice. Pharmacology, surgery, radiology, and now information technology have all had to grapple with the potential problems caused by their use. Information technology has some features that are similar to the other areas of medicine, and some areas which are distinct. What is similar is that the health information tools have genuine utility. They can inform, guide, and enable understanding that can drive effective health care. Conversely they can cause harm in the areas we saw above, in privacy, integrity of information, damage to the doctor-patient relationship, anxiety in patients, and in disparities in health and access.

One of the more interesting distinctions of information technology in health, and especially online health information technology, is the diffusion of these tools outside the traditional practitioners and their professional codes. Complex, detailed medical information is now available to the lay public who never before had access, and the mechanisms of diffusion of this information are coming from those who never before were able to produce, much less deliver health information.

So now more than ever, anyone can give diet advice to hundreds of thousands of people. Or do the same with virtually any condition. Amazingly, some amateurs are able to produce excellent materials that rival in quality and accessibility, those products of the most lauded individuals in the field, and in many cases, surpasses them. Unfortunately, no mechanism currently exists to ensure that these individuals maintain the highest ethical standards that protect the patients they aim to serve.

When looking at health information technology generally, and online health information technology specifically, we must remain humble and admit that we are at a very early stage. Google has been around for less than 10 years. Most other sources and tools of online information technology have not even been around that long.

We are currently discovering how to accomplish the delivery of excellent and useful tools at the same time as we are trying to find how to do it in the most responsible ways. Considering the ethics at every step will be an important ingredient in growing strong and effective health information tools. The stakes are high. These information tools may one day have an even greater role in preserving and restoring health than the medicines, surgeries, and laboratory studies that currently dominate health care. And as such, they will have to command the same highest standards of ethics of their medical forebears.

Reading **7-3**

Bridging the Digital Gap in Emerging Economies

Geetanee Napal

Abstract

While there is a feeling that the construction of an information society could be the key to economic development and modernization, access to new technologies requires high income and reasonable education levels. Where the provision of technological infrastructure is concerned, governments of developing economies draw a distinction between rural and urban areas, under the assumption that inhabitants of villages have no interest in technology and do not need access to information and communication technology. This perception can be challenged, however, as discussed in this paper. Governments of developing nations should invest in technological resources and education if their aim is to contribute to the development of depressed regions and promote global citizenship and human rights worldwide. Having said this, developing economies are at a disadvantage as compared with first-world nations in the field of technology.

How do developed economies expect the less developed world to cope with the challenges facing the global economy? As the priorities of business evolve on the global market, the challenges posed by maintaining standards of business ethics in least developed countries requires growing attention; already the less developed world is vulnerable to ethical issues based on economic exigency. If poor economies were to face ethical issues arising from technological advances which is likely to be the case as they interact on the global scene, notions of ethics need to be strengthened and people educated in order to overcome the problem of knowledge and technology divide between rich and poor.

Introduction

The recognition of digital divide as a significant problem has led several scholars, policy makers and the public at large to realise the "potential of the Internet to improve everyday life for those on the margins of society and to achieve greater social equity and empowerment" (Mehra et al., 2004: 782). While technology revolutionises the nature and speed of communication across nations, the risks that accompany such rapid evolution—cyber crimes; hacking; cyber scams and frauds; Internet defamation; software piracy; copyright infringement—should not be overlooked.

Ideally globalisation should impact people's lives in a positive manner such as enhancing standards of living as a result of consistent economic growth that derives from increased trade and investment. However, do the above statements not solely reflect the impact on developed economies? Is there not a controversial issue if we consider the contrary impact on less developed countries (LDCs) where there is a concentration of power amongst a minority elite who do not consider it quite so profitable to invest in the development of information and communication technology (ICT) for their populations?

If the above statements are restricted to economies that have the means to invest in ICT infrastructure, where do the LDCs fit in? The tendency in LDCs and beyond is to assume that the poor do not need access to technology, hence the slow development pattern that characterises rural areas.

The objective of this discussion is to raise awareness as to the ethical issues likely to affect the developing world as a result of this digital divide. The discussion starts with a definition of the digital divide and a brief outline of the basic factors likely to cause this trend such as gender, social status or age. This is followed by an overview of the issues that are bound to impact on LDCs as a result of the digital divide. These issues include access to ICT infrastructure and education; distribution and use of power in LDCs; corrupt practices in the form of bribery, favouritism and nepotism; infringement of property rights and/or property theft; information gathering through spying. Following this exploration, we address the question of whether 'new ethics' is needed to handle ethical issues associated with technological evolutions. Lastly, we refer to the example of India where attempts have been made to bridge the digital gap by providing traditional village gathering places with Internet-connected computers.

The Digital Divide

'Digital divide' is a term that refers to the gap between those populations who have regular, effective access to digital and information technology and those without equivalent access. The digital divide could be the outcome of various factors worldwide. If gender-based, it depends on whether the female population has access to education. Results of a broad survey of 15 Western European countries demonstrate that—"females, manual workers, elderly and the less educated have less Internet access than males, professionals, the young and the well educated" (Cheung, 2004: 63). If there are discriminatory practices against minority groups, does this not constitute an infringement of people's rights? If the minority are suffering prejudice and are being denied the chance to education and access to ICT, are basic human rights not being violated? If such is the situation in Western economies, we can only imagine how worse off LDCs are. As it is, they already face constraints when it comes to information technology infrastructure and ICT resources in general. In addition to IT infrastructure, transportation infrastructure poses problems in some emerging economies.

As some parts of the global economy experience rapid economic growth, others are characterized by poverty, conflict, corruption, famine, illness and illiteracy (Werhane et al., 2008). Hart (2007) refers to an elite group of executives, employees and shareholders as the sole beneficiaries of the wealth created by multinational enterprises. As the world population grows, a considerable percentage of people of big developing countries like India and China live in utter poverty (cited in Werhane et al., 2008). The same pattern characterises most African economies and Mauritius constitutes no exception (Napal, 2001). In the Mauritian context, the political class denies the existence of poverty in the country although many families have similar living conditions to those as described by Werhane et al. (2008). Such families are often considered as marginal in the Mauritian society. As a response to the difficult conditions facing them, these people have developed feelings of resignation and 'evolve' in their own subculture, which is characterized by feelings of marginality, inferiority, pessimism, and even fatalism. Morally and financially, they feel dependent on others for their survival. They feel excluded from the rest of society and have no interest to compete on the job market. Sadly enough, these are the people who bestow upon the political class the privilege of power and who get brainwashed by the political class at times of elections. Can something be done to get these people out of poverty? A whole educational process needs to take place; but, then again, somehow this marginalized sector of society must be helped to develop a sense of their selves so that they may resist the lure of power from above.[1]

How do we expect less wealthy nations to keep pace with the technological advances taking place globally?

Implications of the Digital Divide

The digital divide is bound to have more serious repercussions on economies that have limited means to invest in ICT. In such an environment, business people are more likely to engage in questionable practices in an effort to 'match' the standard of their business counterparts on the global market. In some LDCs, the problem of the digital divide may be the outcome of an imbalance of diffusion of ICT infrastructure, high online charges, insufficiently trained staff, imperfect network legation and information resource shortage in international languages. Some less wealthy nations may have difficulty achieving connectivity in some LDCs in particular in rural areas. The lack of purchasing power or low population densities in less favourable regions could deter telecommunication providers from investing in broadening their networks.

Inevitably income constitutes a problem for these people. Even if the problem of infrastructure for connectivity is resolved in suburbs, high costs of Internet-compatible computers still have to be faced. Sometimes, market forces push Internet Service Providers to "shy away from investing in these regions that show little promise of short-term profits" (Wilhelm, 2004: 133-134). Wilhelm's findings imply that preference is given to more favourable areas, more than likely urban settings to the detriment of rural ones in LDCs. However, is it fair to quantify returns on a public service in such a way as to hinder the dissemination of knowledge in unfavourable/disadvantaged regions?

Ethical questions that are bound to arise in LDCs include issues relating to access to ICT infrastructure and education; distribution and use of power; corrupt practices in the form of bribery, favouritism and nepotism; infringement of property rights; information gathering through spying.

Access to ICT Infrastructure and Education

Education levels are likely to influence PC and Internet access: those with higher levels of education are more likely to be equipped with information and communication technologies at home and/or at work. Similarly, education is closely correlated to income, which obviously facilitates the purchase of ICTs and inclusion in both home and work settings. However, when income levels are taken into account, those with higher educational achievements may benefit of higher rates of access. It is equally important to note that illiteracy constitutes a major problem in many LDCs. A lack of education contributes to the digital divide in the less developed world as it does between the rural and urban areas of some developing nations. Could we not rationally say that it is the priority of responsible governments to undertake the initiative to improve education in disadvantaged regions if their objective is to build an information society and bridge the digital gap? At least in Mauritian context, this is only legitimate as political campaigns always emphasise such priorities, in an attempt to buy votes.

Other factors influencing the development of ICT are the strength of the telecommunications industry and access to Internet connection in emerging economies. It is understood that income is a key factor at determining whether or not people would have access to information technology. Do governments of emerging economies invest in the development of ICT infrastructure? Do they draw a distinction between urban and rural areas? Do governments discriminate against rural regions when investing in ICT? Is there a balance in telecommunication development between rural and urban areas in LDCs? What about regions that are at a geographical disadvantage?

If public expenditure were manipulated and driven away from growth-promoting areas and essential services like education and ICTs, could public funds be diverted to where bribes are easy to collect? The culture of corruption that prevails in developing nations diverts public goods from ever reaching the poor. In addition, the latter are victimized as they are expected to pay bribes for public services they are entitled to free-of-charge (Werhane et al., 2008). There are even instances where the authorities hold back their services because they have no guarantee of economic pay-off. Already there is evidence of a concentration of public spending in low-productivity projects such as large-scale construction to the detriment of value-enhancing investments like improvements in the quality of social infrastructure and ICTs (Blackburn et al., 2006).

Distribution, Use of Power and Corruption

Would the abuse of discretionary power and monopolistic nature of the state not breed the digital divide? Many LDCs have an individualistic culture where one's immediate obligation goes to one's relations, which may override one's notion of duty as spelled out by basic ethics concepts. This inevitably gives rise to corrupt practices in the form of favouritism and nepotism. What about favouritism and nepotism where access to facilities like ICT infrastructure is concerned? It is a well-known fact that democracy in emerging economies tends to encourage the abuse of power to suit one's vested interests. This is because emerging democracies may not have effective systems of checks and balances, which tends to give way to greater political access coupled with greater flexibility with the way public funds, are dispensed (Mohtadi and Roe, 2001).

Referring to the likely abuse of discretionary power on the part of the political class, if citizens who are at an advantage use their position to avail of access to ICTs while the disadvantaged lag behind, would this not give rise to further inequity with regard to education and IT competencies? What about citizens who do not have the right network to channel their request for such facilities? Is there any scope for them? What about illicit payments effected to gain access to ICT or to secure connectivity? Again, wealthy citizens willing to pay bribes would be at an advantage whereas less wealthy ones would be penalised.

Infringement of Intellectual Property Rights/Theft of Property

Intellectual property may be tangible or intangible. Intangible property can be far more valuable and difficult to protect than tangible assets. It is hard to put a value on intangible assets like the ability to innovate; codified knowledge about products and processes; employee assets in the form of talented people and human capital. While being highly precious to the organisation, these assets are also vulnerable to infringement and theft (Hagan and Moon, 2006). Besides, are intangible forms of property like software, product formulation, formulae, inventions or processing techniques recognised as such? What restrictions can and should be placed on different forms of property including digital information? What exactly constitutes ethical transgression?

Property theft can take the form of insider trading, counterfeit products, or price gouging. Insider trading takes place when one uses privileged information as one's own. A common form of theft is the use of proprietary information to further another firm's ends. Such information is normally accessed through the unauthorised use of company computers and programmes (Fritzsche, 2005).

Information Gathering through Spying

Other factors to consider include the level of education of the population and income levels. If people in LDCs feel that they are not at par with their business partners on the global market, they could engage in unethical competitive behaviour in an attempt to match the performance of their rivals. Crane and Matten (2004) refer to industrial espionage through questionable practices in the normal business settings in European context. However, if this were to apply to LDCs, it could take an even more dramatic turn. What if business people instigate a process of intelligence gathering through spying by having recourse to suspicious means? What if they deliberately flout the legal and ethical practices underlying conventional information gathering or market research? What if spying and information gathering contravene the privacy and confidentiality of competitors and/or other stakeholders in the process? As bribery represents a normal way of doing business in LDCs, what if as a result of differences that exist between rural and urban settings, bribes are offered to induce competitors' employees to access confidential information and trade secrets? If all these issues are taken into consideration, it is obvious that businesses are at risk. In order to protect themselves and to retain their goodwill, they may have to invest in resources to preserve trade secrets, patents, copyrights, trademarks and intellectual property rights including rights on intangible property like software, product formulation, processing techniques to name but a few. The development of new technologies will keep encouraging ethical debates on what exactly constitutes intellectual property (Crane and Matten, 2004; Ghillyer, 2008).

Considering the above, there is a need to acknowledge the seriousness of problems that can potentially be caused by the digital divide. The next part of our discussion focuses on whether we need new ethics to address these issues.

Do We Need New Ethics to Accompany Growing Technological Developments?

So far, increasing replication of digital information and unauthorised accessing and exploitation of intellectual property have accompanied on-going developments in ICTs (Crane and Matten, 2004). As concepts like computer ethics and digital divide continue to grow in importance globally, questions arise as to whether business ethics, as it applies to issues surrounding technology, should be re-visited (Ghillyer, 2008; Hagan and Moon, 2006; Hartman and Desjardins, 2008; Suresh and Raghavan, 2005). Bearing in mind the characteristics of LDCs, notions of ethics need to be reinforced to cope with such changing tendencies as well as to handle basic ethical issues associated with their individualistic culture. Unless a culture of ethics is more effectively instilled, there is potential for harmful business practices leading to serious losses and long-term economic decline.

Ghillyer (2008) lays emphasis on the ten commandments of computer ethics and raises the question as to whether some new code should be adopted for the global community. The fact is that in spite of the existence of the United Nations' Non Governmental Global Compact and the Organisation for Economic Cooperation and Development Guidelines for Multinational Enterprises, ethical misconduct prevails in international business. Ghillyer (2008) proposes a global code of conduct as the solution to moral issues encountered in the context of globalisation. Does the problem not lie with the interpretation of concepts of ethics and codes of ethics that is, with enforcement? After all ethics codes exist worldwide but are subject to varying interpretation, as are universal principles. As they are not legally binding, codes of ethics tend to be regarded as optional while business people have a tendency to underestimate their importance.

While business partners fulfil their responsibility towards their stakeholders, it is the duty of every responsible government to lead by example and breed a culture of ethics at national level. It is equally their responsibility to bridge the digital gap, foster corporate social responsibility and sustain efforts towards the convergence of ethics by providing the necessary infrastructure at national level and this includes putting in place appropriate telecommunication devices. There is evidence that political people in LDCs often welcome corporate investors under 'flexible' terms in the name of economic growth. What if this comprises investment in ICTs and public funds are channelled towards subquality products? If this were the case, would governments not be deliberately inflicting economic and human rights abuses on their people in the name of growth? All this considered ethics is there and should not only be regarded as an academic discipline. While there is no need for new ethics, both private and public sectors should reflect on their mode of doing business and ensure they fulfil their duty towards their stakeholders.

Technology offers a unique opportunity to extend learning support beyond the classroom, something that LDCs have been unable to do until recently. "The variety of functions that the Internet can serve for the individual user makes it 'unprecedentedly malleable' to the user's current needs and purposes" (Bargh and McKenna, 2004: 577). In addition to this view, there is a perception that the building of an information society is the key to economic development and modernization (Dey, 2005), implying that this would naturally pull an economy out of poverty. New technology may bring advantages like contribute to the development of depressed regions and promote global citizenship and human rights amongst other positive things (Argandona, 2003; Richter and Mar, 2004). However, one could argue that there is a bit of a controversial issue there. Does a poor economy have the means of investing in and developing information technology in a way that would enable it to compete with a first-world nation? If competing on the global market, can an LDC compare with a developed one? Are people in LDCs educated and sufficiently well versed in ICTs? The answer could be no, hence the conclusion reached by Hartman and Desjardins (2008), namely that, in economies or contexts where people do not understand technological improvement, they may not be as effectively positioned to benefit as quickly from such advances. This implies that they are also not as adequately prepared to handle the challenges associated with hi tech advancement. In the circumstances, should the priority of major stakeholders—the government, state-owned enterprises, business entities, research institutes, universities—not be to bridge the digital divide at national level?

Bridging the Gap

Telecommunications infrastructure could be developed and sustained in a consistent manner with proper strategic thinking. Should governments of developing nations not pursue reform as part of their national policy to promote their economy on the global market through science and technology? Should they not encourage industrialisation by virtue of IT development and explore means of further developing information technology to accommodate their own needs on economic, social and political fronts? Does the fact that the domestic telecommunication market is gradually opening up to foreign investors and competitors not justify increasing investment in the telecommunication arena in LDCs? Countries that are members of international bodies like the World Trade Organisation are at an advantage. Such affiliation acts as an external drive force for them to persevere at pursuing and sustaining reform in the field of telecommunications and technology. Technological reform should be the priority of all economies involved in global operations, irrespective of how developed they are. India provides a good example of technological progress in the context of agriculture where access to ICT enabled farmers to operate more effectively and profitably.

The example of the *e-Choupal* in India illustrates the potential that technology can bring to rural communities and LDCs in general. The *e-Choupal* demonstrated progress achieved in the field of technology in Indian suburbs. The *e-Choupal* is a new system developed by the Indian conglomerate ITC, whereby farmers are provided with a computer and Internet connection in their traditional village gathering place, which gives them access to many different *mandis* (government mandated marketplaces). Traditionally, farmers went to a single *mandi* and sold their product through ineffective and often dishonest physical marketplaces (Banker and Mitra, 2005). Farmers had no control over the price of their products as they are by and large poor and illiterate. Moreover, commission agents abused of their power to the detriment of farmers who had very limited access to information and education on farming techniques. The introduction of the *e-Choupal* helped rural farmers benefit from easier access to information, better social standing, wider choice and mastery over their lives (Prahalad 2005, cited in Kelley et al., 2007).

The *e-Choupal* has enabled the re-engineering of the old-fashioned export supply chain by giving these people access to digital technology in rural farm villages. The *e-Choupal* is founded on knowledge derived from a combination of technology, sociology and the incentives of the various players involved. This relatively new concept provides farmers with effective methods of price discovery, honest trading and information sharing and is of potential benefit to all stakeholders. The findings of Upton and Fuller (2003) reflect the views of farmers of public marketplaces who claim that before they were introduced to *e-Choupal* by the ITC, they were restricted to selling their produce at low prices in the local mandi, through the intermediary of middlemen who did not necessarily respect their rights. The ITC trained farmers to enable them to manage the Internet kiosk.

There is now a community of e-farmers with access to daily prices of a variety of crops in India and abroad. Access to technology helps these farmers obtain the best price for their produce. They also have access to information on weather forecasts, latest farming techniques, crop insurance, amongst other things. *e-Choupal* has not only changed the quality of Indian farmers' lives, but it has transformed their entire outlook. The strategic intent of the ITC is to develop the *e-Choupal* as a significant two-way multidimensional distribution channel, facilitating the transport of goods and services out of and into rural India. The ITC is transforming the way farmers do business and the way rural markets operate by progressively linking the digital infrastructure to a physical network of rural business hubs and agro-extension services (ITC Limited, undated).

The example of the *e-Choupal* demonstrates that the poor can operate more efficiently if they have access technology, unlike the common belief that they do not need or are not interested in technology (Kelley et al., 2007). The common purpose of such initiatives is to link rural communities to the Internet, give them access to timely price information, disseminate knowledge to producers and allow these producers to execute trades and transactions. The idea is to e-empower the people, eliminate intermediaries, reduce unscrupulous trading and consequently transform the global agricultural supply chain.

Conclusion

As more and more nations with different cultural and historical experiences interact in the global economy, the potential for misunderstandings based on different expectations and poor communication is magnified. As firms either choose to or are forced to compete internationally, ethical questions inevitably arise. There are real communication problems in the developing world and in these conditions, the people have yet to be prepared to contribute to high technology, satellite communication, bulk transport, e-commerce, computerization and robotics.

Problems faced by LDCs include low income, low education/literacy levels, language, disparity in knowledge dissemination and limitations of telecommunications industry amongst other weaknesses. The way power is distributed tends to exempt policy makers from public accountability hence encouraging unethical practices, driving talented people away from productive activities, thereby negatively impacting on growth (Mohtadi and Roe, 2001). Survival in this rapidly evolving global economy requires the acquisition of more relevant competencies like high-level performance in cultivating organisational alliances, partnerships and synergy across frontiers. Referring to the ethical issues likely to result from new technologies in a global era, contemporary ethicists raise the question as to whether 'new ethics' is needed but the verdict is that ethics as a concept remains unchanged. It is the interpretation given to the concept and its application in the context of business and governance that would make a difference.

As traditions of power abuse contribute to widen the digital gap in societies characterised by low standard of living, scarcity of goods, unhealthy competition and spying through the most unscrupulous means, efforts should be directed toward productive means to bridge the divide. The Indian model gives evidence of the power of information technology to generate the potential to bring about higher commodity prices for farmers while reducing unfair trading practices by middlemen to bridge the digital divide. Provided there is a will to invest in technological infrastructure, key stakeholders could undertake to successfully bridge the digital divide which would enable LDCs to interact on the global market and minimise the likelihood of ethical issues, as discussed above.

In addition, we have a global responsibility to encourage those living in poverty to learn about and to acquire ICT skills. While the introduction of computers equipped with Internet facilities has improved the lives of farmers in India, there is no guarantee that this approach would bear the same results in the rural areas, such as Mauritius. Referring to the poor section of the Mauritian population, there may not be a readiness to adapt to this new life style, no matter how beneficial it may be to them in the long term. These people may have become so accustomed to a pattern of life that they feel quite comfortable following the same trend, even though this involves dependency on society. It is that society's responsibility to help to relieve it.

End Note

1. These and later references to the Mauritian con text result from the author's personal experiences.

References

Note: Notes and references removed for publication here, but are available on the book website at www .mhhe.com/busethics2e.

Reading 7-4

The Ethical Use of Technology in Business

Tony Mordini

Abstract

The business environment is dependent upon technology for a range of functions. The potential for communication, data management and business processes are endless but so too are the potential misuses of the technology. This poses problems which often require some ethical perspectives to be considered. In monitoring e-mail, phone and human traffic how much are we encroaching on personal space? In providing employees with technological tools such as lap top computers and cell phones what controls can we legitimately exercise on how they use them? In capturing data from staff and clients what safeguards need to be put in place to ensure information is not misused? There may not be a simple model that fits all contexts but the field of Applied Ethics provides research, frameworks and educational instruments that can help to maximize the ethical use of technology in business and help to articulate the issues, identify what is expected in particular contexts and propose appropriate ways to engender compliance.

Introduction

Technology is embedded in all aspects of our lives to the extent that we would find it difficult to conduct many of our day to day activities without it. The business environment is no different. Technology is used in a myriad of ways including: communication; information and data capture, processing, analysis and storage; monitoring of business performance; electronic commerce; and surveillance.

The developments in information communication technology (ICT) have also resulted in the boundaries between individuals' private and public lives becoming significantly blurred. The cell phone means that people are contactable at almost any time, any where; wireless e-mail communication means faster response rates which can place pressure on individuals to not take a considered, metered approach in decision-making and like cell phones be able to send and receive e-mails almost anywhere and at any time; Web-based social networking can create distractions for individuals in the workplace and surveillance of work sites, Internet traffic and phone usage provide rich data for employers but also present a privacy risk if data is misused.

Ethical Issues with Respect to the Use of Technology

The potential misuse of technology in the business environment is a real risk and presents many challenges for those leading and managing work sites and well as their employees. Technology is an integral business tool with the potential and capabilities to support a range of business functions and create value. However, technology also has the potential to invade individuals' personal lives, distract them from their work, cost businesses significantly if the technology resources are not deployed effectively and requires sound risk management to ensure data is not misappropriated. Some economic projections are explored in a case study that follows. These issues also represent some significant ethical questions for both employers and employees. The problem is that often the issues associated with the use of technology in business environments are not recognized as having potential risks nor that ethical frameworks need to be applied in relation to its use.

Looking at Issues Ethically

Jennifer Jackson (1996) proposes that the difficulties in ascertaining what is ethical and what isn't begins with the notions of *identification and compliance.* Specifically ascertaining what an individual's duties are in a particular situation, how they are expected to perform those duties and how the resources are expected to be deployed in executing those duties need to be articulated in the first instance. Subsequently, the employee needs to actually understand, appreciate and commit to actually doing what they know they ought to do.

Her foundational elements provide a basis for employer and employee to clearly communicate what is expected. Ostensibly employers (often and preferably in consultation with relevant stakeholders) need to work out and subsequently articulate what the job entails and how they expect it to be carried out and what the workplace "rules" will be.

Employees need to clearly understand the "rules" and how these are to be applied. The issue of compliance becomes difficult Jackson notes when the rules are not followed equitably. Where employees see different levels of application (for example, the VP has certain benefits that others don't have), they will at best accept apply the "rules" begrudgingly and at worst find surreptitious ways to "compensate themselves" (p.11).

How do employers work out how best to manage the technology and what frameworks can they use to ensure current and future technologies are approached appropriately? How can they foster an ethical culture in their workplace? Obviously each context needs to be examined on its own merits and models cannot be presumed to be all encompassing but from what has been examined in earlier chapters you have some useful frameworks that you can apply as long as you consider the elements in each case carefully. As John Haldane (1999), suggests that there is a "moral danger in applied ethics" (p.726). Similar to the attack that Socrates made on the Sophists. The Sophists were seen as the "purveyors of moral and political wisdom in the Greek city-states in the fifth century BC". Haldane raises a cautionary note. It is risky to believe that some mechanical formula can be simply applied to all moral issues. Haldane argues it is "a disservice to philosophy" and could lead to a "spread of moral irrationalism" (ibid).

Thus we will proceed with a degree of caution and practicality but at the same time with a degree of confidence that to examine all that we do through an ethical framework has potential for positive personal, professional and business outcomes.

Looking at Business Issues Ethically

Case 1—Who Owns the Technology?

Miranda Rusden is a student liaison officer in the admissions office of a large university. Her main task is to attend to online and phone enquiries and relieve the receptionist when she needs to be away from her post. She has worked in this job for four years and although not overly challenged by the role is not interested in promotion. It suits her family and personal commitments because it is a "nine to five" job and it has few demands out of normal work hours. Furthermore, during semester breaks her days can be pretty quiet.

In the quiet times she will often use the time to catch up on personal e-mails, surf the Web looking at online stores or connect to social networking sites. The university has policies in place on the use of the Internet but Miranda has justified the activity to herself as harmless. Furthermore, she feels that if she has done all that she has been asked to do or is able to answer any enquiries as they come in by phone, fax or e-mail she should be able to make use of the time this way. She feels that if she were to take any initiative to do additional tasks that it would bring attention to the fact that she is not overly challenged. If she is at her computer and appears to be hard at work people will leave her alone.

A recent audit of Internet usage has revealed that a number of university personnel are using work time to access online shopping and social networking. Miranda's manager, upon receiving the report from her Head of Division is amazed at the amount of time Miranda has spent on the Internet engaged in personal activities over the past month. She prepares to call her into a meeting and according to university policy, serve her with a formal written warning and advise her that a subsequent offence could result in a termination of her employment. She finds herself in a difficult situation as she gets on really well with Miranda but knows that it is strictly a business matter and hopes that Miranda will see it that way.

Ethical Analysis

The issues of work time and work equipment are critical factors in assessing and addressing a case like this. Individuals are often entrusted to do a job and act in good faith. Furthermore, the employer provides the "tools" to do the job and expects the employee to use these tools appropriately, and as they are intended to be used.

What Miranda did is common practice and many organizations would find similar evidence if they were to audit the Internet use of their employees. However, what would be even more telling would be if the audit was to also provide the costs of the lost productivity. Imagine for example, that Miranda is one of 3,000 staff and that 10% (300 staff) are chronic abusers of the technology and the audit reveals that they spend approximately 1 hour a day on the Internet in private activities. That amounts to 5 hours of a 40 hour work week, thus 1/8 th of the individual's time is not being used productively. If the average salary for an employee in this sector is $50,000, 300 employees cost $15 million in salaries alone and a loss of productivity of even 1 hour a day equates to $1,875,000 or the equivalent of 37.5 full time staff.

Time for Thinking

Individuals in organizations do not often consider their actions from an ethical perspective, nor do they often do the math as per the previous example to see the impact of such behavior when it is magnified several times over. Examples such as these can be a simple way for teams to work constructively to eradicate losses in productivity but also provide a means of engaging in dialogue that examines behavior from an ethical perspective.

Case 2—Private Lives in the Public Arena

Chat rooms and Web-based social networking such as LinkedIn and Facebook connect individuals from all walks of life and with a myriad of interests. Such networks may have positive business outcomes. Matt Moore, Director of Innotecture, suggests that managed well, social networking and Web-based tools such as wikis and blogs can be turned to an employer's advantage.

> *If used well these tools allow participants to forge relationships with people they might never have found otherwise and do things they couldn't have done before. Social network analysis*[1] *allows individuals to better understand their own networks, as it also allows organizations to better understand the real complexity and power of the networks that form them (2008, p.38).*

However, as Moore, rightly points out, Social Networking Analysis will not identify many of the qualitative aspects of Web-based interactions. For example, how often is the approach a hindrance as opposed to a "helping hand"?

Another factor is that once connected to others in the public domain the lines between public and private become blurred. Blogging on a political site may make it clear what an individual's political leanings are. Participating in wikis means that any text a person writes in this space can be edited by others. Meeting people through Web-based social networks may expose individuals to a variety of risks. In face to face interactions there are a number of visual and audio cues which are hard to pick up through chat rooms and e-mail communication. Nor do individuals have control over information which is in the public domain.

Consider the case of Jonathan, a young finance graduate working for an investment bank. Jonathan is eager to succeed, bright, seen by many of the senior managers as a young guy who will "go places".

Jonathan is reasonably circumspect about his personal life. When at work he is focused on the job. He steers clear of personal chit chat. Like many young gay men he uses social networking sites to keep abreast of events, contact mates and make new friends.

One night, one of the senior staff, Mitch Hendricks is at home surfing the City of Chicago Web site looking up some information on upcoming events. He notices some advertising for Chicago's Gay Pride Week with a photograph of a group of gay men and a hyperlink to the group's Web site. Jonathan is amongst the group of men in the photograph. Although it is not a work related matter, he is concerned of the possible career implications this could have for Jonathan. Many of the senior men in the firm are quite conservative family men. He doesn't know Jonathan that well but hopes that meeting over a coffee will help to map out a strategy should a situation arise that could put Jonathan in a difficult place.

Mitch sends Jonathan an e-mail that night and fortunately Jonathan is online. He responds to the message almost immediately and agrees to a coffee at 10:00 am the next day. Jonathan thinks nothing of it and assumes it is some routine assignment he is being asked to work on. Mitch is uncomfortable about the meeting as he is concerned Jonathan may take it as an intrusion into his personal life. Mitch has grown up in a conservative Baptist family and except for his college years has not been exposed to a wide cross-section of the community. He is also a little anxious what others may deduce from their meeting.

Fortunately, for Mitch the meeting the next day is quite productive. Jonathan agrees with Mitch that although there should not be any problem with how he chooses to live his personal life, the firm and the sector he works in has some very conservative people and he may need to exercise careful judgment in how he balances his personal and professional lives and consider carefully how he might respond if a difficult situation was to arise.

For Mitch, the meeting also gave him a better understanding of how challenging things have been for Jonathan as he has come to terms with his identity and the potential problems it poses in the professional arena.

Ethical Analysis—Finding a Practical, Balanced and Responsible Position

Firms are rarely adequately prepared to respond to such issues. It is impossible to have one clear statement that covers all possible contingencies. Conventions such as freedom of association, freedom of speech, freedom of expression are constitutional rights. However, in practice, they can polarize people and create real tensions in the workplace or the community. Individuals' value systems particularly come into play on issues related to family responsibility, sexuality and religious beliefs and practices.

Workplaces need to be safe (in the broadest sense of the word physically, emotionally, psychologically etc.). Rules need to be in place to ensure that individuals are not marginalized. Individuals however, need to be reminded that what is in the public arena, means exactly that, *information is public* and people can view material, make a range of assumptions based on what they view, can disseminate it as they please and use it in a way that we never intended it to be used.

The technologies associated with social networking sites and other Web-based group activities can have positive outcomes providing networks and a means of accessing people but they can also expose individuals and their workplaces to various risks. However, firms may need to consider policies that clearly articulate their position. For example, institutions may need to consider disclaimers that enable them to clearly demarcate the boundaries between the individual's personal associations and their professional responsibilities. Notwithstanding this, in a number of professional areas such as teaching individuals may need to be reminded that their public and personal activity may impact adversely upon their professional life and that they may come under scrutiny by their employer if there appear to be any conflicts of interest or perceptions of moral impropriety.

Individuals may also need to be reminded that in public domain, Web-based contexts they may be providing people who they don't know with more personal information than they realize and that once it is in the public domain, it will be impossible to control where it is disseminated and who will have access to it.

Case 3—Is Surveillance Always Legitimate?

Many firms have closed circuit television (CCTV) as a deterrent to theft and as a means of providing a safer working environment. For example, if issues arise in a customer service setting, the employee can use digital evidence to defend claims that they may have acted inappropriately.

However, the images captured through the recording of movements on a site need to be stored safely and appropriately. Organizations need to also consider a number of related factors including: how long images will be stored, where they will be stored, in what format and who has the right to view them.

Consider the following scenario. Murray is a rising star in a national retail chain. He has recently been appointed to a small regional centre to manage their store. This is his first management job and we wants to impress. He is very ambitious and sees this appointment as a stepping stone to a bigger role back on the East Coast where he has come from. He knows that head office is very keen to see productivity efficiencies and he is very keen to deliver them. Discussions with senior staff at the store have provided anecdotal evidence that a number of staff are not really pulling their weight and wasting time in certain areas of the business. He decides to use CCTV evidence as a mechanism to provide the metrics he needed to embarrass some staff who are not performing as well as he believes they should be.

Soon after he arrived at his new store he called the manager of the security company monitoring his building and asked if they could meet in a down town coffee shop. On the day they met he stressed that he did not want others to find out about the meeting and that any evidence had to be handed to him directly.

Ethical Analysis

The following week was determined as the week that a specific monitoring would take place. The loading bay and stores area was picked as the area to be placed under closer scrutiny. The evidence was gathered and handed to Murray. He analyzed it as soon as he got it and as he presumed, provided some telling evidence. His initial thought was to call the team of staff in. It was evident that there were some real inefficiencies and time wasting. Murray could use a hard hitting approach challenging the ethical behavior of employees and use it to censure them. He knew however, that this group was heavily unionized. Even if he could justify his actions, he anticipated it could really go against him and the legitimacy of his actions would be questioned.

Taking Action—A Considered Way Forward

He planned therefore, to use the surveillance data to map out a work plan and then take the group through it. By changing some of the rosters which he justified on the basis of the times that goods were delivered across the day, and clearly outlining tasks that could be done in quiet times when there was no stock to unload or process he was able to use the data to help him manage a very ineffectual situation. He was able to use inferences such as: "I assume that in between trucks arriving it might get a bit boring in the stores . . . this will give us a bit of time to do some other tidying up and sort out stock that needs to be returned because it is faulty or broken. . . . I have provided a check list of what we should be trying to achieve on a daily and weekly basis . . .". There was some initial disquiet but Murray was correct in his comments that the group was not showing much initiative in the quiet times and that some clear direction would improve work output.

Some Concluding Remarks

In each of these case studies we see the potential and the possible pit falls of the technology. Used and managed appropriately it provides individuals and firms with the capacity to make better use of their time, network, research, analyze work flows, store information and improve efficiencies. However, technology may not always value add. Technology also increases risk for individuals and firms. Participating in the cyber world removes many barriers. Information in the public domain can injure the reputation of a firm or individual, misused or misappropriated data or information can create significant problems for people. Workplaces need to regularly review how they manage this aspect of their workplace. It is difficult because of the rate at which technology use is developing to have an all embracing policy in place. Policies need to have some level of flexibility, need to be reviewed regularly and need to have a level of flexibility to deal with current, emerging and future issues.

Above all, work places need to be ethical work places and individuals need to be encouraged to work in a manner that is compliant and based on an understanding of what is considered appropriate workplace practice, what are appropriate ways to engage with the technology they are using in the workplace and how they can minimize the risks associated with the use of technology in their day to day lives especially in their personal activities if it could potentially marginalize them or injure their reputation or efficacy in the workplace.

End Note

1. Social Network Analysis (SNA) is an instrument that has been used in Sociology since the 1930s to map relationships and collaborations between people. These maps help to illustrate the networks that exist in organizations and highlight areas where knowledge flow is poor or ineffective.

References

Note: Notes and references removed for publication here, but are available on the book website at www.mhhe.com/busethics2e.

Chapter 8

Ethics and Marketing

Reality is how we felt and saw events, not events as they appeared objectively, because we are not objective.

Anaïs Nin

A magazine is simply a device to induce people to read advertising.

James Collins

I am the world's worst salesman; therefore, I must make it easy for people to buy.

F. W. Woolworth (1852–1919)

Opening Decision Point

Marketing Pharmaceuticals

Pharmaceuticals provide an effective entry into many of the most important ethical issues of marketing. Because all drugs, but especially prescription drugs, involve health risks, the process of marketing pharmaceuticals raises questions of safety and liability for the potential harms caused by these products. Warnings of side-effects, often provided in small print or barely perceptible quickly-spoken side-bars, raise questions of deception. Some marketing practices that involve physicians or other health care professionals have raised questions as severe as bribery and manipulation. Television or magazine advertisements, called "direct-to-consumer" (DTC) advertising, has raised important questions of consumer autonomy and the possibility of exploiting vulnerable populations.

Consider the following aspects of pharmaceutical marketing that might give rise to ethical touch points.

The media and marketing firm, the Nielsen Company, reported that, in the first half of 2009, pharmaceutical companies spent more than $2.1 billion on advertising medications in the United States, an 11 percent decline from the previous year's spending. Only the automotive and fast food industries spent more on advertising than the pharmaceutical industry.

Advertisements promoting prescription drugs have increased significantly within the United States since the Food and Drug Administration (FDA) changed regulations in 1997 to allow DTC advertising. Among the most widely marketed drugs have been Lipitor, Zocor, Prilosec, Prevacid, Nexium, Celebrex, Vioxx, Zoloft, Paxil, Prozac, Viagra, Cialis, Levitra, Propecia, and Zyban. These drug names, literally household names today, were unheard of before the turn of the century; yet, together, they accounted for over $21 billion in sales in 2002.

The medications mentioned above treat the following conditions: ulcers and acid-reflux (Prilosec, Prevacid, Nexium), high cholesterol (Lipitor, Zocor), arthritis pain (Celebrex, Vioxx), depression, panic attacks, and anxiety (Zoloft, Paxil, Prozac), "erectile dysfunction" (Viagra, Cialis, and Levitra), hair loss (Propecia), and cigarette and nicotine withdrawal (Zyban). Ads for these drugs often appeal to such emotional considerations as embarrassment; fear; shame; social, sexual, and romantic inferiority; helplessness; vulnerability; and vanity. Many of these drugs are heavily advertised in women's magazines or during televised sporting events.

By definition, the consumers of prescription drugs have significant medical needs and, in some cases, they face life-threatening illnesses. This fact suggests that such consumers who are the targets for prescription drug advertising are vulnerable to exploitation by those who control access to drugs that promise help. The *Boston Globe* reported one controversial attempt to market pharmaceuticals in 2002 when sales representatives for TAP Pharmaceuticals, makers of Lupron Depot, an analgesic for treating pain associated with prostate cancer, were instructed to attend meetings of a prostate cancer support group to promote the drug directly to cancer patients. While pharmaceutical companies often provide support groups with financial assistance and informational materials, many critics believed that this action crossed the line of acceptable marketing, by directly targeting a population of vulnerable people. (See question number 8 at the end of this chapter for additional activities in connection with marketing this medication.)

Of course, consumers can only obtain prescription drugs legally by first obtaining a prescription from a licensed health care provider. As a result, physicians are a major target for marketing pharmaceuticals; and the sales representatives who work for pharmaceutical companies spend significant time and money trying to persuade physicians to prescribe their company's drugs. In the most egregious cases, marketing to doctors has included barely disguised instances of bribery in which physicians are paid fees as consultants and received expensive gifts. But most marketing to physicians has been more subtle, though no less effective. Small gifts of pens, pads, coffee mugs, mouse pads, calendars branded with the company or drug logo have been common gifts, as have free meals, paid travel to conferences, and various entertainment activities. Most importantly, pharmaceutical companies distribute large quantities of free drug samples to physicians. Pharmaceutical companies have always argued that these activities are all part of an ongoing effort to educate and inform health care professionals about their drugs. Critics claim that they are attempts to unduly influence and manipulate physicians into writing more prescriptions.

In an effort to respond to such criticisms, the Pharmaceutical Research and Manufacturers of America (PhRMA) revised its code of conduct to tighten rules for how sales reps can interact with health care providers. The revised rules went into effect in January 2009 and they prohibits distribution of non-educational items such as pens, mugs and other "reminder" objects to healthcare providers and their staff because such gifts "may foster misperceptions that company interactions with healthcare professionals are not based on informing them about medical and scientific issues." The new code also prohibits providing "restaurant meals" to health care providers, but they allow providing occasional meals in the doctor's office if they are part of an educational or informational presentation.

Critics argue that the gifts themselves are not crucial factor in making this practice ethically suspect. Rather, the access to physicians and the personal relationships between sales reps and doctors are the more important factors. Most importantly, perhaps, is the fact that sales reps regularly provide doctors with free samples of their prescription drugs, an easy and no-cost means for physicians to introduce their patients to specific drugs.

In an effort to control access of sales reps to physicians and avoid such conflicts of interest, the University of Pittsburgh Medical Centers instituted a ban in April 2009 on the delivery of drug samples to doctors' offices in all of its 20 hospitals directly by sales reps. The Medical Center had previously banned their physicians from accepting any gifts and meals from pharmaceutical company sales reps, but extended this policy to avoid actual or perceived conflicts of interests. Doctors can still request samples, and sales reps can provide them; but the transaction now occurs through a computerized system that prevents direct personal contact. "There is a concern that personal relationships can influence decision making," Dr. Barbara Barnes, the associate chancellor of the University of Pittsburgh said when announcing the new policy.

- What facts would you want to know before making a judgment on the ethical appropriateness of direct to consumer advertising of drugs?
- What ethical issues are involved in marketing prescription drugs?
- To what degree, if any, should drug manufacturers be held responsible for the side-effects caused by the drugs they sell?

(continued)

(concluded)

- Who are the stakeholders involved in direct to consumer advertising?
- What are the costs and benefits of marketing prescription drugs directly to physicians?
- What rights or duties might be involved when discussing issues relating to this subject area?
- Are voluntary codes of conduct created by an industry group effective means for establishing and enforcing ethical guidelines?

Chapter Objectives

After reading this chapter, you will be able to:

1. Apply an ethical framework to marketing issues.
2. Describe the three key concerns of ethical analysis of marketing issues.
3. Describe three interpretations of responsibility and apply them to the topic of product safety.
4. Explain contractual standards for establishing business's responsibilities for safe products.
5. Articulate the tort standards for establishing business's responsibilities for safe products.
6. Analyze the ethical arguments for and against strict product liability.
7. Discuss how to evaluate both ethical and unethical means by which to influence people through advertising.
8. Explain the ethical justification for advertising.
9. Trace debates about advertising's influence on consumer autonomy.
10. Distinguish ethical from unethical target marketing, using marketing to vulnerable populations as an example.
11. Discuss business's responsibilities for the activities of its supply chain.
12. Explain how marketing can contribute towards a more sustainable business model.

Introduction

Some believe that the very purpose of business is found within the marketing function. The description of business's purpose offered by marketing scholar Theodore Levitt is a case in point. Levitt suggested that:

> The purpose of a business is to create and keep a customer. To do that you have to produce and deliver goods and services that people want and value at prices and under conditions that are reasonably attractive relative to those offered by others. . . . It was not so long ago that a lot of companies assumed something quite different about the purpose of business. They said quite simply that the purpose is to make money. But that is as vacuous as to say that the purpose of life is to eat. Eating is a prerequisite, not a purpose of life . . . Profits can be made in lots of

> devious and transient ways. For people of affairs, a statement of purpose should provide guidance to the management of their affairs. To say that they should attract and hold customers forces facing the necessity of figuring out what people really want and value, and then catering to those wants and values. It provides specific guidance, and has moral merit.[1]

Similarly, the American Marketing Association defines **marketing** in a way that also suggests that it is at the heart of business activity, "an organizational function and a set of processes for creating, communicating, and delivering value to customers and for managing customer relationships in ways that benefit the organization and its stakeholders."[2]

The concept of an exchange between a seller and a buyer is central to the market economy and is the core idea behind marketing. Marketing involves all aspects of creating a product or service and bringing it to market where an exchange can take place. Marketing ethics therefore examines the responsibilities associated with bringing a product to the market, promoting it to buyers, and exchanging it with them. But this simple model of a seller bringing a product to the marketplace, and the ethics implicit within it, gets complicated fairly quickly.

Even before a product is created, a producer might first consider who, if anyone, is interested in purchasing it. The product might then be redesigned or changed in light of what is learned about potential buyers from market research. Once the product is ready for market, the producer must decide on a price that will be mutually acceptable. At first glance, the minimal asking price should be the production cost plus some reasonable profit. But the producer might also consider who the buyers are and what they can afford, how price might influence future purchases, how the price might affect distributors and retailers, and what competitors are charging before settling on a price. The producer might also consider advertising the product to attract new potential purchasers and offer incentives to promote the product among buyers.

The producer might also consider the lost production that results from the trip to the market and therefore consider hiring someone else, a salesperson, or delegating someone, a "retailer," to handle the actual exchange itself. Producers might be more concerned with cash flow than profit and therefore be willing to ask a price that is below production costs. They might consider where and under what conditions the product is sold, and they might decide that the best chance for a sale will occur only among certain people. The producer might also consider issues of volume and price the product in such a way to insure profit only after certain sales targets are met. The producer might also consider how such factors as price, convenience, reliability, and service might contribute to sustaining an ongoing relationship with the customer. Finally, throughout this entire process the producer might conduct market research to gather information and use that information in production, pricing, promotion, and placement decisions.

All of the factors considered and each decision made throughout this process are elements of marketing. What, how, why, and under what conditions is something *produced?* What *price* is acceptable, reasonable, fair? How can the product be *promoted* to support, enhance, and maintain sales? Where, when, and under what conditions should the product be *placed* in the marketplace? These four general categories—*product, price, promotion, placement*—are sometimes referred to as the **"Four Ps" of marketing.**

Each of the Four Ps also raises important ethical questions. What responsibilities do producers have for the quality and safety of their products? Who is responsible for harms caused by a product? Are there some products that should not be produced, or does consumer demand decide all production questions? Is the consumer's willingness to pay the only ethical constraint on fair pricing? Should the ability to pay be a factor in setting price? Do all customers deserve the same price, or can producers discriminate in favor of, or against, some consumers? What effects will price have on competitors? On retailers? Are deceptive or misleading ads ethical? What ethical constraints should be placed on sales promotions? Is the information gathered in market research the property of the business that conducts the research? What privacy protections should be offered for marketing data? Is it ethical to target vulnerable populations such as children or the elderly? What responsibilities does a producer have when marketing in foreign countries? What responsibilities do producers have to retailers? To competitors? To suppliers?

Ethical Issues in Marketing: A Framework

1 OBJECTIVE

We can take the simple model of a single exchange between two individuals as a useful way to introduce an ethical framework for marketing ethics (see Table 8.1). As in previous chapters, this framework will assist the decision maker in arriving at an ethical decision; but it will not point to the "correct" decision since this is not a normative framework. In other words, it does not determine the right answer but instead the framework identifies rights, responsibilities, duties and obligations, causes and consequences. Once these parameters are clarified, the decision maker uses the framework to effectively analyze the scenario and arrive at the decision that best reflects her or his personal and professional value structure.

This simple situation in which two parties come together and freely agree to an exchange is *prima facie* ethically legitimate. The deontological ethical tradition described in chapter 3 would see it as upholding respect for individuals by treating them as autonomous agents capable of pursuing their own ends. This tradition presumes that each individual will abide by fundamental principles. The utilitarian ethical tradition would take the two parties' agreement as evidence that both are better off than they were prior to the exchange and thus conclude that overall happiness has been increased by any exchange freely entered into.

This assessment is only *prima facie* because, like all agreements, certain conditions must be met before we can conclude that autonomy has in fact been respected and mutual benefit has been achieved. Thus, for example, we would need to establish that the agreement resulted from an informed and voluntary consent, and that there was no fraud, deception, or coercion involved. When

TABLE 8.1
Ethical Issues in Marketing: A Framework

Market Exchange is *prima facie* ethically legitimate because of
- Kantian respect for autonomy
- Utilitarian mutual benefit

This ethical judgment is conditional because
- Informed consent is needed
- Benefits might not occur
- Other values might conflict

Is consent "voluntary"?
- The consumer must have real alternative choices available.
- Anxiety and stress in some purchasing situations
- Price-fixing, monopolies, price gouging, etc.
- Targeted and vulnerable consumers

Is it "informed"?
- Lack of information
- Deception
- Complicated information

Are people truly benefited?
- Impulse buying, "affluenza," consumerism
- Injuries, unsafe products
- "Contrived" wants

Competing Values
- Justice—e.g., "redlining" mortgages
- Market failures (externalities)

these conditions are violated, autonomy is not respected, and mutual benefit is not attained. Furthermore, even when such conditions are met, other values may override the freedom of individuals to contract for mutually beneficial purposes. Thus, for example, the freedom of drug dealers to pursue mutually agreeable ends is overridden by society's concern to maintain law and order.

2 OBJECTIVE

In general, therefore, it will be helpful to keep three concerns in mind as we approach any ethical issue in marketing:

- The Kantian ethical tradition would ask to what degree the participants are respected as free and autonomous agents rather than treated simply as means to the end of making a sale.
- The utilitarian tradition would want to know the degree to which the transaction provided actual as opposed to merely apparent benefits.
- Every ethical tradition would also wonder what other values might be at stake in the transaction.

Let us consider these three issues: the degree to which individuals freely participate in an exchange; the benefits and costs of each exchange; other values that are affected by the exchange.

It is not always easy to determine if someone is being treated with respect in marketing situations. As a first approximation we might suggest two conditions. First, the person must freely consent to the transaction. But how free is "free"? Surely transactions completed under the threat of force are not voluntary and therefore are unethical. But there are many degrees of voluntariness. For example, the more consumers need a product, the less free they are to choose and therefore the more protection they deserve within the marketplace. Consider the use of the *Windows* operating system by the overwhelming majority of computer users. How voluntary is the decision to use *Windows?* Do most people even make a decision to use *Windows?* Or, consider the anxiety and stress that many consumers experience during a car purchase. When an automobile dealer exploits that anxiety to sell extended warranty insurance or road-side assistance, it is not at all clear that the consumer has made a fully voluntary decision. More dramatic cases of price gouging, price-fixing, and monopolistic pricing clearly raise the issue of freedom in marketing. When an insurance company is "too big to fail," one must question if its consumers have any real bargaining power in the marketplace. Practices aimed at vulnerable populations such as children and the elderly also raise questions of voluntariness. Thus, an adequate analysis of marketing ethics challenges us to be sensitive to the many ways in which consumer choice can be less than fully voluntary. (To explore what it means to engage in "voluntary" purchasing decisions, see the Reality Check, "Impulse Buying.")

A second condition for respect requires that the consent be not only voluntary, but also informed. Informed consent has received a great deal of attention in the medical ethics literature because patients are at a distinct informational disadvantage when dealing with health care professionals. Similar disadvantages can occur in marketing situations. Outright deception and fraud clearly violate this condition and are unethical. A consumer's consent to purchase a product is not informed if that consumer is being misled or deceived about the product. But there can also be many more nuanced cases of deception and misleading marketing practices.

The complexity of many consumer products and services can mean that consumers may not understand fully what they are purchasing. Consider, as an example, all that would be involved for a consumer to determine which fuel tank design was most safe for subcompact cars, or which tire design is least likely to cause blow-outs. Consider also the many people who have very weak mathematical skills. Imagine such a person trying to decide on the economic benefits of whole-life versus term insurance, or a 48-month auto lease versus a five-year purchase loan at 2.9 percent financing. In general, while some businesses claim that an "informed consumer is our best customer," many others recognize that an uninformed consumer can be an easy target for quick profits.[3] Serious ethical questions should be raised whenever marketing practices either deny consumers full information or rely on the fact that they lack relevant information or understanding.

The second ethical concern looks to the alleged benefits obtained through market exchanges. Economics textbooks commonly assume that consumers benefit,

Reality Check *Impulse Buying*

Though the cartoon pokes fun at the ability of marketing professionals to "make" us buy certain items, not everyone exercises similar levels of effective judgment necessary to protect themselves from poor decisions about credit and debt, good and bad spending choices. Young spenders in particular may not yet be sufficiently experienced—with shopping, spending or responding to sophisticated marketing campaigns—to adequately protect themselves against strategies designed to encourage impulse buying

Sales pitches that hype the latest and trendiest items, those that must be purchased today and worn tonight, are difficult to resist for some purchasers, who buy in haste and perhaps regret it later. Marketing campaigns are also chastised for creating needs where the purchaser may originally have only sensed a desire. Purchases on impulse are often not reversible, but because they are often so hastily made that the purchaser fails to notice that the product is imperfect or does not match a personal style, they are perhaps most in need of later returns.

In the same way that a hungry person is more likely to buy groceries on impulse than one who has just had her or his meal, we are better off engaging in our purchasing efforts when we are capable of evaluating our options with a clear head (and a full stomach!).

Source: Copyright © cartoonstock.com. Reprinted with permission.

almost by definition, whenever they make an exchange in the marketplace. But this assumption won't bear up under close scrutiny. Many purchases do not result in actual benefit.

For example, impulse buying, and the many marketing techniques used to promote such consumer behavior, cannot be justified by appeal to satisfying consumer interests. (See the Reality Check on impulse buying.) The ever-increasing number of individual bankruptcies suggests that consumers cannot purchase happiness. Empirical studies provide evidence that suggests that greater consumption can lead to unhappiness, a condition called by some "affluenza."[4] So, if simple consumer satisfaction is not a conclusive measure of the benefits of market exchanges, one must always ask about the ends of marketing. What goods are attained by successfully marketing this product or service? How and in what ways are individuals and society benefited from the product?

Both parties to the marketing exchange are also not benefited in situations in which one party is injured by the product. Unsafe products do not further the utilitarian goal of maximizing overall happiness. It would also be the case that consumers are not benefited if the desires that they seek to satisfy in the market are somehow contrived or manipulated by the seller.

The third set of factors that must be considered in any ethical analysis of marketing are values other than those served by the exchange itself. Such primary social values as fairness, justice, health, and safety are just some of the values that can be jeopardized by some marketing practices. For example, a bank that offers lower mortgage rates in affluent neighborhoods than it does in inner-city neighborhoods might be involved only in deals that are mutually beneficial since they do not, in fact, sell mortgages in the inner city. But such contracts would violate important social norms of equal treatment and fairness.

There may be a very strong market for such things as certain body parts of endangered species. There is also, unfortunately, a market for children. But just because someone wants to buy something and someone else is willing to sell it does not mean that the transaction is ethically legitimate. An adequate ethical analysis of marketing must ask who else might be affected by the transaction. How, if at all, are the interests of these others represented? What social goods are promoted, and which are threatened, by marketing this product?

One must also ask what the true costs of production are. An adequate ethical analysis of marketing must consider externalities, those costs that are not integrated within the exchange between buyer and seller. Externalities show that even if both parties to the exchange receive actual benefits from the exchange, other parties external to the exchange might be adversely affected. One thinks of the environmental or health impact of marketing products such as SUVs, pesticides, and tobacco as examples in which a simple model of individual consumer exchange would ignore significant social costs. With these general issues in mind, we can now turn to a closer examination of several major aspects of marketing ethics.

Responsibility for Products: Safety and Liability

3 OBJECTIVE

The general category of business' responsibility for the products and services it sells includes a wide range of topics. Few issues have received as much scrutiny in law, politics, and ethics as has the responsibility of business for the harms caused by its products. Business has an ethical responsibility to design, manufacture, and promote its products in ways that avoid causing harm to consumers.

It will be helpful to review here several different meanings of the word *responsibility* that were introduced in the discussion of corporate social responsibility in chapter 5. Recall that, in one sense, to be responsible is to be identified as the *cause* of something. (See the Reality Check, "The 'Cause' of Obesity," which discusses the possible "responsibility" of soft drinks for childhood obesity.) Thus, we might say that Hurricane Katrina was responsible for millions of dollars in property damages in New Orleans. In another sense, responsibility involves accountability. When we ask who will be responsible for the damages caused by Katrina, we are asking who will pay for the damages. A third sense of responsibility, connected to but different from the sense of accountability, involves assigning fault or liability for something.

The hurricane example demonstrates how these three meanings can be distinguished. Katrina was responsible for (caused) the damage, but cannot be held responsible (accountable for paying for the damages), nor can it be faulted for it. Yet, many think that those who designed, built, or managed the levees in New Orleans were at fault and should be made to pay because their negligence caused much of the harm. In other situations, an automobile crash, for example, a careless driver would be identified as the cause of the accident and held accountable because he was at fault.

Both law and ethics rely on a similar framework when evaluating cases in which business products or services cause harm in the marketplace. The focus for much of the discussion of business' responsibility for product safety is on assigning liability (fault) for harms caused by unsafe products. The legal doctrine of strict liability is ethically controversial exactly because it holds a business accountable for paying damages whether or not it was at fault. In a strict liability case, no matter how careful the business is in its product or service, if harm results from use, the business is liable. We will consider the case of strict liability in more detail in the following section. For the present, let us examine the various standards for holding business liable for its products.

Contractual Standards for Product Safety

4 OBJECTIVE

It is fair to say that the standard of *caveat emptor* (let the buyer beware) is in the background to many discussions of product safety. The ***caveat emptor* approach** understands marketing on a simple model of a contractual exchange between a buyer and seller. This perspective assumes that every purchase involves the informed consent of the buyer and therefore it is assumed to be ethically legitimate. Buyers have the responsibility to look out for their own interests and protect their own safety when buying a product. From this perspective, business has only the responsibility to provide a good or service at an agreed-upon price.

The social contract tradition in ethics holds that all ethical responsibilities can be understood with this contractual model, and that the only duties we have are those that we have freely taken on within a social contract. Individual contracts and promises are the basis of ethical duties. The implication of this within the business sphere is that unless a seller explicitly warrants a product as safe, unless, in other words, the seller promises otherwise, buyers are liable for any harm they suffer.

But even this simple model of a contractual market exchange would place ethical constraints on the seller. Sellers have a duty not to coerce, defraud, or deceive buyers, for example. Consumers who were injured by a product that was deceptively or fraudulently marketed would have legal recourse to recover damages from the seller.

Even in the early years of product safety law, courts recognized an implicit promise, or implied warranty, that accompanies any product that is marketed. What

Reality Check *The "Cause" of Obesity?*

Scholar Regina Lawrence explored where we actually place the responsibility for obesity in our society.[5] Her research sought to determine who is "blamed and burdened in the public debate" surrounding obesity and divided the options between individuals and systemic or environmental causes. Individual causes would limit the causes of the problem to particular individuals, such as eating too much or a lack of exercise, while environmental causes would broaden the focus to government, business, and larger social forces, such as marketing campaigns, a lack of safe places to exercise, or unhealthy food choices in school cafeterias.

To answer the question of where we place responsibility for obesity, Lawrence reviewed the content of *New York Times* page-one stories (from all sections of the paper) and editorials that mentioned obesity over a select period of years. She found that, in 1990, the articles analyzed most often discussed obesity as caused by the individuals themselves (86 percent compared to 14 percent discussing environmental issues as a cause). However, by 2003, only 54 percent discussed individuals as potential causal factors, while 46 percent discussed environmental issues with possible causal links. In other words, our assessment of "fault" for obesity has shifted from a discussion of individual fault to a discussion of responsibility that includes a variety of possible factors. We have shifted the responsibility for obesity from solely those who are obese to a broader view that also includes business, the government and other external forces.

Tara Radin and Martin Calkins explore a similar question in the article "Stakeholders Influence Sales: Soda Companies Stop Selling in Schools," which follows (*adapted with permission of the authors*):

The largest soft drink companies in the United States recently announced that they will stop selling regular soft drinks in school vending machines and cafeterias. By 2008, Coca-Cola, PepsiCo, and Cadbury Schweppes will replace the high-calorie sodas they have been selling with bottled water, natural fruit juice, and diet soda. Specifically targeted are carbonated beverages containing more than 100 calories per serving. While parents and health advocates are thrilled with the success of their concerted efforts, this decision is nothing short of shocking to teenagers around the country.

The decision was motivated in large part by increasing concerns about childhood obesity. It is somewhat myopic, in that it selectively addresses a single possible problem, when there are so many health challenges that children and young adults confront—lack of exercise, smoking, drugs and alcohol, and so on. The decision is also relatively paternalistic in that it effectively removes this temptation from the easy access of children and young adults.

Ironically, this decision runs counter to many past predatory marketing practices. Vulnerable groups, such as children, have traditionally been easy targets for many types of companies. Even though alcohol cannot be sold legally to individuals under the age of 21, it has been claimed time and again that beer manufacturers have featured teenage female models in order to appeal to the young adult market. In the 1970s and 1980s, cigarette companies allegedly focused aggressive marketing campaigns on low-income black males. They initially sold cigarettes with high levels of nicotine to increase their addictiveness, and then gradually reduced the nicotine levels to keep the young men buying more and more cigarettes.

At the same time, this decision calls into question underlying assumptions about freedom of choice. By exerting excessive pressure on soft drink manufactures with threats of litigation, interest groups have removed choice from children and young adults. Is this a positive step? By removing the temptation, are not we in fact depriving children and young adults of a valuable learning experience? Would it not be preferable for us to teach them moderation and resistance to temptation?

The reality is that this is not expected to affect the soft drink industry dramatically—at least not in the short run—considering that the affected sales have accounted for only about 1 percent of total industry revenues. From a business perspective, however, it is somewhat alarming to see the

(*continued*)

extent of stakeholder control over companies. In this situation, parents and health advocates have effectively put an end to a distribution channel for a popular product. Interestingly, it has been labeled a "voluntary" change. This is a shift from customers exercising influence by choosing the products to support through their individual purchases, to interest groups and other stakeholders influencing access to products.

What does this mean for companies? Perhaps this is a signal that, to remain competitive, companies in the twenty-first century are going to have to pay closer attention to the concerns of stakeholders, and they are going to have to cast a wider net around which stakeholders they consider relevant. We are seeing this in the health arena—not just with sodas, but also with the struggles of Krispy Kreme, for example. Other markets, too, are likely to be vulnerable.

At the same time, however, this also reinforces the value of ethics and social responsibility, since vigilant businesspeople and entrepreneurs are likely to identify more growth niches providing products that service socially conscious stakeholders.

the law refers to as the **implied warranty of merchantability,** holds that in selling a product a business implicitly offers assurances that the product is reasonably suitable for its purpose. Even without a verbal or written promise or contract, the law holds that business has a duty to insure that its products will accomplish their purpose. How far does this duty reach? (See the Reality Check, "The 'Cause' of Obesity," for a discussion of that responsibility.)

The ethics implicit within the contract approach assumes that consumers adequately understand products well enough that they can reasonably be expected to protect themselves. But consumers don't always understand products fully and they are not always free to choose not to purchase some things. In effect, the implied warranty standard shifts the burden of proof from consumers to producers by allowing consumers to assume that products were safe for ordinary use. By bringing goods and services to the market, producers were implicitly promising that their products were safe under normal use. The ethical basis for this decision is the assumption that consumers would not give their consent to a purchase if they had reason to believe that they would be harmed by it when used in a normal way.

Of course, if law will hold business liable for implicit promises, a prudent business will seek to limit its liability by explicitly disowning any promise or warranty. Thus, many businesses will issue a disclaimer of liability (e.g., products are sold "as is"), or offer an expressed and limited warranty (e.g., the seller will replace the product but offers no other guarantees). Most courts will not allow a business to completely disclaim the implied warranty of merchantability.

Tort Standards for Product Safety

5 OBJECTIVE

The use of an implied warranty solved one set of problems with the contract law approach to product liability. Consumers would not need complex contracts in order to protect themselves from all possible harms that products might cause. But a second problem remains. If we hold business liable for only those promises

Reality Check *Responsibility beyond Direct Contracts*

During the summer of 2007, the U.S. government issued a product safety recall for millions of children's toys manufactured in China. This recall followed similar safety concerns with Chinese products, including toothpaste, dog food, and automobile tires. In the case of Chinese toys, safety concerns focused on the use of lead-based paints and small magnets embedded in toys that could be swallowed by children.

Of particular concern was the fact that many of the toys were sold by Mattel, the largest U.S. toymaker and a company with an excellent record of safety and a long history of social responsibility, and sold through such major retailers as Target and Wal-Mart. This issue demonstrates the difficulty of tracing responsibility back from a consumer who is injured back through the long supply chain to the party that caused or was at fault for causing the harm. For those companies unlike Mattel who neither own nor operate factories in foreign countries, the links between the consumer and the liable party are significantly more ambiguous.

Unlike many toy manufactures, Mattel actually owned and operated factories in China, which allowed them to closely monitor assembly of toys and manage the chain of suppliers providing the materials that go into their manufacture. In this particular case, it appeared that one of Mattel's manufacturing plants violated policy; either paint was purchased from an uncertified vendor that did not conform to Mattel's standards, or a vendor certified as meeting Mattel's standards violated its own agreements by supplying lead-based paint for use on the toys.

The Consumers Union, a U.S. based consumer advocacy group, estimated that China accounted for 60 percent of all product recalls in the past decade.

made during the market exchange, then as the consumer gets further separated from the manufacturer by layers of suppliers and retailers, there may be no relationship at all between the consumer who gets harmed and the ultimate manufacturer or designer who was at fault. (See the Reality Check, "Responsibility beyond Direct Contracts" and the Decision Point, "When Has a Company's Action Caused Injuries to Its Customers?" for a discussion of the concept of causation or "at fault.")

Negligence, a concept from the area of law known as torts, provides a second avenue for consumers to hold producers responsible for their products. The distinction between contract law and tort law also calls attention to two different ways to understand ethical duties. Under a contract model, the only duties that a person owes are those that have been explicitly promised to another party. Otherwise, that person owes nothing to anyone.

The ethical perspective that underlies tort law holds that we all owe other people certain general duties, *even if we have not explicitly and voluntarily assumed them.* Specifically, I owe other people a general duty not to put them at unnecessary and avoidable risk. Thus, although I have never explicitly promised anyone that I will drive carefully, I have an ethical duty not to drive recklessly down the street.

Negligence is a central component of tort law. As the word suggests, negligence involves a type of ethical neglect, specifically neglecting one's duty to exercise reasonable care not to harm other people. Many of the ethical and legal issues

Decision Point *When Has a Company's Action Caused Injuries to Its Customers?*

One of the most influential cases in U.S. tort law involved a railroad company being sued by a customer who was injured while waiting for a train. In *Palsgraf v. Long Island Railroad,* Helen Palsgraf was standing at a train station awaiting the arrival of her train. As an earlier train was leaving the station, another passenger ran to catch the moving train. Railroad employees helped the man onto the moving train. In the process of being jostled by the employees, the man dropped his package onto the tracks. The package contained fireworks for the upcoming 4th of July celebration, and they exploded, setting off a chain of events. In the mayhem that followed, a scale at the end of the platform was knocked over, striking Helen Palsgaf and causing her injuries. Palsgraf sued to recover damages for her injuries.

The court in this case faced two basic questions: Did the actions of the railroad employees cause her injuries? Were the railroad employees negligent in the way they treated customers and, if so, were they negligent to Mrs. Palsgraf? How would you have decided this case?

- What facts would you want to know before deciding this case?
- What alternatives would a jury face in deciding this case?
- Who are the stakeholders of your decision? What is the impact of each alternative decision on each stakeholder you have identified?
- What rights and duties are involved?
- How would you decide the case? Is it mostly a matter of consequences, or are there important principles involved?

surrounding manufacturers' responsibility for products can be understood as the attempt to specify what constitutes negligence in their design, production, and sale. What duties, exactly, do producers owe to consumers?

One can think of possible answers to this question as falling along a continuum. On one extreme is the social contract answer: Producers owe only those things promised to consumers in the sales agreement. At the other extreme is something closer to **strict liability:** Producers owe compensation to consumers for any harm caused by their products. In between these extremes is a range of answers that vary with different interpretations of negligence. We have already suggested why the strict contract approach is incomplete. In the next section we shall examine the pros and cons of strict product liability. The remainder of this section will examine the important concept of negligence.

Negligence can be characterized as a failure to exercise reasonable care or ordinary vigilance that results in an injury to another. In many ways, negligence simply codifies two fundamental ethical precepts: "ought implies can" (we cannot reasonably oblige someone to do what they cannot do) and "one ought not harm others." People have done an ethical wrong when they cause harm to others in ways that they can reasonably be expected to have avoided. Negligence includes acts of both commission and omission. One can be negligent by doing something

Decision Point — *Liability for Spilt Coffee? A Double Latté!*

In 1992 a 70-year-old woman was severely burned when a cup of coffee she had just purchased at a McDonald's drive-through window spilled on her lap. She apparently held the cup between her legs and tried to pry off the lid as she drove away. The coffee was hot enough (185 degrees) to cause third-degree burns that required skin grafts and long-term medical care. A jury awarded this woman $2.86 million, $160,000 for compensatory damages and $2.7 million in punitive damages. Should McDonald's be held liable for these injuries? Was the restaurant negligent in serving such hot coffee at a drive-through window? Was the consumer negligent in her own actions?

- What facts would you want to know before deciding whether this settlement was fair?
- What alternatives would a jury face in deciding this case?
- Who are the stakeholders of your decision? What is the impact of each alternative mentioned above on each stakeholder you have identified?
- Should *caveat emptor* govern the situation?
- What are the consequences of the jury's decision?
- What rights and duties are involved?
- How would you decide the case? Is it mostly a matter of consequences, or are there important principles involved?

In an interesting 2006 case with somewhat related facts, a woman was awarded more than $300,000 by a jury when a Starbucks Coffee employee caused a cup of coffee to spill on to the woman's foot. In fact, the *barista* (the coffee server at Starbucks) slid the coffee toward the woman; the coffee slipped over the edge of the counter; the top fell off; and the coffee spilled onto the woman's sneaker-covered foot. Her foot suffered nerve damage from the scalding liquid. Starbucks' public statement explained that, while it regrets any injury to Griffin, "we do not believe we are responsible for her injury."

- Do you see a distinction between these two cases?
- Is there any difference between the responsibility McDonald's owes the woman in the first instance and the responsibility Starbucks owes the woman in the second situation, as described above?
- Are the principles involved in the two cases any different?
- Will the decisions in the two cases lead to different consequences?

that one ought not (e.g., speeding in a school zone) or by failing to do something that one ought to have done (e.g., neglecting to inspect a product before sending it to market).

Negligence involves the ability to foresee the consequences of our acts and failing to take steps to avoid the likely harmful consequences (see the Decision Point, "Liability for Spilt Coffee?A Double Latté!").

Decision Point *Foreseeing and Designing for Product Misuse: Can a Manufacturer Be Held Liable When a Product Is Misused?*

Manufacturers can be held legally and ethically negligent if they fail to foresee harms that could reasonably be anticipated in the normal use of a product. Consider this case with the design of a kitchen stove.

A young child is curious about what her mother is cooking on top of the kitchen stove. In order to gain a better view, she opens the oven door and steps up on it to look into the pans on the stovetop. Her weight causes the stove to tip over, spilling the hot food on her and causing severe burns. Was the manufacturer at fault for not designing a stove that would not tip with the weight of a child on the oven door?

Could the stove design team have foreseen a child using the oven door as a stepladder? Could the designers foresee the use of the oven door as a work surface on which to place heavy roasting pans, for example, a turkey pan while basting? If the weight of such a large oven pan is comparable to the weight of a young child, should the oven have been designed to withstand a foreseeable weight being placed on the door? If you were on a jury and had to decide this case, would you hold the manufacturer accountable for the child's injuries?

- What facts would you want to know before deciding this case?
- What alternatives would a jury face in deciding this case?
- Who are the stakeholders of such your decision? What is the impact of each alternative decision on each stakeholder you have identified?
- What rights and duties are involved?
- How would you decide the case? Is it mostly a matter of consequences, or are important principles involved?

The standards of foreseeability, however, raise interesting challenges. One standard would hold people liable only for those harms they actually foresaw occurring (actual foreseeability). Thus, for example, they would be acting negligently if (as was alleged in the famous Ford Pinto case), on the basis of engineering tests, they concluded that a fuel tank placed behind the rear axle would puncture and explode during crashes at speeds below 30 miles per hour, yet still brought the car to market.

But this standard of actual foreseeability is too restricted. If someone actually thinks that harms are likely to result from his acts and proceeds nonetheless, he has committed a serious wrong and deserves harsh punishment. Such a case seems more akin to recklessness, or even intentional harm, than negligence. But this standard would also imply that unthoughtful people cannot be negligent, since one escapes liability by not actually thinking about the consequences of one's acts. "I never thought about that" would be an adequate defense if we used this standard of negligence. Yet this surely is part of what we are after with the concept of negligence. We want to encourage people to be thoughtful and hold them liable when they are not. See the Decision Point "Foreseeing and Designing for Product Misuse: Can a Manufacturer Be Held Liable When a Product Is Misused?" to consider how you might respond.

A preferable standard would require people to avoid harms that, even if they haven't actually thought about, they *should* have thought about had they been reasonable. For example, in the Decision Point, "Liability for Spilt Coffee?" presumably McDonald's did not actually anticipate that customers would be severely burned by coffee. But, had its managers thought about what people who are served coffee at drive-through windows might do to hold their cups when they drive away from the window, they could have foreseen the likelihood of spills. Moreover, the fact that McDonald's had received over 700 prior burn claims involving coffee over a 10-year period suggests that a reasonable person would have concluded that this was a dangerous practice. This "reasonable person" standard is the one most often used in legal cases and seems to better capture the ethical goals of the very concept of negligence. People are expected to act reasonably and are held liable when they are not. In addition, when one has actual notice of a likelihood of harm, such as in this case, the reasonable person expectation is increased. The issue of foreseeability comes up when a product might be misused, as in the Decision Point, "Foreseeing and Designing for Product Misuse."

But even the reasonable person standard can be interpreted in various ways. On one hand, we expect people will act in ways that would be normal or average. A "reasonable" person does what we could expect the ordinary, average person to do. There are problems using this standard for both consumer and producer behavior. It may turn out that the ordinary average consumer is not as smart as we might hope.

The average person doesn't always read, or understand, warning labels, for example. The ordinary and average person may thoughtlessly place a cup of very hot coffee between her legs as she drives out of a parking lot and into traffic. The average person standard when applied to consumers risks exempting many consumers from taking responsibility for their own acts. When applied to producers, the average person standard sets the bar too low. We can expect more from a person who designs, manufacturers, and sells a product than average and ordinary vigilance.

Reasons such as these can lead us to interpret the reasonable person standard more normatively than descriptively. In this sense, a "reasonable" person assumes a standard of thoughtful, reflective, and judicious decision making. The problem with this, of course, is that we might be asking more of average consumers than they are capable of giving. Particularly if we think that the disadvantaged and vulnerable deserve greater protection from harm, we might conclude that this is too stringent a standard to be applied to consumer behavior. On the other hand, given the fact that producers do have more expertise than the average person, this stronger standard seems more appropriate when applied to producers than to consumers.

Strict Product Liability

6 OBJECTIVE

The negligence standard of tort law focuses on the sense of responsibility that involves liability or fault. As such, it asks what the business or person involved had foreseen or should have foreseen. But there are also cases in which consumers can be injured by a product in which no negligence was involved. In such cases where no one was at fault, the question of accountability remains. Who should pay for damages when consumers are injured by products and no one is at fault? The legal doctrine of strict product liability holds manufacturers accountable in such cases.

One classic strict product liability case involved the synthetic estrogen hormone diethylstilbestrol (DES). In the late 1940s, DES was approved for use in the prevention of miscarriages and was widely prescribed for problem pregnancies until the early 1970s. The drug had been widely tested in clinical trials and proved quite successful in reducing the number of miscarriages. However, in the early 1970s a connection was discovered between the use of DES during pregnancy and certain forms of vaginal cancer in the female children of women who used the drug. These cancers did not typically appear until more than a decade after the drug was used. In 1972 the FDA prohibited all marketing of the drug for use during pregnancy. For the experience of another manufacturer, see the Decision Point that follows.

Ethical Debates on Product Liability

6 OBJECTIVE

It is fair to say that the business community is a strong critic of much of the legal standards of product liability. Liability standards, and the liability insurance costs in which they have resulted, have imposed significant costs on contemporary business. In particular, these critics single out the strict product liability standard as especially unfair to business because it holds business responsible for harms that were not the result of business negligence.

In fact, the rationale often used to justify strict product liability is problematic. Defenders of the strict product liability standard, including juries who decide in favor of injured consumers, often reply with two major claims. First, by holding business strictly liable for any harm their products cause, society creates a strong incentive for business to produce safer goods and services. Second, given that someone has to be accountable for the costs of injuries, holding business liable allocates the costs to the party best able to bear the financial burden. Each rationale is open to serious objections.

First, the incentive argument seems to misunderstand the nature of strict liability. Holding someone accountable for harm can provide an incentive only if they could have done otherwise. But this means that the harm was foreseeable and the failure to act was negligent. Surely this is a reasonable justification for the tort standard of negligence. But strict liability is not negligence and the harms caused by such products as asbestos were not foreseeable. Thus, holding business liable for these harms cannot provide an incentive to better protect consumers in the future. See the Decision Point "Who Should Pay for Asbestos-Caused Illness and Deaths?"

Decision Point *Who Should Pay for Asbestos-Caused Illness and Deaths?*

One of the major strict product liability cases involves asbestos, a fibrous mineral used for decades for insulation and fire prevention in homes, industry, and consumer products. When inhaled through long-term exposure, asbestos dust causes a variety of lung and respiratory diseases, including mesothelioma, a particularly fatal form of cancer. Millions of workers have been exposed to asbestos, especially during the middle decades of the 20th century. However, many of the diseases associated with asbestos, including mesothelioma, might take decades before they appear. Thus, it is often difficult if not impossible to identify the exact source of the asbestos that caused the disease. In such cases, the liability focuses on any and all manufacturers of asbestos products. They brought the product to market, the product proved defective, therefore they ought to be held accountable for the damages.

One estimate suggests that 700,000 people have been involved in lawsuits against 8,000 corporations for asbestos-related injuries. Asbestos liability lawsuits have bankrupted several corporations, including the high-profile Johns-Manville. As much as $70 billion has been paid in asbestos claims, and lawsuits continue in every state.

Should manufacturers of asbestos be held accountable for the damages caused by the product they brought to market, even if no direct link can be established between the injury and any specific product they manufactured?

- What facts would you need to know to make a fully informed judgment in this case?
- What alternatives are available? If not the manufacturer, who should be accountable to pay for the damages caused by asbestos?
- Who are the stakeholders who should be involved in this case?
- What are the likely consequences of holding manufacturers strictly liable? Of holding the injured consumer accountable? Of having the government pay?
- What duties do the manufacturers of asbestos have? What does the principle of fairness require in this case?
- If you were on a jury and had to decide who should pay the costs of a worker's mesothelioma, how would you decide?

The second rationale also suffers a serious defect. This argument amounts to the claim that business is best able to pay for damages. Yet, as the asbestos case in the Decision Point indicates, many businesses have been bankrupted by product liability claims.

If it is unfair to hold business accountable for harms caused by their products, it is equally (if not more) unfair to hold injured consumers accountable. Neither party is at fault, yet someone must pay for the injuries. A third option would be to have government, and therefore all taxpayers, accountable for paying the costs of injuries caused by defective products. But this, too, seems unfair.

A third argument for holding business accountable might be more persuasive. Accountability, after all, focuses on those situations where no one is at fault, yet someone has to pay. This might be another way of saying that accountability is not a matter of ethical principle in that no one deserves to pay for damages. But perhaps accountability is best understood as a matter of utilitarian efficiency rather than principle. When business is held accountable, the costs for injuries will eventually fall on those consumers who buy the product through higher costs, especially higher insurance costs to business. This amounts to the claim that external costs should be internalized and that the full costs of a product should be paid for by those who use the product. Products that impose a cost on society through injuries will end up costing more to those who purchase them. Companies that cannot afford to remain in business when the full costs of their products are taken into account perhaps ought not to remain in business.

Responsibility for Products: Advertising and Sales

7 OBJECTIVE

Along with product safety, the general area of advertising ethics has received significant legal and philosophical attention within business ethics. The goal of all marketing is the sale, the eventual exchange between seller and buyer. A major element of marketing is sales promotion, the attempt to influence the buyer to complete a purchase. (See the Decision Point, "Automobile Advertising.") Target marketing and marketing research are two important elements of product placement, seeking to determine which audience is most likely to buy, and which audience is mostly likely to be influenced by product promotion.

There are, of course, ethically good and bad ways for influencing others. Among the ethically commendable ways to influence another are persuading, asking, informing, and advising. Unethical means of influence would include threats, coercion, deception, manipulation, and lying. Unfortunately, all too often sales and advertising practices employ deceptive or manipulative means of influence, or are aimed at audiences that are susceptible to manipulation or deception. Perhaps the most infamous and maligned of all marketing fields is automotive sales, especially in used car markets. The concept of manipulation, and its subset of deception, is central to the ethical issues explored in this chapter and can help organize the following sections.

To manipulate something is to guide or direct its behavior. Manipulation need not involve total control, and in fact it more likely suggests a process of subtle direction or management. Manipulating people implies working behind the scenes, guiding their behavior without their explicit consent or conscious understanding. In this way, manipulation is contrasted with persuasion and other forms of rational influence. When I manipulate someone, I explicitly do not rely on their own reasoned judgment to direct their behavior. Instead, I seek to bypass their autonomy (although successful manipulation can be reinforced when the person manipulated *believes* she acted of her own accord).

Decision Point *Automobile Advertising*

"Below invoice prices." "Cash-back incentives." "Low monthly lease rate." "Late model close-outs." "$500 cash back." "Manufacturer's suggested retail price." "Sticker price." "Factory rebates." "Absolute lowest price guaranteed." "0% interest on selected vehicles." "Factory authorized clearance." "Extended service contracts." "No money down." "Certified pre-owned vehicles." "No reasonable offer refused." "Huge discounts. Save thousands." "We sell wholesale to the public!" "We are dealing. Save $$$." "Credit problems? No problem. Your approval is guaranteed or we'll give you $1,000." "No games, no gimmicks."

All of these claims were found in just a few pages of one local Sunday newspaper. They point to the extraordinary difficulty that consumers face in purchasing a car. Perhaps no other industry suffers as bad a reputation in pricing and sales as the automobile industry.

Do you find any of these claims misleading? Confusing? Deceptive? Which are easily understood? Which are least clear? Who is being targeted by these ads?

- What facts would you want to know before making a judgment about these ads?
- Which ads, if any, raise ethical questions?
- Who are the stakeholders in automobile advertising? What are the potential benefits and potential harms of such advertising?
- What ethical principles have you used in making your judgments?
- What type of people do you think are involved in automobile advertising and automobile sales?

One of the ways in which we can manipulate someone is through deception, one form of which is an outright lie. I need not deceive you to manipulate you, although I would be happy if you falsely believed that you were not being manipulated. We can manipulate someone without deception, as when I get my sons to mow the lawn by making them feel guilty about not carrying their share of family responsibilities. Or I might manipulate my students into studying more diligently by hinting that there may be a quiz during the next class. These examples raise a very crucial point because they suggest that the more I know about your psychology—your motivations, interests, desires, beliefs, dispositions, and so forth—the better able I will be to manipulate your behavior. Guilt, pity, a desire to please, anxiety, fear, low self-esteem, pride, and conformity can all be powerful motivators. Knowing such things about another person provides effective tools for manipulating their behavior.

We can see how this is relevant to marketing ethics. Critics charge that many marketing practices manipulate consumers. Clearly, many advertisements are deceptive, and some are outright lies. We can also see how marketing research plays into this. The more one learns about customer psychology, the better able one will be to satisfy their desires, but the better able one will also be to manipulate their behavior. Critics charge that some marketing practices target populations that are particularly susceptible to manipulation and deception.

Ethical Issues in Advertising

8 OBJECTIVE

The general ethical defense of advertising reflects both utilitarian and Kantian ethical standards. Advertising provides information for market exchanges and therefore contributes to market efficiency and to overall happiness. Advertising information also contributes to the information necessary for autonomous individuals to make informed choices. But note that each of these rationales assumes that the information is true and accurate.

The deontological tradition in ethics would have the strongest objections to manipulation. When I manipulate someone I treat them as a means to my own ends, as an object to be used rather than as an autonomous person in his or her own right. Manipulation is a clear example of disrespect for persons since it bypasses their own rational decision making. Because the evil rests with the intention to use another as a means, even unsuccessful manipulations are guilty of this ethical wrong.

As we might expect, the utilitarian tradition would offer a more conditional critique of manipulation, depending on the consequences. There surely can be cases of paternalistic manipulation, in which someone is manipulated for their own good. But even in such cases, unforeseen harms can occur. Manipulation tends to erode bonds of trust and respect between persons. It can erode one's self-confidence and hinder the development of responsible choice among those manipulated. In general, because most manipulation is done to further the manipulator's own ends at the expense of the manipulated, utilitarians would be inclined to think that manipulation lessens overall happiness. A general practice of manipulation, as critics would charge occurs in many sales practices, can undermine the very social practices (e.g., sales) that it is thought to promote as the reputation of sales is lowered. The example of used car sales, once again, is a good example of such a situation.

A particularly egregious form of manipulation occurs when vulnerable people are targeted for abuse. Cigarette advertising aimed at children is one example that has received major criticism in recent years. Marketing practices targeted at elderly populations for such goods and services as insurance (particularly Medicare supplemental insurance), casinos and gambling, nursing homes, and funerals have been subjected to similar criticisms. (See the Reality Check, "Winners and Losers.")

We can suggest the following general guidelines. Marketing practices that seek to discover which consumers might already and independently be predisposed to purchasing a product are ethically legitimate. So, for example, an automobile dealership learns from its manufacturer's marketing department that the typical buyer of its car is a college-educated female between the ages of 25 and 30 who enjoys outdoors activities and earns more than $30,000. Sending targeted direct mail pieces to everyone within an area who matches these criteria seems an ethically legitimate marketing practice. Marketing practices that seek to identify populations that can be easily influenced and manipulated, on the other hand, are not. Sales and marketing that appeal to fear, anxiety, or other non-rational motivations are ethically improper. For example, an automobile dealer who knows that an unmarried or

Reality Check *Winners and Losers*

The Illinois Lottery Commission came under fire in 2005 for a billboard marketing campaign in downtown Chicago that included signs that read, "How to go from Washington Street to Easy Street—Play the Illinois State Lottery." A boycott of the lottery was organized, claiming that the lottery took advantage of the poor of the inner city. The claim is that the lottery is actually an unfair form of a regressive tax because it draws a disproportionate amount of its revenues from the poor by preying on unrealistic hopes.

To the contrary, argues Edward J. Stanek, the president of the North American Association of State and Provincial Lotteries:

> Big jackpot games are equalizers. Those who were not fortunate in the drawing of genes and inheritance can venture a chance equal to everyone else to benefit financially. . . . Lotteries don't discriminate among their customers. . . . If there is something inherently wrong with allowing less prosperous people the choice to buy a ticket, then the protectionists should seek legislation to prohibit low-income citizens from taking a chance. Why haven't they? Because the folly of their self-righteous protectionism would be exposed. . . .
>
> For a lottery to take "advantage" of the poor would imply that the poor have a "disadvantage." Obviously they have less money, which means that lotteries can benefit them more relative to helping those of greater means. The only way that the poor can be at a disadvantage is if they don't have the same mental capacity to make $1 decisions as those who are wealthier. It follows that those who make such claims are assuming that the poor have a diminished intellectual capacity. But economic status is not a measure of intelligence. Saying that the poor are taken advantage of in this context is an insult to the intelligence of those who play lottery games.

With which side do you agree?

Source: E. Stanek, "Take the High Road and Keep the Upper Hand: A Critique of Lottery Critics," speech to North American Association of State and Provincial Lotteries (Sept. 29, 1997), http://www.nmlottery.com/Miscellaneous/CRITIQUE.HTM.

widowed woman is anxious about the purchase and who uses this anxiety as a way to sell extended warranty insurance, disability insurance, theft protection products, and the like is unethical. (The manner in which this or other information is collected is also subject to ethical concerns; see the Reality Check, "Winners and Losers.")

Marketing research seeks to learn something about the psychology of potential customers. But not all psychological categories are alike. Some are more cognitive and rational than others. Targeting the considered and rational desires of consumers is one thing; targeting their fears, anxiety, and whims is another. See the Reality Check, "New Challenges to Old Problems: From Redlining to E-Lining" and, for more discussion of on-line, viral and other timely marketing techniques, see the reading by Pudner included at the end of this chapter.)

Marketing Ethics and Consumer Autonomy

9 OBJECTIVE

Defenders of advertising argue that despite cases of deceptive practices, overall advertising contributes much to the economy. The majority of advertisements provide information to consumers, information that contributes to an efficient

Reality Check *New Challenges to Old Problems: From Redlining to E-Lining*

by Tara J. Radin, Martin Calkins, and Carolyn Predmore

Today, more than a decade since the Internet became widely and publicly available, we still lack consensus about the degree of ownership and acceptable limits of data gathering and use. In fact, Richard De George's 1999 remark is arguably more valid now than previously: "The U.S. is schizophrenic about information privacy, wanting it in theory and giving it away in practice."[6] Such schizophrenia is problematic in itself, but it has been exacerbated by the questionable applications of data collection that have occurred. E-lining (electronic redlining) represents one glaring example of how data gathering crosses moral boundaries.

Redlining is the practice of denying or increasing the cost of services to residents of certain geographic locations. In the United States, it has been deemed illegal when the criteria involve race, religion, or ethnic origin. The term came to prominence with the discussions that led to the Housing Act of 1934, which established the Federal Housing Authority, which later became the Department of Housing and Urban Development. It occurs when financial institutions (banks, brokerages, and insurance companies) literally draw red lines on maps to distinguish between creditworthy and financially risky neighborhoods.

Although illegal, redlining has not died out completely. It reemerged recently when MCI removed international long distance service via calling cards from pay phones in poorer communities in the suburbs of Los Angeles. It reappeared also in retail sales when Victoria's Secret allegedly tailored its catalog prices along customer demographics (specifically, ethnicity). In this case, two sisters living in different parts of town discovered price differences when discussing items from seemingly identical catalogs. As the two compared prices on the phone, they found that the cost of some items varied by as much as 25 percent. A subsequent and more thorough investigation revealed that Victoria's Secret had been engaging in an extensive practice of price variation according to gender, age, and income. In the end, although Victoria's Secret was vindicated in the court of law, it lost in the court of public opinion.

Finally, it resurfaced when Kozmo.com, an online provider of one-hour delivery services, used zip codes to refuse to deliver merchandise to customers in predominantly black neighborhoods. In all of these cases, companies (to different degrees) "exclude(d) classes of individuals from full participation in the marketplace and the public sphere."

E-lining differs from these more traditional forms of redlining by not drawing a red line on a map, but by using information that Internet users unwittingly leave behind as they surf Web sites. E-liners use "spyware" programs embedded in Web pages to collect information surreptitiously and with little or no outside oversight. They are able to "spy on" surfers in this way without much challenge because, at present, there are few limits on what companies can do with the information they gather.

In recent years companies have used customer information to direct customers to particular products or services. In this way, they have used information in much the same way high-end clothing stores use a Rolodex of customer phone numbers to alert customers about newly arrived items that match or complement prior purchases. At other times, businesses have not acted so benevolently. They have used the data they collected in a discriminatory way to direct customers to particular products or services that fit a profile based on demographics. Amazon has received significant criticism for its use of historical purchase information to tailor Web offerings to repeat customers. Amazon allegedly used data profiling in order to set prices. In September 2000, Amazon customers determined that they were charged different prices for the same CDs. Although Amazon claimed that the price differentiation was part of a randomized test, the result was price discrimination that appeared to be based on demographics.

This sort of discrimination and deprivation of financial opportunities according to demographics

(*continued*)

is exactly what the rules against redlining are intended to prevent. The absence of comparable rules against e-lining is not, as some firms might like to argue, an indication that this sort of behavior is acceptable in e-commerce, but, rather, is a reflection of the lag in time it is taking for the legal infrastructure to catch up with e-commerce. Our current legal infrastructure, particularly in the United States, which is aimed almost exclusively toward brick-and-mortar enterprises, does not account for the tremendous amount of information available through e-commerce or for the numerous ways in which e-merchants are able to exploit customers through misuse of that information. The unfortunate reality is that there is not a clear distinction between acceptable and unacceptable forms of information gathering, use, and market segmentation, and e-commerce provides a cloak that insulates from detection many firms engaging in inappropriate behavior.

There are few if any obstacles to firms engaging in questionable e-commerce business practices in the first place. Public outcries are generally short-lived and do not appear to have a significant impact on e-shopping. If anything, e-commerce continues to attract an increasing number of customers. In the meantime, few generally agreed-upon standards exist regarding the acceptable limits of information gathering via the Internet. Instead, businesses are shaping the expectations of Web users and society in general as they implicitly set standards to guide future marketers through their irresponsible behavior. They are sending the message: "Internet user beware!" to Internet surfers and potential e-customers. As long as the legal infrastructure remains underdeveloped, society remains vulnerable to an increasing number of potential electronic abuses.

Source: Adapted by the authors with permission from work copyrighted © by Tara J. Radin, Martin Calkins, and Carolyn Predmore.

function of economic markets. These defenders argue that over time, market forces will weed out deceptive ads and practices. They point out that the most effective counter to a deceptive ad is a competitor's ad calling attention to the deception.

Beyond this question of what advertising does *for* people, a second important ethical question asks what advertising, specifically, and marketing in general, does *to* people. People may well benefit from business' marketing of its products. People learn about products they may need or want, they get information that helps them make responsible choices, they even sometimes are entertained. But marketing also helps shape culture and the individuals who develop and are socialized within that culture, some would say dramatically so. Marketing can have direct and indirect influence on the very persons we become. How it does that, and the kind of people we become as a result, is of fundamental ethical importance. Critics of such claims either deny that marketing can have such influence or maintain that marketing is only a mirror of the culture of which it is a part.

The initial proposal in this debate was offered by economist John Kenneth Galbraith in his 1958 book, *The Affluent Society.* Galbraith claimed that advertising and marketing were creating the very consumer demand that production then aimed to satisfy. Dubbed the "dependence effect," this assertion held that consumer demand depended upon what producers had to sell. This fact had three major and unwelcome implications.

First, by creating wants, advertising was standing the "law" of supply and demand on its head. Rather than supply being a function of demand, demand

Reality Check *Advertising Spending*

Total spending on advertising in all media for 2005 was estimated by one marketing group to exceed $275 billion. Worldwide, advertising was a $560 billion industry.[7]

In terms of direct marketing, alone, companies spent more than $160 billion in the United States, which, measured against total U.S. sales, generated an estimated $1.85 trillion in increased sales in 2005, or 7 percent of the $26 trillion in total sales in the U.S. economy, and accounted for 10.3 percent of total U.S. GDP in that year.[8]

turns out to be a function of supply. Second, advertising and marketing tend to create irrational and trivial consumer wants and this distorts the entire economy. The "affluent" society of consumer products and creature comforts is in many ways worse off than so-called undeveloped economies because resources devoted to contrived, private consumer goods are therefore denied to more important public goods and consumer needs. Taxpayers deny school districts small tax increases to provide essential funding while parents drop their children off at school in $40,000 SUVs. A society that cannot guarantee vaccinations and minimal health care to poor children spends millions annual for cosmetic surgery to keep its youthful appearance. Finally, by creating consumer wants, advertising and other marketing practices violate consumer autonomy. Consumers who consider themselves free because they are able to purchase what they want are not in fact free if those wants are created by marketing. In short, consumers are being manipulated by advertising.

Ethically, the crucial point is the assertion that advertising violates consumer autonomy. The law of supply and demand is reversed, and the economy of the affluent society is contrived and distorted, only if consumer autonomy can be violated, and consumers manipulated, by advertising's ability to create wants. But can advertising violate consumer autonomy and, if it can, does this occur? Consider the annual investment in this effort (see the Reality Check, "Advertising Spending"). Given this investment, what does advertising do *to* people and *to* society?

An initial thesis in this debate claims that advertising controls consumer *behavior.* Autonomy involves making reasoned and voluntary choices, and the claim that advertising violates autonomy might mean that advertising controls consumer choice. Psychological behaviorists and critics of subliminal advertising, for example, would claim that advertising can control consumer behavior in this way. But this seems to be an empirical claim and the evidence suggests that it is false. For example, some studies show that more than half of all new products introduced in the market fail, a fact that should not be true if consumer behavior could be controlled by marketing. Consumers certainly don't seem controlled by advertising in any obvious sense of that word.

But consumer autonomy might be violated in a more subtle way. Rather than controlling behavior, perhaps advertising creates the wants and desires on the

Decision Point *Advertising for Erectile Dysfunction*

Perhaps no marketing campaign has received as much critical attention as the Viagra, Cialis, and Levitra campaign to counteract erectile dysfunction. Much of the criticism has focused on the ad placements, particularly in places where young children would see them such as during prime time television and during high-profile sporting events. Other criticisms suggest that although these drugs can be used to treat real medical conditions, they are being marketed as little more than recreational drugs and sex toys. Erectile dysfunction can be a problem for older men and especially for men recovering from such medical treatments as prostate surgery. But for younger and otherwise healthy men, the primary causes of erectile dysfunction are alcohol consumption, obesity, lack of exercise, smoking, and the use of other prescription drugs. All these causes are either easily addressed without reliance on pharmaceuticals or, as is the case with alcohol abuse, erectile dysfunction drugs are potentially unsafe.

Arguments in support of direct-to-consumer marketing of prescription drugs are that it provides information to consumers, respects consumer choice, encourages those who are reluctant to seek medical care to do so, gets more people into the health care system, addresses real public health issues, and increases competition and efficiency in the pharmaceutical industry. Opponents claim that these ads increase the unnecessary use of drugs; increase public harms, since all drugs have harmful side effects; increase reliance on pharmaceutical health care treatments and discourage alternative therapies and treatments, many of which have fewer side effects; manipulate and exploit vulnerable consumers; often provide misleading and incomplete information; alienate patients from physicians by bypassing the gatekeeper function of medical professionals; and treat social and behavior problems with medical and chemical solutions.

What is your judgment about the ethics of advertising Viagra, Cialis, and Levitra? Do the reasons for advertising prescription drugs in general apply equally well to these three drugs?

- What alternatives exist for marketing prescription drugs?
- Who are the stakeholders of drug marketing?
- What are the consequences of alternative marketing strategies?
- What rights and duties are involved?

basis of which consumers act. The focus here becomes the concept of *autonomous desires* rather than *autonomous behavior*. This is much closer to the original assertion by Galbraith and other critics of advertising. Consumer autonomy is violated by advertising's ability to create non-autonomous desires.

A helpful exercise to understand how desires might be non-autonomous is to think of the many reasons people buy the things they buy and consume the things they do, and why, in general, people go shopping. After certain basic needs are met, there is a real question of why people consume the way they do. People buy things for many reasons, including the desire to appear fashionable, for status, to feel good, because everyone else is buying something, and so forth. The interesting ethical question at this point is where *these* desires originated, and how much marketing has influenced these non-necessity purchases. These questions and issues are raised in the Decision Point, "Advertising for Erectile Dysfunction."

Marketing to Vulnerable Populations

10 OBJECTIVE

Consider two examples of target marketing. In one case, based on market research supplied by the manufacturer, an automobile retailer learns that the typical customer is a single woman, between 30 and 40 years old; she has an annual income over $30,000, and she enjoys outdoor sports and recreation. Knowing this information, the dealer targets advertising and direct mail to this audience. Ads depict attractive and active young people using their product and enjoying outdoor activities. A second targeted campaign is aimed at selling an emergency call device to elderly widows who live alone. This marketing campaign depicts an elderly woman at the bottom of a stairway crying out "I've fallen and can't get up!" These ads are placed in media that elderly women are likely to see or hear. Are these marketing campaigns on an equal ethical footing?

The first marketing strategy appeals to the considered judgments which consumers, presumably, have settled on over the course of their lives. People with similar backgrounds tend to have similar beliefs, desires, and values and often make similar judgments about consumer purchases. Target marketing in this sense is simply a means for identifying likely customers based on common beliefs and values. On the other hand, there does seem to be something ethically offensive about the second case. This campaign aims to sell the product by exploiting the real fear and anxiety that many older people experience. This marketing strategy tries to manipulate people by appealing to non-rational factors such as fear or anxiety rather than relying on straightforward informative ads. Is there anything to the claim that elderly women living alone are more "vulnerable" than younger women and that this vulnerability creates greater responsibility for marketers? In general, do marketers have special responsibility to the vulnerable?

Are elderly people living alone particularly vulnerable? The answer to this depends on what we mean by particularly vulnerable. In one sense, a person is vulnerable as a consumer by being unable in some way to participate as a fully informed and voluntary participant in the market exchange. Valid market exchanges make several assumptions about the participants: They understand what they are doing, they have considered their choice, they are free to decide, and so forth. What we can call *consumer vulnerability* occurs when a person has an impaired ability to make an informed consent to the market exchange. A vulnerable consumer lacks the intellectual capacities, psychological ability, or maturity to make informed and considered consumer judgments. Children would be the paradigmatic example of consumer vulnerability. (See the Decision Point, "Targeting Vulnerable People?") The harm to which such people are susceptible is the harm of not satisfying one's consumer desires and/or losing one's money. Elderly people living alone are not necessarily vulnerable in this sense.

Decision Point *Targeting Vulnerable People?*

An important case of marketing drugs to targeted populations involves the drug Strattera, Eli Lilly's prescription medication that controls attention deficit disorder and hyperactivity (ADHD) in children. The ad ran in magazines such as *Family Circle* (September 2003) under the simple title "Welcome to Ordinary." The ad pictured two boys holding up a model airplane that they have finished building, a challenging task for a child with ADHD. The ad reads: "4:30 P.M. Tuesday. He started something you never thought he'd finish. 5:20 P.M. Thursday. He's proved you wrong." The ad suggests that, if a child with ADHD is not "ordinary," it is the parents who are "wrong" because all it would take would be Strattera to solve their problem. The same issue of *Family Circle* contained ads for McNeil Pharmaceutical's Concerta and Shire Pharmaceutical's Adderall, the two major competitors to Strattera.

Are these marketing practices ethically responsible?

- What facts would you want to know before deciding this case?
- What alternative marketing practices were open to these companies?
- Who are the stakeholders of your decision? What is the impact of each alternative decision on each stakeholder you have identified?
- What rights and duties are involved?
- How would you decide the case? Would you primarily consider consequences, or are important principles involved?

There is a second sense of vulnerability in which the harm is other than the financial harm of an unsatisfactory market exchange. Elderly people living alone are susceptible to injuries from falls, from medical emergencies, from expensive health care bills, from loneliness. Alcoholics are susceptible to alcohol abuse, the poor are susceptible to bankruptcy, single women walking alone at night are vulnerable to sexual assault, accident victims are susceptible to high medical expenses and loss of income, and so forth. What we can call *general vulnerability* occurs when someone is susceptible to some specific physical, psychological, or financial harm.

From this we can see that there can be two types of marketing that targets vulnerable populations. Some marketing practices might target those consumers who are likely to be uninformed and vulnerable as consumers. Marketing aimed at children, for example, aims to sell products to customers who are unable to make thoughtful and informed consumer decisions. Other marketing practices might target populations that are vulnerable in the general sense as when, for example, an insurance company markets flood protection insurance to homeowners living in a river's floodplain. Are either, or both, types of targeting ethically legitimate?

As an initial judgment, we must say that marketing that is targeted at those individuals who are vulnerable as consumers is unethical. This is a case of taking advantage of someone's frailty and manipulating it for one's own advantage.

Clearly a portion of marketing and sales targets people who are vulnerable as consumers. Just as clearly such practices are wrong.

One way that this issue plays out involves groups who are vulnerable in both senses. Oftentimes people can become vulnerable as a consumer *because* they are vulnerable in some more general sense. The vulnerability that many elderly have with respect to injuries and illness might cause them to make consumer choices based on fear or guilt. A family member grieving over the death of a loved one might make choices in purchasing funeral services based on guilt or sorrow, rather than on a considered judgment. A person with a medical condition or disease is vulnerable, and the anxiety or fear associated with this vulnerability can lead to uninformed consumer choices. An inner city resident who is poor, uneducated, and chronically unemployed is unlikely to weigh the full consequences of the choice of alcoholic beverage.

A number of marketing campaigns seem to fit this model. The most abhorrent (and stereotypical) example is the ambulance-chasing attorney seeking a client for a personal-injury lawsuit. An accident victim is vulnerable to many harms and, while experiencing the stress of this situation, is unlikely to make a fully informed choice about legal representation. Marketing campaigns that target the elderly for such products as supplemental medical insurance, life insurance, emergency call devices, funeral services, and insurance often play on the fears, anxiety, and guilt that many elderly people experience. (See Decision Points, "Targeting Vulnerable People?" and "Marketing in Schools" to consider examples of marketing to specific populations.)

But just as people can be made vulnerable as consumers because they are vulnerable to other harms, there can also be cases in which people become vulnerable to other harms because they are vulnerable as consumers. Perhaps this strategy is the most abhorrent case of unethical marketing. Certain products—tobacco and alcohol are the most obvious examples—can make an individual vulnerable to a wide range of health risks. Marketing campaigns for products that target people who are vulnerable as consumers seem ethically repugnant. This explains the particular public outrage directed at tobacco and alcohol companies that target young people. Companies that market alcoholic beverages in poor inner-city neighborhoods must take this ethical guideline into account. Marketing malt beverages, fortified wines, and other alcoholic drinks to poor inner-city residents must acknowledge that many people in such situations are not fully autonomous consumers. Many people in such situations drink to get drunk; they drink to escape; they drink because they are alcoholics. (For an examination of online marketing that targets children, see the reading from the Kaiser Family Foundation included at the end of this chapter.)

One final form of marketing to a vulnerable population involves potentially all of us as consumer targets. We are each vulnerable when we are not aware that we are subject to a marketing campaign. This type of campaign is called **stealth or undercover marketing** and refers to those situations where we are subject to directed commercial activity without our knowledge. Certainly we are subjected to numerous communications on a regular basis without paying much attention,

company itself. In addition, the consumer is no longer being treated as an end in itself but instrumentally only as a means to the manufacturer's end. Further, if stealth marketing becomes the universal practice, the erosion of trust could become so significant that our commercial interactions would disintegrate under burdens of disclosures that would then be necessary.

Utilitarian analysis also does not support the ethics of these types of practices. When a consumer cannot trust the company's communication, the consumer may also lose faith in the company as a whole and will choose to purchase products and services elsewhere. Neither the company nor the consumer benefits from this result, and a product or service that might otherwise be the most effective or efficient solution may cease production because of a faulty marketing campaign.

Supply Chain Responsibility

11 OBJECTIVE

In creating a product, promoting it, and bringing it to the market, the marketing function of business involves a wide range of relationships with other commercial entities. In recent decades, the ethical spotlight has focused on the responsibility that a firm has for the activities of these other entities, what we shall refer to as supply chain responsibility. Few businesses have received as much attention in this regard as Nike.

Nike is the world's largest athletic shoe and apparel maker. In 1999, Nike held over 30 percent of the world's market share for athletic footwear, and along with Adidas (15 percent) and Reebok (11 percent) controls more than half of the world market. Nike began business in 1964 as Blue Ribbon Sports, an importer and marketer of low-priced Japanese sport shoes. As sales increased, the company began to design its own line of shoes and subcontract the manufacturing of the shoes to Japanese firms, eventually changing its name to Nike. Nike's Web site described its business philosophy decades later in the following words: "Our business model in 1964 is essentially the same as our model today: We grow by investing our money in design, development, marketing and sales and then contract with other companies to manufacture our products."

In the late 1990s, as discussed in chapter 6, Nike was subjected to intense international criticism for the working conditions in the factories where its products were manufactured. Critics charged that Nike relied on child labor and sweatshops in producing their shoes. They charged that workers in these factories were paid pennies a day, were subjected to cruel, unhealthy, and inhumane working conditions, were harassed and abused, and were prohibited from any union or collective bargaining activities.

Nike initially seemed to ignore the critics and deflect any criticism by denying responsibility for the behavior of its suppliers. If local manufacturers treated their workers poorly, that was beyond Nike's responsibility. At one point, Nike's vice president for Asia claimed that Nike did not "know the first thing about manufacturing. We are marketers and designers." Nike soon learned that the public was not persuaded by this response.

Ordinarily, we do not hold a person responsible for the actions of someone else. Assuming that the other person is an autonomous agent, we believe that each person is responsible for her or his own actions. But this is not always the case. There is a legal parallel to the idea that a business should be held responsible for the actions of its suppliers. The doctrine of *respondent superior,* Latin for "let the master answer," holds a principal (e.g., an employer) responsible for the actions of an agent (e.g., an employee) when that agent is acting in the ordinary course of his or her duties to the principal.[9] Thus, in the standard example, an employer can be held liable for damages caused by an accident involving an employee driving the company car on company business.

The justification for doing what might otherwise be considered unfair is that the agent is acting on the principal's behalf, at the principal's direction, and that the principal has direct influence over the agent's actions. Thus, if someone is doing something for you, at your direction, and under your influence, then you must take at least some responsibility for that person's actions. Most of the ethical rationale for business' responsibility for the actions of its suppliers stems from two of these conditions: Suppliers often act at the direction of business, and business often exercises significant influence over the actions of its suppliers.

However, in the multinational apparel and footwear industry, historically the corporate brands accepted responsibility only for their own organizations and specifically did not regard themselves as accountable for the labor abuses of their contractors (see Figure 8.1). This conception changed as multinationals and others became more aware of working conditions in these factories and the lack of legal protections for workers. Today, multinationals customarily accept this responsibility and use their leverage to encourage suppliers to have positive working environments for workers. The new concept of responsibility travels far deeper throughout the entire supply chain system, as is depicted in Figure 8.2. Each element of what should strike you as a tremendously complicated set of interrelationships is based on the potential to influence or exercise leverage throughout the system. The question, however, relates back to our earlier discussion of responsibility. How far down—or across—the supply chain should responsibility travel? Should a firm like Nike truly be responsible for the entire footwear and apparel system? If not, where would you draw the line as a consumer, or where would you

FIGURE 8.1
Historical Responsibility

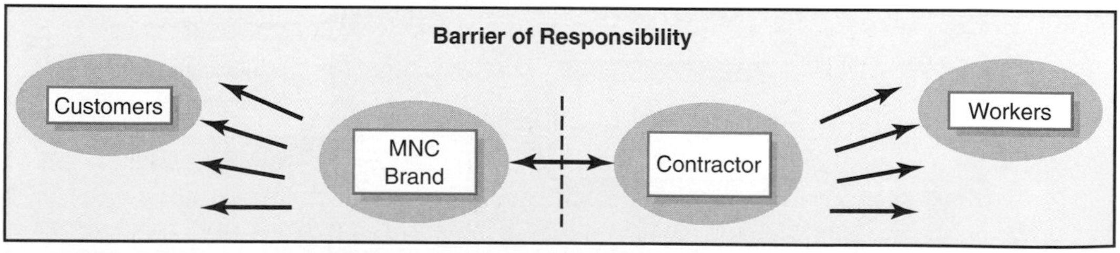

Source: Reprinted with permission from D. Arnold and L. Hartman, "Moral Imagination and the Future of Sweatshops," *Business & Society Review* 108, no. 4 (2003).

FIGURE 8.2 Evolved Concept of Responsibility

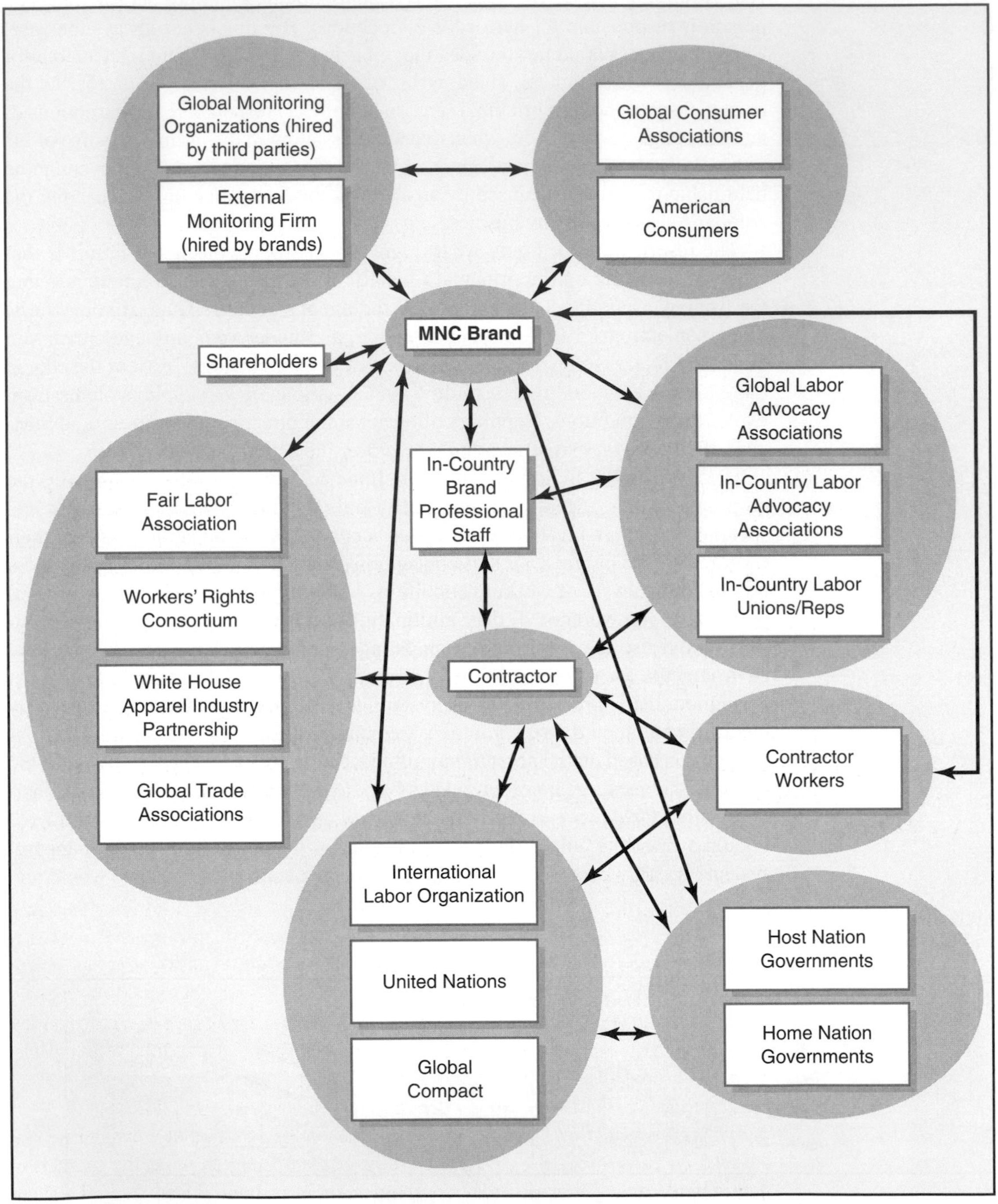

Source: Reprinted with permission from D. Arnold and L. Hartman, "Moral Imagination and the Future of Sweatshops," *Business & Society Review* 108, no. 4 (2003).

draw the line if you were the corporate responsibility vice president for Nike? What response will most effectively protect the rights of those involved while creating the most appropriate incentives to achieve profitable, ethical results? In today's increasingly complicated, globalized multinational systems, stakeholders have yet to resolve this challenging dilemma.

Sustainable Marketing

12 OBJECTIVE

"Sustainability" was introduced in chapter 5 as an approach to Corporate Social Responsibility that is gaining influence in all areas of business. **Sustainable, or green marketing,** is one aspect of this approach that already has changed how many firms do business. The four characteristics of marketing introduced earlier in this chapter—product, price, promotion, and placement—are a helpful way to structure an understanding of sustainable, green marketing.

Product

The most significant progress towards sustainability will depend upon the sustainability of products themselves. Discovering what the consumer "really wants," and developing products to meet those wants, have always been among the primary marketing challenges. Meeting the real needs of present and future generations within ecological constraints can be understood simply as a refinement of this traditional marketing objective.

Consider, for example, the business differences between marketing the physical pieces of computer hardware and marketing computing services. Should Dell or HP be in the business of selling computer components, or are they selling the service to provide consumers with up-to-date computer hardware, software, data storage? Chapter 9 will examine the distinction between products and service in more depth, but the marketing department should be at the forefront of identifying the real needs of consumers so that a business can develop the long-term relationships with consumers that will insure both financial and ecological sustainability.

Another aspect of marketing involves the design and creation of products. William McDonough (see his essay included in chapter 9) has often described environmental regulation as a design problem; a product or production process that pollutes and wastes resources is a poorly designed product or process. Regulatory mandates usually result when business has a poorly-designed product or process. Marketing departments therefore should also be involved in the design of products, finding ways to build sustainability into the very design of each product.

Finally, marketing professionals have an opportunity to influence the packaging of products. Over-packaging and the use of petroleum-based plastics are packaging issues already under environmental scrutiny. Imagine the marketing opportunities if a major soft-drink bottler such as Coke or Pepsi turned to corn-based biodegradable plastics for their bottles. Imagine what the marketing department of major mail-order companies such as Land's End or L. L. Bean could do if their catalogues were printed on recycled paper. Imagine the marketing opportunities, and responsibilities, of a company such as Procter & Gamble moving towards recycled cardboard for its packaging.

These three areas come together clearly within the context of extended producer responsibility and take-back legislation in which a firm is held responsible to take back and recycle all the products it introduces into the marketplace. These regulatory developments, now taking hold especially in Europe, will be seen as barriers to profit by some firms. But more creative firms will see opportunities here for generating entire new markets. Take-back legislation provides strong incentives for re-designing products in ways that make it easier to reuse and recycle. Marketing services rather than products, of course, will be the most efficient means for accomplishing this objective.

Price

A second aspect of marketing is price. Sustainability asks us to focus on the environmental costs of resources, the "natural capital" on which most firms rely, and points out that environmental costs are seldom factored into the price of most products. Marketing professionals should play a role in setting prices that reflect a product's true ecological cost.

At first glance, this might seem a peculiar area in which to expect business to move. Internalizing environmental externalities sounds like a polite way of suggesting that business ought to raise its prices. Such a strategy would seem, at best, unrealistic. Government regulation, rather than voluntary action, is more likely to move business in this direction. Without government mandates across the board for an industry, internalizing the costs of natural capitalism into its products will put a company at a comparative disadvantage.

On the other hand, setting prices in such a way that more sustainable products are priced competitively with other products is a more reasonable strategy for sustainable marketing. Ordinarily, we might think that pricing is a straightforward and objective process. One starts with the costs of producing a product, adds a reasonable rate of return, and the result is asking price. Ultimately, the actual price is whatever buyer and seller agree upon. However, this simple model misses some important complexities. To understand some of the complexities of price, and the role of marketing in this, consider the example of hybrid automobiles.

Like any new product, a hybrid automobile required investments in research, design, production, and marketing long before it could be brought to market. For such a complex product as a hybrid automobile, these investments were substantial, well into the hundred of millions of dollars for each automaker who produces a hybrid. Setting a price for this product involves a complicated process of projecting sales, markets, and a product's life-cycle. In one sense, the very first hybrid cost millions of dollars to manufacture, well beyond an affordable and marketable price. Businesses normally take a loss on a new product until such time as economies of scale kick in to lower costs and market share develops sufficiently to produce a revenue stream that can begin to pay down the initial investment and generate profits. Marketing professionals who are aware of sustainability concerns have much to contribute in establishing prices that protect sustainable products from short-term cost-benefit analyses.

Decision Point

Marketing to the Base of the Pyramid

In his landmark book, business scholar C. K. Prahalad details the business opportunities that exist for firms that are creative and resourceful enough to develop markets among the world's poorest people.[10]

Done correctly, marketing to the 4 billion people at the base of the global economic pyramid would employ market forces in addressing some of the greatest ethical and environmental problems of the twenty-first century.

Obviously, helping to meet the needs of the world's poorest people would be a significant ethical contribution. The strategy involves another ethical consideration as well: A market of this size requires environmentally sustainable products and technologies. If everyone in the world used resources and created wastes at the rate Americans do, the global environment would suffer immeasurably. Businesses that understand this fact face a huge marketing opportunity.

Accomplishing such goals will require a significant revision to the standard marketing paradigm. Business must, in Prahalad's phrase, "create the capacity to consume" among the world's poor. Creating this capacity to consume among the world's poor would create a significant win–win opportunity from both a financial and an ethical perspective.

Prahalad points out that the world's poor do have significant purchasing power, albeit in the aggregate rather than on a per capita basis. Creating the capacity to consume among the world's poor will require a transformation in the conceptual framework of global marketing and some creative steps from business. Prahalad mentions three principles as key to marketing to the poor: affordability, access, and availability.

Consider how a firm might market such household products as laundry soap differently in India than in the United States. Marketing in the United States can involve large plastic containers, sold at a low per-unit cost. Trucks transport cases from manufacturing plant to wholesale warehouses to giant big-box retailers where they can sit in inventory until purchase. Consumers wheel the heavy containers out to their cars in shopping carts and store them at home in the laundry room.

The aggregate soap market in India could be greater than the market in the United States, but Indian consumers would require smaller and more affordable containers. Prahalad therefore talks about the need for single size servings for many consumer products. Given longer and more erratic work hours and a lack of personal transportation, the poor often lack access to markets. Creative marketing would need to find ways to provide easier access to their products. Longer store hours and wider and more convenient distribution channels could reach consumers otherwise left out of the market.

So, too, can imaginative financing, credit, and pricing schemes. Microfinance and microcredit arrangements are developing throughout less developed economies as creative means to support the capacity of poor people to buy and sell goods and services. Finally, innovative marketing can ensure that products are available where and when the world's poor need them. Base-of-the-pyramid consumers tend to be cash customers with incomes that are unpredictable.

(*continued*)

(*concluded*)

A distributional system that ensures product availability at the time and place when customers are ready and able to make the purchase can help create the capacity to consume. Prahalad's approach—tied to moral imagination discussed previously—responds both to the consumers and to the corporate investors and other for-profit multinational stakeholders.

- Do you think that business firms and industries have an ethical responsibility to address global poverty by creating the capacity to consume among the world's poor? Do you think that this can be done? What responsibilities, ethical and economic, do firms face when marketing in other countries and among different cultures? Imagine that you are in the marketing department of a firm that manufacturers a consumer product such as laundry detergent or shampoo. Describe how it might be marketed differently in India.
- What are the key facts relevant to your judgment?
- What ethical issues are involved in a firm's decision to market its products among the world's poor by creating the capacity to consume?
- Who are the stakeholders?
- What alternatives does a firm have with regard to the way in which it markets its products?
- How do the alternatives compare; how do the alternatives you have identified affect the stakeholders?

Consider also how price functions with such business practices as sales, manufacturer's rebates, cash-back incentives to consumers, bonuses to sales staff, and the use of loss leaders in retailing. Obviously price is often manipulated for many marketing reasons, including promotion to help gain a foothold in a market. Short-term losses are often justified in pricing decisions by appeal to long-term considerations. This seems a perfect fit for sustainable marketing goals.

Perhaps nowhere is price a more crucial element of marketing than it is in marketing to the base of the economic pyramid. Small profit margins and efficient distribution systems within large markets, as demonstrated so clearly by large retailers like Wal-Mart, can prove to be a highly successful business model. An ethically praiseworthy goal would be to export this marketing ingenuity to serve the cause of global sustainability. The Decision Point, "Marketing to the Base of the Pyramid," explains the mechanics of this process, and the reading by Prahalad and Hart included at the end of this chapter offers a classic discussion of its marketing analysis. In a subsequent reading, Prahalad responds to his colleague, Professor A. Karnini, who challenges the process, since the concept of a market among those living in poverty is not universally accepted.

Promotion

A third aspect of marketing, of course, is the promotion and advertising of products. Marketing also has a responsibility to help shape consumer demand, encouraging consumers to demand more sustainable products from business. Without question,

Reality Check *Terra Choice's Seven Sins of Greenwashing*

SIN OF THE HIDDEN TRADE-OFF
A claim suggesting that a product is 'green' based on a narrow set of attributes without attention to other important environmental issues. Paper, for example, is not necessarily environmentally-preferable just because it comes from a sustainably-harvested forest. Other important environmental issues in the paper-making process, such as greenhouse gas emissions, or chlorine use in bleaching may be equally important.

SIN OF NO PROOF
An environmental claim that cannot be substantiated by easily accessible supporting information or by a reliable third-party certification. Common examples are facial tissues or toilet tissue products that claim various percentages of post-consumer recycled content without providing evidence.

SIN OF VAGUENESS
A claim that is so poorly defined or broad that its real meaning is likely to be misunderstood by the consumer. 'All-natural' is an example. Arsenic, uranium, mercury, and formaldehyde are all naturally occurring, and poisonous. 'All natural' isn't necessarily 'green'.

SIN OF WORSHIPING FALSE LABELS
A product that, through either words or images, gives the impression of third-party endorsement where no such endorsement exists; fake labels, in other words.

SIN OF IRRELEVANCE
An environmental claim that may be truthful but is unimportant or unhelpful for consumers seeking environmentally preferable products. 'CFC-free' is a common example, since it is a frequent claim despite the fact that CFCs are banned by law.

SIN OF LESSER OF TWO EVILS
A claim that may be true within the product category, but that risks distracting the consumer from the greater environmental impacts of the category as a whole. Organic cigarettes could be an example of this Sin, as might the fuel-efficient sport-utility vehicle.

SIN OF FIBBING
Environmental claims that are simply false. The most common examples were products falsely claiming to be Energy Star certified or registered.

marketing has already shown how powerful a force it can be in shaping consumer demand. Marketing has played a major role in creating various social meanings for shopping and buying. Sustainable marketing can help create the social meanings and consumer expectations supportive of sustainable goals. An often overlooked aspect of advertising is its educational function. Consumers learn from advertising and marketers have a responsibility as educators. Helping consumers learn the value of sustainable products, helping them become sustainable consumers, is an important role for sustainable marketing. For example, see the Reality Check, "Terra Choice's Seven Sins of Greenwashing" as one effort in consumer education.

Certainly one aspect of product promotion will involve the "green labelling." Just as ingredient labels, nutrition labels, and warning labels have become normal and standardized, environmental pressure may well create a public demand for environmental and sustainable labelling. But, past history has shown a tendency for some firms to exploit green labelling initiatives and mislead consumers. "Greenwashing" is the practice of promoting a product by misleading consumers about the environmentally beneficial aspects of the product. Labelling products with such terms as "environmentally friendly," "natural," "eco," "energy efficient"

Decision Point *Examples of Greenwashing?*

Which of the following corporate marketing initiatives would you describe as an example of "greenwashing"?

- An ad for the GM Hummer which describes the truck as "thirsty for adventure, not gas." The Hummer was rated at 20 mpg on the highway.
- A major re-branding of the oil company British Petroleum by renaming itself "BP" for "beyond petroleum."
- An "eco-shaped" bottle for the bottle water brand Ice Mountain. For that matter, any bottled water described as "natural," "pure" or "organic."

Which of the following examples, all taken from the Federal Trade Commission, are cases of misleading greenwashing?

- A box of aluminum foil is labeled with the claim "recyclable," without further elaboration. Unless the type of product, surrounding language, or other context of the phrase establishes whether the claim refers to the foil or the box, the claim is deceptive if any part of either the box or the foil, other than minor, incidental components, cannot be recycled.
- A trash bag is labeled "recyclable"" without qualification. Because trash bags will ordinarily not be separated out from other trash at the landfill or incinerator for recycling, they are highly unlikely to be used again for any purpose.
- An advertiser notes that its shampoo bottle contains "20 percent more recycled content." The claim in its context is ambiguous. Depending on contextual factors, it could be a comparison either to the advertiser's immediately preceding product or to a competitor's product.
- A product wrapper is printed with the claim "Environmentally Friendly." Textual comments on the wrapper explain that the wrapper is "Environmentally Friendly because it was not chlorine bleached, a process that has been shown to create harmful substances." The wrapper was, in fact, not bleached with chlorine. However, the production of the wrapper now creates and releases to the environment significant quantities of other harmful substances.
- A product label contains an environmental seal, either in the form of a globe icon, or a globe icon with only the text "Earth Smart" around it. Either label is likely to convey to consumers that the product is environmentally superior to other products.
- A nationally marketed bottle bears the unqualified statement that it is "recyclable." Collection sites for recycling the material in question are not available to a substantial majority of consumers or communities, although collection sites are established in a significant percentage of communities or available to a significant percentage of the population.
- The seller of an aerosol product makes an unqualified claim that its product "Contains no CFCs." Although the product does not contain CFCs, it does contain HCFC-22, another ozone depleting ingredient.

Opening Decision Point Revisited *Marketing Pharmaceuticals*

Beginning in the summer of 2009, the Obama Administration and the U.S. Congress debated legislation that would create significant health care reform within the United States. Not surprisingly, the pharmaceutical industry has been a major player in health care reform. In June 2009, the U.S. pharmaceutical industry agreed, pending passage of health care reform legislation, to spend $80 billion over the next 10 years to help reduce drug costs for senior citizens. This plan would have pharmaceutical companies paying for what has come to be called the "doughnut hole" in Medicare payments. At the time this agreement was reached, senior citizens were responsible for paying the full costs of prescription drugs that fell within a gap between $2,700 and $6,154 that Medicare pays. This agreement would help pay for President Obama's proposed health care reform plan. In August 2009, the U.S. pharmaceutical industry authorized its lobbying forms to spend up to $150 million to support the President's health care reform package. Most observers saw this as part of the June agreement to support the president's initiatives.

According to some observers, health care reform turned on the question of controlling costs of health care itself, which would include controlling costs of drugs, and controlling costs by regulating the insurance industry and providing government sponsored programs to compete with private insurance companies. Thus, according to these observers, health care reform pitted the insurance industry against the pharmaceutical and medical industry. From this perspective, President Obama sided with the pharmaceutical and medical industry. Critics claimed that the financial contributions to Medicare and spending on political advertising were *quid pro quo* for the pharmaceutical industry's support of the President's policies. By the time the final version of this law was passed in the spring of 2010, it was commonly referred to as "health insurance reform" legislation.

- Do you believe that the pharmaceutical industry was acting ethically when it chose to support the President's health care reform legislation? Would your judgment differ if the President's proposals favored the insurance industry?
- The narrow, legal model of CSR described in chapter 5 holds that business only has an obligation to obey the law. How does this case affect your views of that position?
- In what ways are these activities of the pharmaceutical industry a matter of marketing? In what ways are they not?
- Is political advocacy a legitimate type of marketing? Why, or why not?

"biodegradable" and the like, can help promote products that have little or no environmental benefits. Take a look at the Decision Point, "Examples of Greenwashing?" to see if you can distinguish the green washing claims from the sincere ones.

Placement

The final aspect of marketing involves the channels of distribution that move a product from producer to consumer. Professor Patrick Murphy suggests two directions in which marketing can develop sustainable channels.[11] As typically understood, marketing channels involve such things as transportation, distribution, inventory, and the like. Recent advances in marketing have emphasized just in time inventory control, large distribution centers, and sophisticated transportation schemes. Murphy foresees new sustainability options being added to this model which emphasize fuel efficiency and alternative fuel technologies used in transportation, more localized and efficient distribution channels, and a greater reliance on electronic rather than physical distribution. More efficient distribution channels can also serve the underserved base of the pyramid consumers as well.

Consider, as an example, how the publishing industry has evolved its channels of distribution. Originally, books, magazines, catalogues, or newspapers were printed in one location and then distributed via truck, rail, or air across the country. More modern practices piloted by such companies as *USA Today* and the *Wall Street Journal,* send electronic versions of the content to localized printers who publish and distribute the final product locally. Text book publishers do a similar thing when they allow users to select specific content and create a custom published book for each use. As subscriptions to hard-copy publications decline, many newspapers, magazines, and catalogues are taking this a step further by moving towards on-line publishing.

Murphy also describes a second aspect of the channel variable in marketing that promises significant sustainability rewards. "Reverse channels" refers to the growing marketing practice of taking back one's products after their useful life. The life-cycle responsibility and "take-back" models described in chapter 9 will likely fall to marketing departments. The same department that is responsible for sending a product out into the marketplace should expect the responsibility for finding ways to take back that product to dispose, recycle, or reuse it.[12]

Questions, Projects, and Exercises

1. Are some products too dangerous to be marketed in any circumstance? What regulations, if any, would you place on marketing cigarettes? Handguns? Prescription drugs?
2. Conduct a classroom debate on the McDonald's spilt coffee case. Conduct an Internet search for this case (*Liebeck v. McDonald's*) to find both legal and journalistic comments on this case. One-third of the class should play the role of Mrs. Liebeck's attorneys, one-third the role of McDonald's attorneys, and one-third the role of the judge and jury.
3. Research the case *Pelman v. McDonald's* in which it was alleged that McDonald's was partially responsible for the health problems associated with the obesity of children who eat McDonald's fast food. Should McDonald's and other fast-food restaurants be judged negligent for selling dangerous products, failing to warn consumers of the dangers of a high-fat diet, and deceptive advertising?
4. The Federal Trade Commission regulates advertising on the basis of two criteria: deception and unfairness. How can an ad be unfair? Who gets hurt by deceptive advertising?
5. Collect several sample prescription drug ads from magazines, newspapers, and television. On the basis of location of the ad, what do you think is the intended target

audience? Are the ads in any way misleading? Are the required side-effect warnings deceptive in any way? Do you believe that health care professionals provide adequate screening to ensure that prescription drugs are not misused?

6. Review the Decision Point, "Marketing in Schools" (concerning marketing in the schools and Channel One), and reflect on your own educational experience. Assume you were offered a laptop computer as long as you understood that you would see a commercial every time you turned it on and for two minutes for every fifteen minutes of use. What is your initial reaction to this arrangement? As you consider it in greater detail, what types of restrictions on advertisements do you think the laptop manufacturer (or service provider who is responsible for managing the advertising messages) should impose if the laptops will be given to college-aged students? How would you develop standards for these restrictions?
7. Many salespeople are compensated predominantly on a commission basis. In other words, though the salesperson receives a small base hourly rate, most of her or his compensation derives from a percentage of the price of items sold. Since basically the salesperson makes money only if you buy something and he or she makes more money if you spend more money, do you ever trust a salesperson's opinion? What would make you more likely to trust a commission-based salesperson, or less likely? Is there anything a commissioned salesperson could do to get you to trust her or him? Best Buy, the consumer electronics store, communicates to consumers that it does *not* pay its salespeople on the basis of commissions in order to encourage objectivity. Are you more likely to go to Best Buy as a result?
8. In 2001, TAP Pharmaceuticals pled guilty to participating in a criminal conspiracy with doctors by providing free samples of Lupron for which the doctors later billed Medicare and patients. Federal prosecutors also charged TAP executives and midlevel managers with fraud, alleging that TAP employees bribed doctors and hospitals with cash, free vacations, and free samples as an incentive for them to prescribe Lupron. Defendants argued that the samples and gifts were standard industry practice and did not amount to a bribe. In December 2004, a jury acquitted the individuals involved. TAP itself settled its case with the government by agreeing to pay $150 million restitution to consumers and insurance companies for what the government charged were artificially inflated drug prices. The prices were inflated because of the alleged bribes paid to doctors.

   TAP did not admit to any wrongdoing, claiming that it settled to avoid further legal costs. Studies have shown that samples, as well as small gifts and lunches, can lead doctors to prescribe more expensive brand names when cheaper generic drugs would be as effective. What additional facts might you need to know to make a fully informed judgment in this case? What outcome do you believe the pharmaceutical companies are striving to achieve through these practices? What alternatives might be available to pharmaceutical companies to serve a similar outcome without incurring legal liability or crossing ethical lines? Do the doctors or hospitals bear any ethical responsibility under these circumstances? What duties do the pharmaceutical companies, doctors, or hospitals have? What does the principle of fairness require in this case? What rights are implicated?
9. Go to the FTC Web site (http://www.ftc.gov/bcp/grnrule/guides980427.htm) and review the cases in the Decision Point, "Examples of Greenwashing." You will find the FTC's judgment on each case (and others). Do you agree with the FTC's assessment of misleading environmental marketing examples?

Key Terms

After reading this chapter, you should have a clear understanding of the following Key Terms. The page numbers refer to the point at which they were discussed in the chapter. For a more complete definition, please see the Glossary.

caveat emptor approach, *p. 413*
"Four Ps" of marketing, *p. 408*
implied warranty of merchantability, *p. 415*
marketing, *p. 407*
negligence, *p. 416*
stealth or undercover marketing, *p. 433*
strict liability, *p. 417*
sustainable or green marketing, *p. 439*
word-of-mouth marketing, *p. 435*

End Notes

1. The Levitt quote is taken from Theodore Levitt, "Marketing and the Corporate Purpose: The Purpose Is to Create and Keep a Customer," a speech delivered at New York University, March 2, 1977, available from Vital Speeches of the Day. Similar claims can be found in Theodore Levitt, "Marketing and the Corporate Purpose," Chapter 1 of *The Marketing Imagination* (New York: Free Press, 1983), pp. 5 and 7.
2. The American Marketing Association definition is taken from its Web site: http://www.marketingpower.com/(accessed April 17, 2010).
3. An informal Internet search found over a hundred companies advertising with this slogan. They ranged from real estate companies to antique dealers, and from long-distance phone providers to water filtration systems dealers. Presumably those who disagree do not advertise that fact.
4. See, for example, the PBS video *Affluenza,* produced by KCTS/Seattle and Oregon Public Broadcasting. See also Juliet Shor, "Why Do We Consume So Much?", the Clemens Lecture at St. John's University, in *Contemporary Issues in Business Ethics,* Joseph DesJardins and John McCall, eds., (Belmont, CA. Wadsworth Publishing, 2005); and Jim Pooler, *"Why We Shop: Emotional Rewards and Retail Strategies* (Westport, CT: Praeger Publishing, 2003).
5. Regina Lawrence, "Framing Obesity: The Evolution of News Discourse on a Public Health Issue," Harvard University Working Paper No. 2004-5, 2004, http://www.ksg.harvard.edu/presspol/Research_Publications/Papers/Working_Papers/2004_5.pdf (accessed April 17, 2010).
6. References have been removed but are available from the authors.
7. McCann-Erickson U.S. Advertising Volume Reports and Bob Coen's Insider's Report for December 2005, http://www.mccann.com/news/pdfs/insiders05.pdf, (accessed June 6, 2006).
8. Direct Marketing Association, May 2006, http://www.the-dma.org/cgi/disppressrelease?article=787 (accessed April 17, 2010).
9. This parallel is explained in Michael Santoro, *Profits and Principles: Global Capitalism and Human Rights in China* (Ithaca, NY: Cornell University Press, 2000), p. 161, and is cited as well by Denis Arnold and Norman Bowie, "Sweatshops and Respects for Persons," *Business Ethics Quarterly* 13, no. 2 (2003), pp. 221–242.
10. C. K. Prahalad, *The Fortune at the Bottom of the Pyramid* (Upper Saddle River, NJ: Wharton Publishing, 2005).
11. Patrick E. Murphy, Business and Environmental Sustainability Conference, Carlson School of Management, Minneapolis, MN, "Sustainable Marketing," (2005).

12. Sustainable marketing seems a growing field within both business and the academic community. Two of the earliest books in this field, both of which remain very helpful, are: *Environmental Marketing: Strategies, Practice, Theory, and Research,* Polonsky, Michael J. and Alma T. Mintu-Wimsatt, eds., Binghampton, NY: The Haworth Press (New York, 1995) and Donald Fuller, *Sustainable Marketing: Managerial-Ecological Issues,* (Thousand Oaks, CA: SAGE Publications, 1999). A particularly helpful essay in the Polonsky book is by Seth, Jagdish N. and Atul Parvatiyar "Ecological Imperatives and the Role of Marketing," pp. 3–20. Seth and Parvatiyar are often credited with coining the term "sustainable marketing" in this essay.

Readings

Reading 8-1

The Friendship of Buzz, Blog and Swag

Kalynne Hackney Pudner

Word-of-mouth (WOM) is arguably the biggest trend in advertising since the television commercial. This is not because it is a novel form of disseminating product information (it is rather the oldest), but because the Internet has magnified its reach beyond the most optimistic marketer's imaginings. Where WOM was once restricted by the logistics of proximity and cost, the Internet enables "word explosion," the simultaneous, potentially global transmission of a single message to dozens, hundreds, or even thousands of other Internet users through e-mail, postings, or links; search engines multiply the effect exponentially.[1] Unsurprisingly, the marketing industry is eager to harness this explosive power.

What, precisely, is WOM? The Word of Mouth Marketing Association (WOMMA), the self-appointed industry standard and watchdog, defines it as "the act of consumers providing information to other consumers;" word of mouth marketing, then, consists of "giving people a reason to talk about your products and services, and making it easier for that conversation to take place."[2] Fundamentally, WOM is a marketing strategy that utilizes pre-existing relationships between someone who will advocate the marketer's product (the "advocate") and the marketer's targeted consumers (the "target").

Authentic WOM unhitches the marketing message from control of the marketer, which allows the message to reach targets who may have thrown up a barrier between themselves and the marketer (what one commentator calls a "no-marketing zone"); but which also removes the message from the marketer's direct control.[3] It might be expected that this combination of features places the targeted consumer in a position of vulnerability, particularly toward fraud or deception. For this reason, WOMMA has undertaken to set and informally enforce ethical standards for the practice of WOM. While it also addresses the engagement of minors and respect for venue rules, WOMMA's ethics initiative focuses on transparency, or what it calls "Honesty ROI." It urges WOM marketers and their advocates to be honest and open regarding their *Relationship;* it urges advocates to express only honest and open *Opinions;* and it urges advocates to be honest and open in disclosing their *Identity.*

The intuitive appeal of disclosure is understandable. The ethical red flags were flying high when "Wal-Marting Across America" was exposed as the fake blog ("flog") of a professional journalist couple under paid contract by Edelman, Wal-Mart's public relations firm. Even worse, a second blog called "Paid Critics," which bashed public officials and others who oppose Wal-Mart's expansion and operating practices, was exposed as a flog authored by two full-time Edelman employees.[4] The original flog's Web address, www.forwalmart.com, now bears the Wal-Mart logo and a message reading, "Please check back soon for a new site brought to you by Wal-Mart. For now, please visit Wal-Mart Facts." WOMMA's Code of Conduct would have required the Wal-Mart tour couple to fully disclose their relationship with Edelman, and Edelman's relationship with Wal-Mart, as well as the "Paid Critics" blog authors' identity as Edelman employees. Here, transparency would have benefited readers, the WOM industry and—in light of the scathingly negative publicity backlash—Wal-Mart and Edelman.

WOMMA's disclosure requirement extends beyond blogging and flogging to other forms of word-of-mouth promotion. Think of traditional, person-to-person WOM. The Edelman employees would be required to identify themselves as such before recommending the ten-cent spiral notebooks at Wal-Mart's Back to School extravaganza. This is intuitively odd. Not only is it irrelevant, but it could be off-putting, a superfluous and affected authority claim.

The intuitive oddness may be ascribed to the presupposition that the target either is already aware of the advocate's connection to the marketer, or has reason to trust the advocate's assessment independently of any such connection. I think this is an important observation. But it isn't sufficient to dispel the intuition of awkwardness, because the disclosure would be similarly awkward where there is no such presupposition about the advocate-target relationship. Ditto for the casual acquaintance who urges others to try this tea or that hand cream. To render already-presumed motivation explicit is to render it dubious, it seems, and thereby less effective WOM.

What these considerations suggest is that transparency is not panacea to the ethical tensions of WOM, but rather serves a particular function that varies in importance relative to the particular context of the practice. I would argue that transparency is a subsidiary, and potentially deflecting, aspect of the real crux of the ethical issue: the pre-existing relationship on which WOM seeks to capitalize. If I am correct, then WOMMA's calls for advocate transparency are well-intentioned but misdirected. The relationship that must be made transparent to the target is not that between the advocate and the marketer, but between the advocate and him/herself, the target.

This hypothesis can be supported by comparing the pre-existing relationships utilized by three different forms of WOM: buzz, blog and swag.

Buzz

Departing slightly from WOMMA's usage, the term "buzz" refers here to traditional word-of-mouth communication between particular individuals, regardless of catalyst (advertising, product experience, marketer direction), and regardless of medium (face-to-face, telephone, print or electronic). The essential feature of buzz is that the pre-existing relationship between advocate and target is determinate, between particular and identified individuals.

True buzz (as opposed to the spontaneous product referral it seeks to imitate) is frequently accompanied by product seeding, defined by WOMMA as "placing the right product into the right hands at the right time, providing information or samples to influential individuals." Advocates are given free samples of the marketer's product, to use personally and sometimes to distribute to target consumers as well. BzzAgent (www.bzzagent.com), which bills itself as the leading WOM media network, directs its advocates, or "agents," to disclose to targets that they are receiving free product in exchange for their advocacy.

Note that the very transparency WOMMA thinks will enhance the advocate's credibility actually seems to damage it. The act of disclosure redirects the target's attention from the product, and to the advocacy message itself. Does my friend feel an implicit obligation, grounded on reciprocity or gratitude, to promote this product insincerely? Of course, such promotion would be unethical. But disclosing the receipt of free product doesn't fix the problem.

In addition to raising suspicion of insincerity, buzz transparency raises that of hyperbole; research has established that self-generated advertisements show a marked tendency to exaggerate the positive experience of product use, and that this tendency is recognized and severely discounted by its audience.[5] Even if the disclosure itself is negative ("I'm not getting anything for this"), the very fact that the advocate feels the disclosure is necessary casts aspersion on the reliability of the testimony. Instead, the disclosure raises the question whether product mention is part of an advertising strategy unless explicitly stated otherwise. Nor do the questions stop with product-oriented messages; the target may be led to wonder about the sincerity and motivation of other communication by the advocate, and indeed, about the basis of their relationship itself.

Swag

I want to jump now to the opposite end of the relational spectrum, to "swag." Swag refers in its central cases to free product and other items given by marketers to journalists, editors and public personalities, in the hope that they may be induced to use their regular media platforms to disseminate a positive product message. In some cases, swag is of considerable monetary value, even extravagant.[6] The obvious concern is that the media message not appear to be "purchased," and thus presumably biased. Still, there is a practical argument in favor of swag: how are products supposed to be reviewed unless the reviewer is given no-cost access to the product?[7]

Swag distribution is not limited to product seeding, however, and marketers have strong incentive to pursue positive media coverage by whatever means they can devise. It's almost an advertising truism that negative news can do more harm than the most expensive, expansive advertising campaign can do good. In fact, the downward pull of negative media coverage is so pronounced that subsequent advertising has been shown to be wasted, even if it is an explicit counter to the coverage.[8] Conversely, positive publicity followed by a surge of traditional advertising elicits a stronger, more positive response by consumers than either the publicity or the advertising alone.[9] Because consumers discount positive publicity when it is known to be paid advertising, marketers covet what politicians term "earned media," and swag has proven itself a viable option for generating it. Of course, the value of earned media is imparted by the perception of unbiased, objective, un-self-interested reporting, and this perception is precisely what is compromised when the media is motivated by a sense of obligation to repay the benefit of swag received, or by the hope of future swag. So while a media review of the Kindle is valuable to consumers only if the writer has personal experience with a Kindle, it is considerably less valuable if the writer also has personal experience of, say, the Paris Air Show at Amazon's expense.

In swag WOM, then, advocate transparency does serve the target, and by reinforcing the presumption of unbiased reporting, it serves the marketer as well. Even if stating the obvious ("I was given a free cup of shaved ice to taste before writing this review"), the disclosure does not cloud the advocate-target relationship in the same way it does in buzz. Why?

I would suggest this is because transparency is a natural feature of the relationship itself. As in the case of buzz, swag utilizes a pre-existing relationship between the advocate and the target; but unlike buzz, this relationship is non-particular, generally unidentified, and often invisible. Unlike buzz, the advocate-target relationship in swag consists essentially of one-way dissemination of messages to an indeterminate audience; also unlike buzz, these messages are presumed to be impartial. The target's assumption that the advocate's messages are unbiased, objective, and un-self-interested is necessary for the relationship to work. Transparency is a condition of this assumption.

Blog

Occupying a vast, variegated and ever-evolving relational middle ground between buzz and swag is "blog," in which a particular individual or group of individuals (named or pseudonymous) uses the Internet to disseminate messages to a non-particular, generally unidentified and qualifiedly invisible audience that ordinarily has feedback capability. Although blogs have been around since the mid-90s, they have burgeoned in popularity primarily since 2005, due in large part to the free, user-friendly sites designed to host them. The Pew Internet and American Life Project reports that as of 2006, eight percent of Internet users, approximately 12 million American adults, kept a blog; thirty-nine percent, or 57 million, read them regularly.[10] Although the statistics will certainly have grown further by the time this paper is published, it is projected that the ratio of blog consumption to production will remain constant in the vicinity of 80/20.[11] Marketers who wish to utilize the blogger-audience relationship for WOM are advised to identify bloggers who are passionate about their product or product type, and therefore likely to talk about the product in strong and positive terms, rather than to aim for broader but shallower message dissemination.[12]

One of the more extensive studies on blog activity and the people who engage in it finds that blogs "may function as a personal diary, a daily pulpit, a collaborative space, a political soapbox, a collection of links, or a set of memos to the world."[13] It follows from this range of purpose that the character of blog messages and blogger-audience relationship is anything but standard, and the implications of this variation for blog WOM are enormous. But two generalizations about blogger-audience relationships can be made: first, they are usually derived from contiguous blogger-audience relationships; and second, they are independently defined by the audience.

The overwhelming volume of blog content on the World Wide Web tends to limit the reader's exposure to blog content, as paradoxical as this may sound. The few sites that offer thematically-grouped lists of blogs can be cumbersome as well as vague, and the prospect of browsing for new, relevant and engaging blogs can be daunting.[14] Thus most blog visits are generated by links from other Web sites, especially other blogs. Blogrolls and linked comment sections act as letters of introduction from one blog to another, creating jaggedly overlapping virtual communities of bloggers and their regular, shared readers. The virtual community phenomenon can also be overtly created, as when a blogger links to another blog with explicit instructions to "go here"; and commentators who do so ordinarily credit the referring blog in their feedback.

As I have argued elsewhere, the relationship between blogger and audience, in the absence of further relationship unmediated by electronic communication, is indeterminate, leaving the audience to interpret it as she chooses in order to contextualize both incoming and outgoing messages.[15] This may tip the blogger-audience relationship toward buzz, as it seems to do in the case of "mommy bloggers," or it may tip it toward swag, as in (for example) the blogs of reporter Jeff Jarvis or the Chronicle of Higher Education.[16] Relationship interpretation online is also subject to radical revision, from personal to impersonal, or vice versa.[17]

Just as advocate-target relationships vary across the blog universe, so does the function of advocate transparency. The target is imaginatively constructing the advocate's personality by filling in gaps between advocate disclosures (both related and unrelated to the marketer and its product), and then crafting a relationship with this constructed personality; therefore, the meaning and importance of the transparent information also will be determined solely by the target. Where the advocate-target relationship in blog may be buzz-like, transparency is likely to be disruptive; where swag-like, it is likely to be an asset. But since the relationship is interpreted, frequently revised, and sometimes unilaterally discontinued by the target, transparency's likely effect is ultimately unpredictable.

The Ethics of Transparency

What these comparisons suggest is that the ethical importance of transparency is not intrinsic to WOM as a marketing strategy, but to the relationships that WOM constitutionally employs. As these vary according to WOM type, so does the importance of transparency.

The most intuitively unethical cases of WOM are those in which the target is deliberately and actively deceived, as with the Wal-Mart flogs. Passive deception ("don't ask, don't tell") is marginally better, but still problematic. And the ethical problem is a straightforward one: deception undermines the autonomy of the moral agent at whom it is directed. Intentionally deceptive WOM, whether active or passive, leaves the target with incomplete or erroneous information on which to base his choice; he is therefore not in a position to make his purchase decision autonomously. Transparency, then, protects target autonomy: in Kantian terms, it helps prevent the advocate from using the target as a mere means instead of as an end-in-himself.

All marketing, and indeed much of life, involves using other persons as means: employees are means to profit for owners, teachers are means to learning for students, professional athletes are means to the vicarious thrills of victory and agonies of defeat for inactive spectators. We say that these relationships between employees and owners, teachers and students, athletes and couch potatoes have instrumental value. Yet they are not inherently unethical, as long as each party respects the autonomy of the other, instead of using her as a mere, subhuman, non-autonomous means.

If transparency functions as a kind of ethical insurance policy for the target's autonomy, then its value for swag is obvious. Of all the WOM relationships, swag is the most impersonal and carries the greatest potential for both advocate and target to use each other as mere means. But it is also carries the least potential for alternative relational reward, so the target values his ability to make autonomous decisions about the advocate's message above any personal connection with the advocate. The smart advocate values the target's autonomy as well: the target can just as easily choose not to receive the advocate's publicly disseminated messages, and when a media personality's audience wanes, so does the media personality.

Buzz is very different. The advocate-target relationship is personal, particular and identified, and as such, mitigates against using each other as mere means. Autonomy is generally respected as an integral component of the valued other's personality, and to adopt transparency as an ethical insurance policy introduces the question of its need where it may rightfully be assumed no need exists. Moreover, the relationship itself may require that none exists, and to insert it would change the character of the relationship. What kind of relationship is this, where transparency as a guarantee of autonomy introduces a conceptual third wheel? In a word, friendship.

Friendship and Self-Disclosure

Friendship is a difficult concept to pin down, prompting one contemporary author to recommend abandoning the attempt in favor of a post-modernist "family resemblance" approach. Still, philosophical tradition from Aristotle to Kant and beyond concurs on certain features, notably esteem, well-wishing, and mutuality or reciprocity.[18] These features themselves presume identified particularity:

esteem is esteem for someone in particular, mutuality is between particular persons. Note the neat correspondence with our observations of buzz, blog and swag; central cases of buzz occur between friends, and blog relationships that are interpreted by the audience as virtual friendships lend themselves to buzz strategies, while those that are interpreted as public media lend themselves to swag strategies.

Can the necessarily instrumental relationships of WOM be considered friendships in the philosophical sense? Yes, as long as the instrumentality is subordinate to, and constrained by the necessary features of, friendship properly understood. The philosophical tradition makes a definite (if not altogether clear) distinction between what Neera Badhwar calls "instrumental friendships" and "end friendships," but both types qualify as friendship. That is, they lie within the parameters of esteem, well-wishing and mutuality. On Badhwar's account, instrumental as well as end friendship esteems (i.e., values) the friend as a particular individual, wishes the friend well for his own particular sake, and enjoys the reciprocation of that particular individual; it is "instrumental" only in the sense that it is "based on features that are in some sense *tangential* or *accidental* to the friend and is motivated primarily by each friend's independently defined goals."[19] In an "end friendship," by contrast, it is a connection with the other's own "self" (with all the history, plans, projects, virtues, etc. that this entails) that is one's end.

J.M. Cooper's well-known reading of Aristotle's classification of pleasure-friendship, utility-friendship and virtue-friendship corroborates this view. The charge that friendship can consist of mutual use for pleasure or other self-seeking advantage misconstrues Aristotle, according to Cooper; pleasure, utility and virtue distinguish friendships not by function, but rather by the character and original source of the relationship's bond.[20] It is the friendship itself, and not the friend, that provides the occasion for pleasure, utility or virtue. The friend is always valued and wished well for his own sake, and never as a mere means. "[I]f one is someone's friend one wants that person to prosper, achieve his goals, be happy, and so on, in the same sort of way in which he wishes these things for himself, whatever else one may want as well, and whatever explains one's having this desire."[21]

Applying this analysis to the pre-existing personal relationship of buzz, for example, it would be consistent with morally sound friendship for the advocate to want to benefit herself by connecting her friend with a marketer's product (whatever form this benefit might take) and at the same time want her friend to benefit from the product. Her relationship with the marketer is a means of benefiting her friend at the same time as it is a means of benefiting herself. But both benefits are subordinate to, and constrained by, the necessary features of the friendship between herself and the target, even if this subordination and constraint is not made explicit. Indeed, to make the subordinate and constrained activity explicit is to draw it larger than the relationship to which it is subordinate and by which it is constrained.

We might say that friendship, like politics and sausage-making, is best experienced without poking about behind the scenes. As Christine Korsgaard notes of Aristotle, friendship requires trust in the goodness of the other; but it need not require full transparency of the other's state of mind.[22] Kant, whose conception of friendship is in many ways parallel to Aristotle's, also acknowledges that "men are not transparent to each other," that not every end, reason or intention of one friend can or need be revealed to the other.[23]

Kant concurs with Aristotle, also, that authentic friendship can have varied bases, such as need, taste, or moral attitude.[24] The duties of friendship are complementary love and respect, where love is a practical decision instead of an emotional response (since the emotions, not being subject to the will, are outside the reach of Kant's concept of morality and therefore duty). The positive demands of love, to pursue the friend's good, and negative demands of respect, to refrain from acting in such a way that compromises the friend's autonomy, act in tension of simultaneous attraction and repulsion, keeping persons at the morally appropriate distance.[25]

Kant explicitly addresses transparency in the context of friendship, though perhaps not consistently. In the *Lectures on Ethics,* Kant cautions against fully revealing oneself to a friend, even a moral friend of complete communion, for fear that the friend—who is, after all, only human and subject to changing attitudes—may someday become an enemy. In his later *Metaphysical Principles of Virtue,* he extols the love and trust of moral friendship which allay this fear, thus enabling "complete communion."[26] The very core of this highest form of friendship seems to consist in the mutual confidence of two persons to disclose their most secret thoughts—what Kant calls "free intercourse of mind with mind." But to remain free, mental intercourse must submit to the demands of respect for autonomy, and full revelation of one's thoughts, attitudes, etc. could contravene this respect. In this case, too, friendship itself sets the boundaries of self-disclosure.

Conclusion

The ethical rough edges that transparency is intended to smooth are more clearly visible through the lens of friendship. Whether the advocate's relationship with the marketer ought to be disclosed to the target depends on the advocate's relationship with the target. Transparency may be either a help or a hindrance to the advocate's pre-existing relationship with the target. If the advocate-target relationship is instrumentally valuable to the advocate's WOM intentions, rather than the WOM intentions being merely incidental to the relationship—then transparency will help the target to recognize that instrumentality. Instrumentally valuable relationships, remember, do not necessarily entail one party treating the other as a mere means; they entail an intention to use the relationship itself as a means. This is not necessarily bad. A given relationship may well be a means—to profit, to free product, to social advancement; but also to spiritual fulfilment, to a richer appreciation of art, to a heightened sensitivity to the plight of the poor. It is only when the other party is under the illusion that the relationship is intrinsically valuable, or instrumental to a different sort of end, that the ethical red flags are unfurled. Even then, the illusion may not be anyone's ethical fault so much as a simple misunderstanding.

A "disconnect" between friends in the roles of advocate and target may or may not involve the marketer/advocate relationship. When it does, advocate transparency will improve the situation; when not, not. The dialectic of mutual response in friendship mitigates against this kind of disconnect, as an ongoing series of adjustments maintains equilibrium between advocate and target and their respective perceptions of the relationship. In its highest form, friendship will entail a shared understanding of ends and reasons, of intellectual and moral principles. Not every friendship need adopt this highest form as its goal, but Kant's complementary constraints of love and respect urge every friendship toward a mutual understanding of the friendship itself.

At the other end of the spectrum, the one-way, one-size-fits-all media transmission of swag is ordinarily recognized as such by both parties, and while advocate transparency can be valuable, it is very often unnecessary. The danger of mismatched perception is greatest in blog, where the relationship between blogger and reader is inherently indeterminate and requires reader construction.

In summary, there is no doubt that WOM is appropriately subjected to ethical analysis and can benefit from clearly articulated ethical standards. WOMMA's efforts in this regard are laudable. But they are also somewhat off-target. The ethics of utilizing pre-existing relationships in marketing strategy must first direct attention to the pre-existing relationships themselves, and examine the place of marketing activities within their context.

End Notes

1. Andrea Wojnicki, "Word-of-Mouth and Word-of-Web: Talking About Products, Talking About Me," *Advances in Consumer Research* 33 (2006): 575.

2. http://www.womma.org/wom101/
3. Mike Hofman, "Lies, Damn Lies and Word of Mouth," in *Business Ethics Annual Edition 07/08,* edited by John Richardson (Dubuque: McGraw Hill, 2008), 162–165.
4. CNNMoney.com, "PR Firm Admits It's Behind Wal-Mart Blogs," http://money.cnn.com/2006/10/20/news/companies/walmart_blogs/index.htm. See also Angelo Fernando, "Transparency under Attack," *Communication World* 24 (2007): 9–11.
5. Terence Shimp, Stacy Wood, and Laura Smarandescu, "Self-Generated Advertisements: Testimonials and the Perils of Consumer Exaggeration," *Journal of Advertising Research* 47 (2007): 459f.
6. Weddle, David, "Swagland" (*Business Ethics Annual Edition 07/08:* 178–183).
7. Joshua Trupin, "Bring On the Swag," MSDN Magazine, March 2007, http://msdn2.microsoft.com/en-us/magazine/cc163458.aspx.
8. "Thunder-stealing," proactive admission of the negative news item and announcement of a planned remedy, is the exception to this rule. May-May Meijer and Jan Kleinnijenhuis, "News and Advertisements: How Negative News May Reverse Advertising Effects," *Journal of Advertising Research* 47 (December, 2007): 516.
9. Marsha Loda and Barbara Carrick Coleman, "Sequence Matters: A More Effective Way to Use Advertising and Publicity," *Journal of Advertising Research* 45 (December, 2005): 370.
10. Amanda Lenhart and Susannah Fox, "Bloggers: A Portrait of the Internet's New Storytellers," *Report of the Pew Internet and American Life Project* (Washington: Pew Foundation), 7/19/2006, http://www.pewinternet.org/pdfs/PIP%20Bloggers%20Report%20July%2019%202006.pdf.
11. See also Clay Shirky, *Here Comes Everybody* (New York: Penguin, 2008).
12. Cate Riegner, "Word of Mouth on the Web: The Impact of Web 2.0 on Consumer Purchase Decisions," *Journal of Advertising Research* 47 (December, 2007): 447.
13. Chun-Yao Kuang, et. al., "'Bloggers'" Motivations and Behaviors: A Model," *Journal of Advertising Research* 47 (December, 2007): 473.
14. One site that has addressed the problem of sifting through overwhelming amounts of content in search of worthwhile blogs is StumbleUpon (www.stumbleupon.com), which allows users to identify categories of interest, under which the site has bookmarked blogs and other pages recommended by users with similar interests.
15. "MySpace Friends and the Kingdom of Ends," *Philosophy of Education Society Yearbook 2007:* 273–281. I also find fascinating the phenomenon whereby members of the same blog community are motivated to meet in person, defining and concretizing their relationships (see for example coverage of "BlogHer 2008," a conference of mommy bloggers held in San Francisco in July of that year, at http://www.blogher.com/blogher_conference/conf/2/general/1).
16. Jeff Jarvis' blog is found at http://www.buzzmachine.com/ (note the "disclosures" link, following "about me"); the CHE blog is at http://chronicle.com/news/. The tone of the comments on these blogs is sharply different than those on either of Meehan's.
17. See also Anna Lund Jepson, "Information Search in Virtual Communities: Is It Replacing Use of Off-Line Communication?" *Journal of Marketing Communication* 12 (2006): 248.
18. A. Sandra Lynch, *Philosophy and Friendship* (Edinburgh: Edinburgh University Press, 2005), 21.
19. Neera Badhwar, "Friendship: A Philosophical Reader" (Ithaca: Cornell University Press, 1993), 3. Emphasis in original.
20. John Cooper, "Aristotle on the Forms of Friendship," *Review of Metaphysics* 30 (1977): 633.

21. "Aristotle on the Forms of Friendship": 622 (fn 7); 626f.
22. Christine Korsgaard, *Creating the Kingdom of Ends* (Cambridge: Cambridge University Press, 1996), 190.
23. "Lectures on Ethics," quoted in Pakaluk, 216.
24. Immanuel Kant, "Lectures on Ethics," in Michael Pakaluk, *Other Selves: Philosophers on Friendship* (Indianapolis: Hackett Publishing, 1991), 214. Here, Kant describes friendship of taste as "pseudo-friendship."
25. See H.J. Paton, "Kant on Friendship," in Badhwar, 139–141.
26. Andrea Veltman, "Aristotle and Kant on Self-Disclosure in Friendship," *Journal of Value Inquiry* 38 (2004), 231f.

References

Note: References removed for publication here, but are available on the book website at www.mhhe.com/busethics2e.

Reading 8-2

First Analysis of Online Food Advertising Targeting Children

The Kaiser Family Foundation[1]

Food Company Web sites Feature Advergames, Viral Marketing, TV ads, and Incentives for Product Purchases.

Washington, D.C.—Concerned about the high rates of childhood obesity in the U.S., policymakers in Congress, the Federal Trade Commission, and agencies such as the Institute of Medicine have explored a variety of potential contributing factors, including the marketing and advertising of food products to children. One area where policymakers have expressed interest, but have also noted a lack of publicly available data, is in the realm of online food marketing to children. In order to help fill this gap, the Kaiser Family Foundation today released the first comprehensive analysis of the nature and scope of online food advertising to children, to help inform the decision making process for policymakers, advocates, and industry.

The report, *It's Child's Play: Advergaming and the Online Marketing of Food to Children,* found that more than eight out of ten (85%) of the top food brands that target children through TV advertising also use branded Web sites to market to children online. Unlike traditional TV advertising, these corporate-sponsored Web sites offer extensive opportunities for visitors to spend an unlimited amount of time interacting with specific food brands in more personal and detailed ways. For instance, the study documents the broad use of "advergames" (online games in which a company's product or brand characters are featured, found on 73% of the Web sites) and viral marketing (encouraging children to contact their peers about a specific product or brand, found on 64% of sites). In addition, a variety of other advertising and marketing tactics are employed on these sites, including sweepstakes and promotions (65%), memberships (25%), on-demand access to TV ads (53%), and incentives for product purchase (38%).

"Online advertising's reach isn't as broad as that of television, but it's much deeper," said Vicky Rideout, vice president and director of Kaiser's Program for the Study of Entertainment Media and Health, who oversaw the research. "Without good information about what this new world of advertising really looks like, there can't be effective oversight or policymaking, whether by the industry or by government," she noted. The advertising industry has announced that it is developing more detailed voluntary guidelines for online marketing to children, expected to be released shortly.

The study included detailed analysis of 77 Web sites, including more than 4,000 unique Web pages. Based on data from Nielsen NetRatings, these sites received more than 12.2 million visits from children ages 2-11 in the 2nd quarter of 2005.

About three-quarters (73%) of the Web sites in the study included advergames, ranging from one to more than 60 games per site. In total, the sites in the study contained 546 games featuring one or more food brands, such as the Chips Ahoy Soccer Shootout, Chuck E. Cheese's Tic Tac Toe, the M&M's Trivia Game, and the Pop-Tart Slalom. For example, on Kellogg's FunKtown children can "race against time while collecting delicious Kellogg's cereal," and at the Lucky Charms site they can play Lucky's Magic Adventure and "learn the powers of all eight charms" found in Lucky Charms cereal. To encourage additional time spent at the Web site, many of the games promote repeat playing (71%), offer multiple levels of play (45%), or suggest other games the visitor might enjoy (22%).

Almost two-thirds (64%) of sites in the study use viral marketing, in which children are encouraged to send e-mails to their friends about a product, or invite them to visit the company's Web site. For example, at juicyfruit.com users were encouraged to "Send a friend this fruitylicious site!" and told that if they "send this site to 5 friends" they would get a code that could then be used to access additional features on the site. Other sites encourage young users to invite friends to help them "redecorate" their online "rooms," challenge them to play an advergame on the site, or send them an "e-card" featuring the company's brand or spokescharacters. For example, on Keebler's Hollow Tree Web site, children are invited to send a friend some "Elfin Magic" in a birthday or seasonal greeting.

The report was released today at a forum in Washington, D.C. that featured food industry leaders, government health officials, and consumer advocates. The study was conducted for Kaiser by Elizabeth Moore, associate professor of marketing at the University of Notre Dame. A Web cast of the session is available.

The following are additional key findings from the survey:

Television Advertising Online

- Half (53%) of all sites in the study have television commercials available for viewing. On Kellogg's FunKtown site, children can earn stamps by viewing commercials in the "theater." On the Lucky Charms and Frootloops sites, serialized "webisodes" unveil animated stories featuring brand characters and products. On Skittles.com, users are told they can watch the ads "over and over right now" instead of having to wait for them to appear on TV.

Nutrition Information

- Half of sites (51%) included nutritional information such as that found on a product label, and 44% included some type of nutritional claim, such as "good source of vitamins and minerals."
- Twenty-seven percent of all sites have information about eating a healthy diet, such as the number of servings of fruits and vegetables that should be eaten daily. For example, the Kellogg's site nutritioncamp.com included such features as "nuts about nutrition" and "decipher the secrets of the Food Pyramid."

Incentive for Product Purchases

- Almost four in ten sites (38%) have incentives for the user to purchase food so they can collect brand points or stamps that they can then exchange for premiums (such as gaining access to new games or purchasing brand-related clothing). For example, children are encouraged to purchase specially-marked packages of Bubble

Tape gum and then enter the codes online to get free Nintendo game tips.

Memberships, Registration, and Marketing Research

- One in four (25%) sites offer a "membership" opportunity for children age 12 or younger. Children who sign up on Web sites may be proactively informed about new brands, exclusive offers, and new television commercials available for viewing. Thirteen percent require parental permission, while 12% do not.
- Thirteen percent of sites include polls or quizzes, some of which were used to ask visitors their opinions on products or brand-related items. For example, on cuatmcdonalds.com, visitors are asked to vote for "the dollar menu item you crave the most" and for "your favorite McDonald's IM icon character."

Extending the Online Experience Offline

- Three out of four (76%) Web sites studied offered at least one "extra" brand-related option for children, such as screensavers or wallpaper for a child's computer, printable coloring pages, branded CD covers, or brand logos or characters that can "live" on the child's computer desktop.

Educational Information

- Thirty-five percent of sites offer some type of educational content, ranging from historical facts about dinosaurs to astronomy, sports or geography.
- A third (33%) of sites include what the study has dubbed "advercation," a combination of advertising and education, such as using a brand character to present educational topics, or covering topics such as the history of how chocolate is made on hersheys.com.

Web Site Protections for Children

- Almost all (97%) of the sites in the study provided some information explicitly labeled for parents, such as what type of information is to be collected from children on the site (93%), legal disclaimers (88%), a "contact us" link (87%), statements about the use of "cookies" (81%), and statements of compliance with the Children's Online Privacy Protection Act (COPPA) (74%), or adherence to Children's Advertising Review Unit's (CARU) guidelines (46%).
- On all Web sites where personal data was requested (beyond a first name, screen name or e-mail address for one-time use), mechanisms were in place to ensure that children age 12 and under did not submit any information without parental permission.
- Although CARU's guidelines state that "advertising content should be clearly identified as such" on product-driven Web sites, only 18% of the Web sites studied included any kind of "ad break" or other notice to children that the content on the site included advertising.

Sweepstakes & Promotions

- Two-thirds (65%) of all brands in the study have promotions in which children may participate in some way. They include sweepstakes (such as the chance to win a Nintendo Game Cube system on bubbletape.com or a trip to Nickelodeon studios on pfgoldfish.com), or the chance to get free merchandise related to the food product.

Methods

The study was designed by staff of the Kaiser Family Foundation in collaboration with Elizabeth Moore, Ph.D., associate professor of marketing at the University of Notre Dame. Professor Moore and her colleagues collected and analyzed the data, and she authored the report to the Foundation on the findings. All Web sites were accessed and content was coded during the period from June through November 2005.

Using data from Competitive Media Reports, researchers identified the top food brands advertised to children on TV, and then searched for corporate or brand Web sites for those food products. Any child-oriented brand that was in the top 80% of television advertising spending in its product category was included in the study. A total of 96 brands were identified through this process.

Web sites for these brands were included in the study if they had content for children age 12 and under. In most cases, these were sites whose primary audience was children; in some cases, the primary audience appeared to be either teens or all ages, with content or separate sections likely to appeal to children. Only Web sites sponsored by a food manufacturer and dealing with the branded products identified through the process described above were included; food ads on sites such as nick.com or neopets.com were not included.

A total of 77 unique Web sites were identified through this process. Every page of these Web sites was reviewed and coded by two trained coders (more than 4,000 unique Web pages in total), and more than 400 advergames were played. Screenshots were captured for all pages on each Web site.

End Note

1. The Kaiser Family Foundation is a non-profit, private operating foundation dedicated to providing information and analysis on health care issues to policymakers, the media, the health care community and the general public. The Foundation is not associated with Kaiser Permanente or Kaiser Industries.

Reading **8-3**

Fortune at the Bottom of the Pyramid

C.K. Prahalad and Stuart L. Hart

With the end of the Cold War, the former Soviet Union and its allies, as well as China, India, and Latin America, opened their closed markets to foreign investment in a cascading fashion. Although this significant economic and social transformation has offered vast new growth opportunities for multinational corporations (MNCs), its promise has yet to be realized.

First, the prospect of millions of "middle-class" consumers in developing countries, clamouring for products from MNCs, was wildly oversold. To make matters worse, the Asian and Latin American financial crises have greatly diminished the attractiveness of emerging markets. As a consequence, many MNCs worldwide slowed investments and began to rethink risk–reward structures for these markets. This retreat could become even more pronounced in the wake of the terrorist attacks in the United States last September.

The lackluster nature of most MNCs' emerging market strategies over the past decade does not change the magnitude of the opportunity, which is in reality much larger than previously thought. The real source of market promise is not the wealthy few in the developing world, or even the emerging middle-income consumers: It is the billions of *aspiring poor* who are joining the market economy for the first time.

This is a time for MNCs to look at globalization strategies through a new lens of inclusive capitalism. For companies with the resources and persistence to compete at the bottom of the world economic pyramid, the prospective rewards include growth, profits, and incalculable contributions to humankind. Countries that still don't have the modern infrastructure or products to meet basic human needs are an ideal testing ground for developing environmentally sustainable technologies and products for the entire world.

Furthermore, MNC investment at "the bottom of the pyramid" means lifting billions of people out of poverty and desperation, averting the social decay, political chaos, terrorism, and environmental meltdown that is certain to continue if the gap between rich and poor countries continues to widen.

Doing business with the world's 4 billion poorest people—two-thirds of the world's population—will require radical innovations in technology and business models. It will require MNCs to reevaluate price–performance relationships for products and services. It will demand a new level of capital efficiency and new ways of measuring financial success. Companies will be forced to transform their understanding of scale, from a "bigger is better" ideal to an ideal of highly distributed small-scale operations married to world-scale capabilities.

In short, the poorest populations raise a prodigious new managerial challenge for the world's wealthiest companies: selling to the poor and helping them improve their lives by producing and distributing products and services in culturally sensitive, environmentally sustainable, and economically profitable ways.

Four Consumer Tiers

At the very top of the world economic pyramid are 75 to 100 million affluent Tier 1 consumers from around the world. (See Reading exhibit 8.1.) This is a cosmopolitan group composed of middle- and upper-income people in developed countries and the few rich elites from the developing world. In the middle of the pyramid, in Tiers 2 and 3, are poor customers in developed nations and the rising middle classes in developing countries, the targets of MNCs' past emerging-market strategies.

Now consider the 4 billion people in Tier 4, at the bottom of the pyramid. Their annual per capita income—based on purchasing power parity in U.S. dollars—is less than $1,500, the minimum considered necessary to sustain a decent life. For well over a billion people—roughly one-sixth of humanity—per capita income is less than $1 per day.

Even more significant, the income gap between rich and poor is growing. According to the United Nations, the richest 20 percent in the world accounted for about 70 percent of total income in 1960. In 2000, that figure reached 85 percent. Over the same period, the fraction of income accruing to the poorest 20 percent in the world fell from 2.3 percent to 1.1 percent.

This extreme inequity of wealth distribution reinforces the view that the poor cannot participate in the global market economy, even though they constitute a majority of the population. In fact, given its vast size, Tier 4 represents

READING EXHIBIT 8.1
The World Economic Pyramid

Source: U.N. World Development Reports

Annual Per Capita Income*	Tiers	Population in Millions
More Than $20,000	1	75–100
$1,500–$20,000	2 & 3	1,500–1,750
Less Than $1,500	4	4,000

* Based on purchasing power parity in U.S.$

a multitrillion-dollar market. According to World Bank projections, the population at the bottom of the pyramid could swell to more than 6 billion people over the next 40 years, because the bulk of the world's population growth occurs there.

The perception that the bottom of the pyramid is not a viable market also fails to take into account the growing importance of the informal economy among the poorest of the poor, which by some estimates accounts for 40 to 60 percent of all economic activity in developing countries. Most Tier 4 people live in rural villages, or urban slums and shantytowns, and they usually do not hold legal title or deed to their assets (e.g., dwellings, farms, businesses). They have little or no formal education and are hard to reach via conventional distribution, credit, and communications. The quality and quantity of products and services available in Tier 4 is generally low. Therefore, much like an iceberg with only its tip in plain view, this massive segment of the global population—along with its massive market opportunities—has remained largely invisible to the corporate sector.

Fortunately, the Tier 4 market is wide open for technological innovation. Among the many possibilities for innovation, MNCs can be leaders in leapfrogging to products that don't repeat the environmental mistakes of developed countries over the last 50 years. Today's MNCs evolved in an era of abundant natural resources and thus tended to make products and services that were resource-intensive and excessively polluting. The United States' 270 million people—only about 4 percent of the world's population—consume more than 25 percent of the planet's energy resources. To re-create those types of consumption patterns in developing countries would be disastrous.

We have seen how the disenfranchised in Tier 4 can disrupt the way of life and safety of the rich in Tier 1—poverty breeds discontent and extremism. Although complete income equality is an ideological pipe dream, the use of commercial development to bring people out of poverty and give them the chance for a better life is critical to the stability and health of the global economy and the continued success of Western MNCs.

The Invisible Opportunity

Among the top 200 MNCs in the world, the overwhelming majority are based in developed countries. U.S. corporations dominate, with 82; Japanese firms, with 41, are second, according to a list compiled in December 2000 by the Washington, D.C.–based Institute for Policy Studies. So it is not surprising that MNCs' views of business are conditioned by their knowledge of and familiarity with Tier 1 consumers.

Perception of market opportunity is a function of the way many managers are socialized to think and the analytical tools they use. Most MNCs automatically dismiss the bottom of the pyramid because they judge the market based on income or selections of products and services appropriate for developed countries.

To appreciate the market potential of Tier 4, MNCs must come to terms with a set of core assumptions and practices that influence their view of developing countries. We have identified the following as widely shared orthodoxies that must be reexamined:

- Assumption #1 - The poor are not our target consumers because with our current cost structures, we cannot profitably compete for that market.
- Assumption #2 - The poor cannot afford and have no use for the products and services sold in developed markets.
- Assumption #3 - Only developed markets appreciate and will pay for new technology. The poor can use the previous generation of technology.
- Assumption #4 - The bottom of the pyramid is not important to the long-term viability of our business. We can leave Tier 4 to governments and nonprofits.
- Assumption #5 - Managers are not excited by business challenges that have a humanitarian dimension.
- Assumption #6 - Intellectual excitement is in developed markets. It is hard to find talented managers who want to work at the bottom of the pyramid.

READING EXHIBIT 8.2
Innovation and MNC Implications in Tier 4

Drivers of Innovation	Implications for MNCs
Increased access among the poor to TV and information	Tier 4 is becoming aware of many products and services and is aspiring to share the benefits
Deregulation and the diminishing role of governments and international aid	More hospitable investment climate for MNCs entering developing countries and more cooperation from nongovernmental organizations
Global overcapacity combined with intense competition in Tiers 1, 2, and 3	Tier 4 represents a huge untapped market for profitable growth
The need to discourage migration to overcrowded urban centers	MNCs must create products and services for rural populations

Each of these key assumptions obscures the value at the bottom of the pyramid. It is like the story of the person who finds a $20 bill on the sidewalk. Conventional economic wisdom suggests if the bill really existed, someone would already have picked it up! Like the $20 bill, the bottom of the pyramid defies conventional managerial logic, but that doesn't mean it isn't a large and unexplored territory for profitable growth. Consider the drivers of innovation and opportunities for companies in Tier 4. (See Reading exhibit 8.2.) MNCs must recognize that this market poses a major new challenge: how to combine low cost, good quality, sustainability, and profitability.

Furthermore, MNCs cannot exploit these new opportunities without radically rethinking how they go to market. Reading exhibit 8.3 suggests some (but by no means all) areas where an entirely new perspective is required to create profitable markets in Tier 4.

READING EXHIBIT 8.3
New Strategies for the Bottom of the Pyramid

Price Performance	Views of Quality
• Product development • Manufacturing • Distribution	• New delivery formats • Creation of robust products for harsh conditions (heat, dust, etc.)
Sustainability	**Profitability**
• Reduction in resource intensity • Recyclability • Renewable energy	• Investment intensity • Margins • Volume

Tier 4 Pioneers

Hindustan Lever Ltd. (HLL), a subsidiary of Great Britain's Unilever PLC and widely considered the best managed company in India, has been a pioneer among MNCs exploring markets at the bottom of the pyramid. For more than 50 years, HLL has served India's small elite who could afford to buy MNC products. In the 1990s, a local firm, Nirma Ltd., began offering detergent products for poor consumers, mostly in rural areas. In fact, Nirma created a new business system that included a new product formulation, low-cost manufacturing process, wide distribution network, special packaging for daily purchasing, and value pricing.

HLL, in typical MNC fashion, initially dismissed Nirma's strategy. However, as Nirma grew rapidly, HLL could see its local competitor was winning in a market it had disregarded. Ultimately, HLL saw its vulnerability and its opportunity: In 1995, the company responded with its own offering for this market, drastically altering its traditional business model.

HLL's new detergent, called Wheel, was formulated to substantially reduce the ratio of oil to water in the product, responding to the fact that the poor often wash their clothes in rivers and other public water systems. HLL decentralized the production, marketing, and distribution of the product to leverage the abundant labor pool in rural India, quickly creating sales channels through the thousands of small outlets where people at the bottom of the pyramid shop. HLL also changed the cost structure of its detergent business so it could introduce Wheel at a low price point.

Today, Nirma and HLL are close competitors in the detergent market, with 38 percent market share each, according to IndiaInfoline.com, a business intelligence and market research service. Unilever's own analysis of Nirma and HLL's competition in the detergent business reveals even more about the profit potential of the marketplace at the bottom of the pyramid. (See Reading exhibit 8.4.)

Contrary to popular assumptions, the poor can be a very profitable market—especially if MNCs change their business models. Specifically, Tier 4 is not a market that allows for the traditional pursuit of high margins; instead, profits are driven by volume and capital efficiency. Margins are likely to be low (by current norms), but unit sales can be extremely high. Managers who focus on gross margins will miss the opportunity at the bottom of the pyramid; managers who innovate and focus on economic profit will be rewarded.

Nirma has become one of the largest branded detergent makers in the world. Meanwhile, HLL, stimulated by its emergent rival and its changed business model, registered a 20 percent growth in revenues per year and a 25 percent growth in profits per year between 1995 and 2000. Over the same period, HLL's market capitalzation grew to $12 billion—a growth rate of 40 percent per year. HLL's parent company, Unilever, also has benefited from its subsidiary's experience in India. Unilever

READING EXHIBIT 8.4

Nirma vs. HLL in India's Detergent Market (1999)

Source: Presentation by John Ripley, senior vice president, Unilever, at the Academy of Management Meeting, August 10, 1999

	Nirma	HLL (wheel)	HLL (High-End Products)
Total Sales ($ Million)	150	100	180
Gross Margin (%)	18	18	25
ROCE (%)	121	93	22

transported HLL's business principles (not the product or the brand) to create a new detergent market among the poor in Brazil, where the Ala brand has been a big success. More important, Unilever has adopted the bottom of the pyramid as a corporate strategic priority.

As the Unilever example makes clear, the starting assumption must be that serving Tier 4 involves bringing together the best of technology and a global resource base to address local market conditions. Cheap and low quality products are not the goal. The potential of Tier 4 cannot be realized without an entrepreneurial orientation: The real strategic challenge for managers is to visualize an active market where only abject poverty exists today. It takes tremendous imagination and creativity to engineer a market infrastructure out of a completely unorganized sector.

Serving Tier 4 markets is not the same as serving existing markets better or more efficiently. Managers first must develop a commercial infrastructure tailored to the needs and challenges of Tier 4. Creating such an infrastructure must be seen as an investment, much like the more familiar investments in plants, processes, products, and R&D.

Further, contrary to more conventional investment strategies, no firm can do this alone.

Multiple players must be involved, including local governmental authorities, nongovernmental organizations (NGOs), communities, financial institutions, and other companies. Four elements—creating buying power, shaping aspirations, improving access, and tailoring local solutions—are the keys to a thriving Tier 4 market. (See Reading exhibit 8.5.)

Each of these four elements demands innovation in technology, business models, and management processes. And business leaders must be willing to experiment, collaborate, empower locals, and create new sources of competitive advantage and wealth.

READING EXHIBIT 8.5
The Commercial Infrastructure at the Bottom of the Pyramid

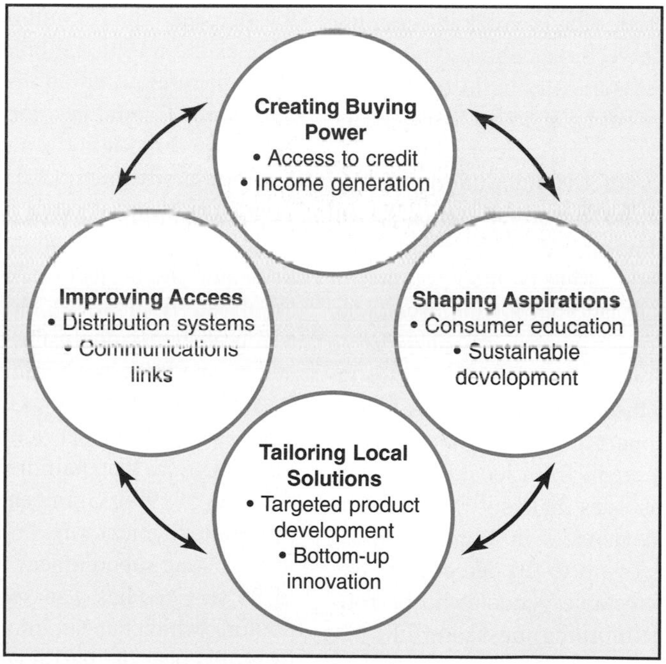

Creating Buying Power

According to the International Labor Organization's *World Employment Report 2001,* nearly a billion people—roughly one-third of the world's work force—are either underemployed or have such low-paying jobs that they cannot support themselves or their families. Helping the world's poor elevate themselves above this desperation line is a business opportunity to do well and do good. To do so effectively, two interventions are crucial—providing access to credit, and increasing the earning potential of the poor. A few farsighted companies have already begun to blaze this trail with startlingly positive results.

Commercial credit historically has been unavailable to the very poor. Even if those living in poverty had access to a bank, without collateral it is hard to get credit from the traditional banking system. As Peruvian economist Hernando de Soto demonstrates in his pathbreaking work, *The Mystery of Capital: Why Capitalism Triumphs in the West and Fails Everywhere Else,* commercial credit is central to building a market economy. Access to credit in the U.S. has allowed people of modest means to systematically build their equity and make major purchases, such as houses, cars, and education.

The vast majority of the poor in developing countries operate in the "informal" or extralegal economy, since the time and cost involved in securing legal title for their assets or incorporation of their microenterprises is prohibitive. Developing countries have tried governmental subsidies to free the poor from the cycle of poverty, with little success. Even if the poor were able to benefit from government support to start small businesses, their dependence on credit from local moneylenders charging usurious rates makes it impossible to succeed. Local moneylenders in Mumbai, India, charge interest rates of up to 20 percent per day. This means that a vegetable vendor who borrows Rs.100 ($2.08) in the morning must return Rs.120 ($2.50) in the evening.

Extending credit to the poor so they can elevate themselves economically is not a new idea. Consider how I.M. Singer & Company, founded in 1851, provided credit as a way for millions of women to purchase sewing machines. Very few of those women could have afforded the steep $100 price tag, but most could afford a payment of $5 per month.

The same logic applies on a much larger scale in Tier 4. Consider the experience of the Grameen Bank Ltd. in Bangladesh, one of the first in the world to apply a microlending model in commercial banking. Started just over 20 years ago by Muhammad Yunus, then a professor in the Economics Department at Chittagong University, Bangladesh, Grameen Bank pioneered a lending service for the poor that has inspired thousands of microlenders, serving 25 million clients worldwide, in developing countries and wealthy nations, including the United States and Great Britain.

Grameen Bank's program is designed to addresses the problems of extending credit to lowest-income customers—lack of collateral, high credit risk, and contractual enforcement. Ninety-five percent of its 2.3 million customers are women, who, as the traditional breadwinners and entrepreneurs in rural communities, are better credit risks than men. Candidates for loans must have their proposals thoroughly evaluated and supported by five nonfamily members of the community. The bank's sales and service people visit the villages frequently, getting to know the women who have loans and the projects in which they are supposed to invest. In this way, lending due diligence is accomplished without the mountain of paperwork and arcane language common in the West.

With 1,170 branches, Grameen Bank today provides microcredit services in more than 40,000 villages, more than half the total number in Bangladesh. As of 1996, Grameen Bank had achieved a 95 percent repayment rate, higher than any other bank in the Indian subcontinent. However, the popularity of its services has also spawned more local competitors, which has cut into its portfolio and shrunk its profits over the past few years.

In addition, Grameen Bank's rate of return is not easy to assess. Historically, the bank was an entirely manual, field-based operation, a structure that undercut its efficiency. Today, spin-offs such as Grameen Telecom (a provider of village phone service) and Grameen Shakti (a developer of renewable energy sources) are helping Grameen Bank build a technology infrastructure to automate its processes. As the bank develops its online business model, profitability should increase dramatically, highlighting the importance of information technology in the acceleration of the microcredit revolution.

Perhaps the most pertinent measure of Grameen Bank's success is the global explosion of institutional interest in microlending it has stimulated around the world. In South Africa, where 73 percent of the population earns less than R5,000 ($460) per month, according to a 2001 World Bank study, retail banking services for low-income customers are becoming one of the most competitive and fast-growing mass markets. In 1994, Standard Bank of South Africa Ltd., Africa's leading consumer bank, launched a low-cost, volume-driven e-banking business, called AutoBank E, to grow revenue by providing banking services to the poor. Through the use of 2,500 automated teller machines (ATMs) and 98 AutoBank E-centres, Standard now has the largest presence in South Africa's townships and other underserviced areas of any domestic bank. As of April 2001, Standard served nearly 3 million low-income customers and is adding roughly 60,000 customers per month, according to South Africa's *Sunday Times*.

Standard does not require a minimum income of customers opening an AutoBank E account, although they must have some regular income. People who have never used a bank can open an account with a deposit of as little as $8. Customers are issued an ATM card and shown how to use it by staff who speak a variety of African dialects. A small flat fee is charged for each ATM transaction. An interest-bearing "savings purse" is attached to every account to encourage poor customers to save. Interest rates on deposits are low, but superior to keeping cash in a jar. The *Sunday Times* also reported that Standard Bank is considering a loan program for low-income clients.

Computerization of microlending services not only makes the overall operation more efficient, but also makes it possible to reach many more people—lending money to individuals with no collateral and no formal address. Since there is lower overhead and little paperwork, AutoBank's costs are 30 to 40 percent lower than those at traditional branches.

At the 1999 Microcredit Summit, the United Nations, in conjunction with several major MNCs, such as Citigroup Inc. and Monsanto Company, set a goal of making basic credit available to the 100 million poorest families in the world by the year 2005. Unfortunately, the success of this undertaking has been slowed by high transaction costs, a lack of automation, and poor information and communications infrastructures in rural areas.

To address these issues and accelerate the development of microlending, French banker Jacques Attali, the founding president of the European Bank for Reconstruction and Development and a former chief aide of French President François Mitterand during the 1980s, has created PlaNet Finance. Its Web site, www.planetfinance.org, links thousands of microcredit groups worldwide into a network to help microbanks share solutions and lower costs.

Ultimately, the development of an automated solution for tracking and processing the millions of small loans associated with microlending should be possible. If processing and transaction costs can be reduced enough, they can then be bundled together and sold in the secondary market to multinational financial institutions like Citigroup. This would greatly expand the capital available for microlending beyond the current pool from donors and governments.

In the United States, microlending has also taken root over the past decade in poor urban neighborhoods. For example, the ShoreBank Corporation, formerly South Shore Bank, has demonstrated the profitability of banking for the poor in Chicago's troubled South Side. Project Enterprise, a Grameen-like program based in New York City, is aimed at minority entrepreneurs.

Several multinational banks are beginning to offer microbanking services in developing countries. Citigroup, for instance, is experimenting in Bangalore , India, with 24/7 services for customers with as little as a $25 on deposit. Initial results are very positive.

Shaping Aspirations

Sustainable product innovations initiated in Tier 4, and promoted through consumer education, will not only positively influence the choices of people at the bottom of the pyramid, but may ultimately reshape the way Americans and others in Tier 1 live. Indeed, in 20 years, we may look back to see that Tier 4 provided the early market pull for disruptive technologies that replaced unsustainable technologies in developed countries and advanced the fortunes of MNCs with foresight.

For example, Unilever's HLL subsidiary has tackled the lack of practical, inexpensive, low-energy-consuming refrigeration in India. HLL's laboratories developed a radically different approach to refrigeration that allows ice cream to be transported across the country in standard nonrefrigerated trucks. The system allows quantum reductions in electricity use and makes dangerous and polluting refrigerants unnecessary. As a bonus, the new system is cheaper to build and use.

Electricity, water, refrigeration, and many other essential services are all opportunities in developing countries. A U.S.-based NGO, the Solar Electric Light Fund (SELF), has creatively adapted technology and applied microcredit financing to bring electrical service to people in remote villages in Africa and Asia who otherwise would spend money to burn hazardous kerosene, candles, wood, or dung for their light and cooking. SELF's rural electrification system is based on small-scale on-site power generation using renewable resources. A revolving loan fund gives villagers the financial means to operate these electrical systems themselves, also creating jobs. Since its founding in 1990, SELF has launched projects in China, India, Sri Lanka, Nepal, Vietnam, Indonesia, Brazil, Uganda, Tanzania, South Africa, and the Solomon Islands.

The success of SELF and other NGOs focused on small-scale distributed energy solutions has begun to attract the attention of Western companies such as the U.S.'s Plug Power Inc. (fuel cells) and Honeywell Inc. (microturbines). They see the logic in moving into a wide-open market in Tier 4 rather than trying to force their technology prematurely into applications for the developed markets, where incumbents and institutions stand in their way. With several billion potential customers around the world, investments in such innovations should be well worth it.

Improving Access

Because Tier 4 communities are often physically and economically isolated, better distribution systems and communication links are essential to development of the bottom of the pyramid. Few of the large emerging market countries have distribution systems that reach more than half of the population. (Hence the continued dependence of the poorest consumers on local products and services and moneylenders.) As a consequence, few MNCs have designed their distribution systems to cater to the needs of poor rural customers.

Creative local companies, however, lead the way in effective rural distribution. In India, for instance, Arvind Mills has introduced an entirely new delivery system for blue jeans. Arvind, the world's fifth-largest denim manufacturer, found Indian domestic denim sales limited. At $40 to $60 a pair, the jeans were not affordable to the masses, and the existing distribution system reached only a few towns and villages. So Arvind introduced "Ruf & Tuf" jeans—a ready-to-make kit of jeans components (denim, zipper, rivets, and a patch) priced at about $6. Kits were distributed through a network of thousands of local tailors, many in small rural towns and villages, whose self-interest motivated them to market the kits extensively. Ruf & Tuf jeans are now the largest-selling jeans in India, easily surpassing Levi's and other brands from the U.S. and Europe.

MNCs can also play a role in distributing the products of Tier 4 enterprises in Tier 1 markets, giving bottom-of-the-pyramid enterprises their first links to international markets. Indeed, it is possible through partnerships to leverage traditional knowledge bases to produce more sustainable, and in some cases superior, products for consumption by Tier 1 customers.

Anita Roddick, CEO of The Body Shop International PLC, demonstrated the power of this strategy in the early 1990s through her company's "trade not aid" program of sourcing local raw material and products from indigenous people.

More recently, the Starbucks Corporation, in cooperation with Conservation International, has pioneered a program to source coffee directly from farmers in the Chiapas region of Mexico. These farms grow coffee beans organically, using shade, which preserves songbird habitat. Starbucks markets the product to U.S. consumers as a high-quality, premium coffee; the Mexican farmers benefit economically from the sourcing arrangement, which eliminates intermediaries from the business model. This direct relationship also improves the local farmers' understanding and knowledge of the Tier 1 market and its customer expectations.

Information poverty may be the single biggest roadblock to sustainable development. More than half of humanity has yet to make a single phone call. However, where telephones and Internet connections do exist, for the first time in history, it is possible to imagine a single, interconnected market uniting the world's rich and poor in the quest for truly sustainable economic development. The process could transform the "digital divide" into a "digital dividend."

Ten years ago, Sam Pitroda, currently chairman and CEO of London-based Worldtel Ltd., a company created by a telecommunications union to fund telecom development in emerging markets, came to India with the idea of "rural telephones." His original concept was to have a community telephone, operated by an entrepreneur (usually a woman) who charged a fee for the use of the telephone and kept a percentage as wages for maintaining the telephone. Today, from most parts of India, it is possible to call anyone in the world. Other entrepreneurs have introduced fax services, and some are experimenting with low-cost e-mail and Internet access. These communication links have dramatically altered the way villages function and how they are connected to the rest of the country and the world.

With the emergence of global broadband connections, opportunities for information-based business in Tier 4 will expand significantly. New ventures such as CorDECT in India and Celnicos Communications in Latin America are developing information technology and business models suited to the particular requirements of the bottom of the pyramid. Through shared-access models (e.g., Internet kiosks), wireless infrastructure, and focused technology development, companies are dramatically reducing the cost of being connected. For example, voice and data connectivity typically costs companies $850 to $2,800 per line in the developed world; CorDECT has reduced this cost to less than $400 per line, with a goal of $100 per line, which would bring telecommunications within reach of virtually everyone in the developing world.

Recognizing an enormous business and development opportunity, Hewlett-Packard Company has articulated a vision of "world e-inclusion," with a focus on providing technology, products, and services appropriate to the needs of the world's poor. As part of this strategy, HP has entered into a venture with the MIT Media Lab and the Foundation for Sustainable Development of Costa Rica—led by former President Jose Maria Figueres Olsen—to develop and implement "telecenters" for villages in remote areas. These digital town centers provide modern information technology equipment with a high-speed Internet connection at a price that is affordable, through credit vehicles, at the village level.

Bringing such technology to villages in Tier 4 makes possible a number of applications, including tele-education, telemedicine, microbanking, agricultural extension services, and environmental monitoring, all of which help to spur microenterprise, economic development, and access to world markets. This project, named Lincos, is expected to spread from today's pilot sites in Central America and the Caribbean to Asia, Africa, and Central Europe.

Tailoring Local Solutions

As we enter the new century, the combined sales of the world's top 200 MNCs equal nearly 30 percent of total world gross domestic product. Yet these same corporations employ less than 1 percent of the world's labor force. Of the world's 100 largest economies, 51 are economies internal to corporations. Yet scores of Third World countries have suffered absolute economic stagnation or decline.

If MNCs are to thrive in the 21st century, they must broaden their economic base and share it more widely. They must play a more active role in narrowing the gap between rich and poor. This cannot be achieved if these companies produce only so-called global products for consumption primarily by Tier 1 consumers. They must nurture local markets and cultures, leverage local solutions, and generate wealth at the lowest levels on the pyramid. Producing in, rather than extracting wealth from, these countries will be the guiding principle.

To do this, MNCs must combine their advanced technology with deep local insights. Consider packaging. Consumers in Tier 1 countries have the disposable income and the space to buy in bulk (e.g., 10-pound boxes of detergent from superstores like Sam's Club) and shop less frequently. They use their spending money to "inventory convenience." Tier 4 consumers, strapped for cash and with limited living space, shop every day, but not for much. They can't afford to stock up on household items or be highly selective about what they buy; they look for single-serve packaging. But consumers with small means also have the benefit of experimentation.

Unburdened by large quantities of product, they can switch brands every time they buy. Already in India, 30 percent of personal care products and other consumables, such as shampoo, tea, and cold medicines, are sold in single-serve packages. Most are priced at Rs. 1 (about 1¢). Without innovation in packaging, however, this trend could result in a mountain of solid waste. Dow Chemical Company and Cargill Inc. are experimenting with an organic plastic that would be totally biodegradable. Such packaging clearly has advantages in Tier 4, but it could also revolutionize markets at all four tiers of the world pyramid.

For MNCs, the best approach is to marry local capabilities and market knowledge with global best practices. But whether an initiative involves an MNC entering Tier 4 or an entrepreneur from Tier 4, the development principles remain the same: New business models must not disrupt the cultures and lifestyles of local people. An effective combination of local and global knowledge is needed, not a replication of the Western system.

The development of India's milk industry has many lessons for MNCs. The transformation began around 1946, when the Khira District Milk Cooperative, located in the state of Gujarat, set up its own processing plant under the leadership of Verghese Kurien and created the brand Amul, today one of the most recognized in the country.

Unlike the large industrial dairy farms of the West, in India, milk originates in many small villages. Villagers may own only two to three buffaloes or cows each and bring their milk twice a day to the village collection center. They are paid every day for the milk they deliver, based on fat content and volume. Refrigerated vans transport the milk to central processing plants, where it is pasteurized. Railroad cars then transport the milk to major urban centers.

The entire value chain is carefully managed, from the village-based milk production to the world-scale processing facilities. The Khira District cooperative provides such services to the farmers as veterinary care and cattle feed. The cooperative also manages the distribution of pasteurized milk, milk powder, butter, cheese, baby food, and other products. The uniqueness of the Amul cooperative is its blending of decentralized origination with the efficiencies of a modern processing and distribution infrastructure. As a result, previously marginal village farmers are earning steady incomes and being transformed into active market participants.

Twenty years ago, milk was in short supply in India. Today, India is the world's largest producer of milk. According to India's National Dairy Development Board, the country's dairy cooperative network now claims 10.7 million individual farmer member–owners, covers 96,000 village-level societies, includes 170 milk producer unions, and operates in more than 285 districts. Milk production has increased 4.7 percent per year since 1974. The per capita availability of milk in India has grown from 107 grams to 213 grams per day in 20 years.

Putting It All Together

Creating buying power, shaping aspirations, improving access, and tailoring local solutions—the four elements of the commercial infrastructure for the bottom of the pyramid are intertwined. Innovation in one leverages innovation in the others. Corporations are only one of the actors; MNCs must work together with NGOs, local and state governments, and communities. Yet someone must take the lead to make this revolution happen. The question is, Why should it be MNCs?

Even if multinational managers are emotionally persuaded, it is not obvious that large corporations have real advantages over small, local organizations. MNCs may never be able to beat the cost or responsiveness of village entrepreneurs. Indeed, empowering local entrepreneurs and enterprises is key to developing Tier 4 markets. Still, there are several compelling reasons for MNCs to embark on this course:

- Resources. Building a complex commercial infrastructure for the bottom of the pyramid is a resource- and management-intensive task. Developing environmentally sustainable products and services requires significant research. Distribution channels and communication networks are expensive to develop and sustain. *Few local entrepreneurs have the managerial or technological resources to create this infrastructure.*
- Leverage. MNCs can transfer knowledge from one market to another—from China to Brazil or India—as Avon, Unilever, Citigroup, and others have demonstrated. Although practices and products have to be customized to serve local needs, *MNCs, with their unique global knowledge base, have an advantage that is not easily accessible to local entrepreneurs.*
- Bridging. MNCs can be nodes for building the commercial infrastructure, providing access to knowledge, managerial imagination, and financial resources. Without MNCs as catalysts, well-intentioned NGOs, communities, local governments, entrepreneurs, and even multilateral development agencies will continue to flounder in their attempts to bring development to the bottom. *MNCs are best positioned to unite the range of actors required to develop the Tier 4 market.*
- Transfer. Not only can MNCs leverage learning from the bottom of the pyramid, but they also have the capacity to transfer innovations upmarket all the way to Tier 1. As we have seen, Tier 4 is a testing ground for sustainable living. *Many of the innovations for the bottom can be adapted for use in the resource- and energy-intensive markets of the developed world.*

It is imperative, however, that managers recognize the nature of business leadership required in the Tier 4 arena. Creativity, imagination, tolerance for ambiguity, stamina, passion, empathy, and courage may be as important as analytical skill, intelligence, and knowledge. Leaders need a deep understanding of the complexities and subtleties of sustainable development in the context of Tier 4. Finally, managers must have the interpersonal and intercultural skills to work with a wide range of organizations and people.

MNCs must build an organizational infrastructure to address opportunity at the bottom of the pyramid. This means building a local base of support, reorienting R&D to focus on the needs of the poor, forming new alliances, increasing employment intensity, and reinventing cost structures. These five organizational elements are clearly interrelated and mutually reinforcing.

- ***Build a local base of support.*** Empowering the poor threatens the existing power structure. Local opposition can emerge very quickly, as Cargill Inc. found in its sunflower-seed business in India. Cargill's offices were twice burned, and the local politicians accused the firm of destroying locally based seed businesses. But Cargill persisted. Through Cargill's investments in farmer education, training, and supply of farm inputs, farmers have significantly improved their productivity per acre of land. Today, Cargill is seen as the friend of the farmer.

  Political opposition has vanished. To overcome comparable problems, MNCs must build a local base of political support. As Monsanto and General Electric Company can attest, the establishment of a coalition of NGOs, community leaders, and local authorities that can counter entrenched interests is essential. Forming such a coalition can be a very slow process. Each player has a different agenda; MNCs have to understand these agendas and create shared aspirations.

  In China, this problem is less onerous: The local bureaucrats are also the local entrepreneurs, so they can easily see the benefits to their enterprise and their village, town, or province. In countries such as India and Brazil, such alignment does not exist. Significant discussion, information sharing, the delineation of benefits to each constituency, and sensitivity to local debates is necessary.

- ***Conduct R&D focused on the poor.*** It is necessary to conduct R&D and market research focused on the unique requirements of the poor, by region and by country. In India, China, and North Africa, for example, research on ways to provide safe water for drinking, cooking, washing, and cleaning is a high priority. Research must also seek to adapt foreign solutions to local needs. For example, a daily dosage of vitamins can be added to a wide variety of food and beverage products. For corporations that have distribution and brand presence throughout the developing world, such as Coca-Cola Company, the bottom of the pyramid offers a vast untapped market for such products as water and nutritionals.

  Finally, research must identify useful principles and potential applications from local practices. In Tier 4, significant knowledge is transmitted orally from one generation to the next. Being respectful of traditions but willing to analyze them scientifically can lead to new knowledge. The Body Shop's creative CEO, Ms. Roddick, built a business predicated on understanding the basis for local rituals and practices. For example, she observed that some African women use slices of pineapple to cleanse their skin. On the surface, this practice appears to be a meaningless ritual. However, research showed active ingredients in pineapple that cleared away dead skin cells better than chemical formulations. MNCs must develop research facilities in emerging markets such as China, India, Brazil, Mexico, and Africa, although few have made a big effort so far. Unilever is an exception; it operates highly regarded research centers in India, employing more than 400 researchers dedicated to the problems of "India-like markets."

- ***Form new alliances.*** MNCs have conventionally formed alliances solely to break into new markets; now they need to broaden their alliance strategies. By entering into alliances to expand in Tier 4 markets, MNCs gain insight into developing countries' culture and local knowledge. At the same time, MNCs improve their own credibility. They may also secure preferred or exclusive access to a market or raw material. We foresee three kinds of important relationships: Alliances with local firms and cooperatives (such as the Khira District Milk Cooperative); alliances with local and international NGOs (like Starbucks's alliance with Conservation International in coffee); and alliances with governments (e.g., Merck & Company's recent alliance in Costa Rica to foster rain forest preservation in exchange for bioprospecting rights). Given the difficulty and complexity of constructing business models dependent on relationships with national or central governments (e.g., large infrastructure development), we envision more alliances at the local and regional level. To succeed in such alliances, MNC managers must learn to work with people who may not have the same agenda or the same educational and economic background as they do. The challenge and payoff is how to manage and learn from diversity—economic, intellectual, racial, and linguistic.

- ***Increase employment intensity.*** MNCs accustomed to Tier 1 markets think in terms of capital intensity and labor productivity. Exactly the opposite logic applies in Tier 4. Given the vast number of people at the bottom of the pyramid, the production and distribution approach must provide jobs for many, as in the case of Ruf & Tuf jeans from Arvind Mills: It employed an army of local tailors as stockers, promoters, distributors, and service providers, even though the cost of the jeans was 80 percent below that of Levi's. As Arvind demonstrated, MNCs need not employ large numbers of people directly on their payroll, but the organizational model in Tier 4 must increase employment intensity (and incomes) among the poor and groom them to become new customers.
- ***Reinvent cost structures.*** Managers must dramatically reduce cost levels relative to those in Tier 1. To create products and services the poor can afford, MNCs must reduce their costs significantly—to, say, 10 percent of what they are today. But this cannot be achieved by fine-tuning the current approaches to product development, production, and logistics. The entire business process must be rethought with a focus on functionality, not on the product itself. For example, financial services need not be distributed only through branch offices open from 9 A.M. to 5 P.M. Such services can be provided at a time and place convenient to the poor consumer—after 8 P.M and at their homes. Cash-dispensing machines can be placed in safe areas—police stations and post offices. Iris recognition used as a security device could substitute for the tedious personal-identification number and card for identification.

Lowering cost structures also forces a debate on ways to reduce investment costs. This will inevitably lead to greater use of information technology to develop production and distribution systems. As noted, village-based phones are already transforming the pattern of communications throughout the developing world. Add the Internet, and we have a whole new way of communicating and creating economic development in poor, rural areas. Creative use of IT will emerge in these markets as a means to dramatically lower the costs associated with access to products and services, distribution, and credit management.

A Common Cause

The emergence of the 4 billion people who make up the Tier 4 market is a great opportunity for MNCs. It also represents a chance for business, government, and civil society to join together in a common cause. Indeed, we believe that pursuing strategies for the bottom of the pyramid dissolves the conflict between proponents of free trade and global capitalism on one hand, and environmental and social sustainability on the other.

Yet the products and services currently offered to Tier 1 consumers are not appropriate for Tier 4, and accessing this latter market will require approaches fundamentally different from those even in Tiers 2 and 3. Changes in technology, credit, cost, and distribution are critical prerequisites. Only large firms with global reach have the technological, managerial, and financial resources to dip into the well of innovations needed to profit from this opportunity.

New commerce in Tier 4 will not be restricted to businesses filling such basic needs as food, textiles, and housing. The bottom of the pyramid is waiting for high-tech businesses such as financial services, cellular telecommunications, and low-end computers. In fact, for many emerging disruptive technologies (e.g., fuel cells, photovoltaics, satellite-based telecommunications, biotechnology, thin-film microelectronics, and nanotechnology), the bottom of the pyramid may prove to be the most attractive early market.

So far, three kinds of organizations have led the way: local firms such as Amul and Grameen Bank; NGOs such as the World Resources Institute, SELF, The Rainforest Alliance, The Environmental Defense Fund, and Conservation International, among others; and a few MNCs such as Starbucks, Dow, Hewlett- Packard, Unilever, Citigroup, DuPont, Johnson & Johnson, Novartis, and ABB, and global business partnerships such as the World Business Council for Sustainable Business Development. But to date, NGOs and local businesses with far fewer resources than the MNCs have been more innovative and have made more progress in developing these markets.

It is tragic that as Western capitalists we have implicitly assumed that the rich will be served by the corporate sector, while governments and NGOs will protect the poor and the environment. This implicit divide is stronger than most realize. Managers in MNCs, public policymakers, and NGO activists all suffer from this historical division of roles. A huge opportunity lies in breaking this code—linking the poor and the rich across the world in a seamless market organized around the concept of sustainable growth and development.

Collectively, we have only begun to scratch the surface of what is the biggest potential market opportunity in the history of commerce. Those in the private sector who commit their companies to a more inclusive capitalism have the opportunity to prosper and share their prosperity with those who are less fortunate. In a very real sense, the fortune at the bottom of the pyramid represents the loftiest of our global goals.

Note: Notes and references removed for publication here, but are available on the book website at www.mhhe.com/busethics2e.

Reading 8-4

Response to A. Karnani

C.K. Prahalad

The document below is a memorandum from C.K. Prahalad to his colleague, Aneel Karnani. It is a response to Professor Karnani's challenge of the concepts in "Fortune at the Bottom of the Pyramid," *written by Professors Prahalad and Hart.*

July 14, 2006
To: Aneel
From: C.K.
Subject: BOP: Mirage

Thank you for your thoughtful piece on "The Fortune at the Bottom of the Pyramid". It appears that you have three basic arguments against it.

1. The measurement problem
2. The distinction between consumption and income generation in poverty alleviation
3. The fallacy of an opportunity at the bottom of the pyramid

The Big Picture

My thesis is simple. Over 80% of the people in the world are ignored as a market by the organized sector (including MNCs and large domestic companies). This was and is the "underserved and the unserved market". This population does not typically have access to world class products or services or to regional and global markets for their effort and production. Awareness, access, affordability and availability continue to be the problems. Yes, I look at *both consumption and production.* The ITC and EID Parry examples are about production. So is the microfinance example. Creation of transparent markets and a market based eco system is also an integral part of the argument. There is a whole chapter on "*transaction governance*" or creating transparent conditions for markets to flourish (chapter 5). So is a *market based ecosystem* including SMEs, single entrepreneurs, NGOs and cooperatives, not just MNCs (chapter 4). I also talk about how to create products and services for the BOP market to be profitable (Chapter 2). Further, most of the case examples are about personal and family productivity. ITC and EID Parry, Cemex, health (Annapurna, Soap, Voxiva). This totality represents the argument on Poverty alleviation. You chose to focus on one aspect of the argument-consumption. I wonder why? The examples of production and income generation—ITC—as a solution that you offer, as an alternative, is in the book. So is the need to create transparent markets. So is the need for new business models and creativity (which you do not cover).

The focus of the book is on 5 billion underserved. They are also poor. But it is naïve to believe that 5 billion represent a monolith (are one segment). Every experiment described in the book does not necessarily have to serve all the segments of the 5 billion underserved. No single business model can do that. My goal was to amplify weak signals and experiments that have potential in this general space. Annapurna and the Soap examples are about the difficulty of educating the poor on health benefits as well as how arduous it is to work with multilaterals. Do firms fail in their experiments? Yes, they do.

Data Inconsistencies

I realize the problems of defining poverty using income and even expenditure assessments. Is there a wide variation in the way the "underserved" is described? Yes. Less than $2,000 per capita, $ 2/day per person are used in the argument. Do 4 billion live below $ 2/day? Al, Stu and I are very aware of the problems of measurement of the underserved and the poor. Al at the World Resources Institute has started a large scale effort, with the IFC to reassess the data from various sources and to arrive at the structure of the Pyramid, by country. It is likely to be the most current and they have used household survey data. It should be out in September, 2006. It shows yet a different view. Let me give you a preview. The data is as follows:

More than $ 21,730 PPP per capita	0.5 billion
3,260–21,730 PPP per capita	2.0 billion
less than $ 3,260 PPP per capita	4.0 billion ($ 2/day)

Add to this the underground economy and the remittances from overseas. (India received $ 21 billion in remittances from overseas last year. Mexico received $ 18 billion). The complexity of the problem defies precise measurement. (I am glad that as a result of my drawing attention to this "forgotten population" to business more people have started to devote their attention to understand this space better. You are a good example). One way to escape this malaise of measurement is to shape this world differently rather than study, in greater depth, its income characteristics. We know that there is a large population out there—be it 4 or 5 billion underserved. (The size of this market does not depend on its income characteristics alone but how we can create the capacity to consume. More of this later). *Shaping the world requires a point of view and some evidence to show that this is possible.* The book is about a point of view. I have tried to apply only one set of tests in my work: Does it change the conversation? Does it show the opportunity? Does it lead to some action?

I respect precision. But to define poverty line as $1.08 or $1.48 is pseudo precision. So is the ability to compute precisely the total number within those income boundaries. In my work I was looking for *dimensionality and directionality.* My goal was never to measure poverty; much less with great precision. There are others who do this well. My goal is to look for an alternative to the tired and tested methods including government subsidies and public sector schemes to remedy this situation.

The broad dimensions of the problem and the opportunity to make a difference is about changing the quality of life of 4–5 billion people who are underserved and most of them are below the radar screen of the organized sector. If it is only 3.5 billion so be it. It is still a large number and worthy of our attention.

Consumption-Income-Production

I am surprised that you fall into the same trap that most do. Consumption can and does increase income.

Can Casas Bahia (and such other examples of consumption) alleviate poverty? I find this a very interesting argument. Let us start with four propositions:

a. The poor live in high cost micro-economic systems (see CKP/AH: HBR)
b. They do not have access to good quality products and services (be it water, food, furniture or credit)
c. They are prisoners of local monopolies; including local moneylenders
d. They have no recourse to law. The local landlords can and do enforce their will on the local population.

Is the ability of someone at the BOP with volatile wages to get access to credit (at 20% rather than 300%), improving income? Does a family of four having a small refrigerator and eating better food improving the quality of life? Is someone becoming independent (one blind person means two people without wages—one who cannot see and one who needs to take care of that person). Is releasing at least one person to do work—even at minimum wages—improving the earning potential of the family? Is helping poor people to avoid diarrhea, helping the family to save on needless costs associated with healthcare, much less, needless death? Is this income? Is this improving the quality of life? Is avoiding mental retardation at an incremental cost, adding to income? The idea of a "poverty penalty" is real. See the report from Brookings. In the USA poor families pay for everything—food, autos, finance,. . . . . Reducing the poverty penalty is adding to real income.

Poverty alleviation is, simply, improving the disposable income for the families—by reducing the costs of services, improving its quality, and releasing their time to do work that is productive.

I also find that you dismiss somewhat easily the cell phone revolution. Did you believe in 1999 that more than 50 % of the cell phones will be sold to the poor in emerging markets including such desperately poor markets as in Sub Sahran Africa (CelTel) or in S Africa (MTN, Vodacom)? Needless to say in India and China. (All cell phone makers are MNCs and the new ones from China are also becoming MNCs). Of course they had to invent new business models from Grammen Phone to "prepaid cards". I am continually humbled by the inventiveness of people who want to serve this population.

Lesson: *Creating the capacity to consume is different from serving an existing market. Creating the capacity to consume can increase disposable income (no different from income generation). Creating the capacity to consume can build new and profitable markets at the BOP.*

There are many ways to do this:

a. single serve (Is Aspirin OK if Shampoo is bad?)
b. monthly payments (Is kitchen Cabinet OK if TV is bad?)
c. pay per use (is Cell phone OK if videogames are bad?)
d. New distribution models (is ITC e-Sagar OK if Shakti Ammas are bad?)
e. Low prices (is a water filter OK if Iodized salt is bad?)

There is another way that consumption leads to income generation. For example, Grammen Phone has 250,000 phone ladies—all entrepreneurs. There are over 100,000 telephone booth operators in Africa and the number is growing. Bharati estimates that it will need about 500,000 individual entrepreneurs to sell "prepaid cards and charge cell phones" for cell phone users in India alone.

I know that you think "Fair and Lovely" is a bad idea. This is an ideological stance. I believe in choice. I believe that the "poor" must have choice. You may believe that the "rich and the elite can decide what is good for the poor, because they cannot decide for themselves". (Fair and Lovely does have moisturizer and sun block). I know you do not approve of single cigarette sales; how about beedis which is more affordable and more deadly? Should a consumer have choice between beedis and cigarettes?

We can also argue that this population does not need PCs. Should AMD, Negroponte, and Intel stop all their efforts to create an affordable PC? Should we fix the drainage in Dharavi before we give them access to global connectivity? I just want you to see how ideology gets so intertwined with our approaches. I am explicit about my preferences. So should you. State your position with respect to "who decides for the poor". I emphasized the consumer side because, as I stated clearly in the book: "We should commence talking about underserved consumers and markets. **The process must start with respect for the Bottom of the Pyramid consumers as individuals** . . . Consumers and consumer communities will demand and get choice. . . . We must recognize that the conversion of the BOP into a market is essentially a developmental activity. . . . **New and creative approaches are needed to convert poverty into an opportunity for all concerned. That is the challenge.**" (Emphasis in the original text. Preface, page xiii)

Is there a Real Market?

Time will tell whether BOP is a market or not. I believe that it is. So do a lot of others (may be foolishly). ICICI just enhanced the role of rural marketing. They believe that the total market for credit in rural India is Rs.15,000 billion (now mostly done by moneylenders at 100% may be). The banks have just scratched the surface with Rs. 40 billion. Even if the organized sector only got to Rs. 10,000 billion and reduced the interest rate from a 100% to 20%, you can calculate the income generated for the poor. Consumption of credit, even to buy a TV, can create income. Obviously ICICI expects to make a profit. This is one of their two corporate initiatives- global and rural!! ITC thinks it can make money. P&G, HLL, Nestle all think so.

The World Is Moving Forward

I believe that the world has moved on. The Inter-American Bank (focused on Latin America) just adopted the Bottom of the Pyramid as their focus. They call it the "business to the majority". Academy of Management calls it "business for the benefit of all". For the last year I have been talking about "democratizing commerce". So the debate is not anymore about how many are really poor; it is about how to bring the benefits of global standards at affordable prices and increase access.

This is a longer letter than I usually write. Because of the high regard I have for you I have taken the time to give a detailed and diligent response. Hope it helps.

Chapter 9

Business and Environmental Sustainability

A thing is right when it tends to preserve the integrity, stability and beauty of the biotic community. It is wrong when it does otherwise.

Aldo Leopold

Growth for the sake of growth is the ideology of the cancer cell.

Edward Abbey

Waste equals food.

William McDonough

Environmental regulation is a signal of design failure.

William McDonough

Opening Decision Point *When is Building Design and Construction an Ethical Issue?*

With only some exceptions, every business operates in and out of a physical location. For even small businesses, constructing a building can represent a multi-million dollar investment, often the largest single investment a company makes. For large multinational corporations, building construction can cost billions of dollars. But based on what grounds, based on what criteria, should a business design and construct its buildings?

One increasingly prominent set of standards are supported by the LEED certification program developed by the United States Green Building Council (USGBC). USGBC is an independent organization of builders, designers, and architects whose mission is "to transform the way buildings and communities are designed, built and operated, enabling an environmentally and socially responsible, healthy, and prosperous environment that improves the quality of life." The USGBC has developed a system of certifying building design and construction called **LEED certification** (Leadership in Energy and Environmental Design) in 1998. LEED certification is now the industry-leading "Green Building" process by which environmentally sustainable standards are applied to building construction and renovation. LEED provides both the standards and the independent third-party verification to certify the environmental quality of a building.

All buildings must meet certain zoning and safety regulations, of course. For the most part, these building codes are established by local governments and typically focus on fire safety, electrical, and plumbing standards, and also include zoning standards for size and building use that is compatible with neighboring sites. LEED standards instead focus on energy usage and efficiency, sustainable and recycled resource use in construction, waste and trash minimization in use, landscaping that restores or protects local habitat, health and safety for building users, indoor air quality, wastewater treatment, and compatibility with alternative forms of transportation.

According to the USGBC, buildings in the United States account for 72 percent of U.S. electricity consumption, 39 percent of energy use, 38 percent of all carbon dioxide (CO_2) emissions, and 30 percent of waste output (136 million tons annually). LEED standards aim to reduce significantly all of these expenditures.

The biggest challenge to the LEED standards involves their costs. Typical estimates suggest that meeting LEED certification standards can add 5 percent to the total project cost, an estimate that can mean hundreds of thousands of dollars to a construction project. For some businesses, this added expenditure to construction costs can be worth it for the longer-term savings in energy efficiency but, for others, the addition can seem too costly.

Other challenges focus less on the LEED standards themselves and more on a movement towards incorporating these standards into existing and mandatory governmental building codes. Critics argue that LEED standards should be left as voluntary guidelines that should be left to individual businesses to follow. Others argue that the social and environmental benefits outweigh the costs and that the standards should be mandatory. Some suggest a parallel with building regulations created by the Americans with Disabilities Act (ADA) which require all buildings to be handicapped-accessible. ADA requirements do add costs to any building

(*continued*)

(concluded)

project, but society has judged these costs acceptable given the social value of equal opportunity. They are simply part of the costs of doing business. So, too, evidently we have determined that the social and environmental benefits of LEED certification should override the initial compliance costs of building to meet these standards.

- Is the decision to meet LEED building standards a business decision or an ethical decision?
- Should every new building project be required to meet LEED standards, or is this best left to individual businesses?
- Who are the stakeholders in this decision?
- Are you familiar with any LEED buildings in your own surrounding community? Are you aware of any controversies that were involved in the project?
- Environmental architect William McDonough and chemist Michael Braungart (see the essay, "The Next Industrial Revolution" included at the end of this chapter) claim that government regulation is evidence of a design problem and a failure to property design a product or building. Can you imagine any regulations that might be avoided by designing a building to LEED certification?

Chapter Objectives

After reading this chapter, you will be able to:

1. Explain how environmental challenges can create business opportunities.
2. Describe a range of values that play a role in environmental decision making.
3. Explain the difference between market-based and regulatory-based environmental policies.
4. Describe business' environmental responsibilities that flow from each approach.
5. Identify the inadequacies of sole reliance on a market-based approach.
6. Identify the inadequacies of regulatory-based environmental policies.
7. Define and describe sustainable development and sustainable business.
8. Highlight the business opportunities associated with a move towards sustainability.
9. Describe the sustainable principles of eco-efficiency, biomimicry, and service.

Introduction

There is a tendency to believe that environmental challenges *always* create a burden on business and that environmental and business interests are *always* in conflict. While it certainly can be the case that environmental regulation can add costs to business operations and restrict business choice, they can also provide opportunities for business. Where one automobile manufacturer sees government mandated fuel efficiency standards as a burden on its ability to sell large SUVs, another company sees it as an opportunity to market fuel-efficient hybrids. Many observers believe we have entered the sustainability revolution, an age in which the race to create environmentally and economically sustainable products and services is creating unlimited business opportunities. As happened in the industrial revolution, there will be winners and losers in this sustainability revolution and, according to supporters, the economic winners will be the firms and industries that do the most environmental good.

As described by geographer Jarad Diamond in his in the best-selling book *Collapse,* human history provides many examples of societies that have run up against the environmental limits of their lifestyles. But the Industrial Revolution of the eighteenth and nineteenth centuries brought with it the ability to degrade the natural environment to a greater extent and at a faster rate than ever before. The industrial model of growth and productive efficiency and seemingly unlimited energy supply continued along almost unchecked by environmental regulation until the latter half of the twentieth century. By the start of the twenty-first century, the earth was experiencing the greatest period of species extinction since the end of the dinosaurs 65 million years ago. Humans are also threatened by global climate change. Each of these monumental environmental events is largely due to human activity, and specifically to our present arrangements of modern industrial society. Simply put, the way we have done business over the last two centuries has brought us up against the biophysical limits of the earth's capacity to support all human life, and it has already crossed those limits in the case of countless other forms of, now extinct, life. Thus, the major ethical question of this chapter is what responsibilities contemporary businesses have regarding the natural environment. For a business leader's perspective on this question, see the Reality Check, "Do Business Leaders Think There Is an Environmental Crisis?" and the reading by Patrick Cescau at the end of this chapter.

It is fair to say that, throughout the history of industrial economies, business most often looked at environmental concerns as unwanted burdens and barriers to economic growth. Nonetheless, the sustainable business and sustainable economic development seek to create new ways of doing business in which business success is measured in terms of economic, ethical, and environmental sustainability, often called the *Triple Bottom Line* approach. The sustainability paradigm sees environmental responsibilities as a fundamental part of basic business practice. Indeed, sustainable business ventures may find that environmental considerations offer creative and entrepreneurial businesses enormous opportunities. The end of chapter reading by Patrick Cescau makes this point persuasively.

1 OBJECTIVE

The environmental research and consulting group The Natural Step uses an image of a funnel, with two converging lines, to help business understand the opportunities available in the age of sustainability. The resources necessary to sustain life are on a downward slope. While there is disagreement about the angle of the slope (are we at the start with only a mild slope, or further along with a sharper downward slope?), there is widespread consensus that available resources are in decline. The second line represents aggregate worldwide demand,

Reality Check *Do Business Leaders Think There Is an Environmental Crisis?*

In a 1997 speech that attracted worldwide attention, John Browne, chief executive of BP, announced:

> [T]he time to consider the policy dimensions of climate change is not when the link between greenhouse gases and climate change is conclusively proven . . . but when the possibility cannot be discounted and is taken seriously by the society of which we are part. We in BP have reached that point . . . there is now an effective consensus among the world's leading scientists and serious and well informed people outside the scientific community that there is a discernible human influence on the climate, and a link between the concentration of carbon dioxide and the increase in temperature. . . . Those are wide margins of error, and there remain large elements of uncertainty—about cause and effect . . . and even more importantly about the consequences. But it would be unwise and potentially dangerous to ignore the mounting concern.

Source: John Browne, group chief executive, British Petroleum (BP America) in a speech at Stanford University, May 19, 1997.

accounting for both population growth and the increasing demand of consumerist lifestyles. Barring an environmental catastrophe, many but not all industries will emerge through the narrowing funnel into an era of sustainable living. Businesses unable to envision that sustainable future will hit the narrowing wall. Innovative and entrepreneurial business will find their way through. The Natural Step's funnel is illustrated in Figure 9.1.

The Natural Step then challenges business to "backcast" a path towards sustainability. We are all familiar with forecasting, in which we examine present data and predict the future. **Backcasting** examines what the future will be when we emerge through the funnel. Knowing what the future must be, creative businesses then look backwards to the present and determine what must be done to arrive at that future. In simple terms, sustainable business must use resources and produce wastes at rates that do not jeopardize human well-being by exceeding the earth's capacity to renew

FIGURE 9.1
The Natural Step's Funnel

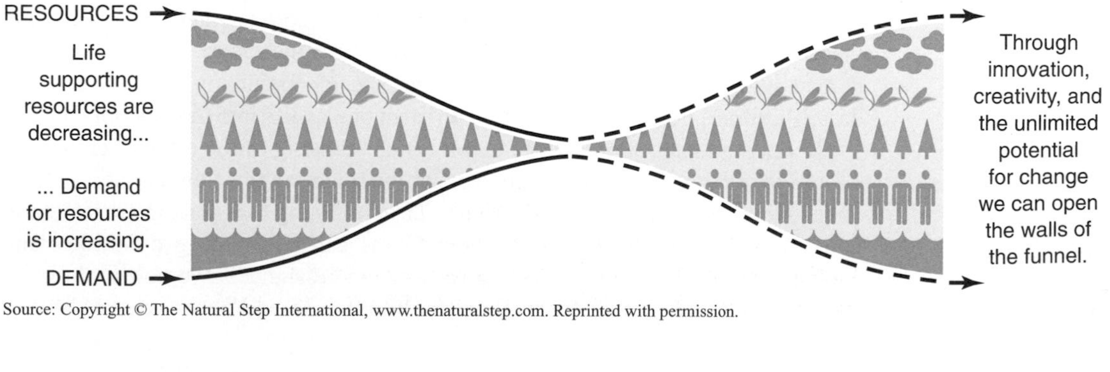

Source: Copyright © The Natural Step International, www.thenaturalstep.com. Reprinted with permission.

the resources and absorb the wastes. Businesses that do so will succeed in moving through the funnel and emerge as successful in the age of sustainability. The "business case" for sustainability will be examined in more detail in the section below.

This chapter will introduce a range of ethical issues that have set the stage for this transition to an environmentally sustainable future. Environmental issues are no longer at the periphery of business decisions, as burdens to be managed if not avoided altogether; nor are they external regulatory constraints in managerial decision making (see the essay, "Taking Sustainability Seriously: An Argument for Managerial Responsibility" by Tara Radin at the end of this chapter for a developed analysis of this view). Environmental sustainability must accompany financial sustainability for business to survive in the twenty-first century. For reasons of both deontological principles of rights and duties and for the overall social good, sustainable business is the wave of the future.

Business Ethics and Environmental Values

2 OBJECTIVE

The opening chapters of this text introduced ethics in terms of practical reasoning. Deciding what we should do is the ultimate goal of practical reason and our values are those standards that encourage us to act one way rather than another. Given this objective, which values and decisions are supported by a concern with the natural environment? Why should we act in ways that protect the natural environment from degradation? Why should business be concerned with, and value, the natural world?

Human self-interest is the most obvious answer to these questions. Environmental concerns are relevant to business because human beings, both presently living humans and future generations of humans depend on the natural environment in order to survive. Humans need clean water to drink, healthy air to breathe, fertile soil and oceans to produce food, an ozone layer to screen out solar radiation, and a biosphere that maintains the delicate balance of climate in which human life can exist. Two aspects of contemporary environmental realities underscore the importance of self-interested reasoning.

As documented in *Collapse,* past human societies have often run up against the limits of the local environment's ability to sustain human life. In these historical cases, environmental degradation has been localized to a particular region and has seldom affected more than a generation. In contrast, some contemporary environmental issues have the potential to adversely affect the entire globe and change human life forever. Global climate change, species extinction, soil erosion and desertification, and nuclear wastes will threaten human life into the indefinite future.

Second, the science of ecology and its understanding of the interrelatedness of natural systems have helped us understand the wide range of human dependence on ecosystems. Where once we might have thought that buried wastes were gone forever, we now understand how toxins can seep into groundwater and contaminate drinking water across great time and distances. We now understand how pesticides accumulate throughout the food chain and pose greatest dangers

Reality Check *Breast Milk Toxins*

Pollutants in the biosphere will tend to accumulate in the fatty tissue of species at the top of the food chain. In mammals, fatty tissue is broken down as a source of energy during lactation. As a result, breast milk is a particularly significant resource for studying toxins that the body has absorbed. The following is a list of synthetic toxins that one study found in human breast milk.

- Chlordane (a compound used in pesticides)
- DDT (a pesticide that has been banned in the United States for decades)
- Dieldrin, Aldrin, and Endrin (insecticides)
- Hexachlorobenzene (a pesticide and an industrial chemical)
- Hexachlorocyclohexane (insecticide)
- Heptachlor (insecticide)
- Mirex (insecticide)
- Nitro musks (used as a fragrance in household products such as detergents and soaps)
- Toxaphene (agricultural insecticide)
- Dioxins and furans (any of a number of polychlorinated compounds produced as by-products from industry and combustion)
- PBDEs (used as flame retardants in clothes and other fabrics)
- PCBs (no longer manufactured, but persistent toxins that were used for a wide variety of industrial purposes)
- Solvents (any of a number of chemical compounds used to dissolve or stabilize other complex chemical compounds)
- Lead, mercury, cadmium, and other metals (can be especially toxic to the developing brain)

not only to top predators such as bald eagles, but to human beings as well. (Consider the basic issue of the environment's impact on breast milk, discussed in the Reality Check, "Breast Milk Toxins.") Where once we thought that ocean fisheries were inexhaustible and the atmosphere too big to be changed by humans, we now understand that a precise environmental balance is necessary to maintain life-supporting systems.

By the late nineteenth century, humans came to recognize the self-interested reasons for protecting the natural environment. The conservation movement, the first phase of modern environmentalism, advocated a more restrained and prudent approach to the natural world. From this perspective, the natural world was still valued as a resource, providing humans with both direct benefits (air, water, food), and indirect benefits (the goods and services produced by business). Conservationists argued against the exploitation of natural resources as if they could provide an inexhaustible supply of material. They made the case that business had good reasons for conserving natural resources, reasons that paralleled the rationale to conserve financial resources. The natural world, like capital, had the productive capacity to produce long-term income but only if managed and used prudently.

Besides these self-interested reasons to protect human life and health, the natural environment is essential and valuable for many other reasons. Often, these other values conflict with the more direct instrumental value that comes from treating the natural world as a resource. The beauty and grandeur of the natural world provide great aesthetic, spiritual, and inspirational value. Many people

Decision Point *Commercialize a Historic Civil War Site?*

Is the market, what people are most willing to pay, the best means to determine land and resource use? Consider the case of a proposed development in Virginia.

The city of Manassas is today a suburb of Washington, DC, in northern Virginia. During the U.S. Civil War, it was the site of two historic battles, the first and second Battle of Bull Run. Thousands of soldiers were killed during these battles and many more thousands injured. Today, Manassas Battlefield National Park and several Civil War cemeteries are located at the site.

In the late 1980s developers announced plans to build a large shopping mall on the land that had once served as Robert E. Lee's headquarters during the battle. Significant public opposition led to a public purchase of the land and its incorporation into the national park. A few years later, Disney Company announced plans to develop a large theme park called Disney's America on land adjacent to the National Park. Disney's America would have included a theme park that would be a tribute to the Civil War, as well as residential subdivisions and commercial developments including hotels and restaurants. Eventually, the national park would have been surrounded by commercial development.

The plan met with vociferous opposition from a coalition of environmentalists, preservationists, historians, and Civil War authorities. Although it was convinced that the project would have been a tremendous commercial success, Disney eventually abandoned its plans to develop this site. Should the company have abandoned these plans?

- What facts would be helpful to know before making a decision?
- What values are in conflict in this case? Take a look at Disney's "environmentality" mission statement (http://corporate.disney.go.com/environmentality/mission_history.html). How might its mission guide its decisions or present conflicts in the current dilemma?
- Who are the stakeholders in this case?
- What would be the consequences if all public land uses were decided by the market?
- What are the rights and duties involved in this case?

view the natural world as a manifestation of religious and spiritual values. Parts of the natural world can have symbolic value, historical value, and such diverse psychological values as serenity and exhilaration. These values can clearly conflict with the use of the earth itself as a resource to physically, as opposed to spiritually, sustain those who live on it.

Aesthetic and inspirational values often play out in public debates about economic development. The 1970s song "Big Yellow Taxi" captured this sentiment with the well-known lyric "they paved paradise and put up a parking lot." Many critics fault business for destroying natural beauty and replacing it with strip malls, neon signs, fast-food restaurants and, yes, parking lots. Consider these debates as you review the Decision Point, "Commercialize a Historic Civil War Site?"

Reality Check *Treatment of Animals in Agriculture*

Some animal farming practices, especially within large-scale industrial factory farms, have been criticized as cruel and heartless. Calves are prevented from exercising and intentionally malnourished so that consumers can enjoy tender and pink veal. Chickens are tightly packed in cages with their beaks cut off to prevent them from pecking each other. Cattle are raised in giant feed lots where they spend their time walking in their own manure.

Opponents have organized boycotts against such fast food chains as McDonald's and KFC (formerly called Kentucky Fried Chicken) to protest how animals in their supply chain are treated. In response to this criticism, McDonald's has become an industry leader in creating policies to ensure the humane treatment of animals. As part of this effort, McDonald's has adopted a set of guiding principles, including the following:

> McDonald's commitment to animal welfare is global and guided by the following principles. These principles apply to all the countries in which McDonald's does business.
>
> **Safety.** First and foremost, McDonald's will provide its customers with safe food products. Food safety is McDonald's number one priority.
>
> **Quality.** McDonald's believes treating animals with care and respect is an integral part of an overall quality assurance program that makes good business sense.
>
> **Animal Treatment.** McDonald's supports that animals should be free from cruelty, abuse and neglect while embracing the proper treatment of animals and addressing animal welfare issues.

Source: McDonald's Corporation, "2006 Worldwide Corporate Responsibility Report; Products: Responsible Purchasing Guiding Principles," http://www.mcdonalds.com/corp/values/purchasing/animalwelfare/guiding_principles.html.

A final set of values that we will consider involves the moral status of animals and other living beings, an environmental value that has raised some of the most widely publicized ethical challenges to business. Variously referred to as the animal rights, animal liberation, or animal welfare movement, this approach attributes a moral standing to animals. According to many people, animals, and perhaps all other living things, deserve to be respected and treated with dignity. Such a status would create a wide variety of distinctive ethical responsibilities concerning how we treat animals and would have significant implications for many businesses.

To defend this perspective, some argue that many animals, presumably all animals with a central nervous system, have the capacity to feel pain. Reminiscent of the utilitarian tradition described in chapter 3, this view asserts an ethical responsibility to minimize pain. Inflicting unnecessary pain is taken to be an ethical wrong; therefore, acts that inflict unnecessary pain on animals are ethically wrong. Raising and slaughtering animals for food, particularly in the way industrial farming enterprises raise poultry, hogs, and cattle, would be an obvious case in which business would violate this ethical responsibility, as one side argues in the Reality Check, "Treatment of Animals in Agriculture."

A second approach argues that at least some animals have the cognitive capacity to possess a conscious life of their own. Reminiscent of the Kantian ethical tradition described in chapter 3, this view asserts that we have a duty not to treat these animals as mere objects and means to our own ends. Again, businesses that use animals for food, entertainment, or pets would violate the ethical rights of these animals.

Business' Environmental Responsibility: The Market Approach

While debate continues to surrounds some environmental values, an overwhelming consensus exists about the self-interested and prudential reasons for protecting the natural environment—humans have a right to be protected from undue harm. What controversy remains has more to do with the best means for achieving this goal. Historically, this debate has focused on whether efficient markets or government regulation is the most appropriate means for meeting the environmental responsibilities of business. Each of these two approaches has significant implications for business.

3 OBJECTIVE

From one perspective, if the best approach to environmental concerns is to trust them to efficient markets, then the responsible business manager simply ought to seek profits and allow the market to allocate resources efficiently. By doing this, business fills its role within a market system, which in turn serves the greater overall (utilitarian) good. On the other hand, if government regulation is a more adequate approach, then business ought to develop a compliance structure to ensure that it conforms to those regulatory requirements.

A market-based approach to resolving environmental challenges is reminiscent of the narrow, economic view of CSR described in chapter 5. Defenders of this market approach contend that environmental problems are economic problems that deserve economic solutions. Fundamentally, environmental problems involve the allocation and distribution of limited resources. Whether we are concerned with the allocation of scarce nonrenewable resources such as gas and oil, or with the earth's capacity to absorb industrial by-products such as CO_2 or PCBs, efficient markets can address environmental challenges.

4 OBJECTIVE

Consider the implications of this model for pollution and resource conservation. In his well-known book, *People or Penguins: The Case for Optimal Pollution,* William Baxter argued that there is an optimal level of pollution that would best serve society's interests.[1] This optimal level is best attained, according to Baxter, by leaving it to a competitive market.

Denying that there is any "natural" or objective standard for clean air or water (as this view would deny there is an objective state of perfect health), Baxter begins with a goal of "safe" air and water quality, and translates this goal to a matter of balancing risks and benefits. Society *could* strive for pure air and water, but the costs (lost opportunities) that this would entail would be too high. A more reasonable approach is to aim for air and water quality that is safe enough to breathe and drink without costing too much. This balance, the "optimal level of pollution" can be achieved through competitive markets. Society, through the activities of individuals, will be willing to pay for pollution reduction as long as the perceived benefits outweigh the costs.

The free market also provides an answer for resource conservation. From a strict market economic perspective, resources are "infinite." Julian Simon, for example, has argued that resources should not be viewed as material objects but simply as any means to our ends.[2] History has shown that human ingenuity and incentive have always found substitutes for any shortages. As the supply of any resources decreases, the price increases, thereby providing a strong incentive to supply more or provide a less costly substitute. In economic terms, all resources are "fungible." They can be replaced by substitutes, and in this sense resources are infinite. Resources that are not being used to satisfy consumer demand are being wasted.

A similar case can be made for the preservation of environmentally sensitive areas. Preservation for preservation's sake would be wasteful since it would use resources inefficiently. Thus, to return to the Manassas Battlefield development plan described previously, preserving open space surrounding the area rather than developing the land as a theme park should be done only if people are willing to pay more for open space than for a park. Since the Disney plan would have been financially very profitable, leaving it undeveloped would be wasting these valuable resources.

5 OBJECTIVE

Challenges to this narrow economic view of corporate social responsibility are familiar to both economists and ethicists. A variety of market failures, many of the best known of which involve environmental issues, point to the inadequacy of market solutions. One example is the existence of externalities, the textbook example of which is environmental pollution. Since the "costs" of such things as air pollution, groundwater contamination and depletion, soil erosion, and nuclear waste disposal are typically borne by parties "external" to the economic exchange (e.g., people downwind, neighbors, future generations), free market exchanges cannot guarantee optimal results.

A second type of market failure occurs when no markets exist to create a price for important social goods. Endangered species, scenic vistas, rare plants and animals, and biodiversity are just some environmental goods that typically are not traded on open markets (or, when they are, they are often traded in ways that seriously threaten their viability as when rhinoceros horns, tiger claws, elephant tusks, and mahogany trees are sold on the black market). Public goods such as clean air and ocean fisheries also have no established market price. With no established exchange value, the market approach cannot even pretend to achieve its own goals of efficiently meeting consumer demand. Markets alone fail to guarantee that such important public goods are preserved and protected.

A third way in which market failures can lead to serious environmental harm involves a distinction between individual decisions and group consequences. We can miss important ethical and policy questions if we leave policy decisions solely to the outcome of individual decisions. Consider the calculations that an individual consumer might make regarding the purchase of an SUV and the consequences of that decision on global warming. The additional CO_2 that would be emitted by a single SUV is miniscule enough that an individual would likely conclude that her decision will make no difference. However, if every consumer made exactly the same decision, the consequences would be significantly different.

This example demonstrates that the overall social result of individual calculations might be significant increases in pollution and such pollution-related diseases as asthma and allergies. A number of alternative policies (e.g., restricting SUV sales, increasing taxes on gasoline, treating SUVs as cars instead of light trucks in calculating **Corporate Automotive Fuel Efficiency [CAFE] Standards**) that could address pollution and pollution-related disease would never be considered if we relied only on market solutions. Because these are important ethical questions, and because they remain unasked from within market transactions, we must conclude that markets are incomplete (at best) in their approach to the overall social good. In other words, what is good and rational for a collection of individuals is not necessarily what is good and rational for a society.

Such market failures raise serious concerns for the ability of economic markets to achieve a sound environmental policy. Defenders of a narrow economic view of corporate social responsibility have responses to these challenges of course. Internalizing external costs and assigning property rights to unowned goods such as wild species are two responses to market failures. But there are good reasons for thinking that such ad hoc attempts to repair market failures are environmentally inadequate. One important reason is what has been called the first-generation problem. Markets can work to prevent harm only through information supplied by the existence of market failures. Only when fish populations in the North Atlantic collapsed, for example, did we learn that free and open competition among the world's fishing industry for unowned public goods failed to prevent the decimation of cod, swordfish, Atlantic salmon, and lobster populations. That is, we learn about market failures and thereby prevent harms in the future only by sacrificing the "first generation" as a means of gaining this information. When public policy involves irreplaceable public goods such as endangered species, rare wilderness areas, and public health and safety, such a reactionary strategy is ill advised. (See the Reality Check, "Supply and Demand for Energy.")

Business' Environmental Responsibility: The Regulatory Approach

3 OBJECTIVE

A broad consensus emerged in the United States in the 1970s that unregulated markets are an inadequate approach to environmental challenges. Instead, governmental regulations were seen as the better way to respond to environmental problems. Much of the most significant environmental legislation in the United States was enacted during the 1970s. The Clean Air Act of 1970 (amended and renewed in 1977), Federal Water Pollution Act of 1972 (amended and renewed as the Clean Water Act of 1977), and the Endangered Species Act of 1973 were part of this national consensus for addressing environmental problems. Each law was originally enacted by a Democratic Congress and signed into law by a Republican president.

These laws share a common approach to environmental issues. Before this legislation was enacted, the primary legal avenue open for addressing environmental concerns was tort law. Only individuals who could prove that they had been

Reality Check *Supply and Demand for Energy*

A recent call from the chairman and CEO of Chevron-Texaco for changes in U.S. energy policy emphasizes the need for partnership between government and business to address the energy market. In a speech delivered in February 2005, David J. O'Reilly claimed that we are now in the midst of what he called a "new energy equation" requiring a broad-based energy policy.

> The most visible element of this new equation is that relative to demand, oil is no longer in plentiful supply. The time when we could count on cheap oil and even cheaper natural gas is clearly ending. Why is this happening now? . . . Demand from Asia is one fundamental reason for this new age of more volatile and higher prices. The Chinese economy alone is a roaring engine whose thirst for oil grew by more than 15 percent last year and will double its need for imported oil between 2003 and 2010—just seven years. This new Asian demand is reshaping the marketplace. And we're seeing the center of gravity of global petroleum markets shift to Asia and, in particular, to China and India. . . . But demand isn't the only factor at play. Simply put, the era of easy access to energy is over. In part, this is because we are experiencing the convergence of geological difficulty with geopolitical instability. Although political turmoil and social unrest are less likely to affect long-term supplies, the psychological effect of those factors can clearly have an impact on world oil markets, which are already running at razor-thin margins of capacity. Many of the world's big production fields are maturing just as demand is increasing. The U.S. Geological Survey estimates the world will have consumed one-half of its existing conventional oil base by 2030. Increasingly, future supplies will have to be found in ultradeep water and other remote areas, development projects that will ultimately require new technology and trillions of dollars of investment in new infrastructure.

Source: David J. O'Reilly, chairman and CEO, Chevron-Texaco Corporation, "U.S. Energy Policy: A Declaration of Interdependence" (keynote address, 24th annual CERA Week Conference, Houston, Texas, February 15, 2005). Available on the Chevron-Texaco Web site: http://www.chevrontexaco.com/news/speeches/2005/ 2005-02-15_oreilly.asp.

harmed by pollution could raise legal challenges to air and water pollution. That legal approach placed the burden on the person who was harmed and, at best, offered compensation for the harm only after the fact. Except for the incentive provided by the threat of compensation, U.S. policy did little to prevent the pollution in the first place. Absent any proof of negligence, public policy was content to let the market decide environmental policy. Because endangered species themselves had no legal standing, direct harm to plant and animal life was of no legal concern and previous policies did little to prevent harm to plant and animal life.

The laws enacted during the 1970s established standards that effectively shifted the burden from those threatened with harm to those who would cause the harm. Government established regulatory standards to try to prevent the occurrence of pollution or species extinction rather than to offer compensation after the fact. We can think of these laws as establishing minimum standards to ensure air and water quality and species preservation. Business was free to pursue its own goals as long as it complied with the side constraints these minimum standards established.

The consensus that emerged was that society had two opportunities to establish business' environmental responsibilities. As consumers, individuals could demand environmentally friendly products in the marketplace. As citizens, individuals could support environmental legislation. As long as business responded to the market and obeyed the law, it met its environmental responsibilities. If consumers demand environmentally suspect products, such as large gas-guzzling SUVs, and those products are allowed by law, then we cannot expect business to forgo the financial opportunities of marketing such products.

6
OBJECTIVE

Several problems suggest that this approach will prove inadequate over the long term. First, it underestimates the influence that business can have in establishing the law. The CAFE Standards mentioned previously provide a good example of how this can occur. A reasonable account of this law suggests that the public very clearly expressed a political goal of improving air quality by improving automobile fuel efficiency goals (and thereby reducing automobile emissions). However, the automobile industry was able to use its lobbying influence to exempt light trucks and SUVs from these standards. It should be no surprise that light trucks and SUVs at the time represented the largest selling, and most profitable, segment of the auto industry.

Second, this approach also underestimates the ability of business to influence consumer choice. To conclude that business fulfills its environmental responsibility when it responds to the environmental demands of consumers is to underestimate the role that business can play in shaping public opinion. Advertising is a $200 billion a year industry in the United States alone. It is surely misleading to claim that business passively responds to consumer desires and that consumers are unaffected by the messages that business conveys. Assuming that business is not going to stop advertising its products or lobbying government, this model of corporate environmental responsibility is likely to prove inadequate for protecting the natural environment.

Further, if we rely on the law to protect the environment, environmental protection will extend only as far as the law extends. Yet, most environmental issues, pollution problems especially, do not respect legal jurisdictions. New York State might pass strict regulations on smokestack emissions, but if the power plants are located downwind in Ohio or even further west in the Dakotas or Wyoming, New York State will continue to suffer the effects of acid rain. Similarly, national regulations will be ineffective for international environmental challenges. While hope remains that international agreements might help control global environmental problems, the failure of the Kyoto agreement suggests that this might be overly optimistic.

Finally, and perhaps most troubling from an environmental standpoint, this regulatory model assumes that economic growth is environmentally and ethically benign. Regulations establish side constraints on business' pursuit of profits and, as long as they remain within those constraints, accept as ethically legitimate whatever road to profitability management chooses. What can be lost in these discussions is the very important fact that there are many different ways to pursue profits within the side constraints of law. Different roads towards profitability can have very different environmental consequences, as is discussed in the Reality Check, "Cap and Trade—A Mixed Approach?"

Reality Check *Cap and Trade—A Mixed Approach?*

One strategy that combines elements of both market and regulatory approaches is the so-called "cap and trade" model that has been proposed as part of U.S. federal legislation to address carbon emissions. Under the cap and trade model, government sets an overall annual target, or "cap," on the amount of CO_2 emissions nationally. Companies then buy government-issued permits to emit pollution. The permits limit the total amount of pollution to the national cap. Individual businesses are free to buy or sell their permits in such a way that an efficient company that emits less pollution than its permits allow can sell its remaining pollution credits to a less efficient company. By thus creating a market for pollution credits, government regulation creates an incentive for individual businesses to reduce its own pollution. Government can then slowly reduce the overlap pollution target annually to achieve its public policy goal.

Defenders see this approach as a powerful way to use market incentives to reduce pollution. Critics see it as government issuing a "license to pollute."

Business' Environmental Responsibilities: The Sustainability Approach

7 OBJECTIVE

Beginning in the 1980s, a new model for environmentally responsible business began to take shape, one that combines financial opportunities with environmental and ethical responsibilities. The concept of **sustainable development** and **sustainable business practice** suggests a radically new vision for integrating financial and environmental goals, compared to the growth model that preceded it (as explored in the Reality Check, "Why Sustainability?"). These three goals, economic, environmental, and ethical sustainability, are often referred to as the **three pillars of sustainability.** Assessing business activity along these three lines is often referred to as the "triple bottom line."

The concept of sustainable development can be traced to a 1987 report from the United Nations' World Commission on Environment and Development (WCED), more commonly known as the Brundtland Commission, named for its chair, Gro Harlem Brundtland. The commission was charged with developing recommendations for paths towards economic and social development that would not achieve short-term economic growth at the expense of long-term environmental and economic sustainability. The Brundtland Commission offered what has become the standard definition of sustainable development. "Sustainable development is development that meets the needs of the present without compromising the ability of future generations to meet their own needs."

Economist Herman Daly has been among the leading thinkers who have advocated an innovative approach to economic theory based on the concept of sustainable development. Daly makes a convincing case for an understanding of economic *development* that transcends the more common standard of economic *growth.* Unless we make significant changes in our understanding of economic activity, unless quite literally we change the way we do business, we will fail to

Reality Check *Why Sustainability?*

Three factors are most often cited to explain and justify the need for a model of economic development that stresses sustainability rather than growth.

First, billions of human beings live in severe poverty and face real challenges associated with the lack of food, water, health care, and shelter on a daily basis. Addressing these challenges will require significant economic activity.

Second, world population continues to grow at a disturbing rate, with projections of an increase from 6 billion people in 1998 to 7 billion shortly after 2010 and 8 billion before 2030. Most of this population growth will occur within the world's poorest regions, thereby only intensifying the first challenge. Even more economic activity will be needed to address the needs of this growing population.

Third, all of this economic activity must rely on the productive capacity of the earth's biosphere. Unfortunately, there is ample evidence that the type and amount of economic activity practiced by the world's economies have already approached if not overshot the earth's ability to support human life.

Given these realities, citizens within developed economies have three available paths. We can believe that developing economies in places such as China, India, and Indonesia cannot, will not, or should not strive for the type of economic prosperity enjoyed in developed economies. Second, we could believe, optimistically, that present models of business and economic growth can be extended across the globe to an expanding population without degrading the natural environment beyond its limits. Third, we can search for new models of economic and business activity that provide for the needs of the world's population without further degrading the biosphere. Sustainable development and the connected model of sustainable business choose this third path.

meet some very basic ethical and environmental obligations. According to Daly, we need a major paradigm shift in how we understand economic activity.

We can begin with the standard understanding of economic activity and economic growth found in almost every economics textbook. What is sometimes called the "circular flow model" (Figure 9.2) explains the nature of economic transactions in terms of a flow of resources from businesses to households and back again. Business produces goods and services in response to the market demands of households; then ships the goods and services to households in exchange for payments back to business. These payments are in turn sent back to households in the form of wages, salaries, rents, profits, and interests. Households receive the payments in exchange for the labor, land, capital, and entrepreneurial skills business uses to produce goods and services.

Two aspects of this circular flow model are worth noting. First, it does not differentiate natural resources from the other factors of production. This model does not explain the origin of resources. They are simply owned by households from which they, like labor, capital, and entrepreneurial skill, can be sold to business. As economist Julian Simon has argued, "As economists or consumers, we are interested in the particular services that resources yield, not in the resources themselves." Those services can be provided in many ways and by substituting different factors of production. In Simon's terms, resources can therefore be treated as "infinite."

A second observation is that this model treats economic growth as both the solution to all social ills and also as boundless. To keep up with population growth, the economy must grow. To provide for a higher standard of living, the economy must grow. To alleviate poverty, hunger, and disease, the economy must grow. The possibility that the economy cannot grow indefinitely is simply not part of this model.

The three points summarized in the Reality Check, "Why Sustainability?" suggest why this growth-based model will be inadequate. According to some estimates, the world's economy would need to grow by a factor of five- to tenfold over the next 50 years in order to bring the standard of living of present populations in the developing world into line with the standard of living in the industrialized world. Yet, within those 50 years, the world's population will increase by more than 3 billion people, most of them born in the world's poorest economies. Of course, the only source for all this economic activity is productive capacity of the earth itself.

Daly argues that neoclassical economics, with its emphasis on economic growth as the goal of economic policy, will inevitably fail to meet these challenges unless it recognizes that the economy is but a subsystem within earth's biosphere. Economic activity takes place within this biosphere and cannot expand beyond its capacity to sustain life. All the factors that go into production—natural resources, capital, entrepreneurial skill, and labor—ultimately originate in the productive capacity of the earth. In light of this, the entire classical model will prove unstable if resources move through this system at a rate that outpaces the productive capacity of the earth or of the earth's capacity to absorb the wastes and by-products of this production. Thus, we need to develop an economic system that uses resources only at a rate that can be sustained over the long term and that recycles or reuses both the by-products of the production process and the products themselves. A model of such a system, based on the work of Daly, is presented in Figure 9.3.

Figure 9.3 differs from Figure 9.2 in several important ways. First, the sustainable model recognizes that the economy exists within a finite biosphere that encompasses a band around the earth that is little more than a few miles wide. From the first law of thermodynamics (the conservation of matter/energy), we recognize that neither matter nor energy can truly be "created," it can only be transferred from one form to another. Second, energy is lost at every stage of economic activity. Consistent with the second law of thermodynamics (entropy increased within a closed system), the amount of usable energy decreases over time. "Waste energy" is continuously leaving the economic system and thus new low-entropy energy must constantly flow into the system. Ultimately, the only source for low-entropy energy is the sun. Third, this model no longer treats natural resources as an undifferentiated and unexplained factor of production emerging from households. Natural resources come from the biosphere and cannot be created ex nihilo. Finally, it recognizes that wastes are produced at each stage of economic activity and these wastes are dumped back into the biosphere.

FIGURE 9.2
The Circular Flow Model

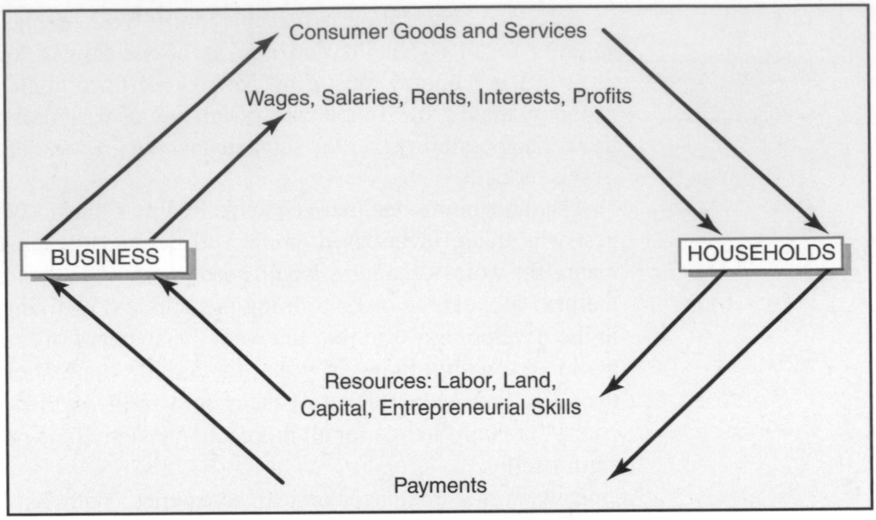

The conclusion that should be drawn from this new model is relatively simple. Over the long term, resources and energy cannot be used, nor waste produced, at rates at which the biosphere cannot replace or absorb them without jeopardizing its ability to sustain (human) life. These are what Daly calls the "biophysical limits to growth.[3] The biosphere can produce resources indefinitely, and it can absorb wastes indefinitely, but only at a certain rate and with a certain type of economic

FIGURE 9.3
A Model of the Economy (or Economic System) as a Subset of the Biosphere (or Ecosystem)

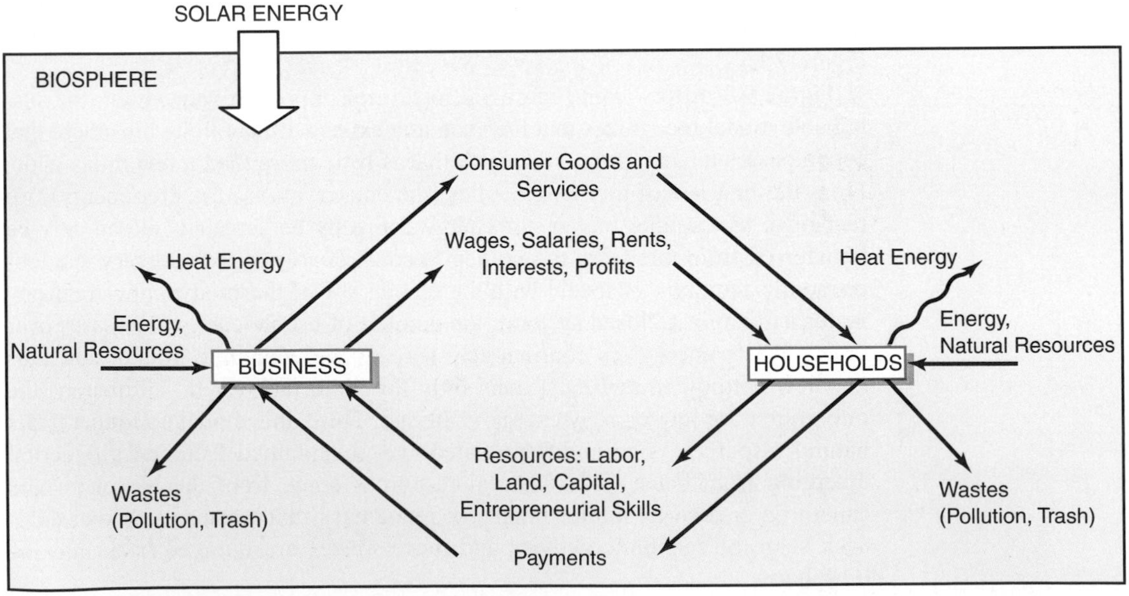

Reality Check *Is Everything Sustainable?*

"Sustainability" has become a somewhat trendy term and can seem to mean all things to all people. When we hear talk about "sustainability," we should always be prepared to ask: *What* is being sustained? *For whom* is it being sustained? *How* is it being sustained? and What *should* be sustained?"

The language of sustainability can be especially attractive to those of us living comfortably in developed economies if it is interpreted to mean maintaining the status quo over the long term. But, not every industry, nor every firm, nor every business practice, nor every consumer product is sustainable. Industrial fishing practices in the North Atlantic have already proven unsustainable, as has or soon will be many agricultural practices such as burning rain forests to increase cropland, tapping underground aquifers for irrigation, and burning fossil fuels to power personal transportation.

activity. This is the goal of sustainable development. Finding this rate and type of economic activity, and thereby creating a sustainable business practice, is the ultimate environmental responsibility of business.

The "Business Case" for a Sustainable Economy

8 OBJECTIVE

While the regulatory and compliance model tends to interpret environmental responsibilities as constraints upon business, the sustainability model is more forward looking and may present business with greater opportunities than burdens. Indeed, it offers a vision of future business that many entrepreneurial and creative businesses are already pursuing. Many observers argue that a strong economic and financial case can be made for the move towards a sustainable future (but also see the Reality Check, "Is Everything Sustainable?").

First, sustainability is a prudent long-term strategy. As the Natural Step's funnel image suggests, business will need to adopt sustainable practices to ensure long-term survival. Firms that fail to adapt to the converging lines of decreasing availability of resources and increasing demand risk their own survival. One can look to the ocean fishing industry as an example.

Second, the huge unmet market potential among the world's developing economies can only be met in sustainable ways. Enormous business opportunities exist in serving the billions of people who need, and are demanding, economic goods and services. The base of the economic pyramid represents the largest and fastest-growing economic market in human history. Yet, the sheer size of these markets alone makes it impossible to meet this demand with the environmentally damaging industrial practices of the nineteenth and twentieth centuries. For example, if China were to consume oil at the same rate as the United States, it alone would consume more than the entire world's daily production and would more than triple the emission of atmospheric carbon dioxide. It is obvious that new sustainable technologies and products will be required to meet the Chinese demand.

Third, significant cost savings can be achieved through sustainable practices. Business stands to save significant costs in moves towards eco-efficiency. Savings on energy use and materials will reduce not only environmental wastes, but spending wastes as well. Minimizing wastes makes sense on financial grounds as well as on environmental grounds.

Fourth, competitive advantages exist for sustainable businesses. Firms that are ahead of the sustainability curve will both have an advantage serving environmentally conscious consumers and enjoy a competitive advantage attracting workers who will take pride and satisfaction in working for progressive firms.

Finally, sustainability is a good risk management strategy. Refusing to move towards sustainability offers many downsides that innovative firms will avoid. Avoiding future government regulation is one obvious benefit. Firms that take the initiative in moving towards sustainability will also likely be the firms that set the standards of best practices in the field. Thus, when regulation does come, these firms will likely play a role in determining what those regulations ought to be. Avoiding legal liability for unsustainable products is another potential benefit. As social consciousness changes, the legal system may soon begin punishing firms that are now negligent in failing to foresee harms caused by their unsustainable practices. Consumer boycotts of unsustainable firms are also a risk to be avoided.

We can summarize these previous sections by reflecting on the ethical decision-making model used throughout this text. The facts suggest that the earth's biosphere is under stress and that much of this comes from the type of global economic growth that has characterized industrial and consumerist societies. The ethical issues that develop from these facts include fairness in allocating scarce resources, justice in meeting the real needs of billions of present and future human beings, and the values and rights associated with environmental conservation and preservation. The stakeholders for these decisions include, quite literally, all life on earth. Relaying on our own moral imagination, we can envision a future in which economic activity can meet the real needs of present generations without jeopardizing the ability of future generations to meet their own needs. Sustainability seems to be just this vision. (The reading, "Taking Sustainability Seriously: An Argument for Managerial Responsibility" by Tara Radin at the end of this chapter offers an additional perspective on the view that the natural environment should be understood as a major business stakeholder.) The next section describes directions in which business might develop towards this sustainable model.

Principles for a Sustainable Business

9 OBJECTIVE

Figure 9.3 provides a general model for understanding how firms can evolve towards a sustainable business model. In the simplest terms, resources should not enter into the economic cycle from the biosphere at rates faster than they are replenished. Ideally, waste should be eliminated or, at a minimum, not produced at a rate faster than the biosphere can absorb it. Finally, the energy to power the economic system should be renewable, ultimately relying on the sun, the only energy that is truly renewable.

The precise implications of sustainability will differ for specific firms and industries, but three general principles will guide the move towards sustainability. Firms and industries must become more efficient in using natural resources; they should model their entire production process on biological processes; and they should emphasize the production of services rather than products.

Versions of the first principle, sometimes called **eco-efficiency,** have long been a part of the environmental movement. "Doing more with less" has been an environmental guideline for decades. On an individual scale, it is environmentally better to ride a bike than to ride in a bus, to ride in a fuel-cell or hybrid-powered bus than in a diesel bus, to ride in a bus than to drive a personal automobile, and to drive a hybrid car than an SUV. Likewise, business firms can improve energy and materials efficiency in such things as lighting, building design, product design, and distribution channels. The LEED building standards described in this chapter's opening Decision Point incorporate many such eco-efficiency ideas. Some estimates suggest that with present technologies alone, business could readily achieve at least a fourfold increase in efficiency and perhaps as much as a tenfold increase. Consider that a fourfold increase, called "Factor-Four" in the sustainability literature, would make it possible to achieve double the productivity from one-half the resource use.[4] When applied to the additional costs for buildings associated with LEED standards, for example, such a return on investment means that companies can quickly recoup this environmental investment.

The second principle of business sustainability can be easily understood by reference to Figure 9.3. Imagine that the waste leaving the economic cycle is being turned back into the cycle as a productive resource. "Closed-loop" production seeks to integrate what is presently waste back into production. In an ideal situation, the waste of one firm becomes the resource of another, and such synergies can create eco-industrial parks. Just as biological processes such as photosynthesis cycle the "waste" of one activity into the resource of another, this principle is often referred to as **biomimicry**.

The ultimate goal of biomimicry is to eliminate waste altogether rather than reducing it. If we truly mimic biological processes, the end result of one process (e.g., leaves and oxygen produced by photosynthesis) is ultimately reused as the productive resources (e.g., soil and water) of another process (plant growth) with only solar energy added.

The evolution of business strategy towards biomimicry can be understood along a continuum. The earliest phase has been described as "take-make-waste." Business takes resources, makes products out of them, and discards whatever is left over. A second phase envisions business taking responsibility for its products from "cradle to grave." Sometimes referred to as "life-cycle" responsibility, this approach has already found its way into both industrial and regulatory thinking. Cradle-to-grave, or life-cycle responsibility holds that a business is responsible for the entire life of its products, including the ultimate disposal even after the sale. Thus, for example, a cradle-to-grave model would hold a business liable for groundwater contamination caused by its products even years after they had been buried in a landfill.

Opening Decision Point Revisited *Building Design and Values*

From the earliest years of the industrial revolution, building design has contributed much to economic growth and economic efficiency. It has also contributed much to environmental degradation and pollution. From giant textile mills in Europe and New England, to Henry Ford's assembly line manufacturing plants, to office buildings with row after row of cubicles and desks, building design has paralleled managerial philosophy. Reflect on how this has changed through the years. Consider how building designs and construction reflect the social values of the times during which they were built.

Can you identify the oldest commercial buildings in your city or town? What are the oldest local manufacturing facilities that are still operating? Can you trace a timeline for types of commercial buildings in your community? What values guided their design? Can you identify the biggest problems with the oldest buildings? Are there any benefits to them? Can you identify any reasons why the oldest buildings continue to function when many building of the same age have long since been torn down? What do the buildings say about workers, management, and business? What do they say about the values that guided their design and construction?

Do the same exercise for the buildings on your own campus. Compare the oldest to the most recent. What are some differences? Were they designed with different values and different understandings of students, teachers, and the educational mission? Does your own campus have any buildings that are LEED certified? How do they differ from earlier buildings? Does your own campus have any buildings in the planning stages? Will they be built to LEED certification? Can you learn why or why not?

Cradle-to-cradle responsibility extends this idea even further and holds that a business should be responsible for incorporating the end results of its products back into the productive cycle. This responsibility, in turn, would create incentives to redesign products so that they could be recycled efficiently and easily.

The environmental design company McDonough and Braungart, founded by architect William McDonough and chemist Michael Braungart, has been a leader in helping businesses reconceptualize and redesign business practice to achieve sustainability. Their book, *Cradle to Cradle,* traces the life cycle of several products, providing case studies of economic and environmental benefits attainable when business takes responsibility for the entire life cycle of products. Among their projects is the redesign of Ford Motor Company's Rouge River manufacturing plant. McDonough and Braungrat provide greater details about their design principles in the reading, "The Next Industrial Revolution" at the end of this chapter.

Beyond eco-efficiency and biomimicry, a third sustainable business principle involves a shift in business model from products to services. Traditional economic and managerial models interpret consumer demand as the demand for products—washing machines, carpets, lights, consumer electronics, air conditioners, cars, computers, and so forth. A **service-based economy** interprets consumer demand as a demand for services—for clothes cleaning, floor covering, illumination, entertainment, cool air, transportation, word processing, and so forth.

The book *Natural Capitalism* provides examples of businesses that have made such a shift in each of these industries.[5] This change produces incentives for product redesigns that create more durable and more easily recyclable products.

One well-known innovator in this area is Interface Corporation and its CEO, Ray Anderson. Interface has made a transition from selling carpeting to leasing floor-covering services. On the traditional model, carpet is sold to consumers who, once they become dissatisfied with the color or style or once the carpeting becomes worn, dispose of the carpet in landfills. There is little incentive here to produce long-lasting or easily recyclable carpeting. Once Interface shifted to leasing floor-covering services, it created incentives to produce long-lasting, easily replaceable and recyclable carpets. Interface thereby accepts responsibility for the entire life cycle of the product it markets. Because the company retains ownership and is responsible for maintenance, Interface now produces carpeting that can be easily replaced in sections rather than in its entirety, that is more durable, and that can eventually be remanufactured. Redesigning carpets and shifting to a service lease has also improved production efficiencies and reduced material and energy costs significantly. Consumers benefit by getting what they truly desire at lower costs and fewer burdens.

Questions, Projects, and Exercises

1. As a research project, choose a product with which you are familiar (one with local connections is best), and trace its entire life cycle. From where does this product originate? What resources go into its design and manufacture? How is it transported, sold, used, and disposed of? Along each step in the life cycle of this product, analyze the economic, environmental, and ethical costs and benefits. Consider if a service could be exchanged for this product. Some examples might include your local drinking water, food items such as beef or chicken, any product sold at a local farmer's market, or building materials used in local projects.
2. Conduct a Web search for ecological footprint analysis. You should be able to find a self-administered test to evaluate your own ecological footprint. If everyone on earth lived as you do, how many earths would be required to support this lifestyle?
3. Research corporate sustainability reports. How many corporations can you find that issue annual reports on their progress towards sustainability? Can you research a company that does not and explore why not (perhaps through its critics), or whether it has plans to change?
4. A movement within the European Union requires that a business take back its products at the end of their useful life. Can you learn the details of such laws? Discuss whether or not you believe such a law could be passed in the United States. Should the United States have similar laws?
5. Apply the concept of sustainability to a variety of businesses and industries. What would sustainable agriculture require? What are sustainable energy sources? What

would sustainable transportation be? What would be required to turn your hometown into a sustainable community?

6. Investigate what is involved in an environmental audit. Has such an audit been conducted at your own college or university? In what ways has your own school adopted sustainable practices? In what ways would your school need to change to become more sustainable?
7. Do you believe that business has any direct ethical duties to living beings other than humans? Do animals, plants, or ecosystems have rights? What criteria have you used in answering such questions? What is your own standard for determining what objects count, from a moral point of view?
8. Investigate LEED (Leadership in Energy and Environmental Design) building designs. If possible, arrange a visit to a local building designed according to LEED principles. Should all new buildings be required by law to adopt LEED design standards and conform to the LEED rating system?

Key Terms

After reading this chapter, you should have a clear understanding of the following Key Terms. The page numbers refer to the point at which they were discussed in the chapter. For a more complete definition, please see the Glossary.

backcasting, *p. 483*
biomimicry, *p. 499*
Corporate Automotive Fuel Efficiency (CAFE) Standards, *p. 490*
cradle-to-cradle responsibility, *p. 500*
eco-efficiency, *p. 499*
LEED certification, *p. 480*
service-based economy, *p. 501*
sustainable business practice, *p. 493*
sustainable development, *p. 493*
three pillars of sustainability, *p. 493*

End Notes

1. William Baxter, *People or Penguins: The Case for Optimal Pollution* (New York: Columbia University Press, 1974).
2. Julian Simon, *The Ultimate Resource* (Princeton, NJ: Princeton University Press, 1983).
3. Herman Daly, *Beyond Growth* (Boston: Beacon Press, 1996), 33–35
4. For the Factor Four claim, see Ernst von Weizacker, Amory B. Lovins, L. Hunter Lovins, and Kogan Page, "Factor Four: Doubling Wealth—Halving Resource Use: A Report to the Club of Rome" (Earthscan/James & James, 1997); For Factor 10, see Friedrich Schmidt-Bleek, Factor 10 Institute, http://www.factor10-institute.org/ (accessed April 22, 2010).
5. Paul Hawken, Amory Lovins, and Hunter Lovins, *Natural Capitalism* (Boston: Little Brown, 1999).

Readings

Reading **9-1**

The Next Industrial Revolution

William McDonough and Michael Braungart

In the spring of 1912 one of the largest moving objects ever created by human beings left Southampton and began gliding toward New York. It was the epitome of its industrial age—a potent representation of technology, prosperity, luxury, and progress. It weighed 66,000 tons. Its steel hull stretched the length of four city blocks. Each of its steam engines was the size of a townhouse. And it was headed for a disastrous encounter with the natural world.

This vessel, of course, was the *Titanic*—a brute of a ship, seemingly impervious to the details of nature. In the minds of the captain, the crew, and many of the passengers, nothing could sink it. One might say that the infrastructure created by the Industrial Revolution of the nineteenth century resembles such a steamship. It is powered by fossil fuels, nuclear reactors, and chemicals. It is pouring waste into the water and smoke into the sky. It is attempting to work by its own rules, contrary to those of the natural world. And although it may seem invincible, its fundamental design flaws presage disaster. Yet many people still believe that with a few minor alterations, this infrastructure can take us safely and prosperously into the future.

During the Industrial Revolution resources seemed inexhaustible and nature was viewed as something to be tamed and civilized. Recently, however, some leading industrialists have begun to realize that traditional ways of doing things may not be sustainable over the long term. "What we thought was boundless has limits," Robert Shapiro, the chairman and chief executive officer of Monsanto, said in a 1997 interview, "and we're beginning to hit them."

The 1992 Earth Summit in Rio de Janeiro, led by the Canadian businessman Maurice Strong, recognized those limits. Approximately 30,000 people from around the world, including more than a hundred world leaders and representatives of 167 countries, gathered in Rio de Janeiro to respond to troubling symptoms of environmental decline. Although there was sharp disappointment afterward that no binding agreement had been reached at the summit, many industrial participants touted a particular strategy: eco-efficiency. The machines of industry would be refitted with cleaner, faster, quieter engines. Prosperity would remain unobstructed, and economic and organizational structures would remain intact. The hope was that eco-efficiency would transform human industry from a system that takes, makes, and wastes into one that integrates economic, environmental, and ethical concerns. Eco-efficiency is now considered by industries across the globe to be the strategy of choice for change.

What is eco-efficiency? Primarily, the term means "doing more with less"—a precept that has its roots in early industrialization. Henry Ford was adamant about lean and clean operating policies; he saved his company money by recycling and reusing materials, reduced the use of natural resources, minimized packaging, and set new standards with his timesaving assembly line. Ford wrote in 1926, "You must get the most out of the power, out of the material, and out of the time"—a credo that could hang today on the wall of any eco-efficient factory. The linkage of efficiency with sustaining the environment was perhaps most famously articulated in *Our Common Future,* a report published in 1987 by the United Nations' World Commission on Environment and Development. *Our Common Future* warned that if pollution control were not intensified, property and ecosystems would be threatened, and existence would become unpleasant and even harmful to human health in some cities. "Industries and industrial operations should be encouraged that are more efficient in terms of resource use, that generate less pollution and waste, that are based on the use of renewable rather than nonrenewable resources, and that minimize irreversible adverse impacts on human health and the environment," the commission stated in its agenda for change.

The term "eco-efficiency" was promoted five years later, by the Business Council (now the World Business Council) for Sustainable Development, a group of 48 industrial sponsors including Dow, Du Pont, Con Agra, and Chevron, who brought a business perspective to the Earth Summit. The council presented its call for change in practical terms, focusing on what businesses had to gain from a new ecological awareness rather than on what the environment had to lose if industry continued in current patterns. In *Changing Course,* a report released just before the summit, the group's founder, Stephan Schmidheiny, stressed the importance of eco-efficiency for all companies that aimed to be competitive, sustainable, and successful over the long term. In 1996 Schmidheiny said, "I predict that within a decade it is going to be next to impossible for a business to be competitive without also being 'eco-efficient'—adding more value to a good or service while using fewer resources and releasing less pollution."

As Schmidheiny predicted, eco-efficiency has been working its way into industry with extraordinary success. The corporations committing themselves to it continue to increase in number, and include such big names as Monsanto, 3M, and Johnson & Johnson. Its famous three *R*s—reduce, reuse, recycle—are steadily gaining popularity in the home as well as the workplace. The trend stems in part from eco-efficiency's economic benefits, which can be considerable: 3M, for example, has saved more than $750 million through pollution-prevention projects, and other companies, too, claim to be realizing big savings. Naturally, reducing resource consumption, energy use, emissions, and wastes has implications for the environment as well. When one hears that Du Pont has cut its emissions of airborne cancer-causing chemicals by almost 75 percent since 1987, one can't help feeling more secure. This is another benefit of eco-efficiency: it diminishes guilt and fear. By subscribing to eco-efficiency, people and industries can be less "bad" and less fearful about the future. Or can they?

Eco-efficiency is an outwardly admirable and certainly well-intended concept, but, unfortunately, it is not a strategy for success over the long term, because it does not reach deep enough. It works within the same system that caused the problem in the first place, slowing it down with moral proscriptions and punitive demands. It presents little more than an illusion of change. Relying on eco-efficiency to save the environment will in fact achieve the opposite—it will let industry finish off everything quietly, persistently, and completely.

We are forwarding a reshaping of human industry—what we and the author Paul Hawken call the Next Industrial Revolution. Leaders of this movement include many people in diverse fields, among them commerce, politics, the humanities, science, engineering, and education. Especially notable are the businessman Ray Anderson; the philanthropist Teresa Heinz; the Chattanooga city councilman Dave Crockett; the physicist Amory Lovins; the environmental-studies professor David W. Orr; the environmentalists Sarah Severn, Dianne Dillon Ridgley, and Susan Lyons; the environmental product developer Heidi Holt; the ecological designer John Todd; and the writer Nancy Jack Todd. We are focused here on a new way of designing industrial production. As an architect and industrial designer and a chemist who have worked with both commercial and ecological systems, we see conflict between industry and the environment as a design problem—a very big design problem.

Any of the basic intentions behind the Industrial Revolution were good ones, which most of us would probably like to see carried out today: to bring more goods and services to larger numbers of people, to raise standards of living, and to give people more choice and opportunity, among others. But there were crucial omissions. Perpetuating the diversity and vitality of forests, rivers, oceans, air, soil, and animals was not part of the agenda.

If someone were to present the Industrial Revolution as a retroactive design assignment, it might sound like this: Design a system of production that

- Puts billions of pounds of toxic material into the air, water, and soil every year.
- Measures prosperity by activity, not legacy.
- Requires thousands of complex regulations to keep people and natural systems from being poisoned too quickly.
- Produces materials so dangerous that they will require constant vigilance from future generations.
- Results in gigantic amounts of waste.
- Puts valuable materials in holes all over the planet, where they can never be retrieved.
- Erodes the diversity of biological species and cultural practices.

Eco-efficiency instead

- Releases *fewer* pounds of toxic material into the air, water, and soil every year.
- Measures prosperity by *less* activity.
- *Meets or exceeds* the stipulations of thousands of complex regulations that aim to keep people and natural systems from being poisoned too quickly.
- Produces *fewer* dangerous materials that will require constant vigilance from future generations.
- Results in *smaller* amounts of waste.
- Puts *fewer* valuable materials in holes all over the planet, where they can never be retrieved.
- Standardizes and homogenizes biological species and cultural practices.

Plainly put, eco-efficiency aspires to make the old, destructive system less so. But its goals, however admirable, are fatally limited.

Reduction, reuse, and recycling slow down the rates of contamination and depletion but do not stop these processes. Much recycling, for instance, is what we call "downcycling," because it reduces the quality of a material over time. When plastic other than that found in such products as soda and water bottles is recycled, it is often mixed with different plastics to produce a hybrid of lower quality, which is then molded into something amorphous and cheap, such as park benches or speed bumps. The original high-quality material is not retrieved, and it eventually ends up in landfills or incinerators.

The well-intended, creative use of recycled materials for new products can be misguided. For example, people may feel that they are making an ecologically sound choice by buying and wearing clothing made of fibers from recycled plastic bottles. But the fibers from plastic bottles were not specifically designed to be next to human skin. Blindly adopting superficial "environmental" approaches without fully understanding their effects can be no better than doing nothing.

Recycling is more expensive for communities than it needs to be, partly because traditional recycling tries to force materials into more lifetimes than they were designed for—a complicated and messy conversion, and one that itself expends energy and resources. Very few objects of modern consumption were designed with recycling in mind. If the process is truly to save money and materials, products must be designed from the very beginning to be recycled or even "upcycled"—a term we use to describe the return to industrial systems of materials with improved, rather than degraded, quality.

The reduction of potentially harmful emissions and wastes is another goal of eco-efficiency. But current studies are beginning to raise concern that even tiny amounts of dangerous emissions can have disastrous effects on biological systems over time. This is a particular concern in the case of endocrine disrupters industrial chemicals in a variety of modern plastics and consumer goods which appear to mimic hormones and connect with receptors in human beings and other organisms. Theo Colborn, Dianne Dumanoski, and John Peterson Myers, the authors of *Our Stolen Future* (1996), a groundbreaking study on certain synthetic chemicals and the environment, assert that "astoundingly small quantities of these hormonally active compounds can wreak all manner of biological havoc, particularly in those exposed in the womb."

On another front, new research on particulates—microscopic particles released during incineration and combustion processes, such as those in power plants and automobiles—shows that they can lodge in and damage the lungs, especially in children and the elderly. A 1995 Harvard study found that as many as 100,000 people die annually as a result of these tiny particles. Although regulations for smaller particles are in place, implementation does not have to begin until 2005. Real change would be not regulating the release of particles but attempting to eliminate dangerous emissions altogether—by design.

Applying Nature's Cycles to Industry

"Produce more with less," "Minimize waste," "Reduce," and similar dictates advance the notion of a world of limits—one whose carrying capacity is strained by burgeoning populations and exploding production and consumption. Eco-efficiency tells us to restrict industry and curtail growth—to try to limit the creativity and productiveness of humankind. But the idea that the natural world is inevitably destroyed by human industry, or that excessive demand for goods and services causes environmental ills, is a simplification. Nature—highly industrious, astonishingly productive and creative, even "wasteful"—is not efficient but *effective.*

Consider the cherry tree. It makes thousands of blossoms just so that another tree might germinate, take root, and grow. Who would notice piles of cherry blossoms littering the ground in the spring and think, "How inefficient and wasteful"? The tree's abundance is useful and safe. After falling to the ground, the blossoms return to the soil and become nutrients for the surrounding environment. Every last particle contributes in some way to the health of a thriving ecosystem. "Waste equals food"—the first principle of the Next Industrial Revolution.

The cherry tree is just one example of nature's industry, which operates according to cycles of nutrients and metabolisms. This cyclical system is powered by the sun and constantly adapts to local circumstances. Waste that stays waste does not exist.

Human industry, on the other hand, is severely limited. It follows a one-way, linear, cradle-to-grave manufacturing line in which things are created and eventually discarded, usually in an incinerator or a landfill. Unlike the waste from nature's work, the waste from human industry is not "food" at all. In fact, it is often poison. Thus the two conflicting systems: a pile of cherry blossoms and a heap of toxic junk in a landfill.

But there is an alternative—one that will allow both business and nature to be fecund and productive. This alternative is what we call "eco-effectiveness." Our concept of eco-effectiveness leads to human industry that is regenerative rather than depletive. It involves the design of things that celebrate interdependence with other living systems. From an industrial-design perspective, it means products that work within cradle-to-cradle life cycles rather than cradle-to-grave ones.

Waste Equals Food

Ancient nomadic cultures tended to leave organic wastes behind, restoring nutrients to the soil and the surrounding environment. Modern, settled societies simply want to get rid of waste as quickly as possible. The potential nutrients in organic waste are lost when they are disposed of in landfills, where they cannot be used to rebuild soil; depositing synthetic materials and chemicals in natural systems strains the environment. The ability of complex, interdependent natural ecosystems to absorb such foreign material is limited if not nonexistent. Nature cannot do anything with the stuff *by design:* many manufactured products are intended not to break down under natural conditions. If people are to prosper within the natural world, all the products and materials manufactured by industry must after each useful life provide nourishment for something new. Since many of the things people make are not natural, they are not safe "food" for biological systems. Products composed of materials that do not biodegrade should be designed as technical nutrients that continually circulate within closed-loop industrial cycles—the technical metabolism.

In order for these two metabolisms to remain healthy, great care must be taken to avoid cross-contamination. Things that go into the biological metabolism should not contain mutagens, carcinogens, heavy metals, endocrine disrupters, persistent toxic substances, or bio-accumulative substances. Things that go into the technical metabolism should be kept well apart from the biological metabolism.

If the things people make are to be safely channeled into one or the other of these metabolisms, then products can be considered to contain two kinds of materials: *biological nutrients* and *technical nutrients.*

Biological nutrients will be designed to return to the organic cycle—to be literally consumed by microorganisms and other creatures in the soil. Most packaging (which makes up about 50 percent by volume of the solid-waste stream) should be composed of biological nutrients—materials that can be tossed onto the ground or the compost heap to biodegrade. There is no need for shampoo bottles, toothpaste tubes, yogurt cartons, juice containers, and other packaging to last decades (or even centuries) longer than what came inside them.

Technical nutrients will be designed to go back into the technical cycle. Right now anyone can dump an old television into a trash can. But the average television is made of hundreds of chemicals, some of which are toxic. Others are valuable nutrients for industry, which are wasted when the television ends up in a landfill. The reuse of technical nutrients in closed-loop industrial cycles is distinct from traditional recycling, because it allows materials to retain their quality: high-quality plastic computer cases would continually circulate as high-quality computer cases, instead of being down-cycled to make soundproof barriers or flowerpots.

Customers would buy the *service* of such products, and when they had finished with the products, or simply wanted to upgrade to a newer version, the manufacturer would take back the old ones, break them down, and use their complex materials in new products.

First Fruits: A Biological Nutrient

A few years ago we helped to conceive and create a compostable upholstery fabric—a biological nutrient. We were initially asked by Design Tex to create an aesthetically unique fabric that was also ecologically intelligent—although the client did not quite know at that point what this would mean. The challenge helped to clarify, both for us and for the company we were working with, the difference between superficial responses such as recycling and reduction and the more significant changes required by the Next Industrial Revolution.

For example, when the company first sought to meet our desire for an environmentally safe fabric, it presented what it thought was a wholesome option: cotton, which is natural, combined with PET (polyethylene terephthalate) fibers from recycled beverage bottles. Since the proposed hybrid could be described with two important eco-buzzwords, "natural" and "recycled," it appeared to be environmentally ideal. The materials were readily available, market-tested, durable, and cheap. But when the project team looked carefully at what the manifestations of such a hybrid might be in the long run, we discovered some disturbing facts. When a person sits in an office chair and shifts around, the fabric beneath him or her abrades; tiny particles of it are inhaled or swallowed by the user and other people nearby. PET was not designed to be inhaled. Furthermore, PET would prevent the proposed hybrid from going back into the soil safely, and the cotton would prevent it from re-entering an industrial cycle. The hybrid would still add junk to landfills, and it might also be dangerous.

The team decided to design a fabric so safe that one could literally eat it. The European textile mill chosen to produce the fabric was quite "clean" environmentally, and yet it had an interesting problem: although the mill's director had been diligent about reducing levels of dangerous emissions, government regulators had recently defined the trimmings of his fabric as hazardous waste. We sought a different end for our trimmings: mulch for the local garden club. When removed from the frame after the chair's useful life and tossed onto the ground to mingle with sun, water, and hungry microorganisms, both the fabric and its trimmings would decompose naturally.

The team decided on a mixture of safe, pesticide-free plant and animal fibers for the fabric (ramie and wool) and began working on perhaps the most difficult aspect: the finishes, dyes, and other processing chemicals. If the fabric was to go back into the soil safely, it had to be free of mutagens, carcinogens, heavy metals, endocrine disrupters, persistent toxic substances, and bio-accumulative substances. Sixty chemical companies were approached about joining the project, and all declined, uncomfortable with the idea of exposing their chemistry to the kind of scrutiny necessary. Finally one European company, Ciba-Geigy, agreed to join.

With that company's help the project team considered more than 8,000 chemicals used in the textile industry and eliminated 7,962. The fabric—in fact, an entire line of fabrics—was created using only 38 chemicals.

The director of the mill told a surprising story after the fabrics were in production. When regulators came by to test the effluent, they thought their instruments were broken. After testing the influent as well, they realized that the equipment was fine—the water coming out of the factory was as clean as the water going in. The manufacturing process itself was filtering the water. The new design not only bypassed the traditional three-R responses to environmental problems but also eliminated the need for regulation.

In our Next Industrial Revolution, regulations can be seen as signals of design failure. They burden industry by involving government in commerce and by interfering with the marketplace. Manufacturers in countries that are less hindered by regulations, and whose factories emit *more* toxic substances, have an economic advantage: they can produce and sell things for less. If a factory is not emitting dangerous substances and needs no regulation, and can thus compete directly with unregulated factories in other countries, that is good news environmentally, ethically, and economically.

A Technical Nutrient

Someone who has finished with a traditional carpet must pay to have it removed. The energy, effort, and materials that went into it are lost to the manufacturer; the carpet becomes little more than a heap of potentially hazardous petrochemicals that must be toted to a landfill. Meanwhile, raw materials must continually be extracted to make new carpets.

The typical carpet consists of nylon embedded in fiberglass and PVC. After its useful life a manufacturer can only downcycle it—shave off some of the nylon for further use and melt the leftovers. The world's largest commercial carpet company, Interface, is adopting our technical-nutrient concept with a carpet designed for complete recycling. When a customer wants to replace it, the manufacturer simply takes back the technical nutrient—depending on the product, either part or all of the carpet—and returns a carpet in the customer's desired color, style, and texture. The carpet company continues to own the material but leases it and maintains it, providing customers with the *service* of the carpet. Eventually the carpet will wear out like any other, and the manufacturer will reuse its materials at their original level of quality or a higher one.

The advantages of such a system, widely applied to many industrial products, are twofold: no useless and potentially dangerous waste is generated, as it might still be in eco-efficient systems, and billions of dollars' worth of valuable materials are saved and retained by the manufacturer.

Selling Intelligence, Not Poison

Currently, chemical companies warn farmers to be careful with pesticides, and yet the companies benefit when more pesticides are sold. In other words, the companies are unintentionally invested in wastefulness and even in the mishandling of their products, which can result in contamination of the soil, water, and air. Imagine what would happen if a chemical company sold intelligence instead of pesticides—that is, if farmers or agro-businesses paid pesticide manufacturers to protect their crops against loss from pests instead of buying dangerous regulated chemicals to use at their own discretion. It would in effect be buying crop insurance.

Farmers would be saying, "I'll pay you to deal with boll weevils, and you do it as intelligently as you can." At the same price per acre, everyone would still profit. The pesticide purveyor would be invested in *not* using pesticide, to avoid wasting materials. Furthermore, since the manufacturer would bear responsibility for the hazardous materials, it would have incentives to come up with less-dangerous ways to get rid of pests. Farmers are not interested in handling dangerous chemicals; they want to grow crops. Chemical companies do not want to contaminate soil, water, and air; they want to make money.

Consider the unintended design legacy of the average shoe. With each step of your shoe the sole releases tiny particles of potentially harmful substances that may contaminate and reduce the vitality of the soil. With the next rain these particles will wash into the plants and soil along the road, adding another burden to the environment.

Shoes could be redesigned so that the sole was a biological nutrient. When it broke down under a pounding foot and interacted with nature, it would nourish the biological metabolism instead of poisoning it. Other parts of the shoe might be designed as technical nutrients, to be returned to industrial cycles. Most shoes—in fact, most products of the current industrial system—are fairly primitive in their relationship to the natural world. With the scientific and technical tools currently available, this need not be the case.

Respect Diversity and Use the Sun

The leading goal of design in this century has been to achieve universally applicable solutions. In the field of architecture the International Style is a good example. As a result of the widespread adoption of the International Style, architecture has become uniform in many settings. That is, an office building can look and work the same anywhere. Materials such as steel, cement, and glass can be transported all over the world, eliminating dependence on a region's particular energy and material flows. With more energy forced into the heating and cooling system, the same building can operate similarly in vastly different settings.

The second principle of the Next Industrial Revolution is "Respect diversity." Designs will respect the regional, cultural, and material uniqueness of a place. Wastes and emissions will regenerate rather than deplete, and design will be flexible, to allow for changes in the needs of people and communities. For example, office buildings will be convertible into apartments, instead of ending up as rubble in a construction landfill when the market changes.

The third principle of the Next Industrial Revolution is "Use solar energy." Human systems now rely on fossil fuels and petrochemicals, and on incineration processes that often have destructive side effects. Today even the most advanced building or factory in the world is still a kind of steamship, polluting, contaminating, and depleting the surrounding environment, and relying on scarce amounts of natural light and fresh air. People are essentially working in the dark, and they are often breathing unhealthful air. Imagine, instead, a building as a kind of tree. It would purify air, accrue solar income, produce more energy than it consumes, create shade and habitat, enrich soil, and change with the seasons. Oberlin College is currently working on a building that is a good start: it is designed to make more energy than it needs to operate and to purify its own wastewater.

Equity, Economy, Ecology

The Next Industrial Revolution incorporates positive intentions across a wide spectrum of human concerns. People within the sustainability movement have found that three categories are helpful in articulating these concerns: equity, economy, and ecology.

Equity refers to social justice. Does a design depreciate or enrich people and communities? Shoe companies have been blamed for exposing workers in factories overseas to chemicals in amounts that exceed safe limits. Eco-efficiency would reduce those amounts to meet certain efficiency would reduce those amounts to meet certain standards; eco-effectiveness would not use a potentially dangerous chemical in the first place. What an advance for humankind it would be if no factory worker anywhere worked in dangerous or inhumane conditions.

Economy refers to market viability. Does a product reflect the needs of producers and consumers for affordable products? Safe, intelligent designs should be affordable by and accessible to a wide range of customers, and profitable to the company that makes them, because commerce is the engine of change.

Ecology, of course, refers to environmental intelligence. Is a material a biological nutrient or a technical nutrient? Does it meet nature's design criteria: Waste equals food, Respect diversity, and Use solar energy?

The Next Industrial Revolution can be framed as the following assignment: Design an industrial system for the next century that

- Introduces no hazardous materials into the air, water, or soil.
- Measures prosperity by how much natural capital we can accrue in productive ways.
- Measures productivity by how many people are gainfully and meaningfully employed.
- Measures progress by how many buildings have no smokestacks or dangerous effluents.
- Does not require regulations whose purpose is to stop us from killing ourselves too quickly.
- Produces nothing that will require future generations to maintain vigilance.
- Celebrates the abundance of biological and cultural diversity and solar income.

Albert Einstein wrote, "The world will not evolve past its current state of crisis by using the same thinking that created the situation." Many people believe that new industrial revolutions are already taking place, with the rise of cybertechnology, biotechnology, and nanotechnology. It is true that these are powerful tools for change. But they are only tools—hyperefficient engines for the steamship of the first Industrial Revolution. Similarly, eco-efficiency is a valuable and laudable tool, and a prelude to what should come next. But it, too, fails to move us beyond the first revolution. It is time for designs that are creative, abundant, prosperous, and intelligent from the start. The model for the Next Industrial Revolution may well have been right in front of us the whole time: a tree.

Source: Published in the *Atlantic Monthly,* October 1998. Reproduced with permission of the authors. See http://www.mcdonough.com.

Reading 9-2

Taking Sustainability Seriously: *An Argument for Managerial Responsibility*

Tara J. Radin

I. Sustainability and Stakeholders

Concern for the natural environment has become a pivotal issue for businesses today. Companies have found that legal approaches only go so far in helping managers deal with the complexity of the environment and they have come to rely more heavily on managerial discretion in dealing with it and the laws governing it. Managers, in turn, increasingly need to be able to interpret and apply laws appropriately. Moreover, they need to develop discretion because there is no formula—no single, universal rule—that will enable them to deal effectively with their problems. Managers must navigate uncharted territory by weighing competing interests to determine the best way to address complex business issues involving the natural world. All this means is that there is less need for regulation and more need for managers to have a clear understanding of ethics and a sense of responsibility for the influence of their businesses on the natural environment. It seems then that responsible organization decision making in response to concerns relating to the natural environment is critical.

During the last 20 years, a number of arguments have emerged in support of the responsibility of business for the natural environment. Throughout this period, appeals have been made to both moral and economic considerations. One of the chief concerns has involved the legitimacy and standing of the natural environment as a stakeholder and the ways the environment relates to business and its various constituents. While the status of the environment as a stakeholder has not been fully resolved, a view of the firm emphasizing the interconnected relationship is helpful in addressing some of the more pressing concerns surrounding the interaction between human beings and the biosphere.

Addressing environmental concerns from a stakeholder perspective demands addressing the so-called "separation thesis," or notion that business and ethics are distinct functions. The term derives from an article by R. Edward Freeman published a decade after his seminal book, *Stakeholder Management.* In the article he asserted that one of the problems in business thinking is the view that functional areas can be isolated (made separate) from one another. In business, for example, marketing is thought to be separate from finance, which is separate from operations, and so on. The result is a mindset that views these entities as discrete and decisions made in each domain as isolated from each another.

While, in many instances, an approach that compartmentalizes the functional areas of business seems to enhance the efficiency of the organization, it nevertheless misses the big picture. More troubling, it can leave out altogether certain functional areas that do not make obvious contributions to the bottom line. One of these is ethics. In terms of business and ethics, the separation thesis would have business and ethics as distinct and non-overlapping, with business concerned with the financial bottom line without consideration of ethics, and ethics concerned with the individual's adherence to moral norms devoid of the contingencies of business.

The separation thesis in regard to business and ethics is mistaken chiefly because the firm's bottom line is influenced by a multitude of interrelated decisions and effects, most of which are embedded with ethical concerns. The same holds true for issues involving the natural environment, where, again, the effects of decisions are multiple, interrelated, and embedded with ethical concerns.

This is particularly relevant as it pertains to the natural environment and concerns for sustainability. As businesses rely on the natural environment, deplete its resources, and interact with the biosphere, it becomes increasingly difficult to separate business concerns from concerns relating to the natural environment. Many of the effects might not be felt on the firm's short-term bottom line, but they nevertheless represent a very real challenge to the firm's long-term stability and success.

A. Three Fundamental Questions

If the separation thesis is false and business and the natural environment are as tightly conjoined as business and ethics, then at least three questions about how firms can and/or should address the environment in their business decision-making arise. Consider the following questions:

Question 1: Is it permissible for firms to contribute resources to environmental efforts?

This question addresses the permissibility of firms considering the environment in their strategic planning, in particular in regard to the environment's influence on short-term profitability. It also introduces topics such as the legitimacy of redirecting funds that would otherwise be channeled toward stockholders or other direct business purposes, as well as the permissibility of investing in research for alternative energy sources, engaging in costly waste reduction procedures, manufacturing lower margin environmentally friendly products, and so forth.

While a stockholder approach to this question might simply focus on the bottom line, a relational stakeholder approach devoid of the separation thesis would charge that firms are morally responsible for the environment as a legitimate stakeholder. It would claim, moreover, that a firm has reciprocal relationships with a wide range of stakeholders who care about the environment and that these concerns warrant the firm's attention to environmental issues.

Question 2: Is it consistent with existing laws for firms to contribute resources to environmental efforts?

This question asks whether or not it is legal for firms to contribute resources to environmental efforts. In doing so, it draws attention to laws related to corporate governance that allow for and require significant managerial discretion.

Since companies hire managers in lieu of robots to access the complex set of values and talents they possess, it is beneficial for the firm's bottom line for decision-makers to be empowered to respond to their inherent moral and strategic intuitions. Firms have found that attention to such concerns is not inconsistent with profit-generation. To the contrary, as numerous examples illustrate, firms increase their profitability and place themselves at a competitive advantage when they take such considerations into account. As George W. Merck stated in 1950: "We try never to forget that medicine is for the people. It is not for the profits. The profits follow, and if we have remembered that, they have never failed to appear. The better we have remembered that, the larger they have been." The same holds true for their concern for the natural environment: it makes good business sense to support laws that encourage managerial discretion and creativity in regard to environmental responsibility.

Question 3: Could it be considered mandatory for firms to contribute resources to environmental efforts?

This question explores the difference between permissibility and obligation. It asks whether or not firms are obliged to support or enhance the environment and whether or not firms need to support other stakeholders who are concerned about the environment. Again, firms are morally and legally responsible to stakeholders based, at least in part, on reliance considerations. Because society relies upon the natural environment and because some natural resources are finite, it is incumbent upon society to carefully steward natural resources. Since firms as an aggregate use substantial amounts of natural resources and because they often have the power, control, and finances to protect natural resources, they are obliged to use their wherewithal to protect natural resources for the benefit of the societies in which the firms are embedded.

B. Three Guiding Principles

The answers to questions such as those above indicate that environmental responsibility on the part of firms is desirable. These answers do not, however, specify how it should manifest itself or to what degree.

Principle 1: Firms are obliged to attend to the natural environment.

The first principle is straightforward: Firms are obligated to pay attention to the environment. How they do this is their choice. At a minimum, they must comply with existing rules, regulations, and industry requirements. The reasons for this mandate are twofold.

First, the pragmatic view: It is important for firms to attend to stakeholder concern to maintain satisfied stakeholders with whom they are engaged in relationships. Second, they have moral duties based on a principle of "do no harm." Since firms are aware of their potential for causing harm and because they typically have the resources to mitigate that harm, they are required to do so.

Principle 2: The nature of a firm's obligation is generally discretionary.

According to this principle, the nature and extent of a firm's obligations beyond compliance is largely discretionary. The manner in which a firm responds to environmental concerns is therefore voluntary. Environmentally responsible efforts on the part of firms tend to be categorized along a spectrum, as displayed in Reading 9.1, which is both normative and descriptive. At a minimum, firms are morally obliged to "do no harm" and remain in compliance with the law. While not specifically definite, this position encompasses the sort of exploitation that leads to tragedies such as Love Canal. It does not mean that firms are not permitted to partake in the earth's resources, but that they should do so moderately and consistent with existing laws.

In the indeterminate middle is the notion that some firms choose to be proactive in deciding to prevent harm while others are merely reactive. The proactive approach considers investments in research, waste management, development of environmentally responsible products, and so forth. A number of companies have engaged in this approach, adopting systemic product and/or process redesigns to make positive contributions to society and the environment. While some companies engage in such undertakings because they consider it their moral obligation, others do so for self-interested reasons, finding that doing so gives them a competitive advantage.

Principle 3: There are circumstances that create mandatory obligations for firm behavior toward the environment beyond mere compliance.

The third principle suggests that there are situations where a firm's obligation could be considered mandatory. Such situations are not the norm, but occur where a particular firm is specially suited for the role.

In general, it is unusual for positive obligations to be assigned—particularly to firms. Firms represent a voluntary contribution to the economy, that is, investors and owners are motivated to participate generally because of the opportunity to profit from certain enterprises. It is therefore generally considered inappropriate to impose correlative burdens that might detract from investment in such enterprises and thereby interfere with the economy.

At the same time, someone must be made responsible when there is harm or potential harm. Economists such as Ronald Coase and Guido Calebresi have argued in favor of efficiency. Coase has argued that firms exist only because of their inherent efficiency. It would seem, then, that coordinated and/or collective corporate initiatives will and should arise when they are recognized as more efficient than costly alternatives. Further, Calebresi has argued that an effective and efficient way of dealing with harm is to impose the burden on the individual or entity who or which is in best position to discover the problem and most cheaply avoid harm.

READING FIGURE 9.1
Shades of Green

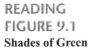

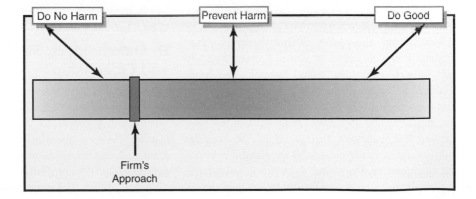

In fact, while it can be argued that we are all aware of the harm, corporations are in the best position to avoid the harm since they are the ones on the front line engaging in the most destructive behavior. It would thus seem logical and appropriate to impose on corporations a mandatory obligation beyond mere compliance when they are specifically in the best position to avoid the harm.

This leads to a set of criteria that can frame those situations in which there can be construed a mandatory obligation for environmental responsibility. First, there must be a specific need for change as manifest in actual or foreseeable harm. Second, there must be proximity through a direct or indirect link. The firm must be a participant in the problem or a direct beneficiary. Third is capability. The firm must have the ability to change products or processes without it becoming overly cumbersome to the firm. Fourth and finally, there exists some sort of comparative advantage. The firm must be particularly situated to address the harm. When these four criteria are met, it can be said that a firm has a specific obligation to engage in environmentally responsible behavior to address harm with regard to the natural environment.

C. Sustainability and Fiduciary Duties

Corporations are often resistant to the imposition of mandatory duties, particularly those that could be construed as conflicting with their other obligations—particularly their fiduciary duty to shareholders. For this reason, it is important to emphasize the connection between sustainability and fiduciary duty. Although it is possible to construe fiduciary duties narrowly in terms of profit-maximization, the reality is that there are many factors that can affect a firm's bottom line—in the long if not short term. Further, shareholders can be held accountable for corporate violations or neglect. On this basis, Professor Cynthia A. Williams and Professor John M. Conley have argued that managers are responsible to consider human rights. In the context of the natural environment, added to this is the recognition that shareholders can be held legally liable for negligence. Since the 1990s, there has been criminal enforcement of American environmental statutes.

The inescapable reality is that corporate responsibilities to the natural environment can no longer be viewed as anything but mandatory—the environment is a business concern. If for no other reasons, corporations have to be mindful of sustainability concerns in light of their reliance on the natural environment. As Bruce Ledewitz warns, "The state of the world is not good, or, since the world will be here long after we are gone, I should say the state of the world upon which people depend is not good. Long predicted and feared environmental problems are now cascading upon us. Not a day goes by, it seems, without news of catastrophic global warming or collapsed fisheries or depleted resources or diminished topsoil or lack of fresh water or diminished biological diversity—and on and on."

While the manner in which a corporation responds to these responsibilities remains voluntary, the presence of a duty must be viewed as mandatory. It can be argued that there is a moral duty to the environment. Beyond that, failure to address environmental concerns can result in financial distress for the firm, including bankruptcy. If it is the fiduciary responsibility of managers to protect the interests (and profits) of shareholders, the only way they can do that is to consider how it affects and is affected by the natural environment because stakeholders affect and are affected by the natural environment. Not only can the corporation's approach to sustainability influence short- and long-term profits, the corporation faces expensive tort litigation and shareholders face criminal sanctions if the corporation does not behave responsibly.

D. Stakeholders, Sustainability, and Citizenship

In addressing environmental responsibility, the term most commonly used today is *sustainability.* Sustainability refers to the integrated, systemic, lasting effect of attention to the natural environment and encompasses everything from the local neighborhood to the planet and the well-being of all living things. The emphasis lies on investments in the future rather than on one-time actions. Sustainability is a process; environmental responsibility is about beginning or participating in this process of addressing environmental concerns. Sustainability is inherently connected to stakeholder thinking (particularly the relationship view) in that both build upon existing relationships, interconnectedness, and synergies.

The key here lies in the notion of "systems thinking," which has recently taken hold in contemporary business scholarship. Systems thinking provides both the rationale for why corporations should be paying attention to sustainability and how they should go about doing so. Each corporation is itself embedded in a web of relationship and at the same time part of a "networked economy."

Stakeholder thinking and sustainability are also connected to the concept of "citizenship." Citizenship emphasizes the responsibilities of individuals in social (community-based) and political systems. An individual derives both rights and responsibilities from his or her affiliation with particular communities or social systems. The protection of the nonhuman, natural environment, as a resource shared by a social system or social systems, becomes a shared responsibility.

Individual citizenship has given way to corporate citizenship. Borrowing from common understandings of individual citizenship, the notion of corporate citizenship suggests that business organizations have rights and responsibilities comparable to those of individuals. This means that corporate citizens are expected to contribute to the communities in which they operate and to be considerate of their interaction with other community members. By implication, this means that, since community members share the environment, corporate citizens should be respectful of them in their use of natural resources and reliance on the environment—if not because of their own feelings toward the environment, then as a result of their community's interdependent and respect for the environment. Progressive interpretations of the law are increasingly reflecting consideration of stakeholder interests.

II. Stakeholders, the Environment, and Good Business Decision Making

The contribution of stakeholder thinking to developing an approach to environmental responsibility is to show how obligations can be assigned to firms. Specifically, firms have legal duties to some stakeholders in some specified circumstances. They have moral responsibilities to stakeholders in general. Whereas it is left to the discretion of firms to determine how they will handle these responsibilities, there is evidence that attention to stakeholders can contribute to profitability.

Specific examples illustrate how environmental responsibility can turn into a competitive advantage. Unpacking fundamental assumptions about business, humanity, and the environment reveals how shifting mental models can open up tremendous new opportunities for business.

A. The Bottom of the Pyramid

C. K. Prahalad argues that the often assumed target of business has been misplaced. He points out that most businesses focus on providing goods and services to the middle and upper class, whereas the poorest socioeconomic group holds the key to tremendous opportunity. In economic terms, the pyramid, as illustrated in Reading 9.2, refers to the distribution of wealth in society. According to Prahalad, the poor represents a virtually untapped resource:

> If we stop thinking of the poor as victims or as a burden and start recognizing them as resilient and creative entrepreneurs and value-conscious consumers, a whole new world of opportunity will open up. Four billion poor can be the engine of the next round of global trade and prosperity . . . . What is needed is a better approach to help the poor, an approach that involves partnering with them to innovate and achieve sustainable win-win scenarios where the poor are actively engaged and, at the same time, the companies providing products and services to them are profitable.

READING FIGURE 9.2
Economic Pyramid

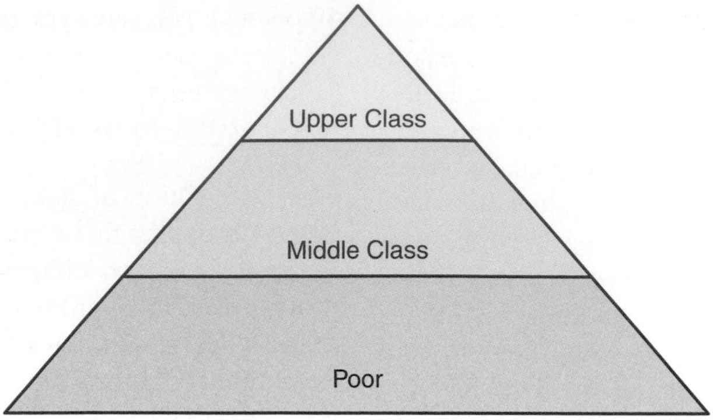

First, there are many more members of this class at the bottom of the pyramid than of the class of wealthy people at the top. Second, particularly from a global perspective, many of the poorest people have fundamental needs that can be addressed without huge capital investments. Third, elevating the standards of the socioeconomic disadvantaged can help to transform societal drains into societal contributions.

Muhammad Yunus has demonstrated the tremendous power of this proposition. In the 1970s, Yunus found the Grameen Bank, a microfinance organization that started in Bangladesh. The purpose of this enterprise is to elevate the status of the impoverished by making small loans without requiring collateral. The underlying premise is that the poor have skills that are underutilized because of their lack of capital.

By infusing capital into poor communities, the Grameen Bank has both elevated local conditions and profited significantly. The bank's assets are experiencing tremendous growth—in the three years between 2002 and 2005 the bank's assets nearly doubled from $391 million to $678 million. The bank boasts 5.58 million borrowers, 1,735 branches, and a 21.22 percent return on equity.

B. Cradle-to-Cradle

William McDonough offers an alternative perspective on how organizations can approach sustainability with an eye toward profits. He advocates what he calls a "cradle-to-cradle" approach. This translates into comprehensive redesign of products and/or processes. The result is far-reaching. In contrast with the traditional "cradle-to-grave" perspective whereby resources are used once and then discarded, the cradle-to-cradle approach advocates the use of perpetually recyclable or compostable materials. According to McDonough, "Pollution is a symbol of design failure."

Small and large companies alike have adopted McDonough's approach to sustainable business. One of his most famous projects in which he was involved was a site restoration of Ford Motor Co.'s historic River Rouge Complex in Michigan. Kodak's single-use camera is another example of cradle-to-cradle product design. Kodak controls the entire lifecycle of the cameras and, even through recovery, keeps most of the materials traveling in a continuous loop.

Cradle-to-cradle design reflects a reconceptualization of what an externality is. Traditional manufacturing has emphasized cost reduction by externalizing nonessential processes. Waste, for example, has traditionally been externalized as pollution. McDonough espouses the exact opposite: he argues that companies should take ownership of their processes and invest in ways to internalize processes so as to minimize waste. Whereas companies fear short-term costs, McDonough argues that long-term profits will follow in addition to positive contributions toward sustainability.

C. Restorative Commerce

An arguably even more dramatic approach lies in aiming for "restorative" commerce. According to Ray Anderson, founder and former CEO of Interface, Inc., a global leader in the design, production, and sale of carpeting, "[B]eing restorative means to put back more than we take, and to do good to the Earth, not just no harm." This is his long-term goal for Interface.

Interface has not always been so "green." Although Interface today is recognized as a leader in sustainable business, it was only about a decade ago that Anderson spearheaded an effort to harness technology and transform processes. The catalyst for this initiative was Paul Hawken's *The Ecology of Commerce*. Hawken's words stunned him into recognizing his company's destructive role toward the environment and he set about reducing his company's petroleum dependence. For Anderson, this sort of approach is not just the morally right thing to do; it is also good for business.

In 2005, Interface introduced a production process that enables the company to recycle old carpeting. Interface considers it a "dream come true. . . . We can now mine the landfill instead of siphoning off more oil. But it's also good business. Now, we're not just willing to take back old carpet, we're eager to take it because Cool Blue [the production equipment responsible for the recycling process] can turn it into profit."

This is Anderson's legacy for Interface: his company has turned a product into a service. Instead of selling carpet tiles, Interface now leases them; as they wear down, they are replaced and the old tiles are remanufactured, as part of an endless loop. Waste has been reduced and this has dramatically decreased the company's reliance on raw materials.

The experience at Interface has been tremendously positive. In the five years between 2000 and 2005, Interface tripled its use of recycled or biobased raw materials and grew its use of renewable energy from 6.4 percent to 21.7 percent. At the same time, it cut its waste (sent to a landfill) by 50 percent. Net sales are growing and the company is looking healthier and healthier.

The experience at Interface underscores the tremendous value—psychically, environmentally, and financially—of the greening of business.

D. Bottom Line

All of these examples reflect the value of sustainable business to the financial bottom line of organizations, communities, and the globe. The bottom line for us is that our businesses do not need laws in order to provide for sustainability; they need good business sense. While laws might have failed businesses, the inherent problem is not the law—it is the reliance of businesses upon laws and the expectation that legislation can and should determine what responsible decision making entails.

Moving forward, it is possible to continue to strive to improve the legal framework, but there will virtually always be an inevitable "lag effect." An alternative is thus to endeavor to influence the norms of acceptable and expected business behavior. Fiduciary duties, prescribed by law, are interpreted according to existing norms. In affecting these norms, then, the fiduciaries of corporations become responsible for living up to and abiding by current societal standards and expectations.

Environmental responsibility is about justice not charity. As a corporate citizen that can and does affect the lives of others, the firm has an obligation to act as a citizen by acting responsibly vis-à-vis the environment. Further, good business decision making (that can translate into profits) demands attention to stakeholder concerns about issues such as the environment.

It is important to keep in mind that, while corporations are legal fiction, the individuals who populate them are very real. While the corporation might not "care" about the environment, its stakeholders are dependent upon its survival. Sustainability is not just the way of the future; it is what will provide a future.

Reading **9-3**

Beyond Corporate Responsibility: *Social Innovation and Sustainable Development as Drivers of Business Growth*

Patrick Cescau, Group Chief Executive of Unilever

It is a long time since I graduated from INSEAD. I return older but, I hope, a little wiser. Of course when I was here in the early seventies, the subjects I will talk about today—corporate responsibility and sustainable development—barely existed. The green movement that was emerging at that time was the province of politics and protest not business.

The idea that companies had responsibilities to society beyond making a few charitable donations did not really start to take shape until a decade later. A lot has changed since then—and I'm not just talking about my appearance! This agenda is no longer about protest and philanthropy, although both still have their place. And businesses and NGOs are no longer automatic adversaries. In many areas, they are partners working together to achieve common goals.

Today social responsibility and environmental sustainability are core business competencies, not fringe activities. We have come a long way since the early eighties when the godfather of free market economics Milton Friedman proudly proclaimed that the only obligation which business had to society was "to make a profit and pay its taxes".

This change has come about for a variety of reasons. Certainly the political context has altered. The laissez faire economics which characterised the Reagan/Thatcher era have been superseded by a more realistic assessment of what the invisible hand of the market can achieve acting alone.

Today there is a growing recognition that the social and environmental challenges facing us in the 21st century are so complex and so multi-dimensional that they can only be solved if government, NGOs and industry work together effectively. It is difficult, for example, to imagine a problem like climate change being addressed without the active participation of Shell, BP and Toyota. Likewise it is hard to see an issue like poor nutrition being effectively tackled without the involvement of the world's major food companies.

Slowly but surely both governments and NGOs are accepting that business has a role to play in the development agenda and that we can be trusted. But perhaps the biggest catalyst for change has been the increasing awareness within business itself that many of the big social and environmental challenges of our age, once seen as obstacles to progress, have become opportunities for innovation and business development.

I believe that we have come to a point now where this agenda of sustainability and corporate responsibility is not only central to business strategy but will increasingly become a critical driver of business growth. I would go further: I believe that how well and how quickly businesses respond to this agenda will determine which companies succeed and which will fail in the next few decades.

I realise that is a bold assertion but it is based on three key premises that I will explore today: Firstly, economic development. Developing and emerging markets will be the main source of growth for many multinational companies in the years to come. Those that make a positive contribution to economic development and poverty reduction in these countries will be better placed to grow than those that do not. I will use the example of Unilever's businesses in Indonesia, Africa and India to illustrate my arguments.

Secondly, social innovation. I will look at how heightened consumer concerns about social justice, poverty and climate change are raising expectations that companies should do more to tackle such issues. The brands that see these challenges as opportunities for innovation, rather than risks to be mitigated will be the successful brands of the future. The examples I will use here are two of our global brands—Dove and Ben & Jerry's.

Thirdly, sustainability. As globalisation accelerates, and as the limits of the planet's resources are reached, large companies and brands will increasingly be held to account on the sustainability of their business practices. The companies that succeed will be those that reduce their environmental impacts and increase the sustainability of their supply chains now, rather than wait until either legislation or public outcry forces them to do so.

First some background about Unilever. Unilever is one of the world's leading consumer goods companies:

- We have operations in around 100 countries and sales in over 150.
- Our products are present in half the households on the planet.
- 160 million times a day, someone somewhere will buy a Unilever brand.
- Our €40 billion turnover is spread across 400 Foods and Home & Personal Care brands.

Corporate responsibility is deeply coded into Unilever's DNA. You can trace its origins to our British and Dutch founders—William Hesketh Lever, Anton Jurgens and Simon van den Bergh—all of whom had an innate sense of social responsibility towards their employees and consumers.

It is from them that we have inherited two enduring principles which have guided our approach to doing business. The first is that the health and prosperity of our business is directly linked to the health and prosperity of the communities we serve. Lever gave substance to this belief by building a garden village for his workforce at Port Sunlight and by his determination to tackle the appalling standards of hygiene and sanitation in late Victorian Britain. He did this by the simple mechanism of making available to millions of people good quality, low cost soap.

The second principle that has been handed down is the simple notion that a successful business is a responsible business. Or if you prefer "doing well and doing good". Central to this is the idea that we can create social benefits through our brands and through the impact which our business activities have on society and, very importantly, still make a good return for our shareholders.

Our commitment to address social and environmental issues has been strengthened over the years by our deep roots in developing and emerging countries. Over 40% of Unilever's business is now in these markets. That makes them bigger for us than Europe and sales there are growing much faster. By 2012 more of our business will come from Asia, Africa and Latin America than from the developed markets of Europe and the USA. Doing business responsibly has served Unilever well. If you look at our share price over the past 25 years and compare it with the S&P 500 you can see that "doing good" and "doing well" are not mutually exclusive.

The Role of Business in Economic Development and Poverty Reduction

Multinational companies can, and do, play a significant role in the development agenda. They stimulate economic growth through international trade and facilitate social progress through the development of human capital. But the positive role of business is rarely talked about in the media. If brands are mentioned at all, it tends to be the ones that have not behaved responsibly, rather than those who have. Part of the problem is that companies do not normally measure their social, economic and environmental footprint in the markets in which they operate and, as we all know, communication without facts is tough. So Unilever has been trying to find out what impacts its operations have in the developing world.

In 2003 we joined forces with Oxfam—an unlikely bedfellow—to research the question. Together we embarked on a project to analyse the impacts of our business in one of our largest markets. The country we chose was Indonesia—a country where I have seen the damaging effects of poverty at first hand.

The report we jointly produced highlighted a number of interesting things. Firstly, it demonstrated that most of the cash value Unilever creates in Indonesia stays in the local economy. This challenges head on the perception which some NGOs have that multinationals are mere extractors of wealth, who make large profits locally that are then immediately remitted to shareholders in London and New York, without benefiting the local economy.

Secondly, the report looked at the impact of our upstream supply chain. It found that some 84% of our raw and packaging materials were sourced from local suppliers thereby creating not just jobs but technology transfer from other Unilever factories around the world.

Finally, our report revealed the extent to which our operations in Indonesia have a major "multiplier effect" on job creation. While Unilever Indonesia itself employs only 5,000 employees, the business supports the full time equivalent of 300,000 jobs, more than half of them in the distribution and retail chain.

Impressive though these figures are, the exercise did also reveal the very limited impact which our operations had in helping the farmers and shopkeepers at the furthest ends of the value chain to lift themselves out of poverty.

Nevertheless, the evidence from Indonesia is that a global company like Unilever with embedded local operations—what we call a multi-local multinational—can have a very positive effect on developing economies.

Encouraged by the Indonesian exercise we have initiated a second study; this time in Africa. Working with Ethan Kapstein—Professor of Sustainable Development here at INSEAD—we are investigating the social, economic and environmental impacts of Unilever's operations in South Africa. Professor Kapstein's report, which will be published later this year, will take the work that we did in Indonesia to a higher level. He will not only measure our footprint in quantitative terms but he will also seek to capture and analyse our "soft' impacts. By soft I mean such intangibles as:

- training and skills transfer;
- support for government capacity building;
- black empowerment initiatives; and
- environmental standard setting.

In a very real sense Ethan is getting a measure of the contribution which Unilever is making to develop a healthy and prosperous South Africa.

Let me give you some examples of how Unilever's presence in the emerging economies of Asia and Africa is contributing to the development agenda. I shall do this under three headings:

- capacity building;
- new business models to generate economic activity at the base of the pyramid; and
- product innovation which addresses specific social needs.

Capacity Building

Capacity building is the jargon that economists use to describe the creation of the skills, physical infrastructure, public health and administrative frameworks that are so necessary for developing countries to prosper. Capacity can be built at both the macro level of the state and at the micro level of individual companies and communities. In Africa, Unilever engages at both levels.

A good example of an intervention at the macro level is the work that Unilever is doing to facilitate cross-border trade on the continent. We were one of the founder members of the Investment Climate Facility, a new public private partnership that aims to address some of the structural bottlenecks holding back investment in Africa. We have committed €1m to getting this going and are concentrating our efforts on working with African governments to rethink their approach to customs and border controls. This is something they have traditionally approached with a revenue mindset rather than a trade mindset.

If Africa is to develop as an economic region there need to be fewer restrictions on crossborder trade. These not only discourage foreign direct investment but also stifle intraregional trade—an important driver of economic growth. In ASEAN, for example, 60% of trade is between neighbours. In Africa it's more like 10–15%.

An example of capacity building at the micro or community level in Africa is Business Action against Chronic Hunger—an initiative we helped to launch last year. This is a programme orchestrated by the World Economic Forum and involving The Millennium Villages Project—a UN initiative pioneered by Professor Jeffrey Sachs. Our shared aim is to help communities lift themselves out of poverty through sustainable income generation.

The pilot programme is in Western Kenya. Agriculture is the primary livelihood there but the land available for farming is less than half a hectare per household—insufficient to produce enough food for the average family. As a result 60 to 70% of the population live below the poverty line.

Agronomists from Unilever's Kenyan tea plantations are helping farmers to convert their smallholdings from commodities like maize to higher value crops—specifically sunflowers and herbs and spices. The land was prepared in January and February. The seeds—which we provided—were planted in March. And in September, they will be harvested.

We have guaranteed to buy their crop at market prices. The sunflower oil will be used in Blue Band margarine and the herbs in Royco—a local brand of bouillon stock cubes. Our aim is for the farmers to make enough money in the first year to be able to feed themselves and to make a surplus for next year. In return for help with training and start-up costs, the farmers have agreed to put 10% of the value of any surplus they make in future years into community projects.

We are in the embryonic phase of this project but plan to scale it up from 30 farmers to 4,000—benefiting some 20,000 people. Again our objectives are clear. We want to work with others to make Kenya a healthy, prosperous society in which businesses like ours can flourish.

New Business Models

Capacity building of this kind is critical for long-term economic development. Of more immediate impact, however, is the ability of the private sector to create new business models. Some of these are designed to reach down towards what C. K. Prahalad has described as "the fortune at the bottom of the pyramid".

An excellent example of this is our Shakti initiative in India. At the end of the 1990's Hindustan Unilever realised that if they were to maintain their growth trajectory then they would need to find a way of selling their products to the rural poor. One in eight people on the planet lives in an Indian village. There are some 650,000 of them. All very isolated. Very few of them served by a retail distribution network.

The solution that we came up with to reach these consumers was to tap into existing networks of women's self-help groups which had grown up on the back of micro-credit schemes. From these groups we recruited and trained our Shakti entrepreneurs who became our local sales representatives. Their role was to go door to door selling our products.

Of course it was not our standard range. We had to re-engineer our products in such a way that they were affordable to people on desperately low incomes. More often than not this implied small pack formats—mainly sachets—which could be sold at prices as low as one or two rupees.

Shakti is at the intersection between social responsibility and business strategy. The social benefits of the scheme are obvious. It creates economic activity at the very bottom of the pyramid. It gives poor people access to products that address their basic needs for hygiene and nutrition. It gives dignity and a sense of empowerment to a large number of rural women.

At the same time the business benefits are huge. Today we have 30,000 Shakti entrepreneurs operating in 100,000 villages serving nearly 100 million consumers. The revenues generated are now close to $100 million per annum and the margins are very similar to those we achieve through our mainstream distribution channels. Make no mistake. Shakti is not a philanthropic activity. It is a serious and profitable business proposition.

Routes to market like Shakti enable Unilever to serve the needs of first time consumers. In turn this gives us the opportunity to address some of the nutrition and hygiene needs of some of the poorest people on the planet.

Products that meet the social needs in the D&E world.

Two examples to illustrate this—one from India and one from Africa. The Indian example is Lifebuoy soap. Every ten seconds a child dies from diarrhoea somewhere in the world. One third of these deaths are in India. Most are children under five. Yet according to the World Bank, something as mundane and simple as washing hands with soap can reduce diarrhoeal diseases by half.

Lifebuoy has been India's leading soap brand for decades. In the late 1990's it launched the largest rural health and hygiene education programme ever undertaken in India. It is called Swasthya Chetna—which means "Health Awakening" in Sanskrit. Piggy backing on the infrastructure created by Shakti, Lifebuoy health education teams visit thousands of schools and communities to teach children about the existence of germs and the importance of washing hands with soap.

Marketing activity of this kind is a classic "win-win". The education programme has a measurable impact on public health. The benefits for Lifebuoy come through in an expanding market for soap which allows strong sales growth—nearly 10% in 2006.

The second example, this time from Africa and from the foods side of our business, is the fortification of basic foodstuffs with micro-nutrients. One of the biggest nutritional challenges in Africa is the absence of certain nutrients in the diet. Iodine deficiency is a case in point. It affects millions of people and can cause mental retardation and brain damage.

In Ghana, for example, simply adding iodine to our Annapurna salt brand helped to nearly double iodine consumption to over half the population. Here our impact was amplified by partnering with UNICEF to create and implement a programme of social marketing. Again this was a win-win. UNICEF and the Ghanaian Ministry of Health achieved their public health goals of increasing iodine consumption. Unilever Ghana was able to open up a new market.

Let me conclude this section by summarising the role which business can play in economic development and poverty alleviation. Unilever's experience is that business can:

- help build human and institutional capacity through activities such as the customs project in West Africa and training subsistence farmers in Kenya;
- develop new business models such as Shakti which allow the creation of profitable economic activity at the very bottom of the pyramid;
- use its R&D and marketing skills to tackle public health problems in areas like nutrition (fortified salt in Ghana) and hygiene (hand wash education in India).

What does business get in return? If it is smart it gets:

- access to new markets;
- new opportunities for innovation and growth;
- new partners;
- and over the long term, it earns the trust and confidence of the community—something without which sustainable growth is impossible.

Social Innovation

By social innovation I mean finding new products and services that meet not only the functional needs of consumers for tasty food or clean clothes but also their wider aspirations as citizens. To some degree both Lifebuoy soap in India and Annapurna salt in Ghana are examples of social innovation.

But in the developed markets of Europe and the United States the opportunities are just as broad. Here we are observing new patterns of consumption. They are being driven by the emergence of what has become known as the "conscience consumer". These are consumers who are worried about social and environmental issues and realise they can influence change through the brands they choose to either buy or boycott.

For Unilever this trend fits neatly with our Vitality mission, which is about feeling good, looking good and getting more out of life. Our market research is telling us that consumers want the benefits of "vitality" products—but not at any price. A growing number, when making their purchasing decision, want to be reassured that the brands they buy will benefit society and the planet, not harm them. In other words, they want brands that not only make them feel good and look good but that also do good. This movement is gathering momentum. In fact we believe this trend has all the hallmarks of ushering in a new age of marketing and branding.

40 years ago brands were all about functional benefits—whether, for example, Persil washed whiter than Ariel. Then advertising agencies, influenced by the social sciences like psychology and anthropology started building in emotional benefits—wash with Lux, the soap the stars prefer, and some of Hollywood's glamour will rub off on you. Now there's a new dimension—brands with social benefits that appeal to consumers as citizens.

I should explain, for those of you who may not be aware, that Dove is a brand whose social mission is to change people's stereotypical views of female beauty. Research shows that 90% of women are not happy with the way they look. Much of the problem lies with the unrealistic way women are portrayed in advertising, fashion and the media. Through the Dove Self-Esteem Fund, Dove is helping women, and young women in particular, to see through the artifice that permeates the world of fashion and, in doing so, build their self-esteem and become more confident about the way they look.

Incidentally it was neither pressure from the NGO world nor legislation that drove the Dove team towards the Campaign for Real Beauty. It was consumer insight. Intelligent interpretation of market research highlighted that this issue resonated strongly with women of all ages around the world. The team realised that by championing the cause they would not only be doing something worthwhile but at the same time strengthening the loyalty of their consumers to the brand. Today we are reaping the benefits of this in rapid rates of growth for Dove all around the world.

Another Unilever brand with strong campaigning credentials is Ben & Jerry's. We acquired the business in 2000 but the values of their eponymous founders, Ben Cohen and Jerry Greenfield, remain the values of the company today. One of Ben & Jerry's key concerns is the environment and, in particular, the devastating effect global warming is having on the earth's polar ice-caps. As Ben Cohen and Jerry Greenfield like to say: "Listen to two old ice cream guys—if it's melted, it's ruined". Their Lick Global Warming campaign and the Climate Change College, which they set up in partnership with WWF, are outstanding examples of how you can make a complex subject accessible to people and relevant to their everyday lives. Last week Ben & Jerry's announced their intention to become a "climate neutral brand"—the first big European food brand to do so.

The examples of Ben & Jerry's with climate change and Dove with its Campaign for Real Beauty are good illustrations of brands picking up issues of concern to millions of people and starting to take meaningful action to raise awareness and change behaviour. Both brands have the credibility to make a difference at a societal level. Both brands, by championing these causes, will cement the loyalty of their consumers. Both are classic examples of brands that are "doing well by doing good".

Sustainability

For Unilever, sustainability covers not just environmental but also social and economic considerations. This is an area we have been addressing with systematic rigour since the early 1990's with programmes to improve the sustainability of our operations and our supply chain.

With over two-thirds of our raw materials coming from agriculture we have had an active programme of sustainable agriculture for more than a decade. Teams of agronomists have been beavering away to learn how to grow crops like tomatoes, tea, palm, peas and spinach without using too much water and with minimal use of pesticide and fertiliser.

But until recently this valuable work never aroused the interest of our brand teams. Now they are beginning to understand that this is an area where there is a convergence between our long-standing expertise in sustainability and consumers' concerns as citizens.

Let me give you an example. Many consumers are increasingly worried about the welfare of the people in developing countries who grow and harvest the food and drink they enjoy. This is behind the phenomenal growth of the fair trade movement. Until now this has largely been the preserve of niche operators. A couple of large companies like Starbucks and Nestle have dipped a toe in the water. Both have introduced Fairtrade versions of their coffees. But these represent just a small fraction of the total volumes they buy.

Coffee companies are not the only ones trying to capitalise on consumer concerns in this area. Countless brands are jumping on the eco-ethical bandwagon. This is an agenda where you are judged by your actions, not by your press releases. Consumers are quick to spot the difference between those brands that are authentic and those that aren't. Companies that try to promote themselves as being ethical in one aspect of their business but who tolerate bad practice in another will come unstuck.

At Unilever we believe this agenda offers huge potential for innovation and brand development. But we believe it will only work for us if it is fully integrated into our way of doing business. To help us do this, we have developed a diagnostic tool called Brand Imprint. It helps our brands take a 360° look at their impacts on society and the environment and gain deep insights into the external forces shaping this agenda.

A number of our global brands have started to use this tool and the first fruits of their work are starting to come through. In fact I can today announce that Unilever has decided to commit to purchasing all its tea from sustainable sources and has asked the Rainforest Alliance, the international NGO, to start auditing the estates from which we buy our tea, including our own in Kenya. Unilever is the world's largest tea company and Lipton is the world's favourite tea brand. We aim to have all Lipton Yellow Label and PG Tips tea bags sold in Western Europe certified as sustainable by 2010 and all Lipton tea bags sold globally certified by 2015.

It is the first time a major tea company has committed to introducing sustainably produced tea on such a large scale and the first time the Rainforest Alliance, better known for coffee certification, will audit tea farms. I have no doubt this decision will transform the global tea industry, which has been suffering for many years from over capacity and falling prices. The decision has the potential to improve the crops, incomes and livelihoods of nearly 1 million tea growers and pluckers in Africa. Eventually, up to 2 million people around the world could benefit—nearly all of them in developing countries, and many of them living on or below the poverty line.

Again this is a win-win. Our consumers will have the reassurance that the tea they enjoy is both sustainably grown and traded fairly. Subsistence farmers will get a better price. Tea pluckers will be better off. The environment will be better protected. And we expect to sell more tea.

This is the way forward for business and brands. At one level it is very simple. It's about:

- brands continuing to provide consumers the functional benefits they seek;
- while at the same time maximising the social benefits and minimising the environmental impacts.

In reality, finding the sweet spot between meeting the needs of society, the needs of the planet, and the needs of consumers as citizens is complex. But it will be a real differentiator for those who do it well and do it with integrity.

So, to summarise, there have been six key themes to my presentation.

- Business can play an effective role in development and poverty reduction, as demonstrated by our subsidiaries in South Africa, Indonesia and Kenya.

- New business models such as Shakti can reach the poorest of the poor and at the same time produce rapid rates of growth at good levels of profitability.
- Brands can be agents of positive social change. Look at Annapurna, Lifebuoy and Dove. Each in its separate way is tackling a social issue—malnutrition, diarrheal disease and women's self-esteem.
- "The conscience consumer" is here to stay. It is a movement that is gathering momentum and will change the face of business and brands. Companies that grasp the opportunity this agenda presents in a genuine and sustainable way will be the ones that succeed in the 21st century.
- Business has to become genuinely sustainable. This is a win-win opportunity. Our decision to buy tea from sustainable sources is good news for farmers, good news for consumers, good news for the environment and makes good business sense.
- Finally and most importantly there is no dichotomy between business doing good and doing well. In fact the two go hand in hand. All of the brands I have talked about are growing rapidly. All are profitable. If they weren't their social and environmental initiatives would not be sustainable. Both parties—business and society—need to benefit.

Conclusion

I started this presentation by saying that social responsibility and sustainable development are no longer fringe activities but are central to our business. And, just as this agenda has become core to business, so it should also become core to management education. It must be moved to the heart of the curriculum. Business schools generally need to give much more prominence to this subject than they have historically. Some are beginning to do so. But many are being slow to integrate this agenda.

Doing business in the 21st century is a much more subtle and complex process than some MBA courses would lead one to believe. Of course there is a place for the financial modelling, the DCF calculations and yield curves. But in the end the big decisions in business are about culture and consumers. It is clear that many business schools are waking up to this. A survey conducted in 2005 found that 54% of schools required one or more courses in corporate social responsibility, sustainability, or business and society, up from 34% four years earlier. This is progress, but not yet enough. The same survey, conducted for the Aspen Institute, found that while students in the top 30 schools covered social and environmental issues in roughly 25% of their coursework, the figure for students in the remaining schools was a disappointing 8%.

From a Unilever perspective, we are already giving increased attention to this in our recruitment policy—and we will continue to do so. Those who come to us with a deep understanding of the area will be at a significant advantage.

So let me finish by offering members of this forum the following advice: For those of you now studying for your MBA, I would say this: get to know this agenda. Understand how it can be a driver of business growth. Build it into your professional skill set. The business world will very soon be divided into those that recognised its potential early on and those who woke up to it too late. Make sure you are an early adopter. For those of you with MBAs who, like me, didn't cover this subject as part of your course, I am sure that you are already grappling with these issues in your various industry sectors. I hope this talk will have stimulated your thinking a little. As was once famously said: "a company that makes only money is a poor company".

Source: This reading is taken from a speech delivered at the 2007 INDEVOR Alumni Forum in INSEAD, Fontainebleau, France, May 25, 2007.

Chapter 10

Ethical Decision Making: Corporate Governance, Accounting, and Finance

Did you ever expect a corporation to have a conscience, when it has no soul to be damned and no body to be kicked?

Edward Thurlow (1731–1806), Lord Chancellor of England

Whenever an institution malfunctions as consistently as boards of directors have in nearly every major fiasco of the last forty or fifty years, it is futile to blame men. It is the institution that malfunctions.

Peter Drucker

Earnings can be as pliable as putty when a charlatan heads the company reporting them.

Warren Buffett

Opening Decision Point *Is Steve Jobs' Health Status a Private Matter?*

What responsibility does a publicly-traded company have to keep the public informed about the health of its key executives? When the executive is as important to a company's success as Steve Jobs, co-founder, CEO, and Chairman of the Board of Apple, this question raises important issues of corporate governance and corporate social responsibility.

While no single individual is ever fully responsible for the success or failure of a company as large as Apple, Jobs has played a central role in virtually every major decision concerning Apple for decades. Jobs has a particular reputation for being an executive who plays an enormously active role in all areas of corporate management. He has been described as both a visionary and a micro-manager; so his health—and related longevity and state of mind—is of interest to investors, employees, consumers, and other stakeholders.

Apple's business was suffering when Jobs returned to the company in the late 1990s after a hiatus. In 2000, the company was worth $5 billion; and, in late 2009, the company was valued at more than $170 billion. For comparison purposes, Apple's stock closed at $8.06 a share on November 1, 2000; nine years later, on November 1, 2009, it closed at $194 a share. In other words, if you bought $1,000 of Apple stock in 2000, it would be worth $24,069 in 2009. Under Jobs leadership and vision, Apple introduced the iMac, itunes, iPod family, the iPhone, the I-Pad, and entered the retail market by opening Apple stores. In fact, Apple Computer dropped "computer" from its corporate name in 2007 shortly after the introduction of the iPhone in recognition of the shift in its business focus.

In 2003, (we later learned) Jobs was diagnosed with a rare but mild form of cancer. Apple informed investors and the wider public about this illness *only* when it simultaneously announced that Jobs had been "cured" of the cancer after successful surgery in 2004.

Questions about Jobs' health arose again in the summer of 2008. In a report on a speech that Jobs had given, the *New York Times* described Jobs as looking "unusually thin and haggard." To quell rumors following this story, various company public relations reports claimed that he suffered from "a common bug" and "nutritional problems." Later statements hinted that he had surgery, but that his health was a "private matter." When Apple announced in late 2008 that Jobs would not deliver the keynote address at the annual Apple Macworld conference in 2009, rumors again spread about the state of his health.

In early January 2009, Apple released a statement from Jobs explaining that his recent weight loss was due to a "hormone imbalance" and a "nutritional problem," the remedy for which was "relatively simple and straightforward." However, he said, "I've already begun treatment. But, just like I didn't lose this much weight and body mass in a week or a month, my doctors expect it will take me until late this Spring to regain it." Jobs went on to say that "for the first time in a decade, I'm getting to spend the holiday season with my family, rather than intensely preparing for a Macworld keynote." Apple's stock price rose 4 percent after this announcement.

Within two weeks Jobs sent an email to Apple employees and explained that "my health-related issues are more complex than I originally thought." He

(*continued*)

(concluded)

announced that he would take a six-month medical leave of absence; but he would "remain involved in strategic decisions while I am out." In response to this announcement, Apple stock dropped 7 percent.

In April 2009, Jobs underwent a liver transplant.

Clearly, public perception of Jobs' health has had an impact on Apple's stock price and real questions can be raised about Apple's transparency, if not its honesty, in its public statements about Jobs' health. Defenders of the company argue that Apple had no legal duty to disclose health matters; the law only requires that information must be disclosed if it is a "material business concern," defined as information that a reasonable investor needs to know to make an informed decision on buying or selling stock.

Critics reply that if Jobs' health was sufficiently poor to move him so quickly to the top of a waiting list of patients needing liver transplants, it was information that investors had a right to know. In an interview, Warren E. Buffett agreed: "Certainly Steve Jobs is important to Apple, whether he is facing serious surgery or not is a material fact."

- What are the ethical issues involved in the factual circumstances discussed above?
- Who are the stakeholders involved?
- What were Apple's alternatives in consideration of these stakeholders?
- From what you have just read, was Apple forthright and honest in its public statements? What facts lead you to this conclusion? What other facts would you want to know?
- If Apple did not have a legal duty to disclose the facts of Jobs' health, would it be ethical to remain silent on the matter? Would it be ethical to issue misleading information?
- Why do you believe that is the disclosure of "material" information a legal duty?
- What responsibilities does the Apple Board of Directors have to the investing public? Do you think that they fulfilled their responsibilities in this case?
- Does Jobs have a responsibility (ongoing? immediate?) to Apple's investors, board of directors, employees and/or customers to inform them about his health?

Chapter Objectives

After reading this chapter, you will be able to:

1. Explain the role of accountants and other professionals as "gatekeepers."
2. Describe how conflicts of interest can arise for business professionals.
3. Outline the requirements of the Sarbanes-Oxley Act.
4. Describe the COSO framework.
5. Define the "control environment" and the means by which ethics and culture can impact that environment.

6. Discuss the legal obligations of a member of a board of directors.
7. Explain the ethical obligations of a member of a board of directors.
8. Highlight conflicts of interest in financial markets and discuss the ways in which they may be alleviated.
9. Describe conflicts of interest in governance created by excessive executive compensation.
10. Define insider trading and evaluate its potential for unethical behavior.

The first edition of this textbook was written in 2006, soon after a wave of major corporate scandals had shaken the financial world. Recall those companies involved in the ethical scandals during the early years of this century: Enron, WorldCom, Tyco, Adelphia, Cendant, Rite Aid, Sunbeam, Waste Management, Health-South, Global Crossing, Arthur Andersen, Ernst & Young, ImClone, KPMG, J.P. Morgan, Merrill Lynch, Morgan Stanley, Citigroup, Salomon Smith Barney, Marsh & McLennan, Credit Suisse First Boston, and even the New York Stock Exchange itself. At the center of these scandals were fundamental questions of corporate governance and responsibility. Significant cases of financial fraud, mismanagement, criminality, and deceit were not only tolerated, but in some cases were endorsed by those people in the highest levels of corporate governance who should have been standing guard against such unethical and illegal behavior.

Sadly, the very same issues are as much alive today as they were several years ago. Consider the rash of problems associated with the financial meltdown in 2007–2008 and the problems faced by such companies as AIG, Countrywide, Lehman Brothers, Merrill Lynch, Bear Stearns, and of the financier Bernard Madoff. Once again, we have witnessed financial and ethical malfeasance of historic proportions and the inability of internal and external governance structures to prevent it. (An insightful perspective on lessons learned, if any, from the Lehman Brothers collapse, is offered by Caux Round Table Global Executive Director Stephen Young in an essay, "Thoughts on Reform: On the First Anniversary of the Collapse of Lehman Brothers" included at the end of this chapter.)

At the heart of the biggest ethical and business failures of the past decade were aspects of financial and accountings misconduct, ranging from manipulating special purpose entities to defraud lenders, to cooking the books, to instituting questionable tax dodges, to allowing investment decisions to warp the objectivity of investment research and advice, to Ponzi schemes, to insider trading, to excessive pay for executives, to dicey investments in sub-prime mortgages and hedge funds, to risky credit default swaps. Ethics in the governance and financial arenas has been perhaps the most visible issue in business ethics during the first years of the new millennium. Accounting and investment firms that were once looked upon as the guardians of integrity in financial dealings have now been exposed corrupt violators of the fiduciary responsibilities entrusted to them by their stakeholders.

Many analysts contend that this corruption is evidence of a complete failure in **corporate governance** structures. As we reflect on the ethical corruption and financial failures of the past decade, some fundamental questions should be asked. What happened to the internal governance structures within these firms that should have prevented these disasters? In particular, why did the boards, auditors, accountants, lawyers, and other professionals fail to fulfill their professional, legal, and ethical duties? Could better governance and oversight have prevented these ethical disgraces? Going forward, can we rely on internal governance controls to provide effective oversight, or are more effective external controls and government regulation needed?

Professional Duties and Conflicts of Interest

The watershed event that brought the ethics of finance to prominence at the beginning of the twenty-first century was the collapse of **Enron Corporation** and its accounting firm Arthur Andersen. William Thomas' essay "The Rise and Fall of Enron" details the steps that led to the downfall of those companies, including using complex special purpose entities to access capital or hedge risk. The Enron case "has wreaked more havoc on the accounting industry than any other case in U.S. history,"[1] including the demise of Arthur Andersen. Of course, ethical responsibilities of accountants were not unheard of prior to Enron, but the events that led to Enron's demise brought into focus the necessity of the independence of auditors and the responsibilities of accountants like never before.

Accounting is one of several professions that serve very important functions within the economic system itself. Remember that even a staunch defender of free market economics such as Milton Friedman believes that markets can function effectively and efficiently only when certain rule-based conditions are met. It is universally recognized that markets must function within the law and they must be free from fraud and deception. Some argue that only government regulation can ensure that these rules will be followed. Others argue that enforcement of these rules is the responsibility of important internal controls that exist within market-based economic systems. Several important business professions, for example, attorneys, auditors, accountants, and financial analysts, function in just this way. Just as the game of baseball requires umpires to act with integrity and fairness, business and economic markets require these professionals to operate in a similar manner by enforcing the rules and attesting to the fundamental fairness of the system.

1 OBJECTIVE

These professions can be thought of as "**gatekeepers**" or "watchdogs" in that their role is to ensure that those who enter into the marketplace are playing by the rules and conforming to the very conditions that ensure the market functions as it is supposed to function. Recall from chapter 3 the importance of role identities in determining ethical duties of professionals. These roles provide a source for rules from which we can determine how professionals ought to act. In entering into a profession, we accept responsibilities based on our roles.

These professions can also be understood as intermediaries, acting between the various parties in the market, and they are bound to ethical duties in this role as well. All the participants in the market, especially investors, boards, management, and bankers, rely on these gatekeepers. Auditors verify a company's financial statements so that investors' decisions are free from fraud and deception. Analysts evaluate a company's financial prospects or creditworthiness, so that banks and investors can make informed decisions. Attorneys ensure that decisions and transactions conform to the law. Indeed, even boards of directors can be understood in this way. Boards function as intermediaries between a company's stockholders and its executives and should guarantee that executives act on behalf of the stockholders' interests. The Opening Decision Point to this chapter raises this question: Was the Apple Board acting in the best interests of its stockholders when it withheld, or opted not to release, information about Steve Jobs' health?

The most basic ethical issue facing professional gatekeepers and intermediaries in business contexts involves conflicts of interest. A **conflict of interest** exists where a person holds a position of trust that requires that she or he exercise judgment on behalf of others, but where her or his personal interests and/or obligations conflict with those of others. For instance, a friend knows that you are heading to a flea market and asks if you would keep your eyes open for any beautiful quilts you might see. She asks you to purchase one for her if you see a "great buy." You are going to the flea market for the purpose of buying your mother a birthday present. You happen to see a beautiful quilt at a fabulous price, the only one at the market. In fact, your mother would adore the quilt. You find yourself in a conflict of interest—your friend trusted you to search the flea market on her behalf. Your personal interests are now in conflict with the duty you agreed to accept on behalf of your friend.

2 OBJECTIVE

Conflicts of interest can also arise when a person's ethical obligations in her or his professional duties clash with personal interests. Thus, for example, in the most egregious case, a financial planner who accepts kickbacks from a brokerage firm to steer clients into certain investments fails in her or his professional responsibility by putting personal financial interests ahead of client interest. Such professionals are said to have **fiduciary duties**—a professional and ethical obligation—to their clients, duties that override their own personal interests. (See the Decision Point, "How to Solve the 'Agency Problem.'")

Unfortunately, and awkwardly, many of these professional intermediaries are paid by the businesses over which they keep watch, and perhaps are also employed by yet another business. For example, David Duncan was the principal accounting professional employed by Arthur Andersen and assigned to work at Enron. As the Arthur Andersen case so clearly demonstrated, this situation can create real conflicts between a professional's responsibility and his or her financial interests. Certified *public* accountants (CPAs) have a professional responsibility to the public. But they work for clients whose financial interests are not always served by full, accurate, and independent disclosure of financial information. Even more dangerously, they work daily with and are hired by a management team that itself might have interests that conflict with the interests of the firm represented by the board of directors. Thus, real and complex

Decision Point *How to Solve the "Agency Problem"*

According to many observers, there is a deep problem at the heart of modern capitalist economies. Modern economies rely on individuals, called "agents," who work for the best interests of others, the "principals." For the system to work, agents must be loyal representatives of their principal's interests, even in those situations when their own personal interest is at stake. For example, a member of a board of directors acts as an agent for the stockholders, executives act as agents for the boards, and attorneys and accountants act as agents for their clients. This agent-principal model assumes that individuals *can* put their own interests on hold and be sufficiently motivated to act on behalf of another. But, this would seem to run counter to a view of human nature that is assumed by much of modern economic theory: individuals are self-interested. Thus, the "agency problem." How can we trust self-interested individuals to act for the well-being of others in cases where their own self-interest must be sacrificed?

Many of the ethical failures described in this chapter can be seen as examples of the agency problem. These are precisely those situations where boards have failed to protect the interests of stockholders, executives have failed to serve their boards, accountants, lawyers, and financial analysts have failed to act on behalf of their clients.

Economics and management theorists have offered several solutions to the agency problem. Some argue that the best solution is to create incentives that connect the agent's self-interest with the self-interest of the principal. Linking executive compensation to performance by making bonuses contingent on stock price means that an executive gains only when stockholders gain. Another approach is to create structures and institutions that restrict an agent's actions. Strict legal constraints would be the most obvious version off this approach. Agents have specific legal duties of loyalty, confidentiality, and obedience and face criminal punishments if they fail to uphold those duties. Professional or corporate codes of conduct and other forms of self-regulation are also versions of this approach.

These two most common answers share a fundamental feature: the agency problem can be solved by connecting motivation to act on the principal's behalf back to the agent's own self-interest. In the first case, motivation is in the form of the "carrot" and the agent benefits by serving the principal; in the second case, motivation is in the form of the "stick," and the agent suffers if she fails to serve her principal.

A third answer to the agency problem denies that there truly is a problem by denying that self-interest dominates human motivation. This third approach points out that, in fact, humans regularly act from loyalty, trust, and altruism. Human relationships are built on trust and reliability; and these motivations are just as basic, just as common, as self-interest. Thus, this approach would encourage corporations to look to moral character and develop policies and practices that reinforce, shape, and condition people to want to do the right thing.

- Can you think of examples in your own experience where someone is required to work as an agent for another, or when you were involved as an agent? How is the agent motivated in this particular case?
- If you were asked to design a policy that would provide a solution to the agency problem in the company that you work, where would you begin?
- Review the section on virtue ethics in chapter 3 and explain how the agency problem would be viewed from that perspective.

FIGURE 10.1 Conflicts of Interest in Public CPA Activity

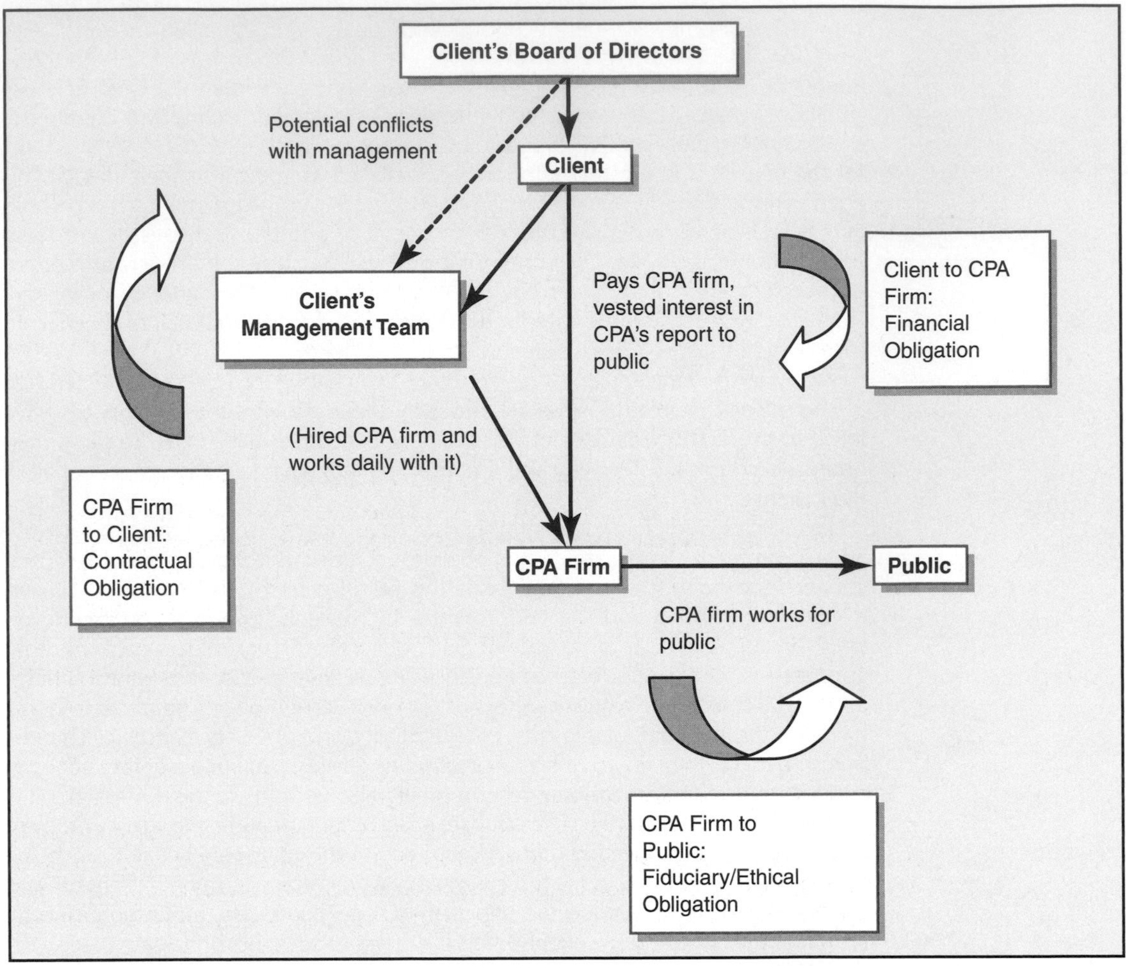

conflicts can exist between professional duties and a professional's self-interest. We will revisit conflicts in the accounting profession later in the chapter. (See Figure 10.1 for an overview of potential conflicts of interest for CPAs).

In one sense, the ethical issues regarding such professional responsibilities are clear. Because professional gatekeeper duties are necessary conditions for the fair and effective functioning of economic markets, they should trump other responsibilities to one's employer. David Duncan's professional responsibilities as an auditor should have overridden his role as an Andersen employee in large part because he was hired *as* an auditor. But knowing one's duties and fulfilling those duties are two separate issues. Consider the conflict of interest involved in the Decision Point, "When Does Financial Support Become a Kickback?"

Decision Point *When Does Financial Support Become a Kickback?*

Consider the case of what is referred to as "soft money" within the securities industry. According to critics, a common practice in the securities industry amounts to little more than institutionalized kickbacks. Soft money payments occur when financial advisors receive payments from a brokerage firm to pay for research and analyst recommendations that, in theory, should be used to benefit the clients of those advisors. Such payments can benefit clients *if* the advisor uses them to improve the advice offered to the client. Conflicts of interest can arise when the money is used instead or also for the personal benefit of the advisor.

In 1998, the Securities and Exchange Commission released a report that showed extensive abuse of soft money. Examples included payments used for office rent and equipment, personal travel and vacations, memberships at private clubs, and automobile expenses. If you learned that your financial advisor received such benefits from a brokerage, could you continue to trust the financial advisor's integrity or professional judgment?

- What facts do you need to know to better judge this situation?
- Who are the stakeholders involved and what values are at stake in this situation? Who is harmed when a financial advisor accepts payments from a brokerage? What are the consequences?
- For whom does a financial advisor work? To whom does she have a professional duty? What are the sources of these obligations?
- Does accepting these soft money payments violate any individual's rights? What would be the consequence if this practice were allowed and became commonplace?
- Can you think of any public policies that might prevent such situations? Is this a matter for legal solutions and punishments
- Compare this situation with the practice, as described in chapter 8, of pharmaceutical companies to supply physicians with small gifts and promotional items. In what ways are they similar? Dissimilar? Are physicians gatekeepers? The pharmaceutical industry voluntarily banned such gifts, should the broker age industry do the same?

Agency responsibilities generate many ethical implications. If we recognize that the gatekeeper function is necessary for the very functioning of economic markets, and if we also recognize that self-interest can make it difficult for individuals to fulfill their gatekeeper duties, then society has a responsibility to create institutions and structures that will minimize these conflicts. For example, as long as auditors are paid by the clients on whom they are supposed to report, there will always be an apparent conflict of interest between their duties as auditors and their personal financial interests. This conflict is a good reason to make structural changes in how public accounting operates. Perhaps boards rather than management ought to hire and work with auditors since the auditors are more likely reporting on the management activities rather than those of the board. Perhaps public accounting somehow ought to be paid by public fees. Perhaps legal protection or sanctions ought to be created to shield professionals from conflicts of interests. These changes would remove both the apparent and the actual conflicts of interest created by the multiple roles—and therefore multiple responsibilities—of these professionals. From the perspective of social ethics, certain structural changes would be an appropriate response to the accounting scandals of recent years.

Possibly the most devastating aspect of the banking industry meltdown of the first decade of this century was the resulting deterioration of trust that the public has in the market and in corporate America. Decision makers in large investment banks and other financial institutions ignored their fiduciary duties to shareholders, employees, and the public in favor of personal gain, a direct conflict of interest leading not only to extraordinary personal ruin but also to the demise of some of the largest investment banks in the world. The fact is that major federal legislation enacted after Enron to provide regulatory checks on such behavior failed to prevent it from happening.

Critics contend that government regulatory rules alone will not rid society of the problems that led to this tragedy. Instead, they argue, extraordinary executive compensation and conflicts within the accounting and financial industries have created an environment where the watchdogs have little ability to prevent harm. Executive compensation packages based on stock options create huge incentives to artificially inflate stock value. (Review the reading on executive compensation in chapter 3 to consider this issue in more detail.) Changes within the accounting industry stemming from the consolidation of major firms and avid "cross-selling" of services such as consulting and auditing within single firms have virtually institutionalized conflicts of interest.

Answers to these inherent challenges are not easy to identify. Imagine that an executive is paid based on how much she or he impacts the share price and will be ousted if that impact is not significantly positive. A large boost in share price—even for the short term—serves as an effective defense to hostile takeovers and boosts a firm's equity leverage for external expansion. In addition, with stock options as a major component of executive compensation structures, a higher share price is an extremely compelling quest to those in leadership roles. That same executive, however, has a fiduciary duty to do what is best for the stakeholders in the long term, an obligation that is often at odds with that executive's personal interests. Not the best environment for perfect decision making, or even for basically decent decision making. Consider the options available in the Decision Point, "But Is Regulation the Answer?"

The Sarbanes-Oxley Act of 2002

The string of corporate scandals since the beginning of the millennium has taken its toll on investor confidence. The more it is clear that deceit, chicanery, evasiveness, and cutting corners go on in the markets and in the corporate environment,

Decision Point *But Is Regulation the Answer?*

Consider your response to the following contentions.

The jury is still out on the costs to corporations of Sarbanes-Oxley compliance; but it is a safe guess that the price is already in the billions of dollars and millions of person-hours. It is arguable that no one doing Sarbanes-Oxley work adds value to any company. They design nothing, make nothing, and sell nothing. They make no improvements to management, marketing, or morale. They meet no demands, satisfy no necessities, and create no opportunities. They simply report.[2]

If Sarbanes-Oxley represents these challenges to business, do alternatives exist through which to address wrongdoing in corporate governance? Is Sarbanes-Oxley our best alternative? What other suggestions might you offer?

- What else might you need to know to determine how to prevent mismanagement of this type?
- What ethical issues are involved?
- Who are the stakeholders in financial mismanagement?
- Whose rights are protected by Sarbanes-Oxley's implementation? What are the consequences of Sarbanes-Oxley's implementation? Is it the fairest option? Is it regulating companies to act in the way a virtuous company would act?
- What alternatives have you compiled?
- How do the alternatives compare; how do the alternatives affect the stakeholders?

the less trustworthy those engaged in financial services become. Because reliance on corporate boards to police themselves did not seem to be working, Congress passed the Public Accounting Reform and Investor Protection Act of 2002, commonly known as the **Sarbanes-Oxley Act**, which is enforced by the Securities and Exchange Commission (SEC). The act applies to over 15,000 publicly held companies in the United States and some foreign issuers. In addition, a number of states have enacted legislation similar to Sarbanes-Oxley that apply to private firms, and some private for-profits and non-profits have begun to hold themselves to Sarbanes-Oxley standards even though they are not necessarily subject to its requirements.

3 OBJECTIVE

Sarbanes-Oxley strived to respond to the scandals by regulating safeguards against unethical behavior. Because one cannot necessarily predict each and every lapse of judgment, no regulatory "fix" is perfect. However, the act is intended to provide protection where oversight did not previously exist. Some might argue that protection against poor judgment is not possible in the business environment but Sarbanes-Oxley seeks instead to provide oversight in terms of direct lines of accountability and responsibility. The following provisions have the most significant impact on corporate governance and boards:

- ***Section 201:*** Services outside the scope of auditors (prohibits various forms of professional services that are determined to be consulting rather than auditing).

Reality Check *Global Consistencies: The European Union 8th Directive*

The **European Union 8th Directive,** effective in 2005 (though member states have two years to integrate it into law), covers many of the same issues as Sarbanes-Oxley but applies these requirements and restrictions to companies traded on European Union exchanges. The directive mandates external quality assurances through audit committee requirements and greater auditing transparency. The directive also provides for cooperation with the regulators in other countries, closing a gap that previously existed. However, contrary to Sarbanes-Oxley, the directive does not contain a whistleblower protection section, does not require similar reporting to shareholders, and has less detailed requirements compared to Sarbanes-Oxley's section 404.

- ***Section 301:*** Public company audit committees (requires independence), mandating majority of independents on any board (and all on audit committee) and total absence of current or prior business relationships.
- ***Section 307:*** Rules of professional responsibility for attorneys (requires lawyers to report concerns of wrongdoing if not addressed).
- ***Section 404:*** Management assessment of *internal controls* (requires that management file an internal control report with its annual report each year in order to delineate how management has established and maintained effective internal controls over financial reporting).
- ***Section 406:*** Codes of ethics for senior financial officers (required).
- ***Section 407:*** Disclosure of audit committee financial expert (requires that they actually have an expert).

Sarbanes-Oxley includes requirements for certification of the documents by officers. When a firm's executives and auditors are required to literally *sign off* on these statements, certifying their veracity, fairness, and completeness, they are more likely to personally ensure their truth.

One of the most significant criticisms of the act is that it imposes extraordinary financial costs on the firms; and the costs are apparently even higher than anticipated. A 2005 survey of firms with average revenues of $4 billion conducted by Financial Executives International reports that section 404 compliance averaged $4.36 million, which is 39 percent more than those firms thought it would cost in 2004. However, the survey also reported that more than half the firms believed that section 404 gives investors and other stakeholders more confidence in their financial reports—a valuable asset, one would imagine. The challenge is in the balance of costs and benefits. "Essentially section 404 is well intentioned, but the implementation effort is guilty of overkill," says one CEO.[3] In response, one year after its implementation, in May 2005, the Public Company Accounting Oversight Board (PCAOB) released a statement publicly acknowledging the high costs and issuing guidance for implementation "in a manner that captures the benefits of the process without unnecessary and unsustainable costs."[4] The PCAOB now advocates a more risk-based approach where the focus of internal audit assessments is better aligned with high-risk areas than those with less potential for a material impact. For a comparison of the application of Sarbanes-Oxley in the European Union, see the Reality Check, "Global Consistencies: The European Union 8th Directive."

The Internal Control Environment

4 OBJECTIVE

Sarbanes-Oxley and the European Union 8th Directive are external mechanisms that seek to ensure ethical corporate governance, but there are internal mechanisms as well. One way to ensure appropriate controls within the organization is to utilize a framework advocated by the **Committee of Sponsoring Organizations (COSO).** COSO is a voluntary collaboration designed to improve financial reporting through a combination of controls and governance standards called the Internal Control—Integrated Framework. It was established in 1985 by five of the major professional accounting and finance associations, originally to study fraudulent financial reporting and later to develop standards for publicly held companies. COSO describes "control" as encompassing "those elements of an organization that, taken together, support people in the achievement of the organization's objectives."[5] The elements that comprise the control structure will be familiar as they are also the essential elements of culture discussed in chapter 4. They include:

- ***Control environment***—the tone or culture of a firm: "the control environment sets the tone of an organization, influencing the control consciousness of its people."
- ***Risk assessment***—risks that may hinder the achievement of corporate objectives.
- ***Control activities***—policies and procedures that support the control environment.
- ***Information and communications***—directed at supporting the control environment through fair and truthful transmission of information.
- ***Ongoing monitoring***—to provide assessment capabilities and to uncover vulnerabilities.

5 OBJECTIVE

Control environment refers to cultural issues such as integrity, ethical values, competence, philosophy, operating style. Many of these terms should be reminiscent of issues addressed in chapter 4 during our discussion of corporate culture. COSO is one of the first efforts to address corporate culture in a quasi-regulatory framework in recognition of its significant impact on the satisfaction of organizational objectives. Control environment can also refer to more concrete elements (that can better be addressed in an audit) such as the division of authority, reporting structures, roles and responsibilities, the presence of a code of conduct, and a reporting structure.

The COSO standards for internal controls moved audit, compliance, and governance from a *numbers orientation* to concern for the *organizational environment*

TABLE 10.1 COSO Definition of Internal Control

Internal control is a process, effected by an entity's board of directors, management and other personnel, designed to provide reasonable assurance regarding the achievement of objectives in the following categories:

- Effectiveness and efficiency of operations.
- Reliability of financial reporting.
- Compliance with applicable laws and regulations.

Key Concepts

- Internal control is a *process*. It is a means to an end, not an end in itself.
- Internal control is affected by *people*. It's not merely policy manuals and forms, but people at every level of an organization.
- Internal control can be expected to provide only *reasonable assurance*, not absolute assurance, to an entity's management and board.
- Internal control is geared to the achievement of *objectives* in one or more separate but overlapping categories.

Source: Committee of Sponsoring Organizations, "Key Concepts," http://www.coso.org/key.htm.

of the Treadway Commission. Reproduced by permission from the AICPA acting as the authorized copyright administrator for COSO.

(see Table 10.1). The discussion of corporate culture in chapter 4 reminds us that both internal factors as the COSO controls and external factors such as the Sarbanes-Oxley requirements must be supported by a culture of accountability. In fact, these shifts impact not only executives and boards; internal audit and compliance professionals also are becoming more accountable for financial stewardship, resulting in greater transparency, greater accountability, and a greater emphasis on effort to prevent misconduct. In fact, all the controls one could implement have little value if there is no unified corporate culture to support it or mission to guide it. As philosopher Ron Duska noted in the Mitchell Forum on Ethical Leadership in Financial Services, "If you don't have focus and you don't know what you're about, as Aristotle says, you have no limits. You do what you have to do to make a profit."[6]

More recently, COSO developed a new system, Enterprise Risk Management—Integrated Framework, to serve as a framework for management to evaluate and improve their firms' prevention, detection, and management of risk. This system expands on the prior framework in that it intentionally includes "objective setting" as one of its interrelated components, recognizing that both the culture and the propensity toward risk are determined by the firm's overarching mission and objectives. Enterprise risk management, therefore, assists an organization or its governing body in resolving ethical dilemmas based on the firm's mission, its culture, and its appetite and tolerance for risk. (Shann Turnbull's essay, "Why 'Best' Corporate Governance Practices Are Unethical and Less Competitive" included at the end of this chapter, offers an innovative analysis of external versus internal mechanisms for ensuring proper board functioning in regulating ethical behavior.)

Going beyond the Law: Being an Ethical Board Member

As suggested previously, the corporate failures of recent years would seem to suggest a failure on the part of corporate boards, as well as a failure of government to impose high expectations of accountability on boards of directors. After all, it is the board's fiduciary duty to guard the best interests of the firm itself. However, in many cases, boards and executives operated well within the law. For instance, it is legal for boards to vote to permit an exception to a firm's conflicts of interest policy, as happened in the Enron case. The Apple Board did not have a legal duty to disclose the specifics of Steve Jobs' health. These actions may not necessarily be ethical or in the best interests of stakeholders; but they were legal nonetheless. The law offers some guidance on minimum standards for board member behavior, *but is the law enough?*

Legal Duties of Board Members

6 OBJECTIVE

The law imposes three clear duties on board members, the duties of care, good faith, and loyalty. The **duty of care** involves the exercise of reasonable care by a board member to ensure that the corporate executives with whom she or he works carry out their management responsibilities and comply with the law in the best interests of the corporation. Directors are permitted to rely on information and opinions only if they are prepared or presented by corporate officers, employees, a board committee, or other professionals the director believes to be reliable and competent in the matters presented. Board members are also directed to use their "business judgment as prudent caretakers": the director is expected to be disinterested and reasonably informed, and to rationally believe the decisions made are in the firm's best interest. The bottom line is that a director does not need to be an expert or actually run the company!

The **duty of good faith** is one of obedience, which requires board members to be faithful to the organization's mission. In other words, they are not permitted to act in a way that is inconsistent with the central goals of the organization. Their decisions must always be in line with organizational purposes and direction, strive towards corporate objectives, and avoid taking the organization in any other direction.

The **duty of loyalty** requires faithfulness; a board member must give undivided allegiance when making decisions affecting the organization. This means that conflicts of interest are always to be resolved in favor of the corporation. A board member may never use information obtained through her or his position as a board member for personal gain, but instead must act in the best interests of the organization.

Board member conflicts of interest present issues of significant challenges, however, precisely because of the alignment of their personal interests with those of the corporation. Don't board members usually have *some* financial interest in the future of the firm, even if it is only through their position and reputation as a board member? Consider whether a board member should own stock. If the board member does own stock, then her or his interests may be closely aligned with other stockholders, removing a possible conflict there. However, if the board member does not hold stock, perhaps he or she is best positioned to consider the long-term interests of the firm in lieu of a sometimes enormous windfall that could occur as the result of a board decision. In the end, a healthy board balance is usually sought. Consider the impact that the composition and training of a board might have on such board decisions as Apple's failure to disclose information about Steve Jobs' health.

The Federal Sentencing Guidelines (FSG), promulgated by the United States Sentencing Commission and (since a 2005 Supreme Court decision) discretionary in nature, do offer boards some specifics regarding ways to mitigate eventual fines and sentences in carrying out these duties by paying attention to ethics and compliance. In particular, the board must work with executives to analyze the incentives for ethical behavior. It must also be truly knowledgeable about the content and operation of the ethics program. "Knowledgeable" would involve a clear understanding of the process by which the program evolved, its objectives, its process and next steps, rather than simply the mere contents of a training session. The FSG also suggest that the board exercise "reasonable oversight" with respect to the implementation and effectiveness of the ethics/compliance program by ensuring that the program has adequate resources, appropriate level of authority, and direct access to the board. In order to ensure satisfaction of the FSG and the objectives of the ethics and compliance program, the FSG discuss periodic assessment of risk of criminal conduct and of the program's effectiveness. In order to assess their success, boards should evaluate their training and development materials, their governance structure and position descriptions, their individual evaluation processes, their methods for bringing individuals onto the board or removing them, and all board policies, procedures, and processes, including a code of conduct and conflicts policies.

Beyond the Law, There Is Ethics

7 OBJECTIVE

The law answers only a few questions with regard to boards of directors. Certainly Sarbanes-Oxley has strived to answer several more, but a number of issues remain open to board discretionary decision making. One question we would expect the law to answer, but that instead remains somewhat unclear, is whom the board represents. Who are its primary stakeholders? By law, the board of course has a fiduciary duty to the owners of the corporation—the stockholders. However, many scholars, jurists, and commentators are not comfortable with this limited approach to board responsibility and instead contend that the board is the guardian of the firm's social responsibility as well. (For one perspective on a board's additional, *ethical* responsibilities, see the Reality Check, "The Basics.")

Some executives may ask whether the board even has the legal right to question the ethics of its executives and others. If a board is aware of a practice that it deems to be unethical but that is completely within the realm of the law, on what

Reality Check *The Basics*

Bill George, former chairman and CEO of Medtronic and a recognized expert on governance, contends that there are 10 basic tenets that boards should follow to ensure appropriate and ethical governance:

1. *Standards:* There should be publicly available principles of governance for the board created by the independent directors.
2. *Independence:* Boards should ensure their independence by requiring that the majority of their members be independent.
3. *Selection:* Board members should be selected based not only on their experience or the role they hold in other firms but also for their value structures.
4. *Selection, number 2:* The board's governance and nominating committees should be staffed by independent directors to ensure the continuity of independence.
5. *Executive sessions:* The independent directors should meet regularly in executive sessions to preserve the authenticity and credibility of their communications.
6. *Committees:* The board must have separate audit and finance committees that are staffed by board members with extensive expertise in these arenas.
7. *Leadership:* If the CEO and the chair of the board are one and the same, it is critical that the board select an alternative lead director as a check and balance.
8. *Compensation committee outside expert:* The board should seek external guidance on executive compensation.
9. *Board culture:* The board should not only have the opportunity but be encouraged to develop a culture including relationships where challenges are welcomed and difference can be embraced.
10. *Responsibility:* Boards should recognize their responsibility to provide oversight and to control management through appropriate governance processes.[7]

basis can the board require the executive to cease the practice? The board can prohibit actions to protect the long-term sustainability of the firm. Notwithstanding the form of the unethical behavior, unethical acts can negatively impact stakeholders such as consumers or employees, who can, in turn, negatively impact the firm, which could eventually lead to a firm's demise. (And good governance can have the opposite effect—see the Reality Check, "Does Good Governance Mean Good Business?") It is in fact the board's fiduciary duty to protect the firm and, by prohibiting unethical acts, it is doing just that.

As author Malcolm Salter warned, perhaps one of the most important lessons form Enron was that "corporate executives can be convicted in a court of law for a pattern of deception that may or may not be illegal." The critical distinction Salter identifies in the Enron jury decision is that "at the end of the day, we are a principles-based society rather than a rules-based society, even though rules and referees are important."[8] Therefore, though our rules and processes offer guidance in terms of corporate decision making from a teleological, utilitarian perspective, if corporate executives breach common principles of decency and respect for human dignity, society will exact a punishment, nonetheless. Accordingly, a

Reality Check *Does Good Governance Mean Good Business?*

Researchers Roberto Newell and Gregory Wilson examined 188 companies from India, Korea, Malaysia, Mexico, Taiwan, and Turkey to determine whether good corporate governance practices resulted in a higher market valuation. They found that companies with better corporate governance had 10 percent to 12 percent higher price-to-book ratios than those with poor practices, indicating that investors do actually reward efforts in these arenas.

Source: Roberto Newell and Gregory Wilson, "A Premium for Good Governance," *The McKinsey Quarterly,* no. 3 (2002): 20–23.

board has an obligation to hold its executives to this higher standard of ethics rather than simply following the legal rules.

Fortune journalists Ram Charan and Julie Schlosser[9] suggest that board members have additional responsibilities beyond the law to explore and to investigate the organizations that they represent, and they suggest that an open conversation is the best method for understanding, not just what board members know, but also what they do not know. They suggest that board members often ignore even the most basic questions such as how the firm actually makes its money and whether customers and clients truly do pay for products and services. That is rather basic, but the truth is that the financial flow can explain a lot about what moves the firm. Board members should also be critical in their inquiries about corporate vulnerabilities—what could drag the firm down and what could competitors do to help it along that path? You do not know where to make the incision (or even just apply a Band-Aid) unless you know where the patient is hurting. Ensuring that information about vulnerabilities is constantly and consistently transmitted to the executives and the board creates effective prevention. Board members need to understand where the company is heading and whether it is realistic that it will get there. This is less likely if it is not living within its means or if it is paying out too much of its sustainable growth dollars to its chief executives in compensation.

Failing in any of these areas creates pressures on the firm and on the board to take up the slack, to manage problems that do not have to exist, to be forced to make decisions that might not have had to be made if only the information systems were working as they should. It is the board members' ultimate duty to provide oversight, which is impossible without knowing the answers to the above questions.

Conflicts of Interest in Accounting and the Financial Markets

8 OBJECTIVE

Conflicts of interest, while common in many situations among both directors and officers as discussed above, also extend beyond the board room and executive suite throughout the financial arena. In fact, trust is an integral issue for all involved in the finance industry. After all, what more can an auditor, an accountant, or an analyst offer than her or his integrity and trustworthiness? There is no real, tangible product to sell, nor is there the ability to "try before you buy." Therefore, treating clients fairly and building a reputation for fair dealing may be a finance professional's greatest assets. Conflicts—real or perceived—can erode trust, and often exist as a result of varying interests of stakeholders. As discussed earlier in this chapter, public accountants are accountable to their stakeholders—the stockholders and investment communities who rely on their reports—and therefore should always serve in the role of independent contractor to the firms whom they audit. In that regard, companies would love to be able to direct what that outside accountant says because people believe the "independent" nature of the audit. On the other hand, if accountants were merely rubber stamps for the word of the corporation, they would no longer be believed or considered "independent."

If you were to look in a standard business textbook, you might find the following definition of accounting: "the process by which any business keeps track of its financial activities by recording its debits and credits and balancing its accounts." Accounting offers us a system of rules and principles that govern the format and content of financial statements. Accounting, by its very nature, is a system of principles applied to present the financial position of a business and the results of its operations and cash flows. It is hoped that adherence to these principles will result in fair and accurate reporting of this information. Now, would you consider an accountant to be a watchdog or a bloodhound? Does an accountant stand guard or instead seek out problematic reporting? The answer to this question may depend on whether the accountant is employed internally by a firm or works as outside counsel.

Linking public accounting activities to those conducted by investment banks and securities analysts creates tremendous conflicts between one component's duty to audit and certify information with the other's responsibility to provide guidance on future prospects of an investment. Perhaps the leading example of the unethical effects of conflicts of interest is manifested in the shocking fact that 10 of the top investment firms in the country had to pay fines in 2005 for actions that involved conflicts of interest between research and investment banking. Companies that engaged in investment banking pressured their research analysts to give high ratings to companies whose stocks they were issuing, whether those ratings were deserved or not. William H. Donaldson, the chairman of the SEC, spelled out the problem on the occasion of a global settlement between those companies and the SEC, NASAA, NASD, and NYSE of approximately $1.5 billion for such breaches.

The ethical issues and potential for conflicts surrounding accounting practices go far beyond merely combining services. They may include underreporting income, falsifying documents, allowing or taking questionable deductions, illegally evading income taxes, and engaging in fraud. In order to prevent accountants from being put in these types of conflicts, the American Institute of CPAs publishes professional rules. In addition, accounting practices are governed by generally accepted accounting principles (GAAP) established by the Financial Accounting Standards Board that stipulate the methods by which accountants gather and report information. However, the International Accounting Standards

Committee, working with the U.S. SEC, is in the process of creating "convergence" between the International Financial Reporting Standards and the GAAP, with compliance required by 2009.[10] It is not an insignificant task; indeed, it poses daunting challenges. Beyond the prospect of the standards simply being translated appropriately and effectively, the standards themselves can be complex, modifying the standards becomes infinitely more complicated, small global firms may realize a greater burden than larger multinationals, and differences in knowledge bases between countries may pose strong barriers. Accountants are also governed by the American Institute of Certified Public Accountants' (AICPA) Code of Professional Conduct. The code relies on the judgment of accounting professionals in carrying out their duties rather than stipulating specific rules.

But can these standards keep pace with readily changing accounting and financing activities in newly emerging firms such as what occurred with the evolution of the dot.coms of a decade or more ago and as occurred in investment banks on recent years? In complex cases such as these, it can take regulators, legislature, and courts years to catch up with the changing practices in business. In any case, would regulatory standards be enough? The answers to ethical dilemmas are not always so easily found within the rules and regulations governing the industry. Scholar Kevin Bahr identifies a number of causes for conflicts in the financial markets that may or may not be resolved through simple rule-making:

1. *The financial relationship between public accounting firms and their audit clients:* Since audits are paid for by audited clients, there is an inherent conflict found simply in that financial arrangement.
2. *Conflicts between services offered by public accounting firms:* Since many public accounting firms offer consulting services to their clients, there are conflicts in the independence of the firm's opinions and incentives to generate additional consulting fees.
3. *The lack of independence and expertise of audit committees.*
4. *Self-regulation of the accounting profession:* Since the accounting industry has historically self-regulated, oversight has been lax, if any.
5. *Lack of shareholder activism:* Given the diversity of ownership in the market based on individual investors, collective efforts to manage and oversee the board are practically nonexistent.
6. *Short-term executive greed versus long-term shareholder wealth:* Executive compensation packages do not create appropriate incentive systems for ethical executive and board decision making. "Enron paid about $681 million in cash and stock to its 140 senior managers, including at least $67.4 million to former chairman and chief executive Kenneth Lay, in the year prior to December 2, 2001, when the company filed for bankruptcy. Not bad for a company that saw its stock decline from $80 in January of 2001 to less that $1 when filing for bankruptcy."[11]
7. *Executive compensation schemes:* Stock options and their accounting treatment remain an issue for the accounting profession and the investment community since, though meant to be an incentive to management and certainly a form

of compensation, they are not treated as an expense on the income statement. They also tend to place the incentives, again, on short-term growth rather than long-term sustainability.

8. *Compensation schemes for security analysts:* Investment banking analysts have an interest in sales; this is how they generate the commissions or fees that support their salaries. However, the sale is not always the best possible transaction for the client, generating potential conflicts.[11]

Similarly, scholar Eugene White contends that, in part based on the above challenges, markets are relatively ineffective and the only possible answer is additional regulation. Though Bahr argues that there may be means by which to resolve the conflicts, such as due notice and separation of research and auditing activities, White instead maintains that these conflicts cannot in fact be eliminated.[12] "Financial firms may hide relevant information and disclosure may reveal too much proprietary information." There remains no perfect solution; instead the investment community has no choice but to rely in part on the ethical decision making of the agent who acts within the market, constrained to some extent by regulation. Moreover, there is not simply just one solution. Karen Hunt Ahmad offers an Islamic perspective on the ethical responsibilities of bankers and financial professionals in her essay, "Islamic Banking and Finance: Moral Beliefs and Business Practices at Work" included at the end of this chapter. Consider how this particular approach might address conflicts differently.

Executive Compensation

Few areas of corporate governance and finance have received as much public scrutiny in recent years as executive compensation. A *Fortune* cover exclaimed: "Inside the Great CEO Pay Heist," and the article inside detailed how many top corporate executives now receive "gargantuan pay packages unlike any seen before." In the words of *Fortune*'s headline: "Executive compensation has become highway robbery—we all know that."[13] (A sophisticated ethical analysis of executive compensation is offered by Jeffrey Moriarty in the essay, "How Much Compensation Can CEOs Permissibly Accept?" reprinted at the end of this chapter.)

In 1960, the after-tax average pay for corporate chief executive officers (CEO) was 12 times the average pay earned by factory workers. By 1974, that factor had risen to 35 times the average, but by 2000, it had risen to a high of 525 times the average pay received by factory workers! (See Figure 10.2.) The most recent figure reports an estimated ratio of 411 times a worker's average pay for 2005. Importantly, these numbers address only the *average* pay; the differences would be more dramatic if we compared the top salary for CEOs and minimum-wage workers. In two of the more well-publicized cases in recent years, Sandy Weill, the CEO of Travelers Insurance, received over $230 million in compensation for 1997 and Michael Eisner of Walt Disney received $589 million in 1998. These numbers continue to rise. In 2005, total direct compensation for CEOs rose

FIGURE 10.2 **Average CEO to Average Worker Pay Ratio, 1990–2005**[14]

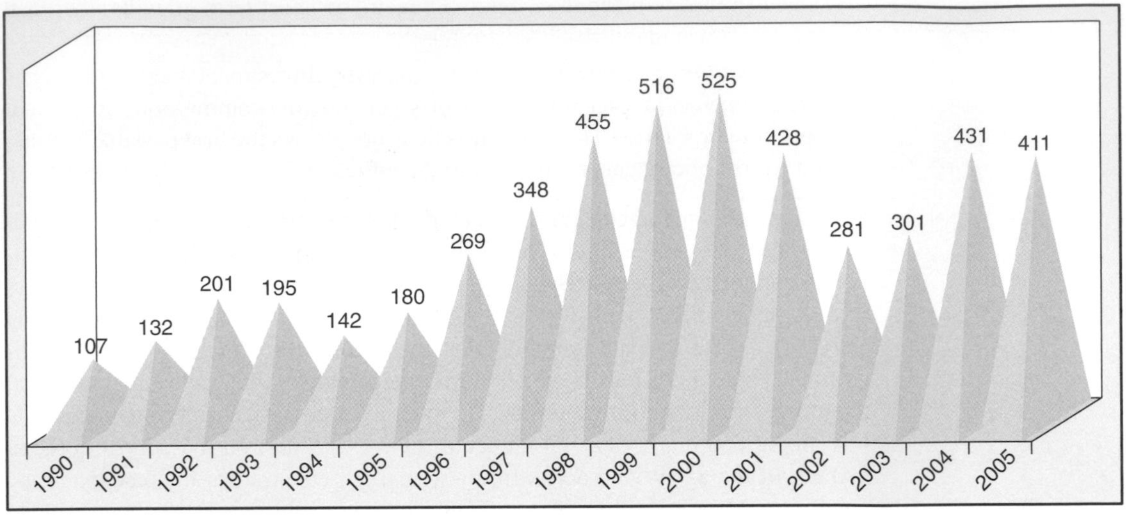

Source: Copyright © United for a Fair Economy, www.faireconomy.org. Reprinted by permission.

by 16 percent to reach a median figure of $6.05 million, not including pensions, deferred compensation, and other perks.[15]

Forbes reported that the CEOs of 800 major corporations received an average 23 percent pay raise in 1997 while the average U.S. worker received around 3 percent. The median total compensation for these 800 CEOs was reported as $2.3 million. Half of this amount was in salary and bonuses, and 10 percent came from such things as life insurance premiums, pension plans and individual retirement accounts, country club memberships, and automobile allowances. Slightly less than half came from stock options.

It is relevant to note in Figure 10.3 that CEO pay and the S&P 500 Index seem to follow similar trajectories. One might expect something along these lines since "pay for performance" is often based on stock price as one element of measurable performance. However, notice that actual corporate profits, not to mention worker pay, have not increased at the same rate as CEO pay. So, though CEOs have seen an increase, the corporations themselves—and the workers who contribute to their successes—have not reaped equivalent benefits. This lack of balance in the distribution of value has led to the perception of unfairness with regard to executive compensation, as we will discuss below.

More recently, compensation packages paid to the top executives of Exxon-Mobil drew harsh public criticism amid rising gas prices and soaring profits. Exxon-Mobil CEO Lee Raymond received total compensation of $28 million, including $18 million in stock in 2003 and $38 million, of which $28 million was in Exxon-Mobile stock, in 2004. In 2005, the year in which he retired, Raymond received $51 million in salary. The interest alone on this three-year salary would,

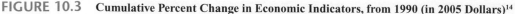

FIGURE 10.3 **Cumulative Percent Change in Economic Indicators, from 1990 (in 2005 Dollars)**[14]

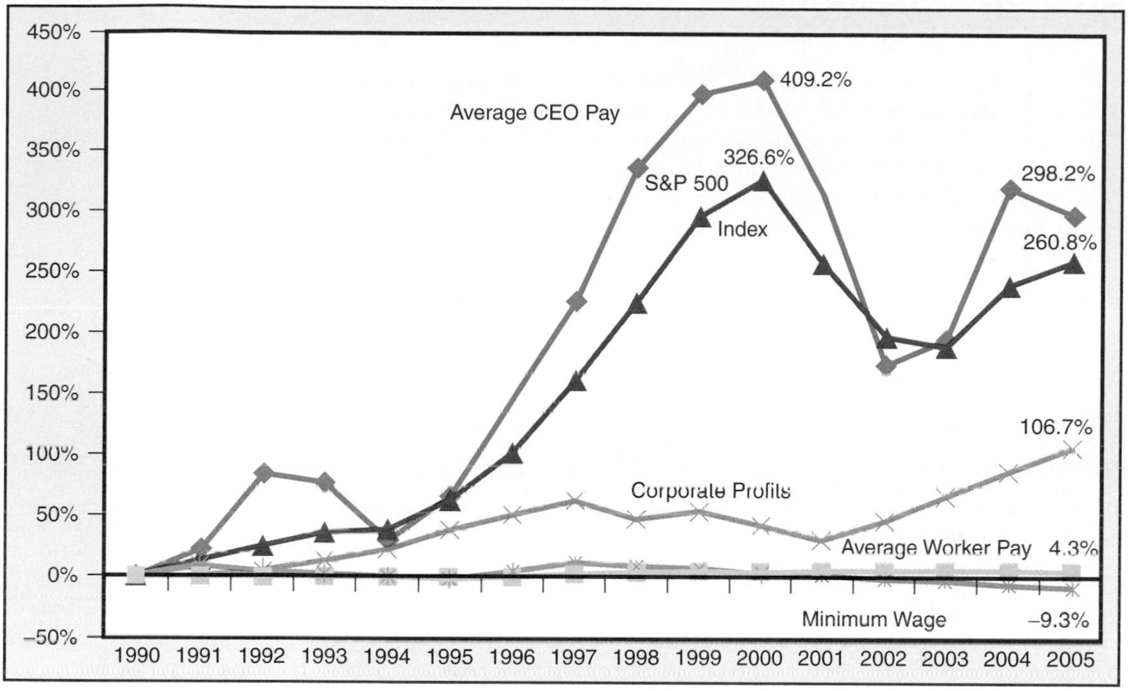

Source: Copyright © United for a Fair Economy, www.faireconomy.org. Reprinted by permission.

at a modest 5 percent rate of return, forever produce $5.85 million annually. Apparently this was not sufficient for Raymond's needs because he also received an additional retirement package with a combined worth of $400 million. When he succeeded Raymond, new CEO Rex Tillerson's salary increased 33 percent to a total of $13 million including $8.75 million in stock. The combined compensation just for these two executives in 2004 and 2005 was in excess of $500 million. During the same period, Exxon-Mobil also achieved record profits, earning more than $25 billion in 2004 and $36 billion in 2005. A few years later, the bonuses of AIG executives came under scrutiny, as you will see in the Reality Check Revisited, "AIG's Bonuses."

These gaps continue to increase. For the decade ending in 2000, the U.S. minimum wage increased 36 percent, from $3.80 per hour to $5.15 per hour. The median household income in the United States increased 43 percent, from $29,943 to $42,680. The average annual salary for a tenured New York City teacher increased 20 percent, from $41,000 to $49,030. During this same decade the total compensation for the Citicorp CEO increased 12,444 percent from $1.2 million to $150 million dollars annually. General Electric CEO Jack Welch's salary increased 2,496 percent, from $4.8 million to $125 million.

Reality Check Revisited *AIG's Bonuses*

One strategy to avoid the agency problem and motivate executives to act for the best interests of their company is to connect compensation with performance. In 1998, *Forbes* magazine reported that there was little correlation between CEO pay and performance. Comparing CEO compensation to stock performance over a five-year period, *Forbes* described 15 CEOs who earned over $15 million while their company's stock lagged well behind the market average of 23 percent. One CEO, Robert Elkins of Integrated Health Systems, received over $43 million during this five-year period while his company's stock valued *declined* by 36 percent. Another report, based on data for 1996, showed that the top executives of firms that laid off more than 3,000 workers in the previous year received an average 67 percent increase in their total compensation package for the year. In 1996, the average gap between CEO pay and the wages for the lowest-paid worker for the top 12 job-cutting companies was 178 to 1. Finally, Pfizer's stock price decreased by more than 40 percent since 2001 when McKinnell became CEO though he has received $79 million in pay during that same period and has a guaranteed pension of $83 million when he retires.

But few cases of executive compensation have caused as much cynicism about the connection between pay and performance than the AIG case introduced in chapter 3. After accepting $180 billion in U.S. federal government bailout money to avoid bankruptcy AIG announced that it was paying $165 million in bonuses to 400 top executives in its financial division, the very unit that was at the heart of the company's collapse. These bonuses came less than a year after former AIG CEO Martin Sullivan resigned as AIG's financial troubles intensified. As his company was headed towards bankruptcy, Sullivan received a $47 million severance package when he retired.

Skyrocketing executive compensation packages raise numerous ethical questions. Greed and avarice are the most apt descriptive terms for the moral character of such people from a virtue ethics perspective. Fundamental questions of distributive justice and fairness arise when these salaries are compared to the pay of average workers or to the billions of human beings who live in abject poverty on a global level. Consider Tyco's Dennis Kozlowski's justification of his salary in the Reality Check, "How Do Salaries Motivate?"

9 OBJECTIVE

But serious ethical challenges are raised against these practices even from within the business perspective. The reading, "How Much Compensation Can CEOs Permissibly Accept?" by Jeffery Moriarty at the end of this chapter details the shortcomings of attempted justifications for such excessive pay packages. Both *Fortune* and *Forbes* magazines have been vocal critics of excessive compensation while remaining staunch defenders of corporate interests and the free market. Beyond issues of personal morality and economic fairness, however, excessive executive compensation practices also speak to significant ethical issues of corporate governance and finance.

In theory, lofty compensation packages are thought to serve corporate interests in two ways. They provide an incentive for executive performance (a consequentialist justification), and they serve as rewards for accomplishments (a deontological justification). In terms of ethical theory, they have a utilitarian function when

Reality Check *How Do Salaries Motivate?*

What motivates executives to seek huge compensation packages? Consider this exchange between a *New York Times* reporter and Dennis Kozlowski, former CEO of Tyco International.

> *Reporter:* It's often said that at a certain level it no longer matters how much any of you make, that you would be doing just as good a job for $100 million less, or $20 million less.
>
> *Kozlowski:* Yeah, all my meals are paid for, as long as I am around. So, I'm not working for that any longer. But it does make a difference in the charities I ultimately leave monies behind to, and it's a way of keeping score.[16]

they act as incentives for executives to produce greater overall results, and they are a matter of ethical principle when they compensate individuals on the basis of what they have earned and deserve.

In practice, reasonable doubts exist about both of these rationales. First, as suggested by Moriarty's essay, and the *Forbes* story mentioned previously, there is much less correlation between pay and performance than one would expect. At least in terms of stock performance, executives seem to reap large rewards regardless of business success. Of course, it might be argued that in difficult financial times, an executive faces greater challenges and therefore perhaps deserves his salary more than in good times. But the corollary of this is that in good financial times, as when Exxon-Mobil earns a $30 billion profit, the executives have less to do with the success.

More to the point of governance, there are several reasons why excessive compensation may evidence a failure of corporate boards to fulfill their fiduciary duties. First, as mentioned before, is the fact that in many cases there is no correlation between executive compensation and performance. Second, there is also little evidence that the types of compensation packages described above are actually needed as incentives for performance. The fiduciary duty of boards ought to involve approving high enough salaries to provide adequate incentive, but not more than what is needed. Surely there is a diminishing rate of return on incentives beyond a certain level. Does a $40 million annual salary provide twice the incentive of $20 million, 4 times the incentive of $10 million, and 40 times the return of a $1 million salary?

Another crucial governance issue is the disincentives that compensation packages, and in particular the heavy reliance on stock options, provide. When executive compensation is tied to stock price, executives have a strong incentive to focus on short-term stock value rather than long-term corporate interests. One of the fastest ways to increase stock price is through layoffs of employees. This may not always be in the best interests of the firms, and there is something perverse about basing the salary of an executive on how successful they can be in putting people out of work.

FIGURE 10.4 Duties of the Board and Senior Executives that May Give Rise to Conflicts of Interest

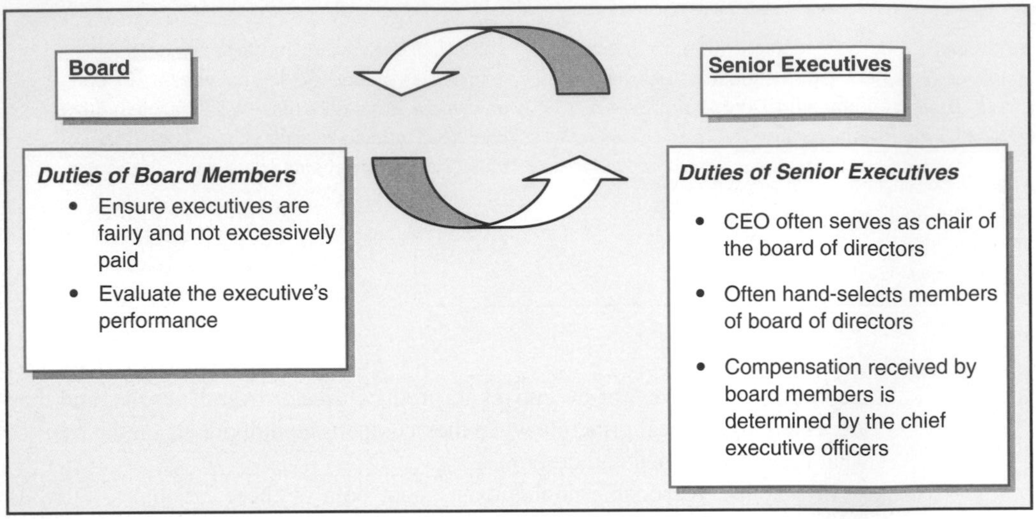

Further, a good case can be made that stock options have also been partially to blame for the corruption involving managed earnings. Two academic studies concluded that there is a strong link between high levels of executive compensation and the likelihood of misstating or falsely reporting financial results.[17] When huge amounts of compensation depend on quarterly earning reports, there is a strong incentive to manipulate those reports in order to achieve the money.

Excessive executive compensation can also involve a variety of conflicts of interests and cronyism. The board's duties should include ensuring that executives are fairly and not excessively paid. They also have a responsibility to evaluate the executive's performance. However, all too often, the executive being evaluated and paid also serves as chair of the board of directors. The board is often comprised of members hand-selected by the senior executives. In addition, the compensation board members receive is determined by the chief executive officer, creating yet another conflict of interest. (See Figure 10.4.)

The cronyism does not end at the boardroom door. One of the larger concerns to have arisen in recent years has been the cross-fertilization of boards. The concern spawned a Web site called www.theyrule.net, which allows searching for links between any two given companies. A search for a connection, for instance, between Coca-Cola and PepsiCo uncovers within seconds the fact that PepsiCo board member Robert Allen sits on the Bristol-Myers Squibb board alongside Coca-Cola board member James D. Robinson III. Though sitting on a board together does not necessarily mean Pepsi's board member will gain access to Coke's secret recipe, it does lend itself to the appearance of impropriety and give rise to a question of conflicts.

In another case involving lesser-known companies, three individuals served on the boards of three companies, with each serving as CEO and chairman of one of the companies, Brocade, Verisign, and Juniper. Unfortunately, the companies were found to have backdated stock options, and each firm found itself subject to either Securities and Exchange Commission inquiries or criminal or civil legal proceedings. Cronyism or basic occurrences of overlapping board members might occur, of course, simply because particular individuals are in high demand as a result of their expertise. However, where the overlap results in a failure of oversight and effective governance—the primary legal and ethical responsibility of board members—the implications can be significant to all stakeholders involved.

Insider Trading

10 OBJECTIVE

No discussion of the ethics of corporate governance and finance would be complete without consideration of the practice of **insider trading** by board members, executives, and other insiders. The issue became front page news in the 1980s when financier Ivan Boesky was sent to prison for the crime of insider trading. Though it certainly has not left the business pages in the intervening years, it once again gained iconic status when Ken Lay and his colleagues at Enron were accused of insider trading when they allegedly dumped their Enron stock, knowing of the inevitable downturn in the stock's worth, while encouraging others to hold on to it. More recent cases involving financiers and bankers such as Raj Rajaratnam, the billionaire founder of the hedge fund Galleon Group (discussed later), and Fidelity Investments employee David K. Donovan Jr., who was convicted in 2009 for giving his own mother inside information on which she then traded.

The definition of insider trading is trading by shareholders who hold private inside information that would materially impact the value of the stock and that allows them to benefit from buying or selling stock. Illegal insider trading also occurs when corporate insiders provide "tips" to family members, friends, or others and those parties buy or sell the company's stock based on that information. "Private information" would include privileged information that has not yet been released to the public. That information is deemed material if it could possibly have a financial impact on a company's short- or long-term performance or if it would be important to a prudent investor in making an investment decision.

The Securities and Exchange Commission defines insider information in the following way:

> "Insider trading" refers generally to buying or selling a security, in breach of a fiduciary duty or other relationship of trust and confidence, while in possession of material, nonpublic information about the security. Insider trading violations may also include "tipping" such information, securities trading by the person "tipped" and securities trading by those who misappropriate such information. Examples of insider trading cases that have been brought by the Commission are cases against: corporate officers, directors, and employees who traded the corporation's securities after learning of significant, confidential corporate developments; friends, business

> associates, family members, and other "tippees" of such officers, directors, and employees, who traded the securities after receiving such information; employees of law, banking, brokerage and printing firms who were given such information in order to provide services to the corporation whose securities they traded; government employees who learned of such information because of their employment by the government; and other persons who misappropriated, and took advantage of, confidential information from their employers.[18]

Because insider trading undermines investor confidence in the fairness and integrity of the securities markets, the commission has treated the detection and prosecution of insider trading violations as one of its enforcement priorities.[19]

Accordingly, if an executive gets rid of a stock he knows is going to greatly decrease in worth because of bad news in the company that no one knows except a few insiders, he takes advantage of those who bought the stock from him without full disclosure.

Insider trading may also be based on a claim of unethical misappropriation of proprietary knowledge, that is, knowledge only those in the firm should have, knowledge owned by the firm and not to be used by abusing one's fiduciary responsibilities to the firm. The law surrounding insider trading therefore creates a responsibility to protect confidential information, proprietary information, and intellectual property. That responsibility also exists based on the fiduciary duty of "insiders" such as executives. Misappropriation of this information undermines the trust necessary to the proper functioning of a firm and is unfair to others who buy the stock. Though one might make the argument that, in the long run, insider trading is not so bad since the inside information will be discovered shortly and the market will correct itself, this contention does not take account of the hurt to those who completed the original transactions in a state of ignorance.

Insider trading is considered patently unfair and unethical since it precludes fair pricing based on equal access to public information. If market participants know that one party may have an advantage over another via information that is not available to all players, pure price competition will not be possible and the faith upon which the market is based will be lost.

On the other hand, trading on inside information is not without its ethical defense. If someone has worked very hard to obtain a certain position in a firm and, by virtue of being in that position, the individual is privy to inside information, isn't it just for that person to take advantage of the information since she or he has worked so hard to obtain the position? Is it really wrong? Unethical? Consider an issue that might be closer to home. If your brother has always been successful in whatever he does in the business world, is it unethical to purchase stock in the company he just acquired? Others don't know quite how successful he has been, so are you trading on inside information? Would you tell others? What about officers in one company investing in the stocks of their client companies? No legal rules exist other than traditional SEC rules on insider trading, but is there not something about this that simply feels "wrong"? Consider the ethical issues surrounding access to information in the Decision Point "The Know-It-Alls."

Decision Point *The Know-It-Alls*

Where does a private investor find information relevant to stock purchases? Barring issues of insider trading, do all investors actually have equivalent access to information about companies?

- What are the ethical issues involved in access to corporate information?
- Where do private investors go to access information about stock purchases? On whose opinion do they rely? Does everyone have access to these same opinions? If not, what determines access to information in an open market? Instead, is there equal opportunity to have access to information?
- Who are the stakeholders involved in the issue of access? Who relies on information relevant to stock purchases?
- Who has an interest in equal access to information?
- What alternatives are available when considering access to information? How can we perhaps best ensure equal access?
- How do the alternatives compare, and how do the alternatives affect the stakeholders?

Some people do seem to have access to more information than others, and their access does not always seem to be fair. Consider how Martha Stewart found herself in jail. Stewart was good friends with Sam Waksal, who was the founder and CEO of a company called ImClone. Waksal had developed a promising new cancer drug and had just sold an interest in the drug to Bristol-Myers Squibb for $2 billion. Unfortunately, though everyone thought the drug would soon be approved, Waksal learned that the Food and Drug Administration had determined that the data were not sufficient to allow the drug to move to the next phase of the process. When this news became public, ImClone's stock price was going to fall significantly.

On learning the news (December 26, 2001), Waksal contacted his daughter and instructed her to sell her shares in ImClone. He then compounded his violations by transferring 79,000 of his shares (worth almost $5 million) to his daughter and asking her to sell those shares, too. Though the Securities and Exchange Commission would likely uncover these trades, given the decrease in share price, it was not something he seemed to consider. "Do I know that, when I think about it? Absolutely," says Waksal. "Did I think about it at the time? Obviously not. I just acted irresponsibly."[20] Waksal eventually was sentenced to more than seven years in prison for these actions.

How does Martha Stewart fit into this picture? The public trial revealed that Stewart's broker ordered a former Merrill Lynch & Co. assistant to tell her that Waksal was selling his stock, presumably so that she would also sell her stock. Stewart subsequently sold almost 4,000 shares on December 27, 2001, one day after Waksal sold his shares and one day prior to the public statement about the drug's failed approval.

In evaluating the causes of the Enron debacle and its implications for change, scholar Lisa Newton analyzes the possible responses we could utilize as a society.[21] Contemplate her arguments that some responses *will not work* and consider whether you agree or disagree:

More regulation: "The people who are making the money eat regulations for breakfast. You can't pass regulations fast enough to get in their way." Regulations are bad for business, she states; they do not have sufficient foresight; and virtual and global business leaves us with little to grasp in terms of regulation.

Business ethics courses: Newton contends that they are ineffective in guiding future action, and they do not sufficiently impact motivations.

Changes in corporate cultures: "What the company's officers do, when they act for good or (more likely) evil, does not *proceed from* the corporate culture, as if the corporate culture *caused* their actions . . . What people do, habitually, just *is* their character, which they create by doing those things. What a corporation does, through its officers, just *is* its culture, created by that behavior. To say that if we change the culture we'll change the behavior is a conceptual mistake—trivial or meaningless."

Does anything work? "Back to those other eras: this is not the first time that, up to our waists in the muck of corporate dishonesty, we have contemplated regulations and ethics classes and using large rough weapons on the corporate culture. And nothing we did in the past worked."

Instead, Newton posits, "capitalism was always known not to contain its own limits; the limits were to be imposed by the democratic system, whose representatives were the popularly elected watchdogs of the economy." Business crime comes not from "systemic capitalist contradictions" or sin; instead it

> . . . arises from a failure of the instruments of democracy, which have been weakened by three decades of market fundamentalism, privatization ideology and resentment of government. Capitalism is not too strong; democracy is too weak. We have not grown too hubristic as producers and consumers [as if the market were, when working right, capable of governing itself]; we have grown too timid as citizens, acquiescing to deregulation and privatization (airlines, accounting firms, banks, media conglomerates, you name it) and a growing tyranny of money over politics.[22]

Newton then explains that "we need, as Theodore Roosevelt well knew (20 years before his cousin presided over the aftermath of the 1929 disaster), democratic oversight of the market, or it will run amok. As it has.

Her conclusion? "Ultimately, our whining and hand-wringing about corporate culture, or executive incentives, or other technicalities of the way businesses run themselves, is useless. Business was never supposed to run itself, at least not for long. We the people were supposed to be taking responsibility for its operations as a whole. We have evaded this responsibility for almost a quarter of a century now, and that's long enough. It is time to remember that we have a public responsibility hat as well as a private enterprise hat, to put it on and put the country back in order."

(*continued*)

(concluded)

Is taking public responsibility the answer to ethical lapses in business?

- What else might you need to know in order to effectively evaluate Professor Newton's conclusion?
- What ethical issues are involved in the challenges she addresses?
- Who are the stakeholders?
- What do you think about her evaluation of the alternatives above?
- How do the alternatives compare? How do the alternatives affect the stakeholders?

Stewart successfully avoided prison for several years, and on November 7, 2003, she explained that she was scared of prison but "I don't think I will be going to prison. "Nevertheless she was convicted on all counts except securities fraud and sentenced to a five-month prison term, five months of home confinement, and a $30,000 fine, the minimum the court could impose under the Federal Sentencing Guidelines.

During the trial, the public heard the testimony of Stewart's friend, Mariana Pasternak, who reported that Stewart told her several days after the ImClone sale that she knew about Waksal's stock sales and that Stewart said, "Isn't it nice to have brokers who tell you those things?" So, to return to the issue with which we began this tale, it appears that some investors do seem to have access to information not necessarily accessible to all individual investors.

A similar, but more far-ranging situation was revealed in November 2009 when the FBI and U.S. Attorneys announced arrests stemming from a large insider-trading operation at the hedge fund Galleon Group. The Securities and Exchange Commission accused the billionaire Raj Rajaratnam and dozens of others associated with the Galleon Group of insider trading that resulted in more than $33 million in profit. They were accused of trading on secret details of corporate takeovers and quarterly earnings leaked to them by company insiders.

Though Stewart, Waksal, Rajaratnam and others involved in these stories were caught and charged with criminal behavior, many believe they were identified and later charged because they were in the public eye. If others are not in the public eye and also engage in this behavior, can the SEC truly police all inappropriate transactions? Is there a sufficient deterrent effect to discourage insider trading in our markets today? If not, what else can or should be done? Or, to the contrary, is this simply the nature of markets, and those who have found access to information should use it to the best of their abilities? What might be the consequences of this latter, perhaps more Darwinian, approach to insider trading, and whose rights might be violated if we allow it?

Consider whether we might have learned anything from the experiences of the past decade, and how we might most effectively proceed, as you review the Decision Point, "The Winds of Change."

Opening Decision Point Revisited *Is Steve Jobs' Health Status a Private Matter?*

In November 2009, Steve Jobs was named *Fortune* magazine's "CEO of the Decade." *Fortune* compared Jobs to Henry Ford except, while Ford revolutionized one nascent industry; *Fortune* credited Jobs with revolutionizing four mature industries: computing, mobile phones, music, and movies. In naming Jobs CEO of the decade, *Fortune* described him as "indispensible," a "visionary," and "irreplaceable."

After having read this chapter, let us return to some open questions from the Opening Decision Point. What responsibilities does the Apple Board of Directors have to the investment community and to the general public? Do you think that they fulfilled their responsibilities in this case? In considering the responsibilities of the Apple Board, reflect on a seemingly simple question: For whom do the directors work, for the investors ("owners" as Milton Friedman might call them) or for the CEO? Consider, also, the definition of materiality offered by Securities and Exchange Commission as information that "the reasonable investor needs to know in order to make an informed decision about his investment." Is the health status of a CEO such as Steve Jobs information that investors need to know in order to make an informed decision?

Reflect, as well, on the various models of CSR that were described in chapter 5 and evaluate how your views on the responsibilities of the Apple Board might have implications for your views on CSR.

Questions, Projects, and Exercises

1. You have been asked by the board of a large corporation to develop a board assessment and effectiveness mechanism, which could be a survey, interviews, an appraisal system, or other technique that will allow you to report back to the board on both individual and group effectiveness. What would you recommend?
2. You have been asked to join the board of a large corporation. What are some of the first questions that you should ask and what are the answers that you are seeking?
3. Scholars have made strong arguments for required representation on boards by stakeholders that go beyond stockholders; such as: employees, community members, and others, depending on the industry. What might be some of the benefits and costs of such a process?
4. You are an executive at a large non-profit organization. Some of your board members suggest that perhaps the company should voluntarily comply with Sarbanes-Oxley. What are some of the reasons the company might consider doing so or not doing so?
5. You are on the compensation committee of your board and have been asked to propose a compensation structure to be offered to the next CEO. Explore some of the following Web sites on executive compensation and then propose a structure or process for determining CEO compensation at your corporation.

   http://www.aflcio.org/corporateamerica/paywatch/ceou/database.cfm
   http://www.ecomponline.com/

http://www.rileyguide.com/execpay.html

http://www.sec.gov/news/speech/spch120304cs.htm

http://www.eri-executive-compensation.com/?TrkID=479-82

http://www.tgci.com/magazine/97fall/exec.asp

6. What are the strongest, most persuasive arguments in favor of a board's consideration of its social responsibility when reaching decisions?
7. A press release has a significant negative impact on your firm's stock price, reducing its value by more than 50 percent in a single day of trading! You gather from conversations in the hallway that the company's fundamentals remain strong, aside from this one-time event. You see this as a great opportunity to buy stock. Is it appropriate to act on this and to purchase company stock? Does it make a difference whether you buy 100 shares or 1,000 shares? Is it OK to discuss the "dilemma" with family members and friends? What should you do if you do mention it to family and friends but then later feel uncomfortable about it?
8. Modify slightly the facts of the previous question. Assume that you are also privy to the annual forecast of earnings, which assures you that the fundamentals remain strong. Stock analysts and investors are also provided this same information. Do your answers change at all?
9. In connection with the two previous questions, assume instead that you think something significant is about to be made public because all officers have consistently stayed late, a special board meeting has been called, you and your boss have been advised to be on call throughout the weekend, and various rumors have been floating throughout the company. You are not aware of the specifics, but you can reasonably conclude that it's potentially good or bad news. You decide to call a friend in the accounting department who has been staying late to find out what she knows. In this situation, do your answers about what you might do change? Is it appropriate to partake in the "rumor mill"? Is it appropriate to discuss and confide your observations with family and friends? Is it appropriate to buy or sell company stock based upon these observations (you may rationalize that it is only speculation and you do not know the facts)?
10. Have you ever been in, or are you familiar with, a conflict of interest situation? How was it resolved? Can you think of any rules or any practices that could have prevented the situation from occurring? Can you think of any initiatives, structures, or procedures that could make it easy to avoid such conflicts in the future?

Key Terms

After reading this chapter, you should have a clear understanding of the following Key Terms. The page numbers refer to the point at which they were discussed in the chapter. For a more complete definition, please see the Glossary.

Committee of Sponsoring Organizations (COSO), *p. 539*
conflict of interest, *p. 532*
control environment, *p. 539*
corporate governance, *p. 530*
duty of care, *p. 541*
duty of good faith, *p. 541*
duty of loyalty, *p. 541*
Enron Corporation, *p. 531*
European Union 8th Directive, *p. 538*
fiduciary duties, *p. 532*
gatekeeper, *p. 531*
insider trading, *p. 553*
internal control, *p. 540*
Sarbanes-Oxley Act, *p. 537*

End Notes

1. C. William Thomas, "The Rise and Fall of Enron," *Journal of Accountancy* (April 2002): 7.
2. Rushworth Kidder, "Combating Ethical Lapses: Why Compliance Is Not the Answer," *Ethics Newsline* 8, no. 16 (April 25, 2005).
3. Colleen Cunningham, president and CEO of FEI, quoted in "Recent Survey Results from the Financial Executives Institute," *NACD Director's Monthly,* March 2005, p. 6.
4. Public Company Accounting Oversight Board, "PCAOB Issues Guidance on Audits of Internal Control," Press Release, May 16, 2005.
5. Criteria of Control, Board Guidance on Control.
6. Ron Duska, "Perspectives in Ethical Leadership," *Mitchell Forum on Ethical Leadership in Financial Services,* January 10, 2004, p. 35. http://www.theamericancollege.edu/docs/79.pdf (accessed April 10, 2010).
7. William W. George, "Restoring Governance to Our Corporations," address given to the Council of Institutional Investors, September 23, 2002, http://www.bus.wisc.edu/update/fall02/ten_step.htm (accessed April 10, 2010).
8. Malcolm S. Salter, "Enron Jury Sent the Right Message," *Harvard Business School Working Knowledge for Business Leaders Series,* July 21, 2006, http://hbswk.hbs.edu/item/5456.html (accessed April 10, 2010).
9. Ram Charan and Julie Schlosser, "Ten Questions Every Board Member Should Ask; And for That Matter, Every Shareholder Too," *Fortune,* November 10, 2003, 181.
10. International Accounting Standards Board, "Accounting Standards: EU Commissioner McCreevy Sees Agreement with S.E.C. as Progress toward Equivalence," Press Release, April 22, 2005, http://europa.eu/rapid/pressReleasesAction.do?reference=IP/05/469&format=HTML&aged=0&language=EN (accessed April 10, 2010).
11. Kevin Bahr, "Conflicts of Interest in the Financial Markets" (Stevens Point, WI: Central Wisconsin Economic Research Bureau, 2002), http://www.uwsp.edu/business/cwerb/4thQtr02/SpecialReportQtr4_02.htm (accessed April, 10, 2010).
12. Eugene White, "Can the Market Control Conflicts of Interest in the Financial Industry?" presentation at the International Monetary Fund, June 4, 2004, http://www.imf.org/external/np/leg/sem/2004/cdmfl/eng/enw.pdf (accessed April, 10, 2010).
13. The Great CEO Pay Heist," by Geoffrey Colvin, Fortune, June 25, 2001, p. 64.
14. Data sources for Figures 10.2 and 10.3: Total executive compensation: 2005 data based on a *Wall Street Journal* survey, April 10, 2006; all other years based on similar sample in *BusinessWeek* annual compensation surveys (now discontinued). Includes salary, bonus, restricted stock, payouts on other long-term incentives, and the value of options exercised. S&P 500 Index: "Economic Report of the President," 2006 Table B-96; 1997, 2000 Table B-93; average of daily closing prices. Corporate Profits: U.S. Department of Commerce, Bureau of Economic Analysis, National Income and Product Accounts, Table 6.16, with inventory valuation and capital consumption adjustments. Average worker pay: Based on U.S. Department of Labor, Bureau of Labor Statistics, Employment, Hours, and Earnings from the Current Employment Statistics Survey (average hourly earnings of production workers × average weekly hours of production workers × 52). Minimum wage: Lowest mandated federal minimum wage, nominal; U.S. Dept. of Labor, Employment Standards Administration, Wage and Hour Division. Adjustment for inflation: BLS, Average Annual CPI-U, all urban consumers, all items.

15. Carol Hymowitz, "Sky-High Payouts to Top Executives Prove Hard to Curb," *The Wall Street Journal,* June 26, 2006, p. B1.
16. William Shaw, "Justice, Incentives, and Executive Compensation," in *The Ethics of Executive Compensation,* ed. Robert Kolb (Malden, MA: Blackwell, 2006), 93.
17. J. Harris and P. Bromiley, *Incentives to Cheat: Executive Compensation and Corporate Malfeasance,* and O'Conner et al., "Do CEO Stock Options Prevent or Promote Corporate Accounting Irregularities?" as quoted in Jared Harris, "How Much Is Too Much?" in *The Ethics of Executive Compensation,* pp. 67–86.
18. U.S. Securities and Exchange Commission, "Key Topics: Insider Trading," http://www.sec.gov/answers/insider.htm (accessed April 24, 2010).
19. U.S. Securities and Exchange Commission, "Insider Trading," http://www.sec.gov/divisions/enforce/insider.htm (accessed April 10, 2010).
20. CBS News, "Sam Waksal: I Was Arrogant," June 27, 2004, http://www.cbsnews.com/stories/2003/10/02/60minutes/main576328.shtml (accessed April 10, 2010).
21. Adapted and quoted from Lisa Newton, "Enron and Andersen: Guideposts for the Future," presentation to the Society for Business Ethics, Annual Meeting, August 2002. Elements adapted by the authors with permission of Dr. Lisa Newton.
22. Benjamin Barber, "A Failure of Democracy, Not Capitalism," *The New York Times,* July 29, 2002, Op-Ed. A19.

Readings

Reading 10-1

Thoughts on Reform: *On the First Anniversary of the Collapse of Lehman Brothers*

Stephen B. Young

One year ago the great Wall Street House of Lehman Brothers filed for bankruptcy, setting off the great global meltdown in financial markets. No one wanted to buy Lehman Brothers, no one wanted to lend it working capital, and neither the United States Treasury nor the Financial Services Authority of Great Britain wanted to save it.

    - the degree to which the remuneration structure aligns executive interests with those of shareholders, including during times of company stress and underperformance.
- Require all equity linked remuneration to be in the form of common equity escrowed for a minimum period of five years, regardless of continued employment.
- Prohibit Board members and key executives from borrowing or hedging against the common equity they hold in the company, unless there is full and timely disclosure of all such borrowing or hedging.
- Cap termination payments at one year's remuneration unless there is prior shareholder approval of a higher amount.

5. **Implement stronger and globally co-ordinated financial and banking regulatory reforms to prevent systemic risk build-up or market manipulation.**

   Proposed reforms:
   - Harmonise regulation and co-operation of financial supervisors/regulators across the G20, including cross-border supervision of globally significant financial entities, to enhance financial system stability and close opportunities for regulatory arbitrage.
   - Broaden regulatory coverage to all financial entities and transactional activities that pose material systemic risk to financial stability.
   - Strengthen capital adequacy of all systemically important financial institutions in line with their underlying risk profiles.
   - Weed out or strictly regulate market products, behaviours and activities that are not consistent with the principles of market stability, long term value creation, and a fully informed market.

6. **Regulate all financial markets instruments and investment activities that materially impact on financial system stability and on superannuation and pension system viability.**

   Proposed reforms:
   - Broaden regulatory coverage to all financial entities, products and transactional activities that pose material risks to financial stability or to superannuation and pension fund viability.
   - Enable regulators to intervene in and control excessive speculation and risk accumulation in all systemically important financial markets and instruments.
     - Market participants, including derivative and hedge funds, required to disclose trading and other information necessary to adequately access market and systemic risk.
   - Establish fully regulated exchanges for credit derivatives and other systemically important instruments.
   - Require registration and ensure regulatory oversight of credit ratings agencies whose ratings materially impact on financial and investment markets.
     - Review the practice of paid ratings and consider possible reform to ensure independence of ratings.

7. **Reform and adequately resource the IMF and other multilateral institutions to ensure they are effective forces for economic and social justice globally.**

   Proposed reforms:
   - Ensure the IMF and other international financial institutions and multilateral development banks are resourced to assist emerging and developing economies in dealing with the flow-on from the global financial crisis.
   - Broaden Financial Stability Forum membership to all G20 members and strengthen its role including via the development of an early warning system for threats to global financial stability.
   - Strengthen measures to oppose and prevent trade protectionism while renewing initiatives within the World Trade Organization towards a global free trade agreement.

Reading **10-2**

Islamic Banking and Finance: *Moral Beliefs and Business Practices at Work*

Karen Hunt Ahmed

The religion of Islam has existed for 1,400 years but Islamic economic theory and its financial institutions emerged as an industry only in the 1970s. Islamic financial institutions (IFIs) are designed to help Muslims conduct business internationally while simultaneously upholding traditional Islamic values related to trade finance and currency movement. The basis for their existence is the Islamic moral prohibition on charging interest—interest is a central component of capitalist banking—yet IFIs conduct billions of dollars of business annually in the world economy and the *de facto* Islamic banking transaction is—in most cases virtually identical to a capitalist banking transaction. Business practices in the industry of Islamic banking and finance (IBF; Maurer 2005) have evolved to reinforce some of the major tenets of a moral belief system based on Islamic principles. This chapter will discuss specific practices put into place by the IBF community that are designed to embody tenets of a belief system based on Islam while at the same time generating profits for the institution and its customers. This chapter will contribute to the discussion of best corporate practices by introducing some of those practices and discussing how those practices contribute to the success of the industry.

Religion and Business Practices

Religion is deeply concerned with the relationship between individuals and society on earth and the implications of that relationship on salvation: therefore, it is crucial for humans to understand the place of material survival in the cosmological scheme of life. That concern has been intertwined with questions of what it means to be a person and how to identify with a certain kind of community or communities. Opposition between religion and economy has arisen at times when a religious community is trying to carve out an identity for itself vis-à-vis the broader society. Individuals and societies change throughout history; therefore, spiritual and material well being must be constantly renegotiated. As such, it makes sense that human beings struggle to find the appropriate balance between material and spiritual matters. These concerns have carried over into contemporary discussions of religion and economy, and have become visible in the form of social movements based on various conceptions of morality. The basic questions and issues are the same as in the past, but the context of globalization (Appadurai 2000, 1996; Sassen 1998; Jameson and Miyoshi 1998; Hannerz 1996; Scholte 2000) has expanded the scope of the meaning of identity and community, especially in the context of competing moralities (Shweder, Minow and Markus 2002; Gupta and Ferguson 1997; Ong 1999).

In the contemporary world, some types of morally driven economic theories—corporate social responsibility, socially responsible investing and, it will be argued throughout this chapter, Islamic finance—are examples of some approaches to economic behavior are based on moral discourse. Regardless of whether or not religion is specifically invoked in the moral discourse, it is clear that discussions about religion and economy are as relevant today as ever before. Economic cultures are sensitive to cultural and religious understandings of the implications of moral belief systems on business practices.

Most economic development textbooks do not take into consideration the effects of moral or religious beliefs on economic behavior (Kuran 2004).

From the Enlightenment until the publication of Weber's *Protestant Ethic,* scholars took it for granted that religion and economy were unrelated spheres of life. Whereas an emphasis on the compatibility of religion and economy may have waned for more than a century, some groups in contemporary society are very much embroiled in the same kinds of conversations about morality and business that occupied the minds of medieval moralists. These conversations may not be based specifically on *religious* morality, but they do call upon an individual's moral inclinations to curb human greed and to form communities around moral beliefs about economic activity.

Introduction to Islamic Finance

The industry of Islamic banking and finance is growing daily. In 2006, the Islamic Development Bank in Saudi Arabia estimated that Islamic financial institutions manage more than USD$800 billion. There are more than 500 Islamic financial institutions worldwide and the world's potential market for Islamic finance consists of more than one billion Muslims, in addition to non-Muslims, who are welcome to participate in Islamic finance. Islamic finance has been compared to an environmental fund in that its policies are based on a certain philosophy of life yet its participants also expect to make a profit on investments. Practitioners in the industry define Islamic finance by the ways in which it objects to conventional financial practices in addition to the ban on *riba,* which is translated from Arabic as interest or usury. Islamic financiers are not allowed to trade in specific goods forbidden under Islamic law, such as pork and alcohol. Islamic finance prohibits taking unnecessary risks or gambling (El Gamal 2000). Islamic financial institutions should adhere to a code of Islamic business ethics and should maintain a *Shari'a* Standards Board composed of Islamic scholars to maintain the purity of the institution's products and conduct (Lewis and Algaoud 2001; Beekum 1997). Ultimately, all features of Islamic finance are designed to uphold theological concepts of God-consciousness (*tawhid*) and social justice (*adalah*) in a business environment.

Framework of an Islamic Economic Theory

The framework of Islamic economic theory was developed in pre-Partition India in the early 20th century by Islamic scholar Mawlana Mawdudi (1903–1979) and expounded upon by one of his students, economist Khurshid Ahmad, who later moved to Pakistan. At the time, Indian Muslims as a group were relatively disadvantaged economically compared with the majority population of Hindus. The British Raj had provided some economic protections to Muslims, farmers in particular, but at the time it was unclear how or if a Hindu-led government would provide the same protection (Kuran 2004). Mawdudi believed that economic activity and technology were crucial to success in the modern world, and he was dedicated to providing Muslims in pre-Partition India with economic opportunities that allowed them both to function in the modern world and to retain their Muslim identity. He and Ahmad believed that it was possible and desirable for Muslims to embrace systems and institutions of modernity while at the same time adhering to the teachings and practices of Islam (Mawdudi 1980; Ahmad and Ansari 1979). One goal of Mawdudi was to redefine Islamic practices to conform to economic changes. Mawdudi's ideas were put into practice in the 1970s in the Arabian Gulf, with the establishment of Dubai Islamic Bank and the Islamic Development Bank in Saudi Arabia.

At first the industry grew slowly. Until very recently Islamic financing was only sporadically available throughout the world, and mostly it was not available at all. Recent developments in the global economic structure due to improved technology and fewer restrictions on capital flows have made world conditions much more amenable to the possibility of IBF making a meaningful contribution to the reformation of business practices to bring them more in line with the Islamic belief system. IBF business practices reflect and reinforce certain key concepts of an Islamic moral economy (Tripp 2006) such as community, partnership and trust. Financial structures and practices provide evidence of adherence to these beliefs.

Business Practices under Islamic Law

The existence of Islamic finance institutions solves a difficult problem for the Muslim desiring to participate in international finance while adhering to Islamic law, or *Shari'a*. Islamic law does not allow for individuals or institutions who lend or borrow money to charge or pay interest on that money. Yet in the early twenty-first century global economy, trade finance and other crucial banking transactions are dominated by capitalist financial practices in which return on investment is based upon charging interest.

The Islamic finance industry intends to improve upon global financial institutions by maintaining their positive features and cleansing them of negative features (Maurer 2002a, 2002b; Al Saud 2000). Islamic banks strive, in the words of a prominent Islamic bank's vision statement, to uphold "deep-rooted traditions in the new world" (Dubai Islamic Bank brochure). Islamic finance professionals claim that an Islamic bank is a conventional bank without its immorality. The framework used to determine morality is based on Islamic text and tradition, yet the institutional framework is, on the surface at least and to the untrained eye, indistinguishable from the capitalist financial structure.

Islamic law is specific about what constitutes permissible trade behavior. Business practices fall under the set of normative relationships between human beings *(muamalat)* that are ultimately governed by the will of Allah, or God (Waines 1995:65). Therefore, banking, finance and trade are regulated by specific rulings found either in the *Qur'an* or in *hadith*.

Discussions of Islamic finance fall into two categories: moral/ethical and social justice concerns. The first category is the better known and involves the prohibition of specific types of transactions: *riba* and *gharar* (El Gamal 2000) as well as more general trading prohibitions regarding goods forbidden under Islamic law such as pork, alcohol and tobacco. *Riba* broadly refers to any goods or services traded in unequal amounts. Muslims cite a well-known *hadith* to support this concept:

> Gold for gold, silver for silver, salt for salt, dates for dates, barley for barley, and wheat for wheat, hand-to-hand in equal amounts; and any increase is *riba*. [El Gamal 2000:147]

The concept of usury may be applied to both monetary and material goods and its prohibition serves a major purpose of keeping relations among businesspeople equitable. This conception of *riba* is, of course, a simplification and its technical properties are widely discussed and debated by Islamic economists (see, for example, Ahmad 1976; for an alternative economic view of *riba,* see El Gamal 2000).

In the area of religious thought Judaism and Christianity, in addition to Islam, have struggled internally throughout history with moral challenges posed by "interest" (Weber 1968). Interest calculation is based on the measurement of time. Foucault (1978) asserts that early Christians viewed time as a gift from God; therefore, it has different value for different people, making the calculation of interest immoral. The original intention of timetables, he asserts, was a religious invention designed to eliminate the dangers of wasting God's gift of time. The move of instituting schedules served to appropriate the use of time in daily human life. In addition, Landes emphasizes the importance of time to the link between Protestantism and the formation of a capitalist subject (Landes 2000). However, Foucault argues that today time is understood as a material possession to be manipulated and shaped at will. The perception of time as a gift has been negated in capitalist society by the "principle of a theoretically ever-growing use of time" (Foucault 1978:154). Islamic thought designates a similar spiritual orientation to the concept of time (Bamyeh 1999; Waines 1998), which some scholars contend has been lost in the modern world (Wilson 1997). Although Islamic practice employs scheduled activities (most notably prayers), Islamic finance intensifies its rejection of the model of interest on the basis of its objectification of time as a material entity (Wilson 1997: see pages 5–7 for a complete discussion). Christianity and Judaism (with similar arguments to those we see in Islamic finance today, see El Gamal 2000) has resolved the moral issue of time in a way that advances capitalist enterprise, where Islam seems to critique capitalism while at the same time advancing it.

Present day IBF institutions avoid the problem of interest by structuring transactions as profit sharing or lease-to-purchase arrangements. Practically speaking, it is challenging for a bank to function without some kind of reference to "interest." This difficulty was made clear when the author decided to open a checking account at an Islamic bank. *Johara* means "jewel" in Arabic. *Johara* is also the name of a bank for women: the stand alone ladies' branch of an Islamic bank in Dubai, United Arab Emirates (UAE) where the author did fieldwork in 2003. The teller was asked to explain exactly how the annual profit sharing payment on the account worked. Immediately, she responded, "Well, it's basically like an interest payment." Although her reference to "interest" may have in part stemmed from the fact that the researcher is American, it was nevertheless hard for her to find the words to explain the payment without reference to the better-known concept of interest, in which she was fully conversant. This is a common tactic employed in Islamic finance, and it is not seen to be at odds with the ban on interest.

Community Financial Transactions

Community discourse permeates discussions about and within the Islamic finance community. From the outset, the industry was meant to address community concerns. The focus on community stands in contrast to a capitalist understanding of economic activity, which is built on the assumption that the individual is the locus of economic activity, as Adam Smith so elegantly noted in *Wealth of Nations* (1976). Islamic economics subverts the neoclassical economic model by asserting that individuals are (or should be) driven to cooperate for the good of society. *This is a very important difference between conventional finance and Islamic finance, and one that is mentioned regularly in conversations with Islamic financiers.* Because the Islamic finance industry defines itself with reference to the conventional finance industry, it is valuable to understand how that difference in meaning is instilled into financial practices.

Classical Financial Structures

One of the first differences one notices between conventional finance and Islamic finance is the structure of financial transactions. This business practice is not visible unless one delves into the minutiae of the financial details. Yet, when Islamic financiers are asked what is the most important difference between conventional and Islamic finance, the most common answer is that the transactions are structured differently. In response to the prohibition against charging or paying *riba,* great attention is paid to how well the cash inflows and outflows are conceptualized. In addition to attention to *riba,* transactional structures are meant to reinforce the idea that the provider *and* recipient of funds share in the risk and return as much as possible. Therefore, the first business practice I will discuss is the practice of structuring the transactions themselves.

There are four classical Islamic financing structures used by the IBF industry intended to avoid *riba* and emphasize the communal nature of business practices. When I began reading about Islamic finance in the early 1990s, these were the *only* transactions available to people who wanted to participate in Islamic finance. Present day Islamic finance transactions are based on these four basic methods; however, there are now countless ways to structure a transaction that adheres to Islamic law but provides competitive returns in the market. They are based on the notion of partnerships, and highlight the importance of business practices that encourage community members to work together as partners. Although each financing structure specifically addresses the concerns of Islamic finance, each is also compatible with conventional banking practices. Knowledge is acquired together with one's fellow community member, rather than autonomously through rote learning. Each kind of transaction will be described below.

The first two structures relate to debt finance. First is a *murabaha,* or trade finance, which accounts for some 80% of Islamic financing (Wilson 1997). This transaction is very formal, and involves a buyer, a seller, goods for trade and a financier. The seller and buyer wish to exchange goods or services and agree upon a price, all according to lawful means. A financier, in turn, provides the money for the goods at their cost plus a predetermined financing fee. The financier then owns the goods (but does not take possession of them) until the buyer pays for the goods in full (Wilson 1997). This method is a short term financing technique, and, except for the predetermined fee, looks and operates like capitalist trade finance.

In other words, say we run a lemonade stand. We need to buy pitchers to serve lemonade to customers and do not have enough cash to purchase those pitchers. We need financing to help us In order to finance the pitchers on a *murabaha* basis, a financial institution would purchase the pitchers from the supplier and immediately resell them to our business for a marked up price based on administrative costs and a profit margin. Remember that there is no prohibition on profit, just the means by which it is acquired.

A second form of debt financing is a lease finance structure. Short term (*ijara*) and long term lease purchase contracts (*ijara-wa-iqtina*) are functionally equivalent to their capitalist counterparts. Both are normally used to finance machinery or other equipment. As under a *murabaha* arrangement, in an *ijara* the bank purchases the goods and the buyer pays the bank through a periodic (usually monthly) fee. At the end of the lease term the purchaser may either purchase the item or let the bank dispose of it. The major difference between a capitalist lease and an *ijara* is that, under an *ijara,* the lessor assumes responsibility for owning and maintaining the asset, whereas that responsibility falls to the lessee under the capitalist tradition (Wilson 1997). This stipulation is consistent with the requirement of a seller's responsibility to take care of merchandise before the sale.

In our hypothetical lemonade stand, another way we can finance the pitchers is via an *ijara.* The financial institution would purchase the pitchers and then lease them to our business. At the end of the lease period, we would either purchase the pitchers outright or return them to the financial institution.

The first Islamic finance structure the author encountered in her professional life was an *ijara.* The company the author worked for in Dubai financed an oil rig, located in Angola. The financial company actually owned the title to the oil rig and received monthly payments as lease payments on that lease. This situation was brought to the author's attention because the cash flow did not look any different from other loans' cash flows, yet the funds were separate from the company's other funds. It was only after looking at the original financing agreement that the author realized the structure was meant to be "Islamic" and the sharing of risk between financial company and lessee were built into the financial plan.

There are two classical forms of equity finance. The first, a *mudaraba,* is a partnership between a provider of capital and a provider of labor. A capital provider may be a bank, individual, or one of many groups of investors (Wilson 1997). Profit and loss sharing are in proportion to the amount of capital invested, and no one except the partners may receive profit (al-Misri 1994) Most importantly, liabilities are limited to the amount of capital invested by each investor (Wilson 1997). This type of arrangement is virtually the same as a limited liability company in capitalism, and is compatible with equity financing through a stock exchange.

Another type of partnership is a *musharaka,* under which both parties supply capital (in contrast to a *mudaraba,* in which only one party or group supplies capital). Losses are not limited to the amount of investment, so risk is greater for all parties. The capitalist equivalent would be a venture capital firm providing capital for smaller ventures (Wilson 1997).

Contemporary Financial Structures

Some contemporary transactions were designed in response to contemporary conventional transactions, but are based specifically on built in partnership arrangements in keeping with the focus on community and cooperation. The most noticeable difference between classical and contemporary Islamic transactions is the presence of an institution called an Islamic bank. If we look closely at the *murabaha, mudaraba, musharaka and ijara* methods of finance, we notice that not one of them requires the existence of an institution. Each form of financing is a partnership arrangement that can easily take place between any entity with available capital and any entity in need of capital. In fact, in the Middle Ages, merchant families themselves financed trade in the Muslim world, not unlike trade finance in Europe at the same time (Udovitch 1979). For example, a neighbor and you could both contribute some money to make a lemonade stand, agree that you will oversee the daily operations of the lemonade stand, and that each person would get a share of the profits according to the relative amounts each of us invested into the project. In this scenario, the neighbor and you have agreed to open a lemonade stand under a *musharaka* agreement. You did not need an institutional intermediary. The transactions discussed below require an intermediary in their financial structure. That intermediary is an IFI or some kind of special purpose investment vehicle. They are more complicated than the classical financial structures.

Salaam *and* Istisna

The *salaam* and *istisna* transactions are both sales contracts used when a commodity is not available for delivery at the same moment financing is needed. A *salaam* contract is used for commodity transactions when the financial institution (on behalf of a buyer) advances the purchase price of goods to the commodity owner. The goods are delivered at a later date to the financier, who then delivers them to the buyer. The buyer pays the financier the purchase price upon delivery of the goods.

An *istisna* works in a similar manner, except that it is used principally for manufacturing and construction finance. The financial institution pays the construction company as work is completed (say, on a building project). The construction company delivers the asset when it is complete. The financier delivers the asset to the customer, who then pays the purchase price to the financier.

The difference between *salaam* and *istisna* is based on the nature of the goods in question. A *salaam* is used to finance goods (commodities) that do not yet exist but are almost assured to exist in the future; e.g., agricultural goods (say, soybeans) that need to be grown during the growing season. The "production process" makes no difference to the transaction: the contract cannot specify how the soybeans are grown, merely that soybeans of a certain quality will be produced. The *istisna,* on the other hand, is tied to goods that would not otherwise be produced, like a commercial office building. The *istisna* is usually tied to a specific production process, which is essential to the final product and which is included in the price as part of the risk structure of the contract (Vogel and Hayes 1998; Bahrain Monetary Agency 2002).

At first glance, there does not seem to be anything particularly "modern" about either of these transactions. After all, it has always been necessary to finance commodities trades or to provide a farmer with financing based upon the anticipated production of agricultural products. Udovitch (1979) points out that trade finance was always prevalent in Muslim societies, just that merchants would provide financing instead of financial institutions. Vogel and Hayes (1998) draw attention to the modern nature of the *istisna* contract: until the Industrial Revolution few goods were exchangeable on a commodity basis as most people produced their own necessary goods. There was little need for manufacturing finance. It was only after the transformation of the nature of goods by the industrial production process that it became necessary to provide long term manufacturing finance (see also

Appadurai 1986 for an extended analysis of the history of the commodity and its uses). The *istisna* is a response to the changing commercial environment. It must be noted, also, that the *istisna* is only valid under the Hanafi legal tradition (Vogel and Hayes 1998). Hanafi was the first legal school to be recognized by Muslims, and is therefore the oldest *madhhab.* Hanafi is generally considered to be the *madhhab* most amenable to modernization. It is also the school most closely associated with the geographical area of South Asia (India, Pakistan, and Bangladesh) that gave inspiration to Mawdudi.

Sukuk

The two most prevalent financing structures in Islamic finance today are the *sukuk* (bond) and *takaful* (insurance). The author does not have any first hand data on either *sukuks* or *takaful*[1] from fieldwork because they were first issued in 2002, when she was in the field. They have since become one of the most popular financing vehicles: therefore, it will be described briefly.

A *sukuk* is a form of bond usually issued by a government, or by a corporation in partnership with a government. It is based on a conventional government bond, and is used for long term financing. A conventional government bond is a method of financing by which a government (local or state/national) sells paper (bonds) to investors in exchange for (1) periodic (usually annual) payments to the investor and (2) repayment of capital at the end of the term. A bond is essentially an IOU from the government to investors. Profit to the investor is based on an interest rate determined by a measure of the stability of the government issuing the bond. The more stable the government—and therefore the better able to repay the funds—the lower the interest rate. Less stable governments must pay a higher interest rate. For example, if a local government wants to build a bridge across the river, it would sell bonds in order to raise cash to pay the contractors. Upon completion of the project, the government would repay the investors from its own capital account.

The cash flow of a *sukuk* looks similar to the cash flow of a conventional bond. The difference, as with most Islamic financial structures, lies with the underlying assumptions and asset structure. Whereas a conventional bond is backed by the goodwill and stability of the government, a *sukuk* is backed by tangible assets. In the example of the bridge financing, the government might pledge the income stream from some government properties or buildings to the *sukuk.* Investor return would be derived from that income. In the event of a government default, investors could theoretically sue the government for the income from its property.

Sukuks are "hot" at this time in the Islamic finance market. On the global market, issues of sukuks increased from $1.9 billion in 2003 to $6.7 billion in 2004 to more than $10 billion in 2005 (www.zawya.com). The largest single *sukuk* issuance on record to date was just issued by Dubai Islamic Bank on December 10, 2006 in the sum of $3.52 billion (www.zawya.com). In July 2007, the government of the United Kingdom agreed to issue the first ever *sukuk* offered by the government of a non-Muslim country.

Takaful

Takaful is Islamic insurance. Insurance is a modern concept and therefore is not found in any of the classical Islamic texts. Insurance means that a person or business (the insured) makes periodic payments (insurance premiums) to an insurance provider so that in the event of loss (of inventory, house, car, etc.) the insurance provider will compensate the insured party for that loss. The concept of insurance is controversial; nevertheless, *Shari'a* scholars have come to recognize the importance of insurance in the international business arena. *Takaful* is one of the fasted growing areas of Islamic finance. I did not interview anyone specifically about *takaful* during my fieldwork because the field is generally considered to be somewhat separate from traditional Islamic finance. It will be described briefly, however, to illustrate how a conventional method of managing risk can have huge implications for the practice of Islamic finance.

What are the problems with insurance? First, the industry is built upon uncertainty about events beyond its control. Insurance deals with an amount of uncertainty (*gharar*) because the outcome of a future event is uncertain in the present. In a sense insurance is gambling (*maysir*), which is forbidden under Islamic law. Because it is highly unlikely that every insured party will incur a loss in the future, insurance companies effectively take a gamble that it will make a profit from insurance premiums even after it pays its insured customers in the event of a loss. This is the second objection to insurance (Lewis and Algaoud 2001). Life insurance presents a particularly difficult challenge to the concept of insurance because of the idea that no one can predict the end of life and that to insure the event shows distrust in God's life plan.[2] A third objection to conventional insurance is that most insurance companies invest their premiums in forbidden *riba* (interest-bearing) investments (Vogel and Hayes 1998). However, this objection can easily be overcome by investing in one of the many Islamic institutions available today.

Conventional insurance operates on a contract basis; i.e., the insured party and the insurance company enter into a contract specifying terms of payment and coverage. The word for Islamic insurance, *takaful,* means "solidarity" and reflects the worldview built into a *takaful* arrangement. In general, a *takaful* agreement is a collective enterprise, in which Muslims pool their resources in order to aid each other in the event of a loss (Vogel and Hayes 1998). Members make periodic payments into the fund and the company invests those funds Islamically. This investment is made on a *mudaraba* basis, with the member acting as the financier and the *takaful* company as the *mudarib* (entrepreneur). This arrangement also helps to mitigate the element of uncertainty about future payments, as the members would expect periodic payments on their capital investment. This arrangement is also consistent with the concept of *tawhid* (unity), because economic actors are pooling their resources to benefit the group.

Partnerships in Business Practice

Just as financial structures reflect an emphasis on partnerships, individuals working in the industry view IBF's business practices as a way to emphasize that same concept. The author interviewed Mohammed, of a government Private Investment Office. He states that what makes an IFI distinct from a conventional bank is that the customer expects to be a partner with the IFI. He emphasizes the situation in which the IFI and the customer have more interaction with each other. In addition, they share the financial risk of the transaction.

> Mohammed: It's more of a partnership . . . if I am your client my relationship with you is by taking the same risk. Any opportunity and any investment if for instance take a decision of making a real-estate investment so in this case the bank and the client take on—sharing the risk. That's the relationship that I expect from the Islamic bank.
>
> Interviewer: Right, so maybe more interaction.
>
> Mohammed: More interaction, more involvement, more of knowing the customer and what I have seen from my own experience, once you get into an Islamic bank you almost get to know everybody.

Partnerships link aspect suppliers and consumers of funds and reinforce the idea of community.

Rania, the general manager of a ladies' branch of a major Islamic bank, states that the partnership aspect of Islamic banking is as important as the actual amount of profit made by the bank or the customer. She believes this is because the bank plays a role in the community of a support system:

> And then they also have the flexibility of supporting you, Islamic banking. It supports you through it in terms of partnerships with you, in terms of management, so that gives you another flexibility and choice so that in case the business fails for some reason, you are not completely left on your own, high and dry, in a sense, not knowing what to do. Children aren't driven out of the house because you owe the bank some money or something like that. We try to help you out in all possible ways to prevent that.

From the customer's perspective, an emphasis on partnership is a positive aspect of Islamic finance. The author talked to a customer about the partnership concept: Manoj is a very successful owner of multiple businesses in Dubai, including marble and tile factories. He had been living in Dubai for over thirty years so he had watched the growth of Islamic finance from ground zero. He is Hindu, from India, but strongly emphasizes that anyone can participate in Islamic banking as he does. Part of what has made him so successful is the fact that he finds the best deal in the market, and he says that, often, Islamic finance provides the best financial deal. In addition to that, he feels that Islamic banks look more at the merits of the project and the customer rather than the interest rate, as the international banks do. The Islamic bank's profit is tied more to the project than the world interest rate. He feels very comfortable with this method of financing and stated that he would rather have a partnership relation with his bank.

Hamad was the director of the Islamic Banking division of the Dubai International Financial Center (DIFC) during the time of my fieldwork. He is a UAE national who was educated (undergraduate and graduate) at a prestigious, socially liberal university in the United States. He is very philosophical about the state of Islamic finance in the Gulf region. The discussion had digressed from the formal questions and were talking about what he sees as strengths and weaknesses of the industry. In addition to what he perceives as a lack of innovation in IBF, he sees the "entanglement of religious behavior" in business to be a weakness of the industry. He sees IBF focuses too much on paperwork where it should be taking the principles of Islam and applying them on a more fundamental level.

> Hamad: I think we have to get rid of this model if we want to have a truly international Islamic finance. We have to separate it. I mean, if you create a truly new industry that does things in a certain way that will be more than just paperwork. So the contractual terms change—this is what you do in Islamic finance—so the contractual term changes and reposition what you are to commercial finance from *lenders to investors to partnership* (italics added). This is what they do. Islam rejected the usury concept, and consider[ing] that most financing is usury, then the contractual terms only change where the *financial institution turns into more of a partner* (italics added).

Hamad's critique of the industry is that it needs more innovation to truly uphold the principles of Islamic finance.

In addition to the emphasis on community building business practices, IBF institutions strive to contribute to the welfare of the Muslim community. For example, Masood of EastWest Bank Corporation (EWBC)—an international, conventional bank with an Islamic division—views his involvement in IBF as a way to promote the Muslim community's welfare:

> Well I always as a Muslim had a passion for this Muslim community welfare as such . . . and I always had a realization that you can't have a strong economy unless you have a strong banking system. And to have a strong banking system you need strong indigenous banks. And I was involved in Islamic banking in supporting Islamic financial institutions in either managing their money or doing transactions for them as a banker.

It appears that the discourse of "IBF as community service provider" is a theme in the offices of EWBC: the idea that banking is providing a needed service for the Muslim community is echoed by Masood's colleague, Peter:

> I mean there are things that you once used to share with the community—for example the building of your house—the whole village comes together. You help me, tomorrow you want to build your house, I'll help you. Now we are living in a different more specialized society and everybody does its own job so we pool our resources in financial institutions, so instead of me going house to house to ask for help to build my house, [I] borrow money, build my house and then I will repay my share to that society so there is a social function—very important.

Peter also recognizes a very important fact in the world today: that institutions have taken over some community functions. If institutions and aid agencies are now providing assistance to the community, then it follows naturally that those institutions should share some of the core values of the community they intend to help.

The Financial Community and Trust

Being part of a community also means being able to trust others members of that community. The author spoke with Hesham, who was born in Pakistan but left when he was a small child. He has lived in the Middle East and in the United States, and now runs a conventional financial management company in the US that also structures Islamic transactions. At the time of the interview, he was relatively new to the field of Islamic finance and was going through the process of introducing an Islamic hedge fund. He had some observations about the function of the Islamic finance industry as a bridge between cultures.

> It's been interesting to create that particular product actually . . . the world view of Islam has changed in my opinion because Islam is truly global today. American Muslims will be very different from European Muslims will be very different from Asian Muslims or Middle Eastern Muslims and so on and so forth because they're American, European, Middle Eastern, Asian and they have their own perspectives in that sense. I never really thought of it as a—as a truly global (religion)—I never really saw it as that.

Hesham became aware of the diversity within Islam only after beginning to work in an Islamic finance space. In conjunction with that diversity, the unity of being part of a Muslim community allows its members to build trust among themselves. It is important for the purposes of looking at the self, though, to understand that Islamic finance does provide a mediating influence in how Islamic practitioners see the role of the industry in their lives. Many IBF practitioners see themselves as part of a community, a role that transcends participation in a mere profession.

Rania, who was introduced earlier in the chapter, also confirms this feeling of trust, and feels it especially in the Islamic banking environment:

> I feel that it's a very fair system. The only thing is that there are no hidden charges; they are very fair with the customers. I mean I worked in foreign banks and when I compare it I know. And people in general have a feeling of more trust and faith and caring. I've seen the compassion in here which I have not seen in foreign banks.

Just as Mandaville (2004) suggests in his analysis of the history of the Muslim community, that many Islamic financiers recall in their imagination the early days of Islam when thinking about Islamic finance. Tony is an accountant who has worked with Islamic finance in the accounting practice run by his father and himself.

> Tony: Islamic banking probably has more because that was probably set as a precedent by the prophet himself because a lot of people entrusted assets to him.
>
> Interviewer: Right.
>
> Tony: Because he's honest, honorable and he would look after those assets—so Islamic financial institutions—probably that is the most important principle that they should adopt—that whatever's entrusted to you, you have to look after in the best possible manner.

Association with this golden era of Islam (Maurer 2005) allows Tony to see IBF as being inculcated with a high level of trust.

Yasir, of Ethical Investing Corporation, raises the issue of trust not only from within the IBF community itself, but as a way to promote interaction with the conventional banking community:

> Yasir: We actually try to tell them [conventional bankers] that "what we do is very, very similar to what you do" but we have a sort of filtering that we have to superimpose over what it is that they do. So we always try and make them feel, especially

> because there is a little bit of aura and, you know you don't trust what you don't know, we want to avoid confusion. A lot of Islamic institutions that I've come across tend like to create a mystique around the whole you know Islamic industry, to make it inaccessible to their Western counterparts. They feel threatened so they say "no no no there's no way you guys can do it"; "you need the *Shari'a* [Board] and it's impossible to talk to them and it's impossible to reach them and you have understand this and that." It's actually not so, it's an accessible market. We've seen that demonstrated by Western institutions that have already set up shop and we take an opposite view. I mean we tell people literally "I do exactly what you do however I have to do it within these guidelines. You have to do it within your guidelines" but amazing similarities.

Yasir sees trust as an important component of the "bridge" function of IBF.

Shari'a Standards Board

Another way of strengthening community through the structuring of transactions is to require *Shari'a* board approval for every transaction, or type of transaction. A *Shari'a* Standards Board (SSB) is composed of Islamic scholars, who are fluent in both Islamic commercial law and international financial principles. The SSB's purpose is to insure that Islamic law is being followed accurately in the business practices and financial arrangements of the IFI. A separate financial standards board evaluates the efficacy of financial transactions, just as it does in a conventional institution, and the two boards often work together.

Islamic scholars must publicly declare that a transaction adheres to Islamic law before a company can go ahead with that transaction. A company's SSB does this by issuing a *fatwa* (religious declaration). A transaction does not adhere to Islamic law if it is not accompanied by a *fatwa,* as Khurram explains: "the *fatwa* is kind of more expected by the retail clients . . . the retail market wants to see a *fatwa.*" The issuance of a *fatwa* makes the transaction Islamic in a way that is recognizable to members of the community, and members trust that transaction will meet their moral criteria for business practices.

Conclusion

The industry of Islamic banking and finance structures its business practices and financial transactions according to a belief system that counts community, partnerships and trust as its highest priorities. Islamic financiers reinforce business practices and financial structures that emphasize the mutual benefits of sharing both profits and losses with fellow humans, rather than a system that focuses attention on profit only. IBF practitioners align themselves morally with corporate social responsibility and socially responsible investing movements in the way they expect to receive profit on investments while at the same time improving upon moral imperatives, such as building community and fostering healthy business practices. IFIs take the additional step of monitoring their own activities through a *Shari'a* Standards Board charged with upholding and monitoring the moral efficacy of the company's activities. Through its financial structures, business practices and corporate governance, Islamic finance provides an example of how business practices can be aligned with moral beliefs.

End Notes

1. The first takaful (Islamic insurance) company was launched in the UAE in October of 2002 (*Khaleej Times* newspaper article, October 12, 2002).
2. Vogel and Hayes (1998) point out that this should not be a concern because insurance protects the living from "adverse material consequences" (p. 151) of death and does not make any prediction about death itself.

Note: Notes and references removed for publication here, but are available on the book website at www.mhhe.com/busethics2e.

Reading **10-3**

Why "Best" Corporate Governance Practices Are Unethical and Less Competitive

Shann Turnbull

1. Introduction

This reading explains why Publicly Traded Corporations (PTCs) are unethical in the US, UK and other "Anglo" type corporate governance countries such as represented by Australia, Hong Kong, India, Malaysia, New Zealand, Philippines, Singapore, Thailand and many others. The reading also identifies how the ubiquitous unethical conflicts expose firms to being less competitive.

The next Section outlines how the modern corporation represent a sub-optimal institution for efficiently and equitably allocating resources by market forces because they allow investors to become overpaid. Investment overpayment is inefficient and so inconsistent with the rationale for a market economy. Accountants do not identity how investors' get overpaid and obscure investment returns. It can be argued that the overpayment of investors is unethical.

Section three considers how the constitutions of Anglo (PTCs) provide directors with absolute power to manage their own conflicts of interests. This gives directors the ability to corrupt themselves and the business and/or harm the interest of stakeholders. It also facilitates excessive payments to executives and unethical corporate behaviour. For this reason bankers and venture capitalists introduce checks and balances on the power of directors so as to protect the funds they advance to a company. Such practices raises the question why stock exchanges, regulators and the law does not require similar checks and balances to be introduced into the constitutions of PTCs.

The concluding Section four describes how abuses of power by directors can be removed and/or ethically managed by shareholders introducing changes in the corporate constitution or charter as found in some non Anglo countries. The concentration of power, ironically denies directors of larger firms the ability to: (a) obtain independently of management, intelligence to evaluate and direct management or the business, and (b) efficiently and effectively control the business.

The reading outlines how additional operating and competitive advantages can be introduced by corporate constitutions also providing formal processes for stakeholders to inform directors on the Strengths, Weaknesses, Opportunities, Threats (SWOT) of the business and its management independently of management.

The reading illustrates why so called "best corporate governance practices" are both unethical and less competitive. It also shows that correcting both problems can be achieved together in a self-reinforcing way by the introduction of "network governance" (Turnbull 2002a).

2. Is Overpaying Investors Unethical as Well as Being Inefficient and Unequitable?

The reasons why modern PTCs are not efficient, equitable or ethical can be traced back to their development as an institutional arrangement for English Sovereigns to raise revenue while at the same time privatising the cost of empire building.

In medieval times "Bodies corporate" were created by Royal Charters to grant English towns some rights of self-government. The progenitor charter of the "City of London Corporation" dates from 1067. The charter granted to the British East India Company in 1601 provided self-governing powers. Its board was described significantly as a "Court of Governors". The company was given monopoly-trading rights in return for paying a tax on the goods imported while also paying the cost of governing the colony established by the merchants.

Consistent with their role of empire building and governing foreign colonies English corporate charters obtained their rights in perpetuity. As a reaction to the failure of the South Sea Company, English law made it illegal from 1721 to 1825 for twenty or more individuals to form an enterprise without a government charter. In continental Europe however, corporations could be established without a Charter from the Sovereign or a Statute. Instead they were established through a common law charter/shareholder agreement that typically limited the life of the enterprise to around 20 to 30 years (Turnbull, 1998).

The commercial incentive for limited life charters was that it allowed investors to obtain a return *of* their investment as well as a competitive return *on* their investment without the need for the enterprise to be publicly traded. Unlimited life allowed both foreign and local investors to get paid for a longer period than that they required for obtaining the incentive to invest. The overpayment of investors with a surplus incentive to invest represents a "surplus profit". Surplus profits are not reported by accountants nor recognised by economists (Turnbull 2000b: 403, 2006: 451).

Besides providing surplus profits, unlimited life charters allow foreign interests to control local economies as occurred in the US colonies before the American war of independence from 1775 to 1782. "Having thrown off English rule, the revolutionaries did not give governors, judges or generals the authority to charter corporations. Citizens made certain that legislators issued charters, one at a time and for a limited number of years" (Grossman and Adams 2003:6). In addition, corporate charters were rescinded if the business created harm. When the US Supreme Court was asked to overrule the right of New Hampshire to revoke a pre-war charter granted in 1769 by King George III, one legislator stated was such an action would accomplish "what the whole power of the British Empire, after eight years of bloody conflict, failed to achieve against our fathers" (Grossman and Adams 1993: 11).

The 20-year charter of the Second Bank of the United States was not renewed in 1836 even after it provided bribes to Congressman, journalists and "men of distinction" (Galbraith 1976: 80). However, later "a handful of 19th century judges gave corporations more rights in property than human beings enjoyed in their persons" (Grossman and Adams 1993: 4) obtaining unlimited life to accumulate wealth. In addition, corporations bribed legislators and "rewrote the laws governing their own creation" (Grossman and Adams 1993: 16).

Terminating the life of the corporation did not mean that its physical operations were also terminated as illustrated by the many privately constructed US Turnpike highways transferred to public ownership. My alternative proposal to further natural justice is to transfer corporate ownership over time from the investors to the "strategic stakeholders" that no firm can exist without like the employees, suppliers and customers (Turnbull 1997, 2000b: 406–8, 2001).

The transfer of ownership rights from investors to the strategic stakeholders of record would limit the over payment of investors while also distributing wealth to many citizens without the need for taxes and welfare (Turnbull 1975: 98, 2000b: 410). Wealth inequality generates a political mandate for governments to increase the size of welfare payments, taxes and so the size and dead weight cost of government.

The overpayment of investors is not reported by accountants because they do not identify for what period of time investors rely on for obtaining returns to make the investment attractive. The higher the risk then the shorter is the investment time horizon. Venture Capitalist use time horizons that may only be a couple of years while mature firms might use a time horizon of up to ten years.

Investors require certainty in the foreseeable future. Even in mature industries the foreseeable future becomes less than ten years because of: competition, changes in markets, technological obsolescence, social and political changes. In any event, the present value of expected future cash received after ten years becomes trivial when discounted back at a compounded equity opportunity rate (Turnbull 2000b: 409).

In addition, accounting profits under-report the cash received by investors by deducting the returns *of* the investment created by depreciation or depletion allowances from the return *on* the investment. If for example an investment was written off over a five year period, the non cash expense introduced to reduce the reported profit would become 20 percent of the investment each year for five years. As a result, if accounting doctrines were ignored and profits were reported in terms of the cash surplus produced each year another 20 percent would be added to the reported returns on the investment[1].

Surplus profits are inconsistent with the rationale of a market economy to efficiently allocate resources. Surplus profits not shared with those who are essential for their creation represent an injustice. Sharing surplus profits with stakeholders also creates a public good by distributing purchasing power in the economy to maintain production. Distributing wealth in this ways provide a more attractive policy initiative for politicians than the alternative of increasing tax, welfare payments and cost of government (Turnbull 1975: 98).

If ethics are determined by whether justice, rights, the public good or utilitarian outcomes are furthered, then corporations that provide investors with surplus profits do not meet the test of being ethical. One would then be forced to conclude that the contemporary system of corporate capitalism is not ethical. Agendas for mitigating this problem that is one of the "seven deadly sins of capitalism" (Turnbull 2002b) are presented in Turnbull (2004).

Speiser (1989) argues that not "sharing a piece of the action" (Speiser 1977) with employees is unethical. This view is consistent with the concept of "Trusteeship" as articulated by Mahatma Ghandi (1979: 7) who said: "Supposing I have come by a fair amount of wealth—either by way of legacy, or by means of trade and industry—I must know that all that wealth does not belong to me: what belongs to me is the right to an honourable livelihood, no better than that enjoyed by millions of others. The rest of my wealth belongs to the community and must be used for the welfare of the community."

Another way in which PTCs become unethical is from the abuse of power. The concentration of power in PTCs creates unconscionable conflicts of interests for directors. Ironically, it also denies directors the ability to carry out their fundamental fiduciary duty to direct and monitor management. To creditably achieve these objectives directors require information obtained independently of management. It is neither responsible nor creditable for directors to rely *only* on information provided by management to evaluate either management or the business. These problems are the subject of the following Section.

3. The Corrupting Power of Anglo Corporate Charters

This Section considers how the problem of directors possessing excessive and inappropriate powers is created by the constitutions of Anglo PTCs.

All corporations that possess only a single/unitary board provide directors with absolute power to manage their own conflicts of interests. Instability is introduced when these conflicts are compounded in firms controlled by their employees, suppliers and/or customers to explain why demutualisation occurs and why so few such firms exist in Anglo cultures.

However, sustainable employee controlled firms do exist in Anglo cultures but these avoid untenable conflicts by introducing a separation of powers (Turnbull 2000c: 177–98). In some European jurisdictions the law requires corporations to have two or more centres of power (Analytica 1992). The US incorporated Visa International, like the Spanish stakeholder controlled Mondragón Corporación Cooperativa (MCC) has over a hundred boards. Both have proved to be highly efficient and competitive. One reason is that multiple boards introduce distributed: intelligence, monitoring and control with also a reduction in information: overload, processing, and complexity in decision making (Turnbull 2000c: 239–49).

As noted by Lord Acton (1887) "power tends to corrupt and absolute power tends to corrupt absolutely". Directors of a unitary board have absolute power to manage their own conflicts of interest to corrupt both themselves and the business. For example they possess the power to control: their own appointment, remuneration, retirement, management of related party transactions and control of the auditors. All of these powers provide ways to divert value from shareholders or entrench the position of directors while none are required to add value for shareholders. For these reasons it makes good business sense for bankers and Venture Capitalists to provide funds on the condition that they can veto any of these activities. Additional "inappropriate powers" are identified by Monks and Sykes (2002: 9) which would be mitigated, inhibited or eliminated when a company was subject to an agreement with a Venture Capitalist.

Other inappropriate powers by which directors can further their own interests but are not required to add value for shareholders is the power to control meetings of shareholders, count the votes for director election and employ the statutory auditors for additional work.

The legal purpose of appointing a UK statutory auditor reporting to shareholders is different from that for appointing the US regulatory Auditor who reports to both the directors and shareholders (Turnbull 2005b: 55). However, the selection, control and remuneration of the Auditor appointed to judge the accounts of the directors is unethical in both jurisdictions for the same reason that it is not ethical for a person being judged in a court of law to select, control and remunerate the Judge (Shapiro, 2004).

The integrity of Auditors and their profession are compromised by being put in the position of judging the accounts of the directors who pay them. Their creditability if then further compromised by the law requiring them to attest that they are "independent" of those who they are judging when in the ordinary meaning of the word "independent" they are not (Turnbull 2007). Why should the public believe an Audit report when Auditors can legally carry out misleading and deceptive conduct to state that they are "independent"?

Likewise, company directors are forced into an unconscionable conflict of interest of paying those that judge their results. All directors are accountable for the results published in the financial statements whether or not a director is classified as being "independent". Requiring companies to constitute audit committees made of so called "independent directors" does not remove the inherent conflict of interest. It acknowledges the problem but makes its worse by giving false comfort while confusing the role of the internal auditor to check on management with that of the external auditor that in the UK is to provide a check on the directors (Turnbull 2005b: 56).

According to Clarke (2006), "The whole purpose of having independent directors is surprisingly under theorized, leading to inconsistent rules". He goes on to say that "important elements of the concept of and rationale for independent directors remain curiously obscure and unexamined". This has led Rodrigues (2007) to refer to the "fetishization" of independence.

Notwithstanding the unconscionable conflict of interest created for both company directors and auditors, this unethical practice has been institutionalised into law by the Sarbanes-Oxley legislation and enshrined in numerous corporate codes and so called "best practices" in many other jurisdictions. In this way conflicts of interests and unethical practices have become "best practice" and mandated by law! The Sarbanes-Oxley Act has been described as "Quack Corporate Governance" (Romano, 2004) and a case study of its failure reported by Turnbull (2008).

The unethical relationships are avoided in a number of European jurisdictions who require the audit committee to be composed of *shareholders* rather than directors. The author organised shareholders of a start up firm to change its constitution to introduce this approach in an Australian company

(Turnbull 2000a). No change in company law was required and this could apply to many other jurisdictions. A model optional constitution published with the English company's Act of 1862 adopted such a provision and this idea was put forward to the UK government in 2004 by the National Association of Pension Funds (*AccountingAge* 2004).

To justify excessive remuneration, directors and their acolytes chant the mantra that the role of directors is to increase shareholder value. However, this objective is not required by company law and I have never discovered such a requirement written into any corporate constitution. Corporations can be set up as non-profit organisations or as a charity that give away value.

The legal duty of directors in both the US and the UK is to further the interest of "the company as a whole" that courts can interpret in many ways. As no operating company can exist without suppliers, employees and customers it provides a basis for directors to be concerned about these stakeholders as well as the shareholders. It also provides a basis for creditors and bond holders to expect that directors will further their interests as is sometimes upheld by the courts.

To allow directors to take into account the interest of stakeholders, other than shareholders, corporate constitutions could be amended to give various stakeholders constituencies a voice. As the operations, sustainability and profitability of a company is dependent upon the support of its strategic stakeholders it is very much in the interest of shareholders that directors not only hear from stakeholders but to become engaged with them to further their mutual business interests. This is why it makes good business sense to formally recognise stakeholders and give them a voice in the governance of the business.

The formal involvement of employees, suppliers, contractors, distributors, agents, customers and host community in the governance of a business can provide manifold benefits as illustrated in stakeholder controlled firms like the MCC for reasons identified by Turnbull (2000c: 239–49). This is outlined in the next Section that considers how to eliminate, mitigate and/or creditably manage conflicts of interest that can lead to the abuse of power and unethical behaviour.

4. Power to Manage Does Not Require also the Power to Govern

This Section considers how the conflicts of interest of directors can be eliminated, mitigated and/or managed in a creditable and ethical manner. It concludes that the law, regulators, stock-exchange listing rules, corporate governance codes and corporate constitutions are irresponsible in perpetuating unethical conflicts of interests.

Many conflicts of interest arise because directors obtain not only the power to manage the business but to also manage the process by which they govern the business. It is because directors have the power to corrupt both themselves and the business that financiers make it a condition of advancing funds that limits are introduced on the power of directors in such way that the ability of the board to add value to the business is not inhibited.

For example, loan agreements with bankers may require that their approval be obtained for: changes in the auditor, board composition, board remuneration, loans to board members, and major investment decisions. Venture capitalists may require additional limitations and may require one or more nominees to attend board meetings and/or become a director. With bankers, these powers become part of the loan agreement and do not normally involve the shareholders. Venture Capitalists obtain their powers through an agreement with all shareholders as they typically require broader safeguards.

The Articles of Association of a company also represents an agreement among all shareholders as to how the company is to be governed. A shareholder agreement can be used to override these arrangements that represent the constitution of a corporation.

Private corporations normally make the transfer of shares subject to the approval of the directors. Stock Exchanges require companies that wish to be publicly traded to change their constitutions to permit the free transfer of their shares. They may also impose other provisions so the practice of stock exchanges determining how a company is governed is accepted. Corporate law also determines the content of corporate constitutions. So this raises the question as to why Stock Exchanges and Regulators permit firms to become PTCs with directors obtaining the power to corrupt both themselves and the business.

A particular puzzle is why Venture Capitalists (VC) who arrange for a firm to become a PTC do not embed the investor protections provisions of their shareholder agreements in the constitution of their investee corporations. In this way the VC would be able to protect their shareholding and that of the public. It is to protect public investors that Stock Exchanges typically forbid a VC to dispose of all their shares when a company becomes a PTC. However, to become a PTC, Stock Exchanges require VCs to dissolve their shareholder agreements so that no single shareholder has any special overriding powers. However this removes the ability of a VC to protect either their or the public interest!

By embedding in the corporate constitution the checks and balances of shareholder agreement no particular shareholder would obtain special powers to allow all investors to obtain superior investor protection. In addition, the company could obtain superior operating and competitive advantages by engaging with its strategic stakeholders as considered below.

One possible answer to the puzzle of why VCs expose themselves to the risk of being subjected to the abuse of power of inexperienced and/or unethical directors is that they simply have not considered the option of amending the corporate constitution. A reason for this is that universities do not have courses on how to design corporate constitutions because they are widely accepted as a culturally determined given and not an operating design variable.

There are two fundamental design flaws in constitutions of Anglo PTCs: (i) Inappropriate and unethical powers of directors and (ii) absence of systematic process for directors to carry out their fundamental fiduciary duty to monitor and direct management and the business for investors with information that is independent of those they are monitoring and directing.

Some of the other mostly related reasons why it is not rational to trust Anglo PTCs are: (iii) Ability of a dominant shareholder to unfairly and covertly extract value through related party transactions; (iv) Ability of directors to unfairly and covertly extract value from the business; (v) Inability of directors to determine when their trust in management might be misplaced; (vi) Inability of any single director to prevent inappropriate or unethical behaviour; (vii) Ability to manage the external auditor to present the accounts in a manner of their choosing; (viii) Ability of directors to control the manner in which they become accountable to shareholders by controlling general meetings including the counting of votes and the exercise of proxy votes; (ix) Ability of directors to use inside information to trades shares in the company without the counter party being informed whether or not the director later make public their trading, and in large complex organisation (x) Information overload to inhibit and/or confuse decision making. These and other 'Corrupting powers of a unitary board' are presented in Table 3.6 of Turnbull (2000c: 115).

To overcome the first two fundamental flaws in Anglo corporate constitutions and many of their derivative problems, two amendments are required to introduce: (a) Checks and balances on the powers of directors and (b) Processes for directors to systematically obtain feedback and feed forward information from corporate stakeholders other than the shareholders, independently of management on the SWOT of the management and the business.

There are innumerable ways in which corporate constitutions can be designed so there is no one size that can fit all situations. There are various approaches by which the power of directors to manage the business can be separated from their power to govern the firm without inhibiting performance. US legal scholar, Dallas (1997) suggested a "Dual board and board ombudsperson". In Australia I introduced a second board described as a "Corporate Senate" in a start up company to allow it to raise funds more efficiently. Details are provided in Turnbull (2000a). It was modelled on the "Watchdog Boards" established in the MCC.

The three member Corporate Senate was elected by shareholders on a democratic basis of one vote per *shareholder* rather than the plutocratic basis of one vote per *share.* This arrangement protected investors by the Senate having veto powers over any action in which any director had a conflict of interest. The executive powers of the Senate were limited to appointing and controlling the auditor and controlling shareholder meetings. The Senate became a shareholder audit committee. Because it could veto any director conflict of interest it could also take on part of the role of a remuneration or nomination committee.

While directors were elected on the basis of one vote per share, each share obtains as many votes as there were vacancies on the board so that votes can be accumulated onto any specific director(s). This form of preferential voting is described as "cumulative voting" that is mandated in some jurisdictions like the Philippines where family controlled PTCs are dominant. Cumulative voting (Bhagat and Brickley 1984) can allow minority shareholders of a PTC, even if it is a subsidiary of another company, the power to elect one or more directors. In this way one of more directors can be elected independently of any parent company or dominant investor.

Cumulative voting provides the basis for a single director to obtain the will to privately blow the whistle to the Corporate Senate on unethical actions. The board still had the power to convene a meeting a shareholders to overturn a veto voting on a one share per vote basis but they would not have the power to control the meeting and there would be an organised and public "loyal opposition" to their actions. If a major shareholder did overturn a Senate veto then market forces could come into play by introducing a discount on the value of their shares.

A necessary but insufficient condition for a director to act independently is to have the: (i) the information to act; (ii) the will to act and (iii) the ability to act. Cumulative voting can provide directors with the will to act to be a whistle blower privately and also secure his re-appointment to the board. With its veto power the Senate can provide a single director with the ability to act privately to prevent her/his colleagues and/or any dominant shareholder making unethical decisions. However, to obtain operational information to act directors also need a systematic process for obtaining information independently of management.

Stakeholders can provide information for the directors, independently of management on both the SWOT of management and the business. To allow strategic stakeholders like employees, suppliers and customers the will and means to inform directors, advisory stakeholder forums are required which can be established independently of management. It is for this reason that the creation of Stakeholder Advisor Councils by stakeholders needs to be embedded in the corporate constitution.

Different stakeholder constituencies require their own separate advisory forums according to the nature of the business and the operating relationships. There are compelling reasons for both directors and shareholders to approve changes in corporate constitutions to allow stakeholders to organise their own advisory councils like Citizen Utility Boards established in the US (Givens 1991) or a Keiretsu Council in Japan.

For Directors, stakeholder councils empower them with information to carry out their fundamental fiduciary responsibility of monitoring and directing management and the business independently of management. They provide directors a way to systematically challenge the hegemony of management information and obtain the other side of management reports. It also allows directors to cross check the information provided by management to detect any biases, errors and omissions that are intrinsic in hierarchical systems as analysed by Downs (1967). For both the reasons it is in the interest of shareholders to support the formation of Stakeholder advisory forums.

Stakeholder forums also provide a framework for managers to work with suppliers to monitor Just In Time delivery of supplies and work with customers on Total Quality Control of goods and services. Research by Hippel (1986) found that most product innovations were contributed by customers rather than the R & D department of a firm. It is in these ways that Stakeholder Councils can improve operations and competitive advantages (Turnbull 1997, 2005a).

The introduction of watchdog boards and stakeholder councils creates "network governance" as found in living systems (Turnbull 2002a). Jones, Hesterly and Borgatti (1997) describe how competitive pressures in complex dynamic industries forces firms to adopt network governance. The reasons why network governance allows ordinary people to achieve extraordinary results as found in the MCC outlined in Section 3 and as explained by Turnbull (2000c: 239–49).

Network governance not only creates a division of power to remove and manage conflicts of interests but also introduces a requisite variety of communication channels, control and decision making processes to minimize errors and improve operations. Network governance as outlined in this reading indicates why so called "best corporate governance practices" are both unethical and less competitive.

End Note

1. It also means that directors can report a profit when a loss results. Consider a company that only owned an uninsured investment described above that was destroyed shortly after a profit was reported for its first year of operation. The return *of* the investment would be less than 40.

Note: Notes and references removed for publication here, but are available on the book website at www.mhhe.com/busethics2e.

Reading **10-4**

How Much Compensation Can CEOs Permissibly Accept?

Jeffrey Moriarty

Executive compensation has received a great deal of attention. This is due, in part, to the large amounts of pay executives, especially CEOs, receive. In 2006, the median total compensation of the top 150 U.S. CEOs was $10.1 million. This is 314 times the $32,142 earned by the median full-time private industry worker in the U.S. that year. This paper examines some moral aspects of executive compensation. It is not the first to do so, but it engages the issue from a new perspective. I focus on the duties *executives themselves* have with respect to *their own* compensation, and argue that CEOs' fiduciary duties place a moral limit on how much compensation they can seek or accept from their firms. Accepting excessive compensation leaves the beneficiaries of their duties (e.g., shareholders) worse off, and thus is inconsistent with observing those duties. Like others who write on executive compensation, I am primarily interested in chief executive officer compensation. By 'executive', then, I mean principally 'CEO'. However, most of what I say applies, with minor modifications, to the pay of other top executives.

1. The CEO's Fiduciary Duty

I begin with the common assumption that executives are fiduciaries. What does this mean? Marcoux explains, "[t]o act as a fiduciary means to place the interests of [a] beneficiary ahead of one's own interests and, obviously, those of third parties, with respect to the administration of some asset(s) or project(s)" (2003: 3). In the CEO's case, the asset or project is the firm. So, CEOs are required insofar as they are fiduciaries to place one party's interests ahead of their own and others' when managing the firm. That is, they have a *fiduciary duty* to do so.

According to some writers, CEOs are fiduciaries for shareholders (Boatright, 1994; Marcoux, 2003). According to others, they are fiduciaries for all stakeholders (Evan & Freeman, 2005). The moral limit I identify exists if CEOs are fiduciaries for *anyone* who stands to lose when CEOs accept excessive compensation. This includes shareholders, stakeholders, and certain other parties. To fix ideas, however, I assume that CEOs are fiduciaries for shareholders.

I further assume that CEOs are fiduciaries in a *moral,* not merely *legal,* sense. To determine whether CEOs' fiduciary duties in law have implications for their pay negotiations with directors, all that is required is to look at the relevant law. My goal is to determine to what, if any, implications CEOs' moral fiduciary duties have for their negotiations with directors.

Assuming that CEOs have fiduciary duties in the moral sense (hereafter, I drop this qualifier), what follows about how they should manage their firms? It is standardly assumed that shareholders want to maximize the monetary value of their investments. Thus, in his classic defense of shareholder theory, Friedman says that a CEO is obligated "to conduct the business in accordance with [his employers'] desires, which generally will be to make as much money as possible" (2005: 8). Let us assume that shareholder value is maximized when firm value, which Jensen defines as "the market values of the equity, debt, and any other contingent claims outstanding on the firm" (2002: 239), is maximized. If so, then executives should manage the firm so as to maximize its value. Managing the firm this way has implications for how much compensation a CEO can permissibly seek or accept from it.

Compensation produces value for the firm by attracting and retaining talented employees, and motivating them to do their best. But compensation is a cost. Other things equal—where "other things" includes the firm's performance—the lower this cost is, the better. It is widely believed that directors have a duty to minimize this cost. I claim that *CEOs themselves* do too. Suppose a compensation package worth $10 million is sufficient to induce a CEO to do his best for the firm, i.e., to maximize its value, so far as he is able. But suppose that the CEO would also do his best if he were paid only $9 million. Then he should refuse the larger package in favor of the smaller one. Now suppose that, if the CEO were paid $8 million, he would not do his best, and the firm would be worse off by more than $1 million. In this case, the CEO is justified in accepting the $9 million package. In general, the optimum amount of compensation for a CEO is the amount that maximizes firm value, taking into account the cost of the compensation. Of course, a CEO is unlikely to work, or work hard, for free.[1] She will require some, perhaps even a lot, of pay. And shareholders are willing to pay for talent. Hiring a talented but expensive CEO, and properly motivating her, produces more net value for the firm than hiring an untalented but inexpensive one, or failing to properly motivate her. But still what is best for shareholders is that they pay the (talented) CEO no more than is necessary to attract, retain, and motivate her. The CEO's fiduciary duty prohibits her from accepting more than this amount.

Let us call this amount—i.e., the minimum necessary to attract, retain, and motivate the CEO to maximize firm value—her *minimum effective compensation,* or MEC. This amount is *effective* because it succeeds in attracting, retaining, and motivating the CEO, and *minimum* because no less would do. Let us further assume, as is standard, that the CEO is motivated exclusively by self-interested considerations, i.e., she is not intrinsically motivated by shareholders' interests. (Later in the paper I examine the implications of relaxing this assumption.) Finally, let us define "excessive compensation" for a CEO as compensation in excess of her MEC.

In economic terms, a CEO's MEC is her "reservation wage" for the job, i.e., the amount necessary for her to accept and retain it, unless, as is often the case, extra pay (e.g., in the form of performance-based incentives) would motivate her to produce an amount of extra revenue for the firm that exceeds the amount of the extra compensation. In this case, the CEO's MEC includes the *minimum amount* necessary to produce that extra revenue. A CEO's MEC will be a function of her next best alternative, including working for another firm, or not working at all. This in turn will depend on her talents, preferences, and market conditions. Note that the CEO's MEC is *not* defined in terms of what she is "worth," understood as how much revenue she adds to the firm (compared to the next most effective available candidate). So it is possible for an amount of compensation to be more than a CEO's MEC but less than her worth. However, the more revenue the CEO adds to the firm, the better alternative offers she will have. So her MEC and worth will tend to converge in a free market.

As I have suggested, the CEO's fiduciary duty entails not only a duty not to *seek* more than her MEC in negotiation, but a duty not to *accept* more than her MEC if it is offered. To illustrate: Richard Grasso, former head of the New York Stock Exchange (NYSE), famously was awarded a $187 million compensation package. In his defense, Grasso said he never had a "two-way dialogue" with the NYSE's directors about his pay. Assuming that $187 million was more than necessary to attract, retain, and motivate Grasso, this does not excuse his behavior. CEOs do not avoid blame by simply staying out of the pay setting process, as they would in a standard conflict-of-interest situation. They are required by their fiduciary duty to be proactive about ensuring that they do not receive excessive pay.

2. Objections and Replies

I have argued for a new moral limit on CEO compensation: CEOs should not accept excessive compensation—i.e., more than their MECs—from their firms. In this section, I defend it against objections.

Objection 1. This moral limit is moot: a CEO will never accept excessive compensation, because it will never be offered to her. Directors will make sure she gets paid no more than is necessary to attract, retain, and motivate her. Market pressures will aid directors in this effort.

Response. This objection assumes that directors are highly powerful and knowledgeable with respect to the CEO. Against this, first, many writers have argued that pay negotiations between CEOs and directors are not carried out at arm's-length, and in particular, that directors do not aggressively represent shareholders' interests at the bargaining table (Bebchuk & Fried, 2004). Second, even if they have the will to achieve the optimal result, directors are likely to be ignorant of what it is. Knowing, as they often do, the average compensation of CEOs of comparable firms does not tell them the precise minimum effective compensation of their *particular* CEO. Thus, we have reason to believe that it is possible for executives to receive excessive pay, and hence that it is worth determining whether or not they are morally permitted to.

Objection 2. When a CEO negotiates her compensation, she is not yet a member of the firm. The employment agreement through which she becomes a fiduciary has not been made. So, she does not yet have a fiduciary duty to the firm's shareholders and, as a result, is not yet forbidden to accept excessive compensation.

Response. This objection does not apply to CEOs who are negotiating *subsequent* compensation packages with their firms. Nor does it apply to CEOs negotiating their *first* compensation packages with a firm who are promoted to the CEO's position from within the firm's top management. Both kinds of CEO are already top managers in their firms, and so have fiduciary duties to their firms' shareholders. The objection applies, then, only to CEOs who come from outside the firm, and only when they are negotiating their first compensation packages. Although the number of outsider CEOs has increased in recent years, approximately 75% of new CEOs are insiders (Jensen, Murphy, & Wruck, 2004). In addition, at least half of CEOs engage in subsequent compensation negotiations while in office. Thus, the substantial majority of CEO compensation negotiations are immune from this objection.

Even given its limited target, however, the objection fails. Whether or not *some* CEOs lack fiduciary duties to shareholders when they negotiate their compensation packages (e.g., because they are outsiders), *all* CEOs have these duties when they receive them. This effectively prevents all CEOs from seeking in negotiation, or accepting, more than their MECs. Consider an example. C, an outsider, is soon to become the CEO of firm F. C negotiates her compensation package before she starts working for F. Call this time T1. She begins to receive the agreed upon compensation once she starts work. Call this time T2. Because C is not a member of F at T1, C does not have fiduciary duties to F's shareholders at T1. However, C will be a member of F at T2, and will have fiduciaries duties to F's shareholders at that time. Thus, at T2, C cannot accept more than her MEC. Given that C will receive the agreed upon compensation at T2, it would be wrong for her to seek more than her MEC at T1.

I am not claiming that, if a person has a duty at T2, and T2 is later than T1, then she has that duty at T1. This claim is easily refuted. Suppose a person who is now 30 will be a parent when she is 31. At 31, she will have a duty to care for her child. But it doesn't follow that she has a duty to care for her (or any) child now, when she is 30. Nevertheless, the fact that the 30 year old *will have* a duty to care for her child at 31 constrains what she can do at 30. She cannot at 30 promise a friend to devote all of her resources and attention when she is 31 to political activism in a distant nation, for she will be obligated, and knows she will be obligated, to care for her child at that time. In the same way, since C is negotiating at T1 the nature of an event that will occur at T2, the duties she will have at T2 constrain her actions at T1.

Objection 3. CEOs are not required *always* to act so as to maximally benefit shareholders. They are only required to do so when they are acting *as managers,* i.e., managing the firm. So, for example, when they are acting *as parents,* i.e., raising their children, they need not act so as to maximally benefit shareholders by, say, trying to persuade their children to buy their firms' products. The same goes for when CEOs are acting as players on a softball team or members of a neighborhood watch. On this objection, when CEOs are negotiating their pay, they are not acting as managers. Put another way, this is not something they need be concerned with in their role as managers. Here they can act *as private citizens:* they are free of the fiduciary duty to shareholders, and so are free to accept excessive compensation.

Response. The claim that CEOs are required to maximize shareholder return only insofar as they are acting as managers is correct. It would be absurd to suppose that they are required to do so in every facet of their lives. However, the claim that, when they are negotiating the terms of their compensation, they are free to act as private citizens and not as managers, is wrong. Surely, the question of how much to pay a firm's workers is a business decision. Attracting, retaining, and motivating talented workers—while not overpaying them—is crucial to a firm's success. So, the CEO's fiduciary duty to shareholders to maximize firm value requires that she concern herself, at some level, with the compensation of the firm's employees. But the CEO is an employee too, so it follows that she must concern herself, *as a manager,* with her own compensation. In examining the firm's payroll to determine whether any cuts can be made to boost firm value, she cannot exclude her own pay from consideration. Much as she might like to be free of the duty not to accept excessive compensation, she is not.

Objection 4. A party to whom a duty is owed can waive its performance, wholly or in part. If they do, the party who owes the duty is not obligated to perform it. I can release you from your duty to drive me wherever I want with respect to, say, driving me to the airport. According to this objection, shareholders—or their representatives, the directors—have done something similar with respect to the CEO's fiduciary duty. While generally leaving it in place, they have waived it in the context of determining the CEO's pay. They have not done so explicitly, by declaring the duty to be waived, but they have done so implicitly, by employing a negotiation to set the CEO's pay. Employing an *adversarial* process signals that, in this context, the CEO's fiduciary duties are suspended: directors are safeguarding the firm's interests, and the CEO can do as she pleases, including accept excessive compensation.

Response. To be clear, the issue is not whether the CEO and directors (merely) *recognize* the application of the CEO's fiduciary duty to the pay setting process. This duty can apply even if it is not thought to apply. The issue is whether directors have *waived* its observance. The objection claims that they have.

In response, it is not clear, first, that directors *can* waive executives' fiduciary duties. Just because one is owed a duty—in the sense that one is the beneficiary of it—does not mean one has the power to waive it. I cannot waive your duty not to enslave me, though I benefit from your observance of it. If your duty to me is based on a contract we have entered into, then I can waive its performance. Thus, if the foundation of your duty to drive me wherever I want is that you have promised me to do so, then I can waive your duty. But it is not clear that the CEO's fiduciary duty to shareholders is contractually based. Boatright, for example, argues that the reason executives owe fiduciary duties to shareholders (as opposed to others) is that this is "the most socially beneficial system of economic organization" (1994: 401). If he is right, then *directors* cannot waive CEOs' fiduciary duties. It does not follow, of course, that they cannot be waived *simpliciter*. But if anyone can waive them, it is society as a whole.

For the sake of argument, however, let us suppose that directors can waive CEOs' fiduciary duties. According to the objection, the evidence that they have done so in the context of setting the CEO's pay is that the process used to determine it is adversarial in nature. This is poor evidence. At present, the CEOs' duties not to accept more than their MECs is not widely recognized, so it would be foolish for directors to allow them a free hand in setting their own pay. Even if this duty were recognized, directors might still wish to retain the negotiation as a way to protect the firm. CEOs will be tempted to seek excessive compensation, even if they know they should not.

Objection 5. According to commonsense morality, while people are sometimes required to benefit others at their own expense, they are not required to make enormous sacrifices for them. For example, this morality would have us give some—perhaps even a substantial amount—of our wealth to the poor, but not so much that we end up impoverished ourselves. Prohibiting the CEO from accepting excessive compensation, according to this objection, places too great a burden on him—i.e., it is too demanding—and cannot be justified by his fiduciary duty.

Response. This is simply implausible. Recall that excessive compensation is compensation in excess of the CEO's MEC, which is in turn of a function of his next best option. Since a CEO's MEC depends on his particular talents and preferences, it is difficult or even impossible to identify what any given CEO's MEC is. But few deny that CEOs are (at least perceived to be) highly talented individuals who can command considerable premiums for their labor. As a result, every CEO is likely to have at least one other very high-paying option for work. This means that their MECs will be very high—far higher than the compensation of the average worker. Given this, it is implausible to suppose that prohibiting the CEO from accepting excessive compensation is too demanding. To be sure, a CEO who refuses to accept more than his MEC might have to refuse a large sum of money. But it doesn't follow that the burden he is under is heavy, given how high his MEC is likely to be.

Objection 6. The prohibition against accepting more than one's MEC discriminates against steward CEOs, i.e., CEOs who are intrinsically motivated by shareholders' interests (Davis, Schoorman, & Donaldson, 1997). Because of this motivation, it takes less compensation, other things equal, to attract, retain, and motivate a steward CEO than an agent CEO, i.e., one who is motivated only by self-interested considerations (Wasserman, 2006). So it seems that the steward CEO accepts more than his MEC at a lower compensation level than the agent CEO. But intuitively, the former is more virtuous than the latter. The prohibition against accepting more than one's MEC thus punishes the steward CEO for his virtue.

Response. This objection misunderstands the definition of MEC. I said that a CEO accepts more than his MEC when he accepts more pay than is necessary to attract, retain, and motivate him to maximize firm value, *assuming he is acting on self-interested motives only.* This assumption is not an empirical conjecture but a normative standard. The MEC is defined relative to the compensation demands of the agent CEO. So, a steward CEO who seeks more than he *actually needs* to be attracted, retained, and motivated does not accept more than his MEC, if that is not more than what he *would need* if he were acting on self-interested motives only.

It is nevertheless true that whether a CEO accepts more than his MEC is in large part a personal matter. It depends on the CEO's particular situation—whether he, given his preferences and options, would work just as hard for the firm for less. This has two important implications. First, one CEO's MEC may be less than another's, even when all else, besides their preferences and options, is equal. One CEO's preference for leisure might be stronger than the other's. Second, it will be difficult or impossible to tell "from the outside" whether a CEO is accepting more than her MEC. The prospects, then, for enforcing a ban on doing so is dim. Some might regard this as problematic for my argument. It might be if my claim were that there should be a *law* against accepting more than one's MEC, so that violators should be subject to civil or criminal penalties. But my claim is that CEOs have a *moral duty* to accept no more than their MECs. The validity of a moral rule does not depend on its enforceability.

3. How Low Should CEOs Go?

Objection 6 raises an important issue which we have so far bracketed. We have measured the CEO's MEC by a partly objective standard, viz., that of the agent CEO. It is the minimum necessary to attract, retain, and motivate him to maximize firm value *assuming he is acting on self-interested motives only.* But, it might be said, while it is desirable to have *some* objective standard for measuring the CEO's MEC, why choose this one? Instead of pegging it to the motivational set of the agent CEO, why not peg it to the motivational set of the steward CEO i.e., the CEO who is intrinsically motivated by shareholders' interests?

If we adopt the steward CEO as our standard, the prohibition on driving a hard bargain becomes more burdensome. As seen, because they are intrinsically motivated by their fiduciary duties, steward CEOs need less money to maximize firm value, other things equal, than agent CEOs (Wasserman, 2006). The more weight the fiduciary duty gets in the CEO's motivational set—i.e., the more of a steward he is—the less money he needs. At the limit, if we choose as our standard the maximally "steward-like" CEO, then it seems the CEO can permissibly accept very little, or even no, pay.

We see now why it makes sense to start, as we did, with the assumption that CEOs are agents. This minimizes the burden imposed on the CEO by the prohibition against accepting excessive pay. If this weak burden cannot be justified, then no stronger one can be. But since the former is justified, it makes sense to inquire into whether the latter can be. Our question is, how much weight should the CEO give to his fiduciary duty in his motivational set, as compared to self-interested considerations? To what extent should he do what is best for shareholders (viz., accept less and less pay), and to what extent can he do what is best for himself (viz., accept more and more pay)? Answering this question requires weighing the force of the CEO's fiduciary duty against moral considerations on the other side.

The CEO's fiduciary duty is thought to have considerable weight. It is appealed to to justify laying off workers and moving plants to foreign countries, despite the burdens these actions impose on employees and communities. It is also thought to justify prohibiting CEOs from shirking, hiring unqualified friends, and empire-building, despite the burdens these prohibitions impose on CEOs.

But if we take seriously, as many do, the idea that morality doesn't require people to take on *enormous* burdens in order to do what is right, then there is a limit to this duty's force. Having to accept a job as a CEO on the condition that one accepts very little compensation is a heavy burden not only on the CEO, but on his family. It is unlikely that the CEO's fiduciary duty requires this level of sacrifice.

Moreover, it is probable that what is best for the firm is not that the CEO accept *very* little compensation. There must be incentives for others, both inside and outside the firm, to aspire to the CEO's position. One such incentive is high pay for the CEO. This is stressed by tournament theory, according to which employees in the firm work hard to win the "prize" of being CEO. In this way, the CEO may be *required* by her fiduciary duty to receive a large amount of compensation. This is not to say that in some cases the CEO is justified in accepting more than her MEC, but that in some cases her MEC, which she may be required to accept, may be de-coupled from the minimum amount necessary to attract, retain, and motivate *her.* The "effectiveness" of compensation is a function of its effects on firm value. We have assumed, consistently with firms' own justifications of their executive compensation packages, that the utility of these packages results from their attracting, retaining, and motivating the very persons who receive them. But if their utility results from motivating *others,* then this must be taken into account in determining the most effective amount of pay.

Finally, it may be good not only for individual firms but for society as a whole if CEOs negotiate in their self-interest, at least to an extent. If CEO compensation is too low, few people will want to become CEOs. They will seek work as, e.g., lawyers or investment advisors. But society as a whole benefits when talented people occupy these important and demanding positions (Jensen & Murphy, 1990). One way to make it more likely that they do is for CEOs to be highly paid. And one way to promote this is to encourage self-interested negotiation by CEOs.[2]

In sum, while the CEO's fiduciary duty exerts downward pressure on her compensation by encouraging selfless negotiation over compensation, it is unlikely to tell in favor of her receiving very little pay. And other considerations tell in favor of (permitting) more self-interested negotiation and thus higher compensation. Determining where the balance of considerations lies—i.e., how self-interestedly the CEO can and should act when negotiating her pay—is a complex inquiry lying outside the scope of this paper. It will be important in this inquiry to identify the foundational moral values that justify the CEO's fiduciary duty, and evaluate the extent to which they are promoted or thwarted by selfless negotiation over compensation. Whatever the outcome, my more modest conclusions seem safe, viz., that CEOs' fiduciaries duties apply in the pay setting context, and imply (minimally) that they should accept no more than their MECs, assuming that they are acting on self-interested motives only. Most people believe only that directors have a duty not to award CEOs excessive pay; I have argued that CEOs also have a duty not to accept excessive pay.

End Notes

1. But, it might be said, *shouldn't* she? After all, this would be *best* for shareholders. I explore this suggestion below.
2. But if this is the reason for high(er) CEO pay, one might wonder why its cost should fall entirely on shareholders, as opposed to the general public.

References

Note: Notes and references removed for publication here, but are available on the book website at www.mhhe.com/busethics2e.

Glossary

A

affirmative action A policy or a program that strives to redress past discrimination through the implementation of proactive measures to ensure equal opportunity. In other words, affirmative action is the intentional inclusion of previously excluded groups. Affirmative action efforts can take place in employment environments, education, or other arenas.

autonomy From the Greek for "self-ruled," autonomy is the capacity to make free and deliberate choices. The capacity for autonomous action is what explains the inherent dignity and intrinsic value of individual human beings.

B

backcasting As developed as part of the Natural Step, involves imagining what a sustainable future must hold. From that vision, creative businesses then look backwards to the present and determine what must be done to arrive at that future.

biomimicry ("closed-loop" production) Seeks to integrate what is presently waste back into production in much the way that biological processes turn waste into food.

bounded ethicality One's tendency to consider one's own actions ethics even though they might condemn those same actions in others, or even in themselves if they were to engage in further reflection or awareness.

C

categorical imperative An imperative is a command or duty; "categorical" means that it is without exception. Thus a categorical imperative is an overriding principle of ethics. Philosopher Immanual Kant offered several formulations of the categorical imperative: act so as the maxim implicit in your acts could be willed to be a universal law; treat persons as ends and never as means only; treat others as subjects, not objects.

***caveat emptor* approach:** *Caveat emptor* means "buyer beware" in Latin and this approach suggests that the burden of risk of information shall be placed on the buyer. This perspective assumes that every purchase involves the informed consent of the buyer and therefore it is assumed to be ethically legitimate.

change blindness A decision-making omission that occurs when decision makers fail to notice gradual changes over time.

character The sum of relatively set traits, dispositions, and habits of an individual. Along with rational deliberation and choice, a person's character accounts for how she or he makes decisions and acts. Training and developing character so that it is disposed to act ethically is the goal of virtue ethics.

child labor Though the term literally signifies children who work, it has taken on the meaning of exploitative work that involves some harm to a child who is not of an age to justify his or her presence in the workplace. The elements of that definition—harm, age of the child, justification to be in the workplace relative to other options—remain open to social and economic debate. UNICEF's 1997 State of the World's Children Report explains, "Children's work needs to be seen as happening along a continuum, with destructive or exploitative work at one end and beneficial work—promoting or enhancing children's development without interfering with their schooling, recreation and rest—at the other. And between these two poles are vast areas of work that need not negatively affect a child's development."

code of conduct A set of behavioral guidelines and expectations that govern all members of a business firm.

Committee of Sponsoring Organizations (COSO) COSO is a voluntary collaboration designed to improve financial reporting through a combination of controls and governance standards called the Internal Control–Integrated Framework. It was established in 1985 by five of the major professional accounting and finance associations originally to study fraudulent financial reporting and later developed standards for publicly held companies. It has become one of the most broadly accepted audit systems for internal controls.

common-law agency test A persuasive indicator of independent contractor status that provides the employer the ability to control the manner in which the work is performed. Under the common-law agency approach, the employer need not actually control the work, but must merely have the right or ability to control the work for a worker to be classified an employee.

compliance-based culture A corporate culture in which obedience to laws and regulations is the prevailing model for ethical behavior.

conflict of interest A conflict of interest exists where a person holds a position of trust that requires that she or he exercise judgment on behalf of others, but where her/his personal interests and/or obligations conflict with those others.

consequentialist theories Ethical theories, such as utilitarianism, that determine right and wrong by calculating the consequences of actions.

control environment One of the five elements that comprise the control structure, similar to the culture of an organization, and support people in the achievement of the organization's objectives. The control environment "sets the tone of an organization, influencing the control consciousness of its people."

Corporate Automotive Fuel Efficiency (CAFE) Standards Established by the Energy Policy Conservation Act of 1975, Corporate Average Fuel Economy (CAFE) is the sales-weighted average fuel economy, expressed in miles per gallon (mpg), of a manufacturer's fleet of passenger cars or light Trucks. The U.S. federal government establishes CAFE standards as a means of increasing fuel efficiency of automobiles.

corporate governance The structure by which corporations are managed, directed, and controlled towards the objectives of fairness, accountability, and transparency. The structure generally will determine the relationship between the board of directors, the shareholders or owners of the firm, and the firm's executives or management.

corporate social responsibility The responsibilities that businesses have to the societies within which they operate. In various contexts, it may also refer to the voluntary actions that companies undertake to address economic, social, and environmental impacts of its business operations and the concerns of its principal stakeholders. The European Commission defines CSR as "a concept whereby companies decide voluntarily to contribute to a better society and a cleaner environment." Specifically, CSR suggests that a business identify its stakeholder groups and incorporate its needs and values within its strategic and operational decision-making process.

corporate sustainability report Provides all stakeholders with financial and other information regarding a firm's economic, environmental and social performance.

cradle-to-cradle responsibility Holds that a business should be responsible for incorporating the end results of its products back into the productive cycle.

culture A shared pattern of beliefs, expectations, and meanings that influences and guides the thinking and behaviors of the members of a particular group.

D

deontological ethics Derived from the Greek word for "duty," deontological ethics stresses the ethical centrality of such things as duties, principles, and obligations. It denies that all ethical judgments can be made in terms of consequences.

descriptive ethics As practiced by many social scientists, provides a descriptive and empirical account of those standards that actually guide behavior, as opposed to those standards that should guide behavior. Contrast with *normative ethics,* below.

diversity Diversity refers to the presence of differing cultures, languages, ethnicities, races, affinity orientations, genders, religious sects, abilities, social classes, ages, and national origins of the individuals in a firm. When used in connection with the corporate environment, it often encompasses the values of respect, tolerance, inclusion, and acceptance.

downsize The reduction of human resources at an organization through terminations, retirements, corporate divestments, or other means.

due process The right to be protected against the arbitrary use of authority. In legal contexts, due process refers to the procedures that police and courts must follow in exercising their authority over citizens. In the employment context, due process specifies the conditions for basic fairness within the scope of the employer's authority over its employees.

duties Those obligations that one is bound to perform, regardless of consequences. Duties might be derived from basic ethical principles, from the law, or from one's institutional or professional role.

duty of care Involves the exercise of reasonable care by a board member to ensure that the corporate executives with whom she or he works carry out their management responsibilities and comply with the law in the best interests of the corporation.

duty of good faith Requires obedience, compelling board members to be faithful to the organization's mission. In other words, they are not permitted to act in a way that is inconsistent with the central goals of the organization.

duty of loyalty Requires faithfulness; a board member must give undivided allegiance when making decisions affecting the organization. This means that conflicts of interest are always to be resolved in favor of the corporation.

E

eco-efficiency Doing more with less. Introduced at the Rio Earth Summit in 1992, the concept of eco-efficiency is a way business can contribute to sustainability by reducing resource usage in its production cycle.

economic model of CSR Limits a firm's social responsibility to the minimal economic responsibility of producing goods and service and maximizing profits within the law.

economic realties test A test by which courts consider whether the worker is economically dependent on the business or, as a matter of economic fact, is in business for him- or herself.

egoism As a psychological theory, egoism holds that all people act only from self-interest. Empirical evidence strongly suggests that this is a mistaken account of human motivation. As an ethical theory, egoism holds that humans ought to act for their own self-interest. Ethical egoists typically distinguish between one's perceived best interests and one's true best interests.

Electronic Communications Privacy Act of 1986 The United States statute that establishes the provisions for access, use, disclosure, interception, and privacy protections relating to electronic communications.

e-mail monitoring The maintenance and either periodic or random review of e-mail communications of employees or others for a variety of business purposes.

employment at will (EAW) The legal doctrine that holds that, absent a particular contractual or other legal obligation that specifies the length or conditions of employment, all employees are employed "at will." Unless an agreement specifies otherwise, employers are free to fire an employee at any time and for any reason. In the same manner, an EAW worker may opt to leave a job at any time for any reason, without offering any notice at all; so the freedom is *theoretically* mutual.

Enron Corporation An energy company based in Houston, Texas, that *Fortune* magazine named America's most innovative company for six consecutive years before it was discovered to have been involved in one of the largest instances of accounting fraud in world history. In 2001, with over 21,000 employees, it filed the largest bankruptcy in United States history and disclosed a scandal that resulted in the loss of millions of dollars, thousands of jobs, the downfall of Big Five accounting firm Arthur Andersen LLP, at least one suicide, and several trials and convictions, among other consequences. Enron remains in business today as it continues to liquidate its assets.

ethical decision-making process Requires a persuasive and rational justification for a decision. Rational justifications are developed through a logical process of decision making that gives proper attention to such things as facts, alternative perspectives, consequences to all stakeholders, and ethical principles.

ethical relativism An important perspective within the philosophical study of ethics, which holds that ethical values and judgments are ultimately dependent upon, or relative to, one's culture, society, or personal feelings. Relativism denies that we can make rational or objective ethical judgments.

ethical values Those properties of life that contribute to human well-being and a life well lived. Ethical values would include such things as happiness, respect, dignity, integrity, freedom, companionship, health.

ethics Derived from the Greek word *ethos,* which refers to those values, norms, beliefs, and expectations that determine how people within a culture live and act. Ethics steps back from such standards for how people *do* act, and reflects on the standards by which people *should* live and act. At its most basic level, ethics is concerned with how we act and how we live our lives. Ethics involves what is perhaps the most monumental question any human being can ask: How *should* we live? Following from this original Greek usage, ethics can refer to both the standards by which an individual chooses to live her/his own personal life, and the standards by which individuals live in community with others (see *morality* below). As a branch of philosophy, ethics is the discipline that systematically studies questions of how we ought to live our lives.

ethics officers Individuals within an organization charged with managerial oversight of ethical compliance and enforcement within the organization.

European Union's Directive on Personal Data Protection E.U. legislation seeking to remove potential obstacles to cross-border flows of personal data, to ensure a high level of protection within the European Union, and to harmonize protections across the European continent and with those countries with whom E.U. countries do business.

European Union 8th Directive Covers many of the same issues as Sarbanes-Oxley but applies these requirements and restrictions to companies traded on European Union exchanges. The updates to the directive in 2005 clarified required duties, independence, and ethics of statutory auditors and called for public oversight of the accounting profession and external quality assurance of both audit and financial reporting processes. In addition, the directive strives to improve cooperation between E.U. oversight bodies and provides for effective and balanced international regulatory cooperation with oversight bodies outside the E.U. regulatory infrastructure (e.g., the U.S. Public Company Accounting Oversight Board).

F

Federal Sentencing Guidelines for Organizations (FSGO) Developed by the United States Sentencing Commission and implemented in 1991, originally as mandatory parameters for judges to use during organizational sentencing cases. By connecting punishment to prior business practices, the guidelines establish legal norms for ethical business behavior. However, since a 2005 Supreme Court decision, the FSG are now considered to be discretionary in nature and offer some specifics for organizations about ways to mitigate eventual fines and sentences by integrating bona fide ethics and compliance programs throughout their organizations.

fiduciary duties A legal duty to act on behalf of or in the interests of another.

"Four Ps" of marketing Production, price, promotion, and placement.

Fourth Amendment protections The U.S. Constitution's Fourth Amendment protection against unreasonable search and seizure extends privacy protections to the public sector workplace through the Constitution's application to state action.

G

gatekeepers Some professions, such as accountant, that act as "watchdogs" in that their role is to ensure that those who enter into the marketplace are playing by the rules and conforming to the conditions that ensure the market functions as it is supposed to function.

H

Health Insurance Portability and Accountability Act (HIPAA) (Pub. L. 104-191) HIPAA stipulates that employers cannot use "protected health information" in making employment decisions without prior consent. Protected health information includes all medical records or other individually identifiable health information.

human rights Those moral rights that individuals have simply in virtue of being a human being. Also called Natural Rights or Moral Rights.

hypernorms Values that are fundamental across culture and theory.

I

implied warranty of merchantability Implied assurances by a seller that a product is reasonably suitable for its purpose.

inattentional blindness If we happen to focus or are told specifically to pay attention to a particular element of a decision or event, we are likely to miss all of the surrounding details, no matter how obvious.

insider trading Trading of securities by those who hold private inside information that would materially impact the value of the stock and that allows them to benefit from buying or selling stock.

integrative model of CSR For some business firms, social responsibility is fully integrated with the firm's mission or strategic plan.

internal control A process, effected by an entity's board of directors, management, and other personnel, designed to provide reasonable assurance regarding the achievement of objectives in the following categories: effectiveness and efficiency of operations, reliability of financial reporting, and compliance with applicable laws and regulations.

Internet use monitoring The maintenance and either periodic or random review of the use of the Internet by employees or others based on time spent or content accessed for a variety of business purposes.

intrusion into seclusion The legal terminology for one of the common law claims of invasion of privacy. Intrusion into seclusion occurs when someone intentionally intrudes on the private affairs of another when the intrusion would be "highly offensive to a reasonable person."

IRS 20-factor analysis A list of 20 factors to which the IRS looks to determine whether someone is an employee or an independent contractor.

J

just cause A standard for terminations or discipline that requires the employer to have sufficient and fair cause before reaching a decision against an employee.

L

LEED Certification Leadership in Energy and Environmental Design is the construction industry "Green Building" process by which environmentally sustainable standards are applied to building construction and renovation. LEED provides both the standards and the independent third party verification to certify the environmental quality of a building.

M

marketing Defined by the American Marketing Association as "an organizational function and a set of processes for creating, communicating, and delivering value to customers and for managing customer relationships in ways that benefit the organization and its stakeholders."

mission statement A formal summary statement that described the goals, values, and institutional aim of an organization.

moral free space That environment where hypernorms or universal rules do not govern or apply to ethical decisions but instead culture or other influences govern decisions, as long as they are not in conflict with hypernorms. In other words, as long as a decision is not in conflict with a hypernorm, it rests within moral free space and reasonable minds may differ as to what is ethical.

moral imagination When one is facing an ethical decision, the ability to envision various alternative choices, consequences, resolutions, benefits, harms.

moral rights Distinguished from legal rights, which are given to individuals by law, moral rights are those entitlements that individuals have in virtue of moral principles.

morality Sometimes used to denote the phenomena studied by the field of ethics. This text uses *morality* to refer to those aspects of ethics involving personal, individual decision making. "How should I live my life?" or "What type of person ought I be?" is taken to be the basic question of morality. Morality can be distinguished from questions of *social justice*, which address issues of how communities and social organizations ought to be structured.

multiculturalism Similar to diversity, refers to the principle of tolerance and inclusion that supports the co-existence of multiple cultures, while encouraging each to retain that which is unique or individual about that particular culture.

N

negligence Unintentional failure to exercise reasonable care not to harm other people. Negligence is considered to be one step below "reckless disregard" for harm to others and two steps below intentional harm.

normative ethics Ethics as a *normative* discipline that deals with norms, those standards of appropriate and proper (or "normal") behavior. Norms establish the guidelines or standards for determining what we should do, how we should act, what type of person we should be. Contrast with *descriptive ethics,* above.

normative myopia The tendency to ignore, or the lack of the ability to recognize, ethical issues in decision making.

norms Those standards or guidelines that establish appropriate and proper behavior. Norms can be established by such diverse perspectives as economics, etiquette, or ethics.

O

Occupational Safety and Health Administration (OSHA) The United States Occupational Safety and Health Administration, an agency of the federal government that publishes and enforces safety and health regulations for U.S. businesses.

P

perceptual differences Psychologists and philosophers have long recognized that individuals cannot perceive the world independently of their own conceptual framework. Experiences are mediated by and interpreted through our own understanding and concepts. Thus, ethical disagreements can depend as much on a person's conceptual framework as on the facts of the situation. Unpacking our own and others' conceptual schema plays an important role in making ethically responsible decisions.

personal and professional decision making Individuals within a business setting are often in situations in which they must make decisions both from their own personal point of view and from the perspective of the specific role they fill within an institution. Ethically responsible decisions require an individual to recognize that these perspectives can conflict and that a life of moral integrity must balance the personal values with the professional role-based values and responsibilities.

personal data Any information relating to an identifiable person, directly or indirectly, in particular by reference to one or more factors specific to her or his physical, physiological, mental, economic, cultural, or social identity.

personal integrity The term 'integrity' connotes completeness of a being or thing. Personal integrity, therefore, refers to one's completeness within themselves, often derived from the consistency or alignment of actions with deeply held beliefs.

philanthropic model of CSR holds that business is free to contribute to social causes as a matter of philanthropy or charity, but has no strict obligation to contribute to social causes.

practical reasoning Involves reasoning about what one ought to do, contrasted with *theoretical reasoning*, which is concerned with what one ought to believe. Ethics is a part of practical reason.

privacy The right to be "let alone" within a personal zone of solitude, and/or the right to control information about oneself.

privacy rights The legal and ethical sources of protection for privacy in personal data.

property rights The boundaries defining actions that individuals can take in relation to other individuals regarding their personal information. If one individual has a *right* to her or his personal information, someone else has a commensurate duty to observe that right.

R

reasonable expectation of privacy The basis for some common law claims of invasion of privacy. Where an individual is notified that information will be shared or space will not be private, there is likely no reasonable expectation of privacy.

reciprocal obligation The concept that, while an employee has an obligation to respect the goals and property of the employer, the employer has a *reciprocal obligation* to respect the rights of the employee as well, including the employee's right to privacy.

reputation management The practice of caring for the "image" of a firm.

reverse discrimination Decisions made or actions taken against those individuals who are traditionally considered to be in power or the majority, such as white men, or in favor of a historically nondominant group.

rights Function to protect certain central interests from being sacrificed for the greater overall happiness. According to many philosophers, rights entail obligations: your rights create duties for others either to refrain from violating your rights ("negative" duties) or to provide you with what is yours by right ("positive" duties).

risk assessment A process to identify potential events that may affect the entity, and manage risk to be within its risk appetite, to provide reasonable assurance regarding the achievement of entity objectives.

S

Safe Harbor exception Considered "adequate standards" of privacy protection for U.S.-based companies under the European Union's Data Protection Directive.

Sarbanes-Oxley Act (Public Accounting Reform and Investor Protection Act of 2002) Implemented on July 30, 2002, and administered by the Securities and Exchange Commission to regulate financial reporting and auditing of publicly traded companies in the United States. SOX or SarbOx (popular shorthands for the act) was enacted very shortly following and directly in response to the Enron scandals of 2001. One of the greatest areas of consternation and debate that has emerged surrounding SOX involves the high cost of compliance and the challenging burden therefore placed on smaller firms. Some contend that SOX was the most significant change to the corporate landscape to occur in the second half of the 20th century.

service-based economy Interprets consumer demand as a demand for services, for example, for clothes cleaning, floor covering, cool air, transportation, or word processing, rather than as a demand for products such as washing machines, carpeting, air conditioners, cars, and computers.

social entrepreneurship A movement that seeks to address social problems through the creativity and efficiency of market forces. Social entrepreneurship involves the standard entrepreneurial characteristics of innovation, creativity, and risk-taking, but marshals these skills to address social needs. Social Entrepreneurship differs from the work of non-profit groups such as NGOs and corporate foundations in that social entrepreneurs explicitly aim to be profitable.

social ethics The area of ethics that is concerned with how we should live together with others and social organizations ought to be structured. Social ethics involves questions of political, economic, civic, and cultural norms aimed at promoting human well-being.

social web model of CSR The view that business exists within web of social relationships. The Social Web model views business as a citizen of the society in which it operates and, like all members of a society, business must conform to the normal range of ethical duties and obligations that all citizens face.

stakeholders In a general sense, a stakeholder is anyone who can be affected by decisions made within a business. More specifically, stakeholders are considered to be those people who are necessary for the functioning of a business.

stakeholder theory A model of corporate social responsibility that holds that business managers have ethical responsibilities to a range of stakeholders that goes beyond a narrow view that the primary or only responsibility of managers is to stockholders.

stealth marketing Also called undercover marketing. Marketing campaigns that are based on environments or activities where the subject is not aware that she or he is the target of a marketing campaign; those situations where one is subject to directed commercial activity without knowledge or consent.

strict liability A legal doctrine that holds an individual or business accountable for damages whether or not it was at fault. In a strict liability case, no matter how careful the business is in its product or service, if harm results from use, the individual or business is liable.

sustainable business practice A model of business practice in which business activities meet the standards of sustainability.

sustainable development Development that meets the needs of the present without compromising the ability of future generations to meet their own needs as defined by the Brundtland Commission in 1987.

Sustainable or green marketing Sustainable or green marketing is the marketing of products on the basis of their environmentally-friendly nature.

sweatshops A term that remains subject to debate. Some might suggest that all workplaces with conditions that are below standards in more developed countries are sweatshops since all humans have a right to equally decent working conditions. (See the discussion in Chapter 6 and D. Arnold and L. Hartman, "Beyond Sweatshops: Positive Deviancy and Global Labor Practices," *Business Ethics: A European Review* 14, no. 3 (July 2005).) In this text we use the following definition: any workplace in which workers are typically subject to two or more of the following conditions: systematic forced overtime, systematic health and safety risks that stem from negligence or the willful disregard of employee welfare, coercion, systematic deception that places workers at risk, underpayment of earnings, and income for a 48-hour workweek less than the overall poverty rate for that country (one who suffers from overall poverty lacks the income necessary to satisfy one's basic nonfood needs such as shelter and basic health care).

T

theoretical reasoning Involves reasoning that is aimed at establishing truth and therefore at what we ought to believe. Contrast with practical reasoning, which aims at determining what is reasonable for us to do.

three pillars of sustainability Three factors that are often used to judge the adequacy of sustainable practices. Sustainable development must be (1) economically, (2) environmentally, and (3) ethically satisfactory.

U

United States Sentencing Commission An independent agency in the United States judiciary created in 1984 to regulate sentencing policy in the federal court system.

Uniting and Strengthening America by Providing Appropriate Tools Required to Intercept and Obstruct Terrorism (USA PATRIOT) Act of 2001 A U.S. statute designed to increase the surveillance and investigative powers of law enforcement agencies in the United States in response to the terrorist attacks of September 11, 2001. The act has been lauded as a quick response to terrorism (it was introduced less than a week after the attacks) and for implementing critical amendments to more than 15 important statutes; it also has been criticized for failing to include sufficient safeguards for civil liberties.

utilitarianism An ethical theory that tells us that we can determine the ethical significance of any action by looking to the consequences of that act. Utilitarianism is typically identified with the policy of "maximizing the overall good" or, in a slightly different version, of producing "the greatest good for the greatest number."

V

values Those beliefs that incline us to act or to choose in one way rather than another. We can recognize many different types of values: financial, religious, legal, historical, nutritional, political, scientific, and aesthetic. Ethical values serve the ends of human well-being in impartial, rather than personal or selfish ways.

values-based culture A corporate culture in which conformity to a statement of values and principles rather than simple obedience to laws and regulations is the prevailing model for ethical behavior.

virtue ethics An approach to ethics that studies the character traits or habits that constitute a good human life, a life worth living. The virtues provide answers to the basic ethical question "What kind of person should I be?"

W

whistleblowing A practice in which an individual within an organization reports organizational wrongdoing to the public or to others in position of authority.

word-of-mouth marketing Efforts by companies to generate personal recommendations by users.

Index